The Witch as Muse

The Witch as Muse

Art, Gender, and Power in Early Modern Europe

Linda C. Hults

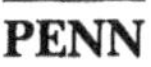

University of Pennsylvania Press
Philadelphia

Copyright © 2005 University of Pennsylvania Press
All rights reserved

10 9 8 7 6 5 4 3 2 1

Published by
University of Pennsylvania Press
Philadelphia, Pennsylvania 19104–4011

Library of Congress Cataloging-in-Publication Data

Hults, Linda C.
The witch as muse : art, gender, and power in early modern Europe / Linda C. Hults.
p. cm.
Includes bibliographical references and index.
ISBN: 978-0-8122-2145-9

1. Witches in art. 2. Witchcraft in art. 3. Gender identity in art. 4. Art, European—16th century. 5. Art, European—17th century. 6. Witchcraft—Europe—History—16th century. 7. Witchcraft—Europe—History—17th century. I. Title.

N8262.7.H85 2005
704.9'4913343—dc22 *2004063823*

In memory of my mother, Ottsie J. Hults

Contents

Illustrations

Preface

This book is not a comprehensive survey of images of witches but a deep reading of artists' engagement with this theme in the early modern period. Toward this end, I chose an episodic treatment in Chapters 3 through 7 that would allow me to explore the various discourses and contextual factors that intersect in the images. As I worked with this material over the last decade, the complexity of this intersection became increasingly apparent. The artists I discuss here are outstanding examples of that complexity.

My methodologies are multiple, shaped over time by my experiences as a scholar and teacher in art history and women's studies. In Chapter 2, making no claims to exhaust possible approaches to images or to history, I give readers an account of that shaping. I was introduced to the European witch-hunts and witchcraft imagery in earlier work on Hans Baldung Grien. My first task was iconographic interpretation, which led me to early sixteenth-century demonological theory and to the historical status of witch-hunting in Baldung's context. My concern to address the understanding of witchcraft and the persecution of witches in specific times and places still lies at the basis of each of my discussions of artists and their works. Even in my initial research on Baldung, however, I could see that his efforts to develop a distinctive style and range of subjects in the wake of Albrecht Dürer's innovative example had much to do with his fascination for the witchcraft theme. Ultimately, my study of these images became not simply a reading of their relationship to the waxing and waning of the idea of witchcraft and to the witch-hunts themselves but also of the construction of artistic identity in early modern Europe, seen through the lens of witchcraft images.

This lens is powerful, revealing the layers and evolution of that construction with particular clarity. Early modern artists' careers and works were shaped by competition for recognition, social status, and economic reward. To compete successfully required alignment not only with various elite patrons but also with elevated theoretical notions of artistic invention, beginning in the fifteenth century with Leonbattista Alberti's intellectual but comparatively modest view (in hindsight) of how an artist creates. Although challenged by ongoing religious and moral scruples, by Baroque currents of naturalism and neoclassicism, and by the academic prestige of history painting, imaginative or fantastic invention survived in the margins to be brought to the center at the end of the early modern period in works by Francisco Goya and others.

Thus, the competitive conditions of artists' careers and the varied elements of artistic self-construction assumed an importance equal to the historical narrative of witchcraft and witch-hunting in my interpretation of the images. Moreover, I found that the discourses surrounding witchcraft were indeed related to the rhetoric of artistic self-presentation. The profound political and intellectual implications of witchcraft and its persecution in early modern Europe (as recounted by Stuart Clark in his cultural history of the idea of witchcraft, *Thinking with Demons*, 1997) weighed heavily on artists' choice of the theme. In ways that often surprised me, the abject image of the female witch (in Chapter 1, I suggest reasons why witches were symbolically if not actually always female) served as a foil for positive masculine identities, including that of artist. My study of these images makes clear that binary notions of gender pervaded early modern culture and society, and that male artists marshaled these polarities to construct identities that overcame the dangers of fantasy, exemplified in extremis by the female witch, with a presumed masculine superiority of reason and virtue, and a control of the senses, the body, and matter. Through the subject of witchcraft—interesting to humanists, theologians, physicians, jurists, officials, and rulers—artists aligned themselves with sites of masculine power and prestige in the early modern period, such as governments, courts, and universities, or the private galleries of wealthy collectors, fascinated not just by the intellectual and moral issues embedded in the theme but also by its capacity to titillate, to shock, and to inspire a sense of the marvelous, the exotic, and the curious.

So this book took shape as an interdisciplinary endeavor, embracing art and literary history, history, and women's and gender studies. What I have most relished about my topic is the way it refuses categorization and closure. In this sense, it clarifies for me my reason for choosing art history as a profession: the opportunity to investigate any aspect of history and culture while remaining firmly tethered to physical objects—a curious combination of freedom and constraint. As the boundaries of my discipline have fallen away, artistic images only seem more significant to me as windows into history and the human condition.

Chapter 1
The Witch as Woman

An Introduction to the European Witch-Hunts: The Place of a Feminist Perspective

Any art historian attempting to establish his or her own interpretive stance on the images of witches I discuss in this book must ultimately grapple with the historiography of the European witch-hunts and with the changing place of gender as an analytical category. Both the methodologies used to understand the European witch-hunts and scholars' assessment of their overall importance have undergone substantial shifts. Some recent historians have been eager to point out the exaggeration of their magnitude on the part of past scholars and writers. Witch-hunting was not pan-European: regions of Europe (most notably Spain, Italy, and the Dutch Republic) remained relatively unscathed. Far from being a sweeping "craze," the result of some collective mental illness, witch-hunting often met determined resistance on philosophical, legal, and humanitarian grounds, and its politics were often highly nuanced.[1] We now know that accusations of witchcraft accounted for a small percentage of criminal prosecutions in Europe.[2] Writing in 1987, Brian Levack estimated the number of trials at about 110,000 and the death count for accused witches at about 60,000—nowhere near the extravagant hundreds of thousands to millions asserted by feminists Mary Daly and Andrea Dworkin, and the trend continues downward, with William Monter recently suggesting Levack's numbers should be reduced by a third. However, feminist historian Anne Barstow asserts that Levack's numbers should be doubled to compensate for tremendous gaps in records.[3] Even then, the European witch-hunts do not begin to approach the Jewish Holocaust of World War II, despite some feminists' embrace of the notions of "gynocide" and a "holocaust of women" in the early modern period to underpin ideas of women's current oppression—an appropriation explored sensitively by Diane Purkiss.[4]

Despite these recent efforts to assess the impact of the witch-hunts on early modern Europe more realistically, an undiminished stream of scholarly books and articles confirms their continuing relevance for European history and historical methodology.[5] Despite the hyperbole of the analogy to the Holocaust, current conservative estimates of the numbers of accused and executed are still remarkable, and the number of families disrupted or ruined in the wake of the trials is sobering. The witch-hunts clearly constitute an important episode in early modern European history. It is not simply that the drama and poignancy of this episode engage us, but also that the questions surrounding it reflect much broader historical issues. Witch-hunting focuses questions about the roles of church and state in forming early modern societies; the causal importance of the demonological beliefs versus war, religious tensions, natural disasters, or economic catastrophes; the interaction of rulers, judges, lawyers, and theologians with the lower classes and how we might understand the agency and subjectivity of the latter; the relationship of urban and rural populations; and, not least, the way early modern societies viewed women.

My discussion of witchcraft images ends with Goya, an artist of the late Enlightenment for whom witchcraft beliefs epitomized both human folly in general and the failure of the Catholic Church in particular. This anticlerical, rationalistic spirit also nourished the earliest historical scholarship on the witch-hunts between the 1880s and World War I. Confident that history revealed the progress of reason, early historians of the witch-hunts, such as the Germans Wilhelm Gottlieb Soldan and Joseph Hansen and the Americans Henry Charles Lea, Andrew Dickson White, and George Lincoln Burr, tirelessly collected the documentary sources that formed the foundation of modern historical inquiry. According to Monter, whose invaluable essay on the historiography of witchcraft studies outlined the major methodological approaches to the problem up to 1972, Soldan's work, continued by his son-in-law Heinrich Heppe, established the basic outlines of the rationalist paradigm. First, the ideas forming the stereotype of the witch originated in the Middle Ages and coalesced at about the time of the *Malleus maleficarum* (Hammer of witches, 1487), written primarily by Heinrich Kramer with Jacob Sprenger listed as its co-author. Second, witch-hunting, based on this stereotype, expanded during the sixteenth century to peak during the Thirty Years War. Finally, the Enlightenment with its scientific cosmology brought an end to most witch-hunting by the early eighteenth century.[6]

These early rationalist scholars believed that witchcraft trials were generated by persistent superstitions fostered by the medieval Catholic Church and the Inquisition's use of torture to extract confessions. Although the Inquisition's role in the codification and early promulgation of the witchcraft stereotype is apparent, rationalist historians could not account for its moderation in executing persons accused of witchcraft, for the zeal often demonstrated by secular courts and by the populace, or for the enthusiasm for witch-hunting in some Protestant contexts.[7] Ultimately, their presentation of the belief in witchcraft and the persecution of witches as remnants of Europe's dark, irrational, medieval past that would finally be dispelled by the Enlightenment rested on a false dichotomy between the ecclesiastical and the secular, between the religious and the rational, during the early modern period.

Despite these shortcomings, the rationalist paradigm cast a long shadow. In his famous essay on the European witch "craze," first published in 1967, British historian Hugh Trevor-Roper dismissed witchcraft belief, which he saw as an unchanging constant inherited by the early modern period from the Middle Ages, as "the mental rubbish of peasant credulity and feminine hysteria."[8] However, his essay was significant for its promotion of the study of social factors affecting witch-hunting. For Trevor-Roper, the Dominican inquisitors who developed the stereotype of witchcraft into its mature form wanted to squelch the social and doctrinal nonconformity that he thought was especially rife in Europe's mountainous regions. Witches were one of a number of marginalized groups scapegoated to relieve social tensions developing after the Reformation, specifically the Wars of Religion.[9] Although Trevor-Roper foregrounded social explanations of witch-hunting in his essay, he nevertheless returned to the rationalist paradigm in his assessment of the concept of witchcraft belief as nonsense and his assertion of the new cosmology of Enlightenment science, for which he offers no social explanation, as the cause of witch-hunting's demise.[10]

We know now that witchcraft beliefs were not a monolith of concretized superstitions inherited from the Middle Ages but an evolving bundle of ideas, often with unresolved internal contradictions, that varied from context to context and did indeed undergo distinct changes in the early modern period.[11] We also know that debate over witchcraft was not a matter of "peasant credulity and feminine hysteria" but constituted a serious intellectual problem, integrally bound up with the early modern worldview, as Stuart Clark has unequivocally demonstrated in *Thinking with Demons* (1997). Concern about witches, expressed with varying combinations of skepticism and credulity, Clark argues persuasively, was normative and eminently *rational*.[12] Despite the widespread critique of many aspects of Trevor-Roper's essay, including its stranger features such as the association of witchcraft beliefs and thin mountain air, his insight into the relationship between the witch-hunts and religious strife after the Reformation continues in more sophisticated and detailed analyses of recent scholars who emphasize the roles of confessionalization and state-building in promoting witch-hunting in the early modern period.[13] However, their work has been subject to critique as well, especially from a functionalist perspective based in anthropology, as I will discuss below.

Trevor-Roper and others who followed the first generation of rationalist historians of the witch-hunts were disabused of the notion of reason's progressive triumph by World War I, and World War II only reinforced that disillusionment. Jonathan Barry expresses how twentieth-century experience underpins Trevor-Roper's thesis: "In a world still darkened by Naziism and mortally threatened by the Cold War, Trevor-Roper chronicled the resurgence of what he saw as an elite irrationality, linked in particular to the Reformation's defeat of Erasmian humanism."[14] Similarly, Norman Cohn acknowledged that his landmark study, *Europe's Inner Demons* (1975), which traced the roots of stereotypical aspects of diabolical witchcraft back through the Middle Ages and antiquity, would "prompt reflections not only about the distant past but about certain aspects of twentieth-century history too."[15] Cohn did not pursue his analysis into the period of the witch-hunts themselves; rather, he described the coalescence of a witch-hunting mentality at the end of the fifteenth century from earlier precedents.

Certainly the European witch-hunts have an affinity with past and modern persecutions (some of the heinous accusations levied upon Jews were simply transferred to witches), but they must also be approached synchronically, as important parts of our understanding of early modern Europe. Cohn, Trevor-Roper, and many other scholars have wrestled with the question of why witch-hunting on a large scale occurred when it did, between 1560 and 1700. Assumptions made by the early rationalist historians that witch-hunting was essentially medieval, in part based on bogus documents exposed by Cohn and Richard Kieckhefer, were simply wrong.[16] For although medieval Europeans believed in witchcraft, demonology owed many of its assumptions to scholastic philosophy, and witch-hunting depended on methods of prosecution developed by the Inquisition, the witch-hunts were a product of the Renaissance, lending that period a distinctly non-Burckhardtian aspect. The demonization of the crime of sorcery by linking it with heresy and the heightened awareness of witchcraft necessary for large-scale hunts are most clear in the *Malleus*, even when one considers its precedents in earlier writings and the relationship between its tenets and the ancient and medieval campaigns against heresy that Cohn discussed.[17] The *Malleus* provided a theoretical foundation, but large-scale witch-hunting lay relatively fallow until the late sixteenth century.

One of the most tenacious explanations of this timing had already been offered in the early twenties by Egyptologist Margaret Murray, a student of Sir James Frazer, who wrote the influential study of fertility myths and cults, *The Golden Bough* (1911–15). Murray's major book, *The Witch-Cult in Western Europe*, was first published in 1921 and has been frequently reprinted; her thesis was repeated in her *Encyclopedia Britannica* article on witchcraft between 1929 and 1968. Like the rationalist historians, Murray blamed Christianity for witch-hunting, but she saw witchcraft as a rival religion: a Greco-Roman fertility cult worshipping a hairy, horned male god and conducting assemblies at which fertility rites involving ritual intercourse were celebrated. (Carlo Ginzburg now argues for the persistence of fertility myths of Eurasian origins in witchcraft beliefs.[18]) According to Murray, Christianity only gradually gained enough influence on the European populace to declare war against this pagan cult in the form of massive witch-hunting beginning in the sixteenth century.

The appeal of Murray's thesis among nonhistorians goes beyond its longstanding accessibility in a standard reference work like the *Encyclopedia Britannica*. Ultimately, Murray's appeal is rooted in the desire to find confirmation of one's own view of the world in the past—a nostalgia based on false premises but nevertheless extremely difficult to dislodge.[19] Like French historian Jules Michelet in his book *La Sorcière* (The witch, 1862), Murray heroized and romanticized the witch as an unfairly maligned and persecuted victim, who partook of a timeless way of life based on the rhythms of nature and bravely resisted the artificial order imposed by church and state. In Michelet's case, the presumed pagan cult was pointedly political and related to his own leftist beliefs in that it represented the economic rebellion of oppressed serfs. For both Michelet and Murray, witchcraft was a woman-centered movement to resist oppression—a concept ripe for romantic fantasy. Listen to Michelet's description of the female serf-witch "with a face like Medea, a beauty born of sufferings, a deep, tragic, feverish gaze, with a torrent of black, untamable hair falling as chance takes it, like waves of serpents."[20] As Purkiss notes, Murray also created an appealing picture of witches as "active worshippers and desiring subjects" that was related to her own stance as an ardent suffragette and pioneer in a male-dominated academic field.[21] Although unconfirmed by historical evidence, the Michelet-Murray witch sustains the modern neopagan movement and this fantasized narrative of the witch-hunts functions as an inspirational martyrs' tale. However, by relegating early modern women to nature—a place fundamentally *outside* the course of western history and culture—the empowering potential of this tale is severely compromised.

Murray never lacked scholarly critics and her arguments, based on an irresponsible use of primary sources that systematically excised fantastic passages in confessions, were resoundingly debunked by Cohn and others.[22] Nevertheless, Murray's fundamental insight may not be entirely wrong. Her assumption of a war between organized, orthodox Christianity and an unconverted populace is related to academically credible attempts to analyze witch-hunting in terms of confessionalization. Efforts by Lutheran, Calvinist, and Catholic authorities to homogenize religious beliefs and practices and to wipe out heterodox beliefs (considered superstitions) among the populations of their various territories were crucial to the integration of early modern states.[23]

In his *Night Battles: Witchcraft and Agrarian Cults in the Sixteenth and Seventeenth Centuries* (1966, with English translation appearing in 1983) and in his more recent *Ecstasies: Deciphering the Witches' Sabbath* (1991), Ginzburg explores the possibility that Murray may have been partly correct about the persistence of non-Christian beliefs at the folk level. Ginzburg follows up this insight by attempting to trace the Eurasian roots of shamanistic beliefs that he thinks formed the basis for the myth of the witches' sabbath.[24] Murray's error, Ginzburg asserts, lay not only in irresponsibly manipulating the texts of confessions but also in assuming that accounts of the sabbath reflected rituals, not myths. Moreover, Murray failed to perceive that the sabbath myth is multilayered—according to Ginzburg, in opposition to those who see it as simple symbolic inversion—with a folkloric core discernible within the demonological interpolations.[25]

In *Night Battles*, Ginzburg followed the fates of Friulian peasants gradually transformed into stereotypical witches by Inquisitorial pressure (not torture) between 1580 and 1650. The peasants were not part of a pagan fertility cult explicitly resisting Christianity, but they did hold beliefs that their educated Christian interrogators could comprehend only through assimilation into their familiar demonology. The *benandanti* ("people who go out to do good") among the Friuli supposedly held beneficent magical powers because they had been born with the caul, which they carried as an amulet throughout their lives. Female *benandanti* were distinguished by their ability to visit and communicate with the dead, and male *benandanti* went forth to *battle* witches and preserve the crops, both in trances. Persuaded by inquisitors, however, the *benandanti* came to understand themselves as devil worshippers going to sabbaths.

Ginzburg's work centers on the crucial question of the basic direction of transmission of witchcraft beliefs—did they move from the "top down" or from the "bottom up?" Did the ideas that constituted the stereotype of witchcraft emerge from learned elites who then imposed this stereotype on the populace, or were the ideas already embedded in a popular consciousness with temporally distant roots? At the heart of this question is also the tug-of-war between particular historical contexts and morphological continuities and parallelisms that resist contextual analyses.[26] Taken together, Ginzburg's two major books on witchcraft suggest a convergence that produced a dialectical interaction of top and bottom. Ginzburg describes exactly how this process operated in the formation of the crucial myth of the witches' sabbath—inquisitors' and lay judges' perception and demonization of conspiratorial sects and folk culture's shamanistic belief in magical flights and transformation into animals.[27] While *Ecstasies* provides the outlines of a folklore that formed the foundation of what inquisitors construed as the diabolical witches' sabbath, *Night Battles* provides support to explanations of witch-hunting in terms of acculturation and confessionalization in the early modern period. Clive Holmes has found a similar dialectical relationship between popular and elite beliefs at work in England, where demonological concepts penetrated unevenly and never as thoroughly as they did on the continent. Even so, Holmes argues, English divines and any judges they were able to influence brought a theological understanding of the demonic pact into a context of English popular belief in harmful magic and control over animals, executed by women who inherited powers through their mothers. Thus, the typical "familiar" of English witchcraft trials, half-pet and half-demon, is a compromise between folklore and demonology.[28]

The specific conditions of the English context—the shallow, sporadic assimilation of continental demonology, the jury system, and the comparative lack of physical torture—inform the functionalist approach represented by Keith Thomas and Alan Macfarlane.[29] Thomas's magisterial *Religion and the Decline of Magic* (1971) dealt with much broader issues than witchcraft, not the least of which was the unity of religion and magic as parts of the same early modern worldview, but his understanding of witchcraft accusations in terms of individual relations at the village level—especially those involving requests for and refusal of charity—was an extremely important insight. Moreover, as Barry notes, Thomas's functionalism, incorporating a sociological, psychological, and intellectual understanding of witchcraft beliefs, was never narrow.[30] Macfarlane's study of witchcraft trials in Essex (1970) focused on three contiguous villages to conclude that it was "normal," "widespread and regular" aspects of village life that sparked witchcraft accusations. In the last section of his book, Macfarlane offered a comparative anthropological analysis of English and African witchcraft beliefs, reinforcing his emphasis on the interpersonal relations of village societies.[31]

A functionalist approach allows us to look at the dynamics of early modern witchcraft and witch-hunting on a pragmatic and situational level. By privileging the way witchcraft accusations operated at the village level rather than how they were theorized and promoted by theologians or judges, it opened the door for more recent inquiries into both the psychology and the agency of non-elite individuals caught up in this phenomenon, such as Robin Briggs's *Witches and Neighbors* (1996). Because many of those individuals were women, this open door might also lead to a more complete history of early modern women. In *Oedipus and the Devil* (1994), Lyndal Roper undertakes a psychoanalytical and historical exploration of how the realities of women's lives as well as their fantasies might have been expressed through confessions of witchcraft. Roper's scholarship attempts to balance women's individual subjectivities and bodily experiences against demonological discourse and exemplifies the value of this reversal of priorities.[32] However, an adequate account of the complex interaction of popular and elite culture seems equally necessary. Robert Rowland argues that functionalist analogies between early modern Europe and African societies were ultimately unconvincing because the latter lacked the "supra-national integration of western Christendom" (i.e., Catholic and Protestant demonology and the drive toward religious homogeneity). Moreover, the intermediate, national structures that operated between the supranational and the local, village levels—the lay courts, the Inquisition, and various other secular and ecclesiastical institutions of the early modern state—were missing.[33]

Although the comparative study of witchcraft in African and English villages yields valuable insights, the differences between England and continental Europe are also important. It is precisely those aspects of English witchcraft most comparable to African witchcraft that distinguish England from continental Europe: the lack of emphasis on flight, on the sabbath, on the demonic pact, and on infanticide. In England, malefice took precedence over heresy; the English familiar, as noted above, often behaved like a pet. African beliefs do contain a figure corresponding to the diabolical witch of continental Europe—the "night-witch," a fantastic, night-flying embodiment of social taboos and of evil itself. That sort of African witch, though—really a metaphor for an inversion of the normal world—was distinct from ordinary witches who inflicted harm on their neighbors. In early modern continental Europe, the two types of witches often merged. This merger could be accomplished only, as Rowland puts it, "by bringing two distinct cultural levels into relation with one another."[34]

Christina Larner and Robert Muchembled, two chief exponents of the theory of witch-hunting as an expression of state-building, acculturation, and confessionalization in the early modern period, would argue that these factors are essential for the formation of large-scale European witch trials, especially in areas other than England. Although it had a highly centralized judicial system, bound by common law and a national system of circuit courts, England was not an absolutist state: Its government was constitutionally restricted, thus limiting the utility of witch-hunting for state-building purposes (or so scholars taking this approach might argue). Larner's research has centered on Scotland, where there was indeed a distinct link between the state (especially in the person of James VI, who believed himself to be the personal target of witchcraft), the judicial system (for example, the commissions from the privy council to local authorities in the 1590s to seek out and punish witches), and witch-hunts. In her major book, *Enemies of God* (1981), Larner stated categorically that the Scottish witch-hunts began with the doctrine of the divine right of kings and ended with the decline of the idea of the godly state.[35]

Muchembled's extensive publications have focused primarily on areas of current France and the Spanish Netherlands, a contested territory held at great expense and difficulty by the Habsburgs where the regents and the judiciary worked in tandem with Tridentine Catholicism to homogenize belief and construct the ideal subject of the absolutist state.[36] Muchembled does not deny the impact of village tensions on witch-hunting: "rapid demographic expansion and economic change" caused a "ferment of social differentiation in the villages" that generated the interpersonal tension and envy leading to witchcraft accusations.[37] For him, however, the more important impetus came from above. The state, allied with the church, sought to enforce Catholic orthodoxy and purge popular customs of immorality. The sabbath myth, an elite inversion of peasant customs, thus diabolizes nocturnal brawls, courting rituals, and dancing; the "plurality of forces" peasants recognized as affecting their lives coalesced in the figure of Satan, reinforcing their need for the salvific power of Christ.[38]

A strong critique of acculturation and state-building as explanations for the witch-hunts emerges from the many instances of centralized authorities acting in response to pressures from local authorities against witches or restraining the excesses of local persecutions. Levack, for example, calls Larner's interpretation into question by pointing out that the commissions from the privy council to persecute witches at the local level were issued because of pressure from local authorities. Moreover, the state abdicated control of the majority of Scottish witchcraft cases, which were conducted by local elders or magistrates rather than by the central criminal or circuit courts. When witchcraft trials were conducted in these latter venues, the conviction rate dropped significantly.[39] Alfred Soman's study of the *Parlement* (high court) of Paris reveals its role in decriminalizing witchcraft in northern and eastern France and its restraint of judicial abuses and public disorder associated with local trials; for these magistrates, moderation reflected the righteousness of the king's justice that they enacted.[40] As we shall see in our discussion of Antwerp artist Frans Francken II (Chapter 4), similar motivations seem to have inspired the attempts of the Habsburg regents of the Netherlands to curb the zealousness of local courts in the wake of the antiwitchcraft decrees of 1592 and 1606, issued by the regents in the name of the Spanish crown. In his exceptionally detailed and illuminating study of witchcraft persecutions in Bavaria, Wolfgang Behringer also draws conclusions about the restraining role of the central authorities: "If the population actively opposed a witch-hunt, it ended quickly. If the authorities opposed a persecution, it never even started."[41] Moreover, as in the regions noted above, efforts were made by Bavarian central authorities to curb excesses of trials.

Careful research on specific regions such as Behringer's on Bavaria makes it impossible now to view witch-hunting as a blunt instrument used crudely by early modern elites to intimidate those who would threaten the divinely sanctioned order of the "godly state." Rather, a much more complex, dialectical interaction between the various levels of early modern society must be assumed, although it seems clear that, without the acceptance and promotion of the stereotype of diabolical witchcraft on the part of religious and secular authorities, witchcraft may have remained, for the populace, mostly a question of discrete acts of black magic. The persecution of witches was not *simply* an instrument of control, though. Rather, persecutions had to reflect not just the power of the absolutist state but also its essential rectitude; to this end, local zealousness, which may indeed have originated from the kinds of social tensions explored by Thomas, Macfarlane and others, needed to be kept within strict bounds. Actions against witches had to be transparently just, with the image of the state's sanctity or the king's divine right to rule clearly visible beyond—that is the reason behind the ostensible paradox of central authorities' double-edged policies of prosecution and restraint.

The role of gender in the European witch-hunts, once largely unexamined, has been extensively debated in the wake of the feminist appropriation of them as a historically and symbolically significant part of the narrative of women's continuous oppression under western patriarchy.[42] It is generally accepted now that between 80 and 85 percent of witchcraft accusations were levied against women (with much regional variation), but why?[43] The question Larner asked—Was witchcraft a sex-specific or a sex-related crime?—has occupied many historians conscious of both the complexity of motivations and circumstances surrounding the witch-hunts and of the misogyny not exclusive to demonological treatises but nevertheless overtly stated or assumed, especially from the *Malleus* on.[44] Briggs points out that Pierre de Lancre, in his *Tableau de l'inconstance des mauvais anges et démons* (Picture of the inconstancy of evil angels and demons, 1612) asserted that women outnumbered men by a factor of ten, and Jean Bodin, in his *Démonomanie* (Demon-mania, 1580), argued that there were fifty female witches for every male witch. The explanations given for the disproportionate involvement of women in witchcraft come from venerable misogynistic rhetoric: women are more imbecilic and more vengeful, their brains are smaller, and their sexual desires more violent.[45] The *Malleus*, of course, declared with resounding finality that "all witchcraft comes from carnal lust, which is in women insatiable."[46]

Larner concluded that witchcraft cannot be defined ultimately as sex-specific, because it did not correspond in every trait to qualities attributable only to women. Yet, as Barstow notes, *Enemies of God* shows a clear sense of the profound importance of misogyny for the witch-hunts.[47] If we looked only at statements by demonologists such as those above, we might believe that "witch" was virtually synonymous with "woman" (or, more accurately, an egregiously deviant woman) and that to hunt witches indeed constituted "gynocide" as feminists have sometimes put it.[48] But arguments that witch-hunting was not equivalent to men hunting women have emerged from investigations of specific trials and executions. First, women often accused other women or were otherwise part of prosecutions (for example, by examining accused female witches for the devil's mark, or as deponents in trials). In *Oedipus and the Devil*, Roper concludes from her research on German witchcraft cases that accusations were not motivated by patriarchal domination but by "deep antagonisms between women" centering on childbirth, suckling, food, feeding, and children's vulnerability.[49] Second, men were also victimized by witchcraft accusations; in some locales, they constituted a large proportion of the accused—for example, the case of the Norman witches investigated by Monter.[50] One of the most moving primary documents from the witch-hunts is imprisoned Bamberg burgomeister Johannes Junius's letter to his daughter Veronica, written with great difficulty because of thumbscrews, explaining that the charges of witchcraft levied on him are entirely false. Junius's letter is a rare opportunity to hear a victim's voice clearly, and we hear that voice primarily because it is male and literate.[51]

Deviations from a proportion of 80 to 85 percent females among accused witches are explicable in a number of ways. Given the assumption of rampant diabolical influence in human affairs that fueled the witch-hunts,[52] it was inevitable that men and even children would be accused. Male victims were often related to or otherwise contaminated by their contact with female witches or had witchcraft tacked onto other felonious charges to make their crimes seem more heinous.[53] Junius's wife had been executed for witchcraft and he was named as a witch by six people under torture during the ferociously snowballing persecutions in Bamberg. There, the bishop confiscated the property of convicted witches—a strong motivation for accusing men.[54] In addition, local variations of the basic witchcraft stereotype might favor crimes more readily attributable to men. For example, the male shepherds in Normandy studied by Monter were particularly vulnerable to charges of witchcraft because of their use of toad venom, the Host, and prayers to protect their flocks from wolves.[55]

Such gendered differences in the popular use of magic may have produced local variations in the basic pattern of witch-hunting, but in the end they also help to explain why most accused witches were female. In her study of witchcraft in the Saar region of Germany, for instance, Eva Labouvie found that men's magic tended to be more "practical and circumscribed," tied to the everyday reality of village life, whereas women's was ambivalent, mysterious, and linked more readily to demonic power. Similarly, Luisa Accati's study of magic among the Friuli suggests that men used "tools and knowledge" that lay *outside* the body to accomplish immediate pragmatic and therapeutic goals (e.g., attracting a woman sexually, healing animals), while women's magic—corporeal, mysterious, centered in the womb—followed the diabolical stereotype promulgated by inquisitors.[56]

Women's seemingly compliant participation in the victimization of other women is also intelligible. Early modern women did not exist outside patriarchal ideology; they too assimilated notions of female vulnerability to evil and the stereotype of witchcraft. As Marianne Hester points out, accusations of witchcraft might be "situated . . . within the women's community, but they were integrally linked to and served to reinforce—or reconstruct—the male status quo."[57] Women might accuse other women of witchcraft out of genuine fear for themselves or their families, they might perceive some economic or social advantage in making an accusation, or they may have been manipulated by male relatives and authorities. Holmes's subtle analysis of women as deponents and accusers in English witchcraft trials suggests that as witchcraft came to be understood more as a crime against human life (as opposed to crops or livestock), women, who tended the sick, naturally became witnesses in cases of supposed bewitchment or possession. In order to function effectively in the judicial system, however, suspicions that may have remained crudely articulated had to be shaped into coherent accusations; in this process, he concludes, female deponents became the tools of the judicial and clerical elite, familiar with the precepts of demonology.[58] Labouvie notes that, although men were accused of witchcraft in the Saar region, they also controlled the process as witnesses and accusers of both women and men—normally men who had "violated male rules of conduct or invaded another man's jurisdiction." Women never had this kind of control.[59]

As feminists have brought gender to the fore, others have subsumed it within the categories of analysis central to their respective approaches. For example, Thomas tended to view women's greater vulnerability to witchcraft accusations in terms of their economic dependence; Muchembled in terms of their close contact with children and their influence in rural society that made them obstacles to the reeducation agenda of church and state.[60] (Hester is quick to point out, however, that such approaches stop short of explaining how pervasive social factors like these reinforced male status and power.[61]) Clark's monumental study of the intellectual, legal, and religious debates surrounding witchcraft and its persecution de-centers gender by emphasizing the binary patterns so important to early modern thought in general and demonology in particular. For this cultural historian demonstrating the broad cultural and intellectual context of the witch-hunts, misogyny was not the driving impetus but a part of an overarching philosophical principle of contrariety:

> At a demonological level, therefore, witches were female because the representational system governing them required for its coherence a general correlation between such primary oppositions as good/evil, order/disorder, soul/body, and male/female; they were females who, by behaviour inspired by the master of inversion, the devil, inverted the polarized attributes accorded to the genders in later medieval and early modern learned culture; and of these subversives, they were thought to be the most extreme and the most dangerous.[62]

Clark argues that the demonologists were relatively unconcerned with the femininity of the witch as an intellectual problem. It was their "presupposition," but they had little interest in "using it to denigrate women."[63]

More recently, in *Demon Lovers: Witchcraft, Sex, and the Crisis of Belief*

(2002), Walter Stephens displaces misogyny as the central factor in the witch-hunts by arguing, through meticulous textual analysis of some early modern demonological writings, that the real motivating force was a crisis of Christian belief.[64] The existence of demons and their active intervention in human life would prove these truths to theologians, but because Christians could not seek contact with demons, they needed witches as expert eyewitnesses to resolve their anxieties. The lynchpin of Stephens's thesis is his detailed account of Kramer's redaction of Part I of the *Malleus*. According to Stephens, Kramer introduced the famous passage on the evil of women (Question 6) only when he realized that it was *logically* necessary to prove why they would copulate with demons. Thus misogyny, for Stephens, is secondary: an unfortunate by-product of Christian anxiety and scholastic logic but not Kramer's true purpose in writing the *Malleus*.[65] Where does this leave a feminist approach to the witch-hunts? Clearly, misogyny is not the sole explanation for the witch-hunts but worked in tandem with village tensions, state-building, philosophical contrariety, and theological anxiety. And, as Clark advises, perhaps we should seek to *interpret* the witch-hunts rather than *explain* them—to "read" early modern phenomena for patterns of meaning rather than causation.[66] However, while putting causation and explanation aside, I would argue for the importance of women and gender within any interpretation of the witch-hunts. Although we have gone beyond simplistic accusations of misogyny, it remains clear that woman-as-witch constituted a fundamental pattern—a presumption that evidently did not require defense.

Interrogating that pattern illuminates early modern history and culture in surprising and profound ways that reach beyond this period into our own. The discourses and practices surrounding the persecution of witches were linked to men's efforts to gain power and status, which were informed, after all, by contemporary ideals of masculinity; the social forces that came into play as witches were accused, tried, and executed were informed by gender at every level (the village, the local court, the state); and the psychological and social impact of this extraordinarily negative female stereotype, although difficult to isolate, was surely enormous. Hester's insistence on framing the witch-hunts within gendered structures of power, and on centering inquiry on early modern women, remains compelling.

Clearly the capacity to act publicly, to argue, to write, or to make artistic images within the binary intellectual system defined by Clark depended on one's gender. How is it possible to say that demonologists did not denigrate women by presuming witchcraft was "natural" to them? How was theological anxiety (not to mention the Christian dogmas and institutions the demonologists desperately wanted to confirm) shaped by gender? By whose criteria is the *logical* function of Part I, Question 6, of the *Malleus* more purposeful than its virulent misogyny, recycled to be sure but now applied with a new and deadly force?

As I see them, the goals of a feminist reading of early modern evidence on the witch-hunts would be to expose the basis of the pattern of woman-as-witch in the theory and rhetoric of witch-hunting, its relation to other forms of social control of early modern women, its effect on women's lives and psyches, and its relevance to global violence against women in our own era (wife battering, rape, bride burning, honor killing, female genital mutilation). Barstow not only asks us to contemplate the psychological impact of witch trials on early modern women by her deliberate foregrounding of the sexual sadism of the witch-hunts, made public through the spectacles of executions; she also asks us to come to terms with this fact: "Among the possible meanings of a woman's life in early modern Europe, the most shocking was that she could stand for all that was utterly evil."[67]

This fact—shocking for Barstow, an intellectual commonplace for Clark—came about by many different means. The discourse of witch-hunting was often verbal, emerging in the form of learned treatises, popular pamphlets, sermons, the reading of sentences at trials and executions, and literature such as the plays and masques in the English tradition. It was also visual, in the form of public spectacles surrounding the torture and punishment of accused witches; illustrations for treatises and pamphlets; theatrical designs and costumes; and paintings, prints, and drawings by prominent artists—the subject of my study. A feminist reading of these images, formally and contextually, yields a number of important insights.

First, the images visualize the presumption of woman-as-witch. Until Francisco Goya's rethinking of the genre of witchcraft imagery in the late eighteenth century, misogyny is absolutely central to them, embedded in their style and iconography. Whether the artists themselves were misogynistic or believed fully in witchcraft, their visual rhetoric made the female witch more plausible. Paradoxically, this is true even when the artist seems to take a skeptical stance, because that stance too was based, as we shall see, on a familiar construction of women as inferior in mind and body.[68] By analyzing and exposing this visual rhetoric within specific historical contexts, I hope to contribute to a recovery of an aspect of women's history, with its ties to second-wave feminism, an inherently political endeavor.[69]

Second, a close study of these images—regardless of their individual contexts—reveals the relational nature of gender. They are as much about men as women. They were demonstrably instrumental in creating and sustaining the inventive authority, and thus professional status, of male artists who made them. The male-generated discourses of witch-hunting and art theory colluded with masculine ideals and with male artists' self-fashioning and self-promotion to produce imagery that valorized artistic invention while it denigrated women. Although critics of the postmodern turn from women's to gender history have pointed out the risk it poses to the political force of feminist scholarship centered on women, I believe it ultimately offers a more complex way of understanding power that is profoundly political because it recognizes the reciprocal interdependence of concepts of gender.[70] This approach does not lay the question of misogyny to rest, but, as Hester's remarks suggest, drives it deeper into complex social structures and relationships.

My analyses of groups of artistic images of witches are specific to distinct historical contexts, but they are consolidated under an examination of gender as a constituent of power and of women as a largely disempowered group in the early modern period. Postmodern theory and identity politics have cautioned us not to trust the universalizing category of "woman," and differences among women—whether in terms of age, economic status, or where they lived—certainly affected their vulnerability to witchcraft accusations. Nevertheless, the idea of the diabolical female witch could level economic and ethnic differences. Simply being female—in the wrong half of Clark's pervasive system of contrariety—implied a greater susceptibility to the devil. This is relevant to our own time. Global violence against women today is manifested in culturally specific ways, but it rests on commonly held and deeply rooted patriarchal assumptions of women's subordination to men and men's property in women. Just as these current practices of violence against women cannot be understood fully without recognizing how they depend on and inform notions of masculinity, so the artistic images of witches I analyze here cannot be comprehended without considering why male artists felt compelled to make them.

Artists' Self-Fashioning and the Visual Discourse of Witch-Hunting

The formulation and perpetuation of the discourse of witch-hunting, whether visual or verbal, and engagement in the debate surrounding witchcraft and its appropriate punishment, were male prerogatives. Witchcraft was the most extreme expression of female deviance: a charge levied not against women in general but against women who were imagined as eluding or subverting patriarchal control. As such, the stereotype of the witch represents early modern Europe's profound fear of female deviance.[71] It was the very banality of misogyny, its complete incorporation into the binary patterns of thought so convincingly elucidated by Clark, and its intensification in the late fifteenth century that made the assertions of the demonologists plausible.[72]

Artistic images of witches fostered misogyny, often directly by engaging the debate about the reality of and the appropriate judicial and social response to witchcraft but always more subtly, I argue, by invoking the early modern ideas of artistic creativity as an exclusively male realm. As recent work by feminist art historians has made abundantly clear, women's near-exclusion from this realm was bolstered by art-theoretical constructs and institutional and social constraints. Women artists who gained prominence in the early modern period had to negotiate the chasm between approved gender roles and ideas of artistic creativity.[73] Although my study does not address these struggles directly, the artistic witch must be seen against this background. An embodiment of the undisciplined and dangerous nature of female imagination, curiosity, and bodily desires, she became an index of the inventive capacity, intellect, and thus the heightened status of the male artist in the early modern period, even though her image was handed down within an iconographic tradition. She stood at the intersection of two discourses—both dependent on notions of male intellectual and moral superiority. She displayed male artists' inventiveness in the competitive context of art's relationship to poetry and the status of both as liberal arts. If this rivalry among artists in this context is already gendered, as Clark Hulse makes so clear in his discussion of the circle of Raphael,[74] then the playing out of this rivalry in an arena defined by such images is even more so.

Artistic witches expose their transgressive sexuality and their folly in glances, gestures, poses, and attributes; they cavort with revolting demonic companions and handle unclean substances; and they concoct their brews and spells as negative foils to the male artistic invention that conceived them. Their magic is a debased version of the transformation of matter into art that the early modern artist effected. This is not to say that male artists understood their inventive power as indomitable or that their efforts toward advancement never met obstacles like obtuse or parsimonious patrons. Early modern artists acknowledged the ambivalence of their efforts in the very choice of the subject of witchcraft, so pervaded with the idea of the devil's influence on imagination and fantasy, the faculties believed to generate artistic images. Artists felt their own moral vulnerability in the face of artistic license: Hans Baldung Grien's *Bewitched Groom* and Goya's *Sleep of Reason* echo warnings about the dangers of fantasy repeated frequently in art theory (see figures 3.13 and 7.2).

However, as males believed to have superior moral and intellectual capacities, early modern artists were thought capable of rising above this vulnerability in ways that women were not. The moral and intellectual inferiority of women is repeatedly asserted in an array of early modern visual topoi, from the "Fall of Man" to "Unequal Lovers" to the "Power of Women."[75] Artistic images of witchcraft are, of course, related to these conceits. However, witchcraft's scatological, taboo and uncanny aspects, as well as its topicality and evolving significance during the early modern period, presented extraordinary opportunities for flamboyant displays of artistic invention that often hinged on an extreme degradation of women.

The concept of the grotesque *female* body is extremely important to my argument. Literary critic Mikhail Bakhtin defined François Rabelais's carnivalesque "grotesque realism" as a renewing social force opposing the dominant class and used without hostility toward the objects of his humor, including women. Bakhtin's "grotesque body" was unfinished, open, impure (i.e., dirty or heterogeneous), eccentric, and disproportionate, and it emphasized gaps or orifices and physical urges and pleasures. In contrast to the "classical body" against which it is defined, the grotesque body was continually transgressive, subverting the rule of reason and the closed-off discreteness of the individual and celebrating the connection of the individual to the material world and to other bodies.[76] Although based in class distinctions, Bakhtin's concept corresponds more closely to *women's* bodies than to men's. In menstruating, giving birth, and lactating, women's bodies are inevitably more open, disproportionate, seemingly more beholden to physical necessity.[77] When linked to the understanding of their wombs as hungry, wandering animals and of their moister and colder physiology, women's bodies are readily interpreted as vehicles of disorder, requiring control by an idealizing aesthetic and by social codes and constant surveillance. In the period of the witch-hunts, Accati observes, elite culture turned from the discipline of the grotesque *phallic* body of the medieval peasantry to the discipline of the grotesque *uterine* body.[78]

The many aged witches in art descend from Albrecht Dürer's famous prototype (see figure 3.4) and carry a range of artistic, social, and psychological implications. Margaret Sullivan has discussed Dürer's figure in terms of its relationship to the old bawd witches of ancient poetry, without addressing the misogynistic content of either.[79] Certainly the hag, whether artistic or poetic, ancient or early modern, offered her creator opportunity for inventive license. She also reflected the social marginalization of old women. In fact, accused witches were often elderly, reflecting the disadvantaged social and economic status of old women, resentment of their requests for charity or their insubordinate scolding or complaining.[80] The endurance and prevalence of the hag, however, suggest deeper reasons for her longevity. Charles Zika interprets Dürer's witch persuasively as a symbol of the inversion of gender roles and, more broadly, of social upheaval and disorder; earlier, Charmian Mesenzeva had interpreted her in relation to Aphrodite Pandemos—the earthly Venus signifying lust.[81] Both iconographic explanations, as we shall see in Chapter 3, illuminate the long legacy of Dürer's figure. The aged female form, presented as an inappropriate, indecorous, and disconcerting spectacle, embodied social and moral disruption.

Swiss artist Niklaus Manuel Deutsch's drawing of an old witch (1518, figure 1.1) brilliantly exemplifies this content. The technique of chiaroscuro drawing, with white highlights on tinted paper, carried great panache among Swiss

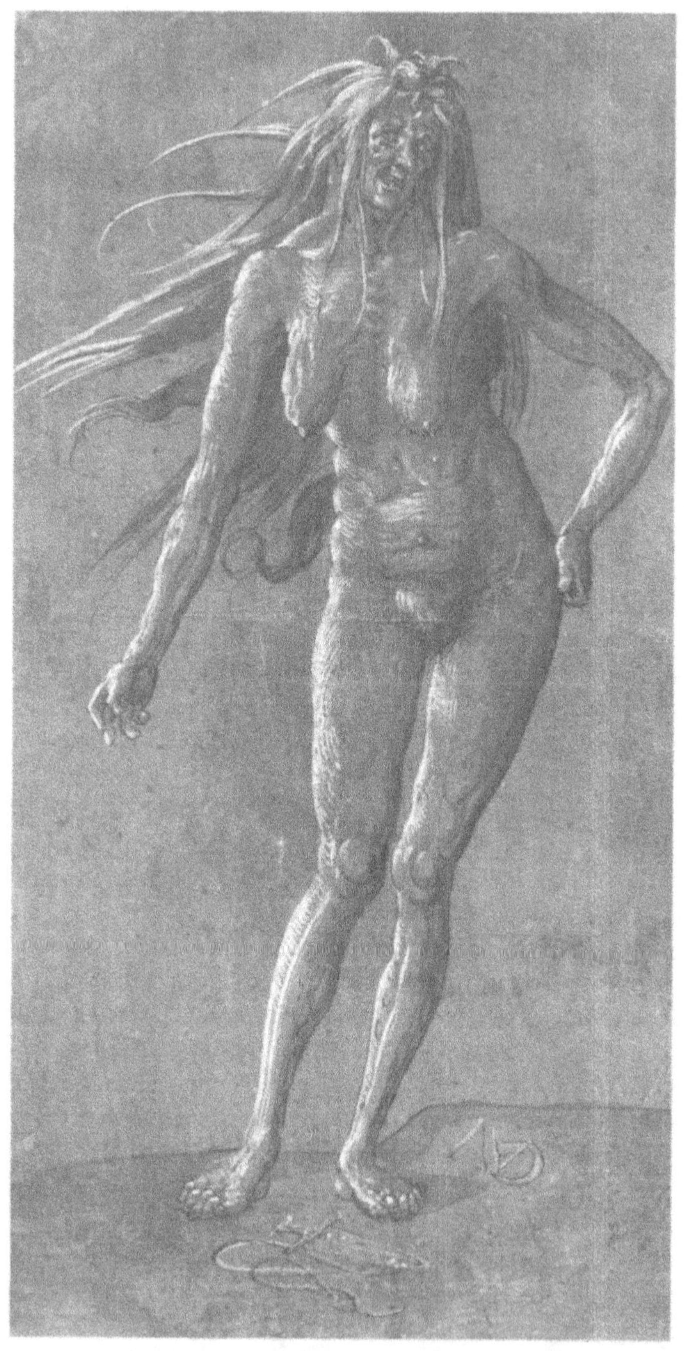

Figure 1.1. Niklaus Manuel Deutsch, *Witch*, ca. 1518. Chiaroscuro pen drawing on red-tinted paper, 276 × 143 mm. Kupferstichkabinett, Staatliche Museen, Berlin. Photo by Jörg P. Anders. Bildarchiv Preußischer Kulturbesitz/Art Resource, New York.

and German artists and collectors, as we shall see. But it is primarily Manuel's subject and his aggressive sabotage of ideal Renaissance form that conveys the audacity of his invention. The witch, her muscular arms betraying her peasant origins, stands in a lurching, hip-shot pose that mocks the chiastic balance and elegant contours we associate with the *contrapposto* stance. We seek but do not find that satisfying vertical axis along which the muscular tensions of the figure are resolved. Instead, Manuel drives his vertical down from the witch's sunken left cheek through her sagging left breast to her navel and pudenda. Along this axis we confront ambiguous bulges, wrinkles, pubic hair no longer curled—in short, the discomforting deterioration of a human body. A symbol of the abject and transgressive, Manuel's hag will not be contained. Her come-on to the viewer is conveyed by her eager glance, coyly inclined head, open mouth with curling tongue, and obscenely cupped hand (as if to grasp a codpiece). Her impact hinges on the preposterousness of her failed attempt at an ideal stance and at sexual seduction. Although her precise identity has been questioned, her wild hair, indecorous sexuality, and grotesque body probably define her as a witch: She descended from Dürer's engraving by way of Hans Baldung Grien's hags (see figures 3.5, 3.7–3.9) and became more grotesque along the way. By 1518, long before large-scale witch-hunts, an iconographic convention for the figure of the witch was established.[82]

Her identity as a witch, though, does not exhaust her meaning, which resides ultimately in her *body*. Perhaps no other artist illustrates the use of the female body as a vehicle of disorder and disruption more consistently than Dürer's pupil Baldung, whose prints and drawings influenced Manuel and whose work vastly expanded the artistic potential of the witchcraft theme.[83] Baldung's *Woman Walking on Balls*, a chiaroscuro drawing on brown-tinted paper done around 1514 or 1515, is not readily seen as a witch or even a goddess like Venus or Fortuna (figure 1.2).[84] Baldung conflated these iconographic conceits into a quintessential embodiment of the instability of female nature. The figure's weight is displaced disconcertingly to walking sticks and to the male child who props up her buttocks. Her grasp on the sticks is infirm; her limbs—swastika-like—deny us the centered vertical axis we instinctively seek. Her lowered head, hunched shoulders, disheveled hair, and expression of intense concentration convey the painful difficulty and ultimate futility of her effort.

Another of Baldung's drawings, even more closely related to his witch images, depicts a woman seated on the ground, defecating (figure 1.3). Carl Koch, who catalogued Baldung's drawings, emphasized the artist's naturalism in this work, but I would argue that other expressive and symbolic imperatives trump mimesis here.[85] Unlike Jacques Callot's *Defecating Peasant* (see figure 2.7), Baldung's woman combines the scatological with an explicit sexuality and bodily instability. Resting uncomfortably on her left hip and with uncertain support from her left limbs, the woman shifts her buttocks toward us so both

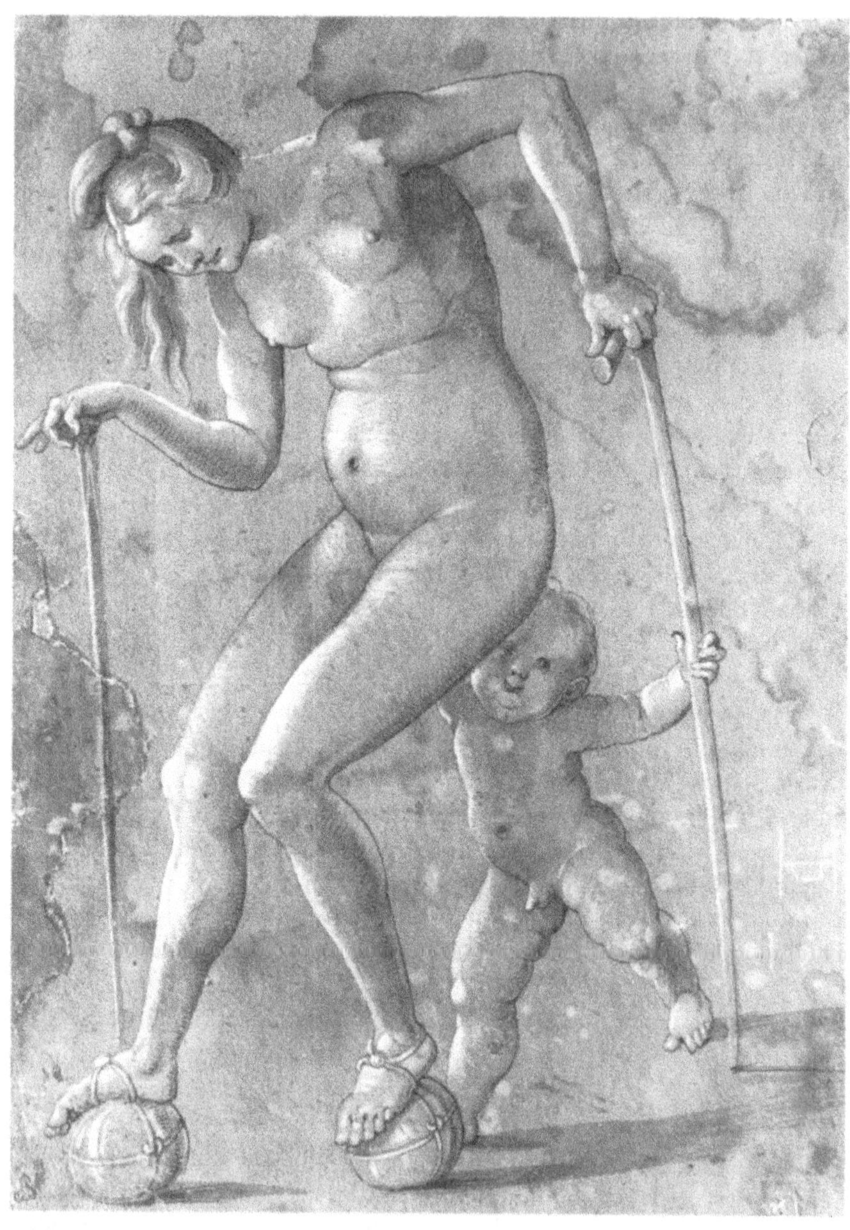

Figure 1.2. Hans Baldung Grien, *Woman Walking on Balls*, ca. 1514–15. Chiaroscuro pen drawing on brown-tinted paper, 270 × 195 mm. Albertina Museum, Vienna.

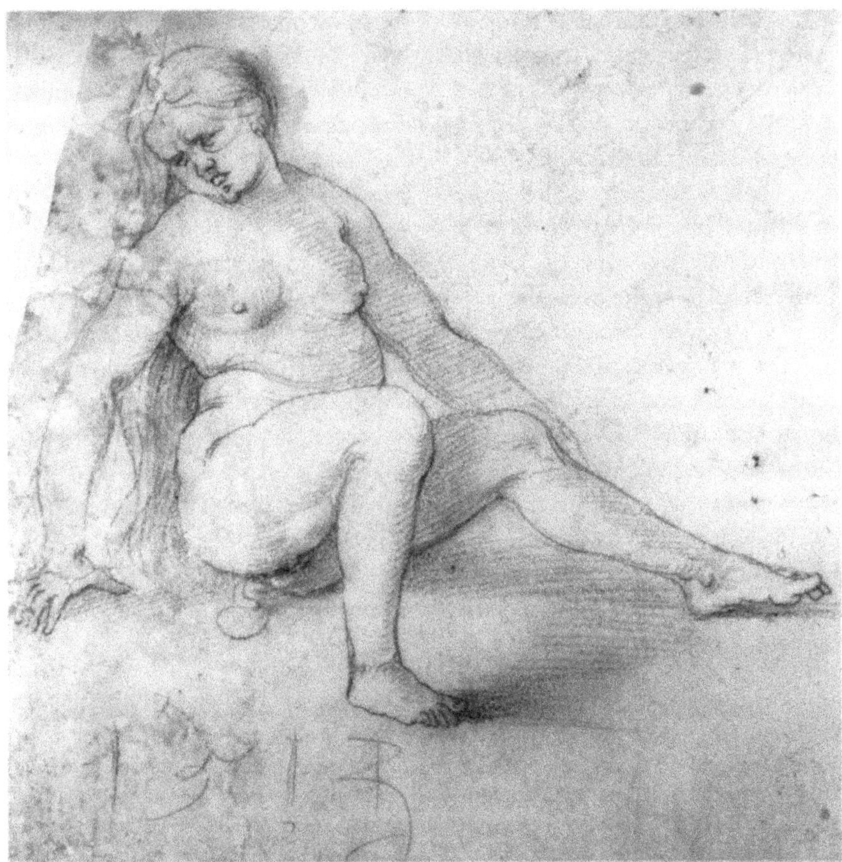

Figure 1.3. Hans Baldung Grien, *Seated Woman Defecating*, 1513. Red chalk drawing, 199 × 199 mm. Kupferstichkabinett, Staatliche Museen, Berlin. Photo by Jörg P. Anders. Bildarchiv Preußischer Kulturbesitz/Art Resource, New York.

anus and vagina are visible. Her face shows distress; the contours of her body are persistently lumpy.

Figures like these may be theorized in both anthropological and psychoanalytic terms. In *Purity and Danger: An Analysis of the Concepts of Pollution and Taboo* (1966), Mary Douglas focused on the need of even highly complex societies (such as those of Renaissance Europe) to set boundaries between clean and dirty, acceptable and taboo, to preserve the status quo. Of its own accord, nothing is dirty or polluted; rather, these are social concepts signaling disruption of some arbitrary order and capable of being represented by bodies or orifices, bodily fluids or excretions.[86] In *The Powers of Horror: An Essay on Abjection* (1982), Julia Kristeva defined abjection in psychoanalytic terms as the process by which individuals separate themselves from the formless, fluid maternal body and emerge as discrete social beings. But the abject is not only that which threatens the boundaries of the individual by evoking the dread of maternal reabsorption, it is also that which "disturbs identity, system, order. What does not respect borders, positions, rules. The in-between, the ambiguous, the composite."[87] The abject is seized upon by civilizations to "build themselves up and function."[88]

I believe that these ahistorical and universalizing concepts are insufficient in themselves to interpret history or images.[89] Combined with specific historical and contextual analysis, however, they help to provide a more complete understanding of the European witch-hunts and why women were their prime targets. The polar opposite of the good housewife and mother intent on keeping dirt at bay, the witch, in Hélène Cixous and Catherine Clément's terms, revels in impurity: "She handles filth, manipulates waste, buries placentas, and burns the caul."[90] Her unabashed, even eager, contact with corpses—the "utmost of abjection," the "most sickening of wastes"—reveals the fear of social chaos and individual dissolution embodied by the witch.[91] Purkiss subtly elucidates how witchcraft itself was a set of activities focused on the dissolving of boundaries and of "counter-exchanges between bodies" that struck at the need for discreteness and for strictly enforced demarcation of the body, the home, the polity:

> Magic and its remedies deal with borders, markers, distinctions, insides and outsides, the limits of bodies, and also what breaches those boundaries; bodily fluids, exchanges of objects through bodies and across thresholds, words that pass through the guard of the ear and enter the mind of the hearer. Women's bodies, by virtue of their reproductive capacities, are seen as more open, more grotesque, less autonomous. The identification of the embarrassing and boundless body with the feminine may be one of the constants of western culture.[92]

Paradoxically, the fear of the witch's formlessness and fluidity also manifested itself in notions of the hardness and dryness of her body—especially the old, withered body of the hag—that must be pricked or otherwise invaded to break her invasive magical power. The witch's inability to cry (tears being a nonpolluting bodily fluid because of their cleansing function[93]) and the failure of insensitive devil's marks to bleed were, like her capacity to breach the bodies and spaces of others, invitations to a violence drastically exceeding what was necessary for mere social control. Beyond the many specific historical factors affecting witch-hunting, the witch seems to have evoked the terror of losing one's self to a controlling and uncontrollable other body.[94]

This is why it may be persuasively argued in psychoanalytic terms that the relentlessly antimaternal figure of the witch expressed the overpowering maternal body, both desired and feared. Witches were thought to focus their vehement hatred of society on procreation, which they sabotaged relentlessly by interfering with conception, successful pregnancies and births, lactation, and the precarious health of young children, or by stealing infants to cannibalize or sacrifice to the devil. The bizarre English notion of the witch's familiar, suckling at some false "teat" to gain nourishment from blood (impure milk in early modern thinking) perversely parodied the nurturing relationship between mother and infant. The witch's body is conceived of as a "poison bag," in Purkiss's words, highlighting the vulnerability of the female body to pollution and focusing the social and psychological anxieties surrounding lactation.[95]

The hag, then, may be understood on historical, anthropological, and psychoanalytic levels, but how should we theorize the application of idealizing aesthetic codes to the figure of the witch, as in the striking nudes of Baldung's *Weather Witches* or the elegantly dressed initiates of Frans Francken II's paintings (see figures 3.12; 4.2–4.4)? Such witches gain their meaning from comparison with hags. The beauty of the witch is deceptive: Underneath lurks the grotesque body of the crone with her implications of social disorder, formlessness, and loss of self. Beautiful witches are defiled by their surroundings, by the polluting substances or creatures they handle, and by the taboo activities in which they engage—all of which signify the suspect, corrupt nature of their beauty. For early modern men, as Gareth Roberts has explored, they evoked the danger of Circean seduction, transformation, and emasculation.[96] The Circean witch's ideal form, like that of Ariosto's Alcina or Spenser's Duessa, is inherently unstable, lapsing into the grotesque to reveal her inner corruption (Ariosto, *Orlando Furioso*, 7.70–74; Spenser, *Faerie Queene*, 8.48). It is the male artist's or poet's capacity either to create (in the form of the female grotesque) or to control (in the form of the idealized nude) matter, without being affected by its corruption or its seductive beauty, that is at issue. As Hulse argues, to succeed in this mastery of the matter of nature is to "resist the feminine," to "become one of the makers or remakers in the course of artistic progress."[97] Whether grotesque or beautiful, the witch's body becomes a particularly charged locus for the display of artistic prowess.

In his discussion of the waning of witchcraft beliefs in England, Ian Bostridge makes the important point that the theory of witchcraft expressed in texts, the actual persecutions, and private belief are three variables that are not necessarily connected and should not be confused.[98] Similarly, artistic images of witches may relate to the texts (and I attempt to demonstrate that relationship in a number of instances) without necessarily defining the artist's private belief or disbelief in witches, or commenting on contemporary persecutions, although at times the alignment of artists with beliefs may be plausibly argued. Moreover, belief and disbelief about witchcraft, as Clark has emphasized, are false polarities: In the early modern period, it is far more accurate to think of varying combinations of credulity and skepticism within the overarching premises of a demonological view of nature.[99]

The way that witchcraft images functioned for early modern artists as displays of invention helps to make their private beliefs especially problematic, although one can sometimes deduce reasonable conclusions about those beliefs from contextual and iconographic analyses. Stephen Greenblatt's concept of literary self-fashioning—those complex social negotiations performed by a writer given the powerful institutions and individuals on which his status and livelihood depended—also proves extremely useful for understanding the motivations and career paths of visual artists.[100] Because they addressed, albeit provocatively or ambivalently at times, a problem that was of great concern to many educated segments of early modern society(physicians, lawyers, judges, theologians, humanists, rulers(images of witches could link artists to these sources of power, prestige, and patronage. Moreover, precisely because witchcraft and its punishment were not viewed with agreement, such images were ideally suited to fulfill what Hulse calls the "ritualized group consumption" of works of art, in which they become meaningful by a "rhetorical process" guided by learned commentary on both their subject matter and on art.[101]

Images of witchcraft helped male artists enhance their status by proving their imaginative and intellectual prowess to peers or superiors and by aligning themselves with the rhetorical and political strategies of elite groups or individuals. Just like the witches of Elizabethan and Jacobean theater, artistic witches tell us more about their creators' professional and social aspirations and their audience's expectations—about the differences between urban and rural people, for example—than about how witchcraft was understood at the level of the populace.[102] The paraphernalia surrounding witches may sometimes inform us about actual magical practices at the folk level, but the primary insight we gain from the images is a greater understanding of the discursive pressures that shaped the consciousness, experience, and actions of early modern people.

With the exception of Goya, whose *Caprichos* (see figures 7.2, 7.5–7.14) perhaps made a bid for recognition and patronage from the Duchess of Osuna and other prominent women of the Spanish Enlightenment, the images I discuss were primarily aimed at male audiences. Dürer wanted to address an elite male audience with his early engravings, including those about witches (see figures 3.2, 3.4), and beginning with Baldung, a tradition of intimate, often erotic drawings of witches that were intended for a small group of male friends develops (see figures 3.7–3.10). Jacques de Gheyn II's drawings of witches may also have functioned this way, not so much for their eroticism but for their articulation of the intellectual aspects of the witchcraft debate in the Northern Netherlands (see figures 5.1, 5.3–5.5, 5.9–5.12). Baldung also offers us what may be the first extant cabinet painting of witches in his Frankfurt panel (see figure 3.12). Such a provocative, meticulously painted work, we may surmise, would have been seen primarily by privileged visitors to the unknown owner's collection. In a typically candid letter by seventeenth-century artist Salvator Rosa, we learn about the value of such works—for example, his spectacular canvas now in the National Gallery in London (see figure fig. 6.10)—as esteemed and titillating curiosities within a collection. Although we have no such evidence about Francken's equally spectacular paintings, we can draw reasonable conclusions about how they fit within contemporary collections. Because his paintings are related to Habsburg antiwitchcraft decrees, their reception by elite Habsburg subjects who delighted in the particular visual and intellectual values of Antwerp art is a crucial question.

Early modern images of witches were made by men mostly for men, but audiences could hardly be so restricted in practice, especially for the cheaper, circulating graphic media (woodcut, engraving, etching), sold, for example, at the Frankfurt trade fair.[103] If only incidentally, early modern women must have encountered artistic images that corroborated the view of witchcraft more publicly espoused in sermons, trials, executions, and theatrical productions. Like Barstow, I would ask readers of my study to contemplate the impact of such negative stereotypes on early modern women and their cumulative legacy over time. In doing so, we may well empathize with women's self-preserving need to distance themselves from witchcraft by cultivating socially endorsed qualities or by projecting its evil onto *other* women—women of a different economic class or religious confession; women without proper Christian virtues. The divisive and isolating effect of the concept of witchcraft on women becomes clear.

Stopping short of Murray or Michelet, some scholars would still argue for the possibility that witchcraft functioned positively as a subversive and empowering concept for early modern women. Indeed, some thoughtful current scholarship tries to recover the agency of accused witches by suggesting how witchcraft could serve as an outlet for women's fantasies and desires or a means of acquiring status and power within a society that offered women few options.[104] Obviously, this is not a direction I can reasonably pursue in this study of artistic images produced by men and functioning within a larger network of antifeminist discursive rhetoric, practices, and institutions. My material is even more constrained in this regard than the trial records and confessions—often edited, coerced, or otherwise compromised—that historians use; in those historical texts, women's voices are sometimes audible, if only faintly. The artistic images tell us mainly about *men's* agency. But beyond the inherent limitations of my material, my broader research on the European witch-hunts has convinced me that any empowerment offered by the persona of witch in the early modern period was severely constrained, and that modern women who fashion the historical witch to suit their own needs are misguided. "In thus helping ourselves," Purkiss states, "we are silencing early modern women anew."[105]

The witch was the ultimate "disorderly woman," but she was fundamentally different from the cuckolding wife or the thieving prostitute in her embodiment of pure evil. In her important essay of 1975, "Women on Top," historian Natalie Zemon Davis recognized a subversive potential for social rebellion and political change within the "disorderly woman's" temporary rule during carnival. She also noted, however, that carnivalesque inversion reinforced the social norms it challenged, and extreme or ferocious representations of disorderly women "preclude fanciful release from, or criticism of, hierarchy."[106] The witch symbolized disorder in extremis, a construction too heinous and vile to function effectively as social critique.

I attempt to read artistic images of witches first in terms of concepts of witchcraft and the history of witch-hunting in specific contexts. But because witch-hunting was an extreme alternative within a spectrum of social controls of women, I also interpret the images more broadly, considering women's roles in any given society. Although, as already noted, witchcraft accusations account for a small percentage of criminal procedures against women in the early modern period, they paralleled an increase in more mundane criminal procedures that *were* undeniably sex-specific, like prostitution and infanticide. The burden of attempts by religious and secular authorities to monitor all forms of sexual behavior in the early modern period fell disproportionately on women.[107]

Early modern societies were determined to regulate many aspects of women's behavior, but the prosecution of witchcraft was a means of control with a demonstrably deadly impact, as Monter noted his in his groundbreaking essay of 1977, "The Pedestal and the Stake: Courtly Love and Witchcraft"[108] Visual art in the early modern period was frequently complicit in the social control of women, not only in the way it presented them in portraits, genre, or religious scenes but also in the way it excluded them from increasingly exalted notions about how art is created. Witchcraft images participate in the doubly antifeminist, reciprocal relationship of male artistic creativity and feminine evil.

Chapter 2
The Witch as Muse

Testing the Limits of Albertian Invention

A constant question in early modern debates about witchcraft concerns the role of imagination and fantasy. These terms for faculties of the human brain that stored sensory impressions and generated thoughts and images were often used synonymously, although fantasy was generally understood as more active and liable to moral corruption.[1] Not only were imagination and fantasy vulnerable to demonic influence in terms of the ideas or images they produced, but also by manipulating the forces of nature (for example, by thickening the air they were made of to produce an illusion), demons could delude unwary humans. This was especially true for women, who lacked the moral strength to resist the sensory appetites and the intellectual capacity to discern illusion from reality—hence the predominance of female witches. Along with danger, however, imagination and fantasy held tremendous power for the male poet or artist. During the early modern period, the value lent to these faculties fluctuated, and there was always a sense of accompanying moral vulnerability, but in general they were ascendant. If properly harnessed, guided, and displayed, the inspiration they provided the early modern poet or artist could be a key to recognition, status, and success.

As a subject already saturated with the notion of corrupted fantasy, witchcraft provided a way for male artists to displace fears about their own vulnerability onto women and to display their control of this unruly beast. In this chapter, I trace how witchcraft images fit within the gendered discourse of artistic creativity in the early modern period. Although they obviously contain some natural elements—humans, animals, landscape—they also contain grotesque distortions of nature and demonic, fantastic forms only tenuously related to what an artist could observe. Thus, perhaps the most "progressive" aspect of this imagery in art-theoretical terms is its critique of the idea that nature is the artist's primary resource: the basis for artistic practice and theory in the fifteenth century as expressed by Leonbattista Alberti (*De pictura*, On painting, 1435, and its Italian translation, *Della pittura*, in 1436).[2] For Alberti, nature was the artist's foundation, but mere imitation was not enough. Nature had to be brought into conformity with higher ideals of beauty, defined in terms of harmony of proportion, although Alberti does not make clear exactly what capacity, beyond practice and training, enables the artist to do this.[3] There is no place in Albertian theory for the grotesque, incorporating bizarre, fantastic, and even frightening elements, and related to but going beyond the ornamental *grotteschi* developed by Renaissance artists from Roman precedents.[4]

Similarly, Alberti does not accommodate imagination. His insistence on the intellectual basis of art and its relationship to poetry and rhetoric was revolutionary but not licentious. As Anthony Blunt characterized it, Alberti's view of art was not defined only by rationalism, classicism, scientific method, and faith in nature but also by the absence of imagination.[5] For Alberti, a work of art is generated through invention (*invenzione*) thoroughly bound up with narratives, or *istorie*, with a distinctly humanistic and literary character. In Book Three of *Della pittura*, Alberti advises the painter to seek the company of poets and orators "who have many embellishments in common with painters and who have a broad knowledge of many things. These could be very useful in beautifully composing the *istoria* whose greatest praise consists in the invention." Poets and other learned men "will give new inventions" or at least help the painter compose the *istoria* on which his renown depends.[6]

Early modern witchcraft imagery is Albertian in that it depends heavily on artists' connection to men of letters, both ancient and contemporary. Witchcraft was not only a current topic debated by theologians, judges, physicians, and political theorists, but—as Margaret Sullivan has emphasized—it was sanctioned as a literary subject by ancient poets: Homer, Theocritus, Horace, Propertius, Ovid, Lucan, Lucian, Apuleius, and others.[7] However, early modern images of witches repeatedly go well beyond any straightforward relationship to particular authors or texts, and thus beyond Alberti. For him, a painter's originality in composing an *istoria* did not consist of making up the subject. He was not an *auctor* (author or originator), a Latin term that relates to *auctoritas*, meaning decision or power. Rather, he finds convincing, beautiful (harmonious) and new ways to depict the subject, and he develops suitable allegorical figures to personify the theme's edifying message. Alberti illustrates this process with Lucian's famous *ekphrasis* of a painting symbolizing calumny (unjust accusation) by the Greek artist Apelles (*De calumnia* 5).[8] In the second half of the fifteenth century, artists challenged the limitations of Alberti's concepts. At the same time, his rational idea of beauty was compromised by the acknowledgment of varying notions of what was beautiful and by the validation of the grotesque as an artistic concern. The role of the artist's inner faculties—imagination and fantasy along with his innate ability or *ingenium*—began to vie with the imitation of nature as the dominant force in making art. The artist's status as *auctor* in the invention of subject matter began to be asserted.

We can perceive the beginnings of this last development in late fifteenth-century works of art. For instance, in his *Calumny of Apelles* in the Uffizi Museum (mid or late 1490s?), Alessandro Botticelli took up Alberti's challenge to produce an allegorical work whose effectiveness depends on his ability to make poses, gestures, attributes, and setting express the content of the story powerfully and clearly. But Botticelli—exceptionally sensitive to the visual expression of classical *ekphrases*—also enhanced Lucian's conception to make the invention his own.[9] He devised complex relief sculptures for *Calumny*'s basilican setting that enhanced the story's moral about the evil of unjust accusation and the need for rulers to exercise good judgment.[10] Additionally, he may have referred to contemporary events. If the painting dates from the late 1490s, it may allude to the downfall of Savanarola, or, as Ronald Lightbown has suggested, to some calumny that the artist himself suffered.[11] In either case, the ancient theme of calumny was brought up to date. In this sense at least, Botticelli himself was *auctor*, even though he was not a humanist and he relied frequently on the advice of humanists.[12] Moreover, the painting was not commissioned but seems to have been a kind of demonstration of the artist's inventive ability given as a gift to his friend Antonio Segni.

This well-known example from Botticelli's oeuvre is a sign of the rethinking of Albertian invention in the late fifteenth century, an insistence on the artist's original contributions to a theme or his own development of new themes. Andrea Mantegna, who provided such an important model for Dürer, exemplified this insistence as well as the use of printmaking as a vehicle for invention. Evelyn Lincoln has suggested that Mantegna patterned his career after that of the successful and erudite court physician of Ferrara, Michele Savanarola, fashioning himself as a supreme artistic inventor within the Gonzaga court of Mantua. He seized on printmaking to extend his fame and elude the restrictions of court patronage.[13] Mantegna's status as unrivaled inventor was confirmed by contemporaries like Lorenzo di Pavia, agent of Isabella d'Este.[14] The *Battle of the Sea Gods* engraving, datable to the 1470s or 1480s, is an especially useful invention for our purposes (figure 2.1).

One of the seven engravings taken by some scholars to be by Mantegna himself, the *Battle* is elaborate and large, printed from two plates. It conspicuously recalls antique reliefs in the sculptural character of its figures and the orientation of its composition to the surface plane.[15] The sea gods fight frenetically but ineffectually, flailing their fish, clubs, and bones in a swamp like unruly children in a bathtub. Lightbown has aptly described the scene as a "mock tourney" and interprets it as a satire of envy, one of Mantegna's preoccupations.[16] Michael Jacobsen has suggested passages in Strabo's *Geography* (14.2, 10.3) dealing with the Telchines, Rhodian sculptors who were notoriously envious and spiteful, as Mantegna's source. The grotesque hag personifying *Invidia* reigns in triumph over their watery tumult.[17] The god Neptune, how-

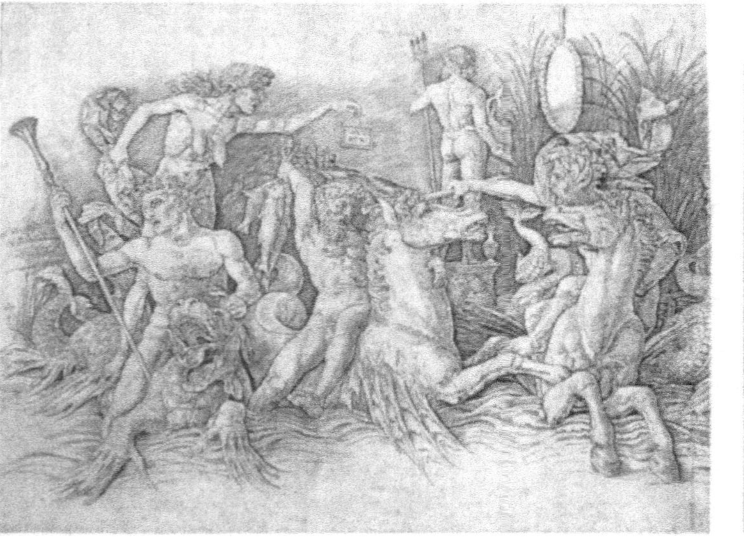
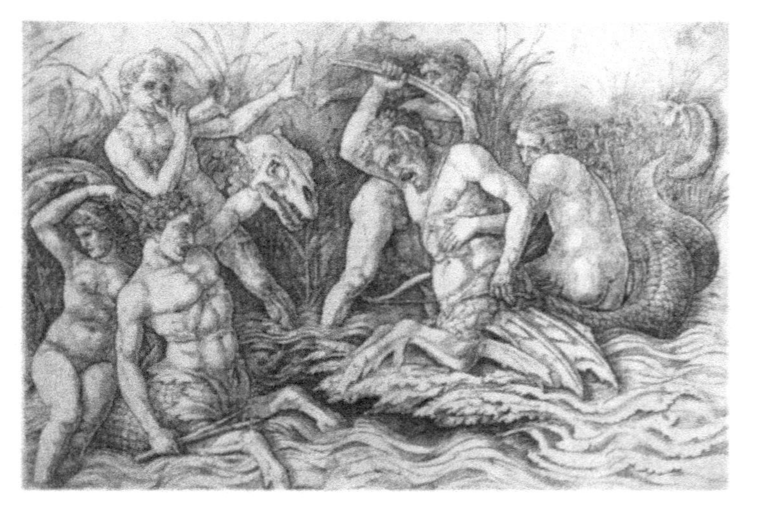

Figure 2.1. Andrea Mantegna, *The Battle of the Sea Gods*, ca. 1475–80. Engraving from two plates, 330 × 431 mm (left half); 268 × 393 mm (right half). © The Cleveland Museum of Art, 2004. Gift of Ralph King, 1924.222, 1924.221.

ever, in the form of a sculpture incongruously placed on a pedestal in a swamp, turns his back on the absurd melee.

More recently, Patricia Emison has viewed the print not so much as a satire on the vice of envy but as a *psychomachia*: a battle between vice, represented by the sea monsters, and virtue, represented by the dolphins (one held by Neptune and one in the water). The theme, she argues, comes from a general context of humanistic allegorical meaning but is not bound rigidly to any text in an Albertian sense. It is Mantegna's invention, although Emison speculates that perhaps Alberti himself could have advised the painter.[18] Given Mantegna's erudition and conscious cultivation of status, though, consultation with Alberti seems unnecessary. *The Battle of the Sea Gods* is Mantegna's bravado display of figural invention, antiquarian knowledge, and burlesque humor. Its allegory, whether it is related to an ancient text or drawn from the humanist vocabulary of symbols, has been redefined in personal terms, as a reference to the envy directed toward him as the reigning north Italian artist. Underneath the main inscription on *Invidia*'s plaque is a mysterious script similar, Jacobsen speculates, to the astrological signs of melancholy, which was beginning to define the exalted nature of artistic creation.[19] As a prestigious artist whose draftsmanship was instantly recognizable and coveted by collectors (the engravings in a sense were substitutes for original pen drawings), Mantegna had little reason to sign his prints.[20] The image itself bore many signs of the artist's unique *ingenium*—credited to poets in antiquity but only beginning to be applied to visual artists. Only Mantegna could be construed as "author" of the particular marriage of form and content evident in *Battle of the Sea Gods*. It is not surprising that Dürer quoted the figure of *Invidia* when he composed *The Witch* (see figure 3.4; ca. 1500–01), because this engraving, like Mantegna's *Battle*, also wittily proclaims the artist's enviable inventive power.

Antonio del Pollaiuolo's *Battle of the Nudes*, perhaps ca. 1470, arguably the most important Italian print of the fifteenth century, is similar to Mantegna's *Battle* but is even more aggressive in its assertion of artist as author (figure 2.2). As if inspired by Alberti's exhortation to artists to seek the company of poets and orators, art historians have searched tirelessly for a literary source for this remarkable image. Is it derived from the story of Jason and the Golden Fleece, from Roman legends, or, most plausibly, from accounts of Roman gladiatorial combat?[21] Emison's interpretation of the print's subject is more convincing than earlier efforts because she recognizes Pollaiuolo's essential freedom from any textual source. She argues that Pollaiuolo constructs himself as author by inventing an allegory centering on the chain held by the two gladiators at the center. The nuances of meaning following from the relationship of the Latin *vincio, vincire* (to fetter or chain), and *vinco, vincere* (to conquer) inform the entire image. The grimacing gladiators, bound to their own flesh

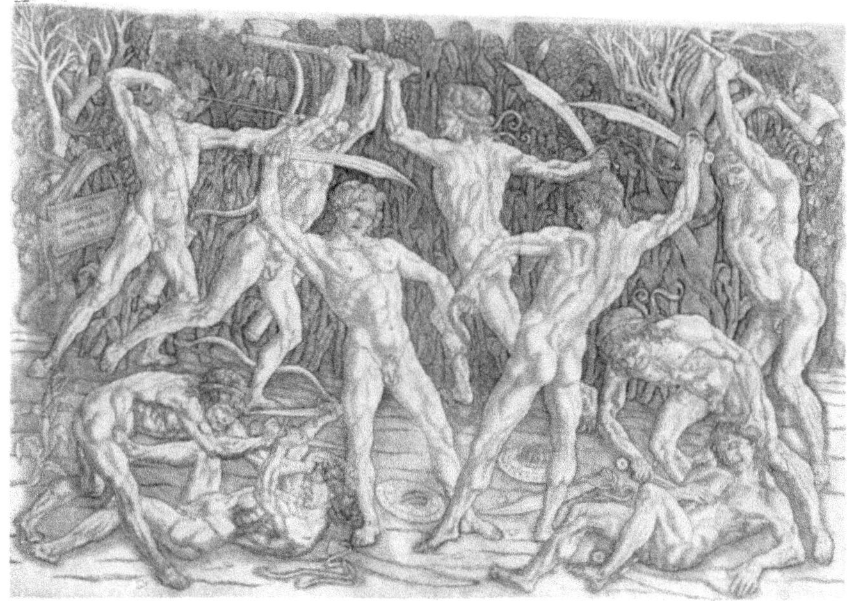

Figure 2.2. Antonio del Pollaiuolo, *The Battle of the Nudes*, ca. 1470–75. Engraving, 420 × 604 mm. © The Cleveland Museum of Art, 2004. Purchase from the J. H. Wade Fund, 1967.127.

and their imminent mortality, are signs of a spiritual vacuum we must rise above with the aid of Christ whose blood is represented by the grapes in the background.[22] In contrast to Mantegna and despite the exaggeratedly muscular, struggling nudes that were his trademark, Pollaiuolo ensured recognition among his learned audience by signing his Latinized name and city proudly on a prominent *tabula ansata*.[23] It was certainly Pollaiuolo's bravado display of anatomical rendering that made this engraving so popular, and hence so rare—only one example of its first state exists.[24] Some of the print's popularity may also have been due to its provocation of discussion and argument regarding meaning. For Dürer, who signed his *Four Witches* (1497; see figure 3.2) not only with a monogram but also with the discussion-provoking conundrum, "O.G.H.," Pollaiuolo's assertion of authorship must have been equally appealing as his representation of the male nude.

The Albertian concept of invention would also undergo revisions in the theoretical writings of the late quattrocento. Leonardo da Vinci at once perfected the mimesis developed in the fifteenth-century Italian tradition and acknowledged a new, more powerful role for imagination and fantasy. His thinking is foreshadowed in Antonio Filarete's treatise on architecture (1464), which in turn had a precocious precedent in Cennino Cennini's *Libro dell'arte* (Book on art), published in Florence or Padua in the early fifteenth century.

Both translate Dante Alighieri's valorization of poetic imagination into the visual arts.[25] To argue for the painter's license, Cennini paraphrased Horace's comparison of poetry and painting in the opening of the *Ars poetica* (see below). Filarete, in turn, interpreted fantasy as a pervasive factor in architectural design: It generates the architect's initial idea and extends and complements his intellect as he completes the design. In painting and sculpture as well, fantasy is also a necessary component of invention, offering miraculous insight into truth and beauty.[26]

Whereas Alberti had virtually excluded imagination from invention, Leonardo wedded the two. Within the context of his anatomical speculations, he relocated the faculty of imagination from the first ventricle of the brain, where sensory impressions were thought to be gathered, to the second, thus making imagination work along with, rather than prior to, the intellective faculty of the second ventricle. This revision of Aristotelian theory, Martin Kemp explains, provided Leonardo with an anatomical foundation for his art-theoretical bonding of imagination and intellect.[27] Moreover, Leonardo's notion of invention was much less literary than Alberti's, emphasizing content *and* form. In his notebooks we find an insistence on the painter's ability to create new forms from the teeming fullness of his imagination. His mental capacity to conceive whatever exists physically *or* imaginatively precedes the skill of his hands.[28] The painter's mental conception engaging fantasy and imagination and intellect comes before the execution of the work of art, as the poet's mental conception comes before the words are written.

As Kemp notes, Leonardo's claims for the infinitude of the painter's works rests rather uneasily with his claims for the infinite variety of nature.[29] Even this latter claim is important for our purposes. Unlike Alberti's, Leonardo's thought offered a place in art for natural forms that were less than ideal. His sense that there were many types of beauty and that nature, as the artist's main guide, offered infinite models and formal possibilities undermines the privileged position of ideal form and harmony within Albertian theory.

We find parallels to Leonardo's views in Dürer's art-theoretical writings, in particular the "aesthetic excursis" at the end of the third book of his *Four Books on Human Proportion*, translated into Latin by his friend Joachim Camerarius in the early 1530s. Although, as Erwin Panofsky noted, the earlier influence of Neoplatonic concepts of the divine nature of artistic creativity had been dampened by 1523, when Dürer, now a devotee of Martin Luther, began reworking earlier schema for his art-theoretical writings and rethinking their contents, the aesthetic excursis still lends the artist considerable freedom. It interiorizes and mystifies the process of making a work of art insofar as piety permits. There is a place in art for the coarse, the ugly, and the monstrous. In his quest for true beauty (which only God can know), the artist relies not simply on rational selection but on an inward intuition that also enabled him to bring forth "new creatures" at will—without the use of natural models.[30] This painting "out of one's head" (*aus der Vernunft*) is replenished by the study of nature, so that—to use Dürer's wonderful phrase—"the stored-up secret treasure of the heart" (*versammlet heimlich Schatz des Herzens*) brings forth new creatures. The great artist's gift is so miraculous that his smallest, rapidly executed sketch is more highly valued (not in monetary terms but in the judgment of those who understand true art) than a big work, labored over for a long time by a less-gifted artist.[31]

Such emphasis on the artist's giftedness and the inwardness of his creative process would become keynotes within sixteenth-century art theory. The early Renaissance notion of invention had begun as the artist's ability to give vivid and varied form to subjects borrowed from the Bible, ancient literature, history and mythology, or contemporary humanism. Toward the end of the fifteenth century, as we have seen, artists began to assert their ability to generate their own subjects; in effect, the artist became an author with images rather than words. Tempered by deep respect for nature as the foremost artistic teacher and a pious desire not to usurp God's privilege to create new things, that artistic authorship became progressively more licentious in the course of the sixteenth century.

The Rise of Fantasy, the License of Ancient Poetry, and Witchcraft

The constant reference to ancient theories of psychology, rhetoric, and poetry in early modern art theory not only elevated the status of visual art by giving it the legitimacy of a theoretical framework borrowed from the ancients but also contributed a larger vocabulary to describe the making of art. Sixteenth-century writers and artists enlisted terms like fantasy and *ingenium* to construct art making as inherently mystical and inimitable. Both imagination and fantasy referred to the mental processing and synthesizing of sensory perceptions that could produce images exceeding the variations and irregularities visible in nature, or entirely new, chimeric forms. Although imagination tended to remain in the realm of general psychology during the Renaissance, fantasy came to be associated with poetic and artistic creation, which in turn took on greater volatility and moral danger along with glory.

Fantasy also came to be allied with the Renaissance concept of artist's melancholy, the development of which is another index of the increasing valorization of artistic creativity during the early modern period. In fact, this study begins and ends with artists—Dürer and Francisco Goya—whose understanding of artist's melancholy contributed to their artistic ambitions and their choice of subjects. As we shall explore further, melancholy was a gendered concept, allowing elite males to assert their productive mastery of bodily humors (and indeed of the body itself and the material world) through the faculty of reason. It defined them over and against women, who lacked such mastery and whose melancholy was unproductive; indeed, melancholy was often thought to afflict female witches. For those males who constructed their subjectivity in terms of this disorder, Juliana Schiesari has argued, the loss of and unrequited desire for the unknowable object that constituted melancholy were made to reflect *back* on the melancholic ego that then represented itself in terms of this privileged loss, distinguished from the mere mourning or sadness associated with women.[32] In his illuminating discussion of Robert Burton's *Anatomy of Melancholy* (begun in 1620 and continually expanded until Burton's death in 1640), Mark Breitenberg argues convincingly for the pervasive significance of the concept for early modern culture. In essence, melancholy was a form of femininity that threatened dissolution and against which masculinity—in the form of individuals, institutions, or the polity—continually defended and defined itself.[33]

Melancholy as a disorder of elite males implied a higher order of being: an innate, heightened sensitivity and insight. Both invention and fantasy as well were related to the artist's *ingegno* or *ingenium* ("natural capacity" in Latin). *Ingenium* was understood as an innate God-given creative capacity—as opposed to skills that could be taught (*ars*)—accessible to us through an artist's style, which carries an *aria* or *aura* unmistakably pointing to him alone.[34] Initially associated with the sensed presence of an individual, as in a portrait, *aria*, when transferred to individual artistic style, implied the mystique, charisma, and inimitability of genius. Michelangelo, of course, was the ultimate exemplar of all of these terms. In the art-theoretical discourse surrounding Michelangelo we find evidence of the increasing importance of the notions of melancholy, genius, *aura*, the divine origins of artistic creativity, and fantastic invention in a grotesque mode as a confirmation of these. The language surrounding Michelangelo's art, analyzed in depth by Summers, is derived not only from the artist's own sonnets but from biographers Giorgio Vasari, whose *Lives* of 1568 included an expanded account of Michelangelo's career, and Ascanio Condivi, whose book was supposedly dictated by the master himself. In addition, Francisco de Hollanda wrote a dialogue in 1548 that may record Michelangelo's attitudes toward art, and Vincenzo Danti's treatise on proportion of 1567 touches on those attitudes as well.[35] A key concept is Michelangelo's *terribilità* (fearsomeness or awfulness), associated by Vasari not only with grandeur but also with awe-inspiring virtuosity and superabundant invention.[36]

This prodigious vision of artistic creativity incorporating the fantastic and the grotesque was supported by ancient poetic examples, particularly satire and invective. In his *Ars poetica* (19–18 B.C.E.), Horace establishes the wide range of the poet's concerns and, in two significant passages, asserts the relationship between poetry and painting. In lines 361–65, he claims for poets the right to work in a broad, impressionistic style, not to be subjected to close scrutiny, as painters do. In the famous opening of the *Ars poetica*, lines 1–13, he asserts the artist's right to make a grotesque hybrid form because poets have that license:

> If a painter chose to join a human head to the neck of a horse, and to spread feathers of many a hue over limbs picked up now here now there, so that what at the top is a lovely woman ends below in a black and ugly fish, could you, my friends, if favoured with a private view, refrain from laughing? Believe me, dear Pisos, quite like such pictures would be a book, whose idle fancies shall be shaped like a sick man's dreams, so that neither head nor foot can be assigned to a single shape. "Painters and poets," you say, "have always had an equal license in hazarding anything."

Of course, this passage ends with a warning about license, which should not go so far that "savage should mate with tame, or serpents couple with birds, lambs with tigers," and the *Ars poetica* as a whole sustains an unresolved tension between fantasy and mimesis, license and decorum, *ars* and *ingenium*. Even as their inventive capacity is celebrated, poets are exhorted to pay attention to the rules of style and to the decorum of characters, and to find consistency within their invention (lines 90–91, 153–77, 119–127). Despite his caution, however, in the end (lines 453–76) Horace's poet is a distracted figure who falls into a pit while gazing at blackbirds, and such self-destructive behavior is his birthright! It is unclear *how* he becomes a verse-monger (that is, poetry is ultimately inexplicable in terms of *ars*); the poet is a mad bear who breaks his cage and startles his audience with his words. In his quest for listeners (and patrons), the poet is also a leech. The double metaphor of the shaggy, mad bear and the slick, bloodsucking leech, Ellen Oliensis points out, is itself a shocking and decidedly indecorous poetic invention by which Horace casts doubt on his own cautions.[37]

Oliensis notes that Horace exemplifies license in the opening of the *Ars poetica* with a hybrid but explicitly female figure: "Rhetorically if not syntactically, Horace's pictured mermaid displaces the centaur-like figure of the opening lines. And it is at this moment that the description thickens and the tone darkens into disgust: *turpiter atrum* [repulsively sordid]. In the end it is the female who makes manifest the gap between form and deformation, outside and inside, surface and depth, fair beginnings and foul endings."[38] For early modern artists and writers as well, the female body could be manipulated to express both the exhilaration and moral danger of artistic license. Gareth Roberts has asserted that the seductive ancient witch Circe was reincarnated frequently in the early modern period—in Spenser's Acrasia and Ariosto's Alcina, for instance—precisely because she represented the emasculating power of sensual pleasure and the poet's manly duty to direct his medium toward reason and truth. The male poet is ideally a magician in control of the transforming power of words, while Circe and her descendants represent the "perilous and unlicensed power to destabilise the relation between fiction and truth."[39]

The old hag-witch of ancient poetry is nothing less than the revolting reality of Circe exposed, as fictive ideal form decomposes into messy matter.[40] Epitomized by Horace's Canidia and Lucan's Erichtho, she expressed not only a fundamental horror of the female body but also the debasement of the poet's verbal magic. Although concerns about actual witchcraft in ancient Greece and Rome might find their way into poetry (for example, Horace's poetry coincides with Augustan legislation against magical practices), the symbolic function of literary witches is paramount.[41] Moreover, they are almost exclusively female, even though the material evidence of ancient witchcraft—for example, curse tablets and "voodoo dolls"—confirms that men were its chief practitioners.[42] Frequently the spells, directed against women who refuse sexual advances, express a violent, misogynistic desire for control.[43] A similar dynamic operated in the early modern period, when artists and poets exploited a topical issue and the inventive elaboration of a negative female stereotype contributed to their identities and self-promotion.

Horace's witch Canidia recurs in the *Satires* (1.8, 2.1, 2.8) and in *Epodes* 5 and 17; she spans the decade of the 30s B.C.E. when the up-and-coming poet enjoyed the patronage of Octavian's adviser, Maecenas. She conjoined a variety of literary, political, and personal meanings in a rich mixture that would have been appealing to early modern sensibilities. Oliensis suggests that Canidia's name recalls the vicious, scavenging dogs that symbolize female violence and desire, as well as the Dog Star Canicula whose pernicious influence provokes female heat and male weakness (Hesiod, *Works and Days*, lines 582–88). Thus she embodies an inversion of the proper order of society. But she also functions as an antitype of the dutiful and loyal poet himself, giving him license to explore his own weaknesses and test the limits of his invention under the protective aegis of a grotesque old hag. Oliensis explains Canidia as an integral part of Horace's self-concept, a projection of his deepest anxieties, and a symbol of sexual and poetic impotence and political disorder.[44]

Canidia both inspires and voices the poetic license that Horace warns against in his later *Ars poetica*. As kind of anti-Muse, she instigates invective by causing the boy she tortures in *Epode* 5 to fling out "Thyestean curses" (lines 91–112), and the wooden statue of Priapus in *Satire* 1.8 to speak. She and her magic charms are debased forms of the poet and his craft; her evil verbal incantations are analogous but oppositional to his socially useful "good verses" (*Satires* 2.1, lines 47–50; 82–86). Nevertheless, in *Epode* 17, Canidia holds the poet in the thrall of a love spell, despite his revulsion and his pleas for mercy, which she receives with a deaf ear. In the end of the *Epode* (lines 74–82) she challenges the poet's power to break her spell:

I'll mount like a knight your unbroken back,
the world give way before my prodigious ride.
Must I, who can animate waxen dolls
(as your curiosity knows), and tear
the moon from the Pole by my spells,
and raise the ashes of the dead,
and nicely mix aphrodisiac draughts:
must I bewail the period of my art,
shall it not prevail over you?

Even if Canidia's threat is a question, the tension between Horace's revulsion and fascination toward the licentious poetics Canidia embodies remains. In *Epodes* 8 and 12—amazingly flamboyant descriptions of the grotesque female body—Horace enjoys, in Richlin's words, "wallowing in the foulness he creates and rejects."[45] Using his poetic gifts to heap invective on hags, Horace makes love to them at the same time. The "deeply rooted kinship" of the witch and the invective poet, Oliensis states, "cannot be so easily dismissed."[46]

Erichtho from Book 6 of Lucan's incomplete *Civil War* is an excruciatingly loathsome, appalling coagulation of horrors, drawn in part from poetic precedents like Seneca's and Ovid's Medea and Horace's Canidia.[47] She expresses the poet's sense of deep corruption and decline in the time of Nero, his patron and nemesis. Before the Battle of Pharsalia, Pompey's son denigrates himself by consulting the "filthy practice of witchcraft" rather than more appropriate and pious augurs (line 467). Erichtho with her matted hair is "scrawny and squalid"; her face "never exposed to daylight" (lines 560–62). She lives in a "dank and fetid cave" with a "sickly coating of mildew" (lines 702–3)—a dwelling reminiscent of descriptions of the old women's vaginas in Latin invective poetry analyzed by Amy Richlin.[48] The shock of Erichtho on the reader deepens as Lucan develops her mutilation of corpses by piling grotesque and scatological details one upon the other in lines 580 to 616. Erichtho tears eyes from sockets, bites the nails from withered fingers, or, in a grotesque and sadistic perversion of a kiss, bites off the tips of tongues by prying dead mouths open with her teeth. Lucan's passages on Erichtho's necromantic rituals form a litany of uncanny, repulsive substances inserted into the corpse of a dead soldier (lines 724–51). In these passages, poetic embellishment achieves a life of its own.

Like Horace's, Lucan's poetic witch would have appealed to early modern writers and artists on many levels. Erichtho echoed the demonologists' conviction that modern witches were implacable and powerful enemies of humanity: She wants nothing less than "the blood of the whole world" (line 632). At another point, however, Lucan wonders about the real power of witches, a question that frequently arises in the early modern period (lines 540–43):

Does control of all Olympians
Rest in the witches themselves, or does their infallible magic

Come from a certain god, himself unconstrained, with the power
Nevertheless to constrain the world?

Erichtho would have provided an ancient precedent for interrogating witchcraft as power and as inversion of social order and state power. Richard Gordon views Erichtho, though drawn from Lucan's knowledge of magic, as a poetic abstraction embodying the inverted values of the Roman civil war—when traditional Roman virtue and piety had been supplanted by their opposites.[49] For the early modern artist or writer, then, the contemporary resonance of Lucan's text would have been multifaceted. It revealed witchcraft's capacity for political and religious meaning and for extraordinarily flamboyant and skillful poetic invention, centering on a hyperbolically grotesque female character.

Just such a complicated kinship also existed between early modern artists and the witches they portrayed. The foulness of female witches simultaneously celebrated artistic license and warned of its dangers. The problem for the early modern artist depicting witchcraft was to bring the same unruly, hybrid, and grotesque forms that announced license and threatened dissolution under the discipline of some adumbrating social purpose; hence, the crucial importance of discrete historical contexts in our understanding of these works. As we shall see, however, the movement from gratuitous, sensationalistic license to vindicating social purpose in these images is often uneasy and obscure, and the acute tensions so apparent in Horace and Lucan's use of the witch are undiminished. Consider the case of the large, elaborate, and enigmatic engraving, *Lo stregozzo* (Witches' procession, or *The Carcass*, early 1520s), and its double relationship to Italian art theory and contemporary debates about witchcraft (figure 2.3).

Witchcraft and Self-Fashioning in the Shadow of Raphael: *Lo stregozzo*

The Italian notion of the grotesque initially developed from the examples of fresco and stucco ornamentation discovered in excavations of the Golden House of Nero (then believed to be the Baths of Titus) in the 1480s, but it rapidly exceeded this ornamental context to embody an extreme artistic license and the free flow of fantasy. These *grotteschi* as they were called (from the Italian *grotta* meaning cave or grotto) focused on the imaginative combination and recombination of fantastic, diverse elements. Raphael and his pupils were especially instrumental in establishing the popularity of such decoration. In his life of Perino del Vaga, for example, Vasari writes of the artist's delight at the novelty of the ancient grotesques and his painting of the staircase of the Doria Palace in Genoa with "decorations of little grotesques after the

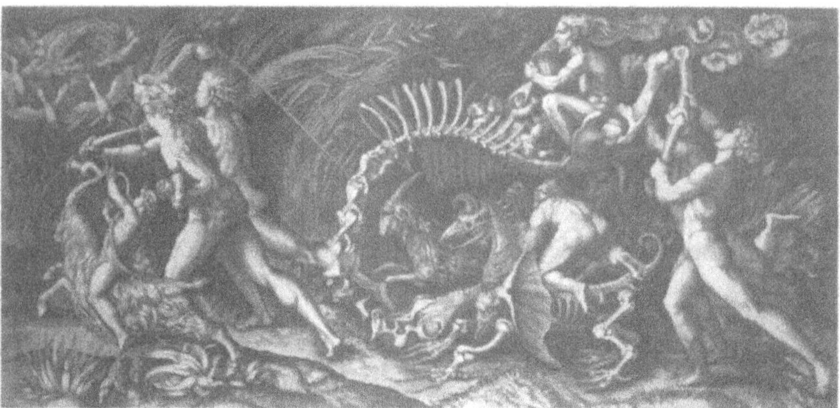

Figure 2.3. Marcantonio Raimondi and Agostino Veneziano after an unknown designer (Giulio Romano?), *Lo stregozzo* (Witches' procession, or *The Carcass*), ca. 1523. Engraving, 302 × 634 mm. Image © 2004 Board of Trustees, National Gallery of Art, Washington, D.C. Rosenwald Collection.

antique that could not be richer or more beautiful, with various scenes and little figures, masks, children, animals, and other things of fancy . . . of their kind they may well be called divine."[50]

Vasari associates the grotesque ornament with the bizarre, marvelous, and divine aspects of artistic creativity, and applies the term in the lives of del Vaga, Filippino Lippi, Taddeo Zuccaro, the weird figure of Morto da Feltre, Raphael, and most of all to Michelangelo, whose *ingegno* was so evident in architectural details such as the grotesque masks of the Medici Chapel.[51] The anecdote told by Vasari and Condivi about Michelangelo as a boy making a marvelous colored pen sketch of Martin Schongauer's engraving of the *Temptation of St. Anthony* (ca. 1470) establishes the centrality of the hybrid, grotesque forms as part of Michelangelo's "divine" creativity. According to Summers, it is likely that the young Michelangelo "admired Schongauer's monstrosities for what they were, creatures utterly of art, illusions of the very kind and with the very meaning writers since Isidore of Seville had warned against, but at the same time examples by which the artist might learn to invent outside the precinct of natural law."[52] Freedom from mimesis apparently outweighed the dangers of such forms, discussed by such diverse writers as St. Bernard and Vitruvius.[53]

As André Chastel points out, the appeal of *grotteschi* was irrepressible, despite their Vitruvian detractors, and their expansion was rapid.[54] Marcantonio Raimondi and his engravers, for instance, made prints after designs for grotesque ornament by Raphael or Giovanni da Udine (figure 2.4). In *Lo stregozzo*, however, hybrid and monstrous elements move from a marginal position in ornament to the central context of *istoria*. In his earlier career in Venice, Marcantonio had already exhibited a penchant for such elements in the so-

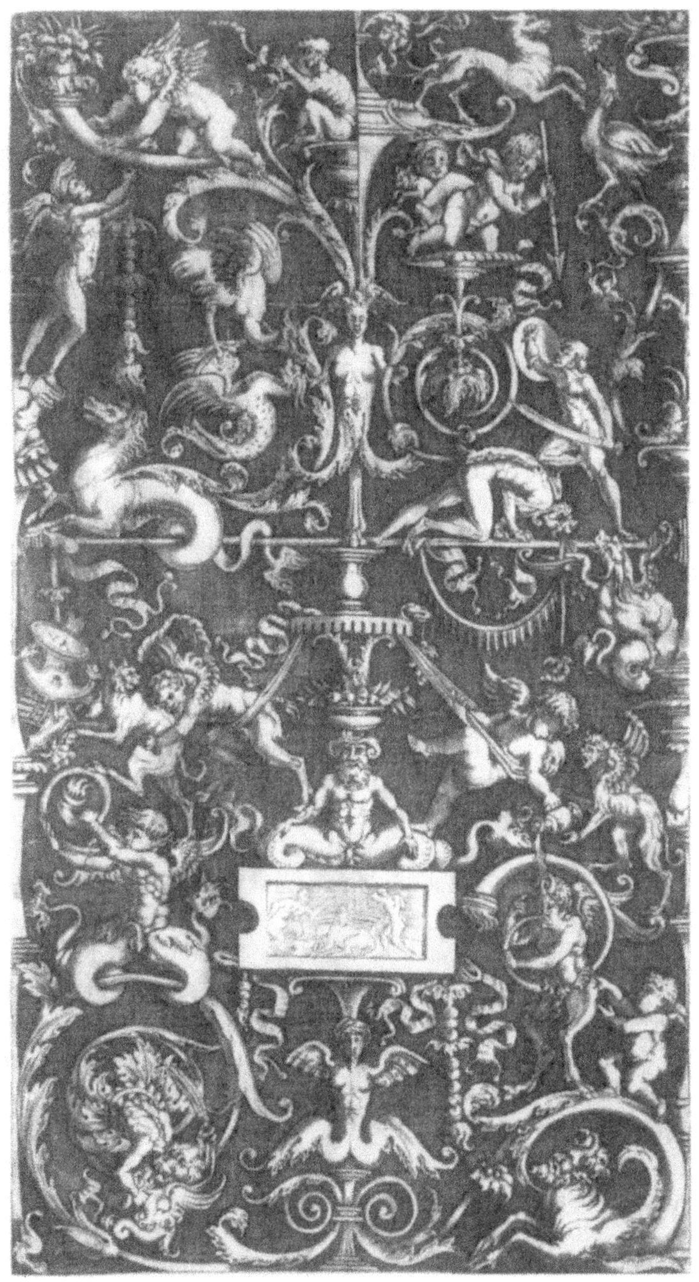

Figure 2.4. Agostino Veneziano after Raphael, *Ornament Panel*, undated. Engraving, 268 × 150 mm. Albertina Museum, Vienna.

called *Dream of Raphael* (ca. 1508) in which Boschian demons and an infernal landscape are conjured up in the dreams of two sleeping female nudes. Although it has been assumed that Marcantonio engraved a design by another artist, Maria Ruvoldt argues persuasively for his role as inventor. He combined and transformed pictorial references from Bosch, Michelangelo, and Giorgione to demonstrate his *ingegno*; the subject of the print depends on the association between dreams and poetic or artistic inspiration. Thus, Marcantonio presented himself as a "protean artist adept in different modes of pictorial expression."[55] *The Dream of Raphael* is, in short, an advertisement of his abilities. *Lo stregozzo*, as well, advertises its engravers.

Above all, this print subverted viewers' expectations of ideal form exemplified in other engravings by Marcantonio and his pupils, such as the majestic and tragic *Massacre of the Innocents*, ca. 1510. Raphael's agent, Baviero di Carrocci or "Il Baviera," the apparent entrepreneurial mastermind behind the marketing of these prints, must have understood the appeal of this work as an innovative curiosity and fodder for learned discussion. *Lo stregozzo* exhibited a provocative inventiveness of form and content that revealed a deeply anticlassical strain within Roman High Renaissance classicism. It is one of a number of works in the early cinquecento discussed by Stephen Campbell that assert artistic license in morbid or nightmarish terms that paradoxically suggest the potentially *un*divine end of divinely given creativity.[56]

Most startlingly, *Lo stregozzo* subjects the heroic male nude—the sine qua non of the artistic accomplishments of Italian High Renaissance art—to the humiliating rule of an aged witch in a kind of self-induced abjection of the male artist that paradoxically proves the brilliance and autonomy of his invention. Descending from the hags of Horace and Lucan, Mantegna's *Invidia* and Dürer's *Witch* (see figures 2.1, 3.4), she rides, open-mouthed with protruding tongue and a cache of sacrificial babies, atop a skeleton pulled by her gorgeous Michelangelesque acolytes, sixteenth-century reprisals of Pollaiuolo's battling nudes (see figure 2.2). *Lo stregozzo*'s rhythmic repetition of curves and diagonals and its momentum from right to left are irresistible. Its fluid juxtaposition and fusion of incongruent forms—heroic nudes, goats, grasses, birds, bones, and terrified babies—echo ornamental *grotteschi* (see figure 2.4). The frisson evoked by the demonic subject matter is heightened by a strong chiaroscuro that reflects changes in Marcantonio's engraving style that in turn responded to Raphael's colorism, beginning with the *Stanza d'Eliodoro* frescoes (1512–14).

The witches' procession shown here relates to but does not duplicate the Italian concept of the "Lady's Game" (*Il gioco della donna*) inherited from the old belief in night flying (riding with Diana or Herodias) censured by the Canon Episcopi and currently being debated in Italy. Indeed, Emison has recently interpreted *Lo stregozzo* as a visualization of Gianfrancesco Pico della Mirandola's affirmation of the reality of the "game" in his Latin dialogue *Strix*, published in 1523 and translated into Italian by Dominican Leandro Alberti the following year.[57] Around 1520, north Italian lawyer Gianfrancesco Ponzinibio had written a skeptical assessment of the legality of witchcraft trials and the bodily reality of the sabbath flight. But Pico was a believer. As the count of Mirandola, he had personally assisted inquisitors in interrogating and torturing accused witches in his domain and in nearby Concordia; of sixty defendants, ten (seven men and three women) were executed.[58] In his dialogue, while retaining the old idea of delusional flight, he attempts to convince his readers and his protagonist Apistius ("the man without faith") of its reality. Phronimus ("the prudent man") and Dicaste ("the judge," an inquisitor) interview an accused witch, an old, ugly woman simply called "Strix" or "Strega" who confirms that she participated in "the game," in *both* body and spirit, that she stole and vampirized infants, made flying unguent from their bodies, desecrated the Host by putting it in a chamber pot, and had pleasurable intercourse with a demon with the disappointingly mundane name of Ludovico.[59] The innovative character of this text lay not only in its dialogue form but also in its insistence on demonic copulation (heterosexual and homosexual) with men as well as women. As Walter Stephens and Tamar Herzig both emphasize, the *Malleus* asserted that demons, angelic in origin, were repulsed by "unnatural" acts like sodomy.[60]

Emison thinks *Lo stregozzo*, allied to Pico's polemical support for the Mirandola trials, was directed mostly if not entirely toward "the masses" to persuade them of the real and present danger of witchcraft. A key aspect of her argument is her separation of artistic invention and content: *Lo stregozzo* is not, she believes, an artist's tour-de-force or fantastic invention but a "tool for molding opinion."[61] I think *Lo stregozzo* was indeed a fantastic invention that exploited the contemporary interest in witchcraft, albeit ambiguously.

There have been many candidates for its inventor—from the minor Umbrian artist Girolamo Genga to the giant Michelangelo; the Dossi of Ferrara to Raphael himself or his protean pupil Giulio Romano.[62] Emison's attribution to one of the Dossi, probably Battista, stems from their interest in magical themes (see my discussion in Chapter 6) and her thesis that the print is propaganda for Pico's dialogue. However, there may be a stronger case for understanding *Lo stregozzo* in the context of Marcantonio and his pupils' Roman print production in the 1520s, as reconstructed by David Landau,[63] and for attributing its design to Giulio, head of Raphael's workshop until his departure to Mantua in 1524. *Lo stregozzo* is intelligible as a bold statement asserting both the Raimondi School's preeminence as purveyors of Roman High Renaissance art, and Giulio's status as heir to Raphael's fertile inventiveness, in which antiquity played a crucial role.

Lo stregozzo's elongated composition, marshy setting, and strident movement recall ancient Bacchanalian processions as depicted on sarcophagi.[64]

Indeed, as a print in the Italian tradition standing for a drawing style, *Lo stregozzo* exemplifies the traits sixteenth-century writers such as Giovanni Armenini in his *De' veri precetti della pittura* (On the true precepts of painting, 1587) praised in Giulio's drawings: his dazzling facility, unimpeded invention, and a complete assimilation of ancient sculpture.[65] Giulio did not merely quote antiquity but absorbed and transformed it into personal inventions expressed in drawings. His *concetti* were, in poet Pietro Aretino's words, "*anticamente moderni e modernamente antichi*" (anciently modern and modernly ancient).[66] Vasari's extravagant praise of Giulio as Raphael's heir emphasized the centrality of drawing in his oeuvre, the immediacy with which Giulio's prolific ideas were set down on paper, and the boldness, versatility, and fanciful nature of those ideas.[67] These are the same traits exhibited in the fertile inventions of *grotteschi.*

A likely date for *Lo stregozzo* is 1523, in terms of both Giulio's own career and the situation of Marcantonio and his pupils. Landau describes the conditions impinging on those engravers after Raphael's death in 1520 and makes sense of the confusion surrounding signatures and replicas among the engravings. With their supply of drawings by Raphael curtailed and the copperplates going to Baviera to support the painter's mistress according to the terms of his will, the engravers tried to salvage their shop by producing new plates of old compositions and by turning to Raphael's painted works or to paintings and drawings by other artists. (Giulio, as head of the shop, essentially assumed Raphael's position with the engravers.[68]) At the same time, the engravers, discouraged by Raphael and Baviera from signing their works, began to assert their own identity by using monograms or, in the case of Marcantonio himself, Landau argues, the deferent "signature" of the empty tablet. As with Mantegna's prints, it was apparently unnecessary for the inventor's name to appear; the engravings were evidently recognized as representations of distinctive styles and *invenzioni.*[69]

Landau's conjectures about Marcantonio School prints may help explain the curious history of the signatures, and lack thereof, on *Lo stregozzo.* Its inventor was never designated, perhaps because the print speaks so clearly to Giulio's style and the bizarre expressiveness he would soon develop further in his works in Mantua. Bruce Davis plausibly reconstructs the print's history in four states. In the first, he thinks, there was probably an empty tablet; in the second, an "AV" for Agostino Veneziano appeared within it. In the third state, the "AV" was burnished out, and care was taken to erase traces of the monogram from the tablet (although in many impressions, the "AV" is replaced sloppily in pen). In the fourth state, the engraved "AV" reappeared on the horn played by the nude riding the lead goat. Such changes corroborate stylistic analysis to suggest that Marcantonio began the print but that Agostino, who was evidently insistent about the inclusion of his monogram, finished it.[70]

Lo stregozzo makes sense as a highly marketable image, exploiting the interest in witchcraft generated by recent Italian trials and publications by Ponzinibio and Pico, exhibiting the inventiveness of Raphael's heir, and asserting the skill of Marcantonio and Agostino. For the engravers, concerned to maintain the shop's viability after Raphael's death, the print's moneymaking potential was of the utmost importance. According to Bette Talvacchia, profit was paramount in publishing *I modi* (The ways), sixteen engravings after Giulio's drawings of coital positions, conceived from antique sources and published in 1524 despite the risk to Marcantonio. When the latter was jailed, Giulio was already safe in Mantua, his appointment with Federico Gonzaga II having been brokered by Baldassare Castiglione.[71] For Giulio, *Lo stregozzo* would have advertised his inventive prowess and announced his independence after Raphael's death. Gian Paolo Lomazzo, attributing *Lo stregozzo* to Michelangelo, emphasized its bizarre inventiveness in his *Trattato dell'arte della pittura, scoltura et archittetura* (Treatise on the arts of painting, sculpture and architecture, 1584), and, unlike Emison, I see no need to understand these remarks as anachronistic.[72] It is no coincidence that *Lo stregozzo*'s muscular nudes, old hag, large rectangular format, and swaying grasses bring to mind Mantegna's *Battle of the Sea Gods*—a paradigm of burlesque invention, evoking antique prototypes (see figure 2.1). Like Mantegna before him, Giulio was shortly to become the preeminent inventor of the Mantuan court.

The print's inventive bravado is obvious; the attitude toward witchcraft it conveyed is more elusive. Papal encouragement of the prosecution of witches remained consistent during the early sixteenth century, with Hadrian VI issuing a bull in 1523 that reiterated earlier exhortations from Julius II and Leo X.[73] In this Roman context, *Lo stregozzo* could be construed as supporting that position, if only because the artist and engravers were wary of reprisal. However, the case for interpreting *Lo stregozzo* as a straightforward endorsement of witch-hunting is less convincing once we realize that the print would circulate widely in and beyond Italy. The artist and engravers surely knew that it would be differently received by a literate audience, including those who disagreed with Pico. Federico, for example, had supported Francesca Trivulzio, duchess of Concordia, when she claimed jurisdiction over the Mirandola trials, and he unsuccessfully sought the release of one of the accused male witches.[74] For this sophisticated and hedonistic duke, the engraving may have been more provocative than propagandistic.

Moreover, *Lo stregozzo* significantly does not depict the mixed procession of men and women, or a procession dominated by women like the "Ladies' Game." Rather, it is a procession of *men* who *serve* an old hag by pulling her bizarre vehicle and trumpeting its progress. As in Pico's dialogue (and despite the predominance of male victims in Mirandola), the symbol of witchcraft is still a grotesque old woman. The ludicrousness of vigorous young men in thrall to a hag—as if bewitched, like Horace by Canidia—suggests a bawdy homage to the leveling power of lust. The indecorous sexual drive of the old witch is conveyed by her coterie of male attendants and goats, and her protruding tongue suggests the vehemence of her appetite. Perhaps the sequence of male buttocks across the engraving even makes a ribald analogy between her lust and sodomy. The uncanny chariot of bones, the doomed babies, and the mire of the swamp (with its old associations of vice[75]) tinge salacious laughter with a frisson of horror. One cannot help but think that this print would have appealed greatly to Giulio's friend Pietro Aretino, whose sonnets accompanying *I modi* shocked not only by the frankness with which sexual practices, including anal intercourse, were described but also by the aggressive sexual appetites of the female participants. In her illuminating study of *I modi*, Talvacchia interprets Aretino's voicing of female desire as an expression of his discomfort with such desires that countered the norms of female behavior.[76]

Geared to shock, confound, and amuse viewers, *Lo stregozzo* is early Mannerist in form and spirit. It corresponds to the contemporary eccentricities of Rosso Fiorentino and Jacopo Pontormo, and of Michelangelo in the ornament of the Medici Chapel, and foreshadowing Giulio's brilliant and often grotesque and lascivious designs for the Palazzo del Te. In this print, the bizarre and ornamental are brought from the margins to the center normally occupied by the *istoria*, and the distinct undercurrent of "terror and violence" in Giulio's art, as Frederick Hartt described it, is explicit.[77] *Lo stregozzo* speaks an artistic counterlanguage, subverting classicism and decorum and corresponding to what Manfredo Tafuri has called the "bipolarism" in Giulio's personality, allowing libertinism and Christian reform to coexist.[78]

Late Mannerist theorists, Lomazzo and Federico Zuccari, championed the freedom and interiority of making art sanctioned in the grotesque and *grotteschi*-like flow of bizarre forms in *Lo stregozzo*. The conceptual distance between Alberti and these Mannerist writers is exemplified by Lomazzo's lack of concern for the imitation of nature, his Neoplatonic mystification of beauty, and his cataloguing of personal artistic styles by astrological types, and by Zuccari's emphasis on the divinely given *disegno interno* in the artist's mind and his hostility to artistic rules. At the same time, theories of poetry—Francesco Patrizi's *Della poetica* (On poetry), published beginning in 1586, and Giordano Bruno's *De gli eroici furori* (The heroic frenzies, 1585)—reassert the poet's capacity for original invention over imitation or adherence to rules.[79] In sixteenth-century northern Europe, this quest for artistic autonomy would follow a different but equally compelling course in which the grotesque demons of Hieronymus Bosch played a central role.

Bosch's Fantastic Inventions in Northern Art and Theory

In the north, the evolution of concepts of artistic creativity is more difficult to trace because of fewer written sources. As I have noted, Dürer's art-theoretical speculations—not to mention his remarkable self-portraits and his lifelong efforts to achieve a higher intellectual and social status for the German artist—had important implications for artistic autonomy. His extant writings are only a small portion of the characteristically overambitious enterprise he planned, however. The most important written reflection on northern Renaissance art is certainly Karel van Mander's *Schilder-boek* (Book on picturing), published in Haarlem in 1604.

In *Het Schilderboek*, van Mander constructed a northern canon that deeply challenged Vasari's: At its beginning was Jan van Eyck, at its culmination Hendrik Goltzius. As Walter Melion has shown, the art-theoretical terms used by van Mander are not simple synonyms for their Italian counterparts; rather, they were differently nuanced according to the history and values of the northern artistic tradition, such as the growth of printmaking and the importance of naturalism. Van Mander's concept of invention (*inventy*), for example, is multifaceted and conceived in a northern European context that valued technical innovation, with van Eyck's use of oil as the paradigm, as well as pictorial construction (*ordinanty*) "out of oneself" (*uyt zijn selven*). In discussing how the artist invents, however, van Mander does not, in Melion's words, "press the claims" of the narrative *istoria*. Rather, the artist's description of the varieties of nature (*versheydenheden*) seems to have equal claim on inventiveness. Similarly, van Mander's valuation of subject matters was more flexible and less hierarchical: He advises the artist who is not so skilled at human figures or in histories to depict a wide variety of subjects, including, for example, genre, landscapes, portraits, and grotesques.[80]

At the core of both van Eyck's and Goltzius's abilities was imitation—van Eyck of nature; Goltzius of the styles of other artists in his reproductive engravings (as humanists would imitate others' styles.[81] Superlative mimetic skill was also a fundamental aspect of northern artists' self-construction: Think, for example, of the way Dürer calls attention to the immaculately painted fur collar in his Munich *Self-Portrait* (1500) or van Eyck's reflection in the armor of St. George in the *Madonna and Canon van der Paele* (Groeninge Museum, Bruges, 1436). Van Mander used the term *nae t'leven* ("after life") to express an artist's immediate recording of sights seen, corresponding most closely to the Italian term *ritrarre*.[82] While *ritrarre* was devalued in sixteenth-century Italian theory (for example, by Danti), it seems to have been privileged in the north. Jan van Eyck's and Dürer's naturalism was renowned, and the Dürer-Renaissance in the late sixteenth century, fostered by Rudolf II at his court in Prague and exemplified by Joris Hoefnagel's nature studies in watercolor, testifies to the continuing valorization of this precise imitative skill.[83] Like Goltzius's uncanny ability to capture the "hand" of other artists in his engravings, subsuming the self in the face of nature was paradoxically the stuff of artistic greatness in the north.

Nevertheless, as we shall see in the discussion of Jacques de Gheyn II in Chapter 5, it is also possible to overemphasize the dominance of imitation in northern art. After all, the northern taste for meticulous nature studies by artists like Hoefnagel and Jacques de Gheyn II was accompanied by an equally enthusiastic taste for the grotesque and fantastic—most notably Boschian imagery and the composite heads of Milanese artist Giuseppe Arcimboldo, who worked for both the Habsburg courts of Maximilian II in Vienna and Rudolf II in Prague. In his life of Antwerp artist Bartolomeus Spranghcr, van Mander tells us that it was Spranghcr's painting of a "magic scene" with witches flying around a ruin—very inventive and containing many *drolleries*—that first attracted the attention of his major Roman patron, Cardinal Farnese.[84] The relationship between the imitation of nature and the creation of fantastic, grotesque imagery is a topic I will explore in more detail in Chapter 5 on de Gheyn, whose witchcraft images exemplify the interrelationship of these two modes of artistic vision. They were not mutually exclusive, as Summers notes. Condivi wrote that in copying Schongauer's hybrid demons, Michelangelo spent time studying nature for the rendering of each part, and de Hollanda advised artists to render each part of their composite monsters perfectly, according to the nature of the animal from which the part is borrowed.[85]

The hybridized demons and monsters that populate northern art from Schongauer to Jacques Callot can indeed be understood partly as syntheses of observations of nature. Van Mander makes it clear that artists work not only after life but from an interior principle he called "*uyt den gheest*" or "*uyt zijn selven*"—terms that Svetlana Alpers and Melion have understood to mean the artist's purely cognitive synthesis of visual memories.[86] Thus, the artist constructing his demon would imitate aspects of nature and combine those remembered aspects. As we shall see, however, van Mander's terms have also been interpreted by E. K. J. Reznicek and Hessel Miedema to refer to a process engaging imagination and *ingenium*—a process implying a greater freedom from nature and a deeper level of interiority, and *uyt den gheest* may also imply a progression from *nae t'leven*.[87] To be sure, Bosch's hybrid forms are constructed from carefully rendered parts of animals and humans; at the same time, his art was described in the sixteenth and seventeenth centuries in terms that insist on its nonmimetic character: "spooks," "phantoms," "visions," and "dreams."[88] Such terms are not easily reconciled with a purely cognitive meaning of *uyt den gheest*.

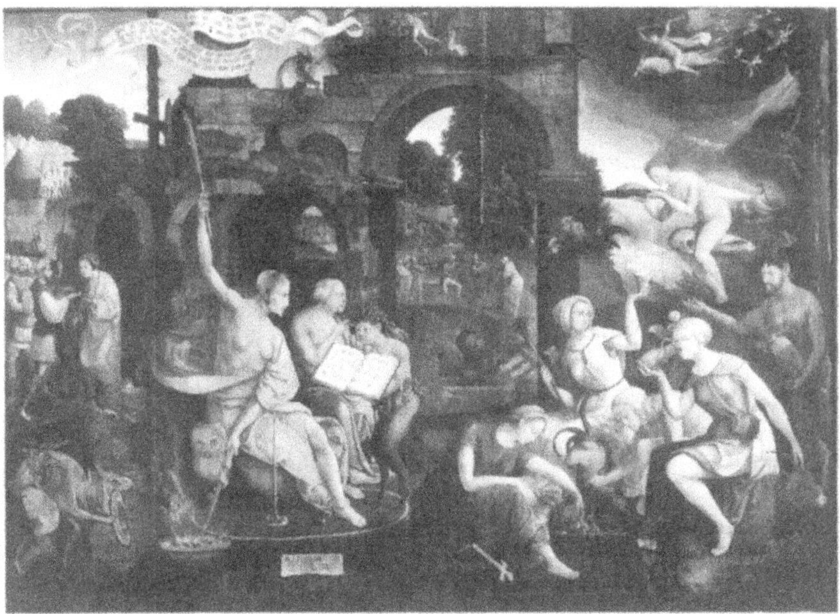

Figure 2.5. Jacob Cornelisz. van Oostsanen, *Saul and the Witch of Endor*, 1526. Oil on panel, 87.5 × 125 cm. Rijksmuseum, Amsterdam. Photo by Collection Rijksbureau voor Kunsthistorische Documentatie (RKD), The Hague.

The northern European diablerie, which centered on the fantastic hybridization of demonic beings set in lurid, infernal landscapes, followed from Bosch's brilliant example.[89] Last Judgments, Temptations of St. Anthony, Descents into Limbo, and other conventional themes provided vehicles for Bosch's legacy, and images of the new topic of witchcraft are closely related to this pictorial genre. In his *Saul and the Witch of Endor* (1526; figure 2.5), with its glowering sky, firelight, ruin, and Boschian demon, Amsterdam artist Jacob Cornelisz. van Oostsanen used the biblical narrative to express contemporary concerns about heresy and witchcraft. Saul's consultation with a female necromancer who conjured up the spirit of Samuel to predict the outcome of a battle against the Philistines (I Samuel 28) was a key, final episode in Saul's long descent. Samuel's ghost predicts the defeat of Saul's army, the death of Saul and his sons, and the loss of the kingdom of Israel to David. Yet the consultation between Saul and the witch is placed inconspicuously in the left background. The painting's foreground contains a scene of her summoning a spirit using a *grimoire* (magic book) and a magic circle at the left, and witches cooking sausages and pancakes (probably derived from Hans Baldung Grien; see figure 3.5) at the right. Satyrs, owls, hens, and the divinatory mirror carried by the Boschian creature at the far left all convey the sexual and heretical nature of the activities. Jane L. Carroll situates the painting within the orthodox Catholic community of contemporary Amsterdam, from which Jacob Cornelisz.'s patronage was drawn and to which he belonged, and its abhorrence of Reformers' denial of the validity of the sacraments. At the right, a cross is turned on its head; and a loaf of bread held by a flying witch and an upheld chalice suggest an abuse of the Eucharist. Saul's interaction with a conjuror of spirits and the witches' mockery of the sacraments both reaffirm Catholic orthodoxy by associating those contemporaries who would question it with witches, diabolical magic, and the impiety of King Saul. Cornelisz. synthesized a variety of topical concerns in this late painting and experimented with Bosch's lurid colors and hybrid forms to appeal to his primary audience of prominent Catholic Amsterdamers.[90]

Cornelisz.'s painting was produced in a spirit of Catholic faith that Bosch himself would have appreciated. Within the extensive diablerie tradition of the sixteenth century, however, the profound religious content of Bosch's symbolic language dissipated; as Silver has noted, it was often the fantastic, visionary character of his art that most fascinated later artists and collectors.[91] Walter Gibson links hybrid, Boschian forms both to the passage in Horace's *Ars poetica*, describing the artist's power to create "idle fancies" like "a sick man's dreams," and also to the Renaissance adaptation of ancient Roman *grotteschi*. In an inscription on an engraved portrait of Pieter Bruegel the Elder, published in a series of artists' *Effigies* by print-publisher Hieronymus Cock's widow in 1572, poet Domenicus Lampsonius wrote that Bruegel brings "his master's ingenious dreams to life once more."[92]

Felipe de Guevara y Lastre's early remarks on Bosch's art in his *Commentaries on Painting* (ca. 1560), reveals that many of the artist's contemporaries responded primarily to its bizarre aspects. Guevara was the half-Flemish, half-Spanish son of Diego de Guevara y Quesada, a high official in the Habsburg courts of Philip I and Charles V who collected Netherlandish paintings that probably included examples by Bosch. Guevara must have had fairly extensive knowledge of Bosch's works through his connections with Spanish and Burgundian nobility who collected them, and we know that Philip II bought six paintings by Bosch from his estate. Guevara writes about Bosch, significantly, in the context of his discussion of ancient *grillen* or "whimsies," a term derived from Pliny's discussion of the grotesque figures painted by Antiphilos of Alexandria (*Natural History* 35.114). Guevara lamented the contemporary misunderstanding of Bosch as an inventor of "monsters and various imaginary subjects." Whereas Bosch himself displayed "wisdom and decorum" in the use of these elements, imitators and forgers now multiply them indiscriminately. The derivative infernos produced by these artists must have satisfied a large market demand, while Bosch's biblical narratives fell on fallow ground. Guevara asserts that there was only one pupil, unfortunately unnamed, who followed his master truly.[93]

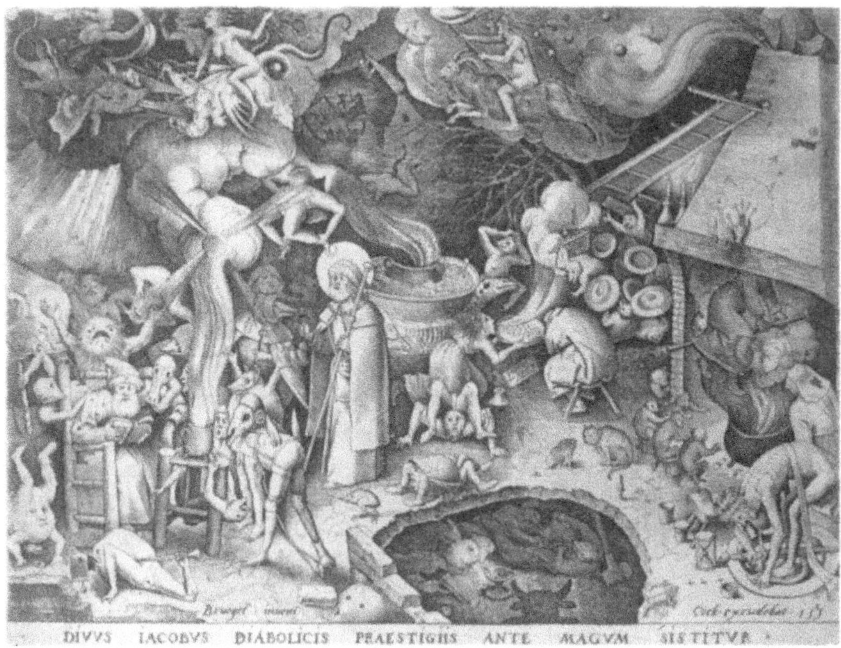

Figure 2.6. After Pieter Bruegel the Elder, *St. James and the Magician Hermogenes*, 1565. Engraving (by Pieter van der Heyden?), 222 × 290 mm. Museum Boymans-van Beuningen, Rotterdam.

Bruegel—the "second Bosch"—designed numerous engravings with Boschian motifs (some were designated as "inventions" of Bosch) for Cock in Antwerp. As Larry Silver points out, such prints were marketed to a specifically Netherlandish audience as "antipodes" to the classicizing prints after Frans Floris and Marten van Heemskerck.[94] Among Bruegel's Boschian prints are St. *James and the Magician Hermogenes* (figure 2.6) and its pendant, *The Fall of the Magician* (1565), both probably engraved by Pieter van der Heyden. Witchcraft is not a major focus of Bosch's works, although there are indications of his knowledge of the *Malleus* and writings on demons by St. Augustine and Cassianus.[95] Bruegel, however, included numerous flying witches, witches casting spells on and under the ground, and a scene of a witch flying up the chimney, all of which influenced the "witches' kitchen" scenes of the Antwerp tradition (see figures 4.3, 4.4, 4.13) as well as images by Jacques de Gheyn II (compare figures 5.4 and 5.5). The strange tale of St. James, the Jewish magician Hermogenes and his assistant Philetus is told in Jacobus da Voragine's *Golden Legend*. After sending Philetus to James to prove the apostle was a fraud and finding that his assistant had been converted to Christianity, Hermogenes ordered demons to summon James and Philetus to him. Instead, being no match for James's power, the demons brought Hermogenes to the apostle, who forgave the penitent magician and ordered him to throw his magic books into the sea. The story is essentially a struggle between apostolic "magic," sanctioned by God, and its heathen counterpart. But the appeal of the tale for Bruegel's contemporaries must have lain in part in the summoning back and forth of magician and saint, carried through the air by demons—a reference to the debates about demonic transport of witches to the sabbath. In the pendant print, Hermogenes is sent hurtling headlong through the air. A horde of Boschian demons, now turning on their former master as they obey a new, saintly one, are eager to tear him limb from limb.

Charles de Tolnay noted the smug clerics behind James who view the magician's punishment with approval, and argued that Bruegel's drawing and the print made from it commented indirectly on the punishment of heretics by the Spanish Inquisition, an instrument of Spanish monarchical power during the revolt of the Netherlands. Citing Dirck Volkertsz. Coornhert on the forgiveness and toleration of those deemed "heretics," de Tolnay saw the print as another one of Bruegel's cryptic comments in favor of religious tolerance and the revolt.[96] In the early stages of the large-scale European witch-hunts, Bruegel perhaps brought the medieval legend of St. James and the magician up to date by incorporating references to the "new" heretical sect of witchcraft and its chief enemy: the Holy Office. The witches, the magician, and the saint may have functioned as codes for deviant religious groups and their oppressors. In a recently discovered second state of the print, a cross on the cloth worn by the man performing magic in the lower right has been burnished out, as if it had been censored because it likened Catholic ritual to magic.[97]

Of course, it is also possible to read *St. James* in completely conventional Christian terms.[98] However, Bruegel's ambivalent allusions to contemporary issues in the context of a biblical theme bears a similarity to Botticelli's reinvigoration of the Calumny of Apelles or van Oostsanen's by the same means: All these works became new inventions out of old themes. Bruegel's use of Bosch's language of hybrid, grotesque forms exemplified most clearly the sixteenth-century understanding of inventiveness in the north. These forms were as malleable in meaning as in physical shape, adapting to the needs of states, churches, or patrons while constantly pointing to the ingenuity of artists.

The *Capriccio*: Fantasy at the Margins

In the seventeenth century, very old moral and religious objections to the fantastic and grotesque took new forms. In response to Protestantism's suspicion of the role of the visual arts in worship, the twenty-fifth session of the Council of Trent (1563) not only reaffirmed the didactic and inspirational utility of the religious image, it also expressed a distrust of artistic invention akin to that of

Protestantism. Its sparse instructions urged artists depicting religious subjects to avoid lasciviousness, doctrinal and historical error, and disorder. Trent's strictures were elaborated by late sixteenth- and seventeenth-century ecclesiastical writers such as Cardinal Gabriele Paleotti of Bologna, whose *Discorso intorno alle immagini sacre e profane* (Discourse concerning sacred and profane images, 1582) helped artists depict religious subjects accurately and with appropriate decorum.

Along with naturalistic trends manifested in international Caravaggism, and in genre and landscape art, especially as developed in the Northern Netherlands, an emerging neoclassical current in Baroque style and theory also worked against the mystification and internalization of the creative process that I have described. Cardinal Giovanni Pietro Bellori, with his ties to the Carracci's reform of art at the turn of the century and his foundational importance for subsequent academic neoclassicism, is a key figure. His *Le vite de' pittori, scultori, ed architetti moderni* (Lives of the modern painters, sculptors and architects, 1672), challenged the Tuscan hegemony of Vasari's *Lives* as well as the latter's narrative approach and his Mannerist delight in licentious fantasy. Bellori was motivated by the need to rehabilitate art and culture in Rome, and his criterion for inclusion in his history was his own critical judgment of quality.[99] Bellori introduced *Le vite* with praise of the beauty of ancient sculpture, concluded with praise of his friend Nicolas Poussin who rivaled that beauty, and discussed only twelve artists in-between. In his first biography, he makes clear that the greatness of Annibale Carracci lies in his rejection of both Caravaggesque naturalism and, as Elizabeth Cropper puts it, "the unnatural liberty of *disegno* bequeathed by the Tuscans"—this second alternative being a much more destructive trend.[100]

Bellori's appropriation into later academic classicism obscured his subtlety. He advocated an idealizing process of selection from nature as Alberti had done, but his process was not a simple averaging of natural traits; rather, it retained something of the sixteenth century's sense of innate artistic gifts. The artist looked inward to perfect what he saw in nature. Bellori's recognition of the diversity of beauty and the sensuality of his *ekphrases* temper his rationalistic classicism. Overall, however, his veneration of Raphael's Vatican frescoes, his scholarly antiquarianism, and his sense of ideal form pointed clearly toward an academic understanding of art in which the imitation of approved artistic prototypes, synthesis, and idealization prevailed.[101]

Art historians continue to debate the ambiguous implications of Poussin's statements on art, conveyed mainly in letters to friends and patrons.[102] His application of the theory of musical modes to painting, for instance, suggests on the one hand that the painter, through his manipulation of artistic *form*, can arouse powerful emotions in spectators that override reason—a strikingly modern idea. On the other hand, as Thomas Puttfarken points out,

Poussin elaborated his thoughts on the modes by turning conventionally to poetic theory, where the *sound* of words was tied to the poet's subject matter. Although he asserted that the end of art was to evoke delight (*délectation*), he also stressed reason as the central principle in both the creation and judgment of art. Having guided the artist, reason enables the viewer to "read" the artist's unequivocal, clear composition of an inventive, ennobling subject: Poussin's term, "*la belle pensée*" (the beautiful idea) incorporates reason, as well as intellectual and formal invention, and it requires attentive viewing.[103]

Charles Le Brun, head of the French Academy, pursued this emphasis on reason and developed a systematic pedagogy in which the imitation of exemplary artistic models rather than nature was central. To the extent that art is understood as teachable, of course, it is acquired rather than innate. Le Brun's categorization of emotions—in essence, bringing mood and feeling into a rationalistic system—had the potential to demystify art for both artists and viewers.[104] It is not that anyone could be an artist by learning rules and being trained, but that rules and training assumed much more importance with respect to innate gifts and the free exercise of fantasy.

These neoclassical currents would seem to preclude or at least dampen the tradition of the fantastic and grotesque that I have traced in this chapter. That tradition continued, though, relocated to the concept of the *capriccio* (caprice, or the Spanish *capricho*) in the seventeenth and eighteenth centuries, drawn from musical theory and applied to figurative art, ornament, and architecture, where it was best exemplified by Francesco Borromini. The *capriccio* was related to sixteenth-century ideas of imaginative invention: In his 1550 edition of *Lives*, for example, Vasari used the term to describe Apelles' *Calumny*.[105] As developed in the Baroque period, however, the *capriccio* was more dangerously licentious. In the name itself was embedded the old moral dangers necessitating control of fantasy: *capo*, meaning "head," was bound oddly to *riccio*, meaning "hedgehog." The combination suggested a wavering, unpredictable impetuousness, codified by the image in Cesare Ripa's *Iconologia* (1603) of a youth in fool's clothing, holding a spur in one hand and a bellows to his head. Another derivation from *capra* (goat) reinforced the *capriccio*'s unpredictability by an analogy to the animal's sudden springing, and the association between goats and Bacchic sexuality, John Ciofalo argues, must have appealed to Goya.[106]

Redolent with the artist's *aura*, the *capriccio* was freely creative to the point of being bizarre. Extremely diverse elements could be included under its aegis. The Florentine art historian and critic Filippo Baldinucci, writing in 1681, described its motley inhabitants as drunkards, plebeians, mountebanks (charlatans), spirits, and demons.[107] In Callot's fifty etched *Caprices*, one set executed in Florence in 1617 and the other in Nancy in 1622, wildly running horses, *commedia dell'arte* figures, views of Florentine festivals, and battle

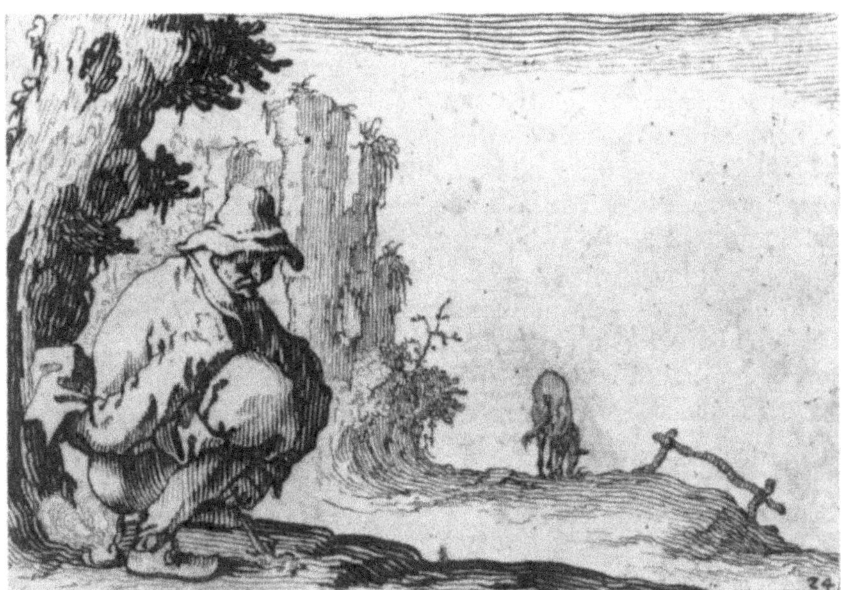

Figure 2.7. Jacques Callot, *Defecating Peasant* from *Les Caprices*, 1617 and 1622. Etching, 53 × 80 mm. Musée des Beaux-Arts, Nancy. Cliché by G. Mangin.

scenes combine with elegantly costumed aristocrats, grotesque dancers, and peasants—one even defecating, like Baldung's witchlike woman (figure 2.7; see figure 1.3). Callot may have composed the series to amuse (with that Tuscan "liberty of *disegno*") Don Lorenzo de' Medici, younger brother of Grand Duke Cosimo II, for whom Callot worked between 1614 and 1621. The naturalism of the peasant (steam rises from his excrement) and the grotesque distortion of other figures vie with the artificial, ornamental quality of many of the *Capricci*, and with Callot's mannered, calligraphic line itself. The result is that the series as a whole suggests, as Werner Busch has aptly observed, the theoretical reconfiguration of the limits and possibilities of art around 1600.[108] One might extend Busch's comment to Callot's entire etched oeuvre, with its remarkable juxtapositions of brutal realism; Mannerism; and fantastic, grotesque, and demonic elements—the last being spectacularly apparent in his Boschian *Temptation of St. Anthony* of 1634.

The *capriccio* was decried by eighteenth-century neoclassical critics such as Francesco Milizia in his *Dictionary of Fine Art* (1797) as arbitrary, whimsical, and divorced from reason and rule: in a word, insane.[109] It was as culpable as the supposedly unselective naturalism of Caravaggesque painters or the *Bamboccianti* (northern painters of low-life genre), all perceived as distinctly anticlassical. The radical freedom of the *capriccio* ultimately extended to the abandonment of readily discernible subject matter, as in Salvator Rosa's etched figural series from the mid-1650s (figure 6.13), dedicated to his friend and patron for the latter's amusement, or Giambattista Tiepolo's "Jokes or Plays of Fantasy" (*Scherzi di Fantasia*; 1743–57; see figure 6.14), a controversial series in which narrative content seems to be tantalizingly suggested but never quite defined, in the manner of a dream.[110] With the *capriccio*, artists' early efforts to invent their own subject matter became, paradoxically, a freedom from any subject matter at all, the creation of subject matter from the artist's inner self, or even that inner self as subject matter. As we will see, Goya's witchcraft images vehemently assert this freedom. Yet at the same time they claim the artist's authorial role in a more traditional sense, for Goya revised the *capriccio* by investing it with serious, complex, and socially relevant content.

Early modern art-theoretical constructs are important aspects of the social and historical context in which the witchcraft genre developed. The discourse of art theory shaped artists' decisions and career trajectories. It is not simply the emergence of the idea of diabolical witchcraft in the late fifteenth century but its applicability of contemporary ideas about art that moved artists to present themselves through the images discussed in this book. It is significant that in the beginning of the witchcraft genre in the late fifteenth century, we find Dürer's multilayered, ambivalent, and provocative engravings, inspired by the fortuitous simultaneity of the stereotype of witchcraft and crucial changes in the notion of artistic invention. At the end, as witch-hunting died, we find Goya asserting the artist's capacity to meld fantasy and social critique. It is only the conjunction of the European witch-hunts and early modern theories of art that made the theme, with its topical urgency, its learned controversies, and above all its focus on the grotesque female body, a particularly telling test of artistic inventiveness.

Chapter 3
Inventing the Witch in the European Heartland: Dürer and Baldung

In hindsight, the psychotyranny of Baldung's witches includes the inquisitor's fires.

—Joseph Leo Koerner, The Moment of Self-Portraiture in German Renaissance Art

Introduction: Germany and the Witch-Hunts

Germany has been understood as the epicenter of the European witch-hunts. Not only was the notorious *Malleus maleficarum* (Hammer of witches, 1487) inspired by Jacob Sprenger and Heinrich Kramer's campaigns in the upper Rhineland in the 1480s, but the worst examples of persecutions during the peak period of the hunts occurred in the German-speaking territories of western Europe. The most recent estimate for German executions between 1560 and 1660 is twenty to twenty-five thousand, a figure dwarfing that of other European territories.[1] These include well-documented episodes, running from the 1580s through the mid-1630s, such as Trier, Ellwangen, Eichstätt, Cologne, Würzburg, and Bamberg. From these disturbing narratives, one envisions a Germany lighted by burning stakes like so many trees in a wood—an analogy applied by one observer at Wolfenbüttel in Brunswick in 1590.[2] In 1636, Cardinal Albizzi, sent from Rome to curb the Cologne witch-hunt, described a similar scene.[3] In the Preface to *Europe's Inner Demons* (1975), Norman Cohn contemplated the relationship between the early modern witch-hunts and the twentieth-century Holocaust, wondering what drove a society to "purify the world through the annihilation of some category of human beings imagined as agents of corruption and incarnations of evil."[4]

As Wolfgang Behringer has explored in detail, however, there are reasons to qualify this characterization of Germany as the heartland of witch-hunting. Most obvious is the ambiguity of the term "Germany."[5] During the early modern period, German-speaking or German-influenced territories (e.g., the Duchy of Lorraine) were politically and religiously fragmented. The Habsburg

Empire in its Spanish and Austrian branches presided loosely over an assortment of entities ruled by both secular and ecclesiastical authorities: duchies, "free" imperial cities, and prince-bishoprics. In the 1560s, when large-scale persecutions began, Habsburg dominion extended through the Lowlands and Holstein at its north; Lorraine and the Franche-Comté at its north and west; the Swiss Confederation, Savoy, Milan, Genoa, and Tuscany at its south; and Austria, Silesia, and Bohemia at its east. By the mid-seventeenth century, this vast area was eroded by the loss of the northern Netherlands, the Swiss Confederation and the north Italian duchies, and confessional differences divided its remaining territories. Moreover, the diversity of local authorities under the broad aegis of the Holy Roman Empire permitted a patchwork of judicial systems that never attained unity even under Charles V's imperial law code of 1532, the *Constitutio Criminalis Carolina*. This judicial fragmentation is one reason for the severity of some German witch-hunts.[6] Wherever the code of the *Carolina* could be enforced, witch-hunting was sharply curtailed. Although the first stirrings of German nationalism were felt in the early modern period, Germany was not a nation. In contrast to Scotland, for instance, Germany experienced no witch-hunt driven by state-building, although regional or local authority was often at issue.[7] Indeed, German territories under the Holy Roman Empire exemplify just how crucial centralized judicial authority could be for *preventing* the large-scale execution of accused witches.

Behringer points out that our notion of the intensity of witch-hunting in Germany must be qualified by consideration of both the geographical and chronological extent of persecutions and the number of executions relative to regional populations. Although many episodes were severe, yielding a high proportion of executions during concentrated periods (a mere five governments account for eight thousand deaths), in many territories this proportion is low and spread over many generations.[8] Such conclusions depend on statistics from current or future regional studies that are crucial to our fuller understanding of the witch-hunts. What has emerged from existing research is a deepening picture of the complexity and diversity of German responses to witchcraft. Scholars' explorations of the social and political dynamics of specific German episodes reveal a variety of social, political, and religious forces driving or hampering witch-hunting; together these illustrate the range of possible responses found in early modern Europe.

Given these qualifications, however, scholars have begun to assemble fundamental reasons for the severity of certain German episodes. As already noted, political and judicial particularism—the capacity of local authorities to escape supervision by a central authority, as in the cases of the prince-bishoprics—is a major factor. Confessionalization is another. Without arguing for religious tension as the major cause, Robin Briggs notes the intensity of witch-hunting in the "dark ribbon" surrounding the Spanish Road, the artery of

Catholic Habsburg power along the Rhine through Switzerland to the southern Netherlands. The worst of the German episodes between 1628 and 1632, Monter states, coincided with religious zeal after the restitution of Catholicism in some areas.[9] Although German Protestant authorities did not eschew witch-hunting, they were less likely than Catholic authorities to execute large numbers of witches, especially when the latter were influenced by an intense Counter-Reformation piety stressing repentance and apocalyptic doom. The impact of Johann Weyer's skepticism on German Protestant territories was great as well.[10] However, Catholic zeal can hardly be blamed for German witch-hunting when Bavaria, as Behringer's major study has decisively shown, exhibited so much resistance.[11]

One of the most important insights of recent German historical scholarship on the witch-hunts has been their relation to climate, weather, and food supply. Behringer makes clear that major persecutions did not occur in German centers of power but in poor, traditional societies with much malnutrition and illness, where witch-hunting worked "functionally" (even though it was dysfunctional in the long run). Poor harvests and famines in German territories triggered the scapegoating of accused witches. In many cases, witch-hunting does not seem to have been driven by authorities' wishes but by their response to the demands of a populace seeking to better its wretched lot by purging witches. Certain common assumptions held in German agricultural regions about the activities of witches—the production of hailstorms and killing of animals, for example—fostered such demands. In particular, Behringer emphasizes the importance of the "little glacial age" between 1560 and 1630, a combination of cold winters and humid summers that increased famine and disease in central and western Europe.[12]

One factor that affected the severity of witch-hunting in some German territories is the early foothold gained by the stereotype of the witch in upper Germany and Switzerland. As early as the Council of Basel (1431–39), an important synod tackling issues of Church reform, Christian unity and heresy, tales of the new sect of witches were shared by attendees and taken back to their respective territories.[13] Writings such as Dominican Johannes Nider's *Formicarius* (The ant colony, 1435–38) and the anonymous *Errores Gazariorum* (Errors of the Cathars, here a synonym for witches, 1437) promulgated a new merger of magic and heresy and made a transition from persecuting medieval heretics to witches. This early, witchcraft was not inextricably linked to women, but Nider explained why women were so often drawn to witchcraft: their weakness of body and faith, and their talkativeness that led to its transmission. As Michael Bailey explains, for him the apostasy of witches was exacerbated by the harm they caused as "surrogate demons."[14] By the 1450s, this new concept of witchcraft is apparent in trials of Els von Meersburg in Lucerne and Margret Jegerin in Lauterburg, Alsace.[15]

Nonetheless, as many scholars have noted, there was considerable resistance to Sprenger and Kramer's inquisitorial activities against witches, beginning in the 1480s in the upper Rhineland. A persecution in Ravensburg near Lake Constance in 1484 and obstacles Kramer encountered in his failed attempt to prosecute a woman in Innsbruck in 1485 inspired the publication of the *Malleus* in 1487, accompanied by Innocent VIII's Bull opening with the Latin words *Summis desiderantes* (desiring with supreme ardor [the flourishing of the Catholic faith]) and a supportive letter from the Emperor Maximilian. Noting that many people in upper Germany and in the territories of Mainz, Cologne, Trier, Salzburg, and Bremen have given themselves to witchcraft, the Bull urges both clergy and laypersons to cease resisting the inquisitors and threatens the uncooperative with excommunication and other penalties.[16] Some, like Georg Golser, Bishop of Brixen, thought Kramer a senile fool who "should go back to his cloister and stay there"—a reaction similar to that of some modern readers of the *Malleus*.[17]

Shortly after the *Malleus* emerged, more moderate views were expressed. In *De lamiis et pithonicis mulieribus* (Concerning female sorcerers and soothsayers), published at Constance in 1489 and in a German edition at Strasbourg in 1493, learned law professor Ulrich Molitor took a relatively skeptical position on witchcraft. His book took the form of a dialogue between himself, the Chief Magistrate of Constance, Conrad Schatz, and Duke Sigmund (or Sigismund) of Austria.[18] Sigmund had been urged to prosecute witches in his territory by Innocent VIII as well as by Kramer and Sprenger. Against the duke's objections to aspects of witchcraft such as bodily flight and metamorphosis into animals, Molitor posits the power of the devil—ultimately serving God by testing the faithful—to deceive foolish women. Although this was a comparatively temperate view, it did not lessen the witches' culpability, for they could never be redeemed from their heresy and deserved extirpation, preferably by fire.[19] The six crude woodcuts in Molitor's text do not show skepticism but depict weather magic, archer magic, a warlock riding a wolf, flying witches partially transformed into animals, witches banqueting, and a witch embracing an incubus (figure 3.1).

The sporadic nature of trials and executions for witchcraft in Germanic territories in the wake of the *Malleus* reflects this initial caution about a new idea. In fact, the *Malleus* was not very influential until the initiation of large-scale hunts after 1560. From 1574 to 1669 it was frequently republished to correspond to the increased fear of witchcraft during the peak period. However, its thirteen Latin editions from French, German, and Italian presses between 1487 and 1520 speak for a contemporary interest in its message, even though we lack precise statistics for witchcraft persecution in southwest Germany before the Reformation.[20] Kramer bragged of over two hundred executions in the region

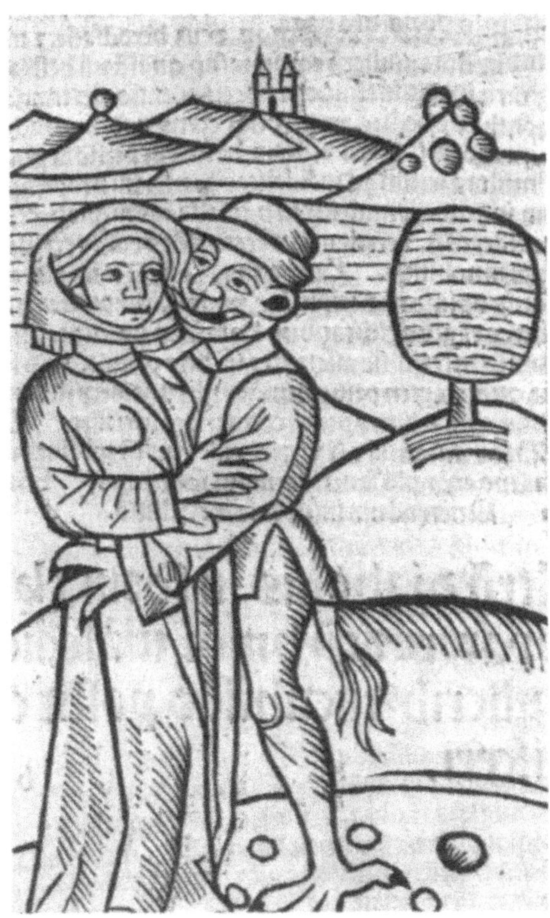

Figure 3.1. *Witch Embracing an Incubus Demon.* Woodcut illustration from Ulrich Molitor's *De lamiis*, Constance, 1489. Division of Rare and Manuscript Collections, Carl A. Kroch Library, Cornell University.

in a letter to the Nuremberg city council, but a zealous inquisitor's assertions are suspect.

Not coincidentally, this period corresponds to the earliest artistic representations of the female witch. In these images, German artists developed visual strategies focusing on the aesthetic novelty of the nude female body that echoed the misogynistic rhetoric of the *Malleus*. These early images, Charles Zika observes, are works in progress—experiments mediating among demonology and popular beliefs, broader moral concepts implicated in witchcraft, and the interests of patrons that artists sought to attract.[21] The concept of the witch was codified in both words and pictures. That Albrecht Dürer and Hans Baldung Grien were personally concerned about witchcraft is uncertain. That they discovered the utility of the sensationalistic image of the witch for their own self-fashioning and that the image they created would serve the later persecutions cannot be doubted, as Joseph Koerner states in the epigraph for this chapter.

Of Hammers: Dürer's *Four Witches* and the Rhetoric of the *Malleus*

Dürer's engraving, *The Four Witches*, or *Four Naked Women*, dated 1497, has eluded interpretation (figure 3.2). In his *Teutsche Academie* published at Nuremberg in 1675, Joachim von Sandrart identified the figures as witches but admitted that some thought they represented the Three Graces. He believed the inscription on the globe, "O.G.H.," must be a shorthand prayer for aid against black magic: "O Gott hüte uns von Zaubereyen" (Oh God, protect us from witchcraft).[22] In his monograph on Dürer (1943), Erwin Panofsky connected the print to the *Malleus*. Although he could not point to a specific aspect of the text that corresponded to Dürer's image, he cited Kramer's account of a magical abortion as the type of activity Dürer meant to suggest.[23]

Despite von Sandrart, many have understood Dürer's image in mythological and allegorical terms. In his free copy of 1500, Nicoletto da Modena assumed that Dürer's subject was a Judgment of Paris, with the three competing goddesses in the front and the figure of Discord at the back.[24] Indeed, Dürer did make classical allusions. The central voluptuous figure apparently wears a wreath of myrtle, a plant associated with Venus, and is viewed from the back in a *pudica* pose recalling the *Capitoline*, *Medici*, and ultimately the *Knidian Aphrodites*. She evokes the pagan goddess of love and the other three figures in circular arrangement around her become the Graces.[25] Modern scholars Jesse Poesch (1964), Eugene Dwyer (1971), and Fedja Anzelewsky (1983) have pursued Dürer's allusion, seeking a solution to his riddle in a humanistic synthesis of classical and Christian thought. For Poesch, the interpretive key was a negative, northern European version of Venus and the Graces; for Dwyer, it was a fluid synthesis of Discord and the Fates, the Four Temperaments and Seasons, as well as Four Witches. For Anzelewsky, Dürer's audience would need to synthesize pagan mythology and Christian apocalyptic thought so that Venus and the Graces could be related to Proserpina and the Fates and the central nude identified as "Queen Mandrake," a sign of the end.[26]

Most recently, Margaret Sullivan (2000) asserts that Dürer, inspired by his close friend Willibald Pirckheimer and other German humanists who knew of treatments of the subject in classical literature, approached witchcraft satirically and skeptically, with the goal of asserting artistic originality rather than concern about contemporary witchcraft.[27] As discussed in Chapter 2, ancient

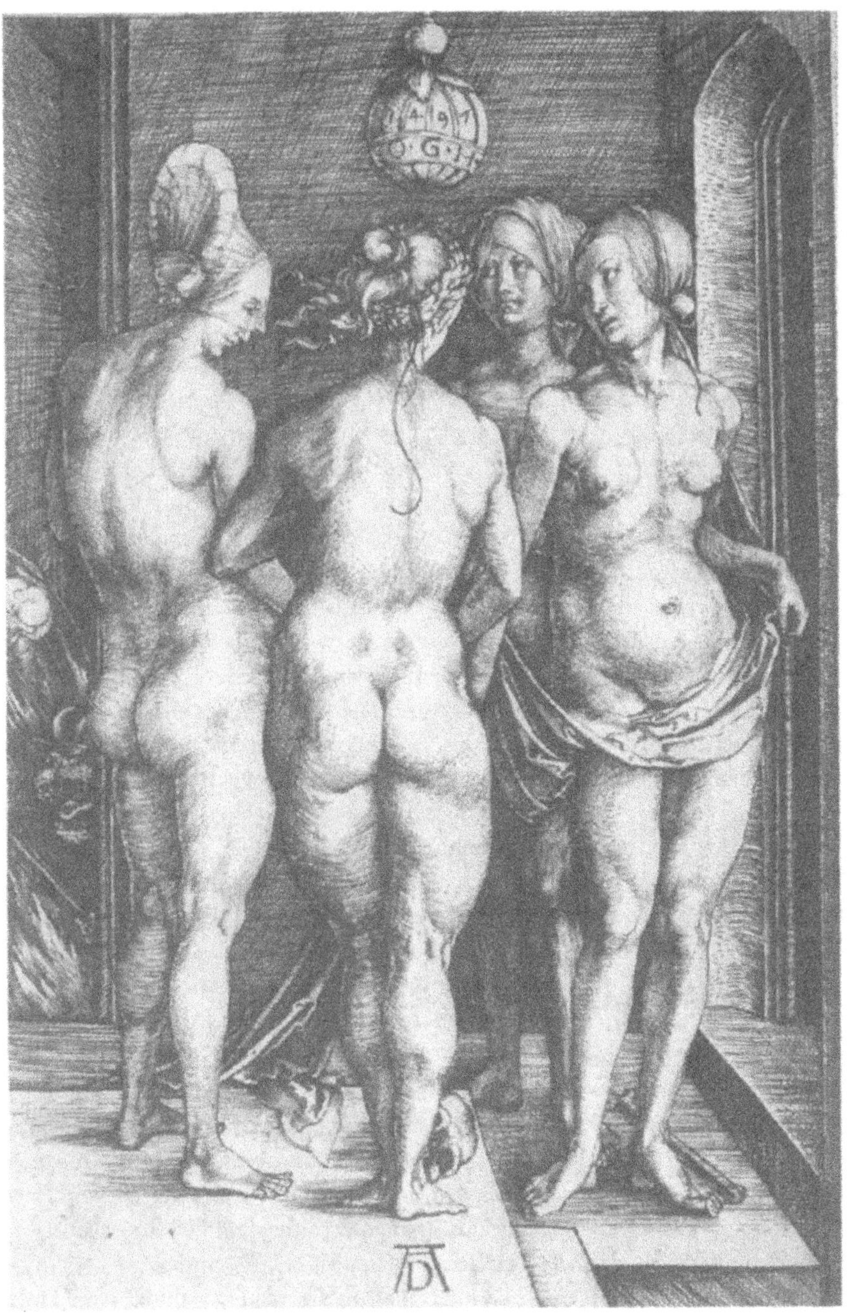

Figure 3.2. Albrecht Dürer, *The Four Witches*, 1497. Engraving, 190 × 131 mm. Kupferstichkabinett, Staatliche Museen, Berlin. SEF/Art Resource, New York.

accounts of witches certainly provided inspiration for early modern artists, who saw them as vindications of their own interests in artistic license and the grotesque. However, Sullivan's thesis rests largely on the untenable premise that witchcraft was not topical when Dürer made his *Four Witches* and *The Witch* (ca. 1500; see figure 3.4). Although it is true that the persecution of witches was sporadic before 1560, the late fifteenth and early sixteenth centuries were the years when the figure of the witch, as Zika states, "was fast becoming critical to the cultural policy and imagination of Europe." As Zika has done for *The Witch*, I argue for the relevance of Dürer's *Four Witches* for "the developing visual language of witchcraft."[28]

The erudite and layered iconography characterizing past interpretations of Dürer's print compromises Sandrart's identification of the four women as witches, while Sullivan circumvents the issue of misogyny by stressing classical influence and artistic originality, as if these were gender-neutral. But no interpretation of *The Four Witches* that subsumes gender can account for its expression. Dürer's arrangement of a few basic elements—female nudes in a conspiratorial huddle, with a demon in the background—held a provocative meaning for the educated males who constituted the audience Dürer most coveted. His allusion to Venus and the Graces was deliberate and emphasized the viewer's role, which was not only to recognize layers of meaning but also to construct meaning from Dürer's clues. *The Four Witches* flirts with the rhetorical strategies of the *Malleus*, also addressed primarily to an audience of educated males. The print's rapport with this text suggests that both tapped common anxieties—broader and deeper than the theological angst Walter Stephens sees as the main impetus behind the *Malleus*.[29]

The *Four Witches* follows a pattern in Dürer's engravings from the last years of the fifteenth and the early years of the sixteenth century. In these remarkable prints, he worked steadily both to improve his skill with the burin and to display his humanistic learning. With their classical and Italianate visual references, and their content often constructed from knowledge of ancient and humanistic texts brought to Dürer's attention by Pirckheimer and his circle, Dürer's early engravings, in contrast to woodcuts which could cut across different social strata, were directed primarily toward educated male viewers of the patrician and middle classes.[30] He impressed them with his technical accomplishment and challenged them with his subject matter.

Despite his middle-class origins in a goldsmith's family, Dürer aspired to an affluent, highly educated circle. His friends, clients, and associates often came from the venerable patrician families of Nuremberg—the Ebners, Holzschuhers, Imhoffs, Kresses, Paumgartners, Pirckheimers, and Tuchers, among others.[31] His prints also circulated widely; in the year the *Four Witches* was published, Dürer contracted an agent to handle "foreign" print sales in other German cities and non-German lands.[32] Certainly the incipient interest in witchcraft both in and beyond his own city influenced his choice and handling of this subject. By his pictorial treatment of the newly defined witch, Dürer visualized a female threat to patriarchal authority and begged the question of authority's response.[33] By hovering ambivalently between his own contemporary world and classical mythology, Dürer gave four nude women a mythic presence.

Put bluntly, Dürer's *Four Witches* expresses men's need to control female sexuality. The engraving's effectiveness is based on what men thought to be ambiguous, secretive, and, most importantly, *shared* about women's activities and knowledge, particularly in the realm of sex. The allusion to Venus and her handmaidens was appropriate because women were being defined in terms of the carnality that Venus embodied. As Cohn established, folk beliefs about the female followers of a pagan goddess, called variously Diana, Herodias, Holda or Perchte, or "Frauw (Lady) Venus," were gradually transformed in the fifteenth century under pressure from learned elites such as inquisitors and judges into the concept of witchcraft.[34]

Poesch recognized the demonic nature of Venus and her companions in northern European thought, even though she minimized Dürer's references to witchcraft. She pointed to the nude in Dürer's engraved *Dream of the Doctor* (ca. 1498) as an example of this northern understanding of Venus not simply as sensuality but also of evil, bestial love. Dürer's conception corresponded to Giovanni Pico della Mirandola's Venus Vulgaris (*amor vulgaris* or "lowly Venus") that appealed only to the senses and the imagination, and, even more negatively, to Marsilio Ficino's *amor ferinus* or bestial love—an insane abandonment to debauchery. Both Giovanni Pico and Ficino were familiar to Pirckheimer and his circle.[35] In *The Dream of the Doctor*, a slothful man sleeping before a warm stove is sandwiched between an imposing Venus and a demon who instill him with lust. Similarly, Poesch asserted that the Graces might be understood as embodiments of the carnal life.[36]

That Dürer was aware of the concept of a demonic Venus connected to witchcraft is also suggested by Charmian Mesenzeva's interpretation of *The Witch* (see figure 3.4) as a contemporary northern Venus figure called Aphrodite Pandemos. Plato contrasted her—the goddess of voluptuousness and daughter of Zeus and Dione—with Aphrodite Urania, embodiment of heavenly love and motherless daughter of Chronos. Dürer's negative conception of Aphrodite Pandemos and the sexuality she embodied is evident in his transformation of her from a beautiful nude into an old woman with sagging breasts, derived from Mantegna (see figure 2.1).[37] In a preparatory drawing, dating about 1496, for a never-finished engraving, Dürer also depicted Aphrodite Urania as she arrived on the shore, awaited by the Horai.[38] Clearly he was interested in the Platonic opposition of heavenly and carnal love.

In the context of contemporary fears about witchcraft, however, carnality was becoming gender-specific. Indeed, this vice *in women* explained witchcraft for Kramer, who intensified a venerable Christian tradition of misogyny. The sexual drive was bound to women, and both were bound to evil. In the *Malleus*, this misogyny was wedded to the apocalyptic mentality defined by Stuart Clark as so important for the early modern idea of witchcraft.[39] As evidence of the implacable opposition of the devil and his army of demons and witches to male Christian authority, Kramer reiterated women's power to incite lust and to control male sexuality through demonic magic, lending a new urgency to old monkish fears.[40]

As Sigrid Brauner points out, the frequent early republication of the *Malleus* indicates a hunger to learn about a new phenomenon, for one of the key aspects of witchcraft as defined by Kramer was its newness.[41] Aimed first at men possessing the ecclesiastical and especially the secular authority to prosecute witches, the *Malleus* embraced a wider audience intrigued by, if variously receptive to, its message. In Nuremberg, Dürer's godfather Anton Koberger published editions in 1494 and 1496. In 1491, at the Nuremberg government's request, Kramer wrote an instructional book in German on the identification and prosecution of witches for officials and judges, although this text apparently had little impact on the city's restrained approach to the crime.[42] In 1496, Kramer also published sermons in Nuremberg, one of which railed against witches and those who committed the heresy of not believing in them.[43]

If Dürer were not made aware of the *Malleus* by these circumstances, he would have known about witch trials occurring more frequently throughout the Rhineland in its wake. Kramer and Sprenger were both natives of the region. Kramer was born in lower Alsace, and Sprenger in Basel. While Sprenger's hub was Cologne, where he was dean of the faculty of theology at the university, Kramer's was Salzburg, where he headed the Dominicans and was a close associate of the archbishop. The *Malleus* cited southwestern German cases and was aimed at the territory in-between.[44] A calendar of witch trials of the 1490s reveals a preponderance of Swiss and South German incidents, in part because of their witch-hunting and preaching activities.[45] These events would not have been lost on Dürer, always attuned to the unusual, as he embarked on his journeyman travels through the Rhineland from 1490 to 1494.[46]

Nuremberg, like many German economic and cultural centers, was quite temperate in its persecution of witches.[47] However, Hartmut Kunstmann's archival research demonstrates some concern about the problem after 1470. In 1486, Barbara Eyrichin and Anna Hansen were discovered attempting to magically animate the corpse of a condemned criminal, but they were let go because it was not clear what harm was done. Els Rutzscherin was permanently banished in 1487 for performing unspecified herbal magic. These cases indicate the still-tentative nature of the concept of witchcraft, but Rutzscherin's indictment was significantly accompanied by charges that she had worshipped a demon "against the Christian order." Kunstmann singles out the trial of Margarete Salchingerin in 1489 as evidence of the influence on Nuremberg's governing authorities of the theological and legal debates about witchcraft set forth in the *Malleus*. For the first time, the Council felt the need to consult local clergy about the punishment of the accused. Forced to wear a cap with a devil's face painted on it, Salchingerin suffered the pillory and permanent banishment.[48]

Dürer's interest in witchcraft in the 1490s, then, was not stimulated just by the knowledge that ancient poets had written about it but by its currency. He added tension and drama to a subject depicted in Molitor's text in a straightforward, naive way (see figure 3.1). Indeed, *The Four Witches* shows a similar relationship to the simple illustrations in Molitor's text as his contemporary *Apocalypse* woodcuts show to their precedents in illustrated Bibles and blockbooks.[49] Moreover, the ungendered character of Molitor's illustrations that Sullivan and Zika note is transformed: *The Four Witches* affirms a special relationship between the devil and women and opposes their world to that of the educated male viewer.[50]

In the words of Gerhild Scholz Williams, witchcraft fascinated learned, rational men because "it was a space to which they had no access"—a situation symbolized by the closed, circular space defined by Dürer's figures. Like the New World, it was an unfamiliar domain whose wonders were to be catalogued and probed by believers and skeptics alike.[51] A masterpiece of insinuation, Durer's image is the perfect embodiment of the status of the concept of witchcraft in the late fifteenth century as it coalesced from ancient beliefs in clandestine, orgiastic nocturnal gatherings, cannibalistic infanticide, and night-flying women who followed a goddess to "Venusberg" for riotous revelry.[52] The *Malleus* forged these beliefs into an apocalyptic misogyny, envisioning an organized conspiracy of witches and the devil against the Christian order—a sure sign of the end.[53] Certainly Kramer thought of contemporary female witches as serious and immediate burdens on humanity ("Onus Generi Humani" is another potential solution to the puzzle of the inscription on the globe) deserving extermination.

In his contemporary, magisterial *Apocalypse* woodcuts, Dürer also capitalized on this eschatological expectation.[54] Like Kramer, he lent an infernal power to female sexuality by alluding to Venus and the Graces to recall old ideas about women who gathered on "Venusberg." He feminized the vice of *luxuria* and negated any positive interpretation of this mythological motif with the demon.[55] Although the Venus figure is central, she is seen from the back; her sexuality is inaccessible. Because we cannot move around her, the *pudica* pose does not function as an erotic tease as in the *Knidian Aphrodite* and her descendants but as an ironic inversion of her true nature. Along with the arms of the other three figures, it calls attention to Venus's unseen pubic area: a symbolic focus and source of power. Through his pictorial choices, Dürer played upon the magical and nefarious associations of the *pudica* Venus-type in the Middle Ages and Renaissance.[56] His emphasis on concealment also echoes early modern descriptions of female genitalia as mysterious and secret. As Lyndal Roper has shown, such descriptions contrast with those of men's genitalia as active, almost separate beings, as well as to the more public display of the phallus—for example, the codpiece.[57]

Despite the ominous quality of this female gathering, Dürer denied his nudes the power of the gaze, for Venus's face is hidden, and even her only handmaiden who faces us averts her eyes. The concept of Renaissance woman as spectacle, discussed by Peter Stallybrass and Patricia Simons among others, is expressed in Dürer's insistent display of naked females who can be scrutinized from many angles by both viewer and demon, but who look at neither. In this respect, Dürer's witches contrast with Baldung's bolder ones. As Koerner has suggested, these later witches often confront male viewers blatantly, implicating them in the very evil and carnality they are supposed to abhore.[58] They seem to exist wholly outside social regulation. The bodies of Dürer's witches are still subject to a controlling surveillance, their female power to authority's regulation.

Not only do Dürer's women lack objectifying gazes of their own but they are naked and arranged decorously, unlike the gesticulating, tumbling witches of Baldung's drawings. The naked female body, Margaret Miles argues, persistently resisted any positive religious connotations that accrued to male nakedness, signifying instead powerlessness and the fallen state, while the nakedness (and/or hairlessness) of the accused witch, Scholz Williams asserts, signified her vulnerability to examination and torture.[59] Roper concludes from her investigation of the use of the term "naked" in documents about sexual encounters in sixteenth-century Augsburg that women were naked more frequently during sex, while men might remain fully or partly clothed. She explains this as a sign of the greater sexualization of their bodies in the early modern period and their lack of "visual mastery." Indeed, Roper continues, women also lacked *words* to describe men's bodies as objects of their own desire. The woman's nakedness expressed not her sexuality, but her capacity to arouse male desire and her vulnerability to it.[60]

Only the demon in Dürer's engraving meets and challenges the viewer's gaze. The *Malleus* emphasized that the new witches were not coerced but entered the pact willingly, intention being an important measure of guilt in Roman and canon law.[61] But the demon really rules this group. In contemporary witchcraft theory, witches' power is subordinated to the authority of the devil (and ultimately of God). Despite Dürer's evocation of conspiratorial female power, his massive nudes are pawns in a struggle for control between demon and viewer. If his most coveted viewer in this case was a patrician or middle-class learned male, his visual rhetoric closely corresponds to the discursive strategy of the *Malleus*. The message of both was clear: Control your women, or the devil will usurp your authority.

Kramer had no doubt that serious harm was occurring as a result of the unholy alliance between the devil and modern women. As Erik Midelfort noted, his emphasis on the enumeration of *maleficia* was innovative, part of his synthesis of heresy and sorcery.[62] Dürer echoed this synthesis by juxtaposing the demon in the doorway with the ominous skull and bones at the nude witches' feet. The viewer knew that the women were carnal, allied with the devil, and murderous. Perhaps the fear that they were not only bewitching but killing men accounts for Dürer's more tenuous allusion to the Fates. The kerchief binding the hair of the right-hand figure extends into a drapery that subtly suggests the skein of yarn they spun, measured and cut to determine human mortality.[63]

The circular arrangement of the figures, recalling the motif of Venus and the Graces, personified voluptuousness and carnal temptations and expressed a conspiratorial mood. We cannot see what the women are doing, but we know that they are up to no good. Evidently, they converse among themselves about a mutually shared, secret knowledge. To paraphrase Dürer's contemporary, Theophrastus Paracelsus, witches are women who turn away from men, not looking them in the eye, shutting themselves in, lying alone, refusing men.[64] When we realize that such an exclusion posits *viewers* as the "other," thus inverting current social order, we can begin to understand how provocative Dürer's *Four Witches* would have seemed to his audience.

To persuade ecclesiastical and secular authorities of the urgent need to prosecute witches, Kramer played upon the notion of female conspiracy, pitting male authority against a presumed female power. Exaggerating common notions of women's speech as dangerously disruptive, he asserted that one of the chief reasons for the rapid spread of witchcraft was the female tongue that passed along evil knowledge: "The third reason [that women are more prone to witchcraft] is that they have slippery tongues, and are unable to conceal from their fellow-women those things which by evil arts they know; and, since they are weak, they find an easy and secret manner of vindicating themselves by witchcraft."[65]

Of course, it was mainly carnality that made women such easy prey for the devil. Part I, Question 6, of the *Malleus* also contains the famous sentence, "All witchcraft comes from carnal lust which is in women insatiable." Kramer followed this with a reference to Proverbs 30 about the mouth of the womb that will not say "enough" and leads witches to have sex with demons—the bizarre mechanics of which concerned Kramer because, Stephens argues, it confirmed the reality of demons and thus his faith.[66] Again, the apocalyptic mentality of the *Malleus* emerges. Because demons could use human procre-

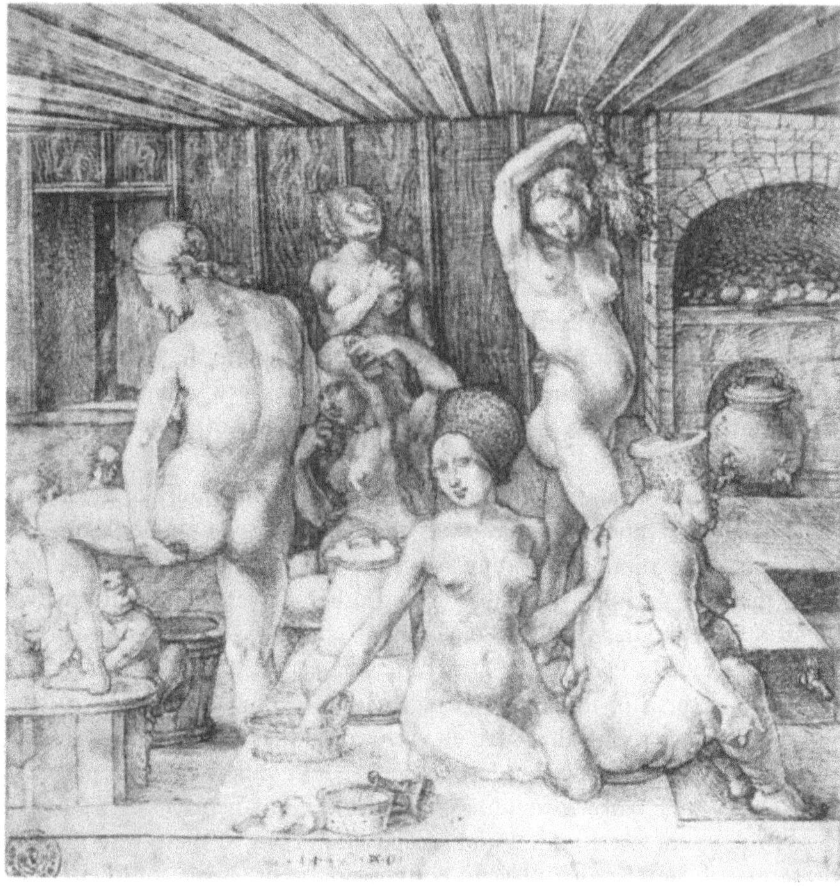

Figure 3.3. Albrecht Dürer, *The Women's Bath*, 1496. Pen drawing in black ink, 232 × 229 mm. Kunsthalle, Bremen.

ation itself to increase their already extensive power, and all women—even the "devout and chaste" who might be drawn into witchcraft by "bawds and hot whores"—were susceptible, the situation in the late fifteenth century was alarming ("O Gott hüte!").[67]

While drawing the male viewer in voyeuristically, *The Four Witches* provoked unease through the figures' secretiveness, ambiguous identity, and undefined setting. Although he hinted at their mythological identities, Dürer also alluded to bathhouse imagery in which women's bodies in closed spaces were voyeuristically perceived (his uneven floor evokes bathhouse benches). Not only have scholars demonstrated the formal relationship between Dürer's witches and figures of his *Women's Bath* in Bremen (figure 3.3), probably a sketch for a woodcut counterpart to his *Men's Bath* of 1496–97, but they have commented on the gendered difference between these two works.[68] A male voyeur and viewers peek from the back and front into the claustrophobic space of *The Women's Bath*. A young woman looks coyly out as she combs her hair; the rest of the diverse, sometimes grotesquely posed or shaped women go about their business. The child in the left corner gazing up at female genitals—a surrogate for the artist and viewer—encapsulates the mood of fascination and repulsion. This type of bath, regarded as unhealthy because it promoted disease, especially syphilis, was currently being displaced by the open-air facilities represented in *The Men's Bath*; in other words, Dürer depicted the contrast between health and disease through gender.[69] Although the nudes of *The Four Witches* may suggest Venus and her Graces, then, this suggestion is never quite fulfilled. These figures are not ideal nudes but naked women.

Sigrid Schade remarks that if nakedness is an attribute of witches, then all naked women are potentially witches when not defined clearly as something else.[70] Very early in the history of witchcraft images, Dürer exploited the ambivalence of female nakedness. Significantly, he also implied that the conspiracy of women bridged economic groups; misogyny subsumed considerations of class. Dürer thus combined bathing women with Nuremberg lady, and goddess of love with mortal females, thereby reducing all women to their sexuality and implying that any woman, by virtue of her sexuality, might be "infected" with witchcraft. Held in place by the demon's gaze from the back and the viewer's from the front, and hemmed in at all sides, the powerful nudes exemplify the transgressive female body only potentially held under control by male authority. Scholz Williams aptly describes this dialectic of women's power and authoritarian control in early modern society: Even as witchcraft was understood to empower women, it also confined them, paradoxically, "in an invisible prison constructed by the everpresent threat of discovery and betrayal."[71] Dürer's image places the male viewer on the brink of discovery, at the moment his authority is threatened. The demon invoked by the women has just arrived, and his unspecified relationship to them is highly charged. The carnality embodied in the nude women is inherently infernal.

Another consequence of lust in women, according to the *Malleus*, was the menacing proliferation of magic relating to amatory matters and reproduction: "And truly the most powerful cause which contributes to the increase of witches is the woeful rivalry between married folk and unmarried men and women." Kramer continues, citing St. Thomas on the devil's desire to control human venereal acts (as opposed to other human activities), and asserting that the worst kind of witches, the lustful and ambitious "adulteresses, fornicatresses and the concubines of the Great," will exterminate the faith through their carnal control of the "mighty ones of the age."[72] Lène Dresen-Coenders points out, however, that Kramer's concerns also reflect social reality. For example, he thought that married women might be seduced by the devil out of fear of desertion and the loss of economic security. Unmarried women (and the marriage age was becoming increasingly older in the early modern period) might succumb out of fear of not finding a husband; jilted women might turn to vengeance when deserted by fiancés in the "clandestine" marriages over which the Church was trying to gain control. Dresen-Coenders emphasizes that the *Malleus* reflects a patriarchal order that wanted to maintain its control over marriage and sexual relationships and felt itself to be losing ground.[73]

In the new witches' presumed manipulation of sexuality and reproduction lies the importance of the globe in Dürer's engraving and its enigmatic inscription. Is the globe an ornament, the Apple of Discord, a terrestrial or celestial sphere or, as many have asserted, an enlarged "male" mandrake berry.[74] In fact, its shape and appearance correspond closely to botanical illustrations of *mandragora*. Based on the mandrake, Gustav Hartlaub (1940) interpreted Dürer's subject as love-magic, and Rudolf Wustmann (1911) as a spell to aid conception.[75] If this is the case, the "begetting of all humanity" (Omnium Generatio Hominum) is a possible solution to the inscription. As a frequent ingredient of love-philters and potions for conception and easy childbirth in which its juice was mixed with sulfur; the mandrake embodied women's seductive power over men and over conception and birth.[76] When enriched by the capabilities of demons, as in the new witchcraft described in the *Malleus*, these female powers could not be tolerated.

Among the group Dürer wanted to reach and to which he aspired were those described in the *Malleus* as the "Great," thought to be especially vulnerable to carnal relations with witches. We might read in *The Four Witches* Dürer's own alarm and participation in the oppositional mentality that set men against women. But it is also possible to understand *The Four Witches* as an instance of the artist's opportunistic timing, his keen sense of the sensationalistic appeal of the rhetoric of the *Malleus* for his contemporaries. In either case, the engraving is an inventive conundrum that hinges on the female nude as vehicle of both a threatening female power and a male artistic authority. Dürer piqued the interest of his audience, challenged their knowledge, and required their participation. Like the chain in Pollaiuolo's *Battle of the Nudes* in Patricia Emison's interpretation, the "O.G.H" is a provocative clue, allowing the viewer to exercise intellectual autonomy (see figure 2.2).[77]

Koerner's analysis of Baldung's witchcraft images as works in which a stunning artistic originality generates in the viewer an abjection, unease, and complicity in lust needs to begin with Dürer's *Four Witches*. Attempts to interpret the print that ignore or subsume gender circumvent its expressive core, for only the contemporary notion of female sexuality can account for the threatening resonance this curious combination of the female nudes, demon, and mandrake fruit would have held for Dürer's most valued audience.

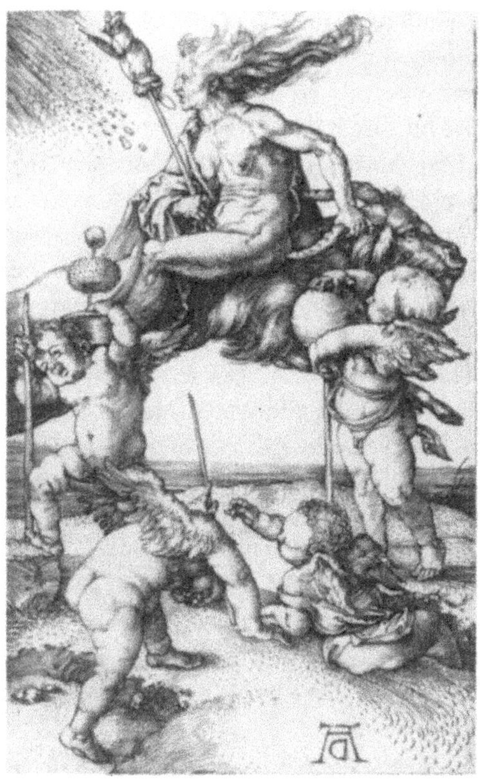

Figure 3.4. Albrecht Dürer, *The Witch* (or *Witch Riding Backwards on a Goat*), ca. 1500–1501. Engraving, 115 × 70 mm. Kupferstichkabinett, Staatliche Museen, Berlin. Photo by Jörg P. Anders. Bildarchiv Preußischer Kulturbesitz/Art Resource, New York.

Of Hags: Dürer's *Witch*

Dürer's *Witch*, or *Witch Riding Backwards on a Goat*—far more significant as a prototype for the witchcraft genre than *The Four Witches*—embodies the inversion and social disorder threatened by unregulated women (figure 3.4). While exemplifying the Renaissance interest in the study of age, like the old woman in the Bremen drawing, she also shows how old age could be gendered. Leonardo's studies of grotesque and often aged figures have been interpreted by Martin Kemp as signs of the inventive capacity of the artist and as challenges to literary *facitie*, ribald farces focusing on human weaknesses.[78] Dürer adapted this motif by drawing on contemporary attitudes toward old women. Often widowed, indigent, sharp-tongued irritants to their neighbors, they were frequently victims of accusations of witchcraft that took many years to accrue. Anne Barstow argues that it was more than their economic and social marginalization in early modern Europe that made them vulnerable, it was the contemporary understanding of their sexuality and their nonideal bodies. The sexual drive was believed to be greater in postmenopausal, widowed women. Their sexuality was especially repugnant not only because of their physical appearance but also because it could not lead to procreation.[79]

As with *The Four Witches*, Dürer's *Witch* has been the subject of complex iconographic interpretations, focusing on the goat as the astrological sign of Capricorn, the nocturnal realm of the planet and god Saturn, with his associations of castration, violence and melancholy.[80] As Zika points out, Saturn's progeny were society's outcasts—cripples, beggars, Jews—or embodiments of evil like cannibals, magicians, and witches. Thus Dürer's figure, read in terms of the astrology and ancient mythology known to an educated audience, was an appropriate symbol of social disorder.[81] This was also legible through more accessible signs such as the backwards ride and the distaff and spindle. Riding backwards, as Ruth Mellinkoff has discussed in detail, signified ostracism and derision (as, for example, of the cuckolded husband or unruly woman).[82] Here, the shrew carries the female symbols of distaff and spindle between her legs like a phallus and rides a goat, a symbol of lust and the animal form most often taken by the devil. Her grasp on the goat's horn, as Zika notes, equally conveys her brazen inversion of gender roles, for as a sign of the fool or the cuckolded husband, the he-goat's horn suggested ridicule of men dominated by women.[83]

The witch's lust is conveyed by her open mouth, her suggestive and readily legible grasp of both the goat's horn and the distaff, as well as more erudite references to Venus. As noted earlier, Mesenzeva connected Dürer's figure to that of Aphrodite Pandemos, ancient goddess of earthly love or voluptuousness, and the four *putti* cavorting below not only allude to Venus but express abandonment to instinctive desire.[84] Compositionally, they bind the witch 's flight to the earth she seeks to escape and negate her momentum by pulling her into their aimless, circular tumbling. Ominous indications of her magical power—the hailstorm and her hair moving uncannily in the opposite direction of her flight—hint at the consequences of the social disorder she embodies. But Dürer's deliberate reversal of his monogram (an unthinkable accident for him) is a reassuring sign of the mastery that holds inversion in check.[85]

Despite the long-lasting impact of his quintessential old hag, Dürer's interest in the theme of witchcraft was short-lived, and misogyny does not dominate his art. It never went beyond what we would expect of any male artist in his culture. Ultimately, Dürer's art was too deeply intellectual and pious, too far ranging and inquisitive, to single out the dangers of sex, women, and witches as major subjects. His opportunism was not lost on his best pupil, however. For Baldung, more attuned to the dark side of the human condition, it would provide a major theme within an oeuvre as astonishing for its inventiveness as for its unrelenting attention to sex, sin, and death.

It's Not Easy Being Grien: Artistic Identity in Baldung's 1510 Woodcut

The young artist whom Dürer probably nicknamed "Grien" or "Grünhans" was uniquely suited to carry on the theme of witchcraft.[86] Born in the mid-1480s into a distinguished family originating from the southwestern German village of Schwäbisch-Gmünd, Baldung entered Dürer's shop around 1503 after a brief apprenticeship to an unknown master, possibly in his Swabian homeland or in Strasbourg, where his father Johann was attorney for the bishop and where the artist himself would eventually settle. Hieronymus Baldung, the artist's uncle who ultimately served Maximilian as honorary physician, had moved to the city in 1496. Baldung's cousin Pius Hieronymus taught law at the University of Freiburg beginning in 1506 and in 1527 would become chancellor of the Tyrol. The artist's brother Caspar, also a professor of law at the University of Freiburg beginning in 1502, succeeded Sebastian Brant as the city advocate of Strasbourg (1521–32?) and eventually became a judge in Maximilian's Imperial Chamber Court.[87] Doctors, lawyers, and judges were all concerned with witchcraft, which they interpreted as an illness, a crime, or both.

It was unusual for someone from Baldung's background to choose art as a profession. Were it not for Dürer's cultivation of humanistic learning and his emphasis on the elevated social status of the artist, Baldung might have chosen a university education and a public career. Dürer must have been eager to enlist an artist with the experience of one apprenticeship and from such a prominent family. The two men seem to have been lifelong friends despite an apparent difference in their temperaments and interests. Upon Dürer's death in 1528, a lock of that famous red hair was sent to Baldung. The nickname "Grien" (to take the more mundane interpretation) might have served as a means of distinguishing him from the other apprentices named "Hans" (Schäuffelein, Süss von Kulmbach, and Dürer's younger brother), or simply as a reflection of color preference. But Gustav Radbruch pointed out that a prominent name for the devil was "Grienhans." Baldung's penchant may have been evident early on.[88]

This hypothesis is strengthened by the fact that the "G" for "Grien" appears prominently, and for the first time, with the monogram in Baldung's first major woodcut, the chiaroscuro *Witches Preparing for the Sabbath Flight* of 1510 (figure 3.5). With this remarkable work, the young artist ensured his own visibility while standing in a big artistic shadow. First, it demonstrated his expressive and technical prowess in the new and originally German medium of chiaroscuro woodcut. Second, its assertive carving-out not just of a wood-

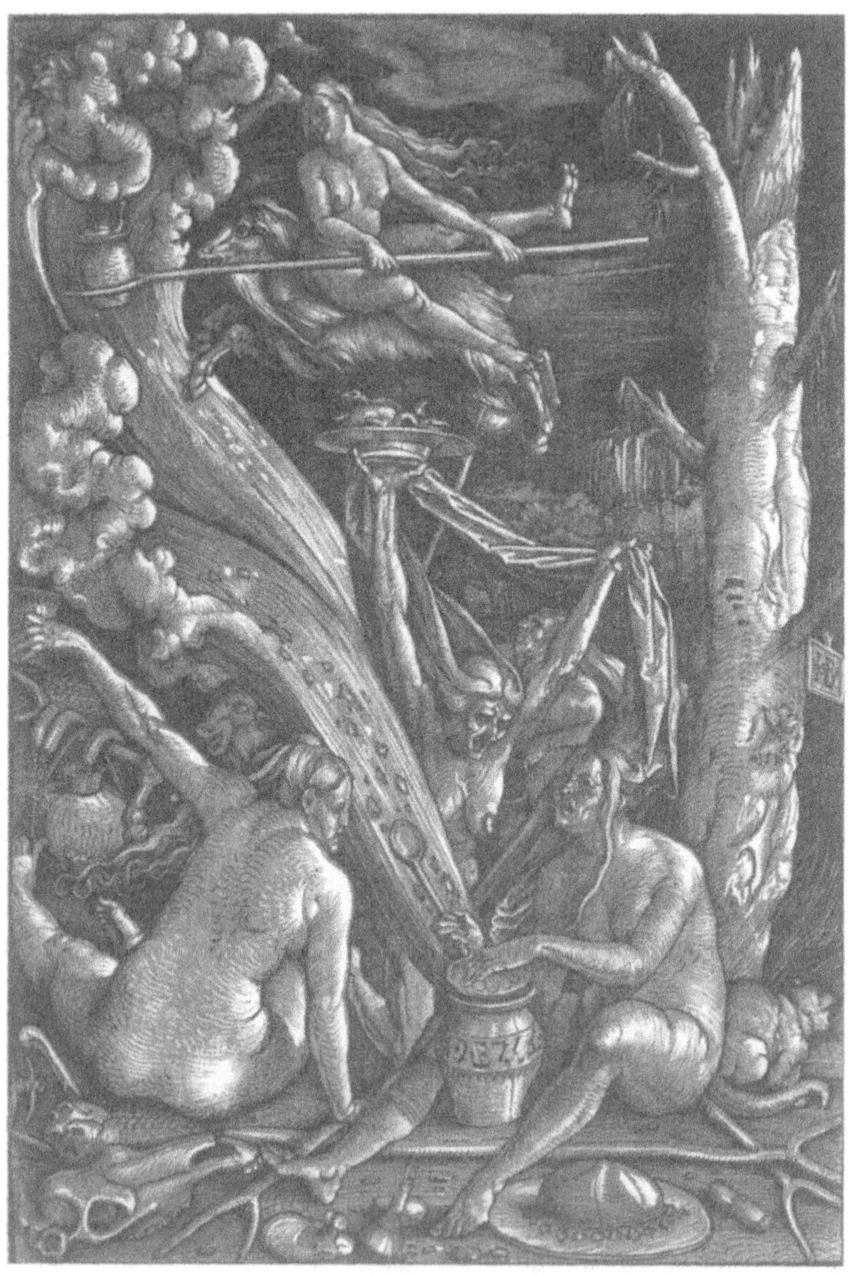

Figure 3.5. Hans Baldung Grien, *Witches Preparing for the Sabbath Flight* (or *The Witches' Sabbath*), 1510. Chiaroscuro woodcut from two blocks, printed in gray and black, 378 × 260 mm. Photograph © 2004 Museum of Fine Arts, Boston. Bequest of W. G. Russell Allen, 69.1064.

block but also of a topical "territory" responded to Dürer's fruitful yet intimidating example. As Koerner emphasizes, Baldung would use witchcraft to implicate his viewers in its abject sexuality as part of his project to undermine the idealizing and stabilizing tendencies in Dürer's art.[89] His use of this theme is one of many Düreresque borrowings that nevertheless set the master's oeuvre on its ear—an oedipal response akin to Italian Mannerist artists' absorption and reworking of Raphael and Michelangelo.[90]

The 1510 woodcut followed Baldung's departure from Dürer's shop, which he probably managed when Dürer went to Venice in 1505, and his 1507 commissions for altarpieces in the city of Halle, including the *Martyrdom of St. Sebastian* (Germanisches Nationalmuseum, Nuremberg). In that work, Baldung appears alongside the saint, confident and resplendent in a green cape, appropriating Dürer's self-portrait in the Uffizi *Adoration of the Magi* of 1504. By 1509, he had moved to Strasbourg; in 1510, he married into a prominent merchant family. Margarethe Herlin was the daughter of Arbogast and niece of Martin Sr., who would be one of Strasbourg's most prominent politicians and a supporter of its militant Zwinglian faction in the Reformation. Her brother Christmann was a mathematician who would teach in the city's classical gymnasium. The marriage brought Baldung citizenship, the right to engage in commerce in the city, and the opportunity to practice his profession. In contrast to Nuremberg, which had no guilds, Strasbourg's guilds gave merchants and artisans a powerful voice.[91] Baldung became a member—and for the last twelve years of his life served on the ruling council—of Strasbourg's large and prestigious guild *Zur Stelz*, which included goldsmiths, engravers, glaziers, printers, and painters. The *Witches' Sabbath* coincides with Baldung's attainment of independent manhood and master's status in his chosen city.

Like Nuremberg, Strasbourg was a free imperial city, a center of trade and publishing, and the major city in the contested region of Alsace, whose Germanic character, fruitfulness, and beauty had recently been touted by historian Jakob Wimpheling in his *Germania* (1501) and *Epitome of German History* (1505).[92] With a population of about twenty thousand, it was a prime place for a young artist to settle. Dürer had almost certainly visited there at the end of his journeyman travels.[93] Not only was Baldung's family already established in the city, but it offered him opportunities for commissions from a strong publishing industry, the Church with its two powerful chapters, the landed nobility, and the wealthy middle class. Baldung could anticipate an excellent living from painting and printmaking and, as Thomas Brady demonstrated, from the investments in annuities, suburban real estate and money-lending to peasants that characterized the local economy.[94] Although Strasbourg society had a well-defined hierarchy, the patricians, merchants, and artisans were interwoven through many familial and economic ties.[95] Prosperity and security beckoned the young artist.

Witches might seem a strange way to mark Baldung's passage into independent professional life, but, like Dürer's *Four Witches*, the 1510 woodcut was a perfect self-fashioning instrument for its historical and cultural moment. Although Dürer and his pupils and associates held sway in Nuremberg until his death in 1528, other German and Swiss artists like Baldung, Lucas Cranach the Elder, Albrecht Altdorfer, Hans Burgkmair, Niklaus Manuel Deutsch, and Urs Graf responded to Dürer's example by self-consciously developing a striking originality in a period of intensely competitive stylistic, technical, and iconographic innovation.[96] Each brandished a distinctive monogram and cultivated a local and regional market: Baldung in the Alsatian capital, Graf in Basel, Manuel in Bern, Burgkmair in Augsburg, Cranach in Wittenberg, and Altdorfer in Regensburg.

Possibly while in Dürer's shop, Baldung had seen Altdorfer's chiaroscuro drawing on pale brown-tinted paper of witches in a forest (1506; Louvre, figure 3.6), an innovative early work in the technique described aptly by Christopher Wood as "one of the great theatres of personal style."[97] The ritual in both works centers on the urn containing flying unguent; the violently upraised arms of Altdorfer's standing witches are used in Baldung's seated witches on the left and in the center; a seated witch with upturned head occupies the right foreground in both works; Dürer's goat-riding witch, now younger, has clearly piqued the imagination of both artists. Like Altdorfer, Baldung set his witches in the German forest: the subject of the first independent landscapes in the European tradition and, as Larry Silver has explored in detail, one that held a range of sometimes antithetical meanings in early sixteenth-century Germany.[98]

Cornelius Agrippa of Nettesheim and other German humanists found a rapport between the human microcosm and the cosmos—a rapport evoked in Altdorfer's oeuvre as figures are absorbed into natural settings. In the Neoplatonic tradition of Agrippa and Paracelsus, the learned male magician sought to use the forces of nature conveyed by landscape, including the beneficent demons he commanded, for good purposes. The dense forests of pine and rock in the paintings of the Danube School also expressed the nascent patriotism evident in the German humanists' response to Tacitus's *Germania*, discovered in the 1420s. Conrad Celtis of Nuremberg, in particular, turned barbarian-bashing on its head to argue for the vigor and simple virtues of the primitive Germans, and scholars of early sixteenth-century Germany (e.g., Pirckheimer, Conrad Peutinger, Beatus Rhenanus, Wimpheling, Aventinus) wrote geographies and histories that shaped German pride in its lands and past, over and against the exploitation and corruption of Rome.[99] The forest was a miraculous and dangerous liminal space for both the mystical experiences and tribulations of saints; according to Tacitus, the ancient Germans worshipped in "woods and groves" (*Germania*, 9). Finally, it was also the abode of lusty,

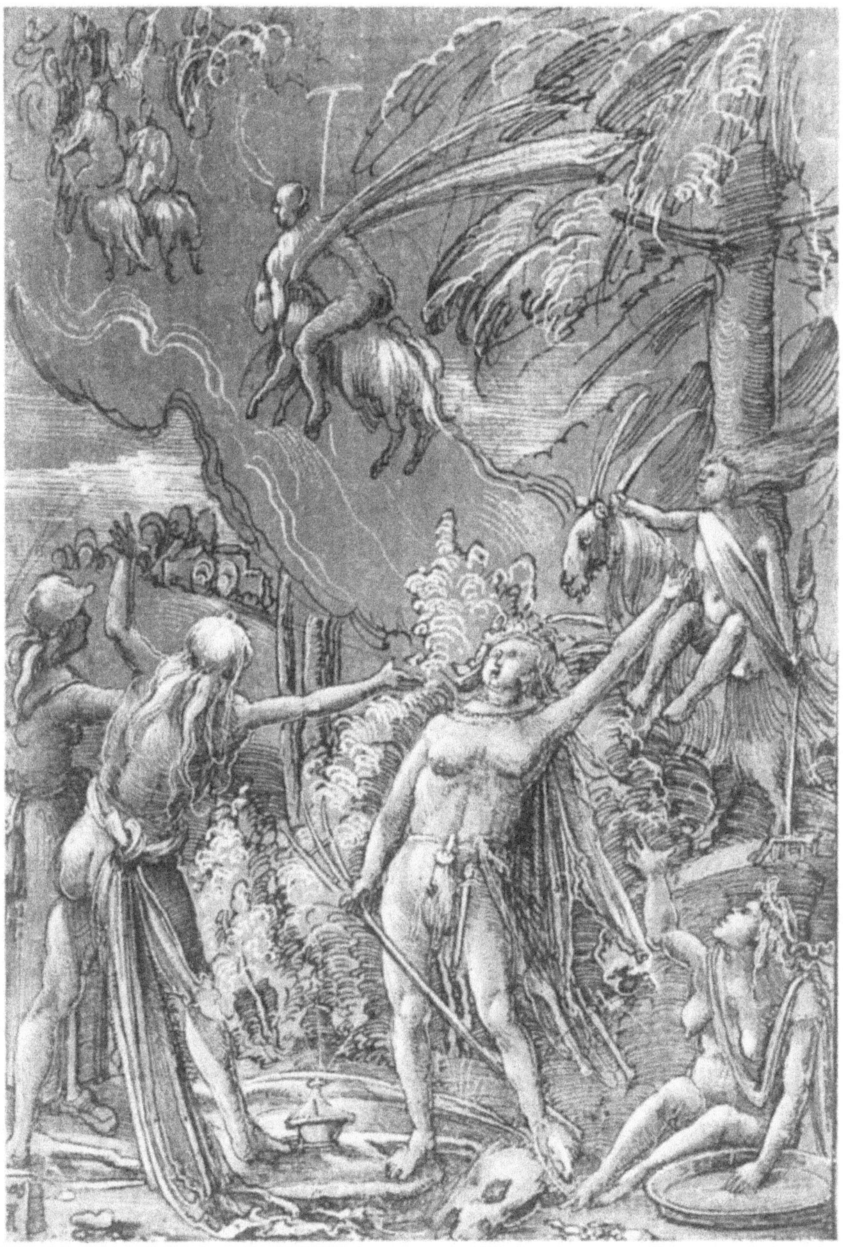

Figure 3.6. Albrecht Altdorfer, *Witches Preparing for the Sabbath Flight*, 1506. Chiaroscuro pen drawing on pale brown tinted paper, 180 × 125 mm. Cabinet des Dessins, Musée du Louvre, Paris. Photo by J. G. Berizzi. Réunion des Musées Nationaux/Art Resource, New York.

primitive wild people and satyrs—all beings grounded in Christian tradition, folklore, and ancient mythology but given contemporary resonance through their association with primitive Germans.[100]

Witches may function in Altdorfer's drawing as symbols of heresy and paganism, like the forest dragon whose battle with St. George served as a metaphor for the conflict between European Christians and the Moslem Turks.[101] Their wild ride, according to Zika, was a complex symbol of social inversion, disorder and emasculation.[102] Theirs is a transgressive female magic, invoking demons (note the markings in the pan at the lower right) who will carry them to their unholy sabbath. Their turbulent, leafy world, like that of the wild people and satyrs, is the antithesis of civilization: a sign, in Wood's words, of the "alliance between wilderness and idolatry," also confirmed by reports from the New World.[103] As a town sleeps unsuspectingly in the distance in Altdorfer's drawing, the civilized viewer (i.e., someone who collected chiaroscuro drawings) comes upon the witches in their forest clearing. Although most of the witches are naked, the woman on the left is dressed in peasant garb. Perhaps we would not be over-reaching to read this image in terms of the artist's middle-class identity and tensions between urban and rural societies.

The differences between Baldung's and Altdorfer's conceptions are extensive, however. Altdorfer staked his claim to originality on his forests and his volatile pen line.[104] Baldung reduced the setting in relation to the bulky, fleshy figures and more sharply delineated iconographic attributes. Objects, bodies, and the oddly plastic stream of vapor strain against the environment that so comfortably embraces them in Altdorfer's drawing. In his *Germania*, Tacitus noted the propensity of the ancient Germans for casting lots and omens and for the particularly female skill of prophesying (*Germania* 8 and 10). But Baldung defines contemporary and more sinister German women, and his deft manipulation of the uncanny and grotesque confronts viewers with an evil that is both spatially and temporally immediate and centered in the female body. The intensity of his images probably reflects a regional concern about witchcraft that came to fruition later: Figures for trials in Alsace, possibly because of the bewildering complexity of its political entities, do not yet exist, although evidence points to about a thousand executions in the peak period.[105]

The technique Baldung chose for his woodcut debut in Strasbourg was brand new, its invention apparently deemed so remarkable that the credit for it was contested. It is now generally believed that Cranach probably back-dated his chiaroscuro woodcuts done around 1509 to 1506 to trump Burgkmair, who, working with his cutter Jost de Negker, Peter Parshall concludes, was probably the first to use the true tone block, the method that ultimately became standard.[106] With its excavated highlights (as opposed to highlights printed positively from light or metallic inks or glue and flocking), this block supplied both middle and high values and, in the finest examples, was conceived along with the line block rather than as an afterthought.

Parshall's discussion of the woodcut in northern Europe in *The Renaissance Print* challenges an older notion of the woodcut as a necessarily poor cousin to intaglio prints. From its inception, the chiaroscuro woodcut, especially, was associated with imperial patronage and an elite audience. Its development confirms what must have been a lively collector's market—difficult to pinpoint but inducible through circumstantial evidence and the works themselves—for the exquisite highlighted drawings on tinted paper that it mimicked. A figure no less important than Peutinger, secretary of Augsburg and counselor to the emperor, fostered the technique's development, and the earliest chiaroscuro woodcuts by Cranach and Burgkmair—equestrian images of St. George and of Maximilian—are luxury prints with imperial iconography.[107]

Surely Baldung was aware of the implications of his medium, lending it a unique style. Whereas his teacher developed a rapport between woodcut and the intricate, velvet tonalities of his engravings, he acknowledged the woodcut's irreducible linearity. Against the insistent boldness of his line, he pitted an equally strident plasticity reinforced by the concentrated massing of highlights in the tone block. Although Parshall raises doubts that Baldung conceived the tone blocks in gray and an eerie, sulfurous orange along with his line block, it seems more likely that the young artist planned every aspect of such an important print.[108] The excavated highlights function to model the powerfully sculptural forms (the tree trunk, the bodies of the three main witches, the curling smoke escaping with uncanny vehemence from the urn) and to create a restless, flickering surface conveying a turgid, nocturnal atmosphere. The 1510 woodcut suggests there was an existing market for Baldung's chiaroscuro drawings and anticipated—or perhaps created—a demand for subsequent drawings among an elite clientele.

Beyond technique and style, however, it was certainly the subject matter—interpreted with Baldung's inimitable combination of élan and perversity—that ensured his print would be noticed. As Sullivan notes, Lucan's *Civil War* and a German translation of Apuleius's *Golden Ass* emerged from Strasbourg presses in 1509, corresponding to a general humanistic interest in ancient accounts of witches that this artist would have known about.[109] But Baldung's witches are not simply humorous, inventive exploitations of ancient precedents—they belong to the "new" sect currently being debated in legal, medical, and humanist circles. This, and not the narratives of Apuleius or Lucan, provided the iconographic content Baldung mustered for his Strasbourg debut. As Schade argues, Baldung created a new provocative synthesis of ideas about witches.[110] In contrast to Sullivan's assertion that his images of witches are irrelevant to witch persecution, I would argue that they are exactly germane. Baldung's 1510 woodcut, along with Dürer's *Witch*, made it possible to visualize a deadly stereotype, regardless of whether artists themselves fully believed in it.

In the foreground, the objects accompanying the oven forks that were flying implements form a catalog of *maleficia*. At the right is a convex mirror for divination and a "witches' bullet," for causing injury—a process illustrated in the "Archer Witch" illustration of Molitor's treatise.[111] Although the bovine skull at the left was supposedly used as a percussive instrument, the human bones suggest murder and grave-robbing. A brush to apply the unguent lies in front of the urn, labeled with a nonsensical script indicating witches' magical use of signs or words—a motif that reoccurs in different forms in Baldung's later drawings (see figures 3.7 and 3.8).

Schade states that Baldung does not explicitly represent demons to emphasize the witches' own powerful manipulation of nature,[112] but this script along with the goat indicates the demonic basis of witchcraft. In the *Malleus*, Kramer critiqued the Neoplatonic view of the instrumentality of language, stating that even if witches use "certain characters of unknown names" as "natural things" beneficently and without expressly calling upon demons, a tacit invocation was still involved.[113] And, as Clark points out, demonologists consistently denied that words or signs alone could function causally: Their efficacy in charms and spells required demonic intervention, for humans *could* not cause effects with them and angels *would* not.[114]

The Hebraic appearance of the script on Baldung's urn draws on a vast reservoir of anti-Semitism—including the myths of Jewish Host desecration and ritual murder of Christian children, usually young boys, for their blood. As R. Po-Chia Hsia's study of these beliefs has demonstrated, early sixteenth-century Germany saw an unprecedented level of debate about Jews and their religion, and a culmination of accusations and executions for ritual murder that had been building since the mid-fifteenth century. Memories of late fifteenth-century cases in Endingen near Freiburg, Regensburg, and Trent in north Italy, with its many connections to Germany, were fresh; the "martyrdom" of the boy Simon of Trent was depicted in woodcuts on a broadsheet in 1498 from Ulm and in the *Nuremberg Chronicle* published by Koberger in 1493. More recently, in 1504, accusations of ritual murder had been the focus of a struggle between Maximilian, following an imperial tradition of protecting Jews in part because of the income they provided, and the burghers of Freiburg who saw the prosecution of Jews as a sign of the autonomy of municipal government and the guilds.[115]

Debates about Jews also engaged the academic world of Baldung's family. Ulrich Zasius, a colleague of Baldung's brother and cousin and a preeminent professor of law in Germany, had published his defense of the forced baptism of Jewish children, even without parental consent, with the Grüninger press in Strasbourg in 1508; manuscript copies were being circulated by 1505 among southwest German humanists, including Wimpheling and Geiler, both of whom praised Zasius's zeal.[116] Also in the years before 1510, academic controversy swirled around converted Jew Johann Pfefferkorn's *Mirror of Exhortation* (1507), urging his people to accept Christ. In 1509, Pfefferkorn convinced Maximilian to issue a mandate for local authorities to collect Jewish books and burn those with anti-Christian content. When influential Jews protested to the emperor, he sought scholarly opinions on the matter. Johannes Reuchlin, who had published a study of the Cabala, a groundbreaking work on the Hebrew language, and who saw knowledge of Judaism as important for understanding the gospel, countered those who sided with Pfefferkorn with a legal brief advocating tolerance in 1510. An Imperial commission formed by Maximilian that same year to control the volatile situation included three of Freiburg's professors, Pius Hieronymus Baldung among them, as advisers: all three condemned Reuchlin's defense of Jewish rights.[117] Reuchlin became the focus of battles among intellectuals, with Maximilian eventually siding with Reuchlin, and the mandate to burn books was never carried out.[118]

Thus Baldung's pseudo-Hebraic script is highly charged. First, it suggests witches' idolatry of demons and word-magic, a trait they supposedly held in common with Jews. Zika argues that Erasmus's deep distrust of this magic pervades his response to Reuchlin, and Luther would later claim that Turks, Jews, witches, and Catholics all venerated letters.[119] Second, the artist's evocation of Jewish child-murder by the script is an early indicator of the importance such charges against witches would assume. Indeed, Hsia concludes that the waning of the discourse of Jewish ritual murder beginning in the 1530s was due not only to an increasing criminalization of child-murder by parents but also to the absorption of this discourse into that of witch-hunting. Witches replaced Jews.[120]

As Richard Kieckhefer argues, these discourses acted in tandem with anxieties about child mortality.[121] The infantile bones in the pot carried by Baldung's gleeful flying witch as well as the implied contents of the urn are horrifying by themselves, but they also seem to visualize a passage, supposedly the testimony of a witch interviewed by Bernese judge Peter von Greyerz, from Nider's *Formicarius* (1435–38):

> [W]ith unbaptized infants, or even with infants already baptized if they are not protected by the sign of the cross and by prayers, we kill by our ceremonies in their cradles, or when they are lying in bed beside their parents, so that they are thought to have been crushed [overlain by their parents] or to have died some other natural way. We then remove them secretly from their graves and cook them in a cauldron until their flesh, cooked and separated from the bones, is made into a powerful liquid. From the solids of this material we make a certain unguent that is useful for our desires, arts, and transformations. From the liquids we fill a container, and from this, with a few additional ceremonies, anyone who drinks immediately becomes a member and master of our sect.[122]

The anonymous *Errores Gazariorum* (1437) also discussed the murder of children and specified that the unguent was used for transformations and greasing staffs, ideas that not only went back to accusations against heretics in late antiquity but were also reasserted in the *Malleus*.[123]

Propelled by the unguent, levitation to their devil-worshipping sabbath is the primary object of the witches' frenetic activity. Although the *Malleus* as an early demonological text does not deal much with the sabbath, it does discuss the question of witches' bodily flight as do other texts the artist must have known about—it was a central issue in the developing concept of witchcraft. A crucial figure for Baldung in this regard would have been the Dominican preacher of Strasbourg Cathedral and humanist Johann Geiler von Kayserberg, who died the year the woodcut *Witches' Sabbath* was published. Baldung was surely familiar with Geiler's ideas. His exact whereabouts in 1508 are unknown, so possibly he even heard Geiler's Lenten sermons that year, published in 1511 as *Die Emeis* (The ant colony, a title borrowed from Johannes Nider) that referred extensively to witchcraft. Baldung almost certainly designed its woodcut illustration of witches, this time enriched by the motif of the "battle for the trousers." As a bare-legged man clings to a tree and watches helplessly, the witches wave his pants in triumph and prepare for their sabbath.[124]

Geiler mocked witches' real ability to fly and focused on their deluded and gullible nature: "I say that they do travel hither and yon, but that they also remain where they are, because they dream that they travel, since the devil can create an impression in the human mind, and thus a fantasy, that they dream with others that they travel, and when they go with each other and see other women and dance, feast and eat, and he [the devil] can do all that to them." He then goes on to describe a woman, observed by a local preacher, who had anointed herself for "flight." His contemptuous words are echoed in Baldung's indecorous and grotesque portrayal of witches' bodies and gestures: "When it was night, and she wished to go, she called him and then lay down on a bench of the kind they have in village houses. Then she sat down and anointed herself with oil and spoke a word that she was used to speaking, and she fell asleep sitting up. Then she began waving her hands and feet around so wildly that she fell off the bench and lay under it and bumped herself badly on her head." For Geiler, the devil lay behind every magical act that the foolish witches seem to do on their own: He gives sorcerers and witches "certain words and signs" by which they can invoke his power.[125]

Geiler's mocking tone helps to explain the burlesque humor of Baldung's 1510 woodcut. Despite all their striving, their flight and their sabbath may occur strictly in their heads, but Geiler's partial skepticism did not imply mercy: He believed that witchcraft was a heinous crime, deserving death. In his text and in Baldung's print, poking fun at witches is accompanied by an intense perception of evil embodied in women. According to Geiler, women were ten times more likely to be witches than men because of their "instability of spirit, because they are understood better by demons, and because of their talkativeness."[126]

For their banquet, Baldung's witches carry foods: the shrunken (bird-like?) bodies on the charger, the pot with children's bones held by the flying witch, and thick sausages slung with a wine canteen over a stick. Along with the pun entailed by the unguent brush (*pinsel* = penis), they convey the witches' lust and the penis-theft through illusion or "glamour," recounted in an outrageous passage of the *Malleus*, describing how they kept and fed the squirming stolen organs (the largest one belonging to a parish priest!) in a nest.[127]

Altdorfer did not sustain an interest in witchcraft, but Baldung reprised it his whole life, quickly dropping any reference to the natural environment to concentrate on the female body in both its Circean and grotesque forms. With the 1510 woodcut, a minor concern for Dürer now became for Baldung a signature topic shaped by a bold style, distinguished by an equal stridency of line and mass. Even with all its grotesque detail, however, the woodcut is a tamer, more public version of witchcraft offered by the chiaroscuro drawings done in Freiburg while Baldung worked on a prestigious commission for the High Altar of the Cathedral that established the financial foundation of his career (figures 3.7 through 3.10).[128]

Law and Visual Order: Baldung's Freiburg Drawings

After the Swabian War of 1499, the small provincial city of over six thousand people in which Baldung resided with Margarethe between 1512 and 1516 as he completed the Altar, became a symbol of imperial power, against the democratic aspirations of the Swiss Confederation, and the intellectual and commercial center of Outer Austria (the Habsburg territories on the Upper Rhine).[129] Maximilian lent support to the University of Freiburg, founded in 1457 by Archduke Albert VI Habsburg, where the artist's brother and cousin taught law. Gregor Reisch, prior of Freiburg's Carthusian monastery and author of the widely read philosophical handbook, the *Margarita philosophica* (Pearl of philosophy, 1503), was the most prominent individual on the arts faculty. The university's most distinguished legal authority was Zasius, the hard-working former secretary of the city and an academic star whose relationship to his fellow professors was often strained. Zasius's defense of the forced baptism of Jewish children (1508), Steven Rowan explains, cemented his ascendancy at the university by demonstrating his political and scholarly connections: Wimpheling wrote a prefatory letter for the treatise, which was dedicated to the rector of the Cathedral (a position occupied by a university

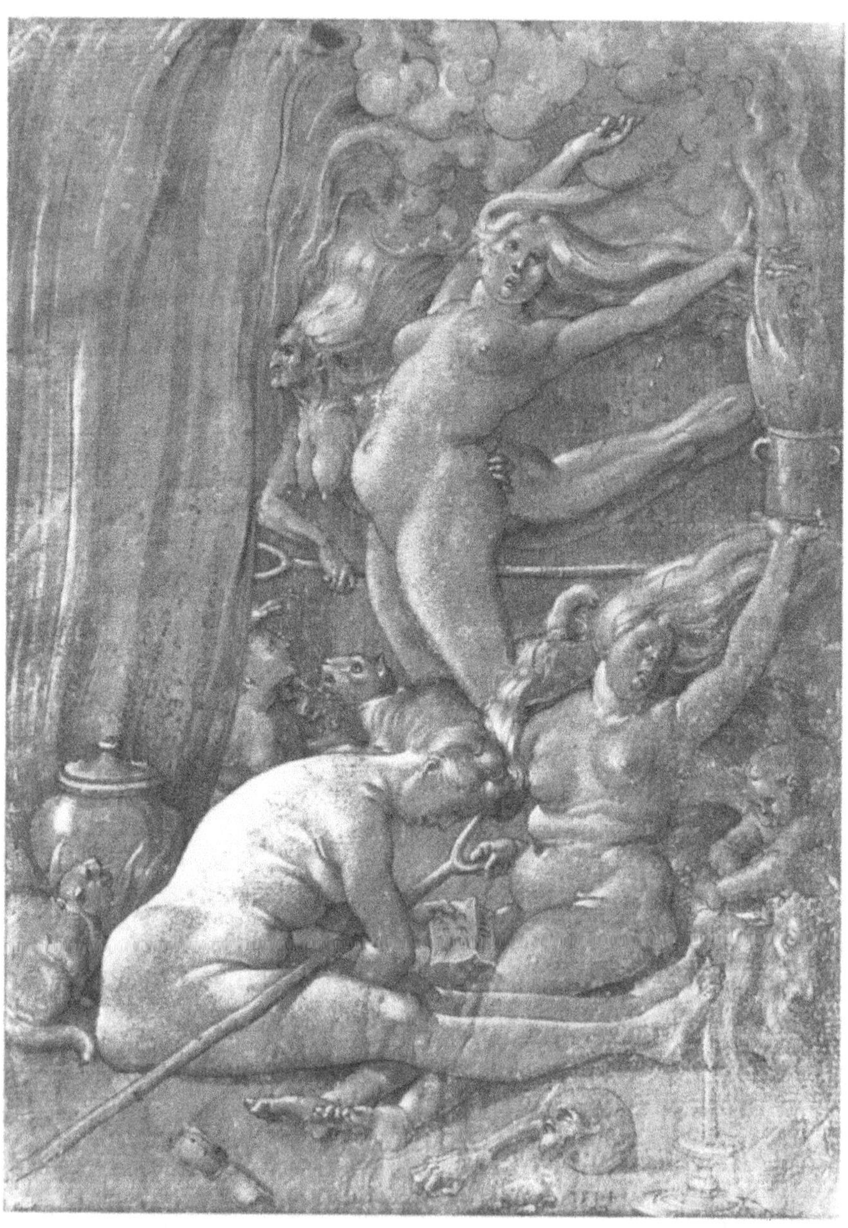

Figure 3.7. Hans Baldung Grien, *Witches Preparing for the Sabbath Flight*, 1514. Chiaroscuro pen drawing on reddish-brown tinted paper, 287 × 206 mm. Albertina Museum, Vienna.

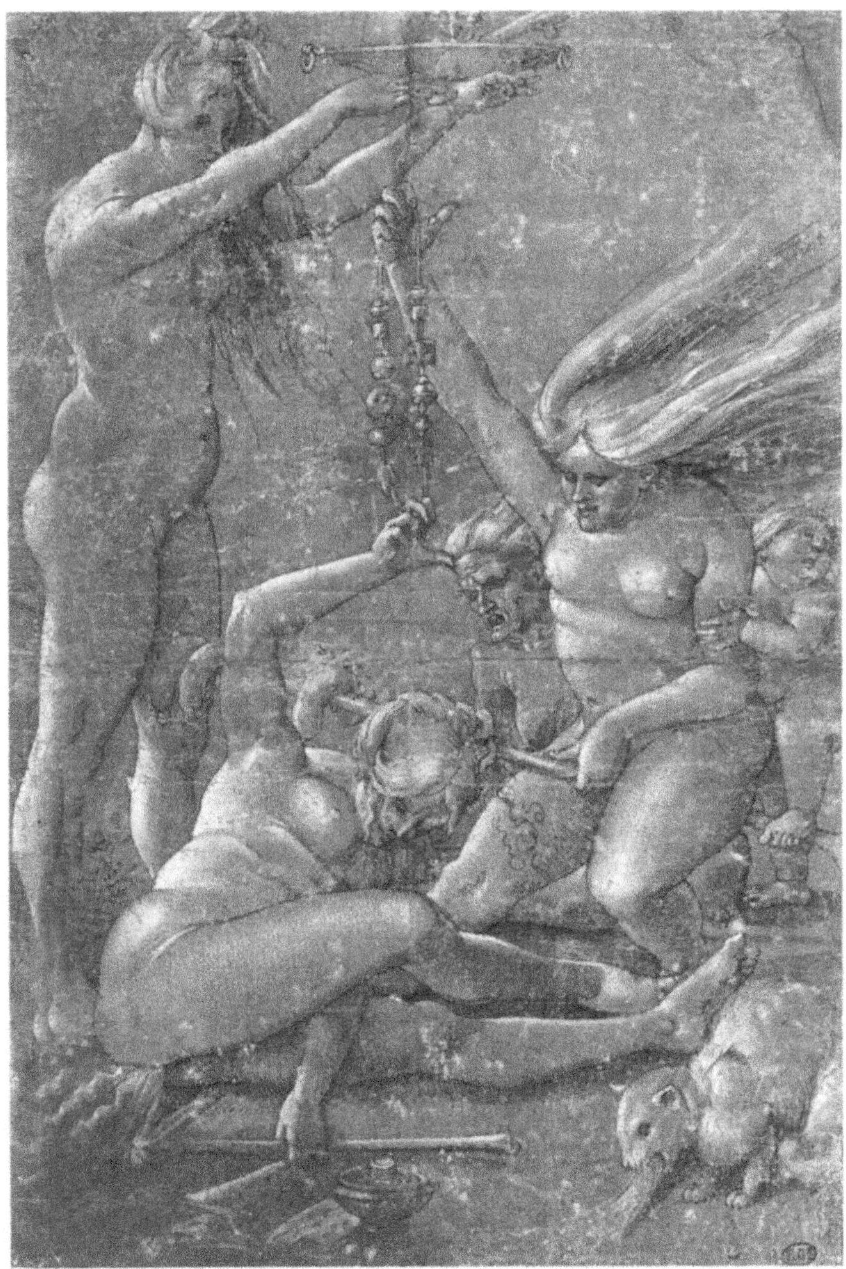

Figure 3.8. Hans Baldung Grien, *Witches Preparing for the Sabbath Flight*, 1514. Chiaroscuro pen drawing on green-tinted paper, 289 × 200 mm. Cabinet des Dessins, Musée du Louvre, Paris. Réunion des Musées Nationaux/Art Resource, New York.

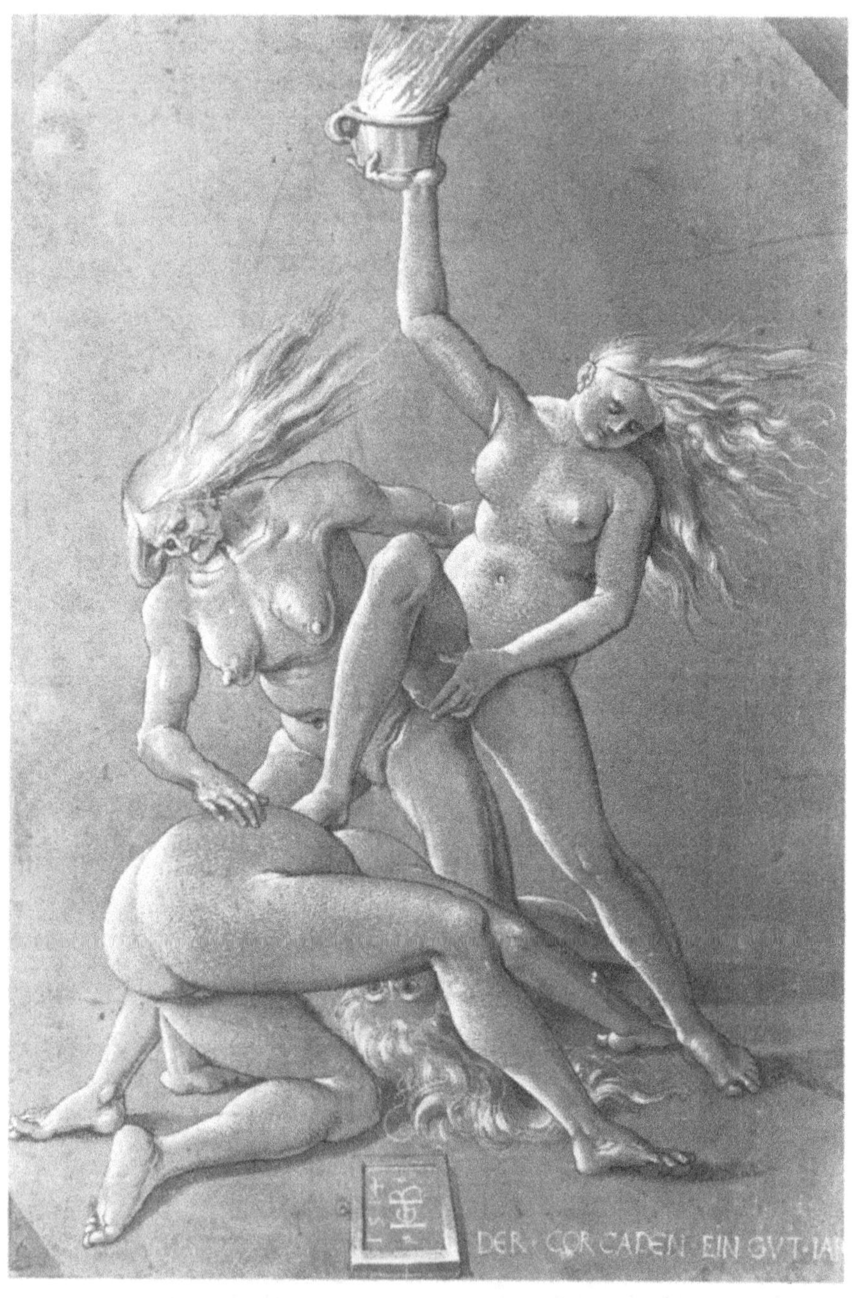

Figure 3.9. Workshop copy after Hans Baldung Grien, *Three Witches* (New Year's Wish), 1514. Chiaroscuro pen drawing on brown-tinted paper, 309 × 209 mm. Albertina Museum, Vienna.

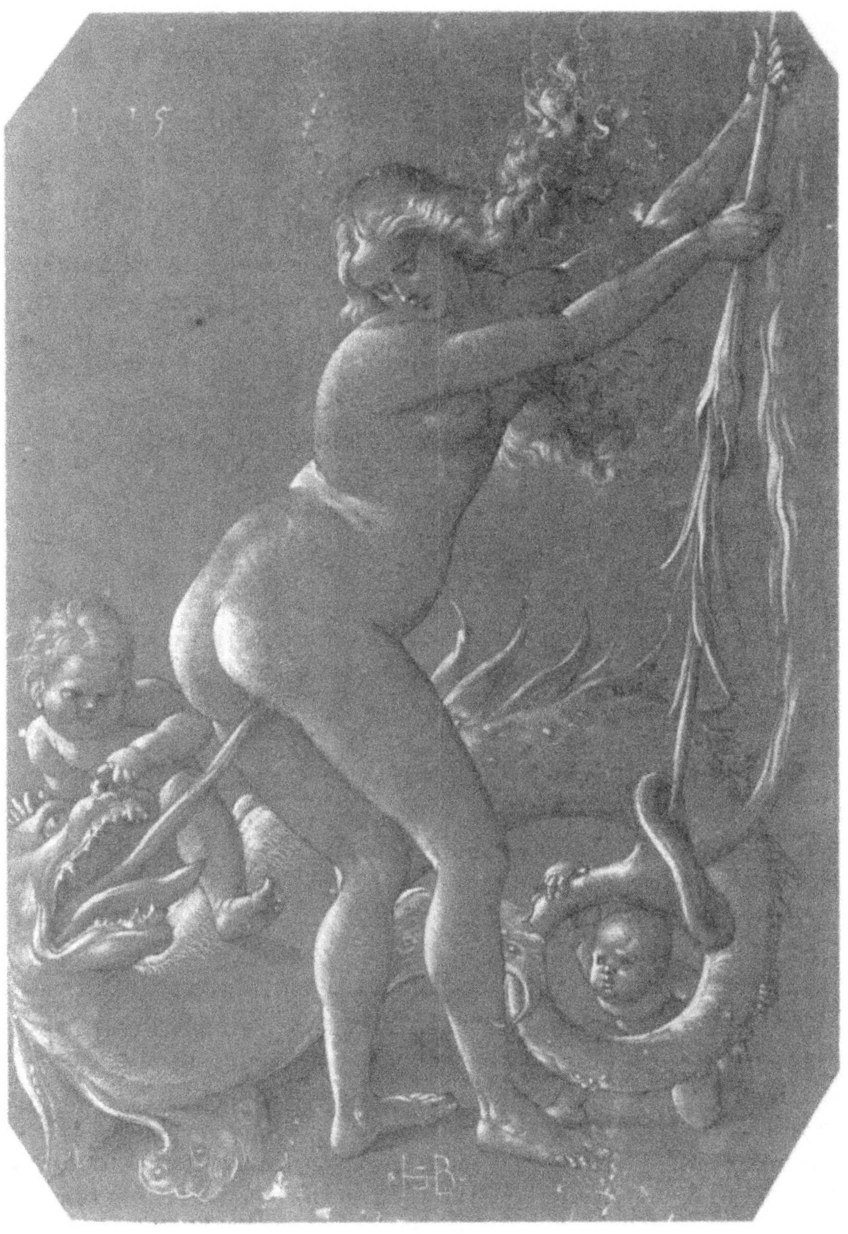

Figure 3.10. Hans Baldung Grien, *Witch and Demon*, 1515. Chiaroscuro pen drawing on brown-tinted paper, 295 × 207 mm. Kupferstichkabinett, Staatliche Kunsthalle, Karlsruhe.

professor and endowed by the emperor); and Baldung's cousin wrote one of the many testimonials following the text.[130] Baldung must have been drawn to this university culture as a source of clients and contacts as well as intellectual stimulation. Academic jurists in particular—highly ambitious, successful men working during a revolutionary period for German law—would have been prime members of the audience Baldung wanted to build.

As Gerald Strauss has explored in detail, law was a privileged profession among wealthy young men or motivated self-starters in early sixteenth-century Germany, despite routine mocking of lawyers for their arrogance, greed, and sophistic manipulation of language. The absorption of Roman law into German legal tradition during the late Middle Ages and early Renaissance, although never complete, created an intense demand for academic jurists to counsel rulers, municipal governments, and regional and local courts; to write the exponentially increasing documentation of cases; and to interpret knotty legal issues within the complex judicial particularism of the Holy Roman Empire. In 1495, Maximilian formed an imperial chamber court (*Reichskammergericht*) comprising doctors of law and bound to Roman law as its first principle, to whose authority decisions of territorial courts were ideally to be subject. The standardization of law codes in the late fifteenth and early sixteenth century—such as the Nuremberg code of 1479, the Bamberg code of 1507, the Freiburg code of 1520 (completed after seventeen years of work by Zasius and his colleagues), and the imperial *Carolina* of 1532—required the expertise of legal scholars to reconcile the patchwork of Germanic law with canon and Roman law. As Strauss emphasizes, everywhere in Germany lawyers' fortunes were tied to authorities claiming legal sovereignty, whether principalities, imperial free cities, or the Empire itself.[131]

The University of Freiburg was not the most prominent of the twenty German institutions offering advanced legal training, but Zasius's presence, as Rowan has made clear, was the focus of international intellectual interchange. He had wide contacts with a variety of legal scholars and humanists, especially Brant, Wimpheling, and Geiler in Strasbourg. Above all, he attracted outstanding students, and the four years Baldung spent in the city were especially rich in such matriculations. Rowan describes the "gilded generation" of Zasius's students, enrolling between 1510 and 1520—young men who would be on the forefront of the Reformation, destined for successful academic and administrative careers.[132] All in all, the university community of faculty, students, and their households, constituted about two hundred people: over a dozen professors and about one hundred fifty students, about fifty of whom studied law. The students' rowdiness and drunkenness (penchants apparently shared by their mentor Zasius) and their shocking dress frequently caused friction with the city council, which also bristled at professors' exemption from municipal taxation.[133]

In contrast to the 1510 woodcut, the Freiburg drawings of witches are paradoxically delicate in their surface details while retaining Baldung's strong bodily plasticity—a legacy of Dürer's training—now hyperbolized without a discernible setting. They were intended to be privately perceived, probably passed among friends: a context recalling the homosocial relationship described by Naomi Zack in which two male subjects, the learned man and the devil, indirectly engaged each other through the medium of the witch—in Zack's terms a *non*identity whose agency was in fact the devil's.[134] Baldung's drawings playfully mocked the men who watch these women—fascinated, repelled, aroused—and yet the artist was also a member of this fellowship. The radical originality of these works is witnessed by copies such as that shown in figure 3.9.[135] If Baldung's High Altar venerated the Virgin, these drawings denigrated her inverse in a pornography that reduced intellectuals, artists, and even clerics to a low level—but never so low as the female witch. For in responding to and rejecting such baseness, the male subject reconstructed himself.

With these works, Baldung integrated his innovations in the 1510 woodcut with a more secure definition of his artistic identity. He pushed the limits of his erotic and scatological expression, and he capitalized on the current taste among elite Germans for chiaroscuro drawing. He challenged and courted his viewers not only with technical and formal skill but also with a vision of a world for them to master. For the jurists who were likely among his audience, the drawings staged a confrontation between the majestic rational clarity and sacred certainty attributed to the reformed law by positing an opposite world with an alien complexity and order.[136] Baldung's rich iconography and compositional finesse gave this world credibility, yet made clear its underlying principles of irrationality, gullibility, bestial sexuality, malevolence, and apostasy. The confrontation staged by these drawings would be echoed in the witch-hunts.

To be sure, persecutions were often initiated by sectors of German society resistant to the reformed law. Moreover, its higher standards of evidence, proof, and documentation, as well as the consultation with higher courts such as the *Reichskammergericht* and learned jurists it fostered, often acted as brakes on witch-hunting.[137] Nevertheless, the new legal framework incorporated procedures that facilitated large-scale witch-hunting. Most significant was the shift from the medieval accusatorial process, in which the injured party initiates prosecution and risks countersuit, to an inquisitorial process, deriving from the interwoven traditions of Roman and canon law, in which officials initiate, investigate, and document a criminal charge. Conviction required two eyewitnesses or a confession. But when eyewitnesses were hard to come by—for example, in occult crimes like witchcraft—torture (sharpened in the Church's

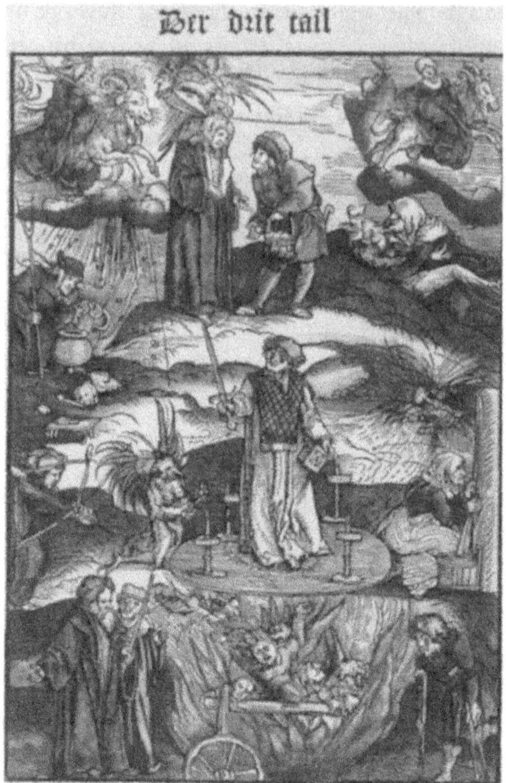

Figure 3.11. Hans Schäuffelein, hand-colored woodcut illustration for Ulrich Tengler's *Der neu Laienspiegel*, Augsburg, 1511. Bayerisches Staatsbibliothek, Munich.

campaigns against heretics) and confession enabled judges to determine "truth."[138]

The Bamberg and *Carolina* law codes were conservative in that they focused on actual harm done by witchcraft rather than on demonic pact that defined it as heresy. In practice, however, *maleficia* and heresy were inseparable by the sixteenth century. In the 1511 edition of Ulrich Tengler's *Laienspiegel* (Mirror for laymen, first published in 1510), which explained the new law for non-Latin readers, a description of the civil crime of witchcraft was added, accompanied by Hans Schäuffelein's didactic woodcut (figure 3.11). Incidents of black magic like storm production, milking a tree-trunk, and causing injury—a witch uses an arrow to cripple her victim, shown on crutches in the lower right—are accompanied by congress with demons. In the center, a magician in a magic circle invokes a demon; at the upper left and right, witches fly to the sabbath and one witch embraces her demon lover; Zika notes she is on top as an indication of social inversion.[139] At the center top, a wealthy man inspired by a demon consults a male soothsayer. At the bottom left, two jurists consign witches to a roaring fire.

This same combination of *maleficia* and heresy is conveyed far more compellingly in Baldung's drawings. The reddish-brown Albertina and green Louvre sheets—of similar size and datable to 1514—are much alike in composition and expression (see figures 3.7 and 3.8).[140] Both describe the exacting yet tenuous choreography of an imagined levitation ritual. Along the central vertical axis of the Louvre work are an unguent jar and paper spell with indiscernible scribbles, a bowl with skull and long bone, held up as an offering, and a "rosary" (easier to discern in the better-preserved copy of this sheet by Urs Graf in the Albertina, Vienna), comprising fool's bells, dice, a rabbit's foot, and a fetal skull. These objects and the witch lighting her flatulence—a motif suggesting being puffed up with pride—convey the notion that witches' efforts to fly bodily on their own power are a foolish gamble. This interpretation is reinforced by a copy after Baldung in Berlin, probably by the Monogrammist Hans Frank of Basel, in which two of the witches are sleeping in the course of their ritual.[141] This partial skepticism conforms to contemporary ideas.

At the same time, however, the drawings show that the witches have resorted to infanticide and murder or grave-robbing to obtain the elements of their ritual, and their bodies—coarse, bulging, posed in fits and jerks—convey a physicality made grosser by its proximity to bones, cats' vomit, the horrific contents of the unguent jars, and fumes. In the Albertina sheet, an old, experienced witch levitates slightly and encourages a voluptuous, entranced young colleague while two other witches, their legs crossing, struggle to read a spell and hold a fire pot aloft. One reaches between her legs (masturbating with the unguent?); the other holds a greased oven fork. Other attributes in the drawings are familiar from the 1510 woodcut: the "witches' bullet," bones, cats, the goat, demonic offspring, and sausages and wine canteen (this time with the coat of arms of the city of Freiburg) slung over an oven fork. This last motif is used to a much bawdier effect in the Louvre drawing, for now the greased stick with its fat sausages (one stroked by an old crone) passes between the legs of two witches. Koerner notes that in Urs Graf's copy, a vein is discernible on the middle sausage![142]

These works would have resonated with their audience through scatology, misogynistic humor, eroticism, and above all their reinforcement of various masculine identities. Beginning in the artist's workshop where they were most likely copied, viewing these intimate drawings must have constituted a male-bonding experience. The completion of a large polyptych like the High Altar necessitated a workshop; the amount of Baldung's payment of gratuities in 1515 indicates that he had several pupils working with him in Freiburg.[143] Exhibiting formal and technical skills as well as an innovative approach to a topical subject, Baldung's drawings of witches were extraordinary examples of male inventive prowess hinging on an intensely negative female stereotype. Merry Wiesner's discussion of the increasing hostility toward women in the craft guilds and journeyman's organizations of early modern Germany, cemented not only in changing corporate regulations but also in social practices and bonding rituals, hints at the drawings' impact on the artists who studied them.[144]

We also know that Baldung gave one image of witches to a cleric friend because an anonymous copy in the Albertina of a New Year's card includes the greeting "*DER COR CAPEN EIN GUT JAR*" (Happy New Year to the captain of the choir; see figure 3.9). Both Schade and Koerner relate the tumbling witches—one looks upside-down from between her legs to symbolize the inverted demonic world—and their confrontation of the card's recipient to the longstanding satire of clerical abuse of the vow of celibacy. The primary expression is ribald humor, but if, as Robert Norman Swanson has proposed, celibate males constituted a third gender ("emasculinity") for whom misogyny was an expression of deep insecurity given their ambivalent status vis-à-vis masculine norms, then Baldung's drawing also confronted this particular viewer with his fears.[145]

Baldung directed his friend's glance along the edges of the figural triangle to experience a mixture of shapely and decrepit legs, buttocks, and breasts. He disrupted the coherence of the female body by a blazoning dismemberment created by the constant overlapping of bodies and body parts, and the elusiveness of the stable vertical axis implied by the monogrammed placard and the fire pot, symbolizing lust's flame at the triangle's apex. Using women's bodies, he condensed and codified a moral disorder barely held in check and threatening to burst out of its fragile triangular confinement. Near the center of the image the voluptuous young witch obstructs the cleric's view of her labia and vagina with a hand pointing downward to the white-haired pudenda of the old hag; the former woman must necessarily become the latter.

Finally, these drawings seem eminently suitable for the academic context of the University of Freiburg. Ruth Mazo Karras describes the formation of male identity in the rituals and celebrations of late medieval German universities as a gradual sloughing off of the bestial, the rustic, and the feminine. The stages of a university career—from the hazing of freshmen, to the expensive banquets they and the masters were expected to provide, to the structure of attack and defense in academic disputation, modeled on honorable individual combat—enabled an ideal of elite academic masculinity. In contrast to the uncontrolled impulses of women, peasants, and animals, academic men were supposedly ruled by reason and moderation. The ritual academic discourse analyzed by Karras is characterized by the overlapping of categories (bestial, female, scatological, uncivilized, Jewish, criminal, worthless, demonic) that are to be purged. For example, in the initiation ceremony described in the *Manuale scholarium* (Scholar's manual), an anonymous late fifteenth-century text, the new student is saluted as a grotesque monster of hybrid animal parts, an ass, a toad, a smelly female goat, and a zero or a figure of nothing to be shat and pissed upon by the devil. Initiates were shaved and bathed, threatened and insulted, false teeth were pulled, and goat-horns on a hat were sawn off.[146]

Jurists may have formed the core of this academic audience. Destined for wealth and political prominence, they were prime future clients for the artist. Baldung engaged them not only with his skilled handling of a prestigious medium but also with a profound understanding of the relationship between witchcraft and the reformed law. His iconography balanced the civil and spiritual aspects of witchcraft, and his compositions constructed an irrational, burlesque antipode, obeying motives and rules all its own, to the massive edifice of the righteous, reasoned law. The drawings illustrate the raison d'être of the reformed law and the academics who explained and administered it precisely, for the new witchcraft was a contemporary crime demanding new applications of the law, new syntheses of existing legal concepts.

It is striking how Baldung appealed to the different components of the audience I attempt to reconstruct here through a profound misogyny, culminating in *Witch and Demon* in Karlsruhe, on grey-tinted paper and dated 1515 (see figure 3.10). Impossibly contorted, a young witch holds onto a curious vine-like projection as she directs her genitals toward the demon's gaping mouth, held open by one of Baldung's uncanny toddlers, sticking his fingers uncomfortably in the monster's nostrils. The witch's vaginal outflow doubles as the demon's tongue in an infernal cunnilingus. Koerner aptly describes the fluid identity of all the components of this remarkable image: "Liquid and gas, influx and efflux, reception and penetration, inside and outside, womb and penis, female and male, human and animal all interchange."[147] Yet, although Baldung's clever visual analogies conflate male and female sexual desires and organs and confuse and connect the two bumpy, wriggling bodies of witch and demon, the grotesque female body drives the image. While the male beholder has the possibility of overcoming the abjection the artist inflicts on him, the grim-faced, irrationally desiring witch does not. She answers only to the deep bodily center that destabilizes her entire form, what Rabelais (also a physician) described as "an animal spirit, a secret part, which men do not have, and this sometimes gives rise to certain spicy impulses, nitrous, brackish, bitter, biting, corrosive, throbbing, fiercely provoking, by means of which painful stinging and quivering (for this hidden organ is highly excitable and exquisitely sensitive) their entire bodies are caught up, every sense swept away in rapture, all affective concerns made intensely subjective, and every thought confused."[148]

Even more than the other Freiburg drawings, this one reads like a dirty joke. If we imagine its reception within the various homosocial contexts I have suggested here, its appeal is more intelligible. Baldung's abject witches confirmed everything that men aspired to by representing all that they struggled to reject.

Of Hailstorms and Horses: The Frankfurt *Weather Witches* and *The Bewitched Groom*

In 1517, when Luther posted his ninety-five theses on the door of Wittenberg Cathedral, Baldung returned to Strasbourg as an accomplished master with a tidy nest egg and was looking forward to a productive career. The Reformation would change the central premises of his profession. Major altars like that of Freiburg's Münster would no more be keys to fame and wealth; private devotional images, prints and book illustrations (especially significant in a great center of publishing like Strasbourg) portraits and secular subjects would fill the gap. Baldung surely knew members of the militant evangelical party of Strasbourg. In 1545, he drew the weary visage of Claus Kniebis whose daughter Barbara was married to Martin Herlin, Margarethe Baldung's uncle; he also knew more moderate Protestants like Wolfgang Capito's protégé Caspar Hedio, whose powerful woodcut portrait Baldung designed in 1543.[149] Baldung does not seem to have been militant in his religious beliefs, and he was too pragmatic to turn down commissions from Catholic patrons. It is clear, however, that his primary allegiances were with the reformers. Indeed, he could not have remained Catholic and experienced the success of his later years, including his service representing *Zur Stelz* in the municipal government the last year of his life.[150]

The year 1523—the date of his *Weather Witches* (Städelsche Kunstinstitut, Frankfurt, figure 3.12)—was a particularly uncertain, divisive year in Strasbourg. Lutheran preaching had begun in 1521; now city officials forbade preaching anything but the gospel to prevent enflaming the public with doctrinal controversies. In effect, this also forestalled criticism of the political and economic status quo.[151] There were popular disturbances in the churches, violence against priests, and support for new preachers sympathetic to Luther's ideas. By 1525, the Strasbourg aristocracy and oligarchy had weathered the crisis but only by making serious concessions dissolving longstanding bonds between wealthy families and Catholic institutions, such as the donation of art to churches, the funding of masses for the dead, the housing of wealthy offspring in convents and monasteries, or the appointment of offspring as canons.[152]

The provenance of Baldung's small, impeccable picture is unknown, although by the time it was acquired by the Frankfurt museum in 1878, it had

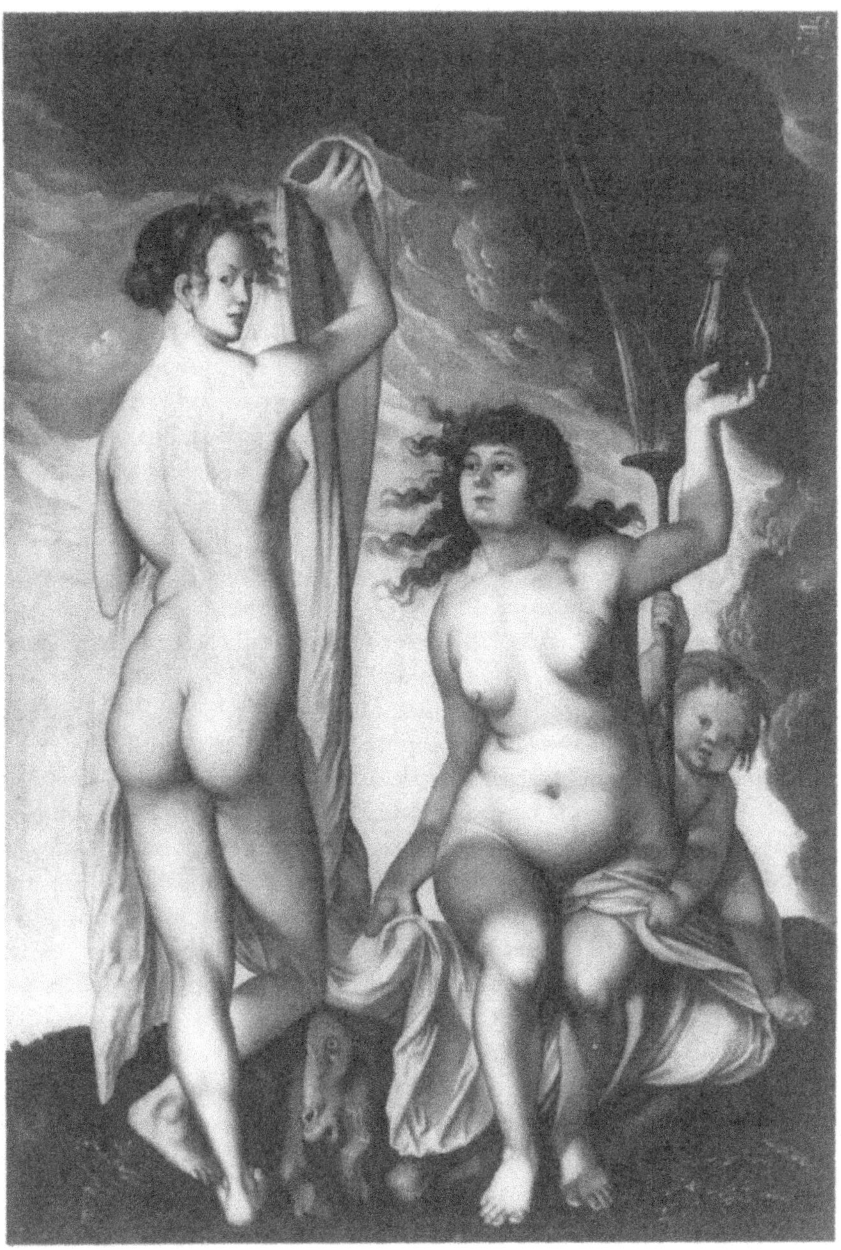

Figure 3.12. Hans Baldung Grien, *The Weather Witches*, 1523. Oil on panel, 62.2 × 45.9 cm. Städelsches Kunstinstitut, Frankfurt am Main.

apparently made its way to Rome.[153] Whoever the patron or buyer was, he was a sophisticated connoisseur, for the panel combines artistic references and a highly charged eroticism with a new twist on the artist's signature subject of witchcraft. It could be the first cabinet picture of witches. The standing nude seen mostly from the back has a long pedigree, incorporating the central figure in Dürer's *Four Witches* (see figure 3.2) and its reference to the *Capitoline Aphrodite* and Dürer's beautiful drawing from 1495 of a nude woman raising a drapery above her head.[154] The seated nude in turn compares with Diana in Dürer's engraving of *Apollo and Diana* (ca. 1505) and with Eve's torso in the engraved 1504 *Adam and Eve.* In general, these Circean witches echo Dürer's preoccupation with the constructed female nude in his proportion studies.[155] The formal references are not merely stylistic, however, for Eve, Diana, and Aphrodite are all appropriate analogies to the witch; indeed, one of Baldung's drawings closely related to the painting is his image of Eve, coyly holding an apple (ca. 1525).[156] In his moral universe, lustful women are simply interchangeable.

Coupled with these highly self-conscious figural references are a spectacular setting and a provocative expression. The standing witch looks out unapologetically and presents her sleek derrière to the spectator. Like Gianfrancesco Pico's contemporary *strega*, who takes on Dicaste and Phronimius with considerable aplomb, Baldung's witch is impossibly brazen.[157] Behind her seated accomplice, who holds their demon captive in a bottle stopped with the fruit of original sin, a robust changeling or demonic offspring also looks out as he climbs aboard the infernal he-goat and holds a torch exuding the corrupting vapors that fill the sky. The witches' magically potent hair blows wildly in opposite directions. Above the hillock, the sky glows from sulfur yellow to a hot red and then to murky brown. Weather magic took many forms, from stirring puddles of witches' urine to overturning pots filled with ashes, excrement, and magical herbs; here Baldung evokes the foul yellow powders blown into the air to initiate storms.[158]

The hailstorms that could devastate crops were a cause of deep economic anxiety in early modern Europe, but given the erudition and eroticism of this panel, the storm is likely metaphorical as well. Few works better express the connection of female witchcraft to the body and to "opaque, ambivalent and mysterious" spells that worked through a sexual bond with demonic power, as Eva Labouvie characterizes female magic.[159] As with all Circean witches, the seductive bodies are but the deceptive exteriors of hags, whose grotesque bodies symbolize the corruption of all flesh. The dynamic, weird flux of sulfurous vapors embodies this threatening female formlessness and leaking effusion that Baldung attempted to shape and delimit with art; hence, his overt formal quotations, the decisiveness of mass and contour. The challenge to the male owner and viewers of this little picture was to resist seduction, the collapse of reason and virtue, emasculation, social disorder. Once again, Baldung plays a game of forced abjection that generates (he hopes) the reconstitution of the patriarchal order and of the male self.

The malaise and uncertainty of that self in the early years of the Reformation may be germane to the appeal of this picture. As an artist, Baldung was surely aware as well of the iconoclastic violence that threatened his livelihood. Strasbourg was soon to experience the destruction of ecclesiastical works of art that rippled through Germany in the 1520s, and, in 1525, during the Peasant Revolt, the city government permitted the orderly removal of works of art from churches and the whitewashing of their interiors.[160] Artists needed new ways to tap into the wealth and prestige represented by ecclesiastical objects; preciously rendered and provocative cabinet pictures could do that.

Baldung's final expression of the witchcraft theme is his enigmatic and powerful woodcut, *The Bewitched Groom*, published around 1544 when he was about sixty (figure 3.13). In a sense, this print is as much of a self-fashioning vehicle for the mature artist as the 1510 *Witches' Sabbath* was for an artist embarking on an independent career. It is, however, a statement of vulnerable masculinity that implicates its author more decisively in the carnality he had long projected on women and witches. As with so many of Baldung's most impressive works, *The Bewitched Groom* engages Dürer's art in a complex dialogue of admiration and self-assertion. The confessional quality of the image is coupled with its enabling function.

There have been many scholarly attempts to find some iconographic framework for what appears to be a narrative or an allegory. The horse, perhaps affected by the witch directing her torch into his stall, has evidently stunned or killed the groom, who has dropped his currycomb. In Baldung's preparatory drawing, a lifted hand makes it even less clear that the groom is dead.[161] Has he been knocked unconscious while trying to curry his frightening charge? Is he asleep and traveling to the sabbath with his witch-companion? Mesenzeva saw a similarity between Baldung's print and the legends of Squire Rechenberger—a robber-knight undergoing penance in a monastery stable when a demonic horse kills him, exactly one year after he sees it, riderless, in a vision. Dale Hoak cited a legend of an Alsatian witch who transformed herself into a horse.[162]

Neither narrative quite matches the picture, nor do they seem to explain its disquieting effect. That *The Bewitched Groom* had some personal meaning for Baldung is made clear by the resemblance of the groom's mustache and beard to Baldung's self-portraits, his family coat of arms on the stable wall, and the insistent pointing of the pitchfork to his monogram. Surely we must look to the artist's works and career for deeper understanding. Baldung's deliberate avoidance of resolution in this image suggests that he did not view it as a riddle to be conclusively solved but as an ongoing challenge to its viewers.

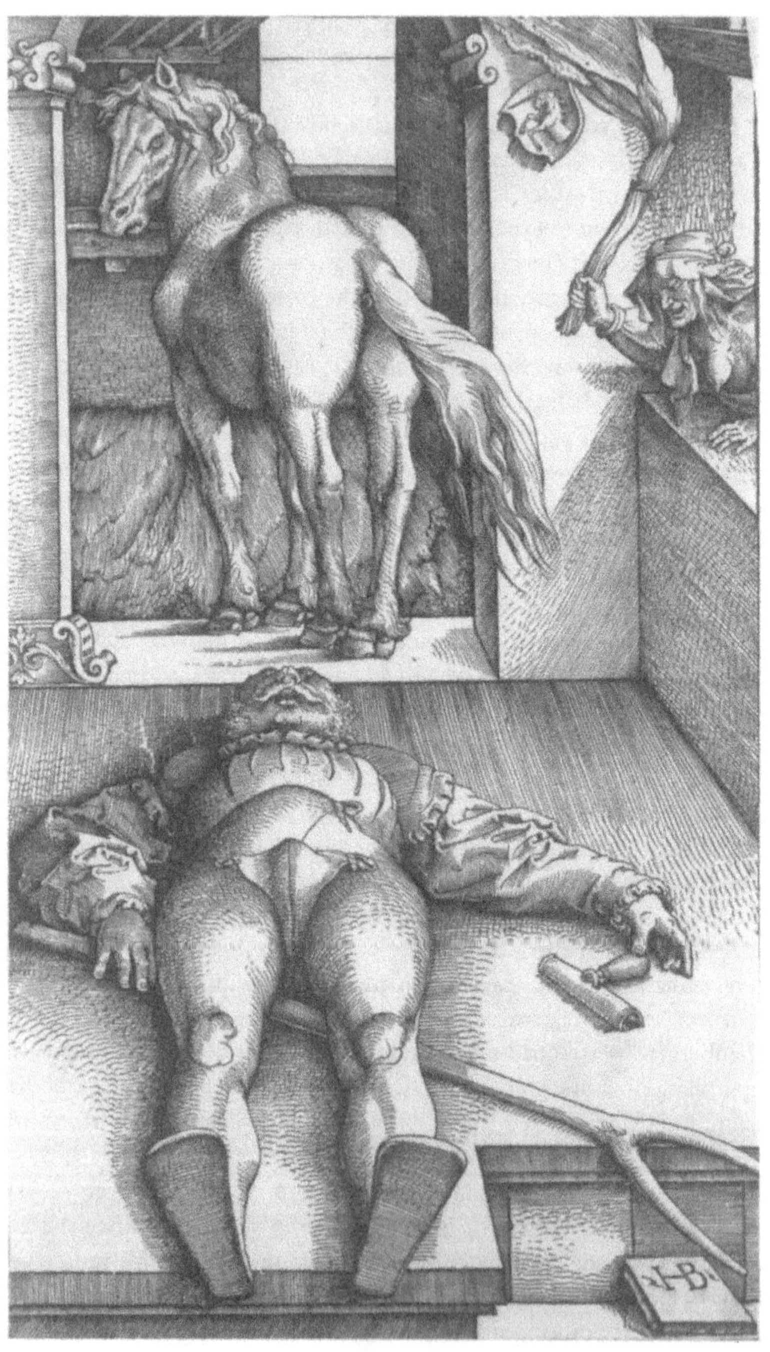

Figure 3.13. Hans Baldung Grien, *The Bewitched Groom*, ca. 1544. Woodcut, 338 × 198 mm. © The Cleveland Museum of Art, 2004. Mr. and Mrs. Charles G. Prasse Collection, 1966.172.

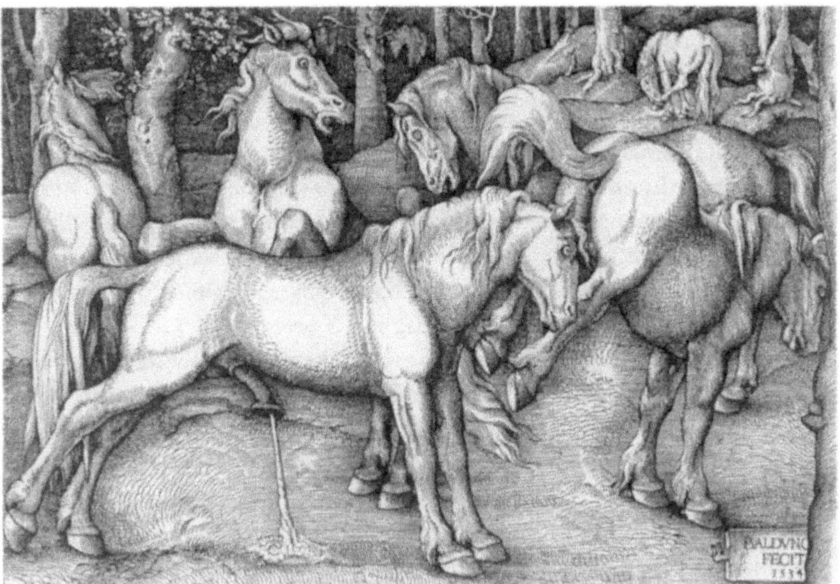

Figure 3.14. Hans Baldung Grien, *Stallion Attempting to Mate*, 1534. Woodcut, 228 × 339 mm. Los Angeles County Museum of Art. Museum Purchase with Los Angeles County Funds.

It is interesting in this regard that the main allegorical interpretations of *The Bewitched Groom* (thus far) complement and enrich each other. In 1984, I interpreted it as an allegorical self-portrait positing the artist's melancholic struggle with carnality and imaginative license, both symbolized by the witch and the horse and subject to diabolic influence.[163] Koerner reads it as a travesty of Dürer's elevated view of the artist and a subversion of "the humanist regimen of visual representation with its clear and bounded categories of artist, model, image and viewer." The artist is a fallen victim, not a masterful observer; his model a dangerously aggressive presence, not a passive object. The image confounds both the intellect and aesthetic sensibility of the viewer. Focusing particularly on Baldung's disorienting lack of spatial cohesion and his abuse of one-point linear perspective to force our gaze over the helpless body of the artist to the horse's anus, Koerner interprets *The Bewitched Groom* in terms of Baldung's project of forced abjection.[164] More recently, Sullivan relates the woodcut to two fragments of Marcus Terentius Varro's *Eumenides*, a satire of madness and furor, that mention an insane groom who cannot control a "wild Damacrine colt" and the female figure of Infamy, with "loose flowing breast, uncut hair, soiled garb and severe mien."[165]

The key element in all three of these interpretations is the horse: a subject Baldung explored in 1534 in woodcuts of wild horses (figure 3.14). As always,

Baldung played upon Dürer's well-known engravings, such as the *Small* and *Large Horses* (1505) and the magnificent steed of *Knight, Death and the Devil* (1513). He gave the gentle, lumbering *Large Horse*, seen from the back, a particularly perverse twist. More generally, he undermines Dürer's ideal equine proportions. Raw energy and appetite, not ideal form, determine the younger artist's horses. In an engraving contemporary with the chiaroscuro *Witches' Sabbath*, Baldung announced his arrival in Strasbourg with *Groom Bridling a Horse* (1510–11)—a parody of Dürer's *Small Horse*—in which a determined groom cannot in fact bridle his mount but is dragged comically along beside the horse's surging body, futilely digging in his heels.

Although he might have been aware of Varro's fragmentary *Eumenides*, Baldung did not need it to compose *The Bewitched Groom*, for he could depend on a common understanding of the horse shared by ancient writers as well as Renaissance humanists: as symbol of the passions (especially lust) that human beings attempt to rein in, bridle, or "curry" (the German *striegeln*, like "to curry" in English, has the idiomatic connotation of beating or ill-using). It is this sort of ungovernable animal who cooperates with the witch, herself an exemplar of unbridled lust, to foil the artist/groom.

In a catalog entry on the 1534 woodcuts, Jay Levenson related them to sources on equine behavior, including Varro's *On Agriculture*, describing both the lustfulness of mares in heat and the bellicose hypersexuality of stallions wanting to mate.[166] Indeed, Baldung may actually have observed wild horses in the Vosges mountains near Strasbourg. Levenson suggested that the woodcuts constituted a series on the mating habits of horses, with the fighting stallions first, and a stallion approaching a mare and then ejaculating on the ground when she rejects him (see figure 3.14) second and third. Koerner follows Schade in placing the scene of approach first, ejaculation second, and fighting third, an interpretation emphasizing the chaos and violence generated by lust.[167] It is equally possible, though, to see the stallion's ejaculation as both literally and figuratively climactic, since the spilling of seed—that rarified, heated masculine blood—was fraught with so much anxiety and significance. Subject to the biblical condemnation of onanism, ejaculation outside the female is unproductive. More than that, it is a symbol of masculine vulnerability, as Mark Breitenberg argues in his essay on Robert Burton's *Anatomy of Melancholy*. In ejaculation, the male sinks to the level of the female, unable to regulate his bodily fluids, but the excess of seed must be evacuated, according to Burton, for otherwise men cannot stop burning with lust.[168]

It may be that Baldung did not imply a particular sequence: Each woodcut is signed separately and could be self-sufficient spatially and compositionally and as a symbol of sexual aggression, arousal, or frustration. Whatever its position, the image of approach and arousal is crucial, for under the stallion's erect penis is a monkey, a symbol of the baser passions, holding the artist's monogram; a human observer, perhaps intended to suggest the artist; and an elk. Given Baldung's foundation in Dürer's art, this elk is most likely a symbol of melancholy; here, it stands in profile behind a tree as it does in Dürer's 1504 *Adam and Eve*.

What has lust to do with melancholy, that condition dominated by black bile, debased when diagnosed in the female yet privileged in the male subject? In early modern thought, as Breitenberg points out, the bodily humors are so intricately interrelated as to present an image of human (especially male) physiology and psychology that is almost infinitely nuanced by virtue of their combinations and mutual influences. For Breitenberg, these complexities are less important than the necessity of constant regulation: "Melancholy," he states, "is linked to so many functions and substances of the body that it is quite impossible to delineate a coherent system, but the central trope in every case is the maintenance of equilibrium over and against the dangers of excess—a homeostatic masculine body."[169] For example, both passion and imagination stimulate the production of blood (the sanguine humor) and black bile (the melancholic humor) by the liver (an organ whose production of fluids is opposite to the brain's housing of reason). Semen is overheated blood whose excess might be found in conjunction with an excess of black bile. Too much black bile may also stimulate the production of air (the "pneuma" that inflates the penis), causing lustfulness and puffiness. And so it goes on: reason and regulation constantly strive to constitute the masculine body and self.

Zika's discussion of Cranach's depictions of melancholy, combined with the motif of night-riding witches, in his paintings from 1532 and 1533, is also relevant here. In a post-Reformation environment—more pessimistic and uncertain for artists—neither Cranach nor Baldung understood the artistic temperament in the exalted intellectual sense of Dürer's *Melencolia I* of 1514. Rather, Cranach combined the Düreresque personification of Melancholy and her attributes with female witches, afflicted with a baser version of melancholy, to suggest the moral danger of the imaginative fantasies of art by comparing them to diabolically induced witches' delusions. By failing to control his fantasy, the melancholic is emasculated—sunk to the level of female witches.[170] This was also a comparison expressed in the dialogue, *On the Imagination*, by Gianfrancesco Pico della Mirandola (1501). For Pico, only when one controls fantasy with reason and invests it with faith can one ward off the devil. For demons "run riot in the phantasies of men, and of women called witches, and most ruinously seize upon their senses." Guided by God, man must strengthen his feeble reason to bring it closer to the pure, disembodied intellect of angels. "He who lacks reason, then, is not a man, but rather a brute to be dragged hither and thither at the beck of the imagination."[171]

In *The Bewitched Groom*, Baldung drew upon the fears common to himself and his audience to produce a richly suggestive image: part moral exhortation, part joke, part puzzle, part personal confession, part artistic triumph. The helpless groom, emasculated by the combined efforts of witch and beast, is a paradigm of collective masculine anxiety, but he is also a brash, enabling gesture of selfhood. The work itself fetishizes and privileges the very condition of struggle and loss it laments, as Juliana Schiesari argued for the concept of melancholy throughout early modern culture. If the very text of Burton's *Melancholy*, according to Breitenberg, takes on the characteristics of the disease through its superflux of detail and its defiance of structure and resolution, so Baldung's woodcut, with its coursing lines and bloated forms competing for pictorial surface and space, epitomizes both the power and vulnerability of artistic imagination. Having dropped his instruments of currycomb and pitchfork, the artist/groom lies indecorously foreshortened and immobilized, the diabolically lusty brute and the evil hag looming above (and in) his head. Yet, in being "dragged hither and thither" by his imagination, he trumped his venerable teacher with his own statement of the melancholic artist.

Swiss Soldier-Artists: Masculine Anxiety Meets Graphic Swagger

Baldung's contemporaries in Switzerland, soldier-artists Urs Graf of Basel (ca. 1485–1528) and Niklaus Manuel Deutsch of Bern (ca. 1484–1530), expressed their artistic identities in lines as flamboyant as the costumes worn by the *Reisläufers* (Swiss mercenaries) and whores who populate their graphic images.[172] Signed with wildly ostentatious monograms and marked by a vigorous linearity, their works express the consciousness of mortality and the shifting winds of fortune. As Baldung condensed his sense of abjection and quest for control into the grotesque or Circean body of the witch, so these Swiss artists often embodied fortune's arbitrary cruelty, sin, and death in female figures—projections of their violent experiences and competitive struggles for status as men.

Neither depicted many witches (that was Baldung's territory) and yet there is an undeniable rapport between his female imagery and theirs. This interchangeability of negative images of women speaks for their overarching function as expressions of male anxieties. Manuel's drawing of a chain-bedecked, floating woman, variously titled *Military Fortune* or *Witch Carrying the Skull of the Artist* (figure 3.15) is a hybrid of Dürer's famous engraved *Nemesis* (ca. 1501–02), the flying witch, and the earthbound whore. No matter; the key is her flippant disregard for the artist's fate. Her smile is reminiscent of that of Graf's insouciant, pregnant camp-follower who happens upon her hanged soldier-paramour too late to save him by presenting the judge with her bulging belly.[173] Manuel's floating figure holds the soldier's skull, still decorated with his familiar sweeping feather, and an hourglass to symbolize the fleeting nature of

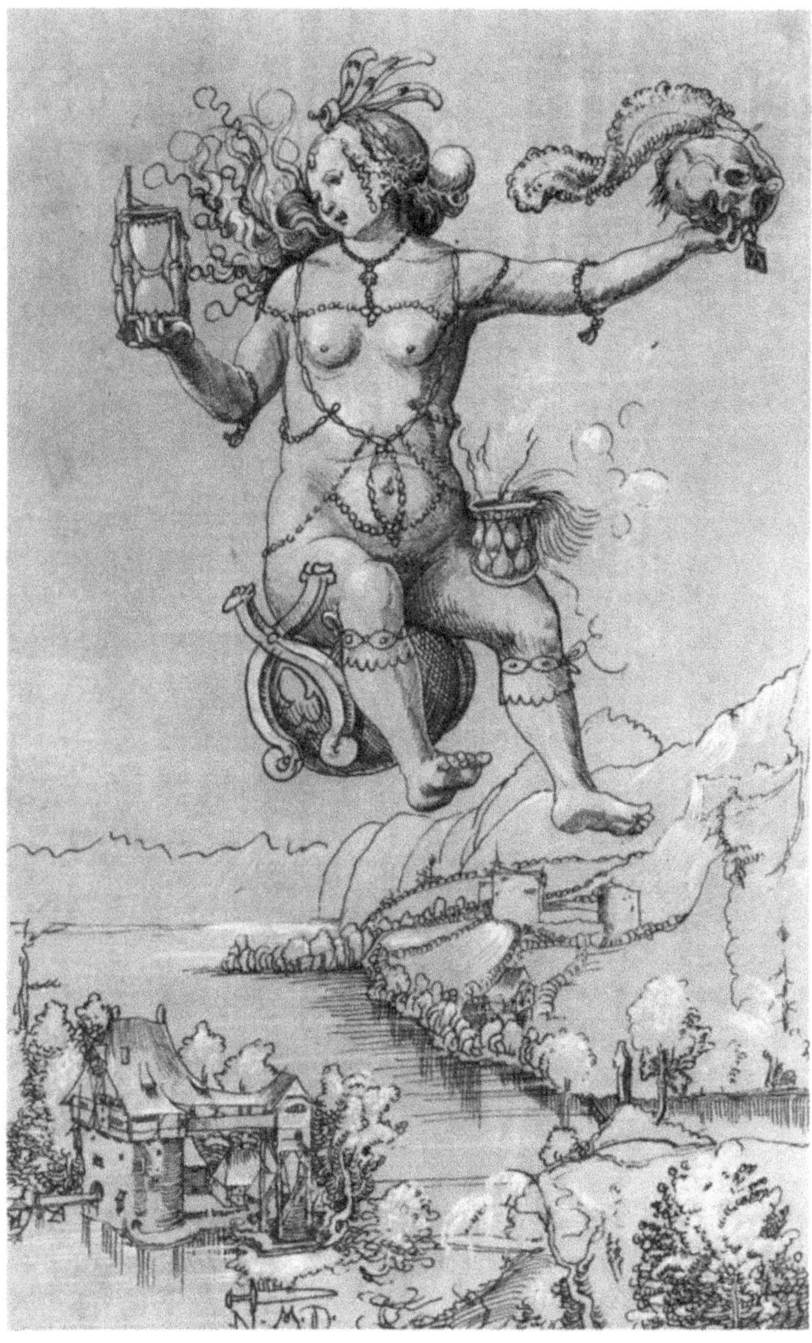

Figure 3.15. Niklaus Manuel Deutsch, *Witch Carrying the Skull of the Artist*, ca. 1513. Chiaroscuro pen drawing on brownish-orange tinted paper, 309 × 209 mm. Kupferstichkabinett, Öffentliche Kunstsammlungen, Basel.

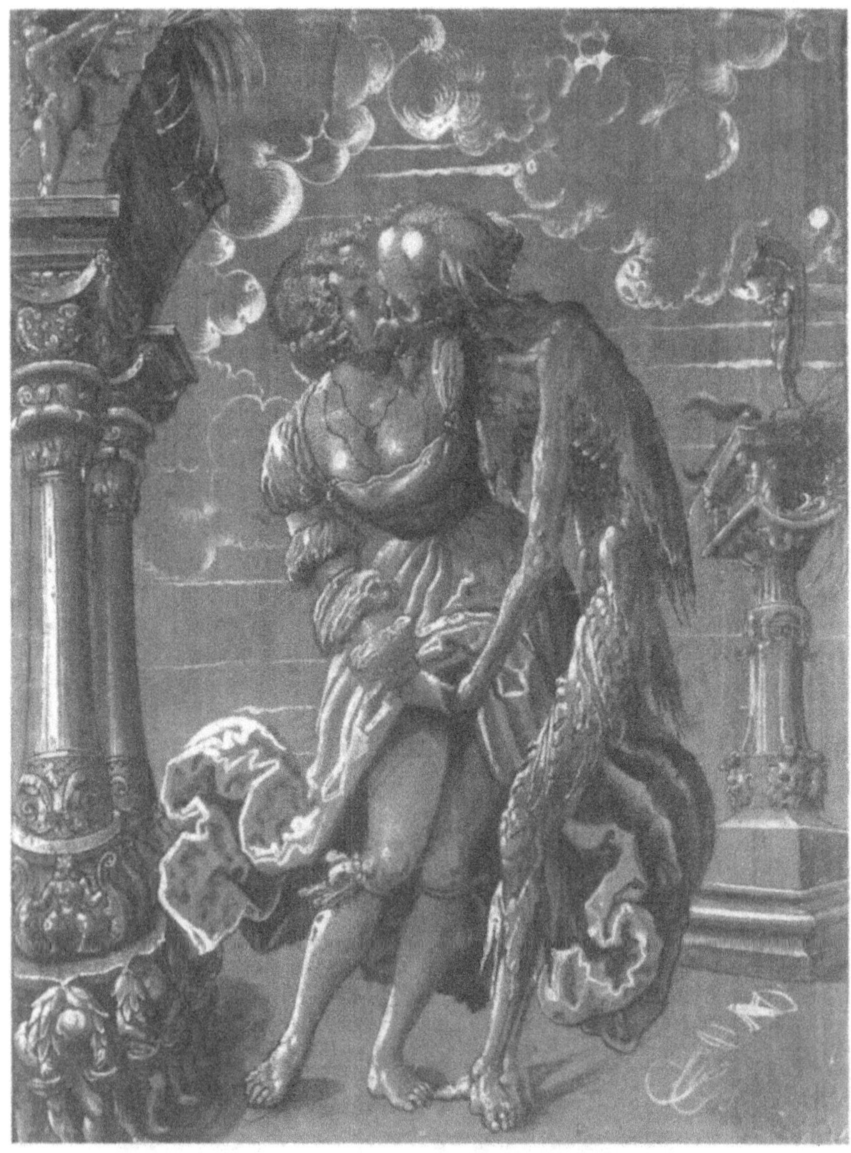

Figure 3.16. Niklaus Manuel Deutsch, *Young Woman and Death as a Soldier*, 1517. Tempera on panel, 38 × 29 cm. Kunstmuseum, Öffentliche Kunstsammlungen, Basel.

fame and glory. Her legs are open to partially expose her genitals; a fire-pot (lust, violence, both?) perches on her left thigh. Her chains encircle her breasts and navel and direct the viewer toward the source of her power.

Manuel's little grisaille panel of *Young Woman and Death as a Soldier* (1517, figure 3.16) pits the *Reisläufer* (his ragged slit breeches are still visible) against the syphilitic whore who destroys him. As she guides his bony fingers to her genitals and he kisses her, he becomes a corpse—a conceit similar to that of Baldung's brilliant, gruesome painting of *Eve, Death and the Serpent* (ca. 1525) in the National Gallery of Canada, Ottawa, in which the sexual stimulation by a sly and uncaring Eve brings death to Adam.[174] Above the column at the left, a cupid impales himself; on the other side of the panel is King David's nemesis—the fateful arousing sight of Bathsheba at her bath.

Eros was just one hazard among many in the life of a soldier. Graf's experience of battle is recorded in a drawing with a corpse-laden foreground and a furious, ongoing engagement in the fields beyond. On the left, amid the carnage, above the broken drum of war and opposite a tree with two hanged men, a vigorous *Reisläufer* drinks from his canteen; his erect sword and impossibly long pike, symbols of an indefatigable masculinity, assert themselves against the surrounding chaos. In his amazing drawing of an armless, half-blind woman with a wooden leg and maimed breast, Graf depicted a camp-follower who has suffered the most egregious occupational hazard (1514, figure 3.17). Caught in artillery crossfire (or mercilessly mutilated by her clientele?) she was one of thousands who traveled in the wake of early modern armies, providing necessities and diversions.[175] Perhaps she was an object of pity to Graf; it is hard for us to believe that he would not pity her. But John Hale, who has written extensively on the military theme in Renaissance art, cautions us about anachronistic pity, and Christiane Andersson, who focuses on Graf's women, interprets the drawing in terms of the perpetual female drive to seduce. For Andersson, the woman (having no other choice, after all) wears her skirt high and her bodice low, and she still proffers herself as an object of lust, for her most essential parts have not been destroyed. Graf's many images of women, Andersson concludes, depict not the actuality of women's lives but the masculine fantasy of the artist.[176] If Andersson's reading is correct, Graf's mutilated woman compares to Manuel's old witch in unexpected ways (see figure 1.1). Both figures apprehend the male viewer as a hoped-for lover; both repel that viewer as a reminder of death or unthinkable violence to the body—surely Graf's major fears. The process of abjection and reconstitution of the male self (this time in its permutation of the soldier-artist) seems equally applicable here.

From Dürer and Baldung's early sixteenth-century images of witches—and their sisterhood with other transgressive women from Eve to camp-whores—we learn that witches *are* indeed women at the symbolic level. We find no simple and necessary correspondence between the images and the chronological peaks of the European witch-hunts; instead, their visual rhetoric (and therefore their deeper relevance for the witch-hunts) is more far-reaching. It emerges from the ideals, fantasies, anxieties, and competitive demands of early modern models of masculinity—in particular, that of the visual artist. In subsequent chapters, I explore this idea further in distinctive historical and artistic contexts.

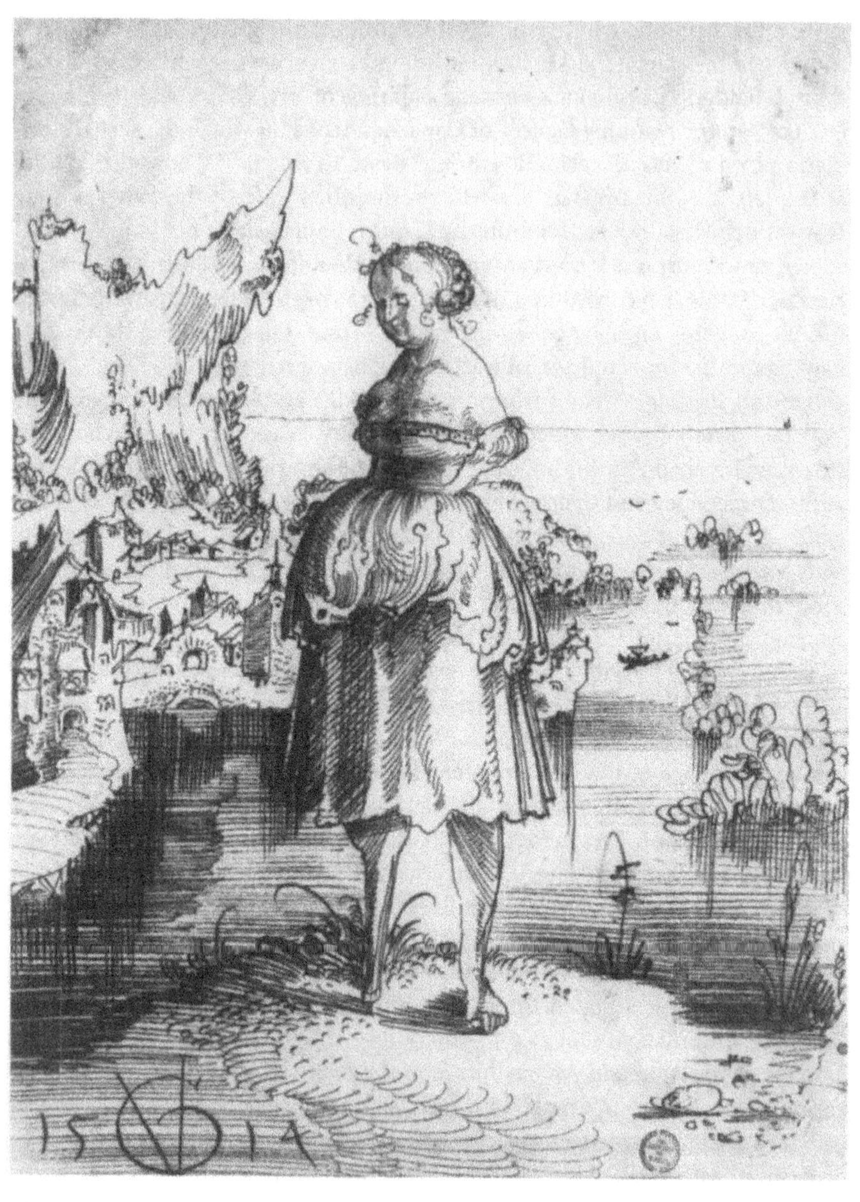

Figure 3.17. Urs Graf, *Armless Camp Follower with Wooden Leg*, 1514. Pen drawing in black ink, 210 × 156 mm. Kupferstichkabinett, Öffentliche Kunstsammlungen, Basel.

Chapter 4
Francken, the Rhetoric of Habsburg Power, and Artistic Invention in Antwerp

"*Pour la Republique*": Pierre de Lancre and Witchcraft as Anti-Kingdom

Sixteenth-century images of witches by Dürer and Baldung depict small pockets of transgressive women and allude to the disruptive or even lethal results of women's congress. The images challenge the male gaze and male control of women, but witchcraft is still seen as an incipient phenomenon. The mood had changed by 1613, when minor Polish engraver Jan Ziarnko made his fold-out illustration, complete with annotated legend, for the second edition of French humanist and magistrate Pierre de Lancre's *Tableau de l'inconstance des mauvais anges et démons* (Picture of the inconstancy of evil angels and demons; figure 4.1).

After the 1520s, concern about witches temporarily waned. Having been reprinted many times, the *Malleus maleficarum* (Hammer of witches) ceased to be issued again between 1521 and 1576. Brian Levack cites a number of reasons for this hiatus: People were distracted from the problem of witchcraft by the Protestant Reformation; many had been persuaded by early sixteenth-century skeptical writers; and the judicial machinery of witch prosecutions underwent alterations.[1] After mid-century, however, various factors came together to strengthen the conception of witchcraft and expand the hunts. The period of 1550 to 1650, the peak of the European witch-hunts, was an era of political and religious turmoil and economic decline that undermined confidence and optimism. Skepticism about witchcraft waned in the face of more detailed arguments in new demonological treatises by Jean Bodin (1580), Peter Binsfield (1591), Nicolas Rémy (1595), Martín Del Rio (1599), Henri Boguet (1602), and Pierre de Lancre (1612). The *Malleus* began to be reprinted again. A general sense of anxiety and instability fed the fear of witches. In his *Demon-Mania* (1580), jurist and political philosopher Jean Bodin repeatedly stressed not only ancient sources on witchcraft but also the accumulation of evidence by early modern authorities and the fundamental agreement of witches' confessions in various countries.[2] The concept of witchcraft had matured. Nothing exemplifies this deadly shift better than the visual rhetoric of de Lancre's illustration.

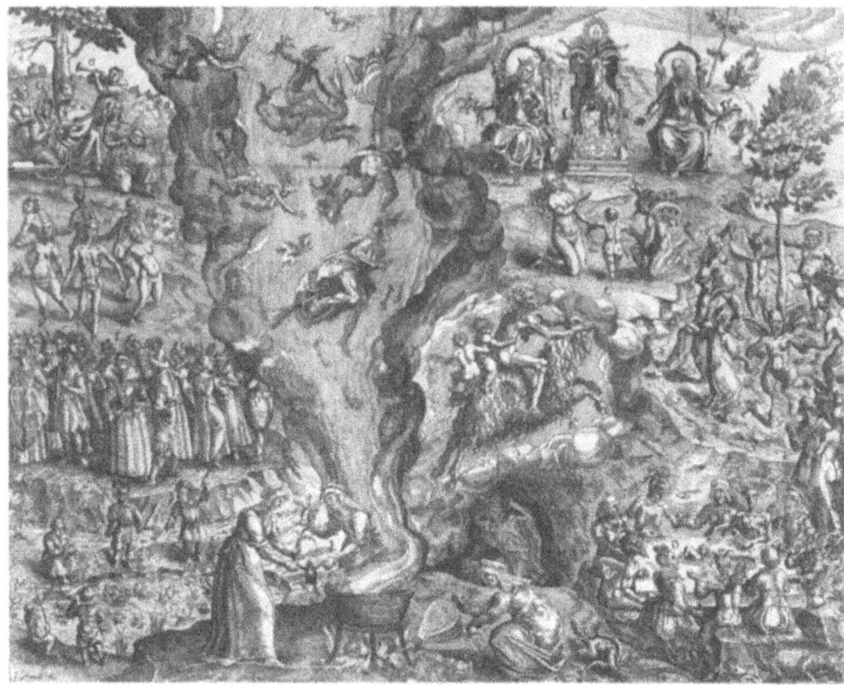

Figure 4.1. Jan Ziarnko, *Witches' Sabbath*, fold-out illustration from Pierre de Lancre's *Tableau de l'inconstance des mauvais anges et démons* (Picture of the inconstancy of evil angels and demons; Paris, 1613 edition). Division of Rare and Manuscript Collections, Carl A. Kroch Library, Cornell University.

In 1609, de Lancre was commissioned by Henry IV to investigate witchcraft in the Basque-speaking Pays de Labourd in southwestern France, an assignment that fomented his contempt for the laxity of judges, religious authorities, and the *Parlement* (high court) of Bordeaux toward witchcraft. For four months, using a translator, he meticulously gathered testimony from hundreds of witnesses, sending some suspected witches to the *Parlement* in Bordeaux or incarcerating them in an auxiliary prison improvised from a local ruined chateau. Ultimately de Lancre executed about eighty people (not the six hundred that is often cited), including two priests.[3] The Labourd campaign focused de Lancre's sense of divine justice and his distrust of the world's inconstancy, as defined by Flemish Neostoic Justus Lipsius in *De constantia* (On constancy, 1584). Inconstancy was exemplified not only by contemporary political and religious upheaval but also by the volatility and dissimulation of demons, and the unrestrained passions of women.[4] This association among demons, women's passions, inconstancy, and political disorder helps explain de Lancre's intense sense of vocation: As a judge, he saw himself as a divine instrument.[5]

De Lancre's commitment to his mission was rooted in his nationalism and France's goal of political and social hegemony. In an insightful analysis of his *Tableau* and other writings, Gerhild Scholz Williams shows how de Lancre's wholehearted adoption of the mythos of the French crown and his belief that royal power transcended ecclesiastical power pervaded his views of Basque society. To de Lancre, the poor Basques (the French-speaking aristocracy of the region largely escaped his purview) were incomprehensible foreigners, with a strange language as well as customs and beliefs he could not fathom. In de Lancre's mind, Scholz Williams suggests, they were akin to the native populations of the New World who must be subjugated. In her equally compelling interpretation of de Lancre, Sophie Houdard also emphasizes his anxiety about the Basques' contamination of the simple, honest French temperament with Spanish duplicity and cruelty. De Lancre was especially astounded by the Basque haughtiness and sense of freedom in the face of poverty. Their mixed geography (mountains and sea) was a sign of their inscrutability and resistance to control. Both Scholz Williams and Houdard note the importance de Lancre lent to the Basque dependence on the sea. Shaped by the fluidity and unceasing movement of the sea, the Basques epitomized inconstancy.[6]

De Lancre scrutinized Basque women with astonishment and desire. For six months out of the year, while the men were at sea, they were without male supervision. He commented on their unruly tresses and brilliant eyes, "*aussi dangereuse en amour qu'en sortilege*" (equally dangerous in love as in witchcraft).[7] De Lancre thought Basque women—fed on apples, the fruit of original sin!—were sexually licentious, a trait manifested in the wild abandon with which they danced. They could also enjoy an unusual degree of religious freedom: Permitted by lax priests, Basque women actually assisted in the mass. For de Lancre, it was not too far a leap from the outrageous customs of the Basques to the witches' sabbath.[8]

De Lancre was chiefly concerned about France's establishment of absolutist authority, but of course this authority was bound to religion. Like Martín Del Rio, whose massive *Disquisitionum magicarum in libri sex* (Six books of investigations into magic, 1599) became the most influential Jesuit demonological text, de Lancre was deeply influenced by the lectures of Jean Maldonat (Juan de Maldonado), a Spanish Jesuit who taught at the College of Clerment in Paris where de Lancre was educated. Maldonat's popular lectures, published in the form of notes taken by his student François de la Borie under the title *Traicté des anges et démons* (Treatise on angels and demons, 1605), clearly established a link between the Huguenot heresy and witchcraft, interpreting both as the devil's work. Jonathan Pearl elucidates the personal and ideological ties among de Lancre, Del Rio, and Maldonat, and the political basis for their demonology, which became a powerful tool for the suppression of Protestantism. This was not simply a rhetorical cloaking of anti-Protestantism in witch-hunting. Rather, Pearl explains, Maldonat thought that Protestantism necessarily degenerated into witchcraft. The two abominations were linked as forms of the devil's deception; people (especially women) were led naturally by sinful curiosity from one to the other. Pearl's analysis establishes how important this linkage was for the gradual suppression of Protestantism in France in the late sixteenth century.[9]

The success of the godly absolutist state depended not on Machiavellian cynicism and dissimulation but on the moral rectitude and piety of its leaders, from the king and court to officials and magistrates, and their ability to mold loyal and pious subjects. As Robert Bireley states, the central principle of this anti-Machiavellian theory of statecraft was that the good and the useful are bound together; virtue yields good reputation, on which power is based.[10] In de Lancre's later treatise *Le livre des princes* (The book of princes, 1617), intended as a moral lesson for young Louis XIII, he argues for the importance of piety and rigorous morality at court to the well-being of the kingdom. The court for de Lancre, Houdard emphasizes, was much like the witches' sabbath: both were theaters of duplicity and cruelty, gatherings of beasts in deceptively elegant guises.[11]

De Lancre must have directed the content of Ziarnko's engraving closely. Witchcraft is no longer visualized as incipient but as a full-blown, alternative social order whose principles are made transparent in a demonic courtly ritual that both mirrors and mocks its counterpart of the royal court. Only an elevated vantage point could fully reveal the scope of this countersociety of witches, demons, and the devil. Individual sections of the engraving, resembling the woodcut vignettes in illustrated demonological treatises, such as the *Compendium maleficarum* (Handbook of witches, 1608) by Milanese friar Francesco-Maria Guazzo, are numbered and labeled for clarity.[12] The he-goat reigns as monarch, with a primary and a less-favored queen (mimicking and mocking the custom of royal concubines?) at the upper right. His court and subjects of various ranks, including "poor witches" marginalized and "pushed into corners" at the middle right, carry out their rituals of music, dance, and feasting. A loyal subject brings tribute to the king and queens in the form of a captive child, while other children are trained in the lower left by herding the toads that were crucial to diabolical magic. In the middle left, aristocratic converts to this anti-court—some masked to avoid being discovered—prepare to conduct the important business of the realm.

From the center spreads a spectacular plume of smoke inspired by Jacques de Gheyn II's master engraving of about 1610 (see figure 5.6), produced in a different context of comparative restraint and skepticism, as we shall see in Chapter 5. It rises from the poisonous brew concocted in the center foreground by the everyday witches whose workaday black magic sustains this anti-kingdom, and embraces witches and their children flying to the sabbath or departing to raise tempests. In its encyclopedic categorizing and summarizing of witches' activities, and in its sense of a world—bursting with energy, fully operative, implacably opposed to our own—Ziarnko's engraving gives visual form to de Lancre's witch-hunting rhetoric and his righteous promotion of the godly absolutist state. Houdard likens the print's episodic structure and sense of the marvelous to the French baroque theater before being disciplined by classicism and its borders and legend to de Lancre's attempt to perceive and contain the mutability of the demonic world. It reads like an attempt to pierce the veil of demonic illusion, to circumscribe inconstancy.[13]

Although de Lancre's loyalty was to France, the principles he advocated applied equally to France's chief rival for European domination, the Habsburg dynasty. In their rebellious territory of the Southern Netherlands, Frans Francken II (1581–1642) produced images of witches that corroborated Habsburg antiwitchcraft rhetoric and the notion of the godly state, both influenced by an intense Counter-Reformation piety and Jesuit thought. Francken's paintings were shaped by these influences, and by Antwerp's unique understanding of artistic invention.

Frans Francken II's Witchcraft Images in Political and Religious Context

Between 1606 and 1610, about the time de Lancre conducted his investigations in the Pays de Labourd and wrote his *Tableau*, Francken painted the most detailed images of witchcraft in the history of the genre. Although little known today, he was one of the most prominent artists working in Antwerp in the late sixteenth and early seventeenth century—a highly competitive artistic milieu, including Jan Bruegel the Elder, Joos de Momper, Sebastian Vrancx, Hendrik van Balen, and, after 1609, Peter Paul Rubens. Francken came from a family of artists: His father Frans I was a painter and had four sons in the profession (Frans II's brothers were Hieronymus, Thomas, and Ambrosius). In turn, Francken trained his younger brother Hieronymus, his son Frans III, and another recorded pupil, Daniel Hagens. There were almost certainly more pupils in Francken's large and active workshop. In 1605, Francken was admitted to the Antwerp Guild of St. Luke as a master and, in 1607, he received a six-month pass to travel to the Northern Netherlands. Exactly when he went or whom he encountered is uncertain; he was back in Antwerp by November of 1607, when he married.[14]

Francken's success may be gauged by his prolific oeuvre, indicating a steady demand for his pictures among collectors, and the amount (four gulden; Rubens left six) bequeathed to the Guild upon his death in 1642. His reputation was based primarily on small, intricate cabinet pictures. Although we know little about Francken as a personality, the iconographic content of his

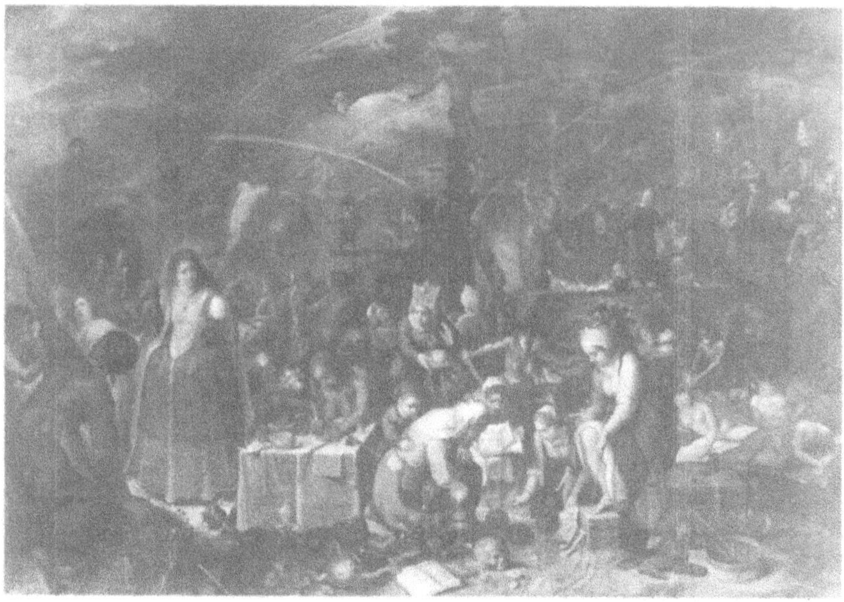

Figure 4.2. Frans Francken II, *Witches' Gathering*, 1607. Oil on panel, 56 × 83.5 cm. Kunsthistorisches Museum, Vienna. Erich Lessing/Art Resource, New York.

art indicates a learned and ambitious artist desiring to upgrade the status of his profession by focusing on the intellectual aspects of invention. He must have been a member of the rhetoricians' chamber in Antwerp, and he apparently had a large library that he used as an iconographic resource.[15] As the inventor of the symbolically laden genre of the "gallery picture," Francken pioneered an understanding of art's intellectual value as a way of diminishing its reliance on manual skill, which nevertheless remained important. This intellectual value was firmly bound to religion in that knowledge of the world constituted understanding of God's creation.[16]

Francken's extant paintings and one drawing of witches date from 1606 through 1610.[17] This period coincided with an intense antiwitchcraft campaign in the Southern Netherlands and with the artist's efforts to augment his professional status after his admission to the Guild in 1605, his marriage, and the purchase of his first house in 1606. The best known and largest of these images is *Witches' Sabbath* or *Witches' Gathering* that hangs in the Kunsthistorisches Museum in Vienna (1607; figure 4.2)—a spectacular outdoor panorama of witches' magical activities that seems to correspond closely to the strident stance against witchcraft taken by Philip II and the Habsburg regents of the Southern Netherlands, Archduke Albert and Archduchess Isabella. Francken also painted Witches' Kitchens—a Netherlandish compositional type, centering on a fireplace, influenced by Pieter Bruegel the Elder's *St. James and the*

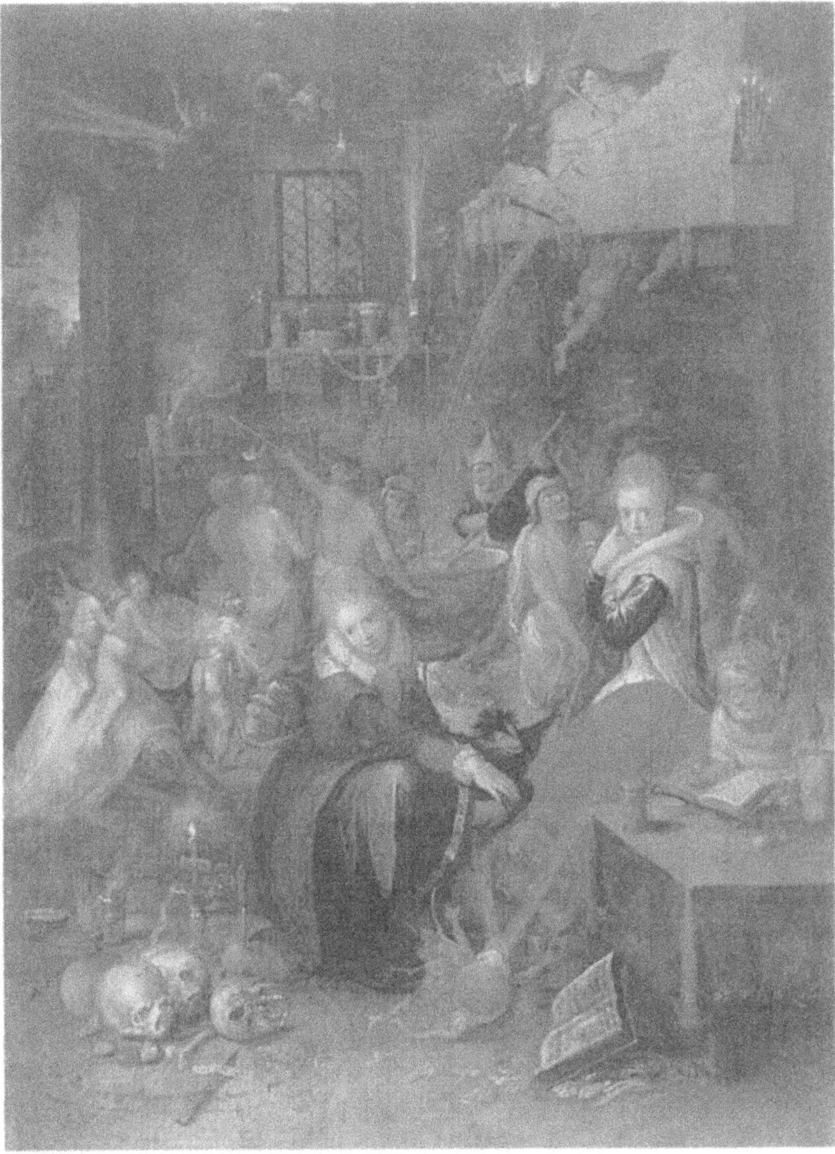

Figure 4.3. Frans Francken II, *Witches' Kitchen*, 1606. Oil on panel, 46.6 × 35.2 cm. Victoria and Albert Museum, London/Art Resource, New York.

Magician Hermogenes (1565; see figure 2.6). The most important of these is a delicately painted vertical panel now in the Victoria and Albert Museum in London (1606; figure 4.3). In keeping with Francken's practice of producing workshop copies, two further versions of this painting exist: one on copper in Frankfurt, dated 1606 on its back, and another undated panel in Berlin—

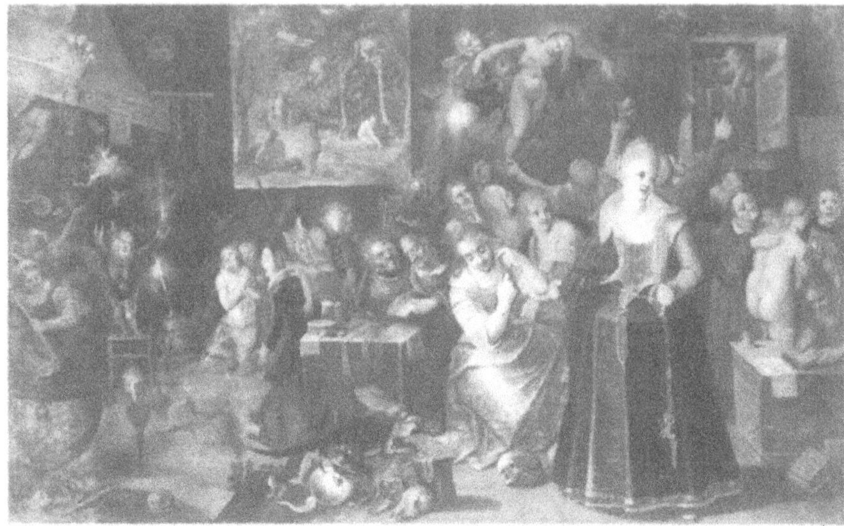

Figure 4.4. Frans Francken II, *Witches' Preparation for the Journey to the Blocksberg*, ca. 1610. Oil on panel, 42 × 69 cm. Alte Pinakothek, Bayerische Staatsgemaauldesammlungen, Munich.

suggesting its appeal to collectors.[18] Francken reworked these two basic images in two additional extant pictures that date about 1610: a *Witches' Kitchen* panel in Vienna, and a so-called *Sabbath* or *Journey to the Blocksberg* in the Alte Pinakothek in Munich. The view through the window and the fireplace in this latter work make it a "kitchen" (figure 4.4).

Many scholars have commented on the extraordinary detail of these paintings.[19] The interiors of the smaller Vienna painting, the London work and its derivatives, and the Berlin and Munich pictures teem with objects, demons, and women of various ages—the wealthy mingling with peasants, the old with the young. The presence of young, beautiful, and well-to-do initiates characterizes all the paintings and is a key to their rhetorical message. Floors and surfaces are cluttered with a bewildering array of paraphernalia of black magic and Boschian demons. In the largest painting in Vienna, the "kitchen" walls of the 1606 London work have dissolved to leave the witches in an apocalyptic nocturnal landscape full of pyrotechnics and observed by an astonished male spectator (his apron suggests he is a worker or an artisan) in the lower left corner.

In their prolific detail and expressive intensity, Francken's paintings exemplify a mature stage in the theory of witchcraft. By the early seventeenth century, demonologists had given the stereotype its full-blown form represented in de Lancre's *Tableau* and urged the prosecution of witches as essential to the preservation of political and social order. Francken's works clearly promulgated these views within the contemporary social and artistic milieu of the Southern Netherlands. Their reach was potentially longer, however, for Antwerp was an artistic center that supplied numerous European courts and wealthy collectors with paintings, prints, sculptures, and tapestries exported as part of the thriving international market for luxury goods. Antwerp art objects and artists found their way to England, the Northern Netherlands, France, and of course to other Habsburg courts in Vienna, Prague, and Spain.[20]

Unfortunately, we have no knowledge of direct commissions for these paintings. However, like much of Francken's oeuvre, they were most likely destined for the *Kunstkammers* (private art galleries) of noble or wealthy bourgeois collectors. With that premise in mind, I argue in this chapter for the paintings' efficacy as political, religious, and moral statements, and as vehicles of self-presentation for the artist and collectors. Francken's paintings of witches affirmed the political and religious order of which he and his clients were a part and functioned in the artist's self-fashioning vis-à-vis that order.

Francken's interest in the theme of witchcraft corresponded chronologically to Archduke Albert and Archduchess Isabella's antiwitchcraft Edict of 1606 (as noted by Reginald Wilenski and others) that in turn followed earlier decrees from Philip II of Spain, Isabella's father and Albert's uncle.[21] The ultimate resting place of two of the paintings in Vienna, where Habsburg collections were eventually funneled, suggests a close connection to the Regents and these decrees.[22] In particular, we might reasonably speculate that the larger Vienna work, measuring 56 × 83.5 cm and with its meticulously executed detail, had a very highly placed patron.

Whether princely or bourgeois, art collections during this period were economic investments and sources of intellectual satisfaction, but above all they functioned to advertise their owners.[23] As Thomas DaCosta Kaufmann has emphasized, princely collections such as those of the Habsburgs in Prague, Innsbruck, and Vienna, worked to support political and dynastic rhetoric. Although audiences for these collections may have been limited, as sites of state visits from other princes, ambassadors, and other high-ranking officials, they were nonetheless important for establishing a princely image.[24] We might speculate that in the context of the Southern Netherlands in the early seventeenth century, Francken would have found an interested audience for his witchcraft paintings among the nobility and government officials or members of the legal profession—people whose occupations gave them reason to be concerned about witchcraft, and whose art collections enhanced their status in a society characterized by rapid upward mobility.[25] The paintings may have appealed to collectors in other Habsburg territories as well, because they affirmed the dynastic effort to combat witchcraft and satisfied the taste for Antwerp art manifested in these very centers.

Although we cannot specify the exact contexts of Francken's witchcraft paintings, it is possible to envision how they might have functioned within an elite *Kunstkammer* of the early seventeenth century. By expressing the elevated artistic taste developed in Antwerp and by engaging the intellectual and judicial aspects of witchcraft, they would have been foci of learned discussion, connoisseurial delectation, and sumptuous display. Moreover, they would have advertised both the owners and the artist as supporters of antiwitchcraft campaigns. They would have functioned didactically to warn viewers of the dangers of witchcraft and the necessity of its prosecution. Because of the connection between witchcraft and heresy, and witchcraft and women, they would have reinforced a broader Counter-Reformation agenda.

Robert Muchembled, historian of the witch persecutions of the late sixteenth and seventeenth centuries in the Southern Netherlands, has argued persuasively that these antiwitchcraft campaigns were tied to the Spanish monarchy's efforts to assert sovereignty over this rebellious territory. Humiliated by their failure to maintain dominance over the United Provinces, the Habsburgs turned the Spanish Netherlands into a bulwark of royal power conjoined with Counter-Reformation Catholicism.[26] In their efforts to forge an orderly Catholic state, one of their tools was demonological theory, aptly described by Alain Boureau as "the last totalizing construction offered by Christianity, the last universal language articulated by the Church."[27]

Muchembled argues for an appropriation of the concept of witchcraft as diabolical heresy by the political realm in the late sixteenth and early seventeenth century. In areas of Europe most affected by the conflict between Catholicism and Protestantism from 1570 to about 1640, witchcraft became a crime of high treason, of lèse-majesté (injury to the sovereign). As the highest of crimes, witchcraft was the most serious threat to the authority of God and to the monarch embodying that authority on earth.

In this context, witchcraft imagined as a collective, conspiratorial activity led by the devil inverted the ideal Habsburg state, especially as conceived by Philip II. Although Charles V wanted his son to preside over a Europe unified under Habsburg control, this dream was foiled by the resistance of Charles's brother Ferdinand, as well as that of the German electors, who did not want a Spanish king. By 1558, two basic spheres of Habsburg sovereignty were clear. Philip was to control Spain and the Southern Netherlands, the North having eluded his grasp. With Spain not only came Naples, Sicily, and Lombardy, but also the New World with untold riches to be harvested and pagan multitudes to be converted to Catholic orthodoxy. Ferdinand I in turn ruled over the German-speaking block of Habsburg lands and when he died in 1564, those lands were not ceded to Philip as Charles wished but to Ferdinand's son, Maximilian II.

Nevertheless, Philip remained captivated by the dream of one Catholic empire. To realize this dream, he used the bewilderingly intricate symbolism of Habsburg sovereignty, described in detail by Marie Tanner.[28] Habsburg genealogy supposedly ran back through Ottonian, Carolingian, and Merovingian rulers and still further into ancient and biblical history. The dynasty was linked not only with Christ himself through his human ancestors of Jesse, David and Solomon, but also to Noah and Adam, to Aeneas, founder of Rome, and to Constantine and the Anicio family, including martyred saints whose bodies were discovered in the early sixteenth century under Charles's auspices.[29] Philip's particular contribution to Habsburg genealogy, Tanner argues, was his assertion of continuous descent from the Eastern emperors, including Heraclius who had taken the Holy Cross from the Persians and restored it to Jerusalem in 627.[30] Devotion to the Holy Blood embodied in the Cross and the Eucharist pervaded Habsburg genealogical mythology, their exalted claims to sovereignty, and their combat against paganism and heresy. Even their pagan ancestor Aeneas was renowned for his piety.

With the help of the new religious orders, and in continuation of his father's practice, Philip II fostered the cult of the Eucharist throughout his territories, including the New World. Habsburg dominion was explicitly associated with Catholic devotion in celebrations of the Feast of Corpus Christi, auto sacramentals (literally, "sacramental acts," short, vivid plays about the Mass fostered by the Jesuits), and in the Forty-Hours Veneration of the Eucharist.[31] This link between state power and the Eucharist helps to explain why witchcraft was so abhorrent. In keeping with the traditional accusations of desecration of the Host levied against Jews or heretics, described in detail by Norman Cohn in *Europe's Inner Demons*, witches were thought to enact a counter-Mass at their sabbaths.[32] In *Demon Lovers*, Walter Stephens not only confirms the importance of demonic copulation in witchcraft theory as established by the *Malleus* as a proof of the Christian faith, but also witches' or Jews' desecration of the Host as proof of the miracle of transubstantiation, the real presence of the blood and body of Christ.[33] This anxious need for proof was only enhanced by the Reformation. Against the frequent Protestant accusation that Catholic sacraments, especially the idea of transubstantiation, were mere magical conjurations, the Church vehemently asserted the truth of its rituals, as opposed to the false ones of heretics, who had always been demonized. The practice of the Catholic sacraments was even said to ward off the danger of witchcraft, advice that seems perilously close to condoning countermagic. As Stuart Clark states, "Theirs [the Catholics'] was an argument based on a simple dualism between God's true church and the devil's false versions, backed up by a reading of history."[34]

This "simple dualism" is visually suggested in Francken's paintings. As Ziarnko's engraved illustration to de Lancre's text presented the reader with witchcraft's threat to the French absolutist state, Catholic Habsburg subjects viewing Francken's paintings were confronted with paradigms of disorder, sacrilege, and inversion. The threat posed by diabolical magic to the godly state is articulated in two important treatises of the late sixteenth century that contributed to Francken's paintings—Bodin's *Démonomanie* (Demon-mania, 1580, with an edition appearing in Antwerp in 1593) and Del Rio's *Disquisitionum magicarum* (translated into French in 1611 and reprinted numerous times until 1747). Both works escalate the perceived scale and threat of witchcraft, consolidate earlier ideas into a more coherent stereotype of the witch, and address their theory to judges with a renewed intensity stemming from a growing understanding of the judiciary as the instrument of state power.

For Bodin—major philosopher and political theorist as well as witch-trial judge—witches were the ultimate enemies of magistrates who, in turn, were the instruments of monarchical power. The majesty of the king is a reflection of the majesty of God; magistrates partake of that descending majesty (that is why, for example, the old question of whether witches could harm judges is answered negatively by Bodin). Remarkably tolerant for his time in his religious views, Bodin nevertheless believed in the fundamental godliness of the state. A state rife with witchcraft is an ill-governed state in which the divine harmony underlying the celestial, natural, and human realms is profoundly disturbed.[35] Although a providential God ultimately sanctions demons and witches, the harmonious state must hold these evil elements in check: "So also a well-ordered Commonweale is composed of good and bad, of the rich and the poore, of wisemen and fools, of the strong and the weak, allied by them which are in the meane betwixt both: which so by a wonderfull disagreeing concord, joyne the highest with the lowest, and so all to all, yet so as that the good are still stronger than the bad; so as hee the most wise workeman of all others, and governor of the world hath by his eternall law decreed."[36] Far from being an aberrant, marginal aspect of his thought, then, Bodin's *Démonomanie* was a complement to his view of the absolute monarchical state.

Although Bodin's *Démonomanie* was well known, a more important text for the artist was probably Del Rio's *Disquisitionum magicarum*. Del Rio was a native of Antwerp, a magistrate, and a Jesuit, and therefore uniquely qualified to express a Counter-Reformation view of witchcraft especially appealing to the rulers and more broadly the dominant culture of the Southern Netherlands. He was born in 1551 of a Castilian father and an Aragonese mother. His father was a Habsburg official whose castle was destroyed in the rebellion. Extremely well educated in classical literature, a variety of languages, and law, Del Rio became the Vice Chancellor and Attorney General for Brabant in his twenties. In 1580, he joined the Society of Jesus to study and teach internationally at various institutions founded by the order. Like de Lancre, Del Rio was deeply influenced by Maldonat's lectures.[37] He died in Brussels in 1608, leaving behind a large body of writings.

After the fall of Antwerp in 1585, the city changed from a center of religious diversity to a Counter-Reformation bulwark. Calvinists moved north in droves. The importance of the Southern Netherlands as an outpost of the intensely Catholic Spanish Habsburgs and an example of their power meant that the country was a choice site for the international religious orders—especially the Jesuits. Indeed, the presence of the Jesuit clergy in the Southern Netherlands increased steadily from 1595 until it came to rival proportionately that of France, Germany, Poland, and Spain. This growth was paralleled by the Jesuits' vigorous enrollment of the laity in sodalities and by the thriving industry of devotional prints. Albert and Isabella's patronage of the Jesuits and other orders was replicated by elite members of society, and Catholic orthodoxy and social discipline (including the persecution of witchcraft) were enforced through provincial councils and secular courts.[38] Artists, including Francken, were strongly influenced by the Jesuit presence.[39]

In the Spanish Netherlands, Tridentine ideals, theories of absolute monarchy and the judiciary as its instrument, and witch-hunting were closely bound together.[40] Muchembled argues that magistrates brought a particularly vivid sense of dualistic confrontation between themselves and witches (or deviants of any kind) to their charge. Like Bodin, Del Rio saw the judiciary and witches as symmetrical systems, serving different masters: the judiciary served the monarch, thus God; witches served the devil. In this battle, the just magistrate, like the just king, partook of the charisma of divine inviolability. Although God might allow witches to operate after they were arrested, their power was sapped after trial—that is, after confrontation with the magistrate. God would surely not allow justice, in the form of the execution of witches, to be impeded.[41]

Francken's paintings immediately follow Albert and Isabella's decree against witchcraft in April of 1606, but this decree followed earlier mandates from Philip II, and the nuances and changes within these royal pronouncements are important for the understanding of Francken's paintings.[42] In 1590, Philip issued a Letter Patent against witchcraft. Although no new laws were needed, bishops and judges were to pursue witches and punish them vigorously as examples for the populace. In 1592, Philip issued a comprehensive royal edict against witches, fully aligned with current demonological theory and outlining procedures for prosecution. This edict would be completed by a 1595 mandate reasserting the need for vigorous prosecution, for although many witches had been burned, it was believed that a great multitude still existed.

The 1595 document shows some interesting qualifications, however. It forbade the water ordeal as a test for witchcraft, following the 1594 judgment on its inefficacy by faculty at the University of Leiden.[43] A pronouncement against "swimming" witches did not necessarily indicate a disbelief in witchcraft or softness toward its severe punishment. Rather, the argument was academic: Because flotation could be affected by other factors, swimming was not a true test of witchcraft and could therefore lead to the mistaken punishment of the innocent. The logic of the royal mandate was that villages were to cease using the water ordeal and conduct witch trials strictly by law. That way, no harm would be done to "delirious persons," or aged and ignorant old women.[44]

What seems to be a softening of persecutory zeal here is better understood as a reinforcement of monarchical control. Clearly local courts had exceeded the control of the authority of the Crown, thus defeating the purpose of the earlier ordinance: to produce a harmonious state under the aegis of a godly monarch who persecuted only the truly guilty. Bodin believed that the authority wielded by the monarch, and the magistrates in turn, conformed of necessity to natural and divine laws. This conformity distinguished mere tyranny and cruelty from legitimate rule.[45]

The construction of witchcraft in Francken's paintings hinges on this conception of the godly state and its manifestation in its treatment of accused witches. The 1606 decree issued by the Regents repeated Philip's earlier mandates but attempted to enforce centralized control over local trials more strictly. To put an end to irregularities in witchcraft trials, the district courts were to appoint a judge to oversee all cases and to report on the courts' actions. Six consulting advocates and a special commissioner were to advise the superior courts on witchcraft cases. A picture emerges of Habsburg Regents who viewed witchcraft in extreme terms, as abjuration of the faith and a crime of lèse-majesté. However, while they wanted to excise it from the kingdom, they wanted to do so only in ways through which their legitimacy was transparent. The visual hyperbole of Francken's paintings conveys both motives, assuring viewers of the true guilt of witches and confronting them with the heightened threat of witchcraft. The abundant magical activities are undertaken with the participants' utter deliberation (and literacy—some of the witches read *grimoires*). Francken's witches are not just guilty, they are guilty of everything the demonologists could think of and they practice their crimes within compositions whose very clutter, disorder, and fluidity reinforce the idea of witchcraft as anti-kingdom and the epitome of inconstancy.

The 1607 Vienna panel especially, with its gesticulating spectator mediating between elite male viewers and the melee of women and demons, presents witchcraft as a vast, formidable new land—replete like the New World with abhorrent yet fascinating customs (e.g., their worship of strange gods and cannibalism)—to be discovered and conquered (see figure 4.2). Scholz Williams's analogy between the early modern effort to comprehend and systematize witchcraft and accounts of the New World is embodied in the scope and expressive character of this painting.[46] Love magic is indicated by a wax figurine right of center and an anthropomorphic mandrake root in the lower left, by the male spectator's hand. In the center of the picture, the lighted fingers of the "Hand of Glory," made from the pickled hand of an executed criminal and able to stupefy victims, burn brightly. Storm production is conveyed by the turgid atmosphere, shot with pyrotechnic flashes; demon invocation by magic circle. At the right near the cauldron is a scale, referring to the practice of weighing suspected witches at Oudewater in the Northern Netherlands (a "normal," not-too-light weight certified one's innocence).[47] The sieve and tongs in the right foreground were used for divining the names of thieves; held with tongs, the sieve shook violently when the thief's name was pronounced.[48] By means of the foul unguent, made from the fat of murdered infants, a witch on a pedestal mounted by bloated toads is transformed into an animal as she begins to fly away.

Levitation takes various forms in Francken's paintings. Witches may be carried bodily by demons or empowered to fly on their own by the unguent, or they may be deluded into thinking they flew. In the right middle ground of the Vienna painting (see figure 4.2), demons feed hallucinogens to slumbering witches. This generous acceptance of different practices corresponds to contemporary thinking. Del Rio believed that the devil sometimes fooled witches, leaving their bodies behind, but this did not mean he always deceived them.[49] As in Baldung's images, the unguent remains a central motif for Francken, embodying the most grotesque and heinous aspects of witchcraft. In the 1603 case of Claire Goessen of Antwerp, the use of the unguent, rubbed on by an older witch named Barbara, to fly to orgiastic sabbaths seemed to weigh more heavily against her than her weak efforts at black magic. She had a skull to conjure demons when she needed to know if someone was bewitched; at one sabbath, a magic powder made from the ashes of a burned goat was distributed, but she did not get any because she didn't attend.[50]

Francken often included an overt scene of demon worship to emphasize witchcraft as a form of heresy—see the far left scene in the Munich painting, and the cave with demons and a worshipping witch at the far left of the Vienna picture (figures 4.2 and 4.4).[51] In the Vienna work, heresy is also suggested by the rosary and priest's stole held and worn by the witches in the right foreground, the disk that might be a Eucharistic wafer on the table and a rosary held by the witch to the left of center.[52] The levitation rituals depicted in all his images imply heresy as well, because levitation was the means of transport to the sabbath, which centered on worship of the devil and violation of the Catholic sacraments. Recalling Maldonat's and Del Rio's causal linkage of Protestantism and witchcraft, we can also understand Francken's pictures as indirect forms of anti-Protestant propaganda. In his Prologue to the *Disquisitionum magicarum*, Del Rio repeats Maldonat's claim that magic follows heresy, and illustrates this causality with global examples: the Muslims of Africa and Asia; the Hindus encountered by the Jesuits in India; the Lutherans of

Germany; but especially the Calvinists of Scotland, England, France, and Belgium, who are second to none in their proclivity toward witchcraft.[53] After all, antiwitchcraft campaigns were only a part of comprehensive programs to solidify confessionalization, improve lay piety, and affirm state authority.[54] When considered in this broader context, Francken's paintings of witches express a range of anxieties about class hierarchy, religious conformity, and women's proper role.

The Infectious Curiosity of Witchcraft

As Sigrid Schade has emphasized, and as the male spectator in the Vienna painting confirms, Francken combined his moralizing message about witchcraft with a voyeuristic eroticism whose objects were young, elegant women, dressed in the Spanish mode, slumming among the old peasant crones and disrobing to be rubbed with unguent.[55] The women appear apprehensive, yet eagerly anticipating the flight and the orgiastic sabbath that will follow. In the Victoria and Albert painting, the young witch at the right looks out with a coy and challenging expression; in the Vienna and Munich pictures, the protagonists are visually linked to scenes of young nude women being rubbed with unguent behind them to the right, as if one of their peers has just preceded them in the levitation process. The eroticism of these pictures engaged elite male viewers familiar with the sexual exploits that supposedly occurred during sabbaths. Ultimately, though, their message was strongly exhortative, exploiting class tensions and fears about the role of well-bred, wealthy women—the wives, sisters, or daughters of Francken's clients—in spreading heresy and witchcraft.

The presence of such women in Francken's witchcraft paintings indicates the spread of witchcraft from the rural sector to the urban elite, the nobility or the wealthy bourgeoisie, and directly corresponds to the rhetoric of contemporary demonologists, who often used the metaphor of sickness or infection to urge prosecution of witches. While discussing the relation between heresy and witchcraft in his Prologue, Del Rio states that witchcraft used to be found "here and there," but now it has "infected even the noble, the well-educated, and the rich."[56] Obviously frustrated by the weak response to his earlier exhortations, de Lancre in his second book on witchcraft, *L'incredulité et mescreance du sortilege plainement convaincue* (Incredulity and disbelief of witchcraft plainly condemned, 1622), takes a highly defensive posture, lamenting skepticism and reasserting that all Europe is affected by the sickness of witchcraft. Remembering his efforts in the Labourd, he insists once again on witchcraft as an active contagion.[57]

The contamination of the upper classes by the lower through the infection of witchcraft reflects the broader class anxieties so evident in early modern Antwerp, characterized by social polarization and inequality accompanying economic growth.[58] The middle class, which included artists, eagerly aspired to nobility through land ownership, dress, and the conspicuous consumption of luxury goods such as art. Spain, always desperate for income, even sold titles to wealthy bourgeoisie.[59]

In her rich analysis of Flemish market paintings, Elizabeth Honig traces the discomfort emerging from the mix of classes inherent in market exchange and the visual and iconographic means used by artists to naturalize and stabilize class distinctions. Upper-class male patrons of market scenes were assured of the propriety of roles of all persons at the market, in particular upper-class female buyers and lower-class sellers, and of his control over them.[60] But by collapsing the classes in crowded pictorial spaces where elite female bodies rub against or (worse) are literally rubbed by old peasant women, Francken exploited his male patrons' class anxieties and exhorted them to vigilance. Elite women are directly implicated by these paintings. Although the wealthy participants do not rub the peasant women in reciprocation, thereby maintaining a semblance of the hierarchy of mistress and servant, Francken's depictions of witchcraft nevertheless level class distinctions among women by demonstrating their equal susceptibility to the devil's power. The reality is that poverty did contribute to women's vulnerability to accusations of witchcraft in the Southern Netherlands and elsewhere.[61] Elisabeth Grutere of Ghent, for example, was a seventy-year-old drummer's widow executed in 1604 "as one would cut off a putrid, gangrenous limb" (*comme on coupe un membre pourri et gangrene*). Elisabeth worked as a maid and sold spiced bread outside churches, but she turned to an evil spirit who helped her perform black magic when she became jealous of prideful women and their fine clothes. According to the prosecutor, she gave herself sexually to the demon "*de vous rendre riche et de vous procurer de beaux habits*" (to get rich and to procure beautiful clothes).[62]

The voyeuristic eroticism, encyclopedic immersion into bizarre and repulsive practices, and the dazzling visual feast provided by Francken's paintings had the potential to compromise their moral purpose. However, when yoked closely to the antiwitchcraft campaign and to the broader Counter-Reformation purpose of restricting women's roles and behavior, the paintings' hyperbolic excess and exposure of women's seductive and disruptive power became permissible, even laudable. Similarly, as Ursula Härting notes, the Catholic religious content of Francken's gallery pictures offered a cloak for collectors' fascination with the exotic and their appetite for treasures.[63] By their gender, male artists and male collectors or viewers could distance themselves from the moral traps to which women were prone to succumb: lust and the highly ambivalent faculty of curiosity. While the former female vice was by now an old article of faith in demonological thought, the latter gained significance in the context of the growth of scientific knowledge, literacy, and exploration of the New World.

Lust was always the vice in women that was most subject to diabolic control. Echoing the old misogynistic pronouncements of the *Malleus*, de Lancre lamented the infinity of women whose licentious appetites could not be curbed by honor or laws.[64] This is evident in Francken's eager young women, disrobing for the debauchery of the sabbath. However, a new emphasis in his elegant young witches is their dazzled amazement at what surrounds them and their curiosity to see and experience more. As their peasant counterparts go about their business as usual, with the same grim application as Baldung's witches (discussed in Chapter 3), the elite women are fascinated by newly discovered places and practices, and actively delight in the freedom from moral, social, and religious conventions that witchcraft offers. Surrounded by a society that is new to them, they look forward to the even more exotic, libidinous, and marvelous world of the sabbath. Their quest for occult knowledge was understood as fundamentally excessive and irreligious: a sensual appetite refusing to recognize that truth had been revealed already. Barbara Benedict notes that unlike religious wonder—passive, reverent, and subordinating the observer as object—curiosity revealed a proactive appetite for knowledge and put the observer in the position of subject, greedily seeking more. In the beginning of the seventeenth century, curiosity was deemed to be out of control, and particularly feminine—the "hubris of Eve."[65]

This heightened sense of curiosity's dangers has great relevance for art. As Christopher Wood has elaborated, the fulsome descriptive detail and meticulously rendered surfaces of many seventeenth-century paintings (like Francken's) satisfied curiosity and were morally dangerous. Through their "centrifugal" tendencies of surplus visual information or ornament, they encouraged sensory appetites and stimulated fantasy.[66] Especially in a context in which Catholic orthodoxy was severely challenged, works of religious art had to convey a clear doctrinal message and curiosity of all kinds had to be kept in check. In *La somme théologique des vérités capitales de la religion chrétienne* (The theological sum of the main truths of the Christian religion, 1625), Jesuit François Garasse, steadfast attacker of heretics, libertines, and atheists, thought it imperative that Christians avoid thinking too much about the tenets of the Catholic faith: "The true liberty of the spirit consists of freely believing what the church proposes to us, without philosophising upon it."[67] The ultimate abomination to which unbridled curiosity could lead was diabolic magic, which challenges divine causation and seeks knowledge belonging properly to God.

Perhaps in response to the anxiety generated by the threatening growth of secular knowledge, pious, educated men projected curiosity on women. Maldonat argued that women were more inclined to curiosity, which contained the seeds of unbelief.[68] Francken's witches display an undisciplined, pointless appetite for new experiences and ideas that threatens the existing social order. Most significantly for this discussion, however, their female curiosity may be regarded as the inversion of the reasoned curiosity appropriate to male collectors.

Both Kaufmann and Wood have discussed how the ambivalence of curiosity applies to *Kunstkammers*, also known aptly as "curiosity cabinets." To avoid the moral pitfall of undirected, purposeless curiosity, the collector or viewer focused on the meaning providing the very structure, not the marginal ornament, of the work. According to Franciscus Junius (François du Jon) the Younger—the German-born, Leiden-educated librarian to the Earl of Arundel—in *The Painting of the Ancients* (1638), it is reason that allows the viewer to discern the core message of a work from its pleasurable but superfluous flourishes that appeal to the senses. Reason is the only real road to truth. Ironically, however, as Wood points out, Junius acknowledged that careful attention to minutiae contributed to the formation of good judgment about art by mimicking the heightened insight of the gifted painter.[69]

Ultimately, the danger of a collector indulging his curiosity was offset by the didactic utility of the works of art and nature in the *Kunstkammer*. Kaufmann notes that Francis Bacon viewed the curiosity giving impetus to collections as justified by their utility not only to learned gentlemen but especially to rulers.[70] Thus, elite male viewers of Francken's paintings of witches could see their own thirst for knowledge and fascination with the exotic against the foil of the misguided curiosity of women. The moral danger presented by the eroticism and the prolific minutiae of these paintings was countered by the urgency of their didactic content. Put another way, Francken deflected potential criticism of these curious pictures by gendering curiosity itself and placing it at the root of women's involvement in witchcraft.

Witches' intensified exemplification of innate female vices of lust and curiosity explains why Francken's witches overlap visually with other kinds of early modern misogynistic imagery. Machteld Löwensteyn has noted how witchcraft images, in which the old instruct the young, recall brothels.[71] In the Vienna, London, and Munich pictures, an old witch wears the twin-peaked cap indicative of a procuress.[72] Härting suggests that Francken's alluring young women relate to the Power of Women theme through their resemblance to Delilah, Salome, and their ilk.[73] Certainly Francken's figures resemble *Luxuria* or "Lady World," and the procuress/prostitute analogy is widely exploited in witchcraft imagery (for example, in Goya's works, albeit with more ambivalence than here). Perhaps an equally significant overlap is with the iconographic conceit of the Idolatry of Solomon (I Kings 11:1–13), also included under the aegis of the Power of Women theme. As the old Solomon's young pagan wives seduce him to worship false idols, so the erotic power of

Francken's beautiful witches threatens to lead to the heresy indicated by burning churches or scenes of idol-worship within his paintings.[74]

Once again, the vices manifested in extremis by witches are those associated with all women—witch-hunting and its associated verbal and visual discourse cannot be divorced from contemporary ideas about women in general. Although they varied from context to context, Counter-Reformation ideas about women were highly traditional and aimed at maintaining carefully defined and monitored roles.[75] For laywomen, marriage and the family were supremely important; even the Virgin Mary and Joseph were reconceived to emphasize their exemplification of proper marriage roles.[76] For nuns, there was renewed emphasis on strict enclosure supervised by male clerics; for *beatas* (pious women who were uncloistered but wished to live a religious life), there was much distrust of the validity of their mystical visions and much concern about preserving their chastity and limiting their freedom.[77] Through a wide variety of institutional and ideological means—ecclesiastical and secular courts, sermons (more frequently published than ever before), confessions, the catechism, devotional books and plays, lay sodalities—the Church and Catholic states sought to systematize and strengthen orthodox beliefs, including those about marriage and sexuality. It was deemed very important that honorable women be clearly distinguishable from the dishonorable, that the hierarchical relationship of celibacy to sex within a Church-sanctioned marriage be maintained, and that deviant sexual behaviors such as sodomy and prostitution be punished. Wiesner notes that chronological patterns of prosecution of sexual crimes like sodomy from the late sixteenth to the early eighteenth century parallel those of witchcraft, although the former was far more widespread geographically than the latter.[78]

The Counter-Reformation efforts on behalf of women's education were focused on producing good Christian mothers and housewives. Girls might be taught to read, but reading materials were mostly devotional (perhaps the *grimoires* of Francken's paintings illustrate the potential end result of unlimited female literacy). Even more threatening than reading was writing, which allowed for expression and circulation of ideas and was not taught simultaneously. Many parents were reluctant to invest in writing materials for girls, and evidence such as clumsy signatures on documents suggest that many literate women were able to write only their names. The focus on women's roles in marriage and the home differentiated the curriculum of the Ursulines, who dedicated themselves to girls' education, from that of the Jesuit colleges, which provided a classical education and theological training for clergy, lawyers, officials, and princes. Thus, while opportunities for women's education may have increased in the Catholic Netherlands during the Counter Reformation, the restrictions that Renaissance humanism had placed on women's learning—women's lack of need for eloquence or for the skills of public office—

were in effect maintained by the gendered separation of the domestic and public spheres. The new importance given to the home as a training ground for the good Christian citizen and subject of the state did not substantively change the content of women's education.[79] The learned content of Francken's pictures and the profoundly intellectual character of artistic invention as defined in early seventeenth-century Antwerp (discussed below) must be viewed within this gendered context.

Francken's paintings of witches are embedded in a complex matrix of interrelated social and religious concerns. In their visual hyperbole and iconographic elisions, we sense the extraordinary connections his society drew among witchcraft and Protestantism, sexual deviancy and the potential collapse of social order. At the core of these connections were anxieties about women's uncontrollable lust, undisciplined curiosity, and innate inconstancy—indeed, the very congestion, heterogeneity, and turbulence of the paintings are metaphors for the disorder and disruption against which the Neostoic, nurtured by patience and guided by reason, strove to attain tranquility. The abrupt juxtaposition of young, wealthy, beautiful women and old peasant crones convey the potential slippage of distinctions between classes and between the honorable and dishonorable as well as the instability and danger of the Circean witch discussed in Chapter 1.

Thus the eroticism and curiosity of Francken's images was chastised, safely subsumed under an urgent ideological content. The artist's self-promotion, too, was contained and acceptable within the didactic and exhortative content of these pictures, which melded fully with the state's position and with Jesuit thinking about witchcraft from Maldonat to Del Rio. While reinforcing the ideals of the Catholic state, Francken's spectacles of witches' activities capitalized on a local understanding of artistic invention and were a particularly effective means by which the artist reached his coveted audience.

Francken's Witches and Artistic Invention in Antwerp

Erotic and preciously detailed, Francken's witchcraft paintings are relatively small cabinet works most likely intended as objects of discussion and delectation among a limited elite audience. The location of two of the paintings in Vienna, where Habsburg collections were eventually funneled, suggests a connection to the court and officials, although clearly the visual rhetoric of the works could have served to promote strident yet by-the-book prosecution of witches in other noble or bourgeois contexts as well. To be considered morally acceptable and socially useful, that visual rhetoric had to balance its "centrifugal" tendencies—its incitement to erotic response and pointless curiosity—with an unrelenting message. Francken confronted the *Kunstkammer* audience with a dazzling display of the heinous crimes and heretical, treasonous intent of witchcraft, in part to convince them of the necessity and rectitude of the state's antiwitchcraft stance—a stance that transparently revealed the state's godly nature.

This political rhetoric against witchcraft—based ultimately on the idea of the transgressive woman and related more broadly to the Counter-Reformation effort to circumscribe women's social roles and supervise their morality—was intertwined with an artistic rhetoric in which women's immersion in a grotesque, demonic realm became an index of inventiveness. Signed with *invenit*, or *invenit* and *fecit*, Francken's paintings of witches are to be understood as proclamations of a type of invention that grew out of the specific context of early seventeenth-century Antwerp. As Zirka Filipczak has shown in detail in *Picturing Art in Antwerp*, the city's artists, although never abandoning the value of execution (*fecit*), emphasized the intellectual activity preceding execution (*invenit*) beginning in the second half of the sixteenth century.[80]

As poets enjoyed creative license, painters should too, as conveyed by this oil sketch for an engraving by Otto Van Veen (ca. 1595; figure 4.5), done for a book of allegorical emblems visualizing quotations from Horace. As the poet writes, the painter paints a sphinx—significantly, a monstrous, hybrid form—on an easel. Poet and painter together overshadow a physician and smiths in the background, and selected and edited quotations from Horace's *Ars poetica* on the poet's scroll and the artist's canvas convey the poets' and painters' rights to creative license. As Filipczak points out, in the final engraving, Van Veen tempered his assertion of artistic license by deleting the inscription from the poet's scroll altogether and reducing that of the painter's canvas to "*pictoribus atque*" (to painter and [to poets]). In the context of the overarching meaning of Van Veen's book—living a good life—a too-aggressive claim to artistic freedom may have seemed out of place.[81] However, the equation between the two art forms remained and it is painting's claim to equality with poetry that fostered an understanding of the former as an intellectual exercise, whatever it included of manual skill.

Francken was certainly one of the engineers of this campaign for enhanced artistic status. His allegorical drawing of Painting shows the artist as equivalent to and even overshadowing the poet by his spatial position (ca. 1618; figure 4.6). On the easel, a nude Geometry conquers Ignorance; the inscription advises painters to "learn good art" while they are young (that is, to go beyond mere talent by study). The drawing summarizes the studious inventiveness for which Francken wanted to be known.[82] As a learned topic that nevertheless admitted many fantastic motifs, few themes worked better than witchcraft to prove an artist's inventiveness.

In Chapter 2, I touched on the importance of demonic scenes for the Antwerp tradition; Francken's paintings of witches form a subset of this genre and

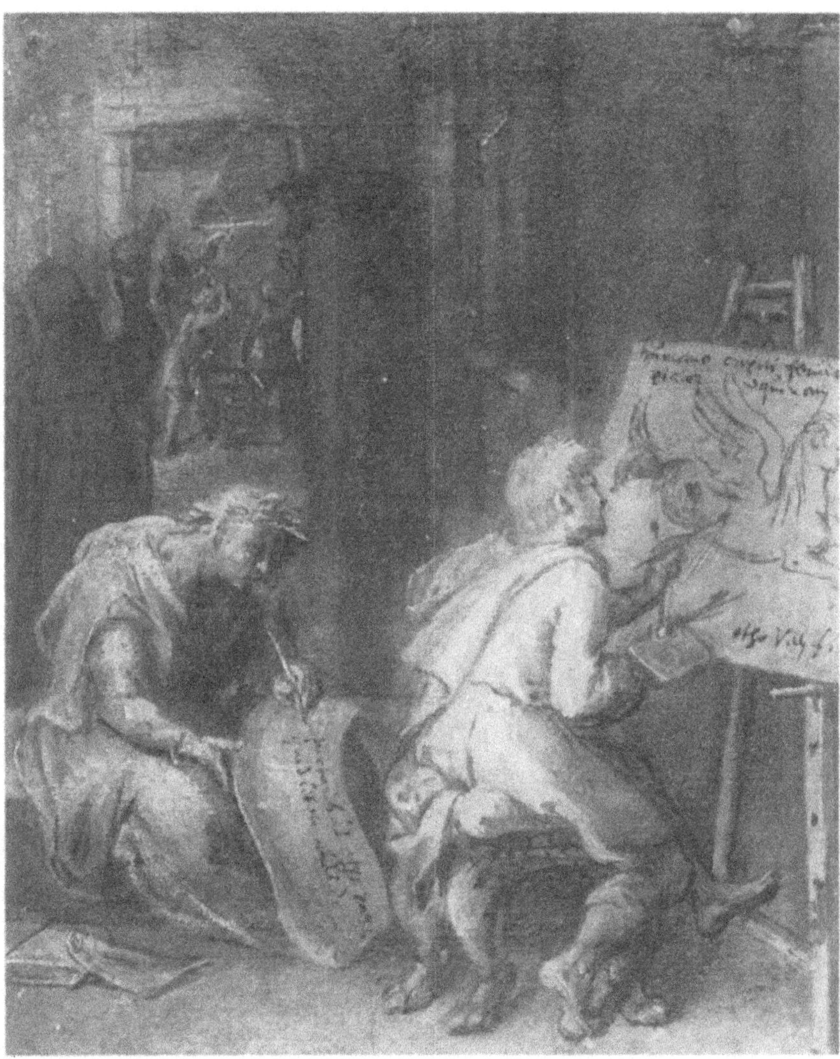

Figure 4.5. Otto van Veen, *Painting and Poetry*, ca. 1595. Grisaille oil sketch, 17.5 × 14.5 cm. © The British Museum, London.

indicate the artist's inventiveness, circumscribed by this local tradition. In his life of Bosch, van Mander stresses the incomprehensibility and copiousness of Bosch's weird and strange ideas as the bases for his artistic preeminence. In Domenicus Lampsonius's verse included by van Mander, Bosch is imagined seeing monsters flying around his ears.[83] And, according to van Mander, Antwerp artist Bartholomeus Spranger's introduction to his patron Cardinal Farnese was accomplished by his (now lost) paintings of witches shown to the cardinal by the illuminator Giulio Clovio. Van Mander describes the cardinal's

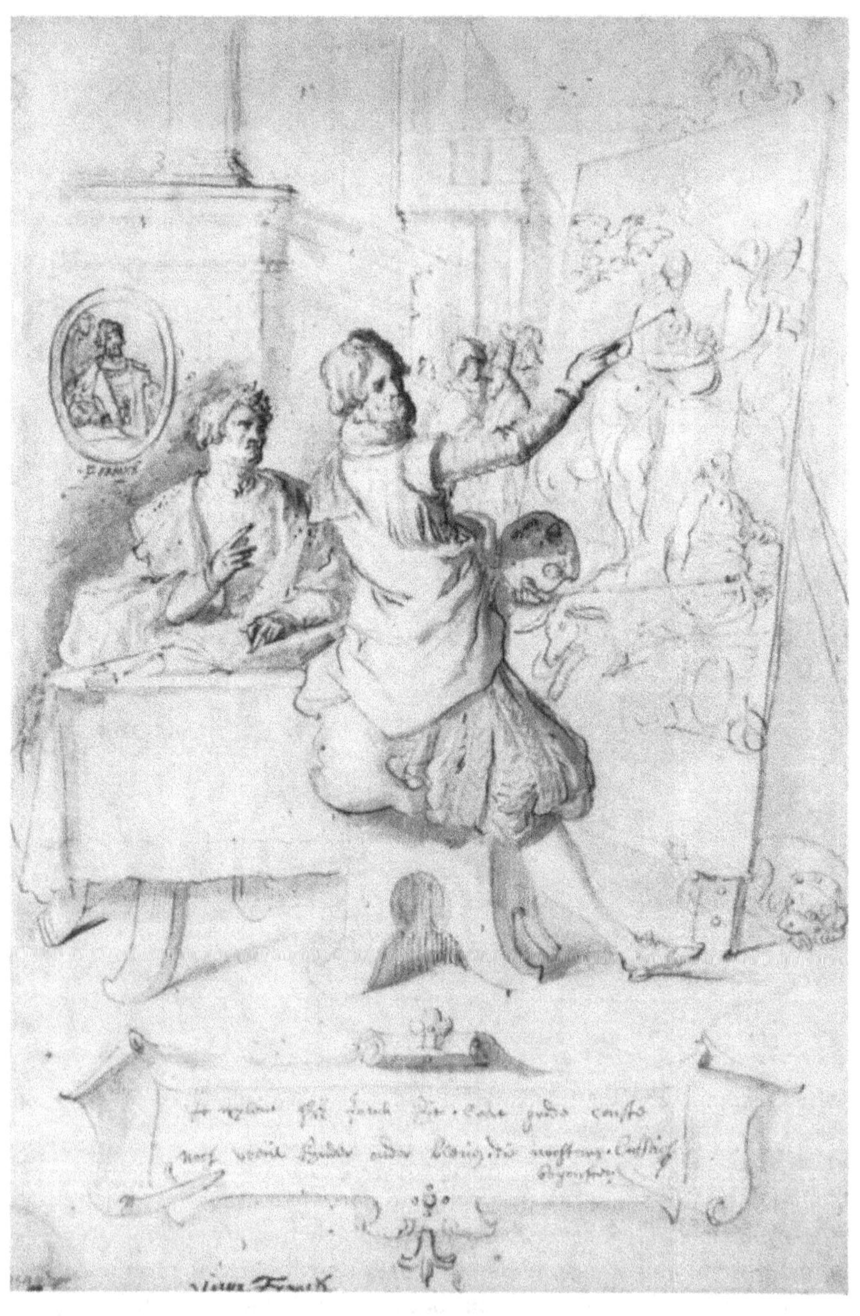

Figure 4.6. Frans Francken II, *The Painter at His Easel*, ca. 1618. Ink and wash drawing, 292 × 198 mm. Cabinet des dessins, Musée du Louvre, Paris. Réunion des Musée Nationaux/Art Resource, New York.

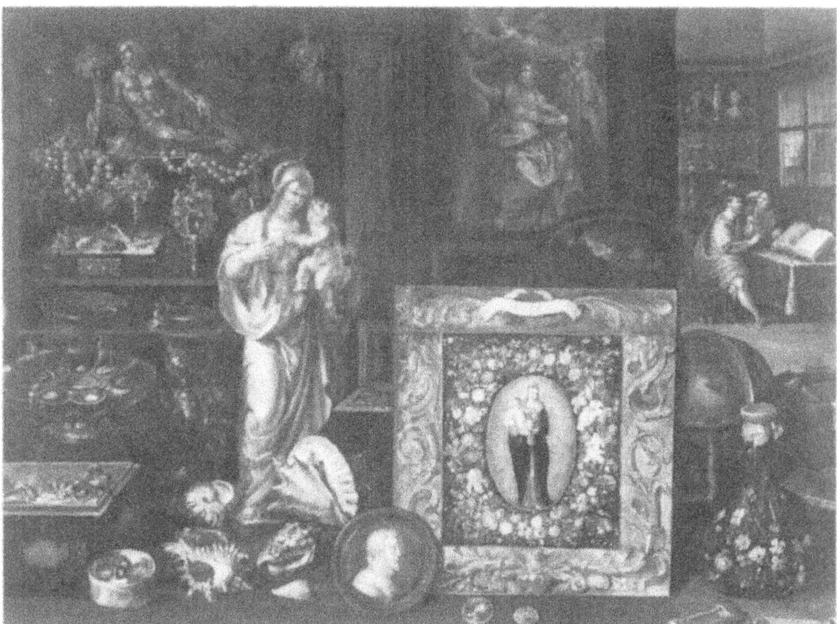

Figure 4.7. Frans Francken II, *Collector's Cabinet*, ca. 1615. Oil on panel, 49 × 64 cm. Historisches Museum, Frankfurt am Main.

ability to discern the virtue and subtlety of artistic talent, and the paintings of witches evidently proved that.[84] Sprangher, of course, was to be employed as the foremost painter working for Rudolf II of Prague whose court fostered a highly subtle, intellectually and visually complex approach to art.[85]

Francken not only appropriated the theme of witchcraft to align himself with his sovereigns' concerns about its proliferation and severity but also with the notion of art as an intellectual activity and with a Netherlandish tradition of grotesque infernal imagery founded on Bosch. For aristocratic or newly wealthy middle-class collectors in early seventeenth-century Antwerp and elsewhere, these would have been highly marketable traits. As we have seen, paintings were part of Antwerp's thriving market for luxury goods, for consumption both by abundant local collectors and for export. Collectors did not serve art simply by purchasing it, however, but also by appreciating it and confirming its status as an intellectual endeavor. Their importance for the promotion of the status of painting is witnessed by the admission of *liefhebbers van schilderijen* (lovers of art) into the Antwerp Guild of St. Luke as early as 1602.[86] Paralleling this recognition of collectors was Francken's invention of an artistic genre, depicting model collections (figures 4.7 and 4.8). Although they usually portray purely imaginary collections, such pictures tell us what collectors valued and the functions they assigned to works of art and other objects.

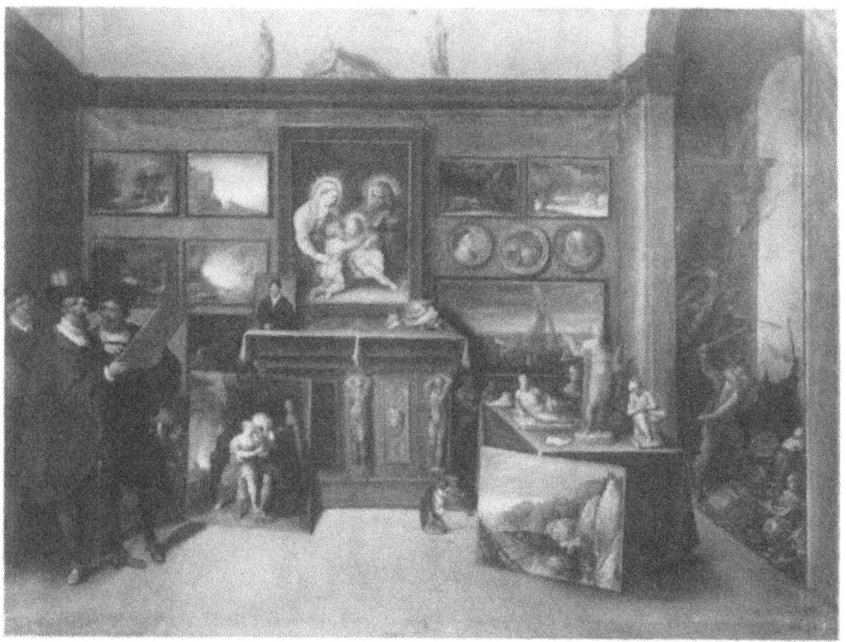

Figure 4.8. Frans Francken II, *Gallery Interior with Iconoclastic Donkeys*, mid-1620s. Oil on panel, 54 × 63 cm. Alte Pinakothek, Bayerisches Staatsgemäldesammlungen, Munich.

Early seventeenth-century collectors clearly valued the range of knowledge represented by the assembled works of art and objects and viewed collections as signs of their own hunger for knowledge and as educational instruments. Shells, classical coins, medals, and scientific instruments such as telescopes mingle with sculptures and paintings. Francken often stressed the association of art with knowledge by allegorical elements. In figure 4.7, scholars, one gesturing toward his intellect, are engaged in discussion in the right background; globes function as symbols of universal knowledge and, in this Jesuit context, symbols of the universal Catholic faith. In figure 4.8, men with donkeys' heads, symbolizing Ignorance, attack art and learning outside the safety and edification of the collector's cabinet. The connection of art to the Catholic faith is repeatedly fostered in gallery pictures by traditional religious themes, such as the Madonna in a floral wreath in figure 4.7. Francken's *Allegory of Sacred Painting* in Budapest (ca. 1616–20), related compositionally to the gallery pictures, conveys an utterly Tridentine message. The most elevated function of art is the depiction of the life of Christ and the promulgation of the Christian message. The figure of Sacred Painting paints an Adoration of the Shepherds but looks toward Christ who miraculously appears in her studio; Christ guides her work in every sacred subject. Like the angelic music that intrudes into the space above her, visual art has the primary task of sustaining faith.[87]

Undoubtedly, images of witchcraft could have fulfilled this didactic function within early seventeenth-century collections, for, as we have seen, witchcraft was a learned topic despite its sensationalistic potential. Debates surrounding the nature and activities of witches did not simply indulge a taste for the exotic, the erotic, and the fantastic but were an integral part of the early modern understanding of the world. These debates engaged philosophical questions regarding God's permission of evil, the extent of demonic power, the limitations of the human will and understanding, and the very nature of the times: Did the new sect of witches signal the end of the world? Magistrates and lawyers were deeply concerned about what constituted proof of witchcraft, what its appropriate punishment should be, and who held primary responsibility for punishment. And what of the views of radical skeptics such as Dutch physician Johann Weyer or English country gentleman Reginald Scot? Was witchcraft an impossible crime, an old woman's delusion best handled by spiritual counseling and forgiveness rather than the stake? Or were writers like Scot and Weyer themselves agents of the devil by giving succor to witches? Through the hyperbolic visual rhetoric of his paintings, Francken strove to give viewers an encyclopedic understanding of the true witchcraft that was ideally the target of the Habsburg edicts.

Francken's paintings of witches certainly could have fueled learned discussion, but collectors were also cultivating a new concern for individual style and connoisseurship; *liefhebbers* in Antwerp were increasingly interested in displaying the cachet symbolized by the discerning eye along with intellectual knowledge. In Honig's analysis, an idea of a model collection that developed in Antwerp by the early seventeenth century was based on a canon that was local and conservative; the taste displayed in collectors' acquisitions were a sign of civic pride and a reassertion of Antwerp's past glory.[88] The progress of artistic status in Antwerp traced by Filipczak is also reflected in the emphasis on this local canon, which included contemporary artists such as Francken, Jan Bruegel the Elder, and Rubens, as well as sixteenth-century painters such as Quentin Metsys and Pieter Bruegel the Elder.[89] Francken's paintings of witches not only expressed contemporary fears about witchcraft and broader anxieties about class, gender, and social order, they also displayed their inventiveness within Antwerp's unique pictorial tradition.

Epilogue: David Teniers II, Witchcraft, and the Status of the Artist

As an artist of the next generation, David Teniers II (1610–90) benefited from the efforts of earlier Antwerp artists such as Francken to enhance the esteem in which his profession was held. Trained by his father, Teniers became a master in 1632/33 and exhibited a pronounced, lifelong personal ambition and a dogged concern for the status of artists. In part, his determination to succeed was affected by his father's financial reversal in 1628, but Teniers sought more than economic security.

An early step in his upwardly mobile progress was his marriage to Jan Bruegel the Elder's daughter Anna (pictured in figure 4.13) in 1637. This marriage, witnessed by Rubens, Anna's guardian, not only linked Teniers to one of Antwerp's preeminent artistic dynasties, it also brought him paintings and drawings by the Bruegel family.[90] After this auspicious union, Teniers's rise was rapid and steady. He became dean of the Guild of St. Luke in Antwerp in 1645/46 and was employed by the new Regent of the Southern Netherlands, the Archduke Leopold Wilhelm, beginning in 1647, probably through the influence of Bishop Antonius Triest of Ghent, a major art connoisseur who had commissioned several works from the artist. Teniers would serve the archduke in Brussels as court painter and curator and then in the high office of *ayuda de cámara* (royal valet) also held by Diego Velasquez under Philip IV of Spain. Shortly after Anna's death in 1656, Teniers married Isabella de Fren, daughter of the secretary to the Sovereign Council of Brabant; as a sign of his elite status, he also purchased a country house that was owned by the second husband of Hélène Fourment (Rubens's widow). By this time, Teniers's patrons included not only Leopold Wilhelm but also Willem II of Orange, Queen Christina of Sweden, the Duke of York (later James II), and Louis II of Condé, the Prince of Bourbon.[91]

Teniers was eminently successful at furthering the intellectual status of art. One of his most remarkable achievements was his conception and direction of the *Theatrum pictorium* (Theater of paintings), 243 engravings of the Italian pictures in the Duke's collection—the first catalogue of a collection—published at his own expense in 1660. Teniers used his favor with the Habsburgs to petition Philip IV of Spain for permission and funding to found the Antwerp Academy of Art in 1664, a year after he attained noble status, which fully legitimated the profession of artist.[92]

Teniers's extensive exploration of witchcraft, evident in about a dozen paintings of the theme, linked him to the Bruegel family, which in turn tied him to Bosch, that paradigm of Netherlandish fantastic invention. With this and other favorite themes such as the Temptation of Anthony and alchemy, Teniers promoted himself as inventive within this distinctly Flemish tradition. Because the dating of his works is often uncertain, it is difficult to correlate all of them precisely with points along his career trajectory, but a broad correspondence between witchcraft paintings and Teniers's claims for a more elevated status may be sketched. His first image of witches, a painting in the Musée de la Chartreuse in Douai that is greatly indebted to Francken, coin-

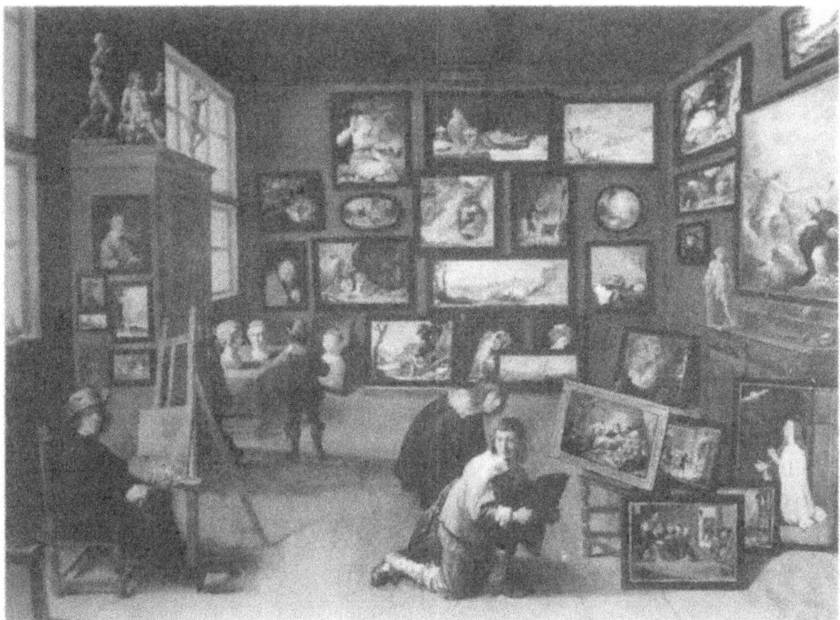

Figure 4.9. David Teniers II, *The Artist in His Studio*, 1635. Oil on panel, 54.6 × 77.5 cm. Location unknown.

cided with his becoming a master. As a fledgling master in 1635, he painted a remarkable image of himself in his studio whose walls are covered with existing works by himself and others, including Rubens, Adriaen Brouwer, Francken, and Teniers's future father-in-law Jan Bruegel the Elder (figure 4.9). In the middle of the wall is his own painting of a witch with flowing hair stirring a cauldron—an image influenced by Dutch artist Jan van de Velde's engraving of a witch from 1626 (figure 4.10).

Through the assortment of paintings, Teniers proclaimed his artistic pedigree—the influence of his father and Adriaen Brouwer—as well as his versatility in painting many subjects. Landscapes flank the painting of the witch and cauldron and mingle with still lifes, mythologies, and religious pictures. The inclusion of works by the learned and acclaimed Rubens makes a strong statement of the young Teniers's ambition, corroborating his claim to the title of *pictor doctus* (educated painter). The empty canvas, awaiting inspiration in front of the artist, signifies invention.[93] Near the connoisseurs at the lower right are paintings that celebrate grotesque invention in the style of Bosch and Bruegel: two scenes of apes, a Temptation of Anthony, and a peasant scene by Brouwer. These works allude to Teniers's particular strengths within Antwerp tradition, and their juxtaposition to a *Vision of Theresa* by Rubens might even suggest equivalence between this tradition and the grand Italianate manner exemplified by the latter.

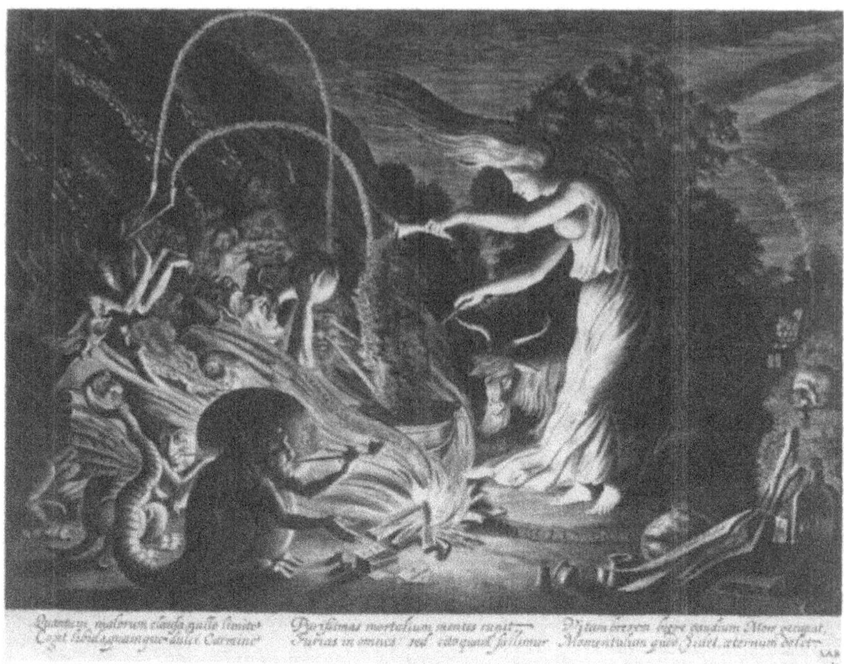

Figure 4.10. Jan van de Velde, *The Sorceress*, 1626. Engraving, 216 × 288 mm. Photograph © 2004 Museum of Fine Arts, Boston. Bequest of Eleanor A. Sayre, 2002.595.

Van de Velde's engraving after which Teniers's painting was modeled was done in the innovative "black manner" initiated by Hendrik Goudt in his engravings after Adam Elsheimer's nocturnal scenes, meticulously rendered and often on copper. Dutch printmakers excelled in the production of these dark prints, which were highly praised and coveted for their light effects by contemporary collectors and connoisseurs.[94] Teniers's quotation of van de Velde's *Sorceress* thus appropriates the connotation of pictorial skill and technical innovation represented by Elsheimer's works and black-manner prints. Moreover, the ring of demons in both engraving and painting announce their Boschian origins.

Although van de Velde's witch is Circean, Teniers's is an old hag—a familiar dichotomy whose poles are linked by the perceived instability of woman's nature, as I have discussed in Chapter 1. And while Teniers's demons lurk in the murky enveloping darkness, van de Velde's are more sharply lit and clearly distinguishable. Smoking and drinking like boorish peasants, they reinforce the bland moralizing of the inscription reducing witchcraft to a confirmation of the vanity of worldly pursuits and the lust embodied in the Circean figure—an interpretation perhaps appropriate to a Dutch context in which judicial restraint and skepticism about witchcraft prevailed.[95] The meaning of Teniers's witch may not have been so innocuous, given his Southern Netherlandish context in which witchcraft still constituted a heinous crime against the Church and state.

When surrounded by a botanical wreath, probably by another artist, in a painting in the Hamburg Kunsthalle, moreover, Teniers's witch and her associates take on more specific connotations revolving around the contemporary view of countermagic (1640s; figure 4.11). The wreath contains a mix of common specimens like clover, hops, burdock, thistle, and wild blackberries and acorns. According to Jane Davidson, the wreath does not suggest witches' use of hallucinogens. Some of the plants, like the ivy and mushrooms, are potentially harmful; others, such as the wood fern, used apotropaically against the devil or witchcraft, and the tiny yellow Potentilla, used as an astringent and to assuage menstrual pain, are medicinal or beneficent. Diedrich Roskamp, focusing largely on the use of the wood fern in popular spells, concluded that Teniers's witch practiced "white" magic.[96]

According to both Protestant and Catholic authorities in the early modern period, however, such magic was just as insidious as magic that caused harm, for each entailed a lack of faith in the providence of God by trusting in the devil. The Counter-Reformation church, moreover, was concerned to defend its sacraments, most significantly the Eucharist—absorbed, as we have seen, into the ideology of Habsburg sovereignty—and rites such as exorcism against Protestant accusations of magic.[97]

The Hamburg work might be considered not only as a condemnation of popular magic but also as an inversion of the wreath paintings fostered by the Jesuit order. Through their dazzling visual effects, these works asserted the truth of transubstantiation against the Protestant claim that the bread and wine had only symbolic value and that the laity should have access to both. Jan de Heem's *Eucharist in Fruit Wreath* in Vienna (1648) was one of many wreath pictures influenced by the Jesuit painter Daniel Seghers of Antwerp, where de Heem, a native of Utrecht, spent much of his life (figure 4.12). The painting shares Seghers's recovery of the Christian symbolism of fruit and flowers, while perhaps divesting them, in this Counter-Reformation context, of any old associations with popular magic.[98] As Norbert Schneider has noted, de Heem's tall and ornate chalice affirms the Church's position that the priest alone should receive the wine, while the luminous Host appears to transubstantiate before our eyes. Miracle is distinguished from magic; reverent wonder from curiosity. Together, he argues, the chalice and Host are "remote objects of awe," a "miracle performed by the clergy."[99] Understood in conjunction with such contemporary works, Teniers's *Witch's Scene* in Hamburg contrasts the misguided magic undertaken by the ignorant laity with the "magic" of transubstantiation that is truly miraculous because it derives from

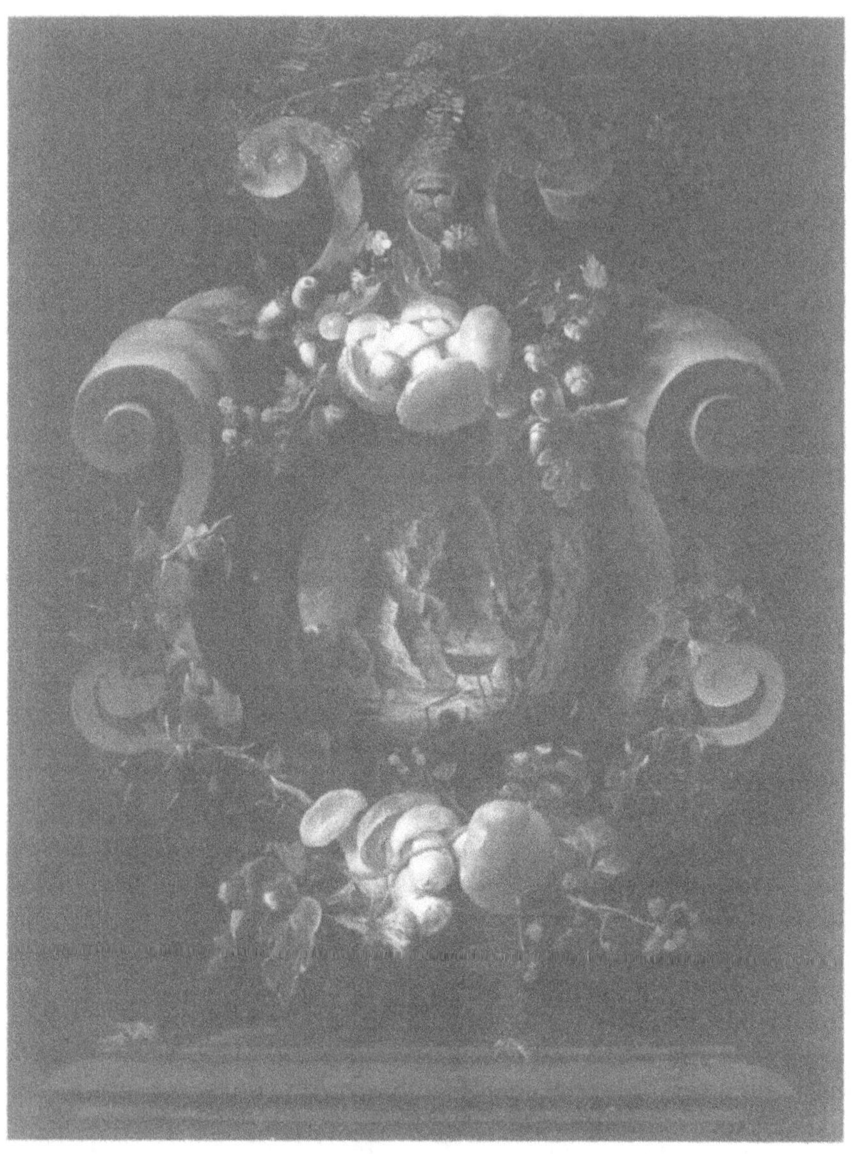

Figure 4.11. David Teniers II (wreath by an unknown artist), *Witches' Scene*, 1640s. Oil on panel, 64.2 × 48.5 cm. Kunsthalle, Hamburg. Bildarchiv Preußischer Kulturbesitz/ Art Resource, New York.

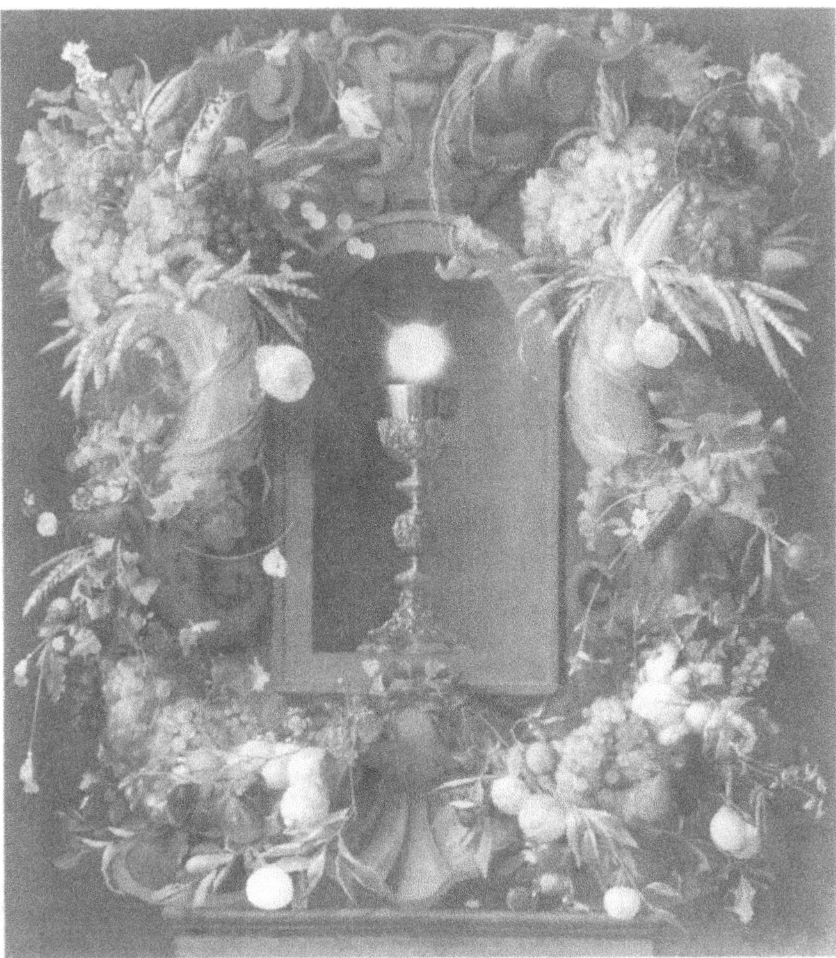

Figure 4.12. Jan Davidsz. de Heem, *Eucharist in Fruit Wreath*, 1648. Oil on canvas, 138 × 125.5 cm. Kunsthistorisches Museum, Vienna.

God. The theme that unites both de Heem's painting and Teniers's is the truth and power of the eternal Church, whose clergy must maintain the power to administer the sacraments and to shepherd the laity to bring them to right belief and conduct.

Jane Davidson and Marijke Lucas have speculated that Teniers probably accepted witchcraft as a reality. It is especially likely that he knew about trials in Malines, which was near his country estate, between 1544 and 1663, in the course of which thirty-three accused witches were executed.[100] Certainly there is no evidence to the contrary. However, in the shift from Francken's encyclopedic and agitated compositions to Teniers's calmer and less detailed works, there is a change in tone. The mood becomes less urgent, stressing the futility

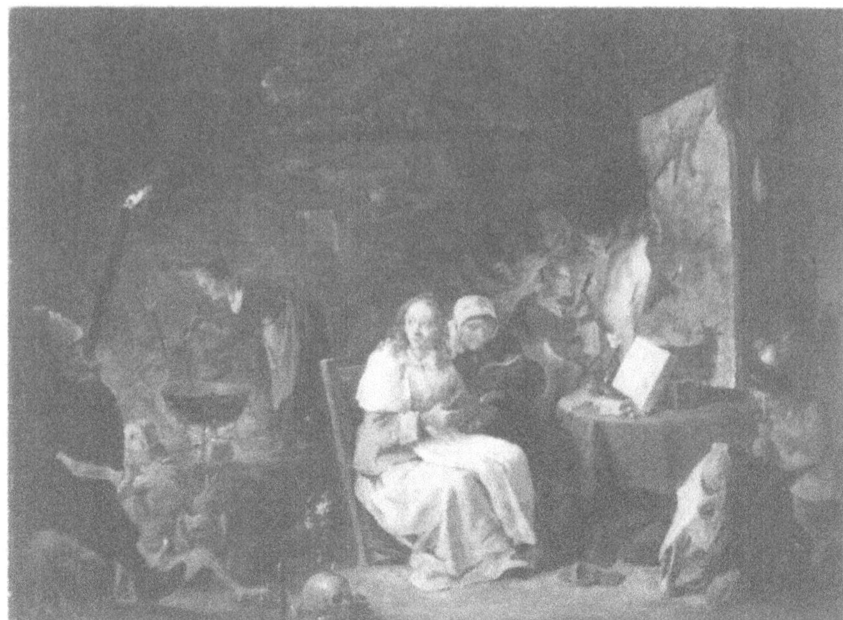

Figure 4.13. David Teniers II, *Incantation Scene*, early 1650s. Oil on copper, 36.8 × 50.8 cm. Collection of the New York Historical Society, 1867.175.

and folly of popular and ignorant beliefs such as those illustrated in Teniers's Hamburg wreath. Concomitantly, the triumph of the Eucharist proclaimed in de Heem's painting is more assured. In Teniers's *Incantation Scene* (early 1650s; figure 4.13), a young woman modeled on Anna Bruegel looks anxiously over her shoulder at the recycled cauldron scene (compare figs. 4.11 and 4.12) as if distracted from reading her *grimoire*. An older witch, her hand on "Anna's" shoulder, gently prompts her as a nude companion is anointed in front of the chimney at the right. The leitmotifs are familiar, handed down from Francken. However, the central initiate played by Anna does not disrobe, virtually defusing the intense erotic charge of Francken's images. Moreover, the "kitchen" seems to have undergone a housecleaning: Francken's mind- and eye-boggling clutter is replaced by clearer surfaces, with sparser objects neatly displayed—the menacing presence of the skull in the foreground is assuaged by an adjacent, pretty floral still-life. The demon in the right corner with a rooster perched on his head seems like some rustic artisan intent on his work.

Although Davidson interprets Teniers's attitude toward witchcraft as "straightforward and serious," it is difficult to apprehend these players as imminent threats to the stability of the godly state.[101] Francken's jeremiads on the urgent necessity of class, gender, and doctrinal conformity have been replaced by a more urbane and condescending perception of quaint peasant beliefs—a perception that indeed constituted the basis of the tremendous appeal of Teniers's works, and numerous engravings after them, in eighteenth-century France.[102]

Both Davidson and Lucas note that artists' wives and other family members were often used as convenient models, so we need read nothing insidious into Anna's presence in this painting.[103] I would argue, however, that Anna's recognizable figure, strongly lighted against the murky interior, does have a specific function—advertising Teniers's artistic status. For it is not just iconography and style that confirm the Bosch/Bruegel lineage here but also a son-in-law's inheritance of artistic pedigree through marriage. At the same time, the threat presented by witchcraft is decisively tamed. Put differently, perhaps artistic license is no longer quite so firmly yoked to the joint purposes of religious orthodoxy and state power.

The early 1650s was a time of high achievement for Teniers, who had entered the service of Archduke Leopold Wilhelm in 1647 and been appointed court painter in 1652. In 1651, he went to London on behalf of the archduke, presumably in connection with the purchase of over four hundred paintings owned by the Duke of Hamilton but formerly belonging to King Charles I. The Italian works that appear in Teniers's gallery pictures in Brussels, Vienna, and Petworth, all dated 1651, are from Hamilton's collection.[104] Teniers's instrumentality in the formation of Leopold Wilhelm's world-class collection and his gallery pictures documenting it attest not merely to his artistic skill but to his status as a learned connoisseur, setting the stage for his work on the *Theatrum pictorium* in the mid-1650s; his second marriage, to Isabella Fren in 1656; and his subsequent attempt to become ennobled; Cornelis de Bie's encomium of 1661; and finally the formation of the Antwerp Academy. Viewed in the light of Teniers's career trajectory, Anna Bruegel's appearance in the New York *Incantation Scene* does not seem merely convenient.

This shrinking of the witches' world and its absorption into a quaint and amusing rural genre that we might read in the picture might correspond to a general dampening of witch-hunting zeal toward mid-century.[105] In 1631, Jesuit Friedrich Spee's *Cautio criminalis* (Precautions for prosecutors), one of the most eloquent protests against the witch trials, was published anonymously in the Protestant city of Hameln, but Spee had circulated the manuscript earlier. Spee had worked as a confessor to accused witches during the trials in the prince-bishopric of Würzburg in the late 1620s, one of the most violent episodes of witch-hunting. While never denying the possibility of witchcraft and with a poet's gift for language, Spee courageously exposed the fraudulence of accusations by rumor, confessions extracted under torture, and the manic escalation of trials brought about by the extortion of additional witches' names from the accused. By focusing on the inevitability of an accused witch's execution, he advanced the cause of judicial restraint and mercy. According to

Marie-Sylvie Dupont-Bouchat, he had a decisive impact on Jesuit enthusiasm for witchcraft trials.[106]

Nevertheless, Albert and Isabella's decrees were repeated in the Southern Netherlands until 1660.[107] The official Habsburg rhetoric against witchcraft lingered, even as the artistic status Teniers asserts in his witchcraft pictures became less dependent on its corroboration and more grounded in individual artistic prowess. The specifically northern pedigree of invention he claimed, based on Bosch, Bruegel, and the artistic tradition of Antwerp, was equally important in the Northern Netherlands, where so many immigrants from the south—including Jacques de Gheyn II, the subject of the next chapter—relocated. The intersection of that artistic tradition with the new context of Dutch attitudes toward witchcraft in de Gheyn's fascinating works produced a paradoxical blend of rational skepticism and inventive fantasy.

Chapter 5
The Art of Describing Delusion: De Gheyn and the Dutch Variant

An Approach to de Gheyn's Witchcraft Images

Along with Frans Francken's paintings, the witchcraft images of Jacques (or Jacob) de Gheyn II (1565–1629) form the most important early seventeenth-century record of witchcraft beliefs in art. But unlike Francken's works that seem to correspond closely to Habsburg political and religious goals, de Gheyn's images have puzzled scholars, and opinions on their meaning range widely. In his catalog of the de Gheyn family of artists (published in 1983 and based on the author's research in the 1930s), I. Q. van Regteren Altena, persuaded by de Gheyn's intellectual connections and his probable knowledge of skeptical writers such as Johann Weyer and Reginald Scot, believed that de Gheyn intended to satirize belief in witches.[1] Writing in 1973, J. Richard Judson speculated that de Gheyn, moved by the spirit of scientific study that so clearly pervades much of his art, visited witches' gatherings.[2] This statement rests in part on the mistaken premise, ultimately traceable to Margaret Murray's influential thesis discussed in Chapter 1, that such gatherings took place. Other scholars have remained reticent about de Gheyn's view of witchcraft, interpreting his images of witches as moralizing allegories of the vices as well as the Power of Women.[3]

Because allegorical meaning does not preclude belief in witchcraft—social realities, after all, were saturated with allegorical potential for early modern observers—this iconographic reading of de Gheyn's witchcraft images can tell us little about his attitude toward witchcraft. However, if we keep in mind the distinctive historical context that shaped de Gheyn and the idea of witchcraft as an aggregate of separable components, we can come to reasonable conclusions about what his images conveyed to his audience. *The Parable of the Devil Sowing Weeds* (1603; see figure 5.1), in particular, can be interpreted in terms of a contemporary and characteristically Dutch stance on witchcraft, as we shall see below.

This stance can be described as comparatively reticent and restrained. The Dutch tended to seek other explanations (such as medical causes) for apparent witchcraft and to prosecute the crime cautiously. Although Marijke Gijswijt-Hofstra qualifies what she calls the "Dutch variant" by noting that the proverbially low intensity of persecutions applies only to the period after 1600 (roughly when Dutch executions stopped), it remains true that the Dutch Republic *was* fundamentally different from Germany, the Southern Netherlands, and France in its response to witchcraft at the very height of the hunts. The essential ingredients for witch-hunting—the judicial mechanisms for punishment, the popular beliefs in magic, the accessibility of elite demonological theory—were present in the Northern Netherlands as elsewhere in early modern Europe, so how do we explain this difference?[4]

The reasons are multiple. Dutch prosperity lessened the need to prosecute witches as scapegoats for economic tensions. Also, witch-hunting could not be incorporated into intensive campaigns for religious conformity where there was tolerance (in the pre-Enlightenment sense of sufferance) for a certain level of religious pluralism.[5] In keeping with his association of Habsburg monarchical control, Counter-Reformation ideology, and witch-hunting for the Southern Netherlands, Robert Muchembled argues that it was this profound political difference that caused the Dutch to take a different path. Concepts of sovereignty developed by Jean Bodin and later Thomas Hobbes did not appeal to this nation with its long tradition of local autonomy; although Calvinism was dominant, Catholicism and variant forms of Protestantism could exist without violent extirpation. Demonological theory was not co-opted in the Dutch Republic by the drive toward religious and monarchical hegemony that fostered witch-hunting elsewhere.[6] In Willem Frijhoff's terms, religious unity was replaced by the *concordia* of a secular community based on the principles of public order and political reason.[7]

In his thorough analysis of the distinctiveness of the early modern Dutch state, Heinz Schilling also discusses the pervasive rationalization of Dutch society, exhibited, for instance, in the Dutch approach to midwifery. Dutch midwives were detached from their responsibilities for emergency baptism and indeed from all ecclesiastical control. They were defined not by piety but by pragmatic anatomical knowledge and obstetrical skills, concentrating on the physical well-being of mother and child rather than the eternal salvation of the child. Schilling argues that the rational, secular, and pragmatic concerns driving this small change ultimately characterized the entire ethos of the Dutch Republic.[8]

De Gheyn was a child of this Republic. Although born in the south, he became an eager citizen of the north, like so many other artists drawn to the pluralistic intellectual milieu and the opportunities for entrepreneurial printmaking and publishing it provided. From his teacher Hendrik Goltzius, who was trained in turn by the remarkable humanist, engraver, and patriot Dirk Volkertsz. Coornhert, de Gheyn may have inherited an Erasmian tolerance of various religious confessions.[9] De Gheyn's engagement with the elite, highly individualistic scholars at the University of Leiden is apparent, as is his eagerness to serve the States General and the House of Orange. It would be surprising if his attitude toward witchcraft did *not* follow the Dutch propensity for questioning the theoretical premises of demonology, and for pragmatic concerns about legal proof of the crime and how witchcraft might be eliminated from society. These issues would have made de Gheyn's images eminently fascinating for his contemporaries.

Indeed, these images may frustrate conventional interpretation precisely because they were so subtly nuanced in deference to de Gheyn's audience. Historians of the Golden Age have begun to ask new questions that can inform art history. For example, rather than attempting to ascertain individual levels of religious commitment in understanding Dutch tolerance (who believed what), Benjamin Kaplan prescribes an investigation of the social realities of confessional coexistence.[10] As Judith Pollmann notes, recent research indicates that a larger proportion of the Dutch population than previously thought did not identify with a confession and that, despite the efforts of religious authorities, Dutch society was not so segregated by confession in practice as we have assumed. Her analysis of the writings of jurist Arnoldus Buchelius (Arend van Buchell), who probably sparked de Gheyn's interest in witchcraft, suggests that civil intellectual discourse, the *concordia* of the Republic, and a respect for individual conscience (within the limits of Christian piety) could trump confessional identity in certain literal and figurative spaces where different beliefs intersected.[11] The learned discussion of witchcraft that surely took place around de Gheyn's drawings could well have been such a space. At the same time, the restrained Dutch approach to the problem of witchcraft was a matter of national pride. As stakes continued to flare in neighboring France, Germany, and the Southern Netherlands, de Gheyn's master engraving of about 1610, in the wake of the Twelve-Years Truce with Spain, may have evoked the Republic's rejection of this destructive path (see figure 5.6). In his old age the poet and statesman Jacob Cats recalled proudly that, around this time, witchcraft was banished from the land.[12]

The Layers of de Gheyn's Artistic Identity

The art-theoretical dimension of de Gheyn's witchcraft images is equally nuanced because his artistic identity, centered on the paradoxical relationship of mimesis and fantasy, was particularly complex. The theme enabled de Gheyn to present himself as a distinctive artist in terms praised by his longtime friend Karel van Mander—artist, poet, art theorist, and historian—in *Het Schilder-Boek* (Book on picturing, 1604), a series of biographies of northern artists prefaced by a long didactic poem on the principles of art. Van Mander lauded de Gheyn as a successor to Jan van Eyck by virtue of his brilliant powers of observation (working *nae t' leven*, "from life"). But, significantly, these naturalistic powers are complemented by de Gheyn's ability to work "*uyt den gheest*"—variously translated as "from the memory of things seen," "from the mind or spirit," or "from the imagination."[13] Van Mander associated de Gheyn's decision to work more from *gheest* with the artist's shift from engraving and printing to the more privileged medium of painting after 1600.[14] I argue in this chapter that de Gheyn's interest in and development of the theme of witchcraft exactly correspond to this evolution.

How exactly did de Gheyn and van Mander understand *uyt den gheest*? E. K. J. Reznicek saw "working from the imagination," as he translated it, as one ideal or mannered branch of a forked path in Dutch art around 1600, and Hessel Miedema's philological studies of van Mander emphasize his indebtedness to Italian artistic and poetic theory, relating *gheest* to the Latin *ingenium* so that it suggests an irreducible individuality of style. More recently, Claudia Swan has pointed out the "academic logic" of understanding the two terms not just as alternative but as sequential modes of working, so that an artist could progress from mastery of life to creation from his imagination.[15] Svetlana Alpers and Walter Melion, however, have interpreted *uyt den gheest* in a purely cognitive, perceptual sense to refer to the artist's mental storing and synthesizing of remembered observations into a new work of art, as when van Mander describes Pieter Bruegel the Elder's swallowing up the Alps to spit them out later onto canvases and panels.[16]

Undoubtedly, de Gheyn often followed the mnemonic synthesis suggested by this latter understanding of *gheest*: Even in his most fantastic works such as the late design for a grotto for Prince Maurice, a foundation in natural observation may still be sensed (see figure 5.13). De Gheyn's witchcraft images, too, depend on his synthesized observations of plants, animals, landscape, and human figures. They also contain and at times consist entirely of sketchy, fluid lines that call a purely cognitive interpretation of *gheest* into question; if such drawings are late, they would confirm Swan's idea of progression (see figures 5.9–5.12). More than any other works by de Gheyn, his witchcraft images reveal a profoundly naturalistic artist paradoxically captivated by the fantastic and the grotesque. It is worth noting once again the fundamental question of witches' delusions. Witchcraft *as a subject* engaged the issue of the power of imagination and fantasy that de Gheyn's images exemplify. It is also important to recognize that van Mander was much more inclusive than Alberti in his views of worthy artistic subject matter: "If [your] perfection is not in figures and histories, so may it comprise animals, kitchens, fruits, flowers, landscapes, masonry, perspectives, [views into] rooms, *grotesques*, night-scenes, fires, portraits after life, sea-scenes, and ships, or the painting of other such things" (emphasis mine).[17]

In the early seventeenth century, witchcraft was also a relatively new subject that afforded de Gheyn considerable freedom of invention, in two of the major ways van Mander used the Dutch version of this theoretical term, according to Melion. *Inventy* could signify technical breakthroughs such as van Eyck's paradigmatic discovery of oil pigments and the skills needed to use them. Or, it could refer to an artist's departure from pictorial precedents, either in subject matter or aspects of composition—in this latter respect, that of ordering a compelling picture (*ordinanty*) of a new subject, de Gheyn's witchcraft images clearly excel (see figure 5.6 especially).[18] In addition, however, artists could announce their inventiveness by their personal manner of rendering, or *handelingh*—that quintessential uniqueness of an artist's hand.[19] It is perhaps to this kind of inventiveness that de Gheyn aspired in his witchcraft drawings that emphasize the rapid, fluid character of his pen-stroke (see especially figures 5.9–5.12). As Melion points out, van Mander's insistence on the importance of manual skill, the "virtuosity of the hand," to the nobility of art is one of the things that distinguishes his notion of *teyckenconst* (conception or the artistic image and execution) from the corresponding Italian notion of *disegno*.[20]

All these art-theoretical constructs, as well as their gendered implications, are part of de Gheyn's artistic identity, which embraces both *leven* and *gheest* as two poles that might be differently combined along a spectrum. As a son of Antwerp, de Gheyn carried with him the inventive tradition of Bosch and Bruegel, in which the uncontrolled imaginative license exemplified by the witch is ideally brought under control by *ingenium*, reason, and artistic skill. However, his engagement with natural science during his Leiden years may have added another layer, borrowed from the naturalists. As Paula Findlen notes, the early modern naturalist cultivated a persona of fluid movement among elite academic, courtly, and urban cultures; as his specimens became luxury goods and sites of patrician social intercourse, he catered to wealthy patrons in the manner of a courtier.[21]

The study of nature was also gendered, defined as a masculine mastery and potency vis-à-vis a feminized nature. De Gheyn's artistic naturalism finds an analogy in what Mark Breitenberg calls the "linguistic transparency"—the equation between words and things—that represented the ideal mode of scientific discourse for Francis Bacon.[22] The substitutability of de Gheyn's plant and animal studies with the object or specimen, as Swan has argued, was part of an "aesthetics of possession." But even as they were mediated by de Gheyn's artistry, she argues, his lifelike images were paradoxically part of a selfless and style-less "mimetic performance."[23] In his discussion of Goltizius's and de Gheyn's naturalistic landscapes, Lawrence Goedde also notes that they paralleled the "non-rhetorical rhetoric" of Bacon, Michel de Montaigne, and Thomas Brown. Adopting a Senecan or Attic approach to writing, these authors strove for effects of uncalculated structure and spontaneity.[24] At the end of de Gheyn's Leiden period, this rhetorical naturalism was enriched and complicated by the imagination evident in a remarkable series of witchcraft drawings.

De Gheyn's Early Career

Throughout his career, de Gheyn moved within a circle of educated, elite clients and friends. He was born in Antwerp in 1565, son of an Utrecht patrician who had become an artist, designing stained-glass windows and joining the Antwerp painters' guild in 1558. When Jacques II was fifteen, his family went back to Utrecht, a city where a substantial population of "libertines" (those who rejected ecclesiastical discipline and confessional uniformity) existed alongside Catholics, Lutherans, and Calvinists.[25] After his father's death, de Gheyn's artistic ambitions led him to enter the Haarlem atelier of famed engraver Goltzius around 1585, also the date of the fall of Antwerp. In 1587, de Gheyn became Goltzius's assistant, remaining in this capacity until Goltzius left for Rome in 1590. It was also in Haarlem that de Gheyn first met van Mander, whom he drew on his deathbed in 1606.[26]

The impact of van Mander and Goltzius on de Gheyn's own artistic ambitions must have been extraordinary. In his development of an art history and theory that were alternatives to Vasari's, van Mander established Goltzius—like de Gheyn a brilliant draughtsman and engraver—as the embodiment of northern values.[27] As Larry Silver has traced in detail, Goltzius had taken major steps in 1583 to assert his artistic independence.[28] Beginning his career as a reproductive engraver working for Coornhert and then for Philips Galle, Goltzius established his own print-publishing firm in Haarlem and, facilitated by van Mander, initiated a working relationship with Bartolomeus Spranger, a native of Antwerp then employed by Rudolf II at his court in Vienna (and, as discussed in Chapter 2, also a painter of witchcraft scenes). Goltzius's engravings after Spranger's drawings and his inventions based on Spranger's Mannerist figural style revealed Goltzius's boldly swelling burin lines that conveyed both a powerful plasticity and chiaroscuro as well as his astonishing ability to assimilate another artist's *handelingh*—for van Mander, part of the evidence of Goltzius's superior *teyckenconst*.[29] In 1586 and 1587, Goltzius's engraved series of *Roman Heroes* and his spectacular *Wedding of Cupid and Psyche* combined lofty themes, figural invention, and virtuoso engraving to assert the artist's independence and inventiveness. Silver also argues that between 1585 and 1590, the very period in which de Gheyn worked with Goltzius, the latter's use of Latin inscriptions on his engravings (following van Mander's moralization of Ovid) were part of a campaign to elevate his art to a high level of moral seriousness.[30]

After Goltzius went to Rome in 1590, de Gheyn set out on his own, moving to Amsterdam in 1591 to establish a print-publishing enterprise. Goltzius would continue with his upward career trajectory, ultimately putting aside the burin for the paintbrush, thus totally assuming the role of inventor who leaves the engraving of compositions to others.[31] De Gheyn seems to have taken Goltzius's model to heart. In Amsterdam, he engraved works by other artists (e.g., van Mander and Abraham Bloemaert), but around 1592 he began to publish works of his own invention to be engraved by his assistants—an upward move, replicating Goltzius's career path.[32]

In 1595, de Gheyn married wealthy aristocrat Eva Stalpaert van der Wielen whose father was a burgomaster in The Hague, thus facilitating the artist's connections to Prince Maurice's court, the States General, and Dutch Regent families in general. The van der Wielens were Catholic, although the evidence about his religious views, as for Goltzius, is ambiguous. No priest appears to have been called at his death, and an interconfessional marriage is quite possible. As we shall see, *The Pious Family* (see figure 5.14) has been interpreted in terms of a Reformed ideal of the family, yet de Gheyn also made altarpieces and prints with traditional Catholic iconography.[33] Although the debate about witchcraft was often bound up with confessional polemics, it seems impossible to draw any absolute conclusions about de Gheyn's confessional stance from his witchcraft images. It is worth noting, however, that de Gheyn's view of witchcraft seems to have been influenced by both Weyer and Scot, two skeptical writers who viewed witchcraft beliefs from a Protestant perspective.

Shortly after his marriage, de Gheyn moved with Eva to Leiden, where the university brought him into contact with prominent scholars in various academic fields. One of de Gheyn's first collaborations in Leiden was with child prodigy Hugo de Groot (Grotius), destined to become the Dutch Republic's preeminent historian, as well as legal and political theorist, who supplied elevated Latin inscriptions for de Gheyn's prints.[34] De Gheyn's stay in Leiden could not have come at a more opportune time. Only a quarter-century old in 1600, the university had been founded in part as a reward to the city for its bravery and suffering during the Spanish siege. Viewing itself as *the* elite institution of higher, specialized learning in the Dutch Republic, Leiden fostered a climate of scientific inquiry, humanistic culture, and religious tolerance, and attracted the most progressive minds in Europe.[35] Besides Grotius, de Gheyn's contacts there included Carolus Clusius (Charles de l'Écluse), philologist, historian, philosopher, jurist, zoologist, and botanist who founded the Leiden Botanical Gardens; medical historian and anatomist Pieter Pauw, who directed the Leiden anatomical theater; and mathematician and engineer Ludolf van

Collen, who headed the engineering school founded at Leiden by Prince Maurice.[36] Even when he moved to The Hague, de Gheyn maintained his Leiden connections, and the scientific and humanistic interests he fostered there were never abandoned.

Given the intellectual and cultural appeal of Leiden, de Gheyn's move—perhaps shortly after 1601, when his testimony as an "engraver in Leiden" before a notary is recorded—might seem odd.[37] The Hague, however, was the site of Prince Maurice's court with which de Gheyn had been associated since 1593 when he designed, engraved, and published a map of *The Siege of Geertruydenberg*, a victory of Prince Maurice over the Spanish, for the Amsterdam Admiralty. By 1598, de Gheyn had already registered with the Guild of St. Luke in The Hague as an engraver and a painter; by 1615, significantly, he was registered only as a painter.[38] Undoubtedly, the early death in or shortly after 1601 of Zacharias Dolendo, de Gheyn's talented pupil who had engraved designs by de Gheyn and others, was a pragmatic reason for this shift.[39] Ultimately, though, de Gheyn's move to The Hague signals his turning away from engraving and publishing prints to drawing and painting: that is, to autonomous invention.[40] Van Mander writes of de Gheyn's increasingly ardent desire to become a painter—again, following Goltzius's career model.[41]

It is no coincidence that de Gheyn's witchcraft images begin appearing about the time of his move to The Hague and his desire to reinforce his status as inventor by taking up painting. A corollary of this desire was an increased concentration on themes of his own invention in his drawings, a further distancing from Goltzius's legacy of mythological and biblical scenes, portraits, landscapes, and nature studies.[42] In *The Parable of the Devil Sowing Weeds*, a drawing in Berlin dated 1603, de Gheyn introduced witchcraft into a rural landscape that also illustrates the parable in Matthew 13:24–30 (figure 5.1). Having sown good seeds, a farmer has his field ostensibly spoiled by an enemy's (i.e., Satan's) sowing of tares (weeds), "while men slept" (verse 25). When his servants question the farmer about rooting up the tares, he replies that the wheat would be torn out of the ground with them. Therefore, "Let both grow together until the harvest: and in the time of the harvest I will say to the reapers, Gather ye together first the tares, and bind them in bundles to burn them: but gather the wheat into my barn" (verse 30). Although the parable was assimilated to the exhortation against Acedia (Sloth), a common theme in Netherlandish prints of the period, its main point is the Last Judgment.[43] Then, the problem of the existence of evil in a world created by a provident God will be resolved—the tares will be burned (hell) while the wheat will be taken to the barn (heaven). Human judgment before this final moment is necessarily fallible. We do not always have the wisdom to distinguish wheat from tares.[44]

An earlier drawing by Hans Bol depicts peasants sleeping under a tree as

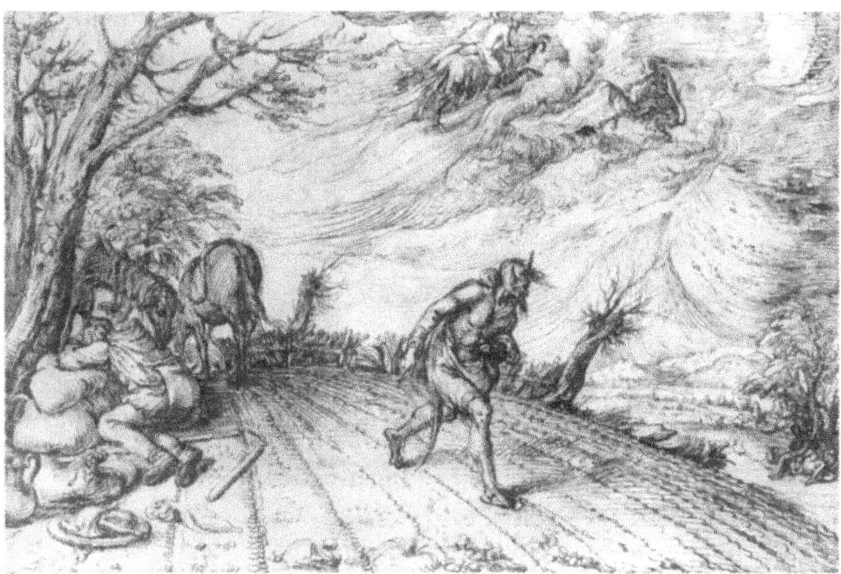

Figure 5.1. Jacques de Gheyn II, *The Parable of the Devil Sowing Weeds*, 1603. Pen and brown ink on buff paper, 263 × 417 mm. Kupferstichkabinett, Staatliche Museen, Berlin. Photo by Jörg P. Anders. Bildarchiv Preußischer Kulturbesitz/Art Resource, New York.

the devil sows the weeds in the field: an image illustrating the dangers of Acedia (figure 5.2). But de Gheyn translated the parable into terms specific to contemporary debates surrounding witchcraft and its punishment. As the devil sows tares in a ploughed field, peasants slumber to the left and a troupe of witches fly to the sabbath on goats in the sky. Clearly, the tares that the devil has sown in the slumbering minds are delusions of the flight to the sabbath and, by extension, the sabbath itself. Here de Gheyn echoes old skeptical views of bodily flight to and participation in the sabbath. By doing so, he calls into question an important principle of the witchcraft stereotype as promulgated in current demonological texts by Nicolas Rémy, Bodin, Martín Del Rio, and others. Equally as important as skepticism about bodily flight and the physical reality of the sabbath is de Gheyn's affirmation in this drawing of divine providence as it pertains to witchcraft. As God permits the devil, demons, and witches to do evil, He alone will punish them.

The parable had long been adduced in arguments against the punishment of heretics, and it figured frequently in discussions of the punishment of witchcraft. Both Erasmus and Johann Weyer, skeptical Dutch Lutheran physician to the Duke of Cleves, had argued in his *De praestigiis daemonum* (On the tricks of demons, 1563) that the "weeds" should be tolerated on the chance they might repent, thus changing into wheat.[45] Jesuit confessor Friedrich Spee,

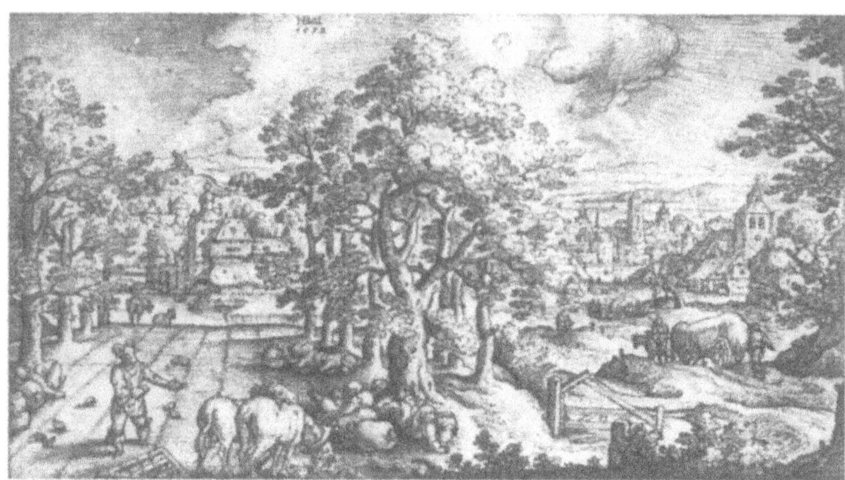

Figure 5.2. Hans Bol, *The Parable of the Devil Sowing Weeds*, 1572. Drawing in brown wash, 87 × 117 mm. Rikjsprentenkabinet, Rijksmuseum, Amsterdam. Photo by Collection Rijksbureau voor Kunsthistorische Dokumentatie (RKD), The Hague.

in his *Cautio criminalis* (Precautions for prosecutors, 1631), cited St. Augustine's and St. Thomas Aquinas's exegeses of the parable in terms of the toleration of evildoers for fear of mistakenly punishing the good.[46] Relying on such evidence as the testimony of minors, enemies of the accused, rumors, or confessions extracted under torture, and based on actions that clearly contravened natural law, witchcraft was difficult if not impossible to prove in the minds of many skeptics of the hunts. The fallibility of human judgment was frequently invoked to protest the witch trials, perhaps most eloquently by Montaigne in his essay "Of Cripples" (that is, of crippled human reason): "After all, it is putting a very high value on one's conjectures to cause a man to be roasted alive on the strength of them."[47] Writing in 1635, Lutheran pastor Johann Matthäus Meyfart also argued against the procedural injustices in witch-trials, calling for their cessation until the practical difficulties of evaluating the reliability of evidence and testimony could be overcome.[48]

Given de Gheyn's social and intellectual context, especially his Leiden connections, the cautious view of witchcraft he expresses in *The Parable of the Devil Sowing Weeds* is not surprising. This was not a denial that witchcraft was possible but a sense that much of it was constituted by the delusions of the ignorant or mentally disturbed, and a judicial wariness about extreme punishment. Such caution was common among Dutch humanists and Reformed ministers, for example, and, increasingly during the course of the seventeenth century, witchcraft beliefs were associated only with the poor and uneducated.[49] Sixteenth- and early seventeenth-century Dutch physicians (e.g., Pieter van Forrest, Johannes Heurnius, Johannes van Beverwijk), following Weyer, recognized that illness played a part in suspected cases of witchcraft and, by the next generation, they would deny the reality of the demonic pact. As Hans de Waardt points out in his discussion of Dutch physicians' views on witchcraft, their powerful influence on jurists distinguished the Dutch Republic from France and the Holy Roman Empire.[50]

Dutch judicial authorities were increasingly reluctant to inflict severe punishments for witchcraft; as noted above, executions in the northern provinces of the Netherlands ceased around 1600. The opinion offered in 1594 by the philosophical and medical faculties of the University of Leiden against the efficacy of the water ordeal in determining witches' guilt, signed by de Gheyn's friend Dr. Pieter Pauw, did not indicate disbelief in witchcraft but showed concern about establishing valid proof.[51] For our purposes, the controversy over the water ordeal confirms the topicality of witchcraft in Leiden during the period de Gheyn was there.

Even as early as 1591, during his stay in Amsterdam, de Gheyn was visited by Buchelius, an Utrecht art connoisseur, jurist, and historian whose interest in witchcraft cases began about this time. In his *Commentarius rerum quotidianarum* (Commentary on daily events), an autobiographical journal written in the 1590s, Buchelius informs us about the concerns of a highly educated Dutch jurist vis-à-vis witchcraft. He noted the difficulty of proving witchcraft, and, comparing Bodin to Weyer, he argued as Weyer did that it is better to release the guilty than to condemn the innocent. Although Buchelius became increasingly convinced of the reality of witchcraft through the 1590s, moving from relative skepticism to relative belief as he noted the details of local cases, he remained deeply concerned about lawyers' ability to discern the truth in such matters. He came to understand witchcraft as a problem of moral education to be resolved by religious guidance provided by the Reformed Church.[52]

It may have been Buchelius who introduced de Gheyn to the literature of witchcraft; in his will, de Gheyn left an extensive library and, unlike many artists, he seems to have known Latin, the original language of many treatises on witchcraft.[53] Among available authorities, the two singled out by Buchelius represented for contemporaries two poles of opinions about witchcraft. As we have seen, Bodin's *Démonomanie*, translated into Dutch in 1596 by Leiden professor of theology Franciscus Junius (François du Jon) the Elder, argued for the reality of witchcraft and urged vigorous persecution. Bodin's immediate goal was to refute Weyer, who argued first in *De praestigiis daemonum* and later in *De lamiis* (On witches, 1577) that accused witches were old women deluded by the devil or suffering from melancholy, meriting compassion and medical and spiritual help more than the stake; Bodin, while also recognizing the wretched social and economic status of the witch, advocated merciless prosecution.[54]

Primarily motivated by pity for accused women and an evangelical anti-

Catholicism (for instance, how could witches commit sacrilege against the Eucharist when it was not truly a sacrament?), Weyer nevertheless argued from within the demonological tradition. He believed ardently in the power of the devil, and much of his book is dedicated to the true guilt of demon-worshipping *male* magicians, contrasting male deliberation and guilt for contracting with demons with female delusion and innocence. Despite his fundamental conservatism, however, Weyer made some significant points against witch-hunting. He denied the credibility of confessions obtained by torture and recognized that imprisonment itself was a form of torture.[55] He favored the removal of witchcraft cases from the jurisdiction of secular courts on the grounds that witches could not really do harm—a radical assertion for its time.[56] Because there is no crime and no justification for criminal punishment, the witch should be given over to religious authorities, whose proper response includes forgiveness, counseling for religious error, and perhaps moderate punishment, but never the death penalty.[57] Weyer also challenged jurists to contemplate the omniscience of the one true judge:

> But when He finally appears Whom nothing escapes—the searcher of hearts and reins [i.e., the controlling or guiding power] Who knows and judges the most hidden truth—your deeds will be made public, you stubborn tyrants and bloodthirsty judges stripped of humanity and far removed from all mercy because of your blindness. I challenge you to appear at the most just tribunal of the Supreme Judge Himself, Who will decide between you and me when the truth that has been buried and trampled under foot will rise again and oppose you to your face, exacting vengeance for your villainy.[58]

In 1584, *The Discoverie of Witchcraft* by English country gentleman Reginald Scot, who had personally witnessed the execution of the St. Osyth witches in 1582, reprised and amplified Weyer's arguments with a caustic, vehemently anti-Catholic satirical turn, even going so far as to doubt the activity of demons in nature.[59]

Scot's *Discoverie* was published in Dutch by English emigrant Thomas Basson of Leiden in 1609, but Basson had considered the project as early as 1602. De Gheyn was related by marriage to the Basson family when his widowed sister Anna married Govert Basson in 1608. Govert was to take over his father Thomas's publishing business upon Thomas's death in 1612. According to Thomas Basson's biographer, J. A. van Dorsten, it is likely that de Gheyn and Thomas knew each other fairly well. In the preface to his Dutch translation of Scot, Thomas noted that it was the encouragement and support of "a certain good gentleman"—probably historian Petrus Scriverius (Pieter Schryver)—that led to the first Dutch edition of Scot's *Discoverie*.[60] A poem included in the 1609 edition and addressed "To the Thoughtless Witch-Judge" by Tuningius (Gerard Tuning), professor of law whose stay at the University of Leiden (1590–1610) overlapped de Gheyn's (1595–1601 or 1602), gives us a sense of the meaning Scot's text held for many Dutch jurists:

Judges! If thyselves art free
Of this supposed sorcery,
With compassion as thy guide
Look with both eyes open wide,
Black magic raises doubts in Scot,
To innocence he'll worth allot,
Do not sully his good fame
Or as unchristian slur his name,
The blindness is so monstrous great
Which sends so swiftly to their fate
The simplest souls that God did make
Whom we see burning at the stake;
Why be so vicious, cruel at heart,
As if thyselves bewitched art?
Only in the blinded mind
Do we harmful witchcraft find.[61]

An understanding of this context can help us read de Gheyn's witchcraft images, even when the iconographic clues are less clear than they are in *The Parable of the Devil Sowing Weeds.*

For example, a drawing on two sheets in Christ's Church, Oxford, perhaps one of de Gheyn's earliest images of witches, could well be interpreted in terms of the devil's delusion and seduction of pathetic and powerless old women—the heart of the anti-witch-hunting arguments of Weyer and Scot (see figure 5.3).[62] At the right, a naked hag with sagging breasts rides a demon and is caressed tenderly by a younger male companion, his leg slung lasciviously over hers. De Gheyn's less detailed rendering of this dark lover as well as the flurry of cloudlike marks surrounding him suggest his illusory nature as an incubus formed from thickened air.[63] The hag and her young lover recall the popular genre motif of the *ungleiches paar* (unequal couple) whose point is the folly of the aged partner, whether male or female.[64] At the left, witches prepare unguents as one of their companions in a ruined building sits in a stupor, inhaling the vapor from a hanging lantern. The mournful demeanor of the huddled witch in the left foreground and the longing gaze of the seduced woman on the monster suggest the mental state of melancholy inspiring witchcraft in women.

The fantastic mount of the lovers is particularly indicative of de Gheyn's pictorial process. A huge, hybrid creature uncannily resembling a dinosaur, he is in fact drawn in part from one of de Gheyn's studies of a dead bird.[65] His neck arches gracefully toward the center of the image, linking the composition's two sides and drawing our attention to familiar paraphernalia below: a

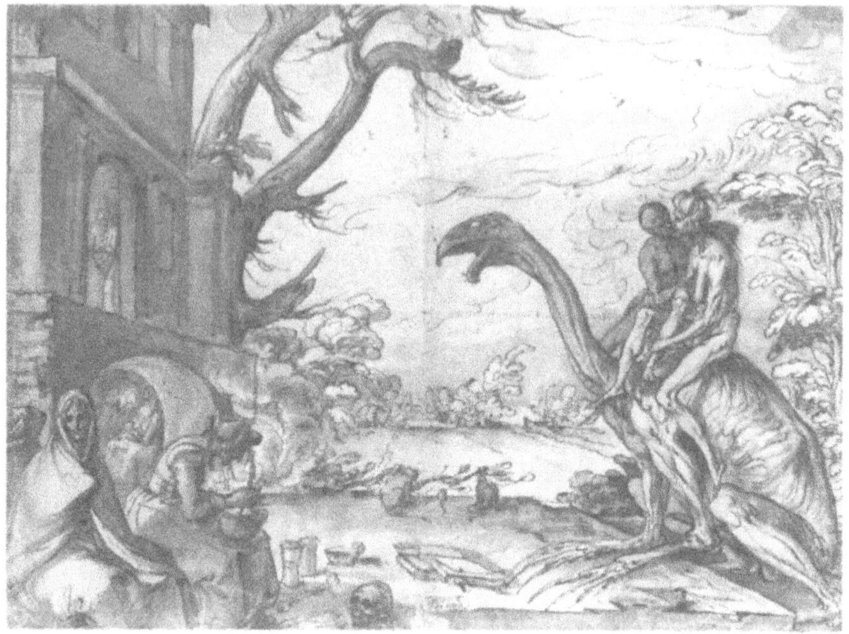

Figure 5.3. Jacques de Gheyn II, *A Witches' Sabbath* (or *Landscape with Witches*), undated. Black chalk drawing with pen and brush in gray ink, heightened with white, 380 × 544 mm. The Governing Body of Christ Church, Oxford.

cat, rat and frog; containers for foul concoctions; a long bone and skull; *grimoires*; and the artist's signature beneath. The imaginative license suggested by the marvelously transformed and resuscitated bird would assume an increasingly important role for de Gheyn.

Witchcraft *nae t'leven* to *uyt den gheest*

In two drawings, in Berlin and the Ashmolean Museum in Oxford, de Gheyn escalated the inventive resonance of his theme while retaining evidence of his consummate naturalism (figures 5.4, 5.5). The sheets are dated 1604, one year before an elaborate drawing of *Orpheus in Hades* in which flying witches (*Christian* heretics) also appear with the devils and the damned in the skies above the Styx.[66] The Berlin drawing purposefully recalls Bruegel's *St. James and the Magician Hermogenes* (1565; see figure 2.6) by the motifs of the cutaway "cellar" view and the witch flying up the chimney, and contains female allegorical figures suggestive of the Power of Women theme entering the room ceremoniously from the right. The second woman in particular is reminiscent of Salome and the lust and greed she represents. The Oxford drawing of witches depends less on visual and iconographic prototypes.

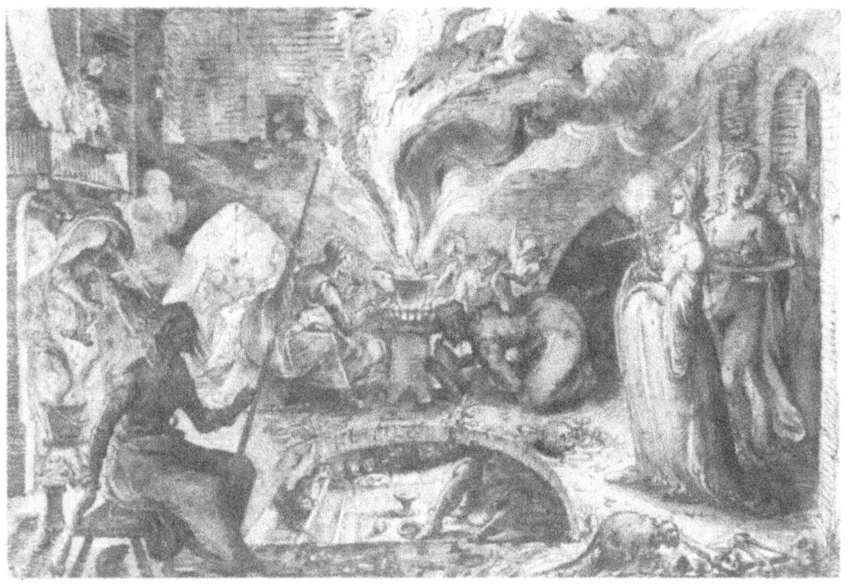

Figure 5.4. Jacques de Gheyn II, *Witches' Kitchen*, 1604. Pen and brush drawing with grey and brown ink on grey paper, 267 × 415 mm. Kupferstichkabinett, Staatliche Museen, Berlin. Photo by Jörg P. Anders. Bildarchiv Preußischer Kulturbesitz/Art Resource, New York.

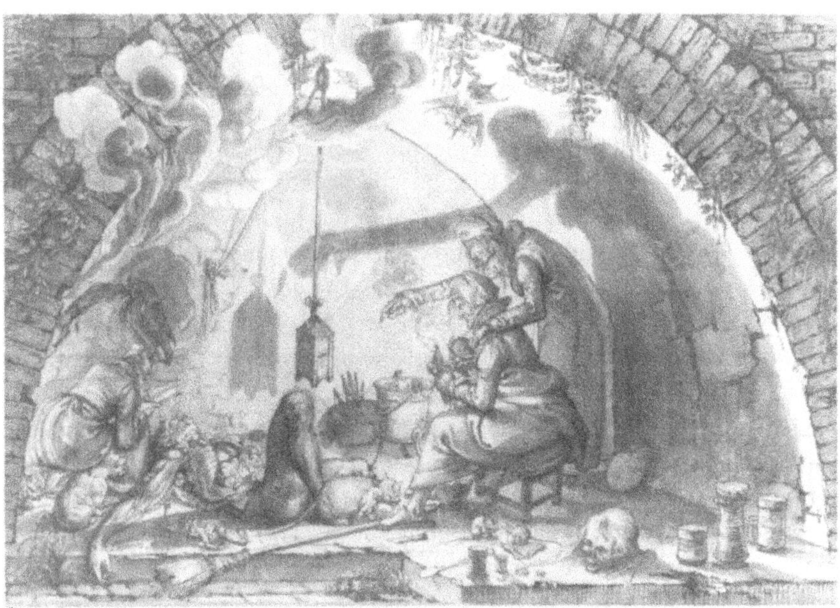

Figure 5.5. Jacques de Gheyn II, *Witches at Work under an Arched Vault*, 1604. Pen and brush drawing in brown and gray ink, 282 × 410 mm. Ashmolean Museum, Oxford.

Both drawings reveal de Gheyn's concern for light effects: In the Berlin example, the witch in the left foreground is backlighted, while witches in an illuminated room to the rear seem to be intoxicated by the lantern's smoke. In the Ashmolean drawing, the witches occupy a decaying arch, and their lantern casts eerie shadows across its surface. Both drawings are littered with witches' paraphernalia: skulls, specimen jars, frogs, cats, and brooms. Hands of Glory, amputated from corpses to stupefy victims or locate buried treasure, are found above the mantel in the Berlin sheet and at the center of the Ashmolean sheet. Machteld Löwensteyn has argued that the activity depicted in the Ashmolean drawing is treasure-hunting, motivated by one of the main vices of witches: greed.[67] But a purely iconographic reading alone is too narrow.

In these two drawings, de Gheyn combined his renowned naturalism and his capacity for fantastic invention with spectacular bravura. In an intellectual milieu that considered the reality of witchcraft and the proper responses of authorities to it to be matters of significant debate, the drawings must first have been intended to sustain learned discussion. As with Hans Baldung Grien's drawings, we can readily imagine them being passed around to friends for delectation and argument. And, like Baldung's, these would have provoked some unease in de Gheyn's circle. For Charles Zika, the foreshortened and cut-open male corpses that appear in the Berlin and Ashmolean works suggest images of cannibalism in the New World, such as a Coornhert's *Battlefield in America*, engraved after Marten van Heemskerck for the series, *The Victories of Charles V* (1555). In addition, Valerie Traub's rich discussion of early modern images of dissection in the anatomy theater, such as de Gheyn's *Anatomical Lesson of Professor Pauw*, engraved by Andreas Stock in 1615, offers further interpretive possibilities.[68]

Because Dutch men were leaders in science as well as colonial exploration, such disturbing visual allusions begged for reconstruction of their national and gendered identity. Traub interprets dissection images as evidence of early modern masculine anxiety. In effect, the illustrations conflated the male corpse—"rendered open, vulnerable, the object of a (masculine) gaze that it cannot evade or control"[69]—with anatomists like Professor Pauw. The resulting abjection and mortification provoked mitigating visual strategies such as eroticized female corpses and classical male figures to contain, literally and figuratively, the grotesque vision of the male body's interior. Placed in the gendered context of early modern science, such compensatory efforts were motivated, Traub argues, by the image of the violated male body.

Perhaps de Gheyn's own mitigating strategy lay not only in the grotesque bodies of his female witches but also in his assertion of both imaginative invention and scientific objectivity—of naturalistic skill inserted into the context of female witchcraft. His elaborate engraving, after a drawing of witches preparing for the sabbath in Stuttgart, dated about 1608, incorporates elements

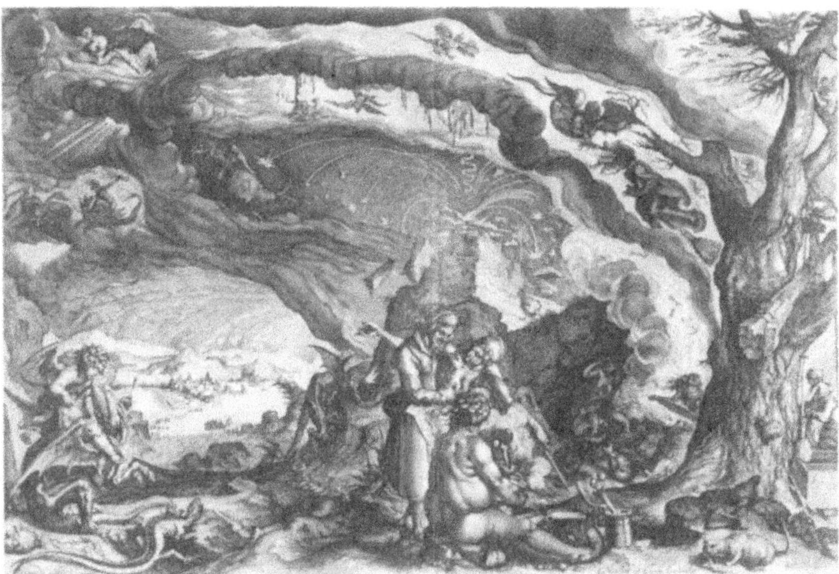

Figure 5.6. After Jacques de Gheyn II, *Preparations for the Witches' Sabbath*, ca. 1610. Engraving by Andreas Stock from two plates, 435 × 658 mm. Prentenkabinet, University of Leiden.

traceable to his meticulous botanical and zoological studies (figure 5.6). For example, the salamander at the left and the tree trunk are related to nature drawings in Frankfurt and Rotterdam.[70] The nailed-down frog in *Witches at Work under an Arched Vault* also corresponds to a frog in a drawing in Amsterdam.[71] De Gheyn's studies of frogs, in particular a drawing of a frog and a stuffed rat dated 1609 in Berlin, also lie at the basis of his creepy drawing of the attributes of witchcraft in the Netherlandish Institute in Paris (figure 5.7).[72] Here the frogs have metamorphosed into demonic familiars with human genital organs, crawling eerily past a *grimoire* open to an illustration of the "Hand of Glory," supported by a second *grimoire* and topped by a skull. Although a common attribute of witchcraft, the skull on top of a pile of books inevitably calls to mind the Dutch *vanitas* still life and its broader message: the worthlessness of worldly experience and knowledge without God. By combining the skull in such a way with the attributes of witchcraft, de Gheyn inventively conveyed the vanity of the witches' false knowledge.

Indeed, when they are considered collectively, de Gheyn's drawings fit comfortably into an understanding of the witch as a pathetic, ignorant, and often old woman, susceptible to vice and to the wiles of the devil. Her attempts at magic are vain, and her fate should be left ultimately to God rather than to the judicial system. Anne Barstow reminds us, however, that even an ostensi-

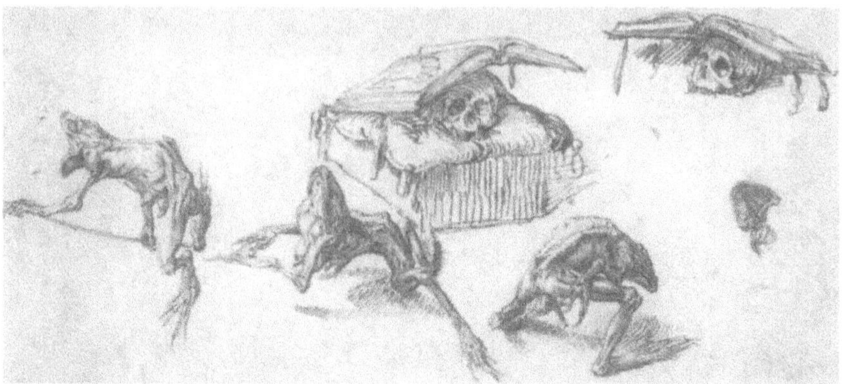

Figure 5.7. Jacques de Gheyn II, *Attributes of Witchcraft*, undated. Pen and brown ink, 94 × 353 mm. Collection Frits Lugt, Institut Néerlandais, Paris.

bly sympathetic concern about accused witches still denigrates women, particularly of the lower class.[73] Scot, for example, describes witches as

> women which be commonly old, lame, bleare-eied, fowle, and full of wrinkles; poore, sullen, superstitious, and papists; or such as knowe no religion: in whose drousie minds the divell hath gotten a fine seat; so as, what mischeefe, mischance, calamitie, or slaughter is brought to passe, they are easilie persuaded the same is doone by themselves; imprinting in their minds an earnest and constant imagination thereof. They are leane and deformed, shewing melancholie in their faces, to the horror of all that see them. They are doting, scolds, mad, divelish. . . .[74]

In this passage, Scot paraphrases language in Weyer's preface and repeats the latter's emphasis on the melancholy of accused witches.[75] Scot's frequent references to the cruelty of "popish" inquisitors toward their weak and ignorant victims is rooted in Weyer, who summoned a variety of ancient sources to advocate merciful treatment of women, based on their inferiority: "It is commonly said that in the same type of offense, women sin less than men and should be punished less than men, all other things being equal. This is of course because of their weakness of spirit, mind, and natural disposition."[76]

In de Gheyn's world, then, witchcraft—the wicked, vain, and ineffectual practice of ignorant, deluded women whose fantasy escaped reason's control—could be understood as the inversion of true science, practiced by many of his patrons and friends, and of his own art, a deft blend of the fantastic and the mimetic. In her study of the complex identities of early modern scientists, Naomi Zack notes that a scientific approach to witchcraft still retained the gendered hierarchy of demonology: The female witch was at the lowest rank of knowers, with the male scientist displacing the elite male magician at the highest. From either perspective, the witch had no real occult agency and, Zack argues, no identity of her own.[77] Class and gender distinctions as well as male professional identity worked to distance de Gheyn and his audience from women accused of witchcraft. Pity hinged on contempt.

The Paris *vanitas* drawing was numbered at the top, indicating its position in an album (see figure 5.7). Judson thought that the sheet was torn from an album devoted to witchcraft images, but its provenance shows that it was combined with drawings from life of various subjects, including studies of an ass, and of gypsies, as well as a portrait likely to be of his wife Eva.[78] The mixed composition of the album suggests that de Gheyn's witchcraft images were understood as part of his repertory as an accomplished draughtsman, a complement to his portraits and nature studies. Moreover, the references to his nature drawings found in these images suggest that de Gheyn understood invention as a distillation of memories of visual experiences, inscribed in the mind of the artist by the act of drawing from nature. The artist's observation of nature and his exercise of imagination are not mutually exclusive but work in a dialectical and complementary fashion to reveal his artistic prowess.

The engraving after the Stuttgart drawing proudly announced this prowess to a wider public than drawings could reach (see figure 5.6). The careful blocking out of tones in the drawing, the existence of tracing marks, as well as reversal, resulting in *appropriately* left-handed witches indicate that it was certainly made to be engraved.[79] The print was published by Nicolas de Clerck, active in Delft and The Hague, probably around 1610, and is of such size (435 × 658 mm, on two sheets) and elaboration that it rivals Goltzius's *Cupid and Psyche* of 1587 (432 x 857 mm). De Gheyn is designated as the "inventor" in the inscription, and no engraver is indicated, although it was probably Stock.[80] In 1613, Polish artist Jan Ziarnko relied heavily on de Gheyn's print in his comprehensive fold-out illustration for Pierre de Lancre's treatise (see figure 4.1), even though his image was used to support the vehement pro-witch-hunting stance of the author. The meaning of de Gheyn's image has been more controversial.

Löwensteyn argues that if the Stuttgart drawing and its engraving were to be taken as anti-witch-hunting propaganda, then Basson would have published the print.[81] However, de Gheyn chose de Clerck to publish other important inventions around the same time—for example, *The Fortune Teller, The Crossbowman,* and the *Landscapes*—all of which are signed with "*in.*" or "*Inventor,*" but not "*fecit.*" Clifford Ackley has grouped these prints together as self-conscious displays of both de Gheyn's inventiveness and his calligraphic line.[82] The emphasis on the invention of the image rather than the carving of the plate in the inscriptions tells us something about how de Gheyn wanted these images to be received (*The Crossbowman*, especially, demands the viewer's attention literally by the aim of its main figure!). In publishing the print after the Stuttgart drawing, de Gheyn may have chosen de Clerck to ensure the print's audience. De Clerck rented a stall in the Binnenhof, the inner court of the Princes of Orange and the meeting place of the States General, in an area used by book- and print-sellers, especially on holidays and fair days.[83] De Gheyn could be assured that de Clerck would market the print successfully to an audience of residents of and visitors to The Hague.

I think it is no coincidence that de Gheyn's master engraving of witches emerged about the same time as the Dutch translation of Scot. De Gheyn may have known about Basson's plans for the translation and perceived that the Dutch text was certain to increase discussion of witchcraft in The Hague and elsewhere. The engraving would challenge the audience's knowledge of the witchcraft debate as well as their knowledge of art, for de Gheyn orchestrated the repertory of motifs within the witchcraft genre into a superbly realized, grandiose conception. The fat witch in the center and her stridently gesticulating companion are reminiscent of Baldung's woodcut prototype from 1510 (see figure 3.5); the figure to the upper right of Dürer's engraved *Witch* of 1500 (see figure 3.4). Turbulent clouds suggest weather-magic as does the steam spewing from a cauldron in the right middle ground; a well at the far right suggests witches' poisoning of wells. In the center, witches prepare their unguent while others fly to the sabbath. At the left is a cupid climbing on and prodding a demon with his arrow, a motif recalling Baldung (see figures 3.7, 3.10, 3.12). This motif also relates closely to de Gheyn's designs for emblems for poet Daniel Heinsius's (Heins) *Emblemata Amatoria* (Love emblems, before 1607).[84] Its caption reads "Love Conquers All," and the cupid mounts a lion.

The prominent presence of this emblematic motif in a witchcraft image is intriguing because of the circle of literati it suggests. According to Scriverius in the 1616 edition of the emblem book, the subjects had been selected, perhaps by Scriverius himself ("a certain amateur"), from the collections of Haarlem humanist Hadrianus Junius (Adriaen de Jonghe) and others.[85] Grotius, moreover, provided some of the captions. Although Löwensteyn points out that the borrowed cupid may simply indicate witches' lust as well as amatory magic (e.g., causing impotence, or inspiring passion with potions or glances), one wonders what else it may have suggested to the circle of intellectuals familiar with Heinsius's emblem book.[86] As noted earlier, Scriverius was also probably that "certain gentleman" whose support led Basson to publish the Dutch translation of Scot's *Discoverie*. And Scot ends his text (Chapter 10), rather curiously, with an explanation of how love magic supposedly accomplished through the bewitching glance may be understood in natural, humoral terms. As the "bewitcher's" eyes emit beams or vapors toward the beloved, the blood of the latter is moved and love is kindled. The chapter ends with a Latin poem by Lucretius, translated by Scot's English publisher Abraham Fleming, about blushing.[87]

Scriverius's sonnet to Basson, echoing Tuningius's poem promoting the providential view of witchcraft cited earlier, was published with the Dutch translation of Scot. The last line reads "If all Judges were to share our defiance of ancient myth, fewer humans would suffer injustice; some things are hidden on purpose, one should submit to God's ultimate verdict."[88] For those familiar with the emblem book, the cupid mounting the demon might have pointed to Scriverius, and thus to the skeptical stance on witchcraft epitomized by Scot. Despite the legibility of the cupid motif in conventional moralizing terms, as the lust that fuels witchcraft, it may have raised associations for the members of this intellectual circle.[89] With this engraving, de Gheyn aligned himself with this circle of Dutch intellectuals. He also created a work that proclaimed his inventive capacity but held reminders of his incomparable mimetic skills in details such as the lizard, frogs, and tree trunk. In its scope, detail, and energetic conception, the engraving proclaimed the consummate artistic accomplishment of its inventor.

This claim was echoed in a portrait of de Gheyn, designed by the artist and engraved by Stock for a series of seventy-two northern artists' portraits published by Hendrik Hondius in 1610 (figure 5.8). Here, the artist's elevated status is based on the range of his skills, his inventiveness, and his service to the prince. In front of the distinguished, serious, middle-aged artist are implements indicating the impressive variety of his abilities: a burin for engraving, brushes for painting, and quills for drawing. The scene in the background, however, shows de Gheyn in front of a painting of a vague mythological scene and a shelf holding sculptures, working on an easel from a nude female model, thus privileging his activities as a painter of elevated subjects, involving knowledge of the human figure. The inscription itself proclaims him first as a *pictor*, and it singles out his work on war and peace and his favor with Prince Maurice. He points to a miniature of his wife Eva—at once a gesture of affection and a reminder to the viewer of the status of her family. The symbols on the cube beneath his elbow speak of the artist's fame that is gained from his constant toil and outlives him (the hourglass with bird and bat wings symbolizing day and night). Yet that assertion is tempered with the transience suggested by the tulips: symbol of fleeting beauty and, in a Dutch context, of the humility and piety necessary to the human condition.[90]

Witchcraft and de Gheyn's Fantasy

Although it would seem difficult for de Gheyn to surpass the imaginative qualities of his master engraving and its preliminary drawing, many of his witchcraft drawings, most undated, are indeed more fantastic and very freely executed in swirling pen lines. Meticulous natural details fall away and swift pen lines create an energetic, sweeping vision of witchcraft, suggesting that the

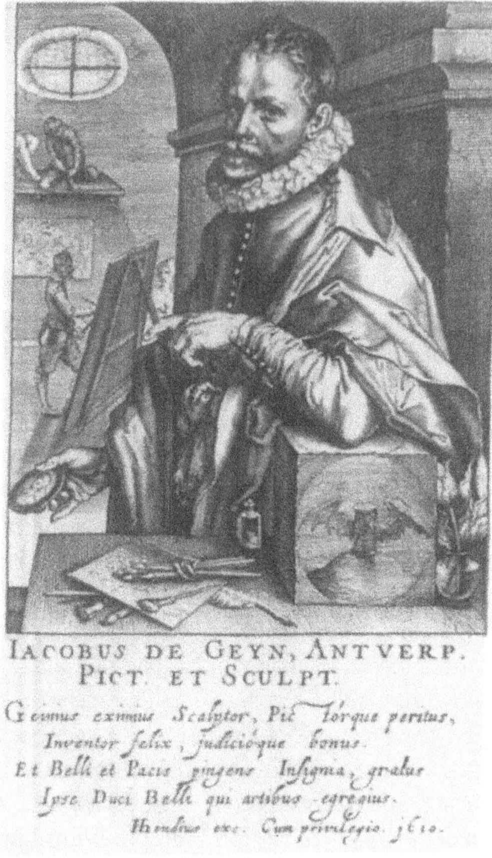

Figure 5.8. After Jacques de Gheyn II, *Portrait of Jacques de Gheyn II*, ca. 1610. Engraving by Andreas Stock, 200 × 123 mm. Bibliothèque Royale de Belgique, Brussels.

balance between *nae t'leven* and *uyt den gheest* has shifted in favor of the latter. Two drawings in particular startle us with their gruesome violence and intensely expressive draftsmanship (figures 5.9 and 5.10). The sheet in the National Gallery in Washington depicts a witch vampirizing a limp infant, as an evidently ineffectual string of garlic hangs in the doorway. Here de Gheyn combines diabolical witchcraft (note the magical scribbles on the wall and the owl) with "white" countermagic, which was of equal if not greater concern as witchcraft, especially in Protestant countries. Popular superstitions, while well intentioned, also showed a lack of faith in divine providence and illustrated the need for religious education. In the Northern Netherlands, the concern of both magistrates and clergy over white magic continued long after the execution of witches ceased.[91]

The drawing in the Metropolitan Museum shows witches preparing the flying unguent in a cauldron as one witch rubs her legs with the foul concoc-

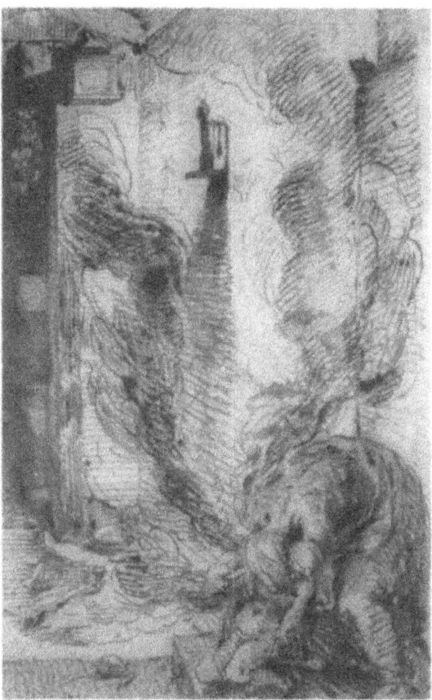

Figure 5.9. Jacques de Gheyn II, *Interior with Witchcraft Scene*, undated. Pen and brown ink over black chalk, 323 × 206 mm. Image © 2004 Board of Trustees, National Gallery of Art, Washington, D.C. Ailsa Mellon Bruce Fund.

tion (figure 5.10). As another witch brings a platter of body parts to the cauldron, the nipples of her sagging breasts tickle the platter's rim. The witches' hair, billowing garments, and smoke from the fire are analogous, freely drawn forms. In an astonishing composition in Dresden, oddly suggestive of Giovanni Battista Piranesi's fantastic architectural *capricci* over a hundred years later, witches fly overhead, occupy the rooms and corridors of ruined architecture, and looking somewhat stupefied, sail on canals under bridges (figure 5.11). At the bottom right, one witch strikes the pose of melancholy, the mental illness that, according to Weyer, drove women to witchcraft. An elephant, too big for its spatial niche, is presumably a transformed witch or demon. This drawing, in particular, seems to exceed the notion of a synthesis of perceptions of the visible world and move into the realm of fantasy.

In a drawing in Leiden of witches (three female and one male) riding to the sabbath on a cart pulled by a goat, de Gheyn reprises *Lo stregozzo*, discussed in Chapter 2 (figures 5.12 and 2.3). The background of tall, grassy plants, swaying rhythmically; the goat with long, curving horns; and the primary witch with sagging breasts all suggest that de Gheyn composed his own invention based on the Italian engraving that, as I have argued, embodied the inven-

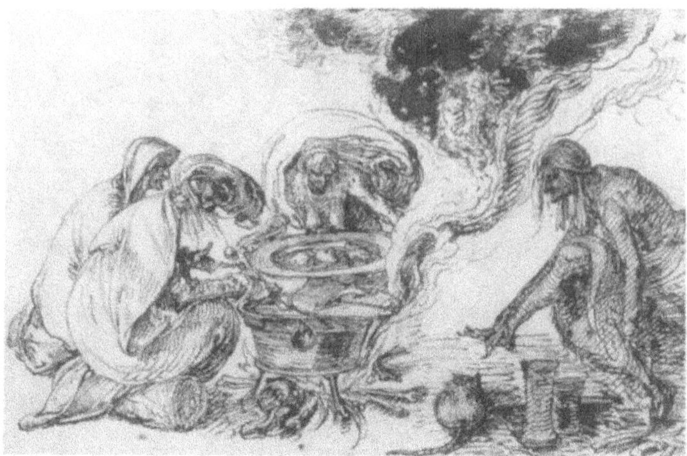

Figure 5.10. Jacques de Gheyn II, *Preparations for the Witches' Sabbath*, undated. Pen and brown ink, brown wash, 235 × 367 mm. Metropolitan Museum of Art, New York. Purchase, Joseph Pulitzer Bequest, 1962 (62.196). All rights reserved, The Metropolitan Museum of Art.

tive potential of this theme in the early sixteenth century. Most provocative is the fact that the male figure holds a cross and dish, possibly suggesting a paten with the Host. This detail may refer to the perversion of the Catholic Mass that witches were supposed to undertake at their sabbaths—a pointed reference in the context of the confessional aspects of the contemporary debate about witchcraft. Catholic writers, following the logic of inversion within demonology, might use the "black mass" aspect of the sabbath as proof of the divinity of the sacrament, about which, according to Walter Stephens, they had plenty of anxiety. Skeptical Protestants like Weyer and Scot, however, critiqued the Catholic sacraments as forms of magic and, therefore, impossible for witches to desecrate.[92]

Was de Gheyn expressing a concern about the abuse of the sacrament, mocking such a concern, or merely playing to his audience's awareness of the debate? It is difficult to read a confessional meaning into this drawing. Extrapolating from his early *Parable of the Devil Sowing Weeds* (see figure 5.1) we can conclude, however, that the wild ride shown here is a frenzied and foolish quest. Indeed, the very style of these last four drawings under discussion—their impetuous, fluid, indefinite rendering, and their combination of bizarre and grotesque motifs—suggests that de Gheyn, informed by the controversies he read and heard about witchcraft, now extemporized on a theme he regarded as fantastic in order to display the power of his own fantasy. The negative fantasies of female witches are thus transformed by a male artist, renowned for his mimetic skill, into dazzling proof of inventive prowess.

Whether we can confirm a developmental movement in de Gheyn's work

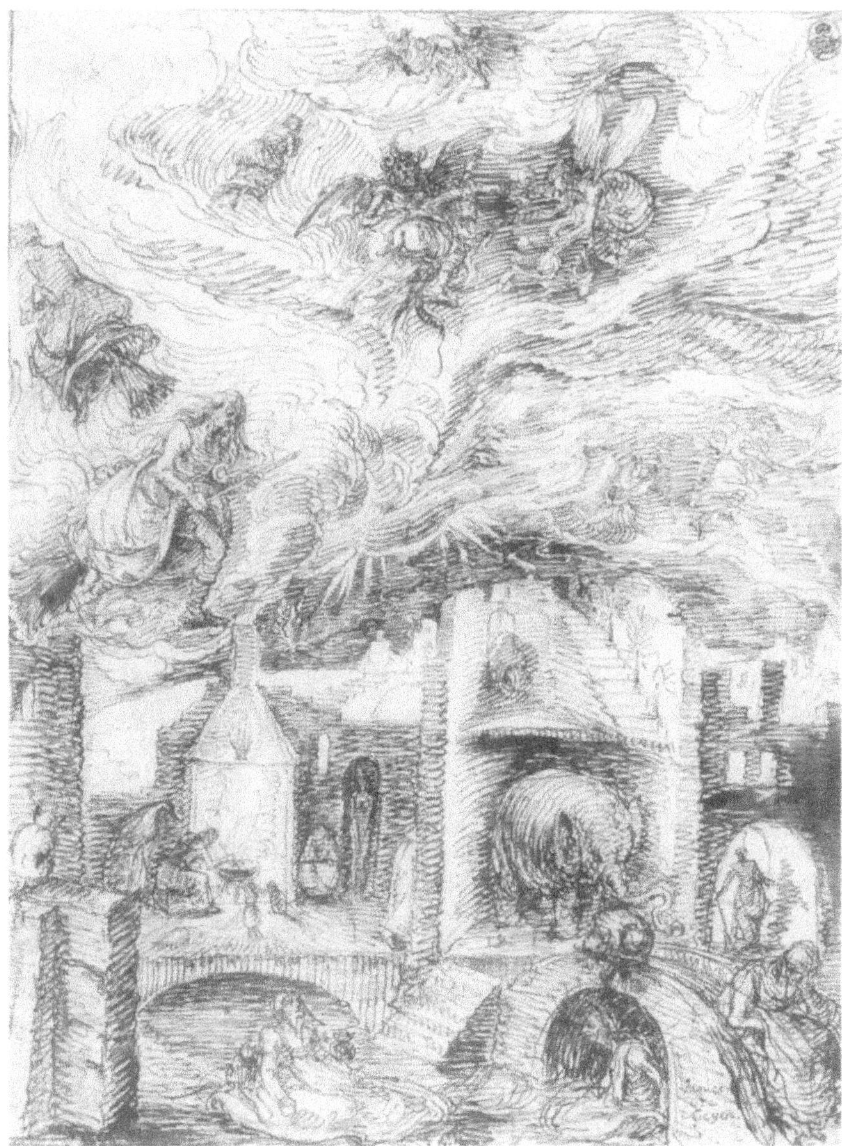

Figure 5.11. Jacques de Gheyn II, *Scene of Sorcery*, undated. Pen and brown ink, 382 × 285 mm. Kupferstichkabinett, Staatliche Kunstsammlungen Dresden.

from tighter to looser handling, and from a purely cognitive understanding of *uyt den gheest* to one that embraces an autonomous fantasy emerging solely from the artist, is an open question because of the uncertain dating of many of his freely drawn images. Although he noted that it is tempting to read such images as evidence of a late "old-age" style, van Regteren Altena cautioned

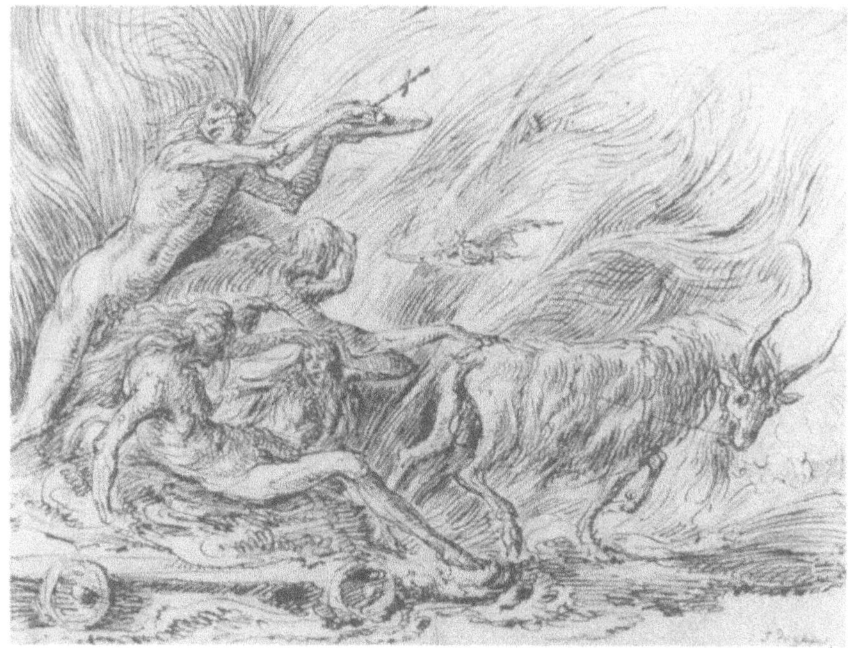

Figure 5.12. Jacques de Gheyn II, *The Journey to the Witches' Sabbath*, undated. Black chalk, pen and brown ink, 283 × 375 mm. Prentenkabinet, University of Leiden.

against this, suggesting that de Gheyn worked deliberately in different modes—a caveat reflecting the ambiguity of *nae t'leven* and *uyt den gheest.*[93] Perhaps the aging and successful de Gheyn simply felt freer to engage in the loose manner that was also evident at times in his earlier career, but this freedom, I would argue, was in part the result of his status. Perhaps his brilliant work "from life" had earned him the right to work "from the imagination."

The epitome of inventiveness in de Gheyn's late period, and of his success as a court artist, is undoubtedly his design for a grotto and fountain, made of plaster, mortar, shells, and coral, and commissioned by Prince Maurice for the Buitenhof in the early 1620s.[94] The execution of the work continued beyond the prince's death in 1625 and de Gheyn's own death in 1629 to be completed by Jacques III. The most elaborate drawing in London seemingly depicts a kingdom of Neptune, the old man in the center, as if to pay homage to the Dutch mastery of the sea (figure 5.13). Certainly the loving attention given to shells and marine creatures bears comparison to the use of those elements in seventeenth-century Dutch still lifes. The grotto probably rested against the back of a gallery with Doric columns; as water spilled into the basin from the grotto, the viewer would have been dazzled by the combination of actual and sculpted natural specimens, of naturalism and fantasy. Monstrous heads emerge from the coalescence of other forms; oversized lobsters face off with

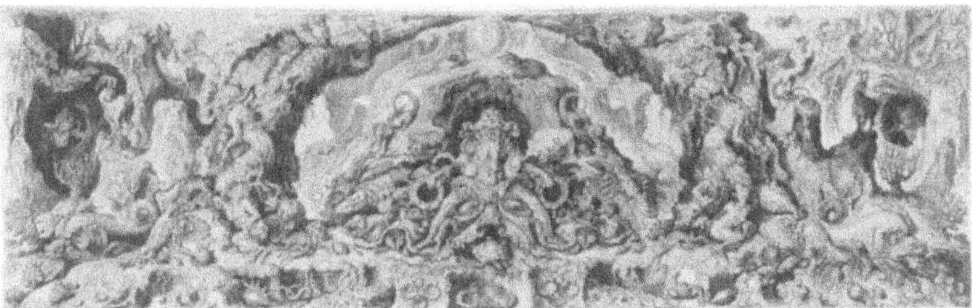

Figure 5.13. Jacques de Gheyn II, *Large Design for the Rear Wall of a Garden Grotto*, ca. 1625. Pen and brush with watercolor on four sheets of paper, 228 × 742 mm. © The British Museum, London.

chimeras; owls and goats are incongruously found among Neptune's menagerie. The grotto design offers the same combination of precise observation of natural forms and inventive license that is found in the witchcraft drawings that can be dated in the early years of the century. But the balance has shifted toward license.

Dutch Witches—Dutch Women

Taken together and in context, de Gheyn's drawings speak to the measured, cautious stance on witchcraft that ultimately prevailed in the Northern Netherlands. When discovered, incidences of witchcraft called for pity, spiritual guidance, and education. The devil probably existed for the artist but ruled no anti-kingdom. Witchcraft was possible, but witches were not an overwhelming army of women truly empowered by the devil. Rather, they were melancholic or otherwise deranged, susceptible to those vices and weaknesses that most afflicted the so-called weaker sex—particularly lust and a readily corrupted imagination. Only men of reason like de Gheyn could harness the power of imagination and make it productive. Similarly, witches' muddled attempts at experiment parodied the true knowledge sought by de Gheyn and the scientists and humanists whose patronage and friendship he avidly cultivated. The witch, in Zack's terms, lacked any positive identity. Whether demonological or skeptical, the elite interest in witchcraft described a "homosocial triangle of learned men, lowly women, and the Devil."[95]

For de Gheyn, women likely to be accused of witchcraft were a distinct type. His broader view of the role of women in society conformed fully to his Dutch context, in which the long western tradition of misogyny was tempered by a degree of independence for Dutch women, and a positive understanding, fostered by the value placed on marriage within Protestantism, of their crucial significance within the family and the Republic (figures 5.14 and 5.15).[96] The

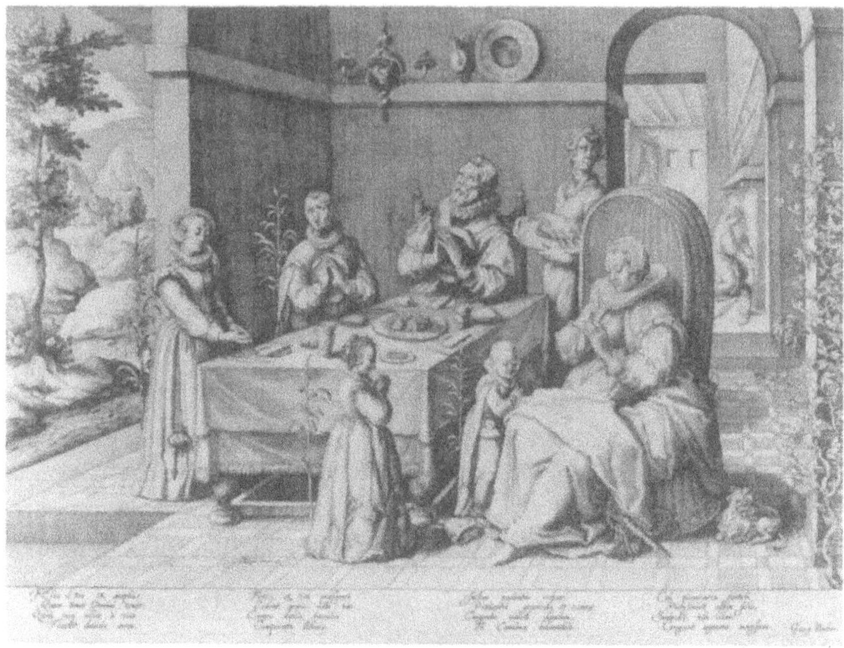

Figure 5.14. After Jacques de Gheyn II, *The Pious Family* (or Grace *before the Meal*), ca. 1595. Engraving (by Zacharias Dolendo?), 307 × 410 mm. Museum Boymans-van Beuningen, Rotterdam.

early *Pious Family* in Brunswick, engraved about 1595, perhaps by Zacharias Dolendo, may be based on de Gheyn's own family with himself as the eldest son.[97] The mother is clearly subordinated to the father who heads the table and leads the family in saying grace. Yet her position is an important one, confirmed visually: Although she sits lower than the father, she is in front of him spatially and has great weight within the composition. Significantly, the two younger children look to her, while the older son is near the father and mimics his pose. The wife is, of course, the doyenne of the home whose piety she guards and fosters.

While the drawing and resulting engraving are generally applicable to all families in the early modern period, Pieter J. J. van Thiel has interpreted them in terms of Calvinist ideals.[98] The drawing, with its prominent vine at the left and olive plants sprouting incongruously from the floor, is not a portrait but a visualization of Psalm 128 on God-given blessings. The inscriptions under the engraving are poems based on the Psalm: one in Latin by Scottish Calvinist George Buchanan and one in Dutch. The section of the Psalm describing a man's wife and children explains much of the botanical symbolism in the image: The wife is a well-rooted vine, laden with sweet grapes and swiftly

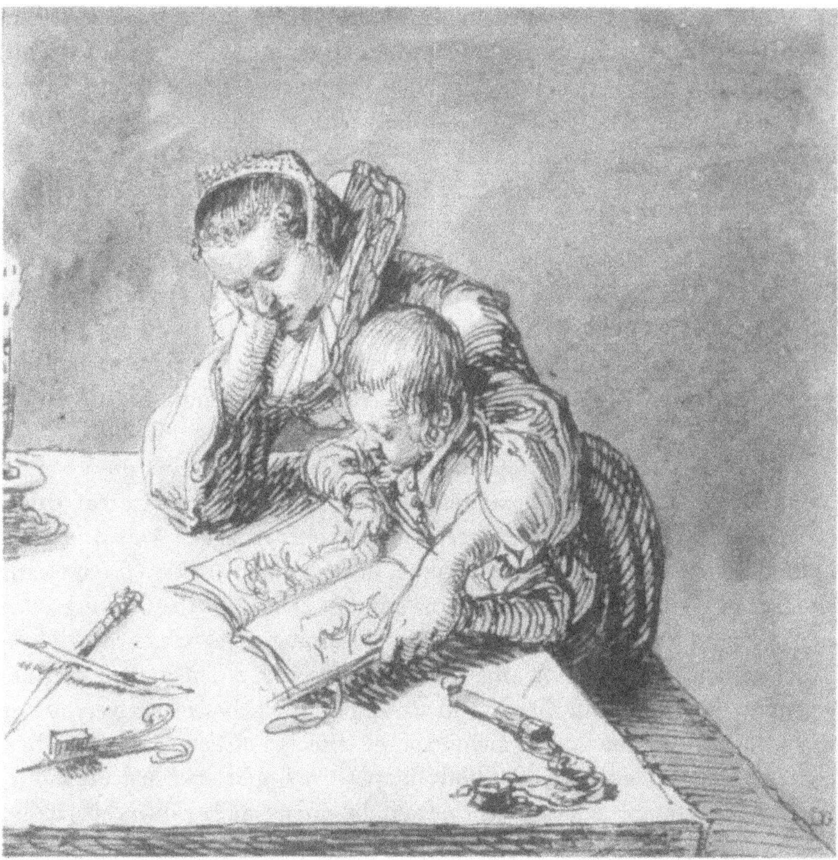

Figure 5.15. Jacques de Gheyn II, *A Mother and Her Child Looking at a Picture Book*, ca. 1600? Pen and brush with brown ink, 147 × 177 mm. Kupferstichkabinett, Staatliche Museen zu Berlin. Photo by Jörg P. Anders. Bildarchiv Preußischer Kulturbesitz/Art Resource, New York.

bringing forth fruit, and the children cleave like olive plants to the father's table.

In another, wonderfully intimate and ostensibly naturalistic drawing in Berlin, foreshadowing Rembrandt, de Gheyn may have depicted his wife Eva and their son, Jacques III (see figure 5.15).[99] Whoever his models were, the woman here plays a vital role in the instruction of her very young child, which she undertakes with obvious tenderness and patience. The candle, pen, penknife and case serve as still-life objects but also as allegorical symbols of industrious study, and memory; the snuffer as a reminder of the transitory nature of worldly accomplishment.[100]

There are two major contradictory interpretations of the Berlin drawing, both hinging on the role of visual observation in knowledge. In his heavily allegorical reading, Hessel Miedema emphasizes the early, incomplete stage of the boy's knowledge, as the natural aptitude given to him by Mother Nature, personified by the woman, is developed by the practice of looking at a picture book and naming its depicted objects. This early perceptual stage needs to be developed by diligent study to attain true insight and reason. Alpers, however, taking Miedema to task for his dichotomization of realism and allegory, sees the drawing less in terms of successive and increasingly profound stages of knowledge, gradually leaving observation behind, and more in terms of the identity between knowledge and representation of the visible world. She compares de Gheyn's drawing to Moravian clergyman and educational theorist Johann Comenius's insistence on the material basis of knowledge in his *Orbis sensualium pictus* (The visible world pictured, 1658) and more broadly to the Dutch affirmation of representation as a means of knowing.[101]

Comenius was also a progressive advocate of women's education—in his *Opera didactica omnia* (The great didactic, 1657), he even suggested that education could prepare women for careers other than marriage.[102] This would not become reality for a long time to come, however, and for de Gheyn's early seventeenth-century context, Miedema's interpretation of the drawing as an allegory of an early and incomplete stage of learning, albeit couched in a brilliant "mimetic performance," may be more appropriate. The mother may not personify Nature, but de Gheyn's focus on her as teacher of her very young son as he strives to name and memorize the depicted objects is informed by a contemporary understanding of both the positive importance and the limitations of the mother's educational role and, by extension, her own capacity for intellectual endeavors.

As a male child, Jacques III would leave his picture book and his mother's instruction behind as he worked toward professional status as an artist—van Regteren Altena points out that his classical education was ambitious, including instruction in Greek along with Latin.[103] In contrast, most girls in the early modern period were destined for marriage and were educated only enough to provide suitable companionship for their husbands and the most basic, early instruction for their children, or to offset boredom that led to idleness and vice.[104] Erika Rummel characterizes Erasmus's attitude toward women's learning as liberal for his time (Henry's More's daughters had changed his early opinion on the worthlessness of education for women) but by no means feminist. In a letter to Guillaume Budé, for example, he wrote that reading and study protect the mind from idleness and lead to virtue. Moreover, educated women make better company for their husbands. The idea that a woman should pursue learning for herself is mocked in Erasmus's *The Abbot and the Learned Lady*, where Magdalia's quest for knowledge is evidence of the topsy-turvy world.[105]

In his remarkable *On the Excellence of the Female Sex* of 1639 (ten years after de Gheyn's death), Dordrecht physician Johann van Beverwijk championed women's intellectual capacity. He based his argument partially on his empirical anatomical observations—women have just as large a brain as men—but also on historical examples of learned and virtuous women, and on an unusual interpretation of Galenic medicine. Although women's coolness and wetness were usually assumed to hamper their intellectual abilities, van Beverwijk thought that these qualities were necessary to steady the senses. Nevertheless, he still saw women's learning primarily in the context of their ideal state of marriage, and he soothed men's concerns about their wives' learning by arguing that it neither disrupted domestic work nor inspired disobedience. He had no fear that his educated daughters would be lesser housekeepers or disobey their husbands, for stubbornness is epitomized by ignorance.[106]

Intellectually accomplished women were still considered exceptional. The most remarkable Dutch female intellectual of the Golden Age—poet and scholar Anna Maria van Schurman, praised by van Beverwijk, Cats, and Constantijn Huygens—argued boldly that learning could be an end unto itself, even for women. She felt it necessary to justify her own intellectual accomplishments, however, by pointing out her unmarried state and by claiming that learning promoted political stability.[107] Laurinda Dixon has shown that, despite the remarkable similarity between symptoms of the female malady of hysteria and the male scholarly disease of melancholy, Dutch medical theory was reluctant to equate the two and continued to emphasize the dangers of too much study for women's health. The malady of *furor uterinus*, caused by the hunger of the womb for intercourse, Dixon argues, fascinated the budding medical field of gynecology, fostered particularly at the University of Leiden, because it provided a medical reason for keeping women married and at home.[108]

De Gheyn's contented young mother instructing her son with a picturebook is of course distinguished from his witches by her economic and social class, her degree of education, and her display of maternal virtue. However, she too must be understood within the context of the early modern belief in the intellectual limitations of women. Whereas the mother provides the foundations for her son's further learning, de Gheyn's witches—female embodiments of ignorance, moral weakness, and fantasy uncontrolled by reason—invert the true knowledge pursued by the artist and his friends. At worst, women invert reason; at best, they foster the education of their children and ultimately the well-being of the family and state. Given such limitations on their intellectual capacity, it is not surprising that early modern women were excluded from universities and scientific academies, and restricted in their production of culture by the age-old injunctions to silence, humility, and obedience.[109]

Chapter 6
Rosa: Witchcraft and the Fiery Painter

Sincere, free, fiery painter and equable, despiser of wealth and death. This is my Genius. Salvator Rosa.

—Inscription from Rosa's Genius *etching, ca. 1662*

Witchcraft and *Libertà*

Within the history of witchcraft images, Neapolitan artist Salvator Rosa (1615–1673) holds a crucially important place. Although his use of the theme is limited to several pictures done at mid-century, it tellingly underscores his break with traditional forms of patronage and his quest for an absolute artistic autonomy. His witchcraft pictures also expose a fundamental and unresolved tension—between what Rosa did well and what he most esteemed—that took different forms during his career. While collectors coveted his dark, wild landscapes, his violent battle scenes and his low-life genre pictures (*Bambocciate*, after Dutch artist Pieter van Laer, nicknamed "Il Bamboccio," meaning dolt or puppet), Rosa longed unrequitedly for the respect due an intellectual history painter like Nicolas Poussin. Forever plumbing the mind of his friend Giovanni Battista Ricciardi, a scholar, playwright, and poet, for new, obscure narratives, Rosa's real talent lay in the very subjects he shunned.[1] As his landscapes were crucial to the formation of the picturesque aesthetic in the eighteenth century, his witches, bandits, and soldiers emerged from the Baroque tradition of the *capriccio* but asserted inventive license more boldly. Rosa always knew he was an important artist, even if he did not understand why.

Rosa's thoughts on art can be reconstructed with some precision. His remarkably candid correspondence, his poetry, his self-portraits, and his allegorical images are rich sources regarding his life and his artistic goals.[2] It is possible, then, to situate his witchcraft images in both biographical and art-theoretical contexts. His lifelong striving to fashion himself as a satiric painter is indicated by his term, *pictor succensor*, or "fiery painter," inscribed in *The*

Genius of Salvator Rosa, his etching of about 1662 (figure 6.1). The word *successor* does not exist in classical Latin: Rosa coined it by combining the word *censor*, corrector of morals, with a prefix to fit his meter.[3] This "fiery" nature of the artist who castigates human folly is evident not just in the subject matter of his poetry and art but also in his extraordinarily uncompromising and self-assertive behavior with patrons, who were to have no say about a painting "after the measurements."[4] Among the figures defining his artistic goals in *The Genius of Salvator Rosa*—the satyr for Satire, Painting at the left, and Sincerity in the center, with the toga-clad figure of Stoic Equability and Self-Knowledge behind—is *Libertà*, or Freedom, who bestows cap and scepter on the artist's genius.[5] Rosa's images of black magic, analogous to his literary creations such as his poem *La strega* (The witch) of the mid-1640s, assert this brash version of pictorial freedom. In addition, however, witches and magicians held allegorical meaning for Rosa as symbols of the dangers of artistic and poetic creation.

Rosa's humble origins help to explain the vehemence of his later assertions of status and honor. His grandfather built houses; his father was a builder and surveyor. His mother, the daughter of an insignificant artist, bore two other children, Giuseppe and Giovanna. During his father's long illness before his death in 1621, the family was in such bad financial straits that Rosa's mother pawned her best dress and her jewelry. When she remarried, she entrusted her children to her father, who sent the two boys to a crowded school for the Neapolitan poor, characterized more by strict religious discipline than by a good education. Rosa followed his older brother into the novitiate but soon left (not surprisingly, given his volatile temperament) and went to live with his mother's family. Giovanna's marriage to Francesco Francanzano, a good painter who encouraged Rosa's artistic efforts, was crucial for the young man's development.

Glimpses into Rosa's early career reveal how closely he connected subject matter, status, and reputation. When he first went to Rome in 1635, he stayed in the house of Cardinal Francesco Maria Brancaccio, a fellow Neapolitan who would employ him in 1638, along with Pietro da Cortona, to decorate his palace at Viterbo. Giovanni Battista Passeri, in his *Lives* of seventeenth-century Roman artists (1673–79), noted that, eager to make a name, Rosa sold dealers small pictures of various "humble" but "witty and spirited" subjects like lime burners, cardsharps, beggars, and fishermen—in other words, the *Bambocciate* that he would later repudiate.[6] Back in Naples, he decided to develop a reputation for battle scenes that he came to despise subsequently as well. The violence of these pictures was condensed into a life-sized, now lost painting of the giant Tityus with his entrails being torn out by an eagle. Rosa proudly sent this gruesome picture to Rome, where it was placed by dealer Niccolo Simonelli in the public exhibition at the Pantheon, accompanied by Simonelli's poem lik-

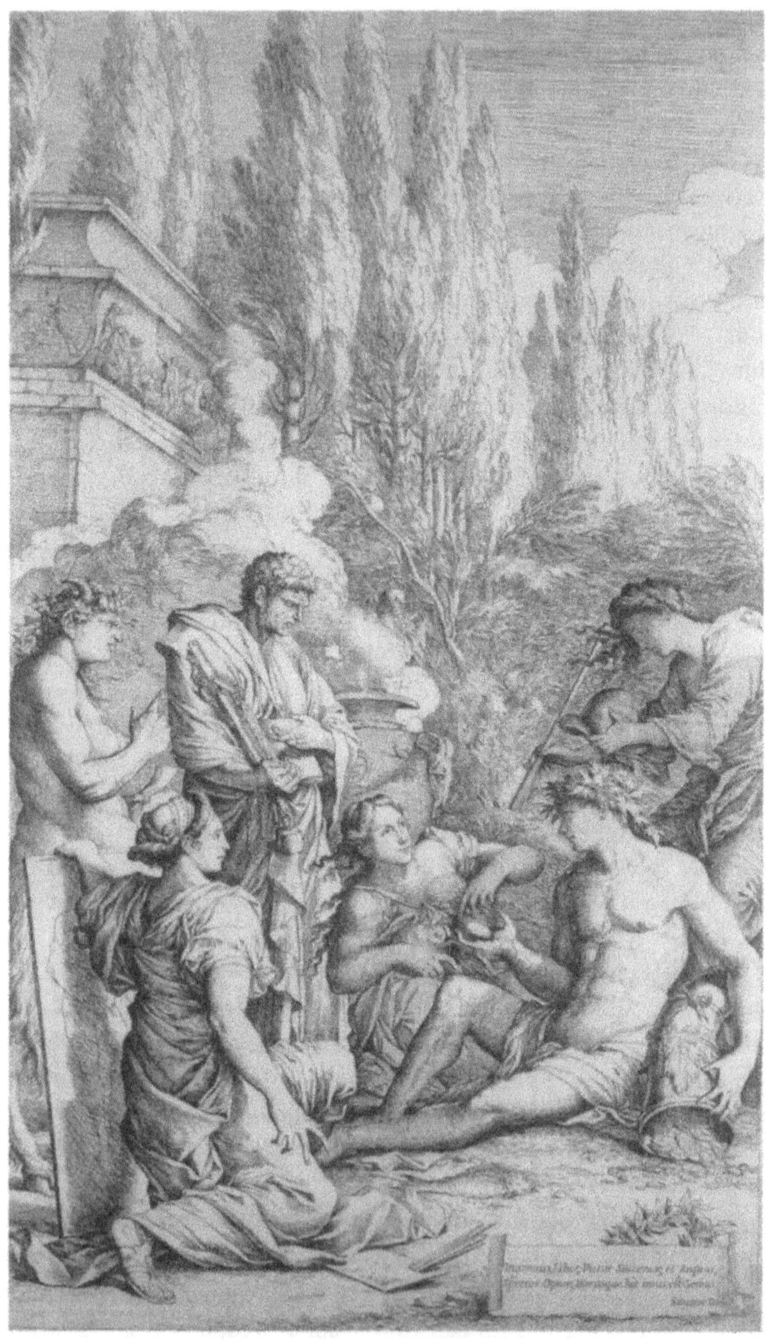

Figure 6.1. Salvator Rosa, *The Genius of Salvator Rosa*, ca. 1662. Etching, 457 × 275 mm. Image © 2004 Board of Trustees, National Gallery of Art, Washington, D.C. Ailsa Mellon Bruce Fund.

ening young Salvator to the ancient Greek orator Demosthenes, famed for his acrid denunciations of his political enemies.

When the painter moved to Rome in 1639, encouraged by the reception of *Tityus*, he hung four paintings over the door to his house to proclaim his accomplishments: two landscapes, a *Bambocciata*, and a battle scene. His theatrical efforts were more suggestive of things to come, however. He made an ostentatious impact at the Carnival in Rome—a bellicose city characterized by street brawling and a culture of ritualized insults, shame, and honor—by organizing a troupe of friends disguised as charlatans hawking medicines for imaginary ailments. Rosa's weapon of choice, satire, was already evident. His portrayal of the quack doctor's servant, Formica, in improvised comedies gained the attention of his Roman audience, including the reigning artistic giant Gianlorenzo Bernini, whose stagecraft containing realistic genre elements for the *intermezzo* for Marco Marazzoli's opera *Chi soffre, speri* (Who suffers, hopes, 1639) was brashly lambasted by Formica.[7]

When Prince Gian Carlo de' Medici, younger brother of the Grand Duke of Tuscany and an avid lover of art and the theater, invited Rosa to Florence in 1640, he probably did not know or care about the young artist's discontent.[8] Even though he was only in his mid-twenties, Rosa was deeply disappointed with his progress in the eternal city. His comedy had brought him notoriety, but the reception of his pictures had not been enthusiastic enough for the ambitious artist. One work of this period, *Painting in the Wilderness*, now lost, expressed Rosa's disgust via an *ekphrasis* by his friend, poet Antonio Abati. The personification of Painting has fled the city and cast away her artist's tools because she can no longer endure the disrespect of the rabble or the elite. From now on, she declares, she will endeavor to please herself.[9]

Rosa's Self-Fashioning in Florence and the Cleveland Tondi

The four tondi of black magic scenes in the Cleveland Museum of Art (figures 6.2–6.5) probably constitute Rosa's earliest paintings in the witchcraft genre. They were mentioned by Francesco Bocchi in his *Bellezze della Firenze* (Beauties of Florence, 1677) as being in the Palace of the Marquis Giovanni Niccolini, who also owned a landscape now in the Methuen Collection, Corsham Court. We cannot assume a commission from Niccolini, however, for Rosa's favored practice was to display works in his studio for purchase,[10] and, as we shall see below, the pictures speak to artistic issues important to him. Two equally remarkable works from Rosa's Florentine period, pendant personifications of Philosophy and Poetry usually identified with Rosa and his mistress Lucrezia Paolino, a young artist's model whom he met soon after he arrived in Florence, were also owned by Niccolini: *Self-Portrait as a Philosopher* in the

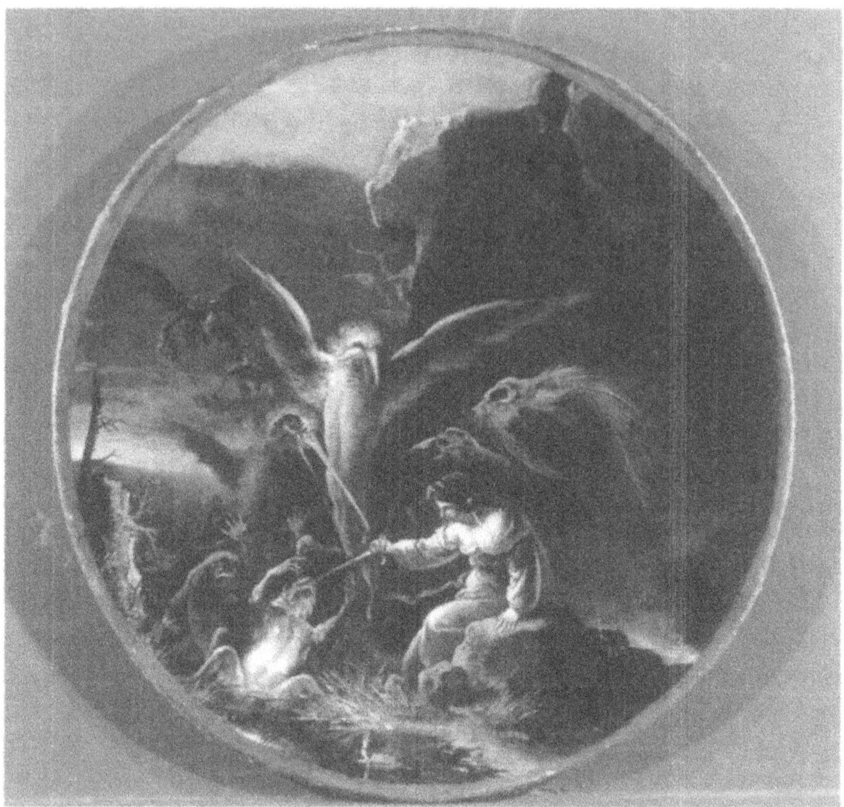

Figure 6.2. Salvator Rosa, *Scene with Witches: Morning*, mid-1640s. Oil on canvas, 54.5. cm diameter. © The Cleveland Museum of Art, 2004. Purchase from the J. H. Wade Fund, 1977.1.

National Gallery, London, and *Lucrezia as the Personification of Poetry* in the Wadsworth Atheneum, Hartford, Connecticut (figures 6.6 and 6.7).[11]

In the mid-1640s, Rosa was steeped in the heady Florentine atmosphere of art, poetry, and drama, and he cultivated the image of Cynic-Stoic philosopher and satiric poet expressed in the Niccolini pendants. In the Wadsworth painting, Lucrezia appears as the Muse of satiric poetry, scowling and disheveled; in the London picture, the figure of Philosophy takes on Rosa's swarthy, frowning countenance and presents an inscribed tablet. Its withering inscription, "Be silent, or say something better than silence" (AUT TACE AUT LOQUERE MELIORA SILENTIO), aligns Rosa, despite his loquaciousness, with ancient philosophers such as Zeno, Pythagoras, and Seneca who found virtue in brevity of speech.[12] Rosa's contemporary interest in witchcraft must be understood as part of this mocking vision of human folly that the artist-poet rises above with the proper use of brush or pen.

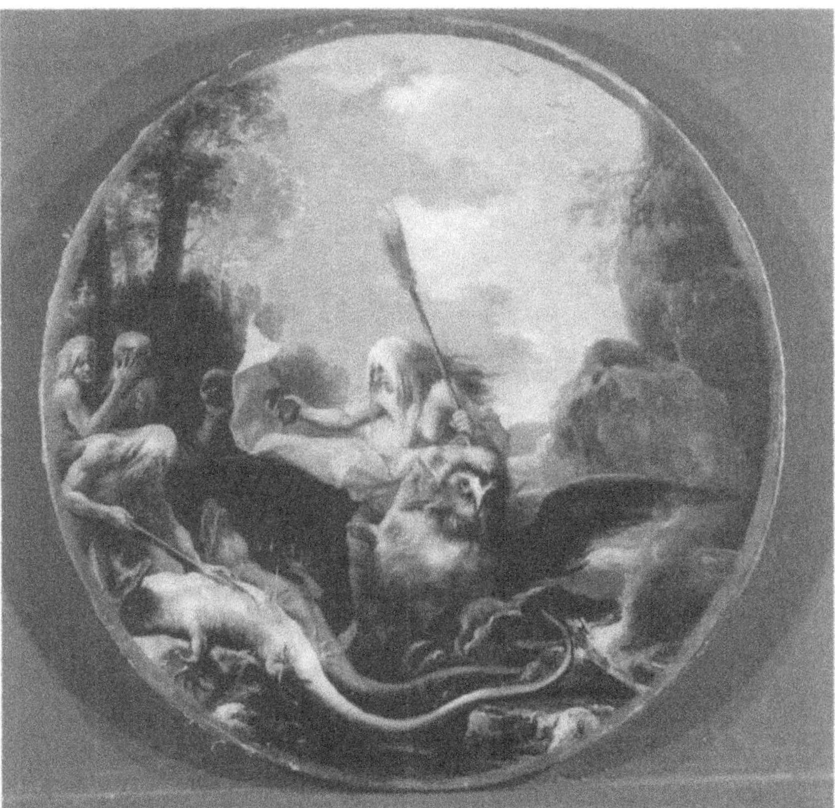

Figure 6.3. Salvator Rosa, *Scene with Witches: Day*, mid-1640s. Oil on canvas, 54.5 cm diameter. © The Cleveland Museum of Art, 2004. Purchase from the J. H. Wade Fund, 1977.2.

Rosa's witchcraft imagery includes the Cleveland tondi; an oval painting of witches and magicians in the Capitoline library; two drawings in the Metropolitan Museum of Art; a painting in the Corsini Collection in Florence (see figure 6.9); a seated witch pendant to a seated soldier, both owned by Cardinal Pio in Rome; and a spectacular painting in the National Gallery in London (see figure 6.10). Scholarship on these works has revealed more about the artistic and literary value Rosa invested in the theme than any precise connection to contemporary concerns about witchcraft. It is clear that Rosa intended his witchcraft paintings as satire, but who exactly was the target of his venom? Rosa wrote in *La poesia* (Poetry, ca. 1642), "Oh! take up the whip, close your eyes, and whoever gets hit gets hit: Let this uncouth rabble feel the scourge."[13] This "uncouth rabble," as we shall see, was likely to have comprised writers and artists, even though the buyers of such paintings, happy to have examples of Rosa's bizarre genius, may have been oblivious to their satirical undertones.

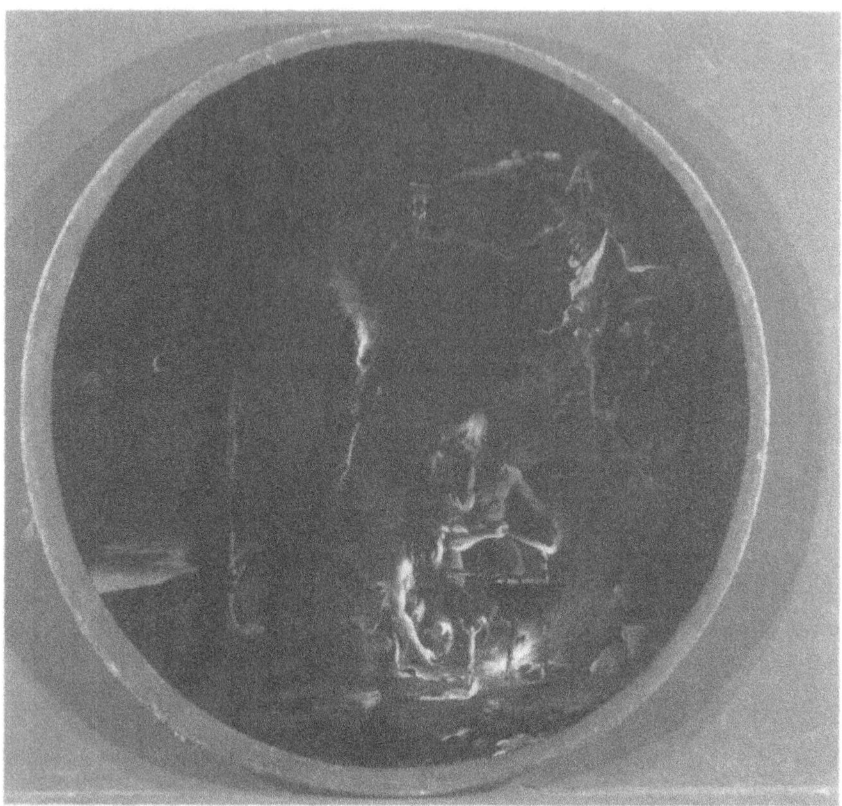

Figure 6.4. Salvator Rosa, *Scene with Witches: Evening*, mid-1640s. Oil on canvas, 54.5 cm diameter. © The Cleveland Museum of Art, 2004. Purchase from the J. H. Wade Fund, 1977.3.

As early efforts, the Cleveland tondi establish the iconographic parameters of Rosa's interest in witchcraft. Indeed, they constitute a typology of the subject. In these paintings, Rosa focused on four fundamental activities in black magic (transformation, levitation, love magic, and the invocation of demons). They also combine "high" examples of the black arts (*negromanzia*)—transformation of men into animals by a Circean figure and the invocation of demons by a male magician (see figures 6.2 and 6.5)—with "low" examples (*scongiurazioni*)—levitation and love magic performed by ignorant hags (see figures 6.3 and 6.4). They blend Italianate compositional and figurative traits with Rosa's knowledge of northern European witchcraft imagery, most likely transmitted through Albrecht Dürer's engraved *Witch* of about 1500 or Hans Baldung Grien's 1510 woodcut (see figures 3.4 and 3.5) and the engraving after Jacques de Gheyn II published by Nicolas de Clerck (ca. 1610; see figure 5.6). Once again, paradoxically, an artist built on these traditional sources to produce works announcing his inventiveness.

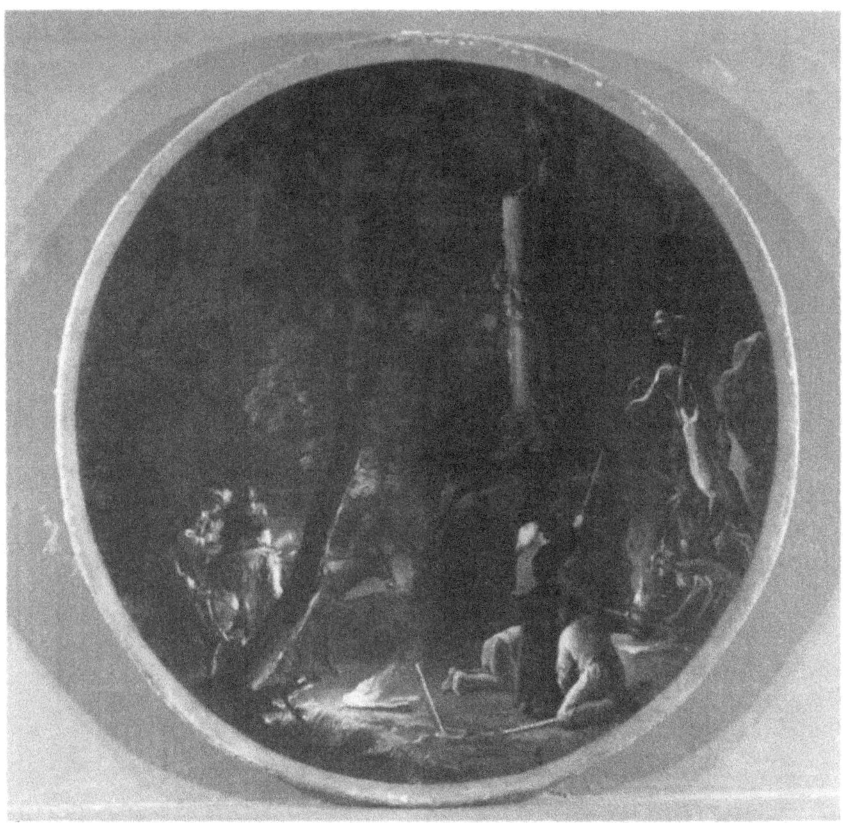

Figure 6.5. Salvator Rosa, *Scene with Witches: Night*, mid-1640s. Oil on canvas, 54.5 cm diameter. Photo © The Cleveland Museum of Art, 2004. Purchase from the J. H. Wade Fund, 1977.4.

With their references to classical literature and to Rosa's own contemporary poem, the tondi were clearly intended as visual counterparts to poetry. Their connection to contemporary demonological writings that made the intensive witch-hunting in areas of Europe during the seventeenth century possible is much less clear. Although, like most of his contemporaries, Rosa probably did not deny the possibility of witches and demons, there is no evidence to suggest that he, unlike Guido Reni (1575–1642) who had a neurotic fear of being bewitched,[14] was concerned with witchcraft. Rather, Rosa's engagement with witchcraft accomplished key goals related to his artistic and poetic self-fashioning in the 1640s.

Although the practice of magic was widespread in Italy as it was in the Iberian Peninsula, several factors worked there to lessen the number of executions and to avoid the devastating witch-hunts that characterized parts of northern Europe. The centralized control of the Roman and Spanish Inquisi-

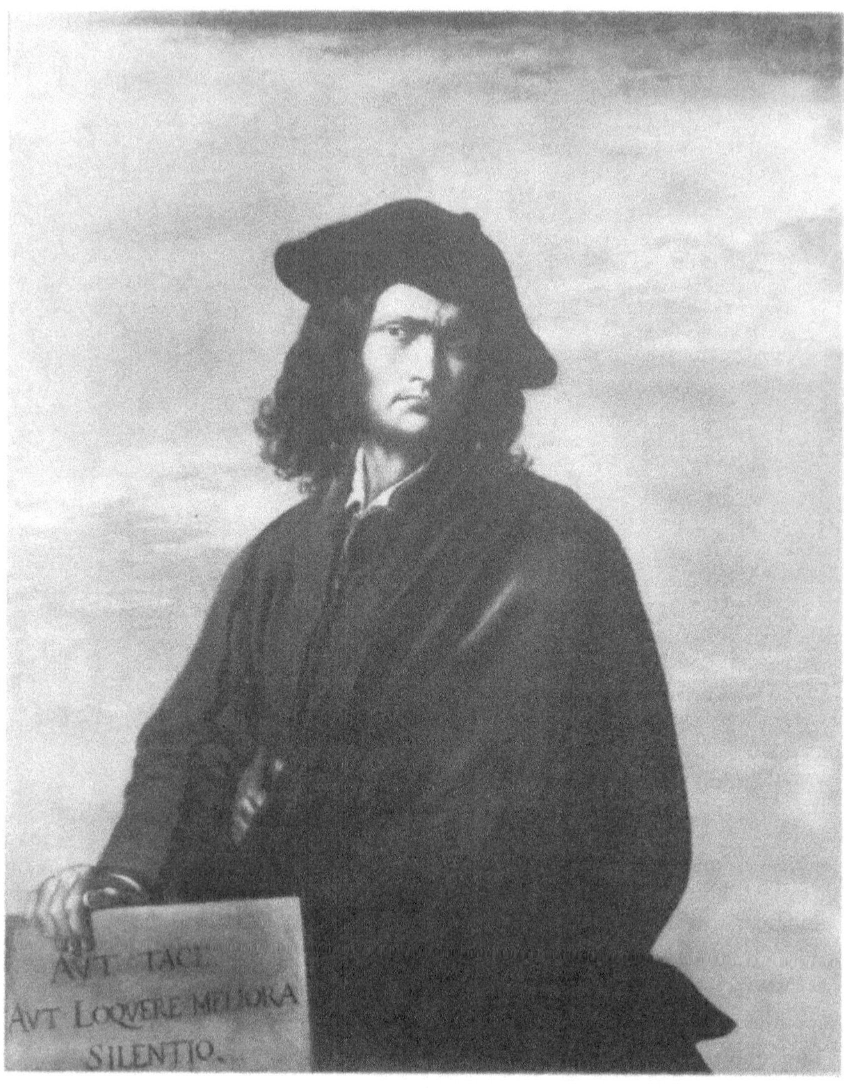

Figure 6.6. Salvator Rosa, *Self-Portrait as a Philosopher*, 1640s. Oil on canvas, 115 × 92 cm. National Gallery, London.

tions over crimes of magic meant that restrictions against the use of torture and the types of testimony accepted were stronger. Ironically, although the full-blown stereotype of witchcraft with the demonic pact and sabbath emerged from Dominican writings such as the *Malleus maleficarum* and had papal endorsement, it failed to take firm hold in Italy or the Iberian Peninsula as it did in northern Europe. Witchcraft was conceived much more in terms of the specific harms, or *maleficia*, with amatory magic and divination—both

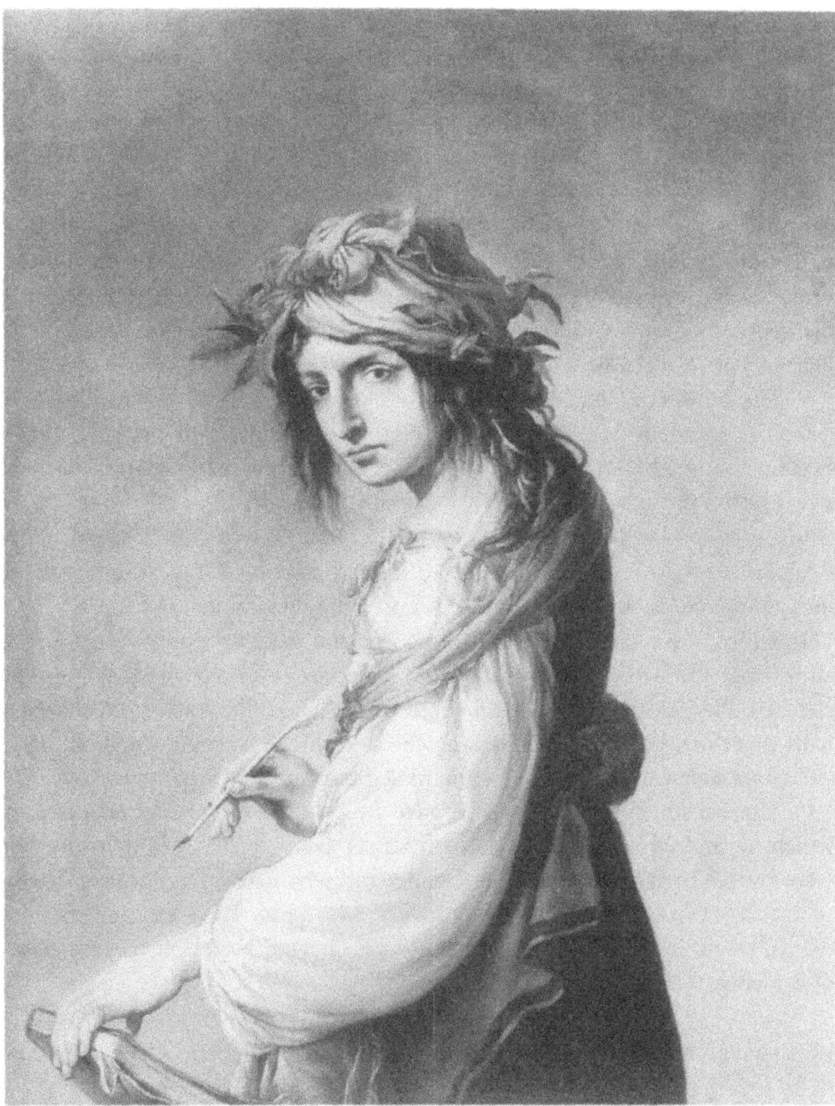

Figure 6.7. Salvator Rosa, *Lucrezia as the Personification of Poetry*, 1640s. Oil on canvas, 116 × 94 cm. Wadsworth Atheneum, Hartford, Conn. The Ella Gallup Sumner and Mary Catlin Sumner Collection Fund.

of which are featured prominently in Rosa's works—topping the list.[15] Also, the greater impact of classical concepts of witchcraft (most importantly, the figure of Circe) in the artistic tradition of Italy may have tempered the concept of the witch. In Rosa's Cleveland tondi, these classical concepts are blended with the more grotesque and horrific aspects of witchcraft depicted in northern European sources. As he tried to surpass the shock value of earlier works in slightly later paintings (see figures 6.9. and 6.10), Rosa dropped references to Circe and to the elite male magician, relying more fully on northern prototypes.

Prince Gian Carlo paid Rosa a smaller than normal salary, but in compensation agreed to allow him to live in his own quarters; already, Rosa, the reluctant courtier, was negotiating his independence. Gian Carlo became a cardinal in 1644 and dismissed Rosa by 1646, for what reasons we can only guess. Financially strapped and embittered by the "cancellation of my fortune," Rosa then moved between Florence and Volterra, where he stayed with his generous friend Giulio Maffei, a wealthy merchant, and his family until February 1649 when he and Lucrezia went to Rome.[16]

The context of late-Medici Florence of the 1640s and Rosa's efforts to establish an identity as a boldly satirical and independent artist and poet explain the witchcraft paintings. No longer a major artistic center, Florence nevertheless provided Rosa with the opportunity to shine as a painter of wild landscapes and battle scenes, as well as with noble collectors, whose patronage Rosa cultivated even as he attempted to maintain his financial and artistic independence. In this effort, he was uniquely determined and audacious.[17] Ultimately, Rosa came to resent his Florentine patrons' appreciation of his landscapes and battle scenes deeply, and his desire to be recognized for a more elevated allegorical and historical subject matter led him back to Rome, perhaps eager to compete with Poussin, who had gained a reputation as an intellectual painter with the kind of enlightened patrons that Rosa coveted.[18]

The decade spent in Florence gave Rosa an intellectual atmosphere in which he thrived on his contacts with artists, poets, actors, and patrons who were riveted by his works and his flamboyant personality. Florentine connoisseur and art historian, Filippo Baldinucci, who knew Rosa and collected his works, wrote in his *Notizie de' professori del disegno* (Notes on the professors of drawing, 1681–1728):

> [Rosa] found many such people at that time who were admirers of the work of his brush and of his new and charming manner of painting landscapes and marine views, which had certainly not been seen before in Italy; they were also attracted by his lively conversation and by the vivacity and, at the same time, by the grace of his arguments, which are hard to explain to those who never had personal experience of them; and so people flocked around him and considered themselves fortunate if they won a place among his intimates. He was often visited at home by cardinals and princes who wanted to see him at work. . . .[19]

The Florence of Grand Duke Ferdinando II de' Medici would have been attractive to any up-and-coming artist or intellectual interested in the latest scientific knowledge and artistic and literary trends. His brothers—Mattias, who handled the military affairs of the duchy; Leopoldo, who handled political affairs; and Gian Carlo, in charge of finance—all had their own courts offering opportunities for patronage. Edward Goldberg points out that the brothers' artistic interests overlapped and it is often difficult to determine which Medici was the intended recipient of purchases. The gifted Leopoldo was an antiquarian and a collector and patron of art, but his scholarly and scientific interests were just as remarkable. He represented the Medici in the *Accademia della Crusca* (Academy of the chaff, symbolized by a complex iconography of grain and flour), whose purpose was the preservation of the Tuscan language and fostering of Tuscan scholarship and literature. In the 1640s, Leopoldo joined Ferdinando in conducting and sponsoring scientific experiments with the hopes of disproving Aristotelian assumptions (because demonology was associated with scholasticism, satires of witchcraft might have appealed to this circle). In 1657, Ferdinando and Leopoldo's goals were solidified in the formation of the *Accademia del Cimento* (Academy of risk, or of the test). Adopting Galileo (whose disciples had tutored Leopoldo) as their hero, the *Cimento* nevertheless tried to avoid offending the church.[20]

Rosa himself organized an academy that gathered at his house: the *Accademia dei Percossi* (Academy of the smitten). Members included the scientist and mathematician Evangelista Toricelli; art collector and author Andrea Cavalcanti; John Milton's friend Carlo Dati (dubbed by Rosa as the "Plato of Florence" and also Vice Secretary of the *Crusca*); Venetian ambassador to Florence, Paolo Vendramin; composer of oratorios, Giovanni Filippo Apolloni; satirist Pietro Salvetti; poet and Cardinal Volunnio Bandinelli; secretary to Mattias de' Medici, Paolo Minucci; art dealer Francesco Cordini; and poet, playwright and longtime close friend of Rosa, Giovanni Battista Ricciardi. Almost certainly, Rosa's neighbor Lorenzo Lippi, poet and painter, was also included.[21] Lippi wrote a parody of Tasso's *Gerusalemme liberata* (Jerusalem liberated), *Il Malmantile racquistato* (Malmantile retaken), for which Paolo Minucci wrote a commentary. A central character in Lippi's poem is the grotesque witch Martinazza, who visits an inferno of gruesome design: the walls are covered with human skin, drink is served in skulls, skeletons hang from trees, and gibbets and statues made of mummies with heads of criminals ornament the garden. As Helen Langdon and others have noted, the mixture of comedy and horror in Lippi's poem is very close to the mood of Rosa's paintings.[22]

The elaborate dinners provided for the *Percossi* by Rosa were accompanied by various orations, and the Academy used the garden of Gian Carlo de' Medici's Casino to stage plays—dramas based on classical models and written by members of the *Percossi* and extemporaneous comedies using the stock characters of the *commedia dell' arte.*[23] Rosa posed for one self-portrait as the *commedia* character, Pascariello, a down-and-out gentleman-turned-servant.[24] By all accounts, Rosa was an outstanding comic actor, embellishing his dramatic performances or recitations of his own poetry with superb control of accent, gesture, and facial expression.[25] As head of the learned literary *Percossi*, Rosa promoted jocular humor and a rivalry of the burlesque. While evoking sensations of horror, Rosa's paintings of witches along with the poetic descriptions of witchcraft by himself and others were apparently taken as burlesque and grotesque examples of the painter or author's vivid inventive capacities. Within this circle of learned men, the frisson derived primarily from gruesome or scatological details. The prominence of love magic in Rosa's paintings as well as in *La strega* not only corresponds to the emphasis on this activity in Italian witchcraft beliefs, but also suggests the provocation of mock fear among his male audience. Who were the unsuspecting philanderers who would become targets of witches' amatory philters or spells of revenge?

The Cleveland tondo focusing on a beautiful Circean figure in a dawn landscape (figure 6.2), for instance, plays on the transformative and emasculating powers of this character in ancient and recent literature and art. The sword held by Rosa's protagonist points toward a huge frog spewing blood from its mouth, and oversized birds surround her: We are probably to understand these animals, following the ancient story of Circe's transformation of Odysseus's men into pigs, as transformed men. Dosso Dossi may have depicted Circe in a painting in the National Gallery in Washington (ca. 1511–12), probably produced for the Gonzaga court of Mantua, and in another in the Borghese Gallery in Rome (ca. 1515–16; figure 6.8), perhaps destined for the Este court in Ferrara.[26] Later, Rosa's contemporary Giovanni Benedetto Castiglione depicted Circe as a beautiful woman surrounded with animals in a landscape setting in drawings, paintings (the most famous of which is in the Pitti Palace in Florence), and in an etching dated in the early 1650s.[27]

Renaissance literature offered new incarnations of Circe—young witches with transforming powers whose exquisite beauty ensnares men while disguising the rotten, horrific appearance underneath their gorgeous facades. The classical witches in Dosso's Borghese and Washington paintings have been identified by some scholars as Circe and by others as Ludovico Ariosto's witch Alcina from *Orlando Furioso*, first published in 1516. For the Borghese work, possibly coinciding with the publication of *Orlando*, a plausible case has been made for Alcina's good counterpart, Melissa, who rescued knights from the transformed states in which Alcina put them, and restored their weapons (*Orlando Furioso* 8.14–15). The armor in the lower left of the Borghese painting, the soldiers in the middle ground, and the preoccupation of Duke Alfonso d'Este and the Ferrara court with Ariosto's poem, in which Melissa foretells the descent of the Este from Ruggiero and Bradamante (2.27), speak for the identification of the figure as Melissa. However, scholarly arguments surrounding her identity are compromised by the description of the painting in

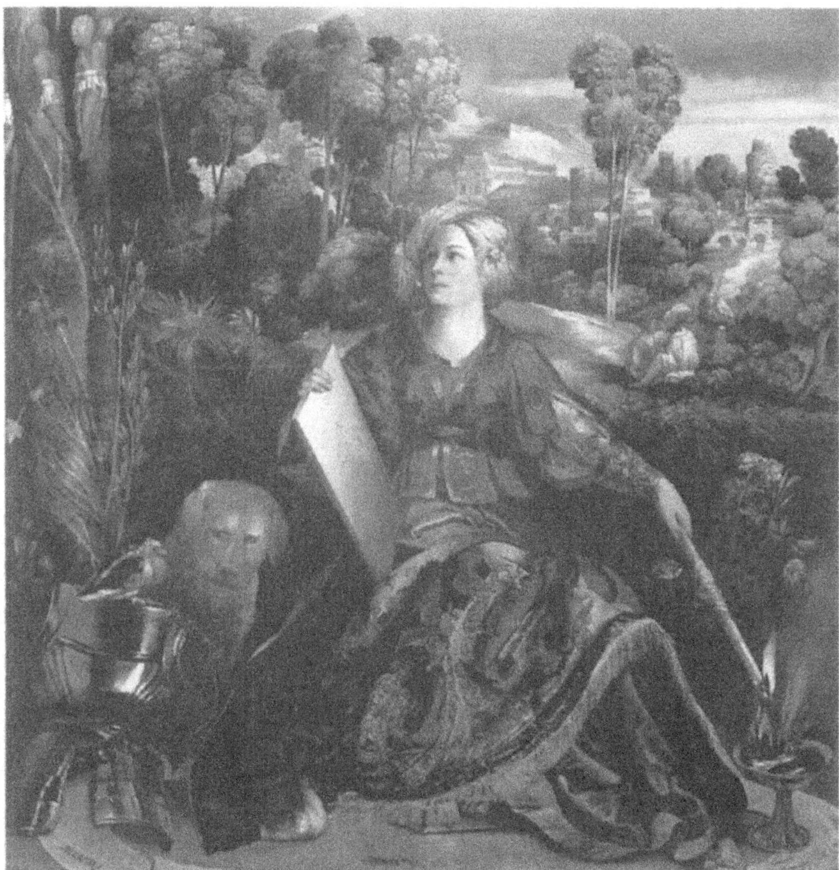

Figure 6.8. Dosso Dossi, *A Sorceress* (Melissa, Alcina, Circe?), ca. 1515–16. Oil on canvas, 176 × 174 cm. Borghese Gallery, Rome. Scala/Art Resource, New York.

seventeenth- and eighteenth-century documents as a sorceress casting spells or even as Circe herself.[28]

It is very likely that Dosso's figure is poetic and evocative rather than specific, in the Giorgionesque tradition: X-ray evidence shows that an armored man once stood where the dog is now.[29] Like Rosa's figure, she is Circean, and her provocative effect depends on the danger lurking in her beauty. Above all, she is a beautiful woman whose power, although benevolent in Melissa's case, is nevertheless dangerous and transgressive and requires containment precisely because it is located in a woman.[30] As she casts her spell, Dosso's sorceress glances toward manikins—looking brown, dried, and vaguely phallic—strapped to a tree. One holds his tiny hand up as if frozen in the act of imploring her. The manikins have been taken as Melissa's knights in an intermediate state of transformation,[31] but if the main figure is read generally as a sorceress, the manikins are more ominous. Indeed, they resemble the wax figurines or mandrake roots seen in images of love magic (clearly visible in figures 6.4 and 6.10) or they could be men victimized by female sorcery. In either case, the message to male viewers would have been to urge caution in the face of beauty: Gareth Roberts points out that Andrea Alciati's emblem of Circe (1621) read "*Cavendum a meretricibus*" (One must beware of whores).[32]

Rosa's Circe tondo must be understood also in conjunction with figure 6.3, in which the similarly posed main figure is a hideous hag of northern descent. If not convinced by the ambivalence of Circe herself, Rosa's audience could acknowledge the possibility of one form of witch changing into the other—of the classical witch inspiring the modern, of beauty disguising horror. The story of Circe was indeed used by some demonologists as proof of the existence of contemporary witches and their power to transform.[33] Perhaps more significant, however, was Circe's overall symbolic meaning for the Renaissance and Baroque periods. She or her various incarnations appear regularly in court festivals as threats to divinely ordained royal power and are banished by the same.[34] As Roberts asserts, the fascination with Circean figures in Renaissance literature is ultimately rooted in the problematic relationship between pleasure and virtue, and the male fear of loss of authority and reason.[35] The beautiful witch—Tasso's Armida, Ariosto's Alcina, Spenser's Acrasia—tempts the hero, emasculating him by immersing him in sensual delights, as Circe rendered him ridiculous by transforming him into an animal, until her true nature is uncovered and he is restored to manly reason and virtue. The lush passages of Spenser's *Faerie Queene* in which Acrasia ensnares the hapless Verdant in the Bower of Bliss (*Faerie Queene* 2.12, 42–87) are the most brilliant example of the Circean narrative in Renaissance literature. In the end, Acrasia is brutally chained by the Palmer and Guyon (i.e., sensuality is subjected to the bonds of reason and temperance).[36] In *Orlando Furioso*, Ariosto's formidably seductive Alcina makes Ruggiero her helpless love-slave until, through Melissa's intervention and a magic ring that restores his reason, her true appearance is revealed. Alcina becomes "a woman so hideous that her equal for ugliness and decrepitude could be found nowhere on earth. She was whey-faced, wrinkled, and hollow-cheeked; her hair was white and sparse; she was not four feet high; the last tooth had dropped out of her jaw; and she had lived longer than anyone on earth, longer than Hecuba or the Cumaean Sibyl" (*Orlando Furioso* 7.70–74). Ariosto explicitly attributed Ruggiero's rescue from the clutches of Alcina to the restoration of reason by the ring: "You [sorcerers and sorceresses] work your magic not by virtue of obedient sprites or by conning the stars for signs: by trickery, lies, and dissimulation you bind the hearts of others with knots that cannot be untied. Those of us who possessed Angelica's ring—I mean the ring of Reason—could descry each person's true face, undisguised by cunning artifice" (*Orlando Furioso* 8.1).

The hag of figure 6.3 is the true face of Circe in figure 6.2, "undisguised by cunning artifice." Her flight conjures up the most scurrilous and controversial of witches' activities: the orgiastic sabbath. Although Rosa's old witch, now in a daylight landscape, rides an owl instead of a he-goat and carries a broom, she is nevertheless a recognizable descendant of Dürer's witch (figure 3.4). The owl certainly recalls ancient literature as well, including Pamphile's own transformation into an owl in Apuleius' *Golden Ass* or *Metamorphoses* (2.22), and Ovid's association of owls with evil and vampirism of children (*Fasti* 6.131–34).[37] Her companions at the left hold up skulls, evidence of the murder or nefarious use of corpses to attain flight, and disembowel crocodiles. The main witch offers up a dripping, reddish-brown organ, possibly a liver. As the seat of imagination, sexual passion, and "feminine corporeality," in Mark Breitenburg's words, the liver was opposed to the ethereal masculine brain, which had to regulate its production of fluids. It functioned as an aphrodisiac, as in Horace's *Epode* 5 about Canidia's torture of the Thracian boy by starvation, in part to obtain his liver for spells (lines 42–44).[38]

As in the much more intricately choreographed levitation rituals of Baldung's witchcraft drawings and his famous 1510 woodcut that Rosa certainly knew—perhaps through Italian copies, such as a reversed engraving by Lucantonio de' Uberti (1516)—the main purpose of this collective activity might be to get the central witch off the ground. As we have seen, although explicitly labeled as a delusion in canon law, bodily flight and the physical reality of the sabbath were intensely questioned and debated early on in the development of the witchcraft stereotype. Only briefly mentioned in the *Malleus*, these had become routine features in demonological literature by Rosa's time. In Italy, as elsewhere, bodily sabbath flight and its attendant concepts were not universally accepted. As discussed in Chapter 2, in the early sixteenth century Gianfrancesco Pico della Mirandola confirmed the reality of bodily flight in his dialogue, *Strix* (The witch, 1523), translated into Italian the following year. About the same time, however, north Italian lawyer Gianfranceso Ponzinibio argued in his *Tractatus de lamiis* (Treatise on witches, 1520) that witchcraft, including the sabbath flight, was a delusion. Belief in bodily flight and the reality of the sabbath was not a given: It had to be nurtured, promoted, or coerced. Carlo Ginzburg demonstrated that the Inquisitors who prosecuted the Friulian peasants for heresy in the late sixteenth and early seventeenth centuries had to transform their harmless belief in dreaming, night-flying *benandanti* ("well-farers") into the myth of the bodily sabbath flight.[39] The demonological treatises of the late sixteenth and early seventeenth centuries, insisting on the physical reality of the flight and the sabbath, belie a deep reservoir of skepticism. The humanistic tradition with which Rosa was aligned often resisted the ideas promulgated by the witch-hunters.[40]

By introducing the theme of the Düreresque flying witch into his series,

Rosa emphasized his knowledge of northern European witchcraft imagery, in which this motif is absolutely central. And, like artists before him, Rosa understood the implications of witches' flight for suggestively escalating the frisson generated by his images. Because flight not only implied the devil worship, sexual taboos, and cannibalism associated with the sabbath, it also brought to mind the horrific contents of the levitation ointment, whose base was baby-fat. Figure 6.3 would have combined powerfully with figure 6.2 to suggest to Rosa's audience the grotesque horror underlying Circe's beautiful facade.

This is not to say, however, that Rosa took demonological concepts such as the flying ointment and sabbath orgy as truths; indeed, his rebellious and sarcastic nature might have favored a pronounced resistance to these beliefs. We can perhaps gauge his own attitude toward the issue of flight as well as other claims of the demonologists from that of his closest friend, Ricciardi, writer of comedies and burlesque poetry and later a Reader in Moral Philosophy at the University of Pisa. Rosa was in close contact with Ricciardi in Florence between 1640 and 1649 and continued an intimate correspondence with him until his death. In a letter of 1652 to an unknown recipient, Ricciardi gave a list of treatises dealing with magic, including Neapolitan Giambattista della Porta's *Magia naturalis, sive de miraculis rerum naturalium* (Natural magic, or whether miracles are natural events, 1558), and Leonardo Vairo's *De fascino* (On casting spells, 1589). Ricciardi singled out Martín Del Rio's treatise on magic, discussed in Chapter 4, as offering a particularly complete account of magical activities. Ricciardi's attitude toward such subject matter is summed up at the end of the letter by the phrase "*diversi capricci*" (diverse caprices).[41] He seems to view magic primarily as an interesting curiosity. Similarly, Rosa found in magic and witchcraft a pictorial resource that suited his relentless quest for "singular and extravagant material" which Ricciardi, as a humanistic advisor to the painter, tried his best to supply.[42]

That Rosa appropriated witchcraft in an effort to align painting with poetry and to appear as a satiric, inventive genius becomes more evident in the two remaining Cleveland tondi. If Circe is contrasted with the old witch on the owl, then the grotesque female witches performing love magic are contrasted with an ostensibly dignified male magician, surrogate for the artist-poet, in these two paintings. Figure 6.4, an evening scene, closely evokes Rosa's own *La strega*, set to music by his lifelong friend, leading composer Marcantonio Cesti, for whom Rosa sometimes wrote lyrics.[43] Both the poem and painting echo narratives of love magic from ancient literature. Rosa's witch Phyllis has been rejected by a lover and vows to take revenge by black magic: The forces of hell will move him if heaven has not. The most effective section of the poem is the marvelous list of ingredients for her spell:

A magic ring,
Icy streams,

Fish of sorts,
Alchemic draughts,
Black balsam,
Ground powders,
Mystic gems,
Snakes and owls,
Stinking blood,
Oozing guts,
Dried mummies,
Bones and grubs,
Fumigations
that will blacken,
Horrid cries
that terrify. . . .

The English lacks the poetic rhythms of the Italian, which form a mesmerizing incantation:

mago circolo,
onde gelede,
pesci varij,
acque chimiche,
neri balsami,
miste polveri,
pietre mistiche,
serpi, e nottole,
sangue putridi,
molli viscere,
secche mummie,
ossa, e vermini,
suffumigij,
ch'anneriscano,
voci horribile
che spaventino. . . .[44]

Rosa's verbal evocation of the heterogeneous, often revolting elements of the witch's practice is analogous to the messy visual piles of discrepant paraphernalia in his own and other artists' images, a quintessential anticlassical device that Tiepolo would perfect in his *Capricci* and *Scherzi* series.[45]

Phyllis's magic culminates in the burning of a wax figure of her lover along with a cypress, the moment evidently depicted in the tondo. Two companions, one holding a mirror to the cauldron, assist her, as well as two of the "mob of hell" (*la turba inferna*) she has called down. The largest demon is a fantastic skeletal monster derived from the *Indian Cock* etching in the series of animal skeletons by Filippo Napoletano (1620–21). It is also reminiscent of the various fantastic monsters and demons of northern prints from Martin Schongauer to Jacques Callot: a tradition that appealed greatly to the Florentine context in which Callot worked for part of his career, as discussed in Chapter 2. He is swathed in a bright red drapery and holds an hourglass and architect's plumb line that emphasize the preposterous precision and timing necessary for the spell. The firelight, torch, and burning cypress illuminate the witches' bodies and the demon's draperies with a flickering brilliance—metaphor for the witch's burning love, now turned to burning hatred.

Rosa's tondo and poem have a close affinity to ancient tales of love magic, especially to Theocritus's *Pharmaceutria*, a beautiful poem suffused with moonlight and lovesick reverie, in which the seduced Simaetha with the help of an assistant, Thestylis, seeks to bind her lover Delphis through magic. That having failed, she vows to murder him with poisons. In Virgil's eighth *Eclogue*, the lovesick Alphesiboeus with the help of Amaryllis uses magic rites "to turn to fire my lover's coldness of mood" (lines 66–67). Both poems, among other acts, involve the burning of wax dolls, as does Horace's famous eighth *Satire* from Book I. The burlesque mood of this last poem would have appealed greatly to Rosa and his Academy. The attempts of the witches Canidia and Sagana to conjure the spirits of the dead in a burial ground on the Esquiline Hill are witnessed by a wooden statue of Priapus with a large crack in his posterior—the source of a loud fart that banishes the witches at the end of the poem. Throughout the poem, the ineffectual, shrieking witches are objects of ridicule; in the end, Canidia loses her teeth; Sagana's high wig falls down, and the herbs and love knots fall from their arms (lines 47–50).

In contrast to the grotesque witches of Rosa's love-magic tondo, the male protagonist of figure 6.5 is an ostensibly noble figure, holding a wand and closely resembling Moses Striking the Rock. Deep in a midnight landscape with a barely visible moon, he invokes a crowd of distinctly Boschian demons while two mounted soldiers who have apparently stumbled upon this scene look on in fascination. Clearly Rosa intended to contrast the learned male magician of the Neoplatonic tradition with the coarse female witches performing amatory magic with the help of charms, incantations, and even demons. In contemporary Italian terms, the distinction is between the high art of necromancy (*negromanzia*) and the nonacademic, corrupt attempt to invoke demonic spirits, conjuration (*scongiurazione*).[46]

These class and gender distinctions are important. Indeed, practitioners of learned magic were often skeptical of witch-hunting precisely on the grounds that witchcraft was a delusion of ignorant old peasant women (as opposed to their own learned or mystical attempts to use hidden natural forces). We are reminded of Cornelius Agrippa's defense of an accused witch in 1519, based on the idea of witchcraft as a delusion influenced by a "vehement libido." Perhaps more important for Rosa as a Neapolitan would have been della Porta's experiments to prove that the sabbath was a delusion induced by the natural components of the flying unguent, published in *Magia naturalis*, with which Ricciardi was familiar.[47] We may be justified, then, in seeing a gendered and classed contrast of "high" with "low" in Rosa's tondi that banishes uneducated women (in effect, most women) from the intellectual and creative realms. In Rosa's satire *Invidia* (Envy, 1654), the artist must seek out the secrets of nature as rigorously as the magician: "If you look at the books of Vasari you will see that of the painters, the best ones are famous for their poetry. And not only were these painters poets, but also great philosophers, and were demons in seeking out the great secrets of nature."[48] Rosa, satirist to the core, was aware of the ambiguity of the male magician, understood as surrogate for the poet or artist, and warned his primary audience of male literati of the moral dangers associated with the exercise of imagination. It might be significant that Rosa's signatures in the Cleveland tondi are closely aligned with all the performers of magic but especially with the necromancer: As poet and artist, Rosa implicated himself and his fellow poets and artists in this moral danger.

The male magician in Renaissance and Baroque literature ultimately derived from the Celtic and medieval legends of Merlin and was complicated by the Renaissance tradition of Neoplatonic magic. In deference to Christianity and despite Merlin's father having been an incubus (!), Geoffrey of Monmouth's (1100–ca. 1154) account of the benevolent magician has him acting without demonic pact. Similarly, the "natural magic" of the Renaissance Neoplatonic tradition, it was argued, had no necessary consort with demons. But because the natural forces magicians attempted to manipulate included demonic spirits, natural magic was ultimately difficult to defend in an atmosphere of increasing concern about demonic interference in human affairs. Although based on the same assumptions about the interconnectedness of natural phenomena and the descent of spiritual influences into the heavenly world, thence to earth, natural and demonic magic were distinguished morally by the presence or absence of demonic intervention.[49]

Like the magician, the poet or artist must also choose to use his transforming powers for good or ill because his imagination and *invenzione* are also vulnerable to demonic influence. In Spenser's *Faerie Queene*, Merlin's main creation is a magic mirror that, like good poetry, reflects only the truth. In contrast, Spenser's black magicians such as Archimago abuse their powers of magic and language to deceive and delude; Archimago's tongue was filed as smooth as glass (*Faerie Queene* 1.1.35). In Ariosto's *Orlando Furioso*, Merlin is more specifically a symbol of the visual artist who commands demons to raise a painted dining hall for King Paramond (33.4). The prophetic paintings predict a war and are compared to ancient works of art and the masterpieces of Renaissance Italy (33.1–2).[50]

For Ariosto, however, magicians could also be comic characters—for example, Jachelino as described by his servant Nibbio in Act 1, scene 2 of the play, *Il negromante* (The necromancer, 1520):

My master, Jachelino, certainly has great confidence in himself; for while he hardly knows how to read and write, he nevertheless professes to be a philosopher, an alchemist, a doctor, an astrologer, a magician, and even a conjurer of spirits. Although he's called the Astrologer/par excellence, just as Vergil is known as the Poet and Aristotle as the Philosopher, /he knows as much about these and other sciences as a donkey or an ox knows about playing an organ. But with a face as motionless as marble, with stories and lies, and no other skills, he swindles people and confounds their minds. Thus, he benefits and makes me benefit from the world of others—with the help of folly, which abounds in the world.

Thus Rosa's magician (poet-artist) could be interpreted as the learned counterpart of the ignorant, deluded witch, but he was also subject to negative interpretation. In particular, the greed embodied by Ariosto's Jachelino was anathema to Rosa, who disdained wealth rhetorically if not actually. In *The Genius of Salvator Rosa* (see figure 6.1), the genius figure holds an overturned cornucopia to symbolize a Stoic-Cynic indifference to wealth, expressed in the inscription by the phrase "*Spretor opum*," despiser of wealth).[51] The false poets and artists who might be symbolized by the charlatan magician would be the object of Rosa's satirical darts in the poems on poetry and painting, *Poesia* (1642) and *Pittura* (1650). Within his Florentine audience, there were many who could have been the targets of Rosa's moralizing warning about the proper use of the poet or artist's gifts, even if they were the artist's esteemed friends. Rosa also saw himself as Diogenes, who reportedly said, "Other dogs bite their enemies; I bite my friends, for their salvation."[52]

Rosa's choice of Diogenes as an alter ego is telling. The legendary Cynic philosopher's contempt for luxury and his outspoken disregard for convention—all to expose the follies of society and advance an ideal of self-sufficiency and autonomy—fit Rosa's obstreperous personality like a glove. The disadvantage of such a paradigm for an early modern artist was the loss of steady patronage and protection that subservience and conventionality could bring: By his dependent relationship to patrons, the courtier-artist or poet was feminized. The bellicose paradigm, however, dovetailed with masculine ideals. All Diogenes's biting dogs were male. To understand the intensity of Rosa's blustering, we must recall the gendered nature of early modern artistic discourse. Rosa's battles over matters of artistic and poetic form constituted a defense of his integrity and manhood as an artist. The wonderful Niccolini pendants, allegorical portraits of Rosa as a Philosopher and Lucrezia as the Personification or Muse of Poetry (see figures 6.6 and 6.7), also reveal the degree to which Rosa's self was constructed in gendered terms. While Lucrezia—lovely, glowering, and unkempt—*inspires* her lover's satiric poetry, Rosa *is* the stern figure of the Stoic philosopher, clad solemnly in black and silhouetted heroically against the sky. The dismissive Latin inscription emasculates his rivals by telling them to shut up. The self-construction that Rosa forged in Florence was developed in a context of artistic rivalry in which, Philip Sohm has argued, style constituted self, and stylistic controversies were colossal battles among great men.[53]

Witches as Artists: The Corsini and London Paintings

In Rosa's subsequent witchcraft paintings (figures 6.9 and 6.10), he dropped references to the classical Circe and minimized the presence of the male magician in favor of northern European motifs, signaling his increasing interest in the satiric potential of the theme. A canvas bought by the Marchese Bartolomeo Corsini for sixty *scudi*, a moderate but not paltry sum,[54] reiterates the skeletal apparition of figure 6.4, and the witches' attention also focuses on the magic paraphernalia at the center of the picture. This work was copied at least twice, a fact testifying to its novelty.[55] The Niccolini tondo on love magic is expanded here to include a full cast of shrieking hags who converge energetically on the spell being performed at the center of the picture. A preparatory drawing for the painting in the Metropolitan Museum shows that the kneeling figure at the right was originally conceived as a monk.[56] Rosa's decision to replace that figure with a female witch is probably an indication of exactly how scandalous such depictions were seen to be, even in Florence. Indeed, clerics made up 40 percent of the accusations of witchcraft in Venice between 1550 and 1650, the period analyzed by Ruth Martin. Their interest usually lay in invoking demons to seek treasure.[57]

Witches at their Incantations (Baldinucci's title), now in the National Gallery, London, formerly in the collection of Lord Spencer at Althorp, originally belonged to Carlo de' Rossi, Rosa's loyal Roman friend and patron, who bought the work in Florence around 1646. Rosa could always count on de' Rossi, a merchant and banker, as an obliging supporter whose generosity gained him "two rooms full of landscapes, those dark country views, full of witches, and a thousand other fantasies of that great virtuoso, as well as life-size figures."[58] For the London picture, we have Rosa's testimony as to its value in a letter of 1666 to Ricciardi: "Of the one about witches, its length is two *braccia* and a fourth, and the height one and a little over a half. His present was worth fifteen *doble*, and it is now twenty years since I made it. Anytime that Mr. Rossi wants to dispose of it, he could get four hundred *scudi*; and I have predicted to him that after I die the price will be a thousand *scudi*, since it goes beyond the limits of the curious, and therefore is shown last, and is kept covered by a taffeta cloth. . . ."[59] This spectacular picture certainly vindi-

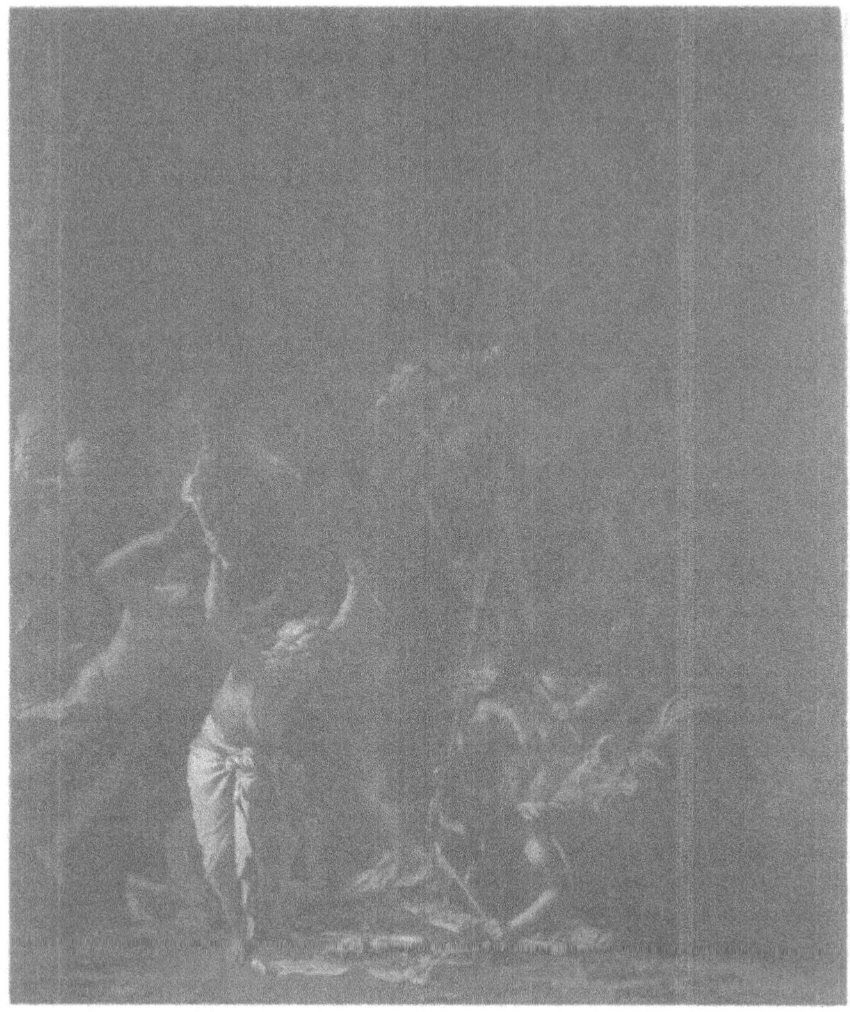

Figure 6.9. Salvator Rosa, *Scene of Witchcraft*, mid-1640s. Oil on canvas, 76 × 65 cm. Corsini Collection, Florence. Scala/Art Resource, New York.

cates Rosa's evaluation as the rare pièce de résistance of the collection, to be presented as a kind of grand finale.

Considered so bizarre that it needed to be covered by a curtain to avoid offending certain visitors, especially clergy, the image centers on the repulsive unguent stirred by a fat witch taken directly from de Gheyn's engraving (see figure 5.6; note the bones used as stirring implements). From the central dead tree hangs a corpse fumigated by one witch and robbed of his toenails by another. To the left of center, witches use a wax manikin and mirror to perform love magic. Further to the left, necromancers raise a skeleton from a cof-

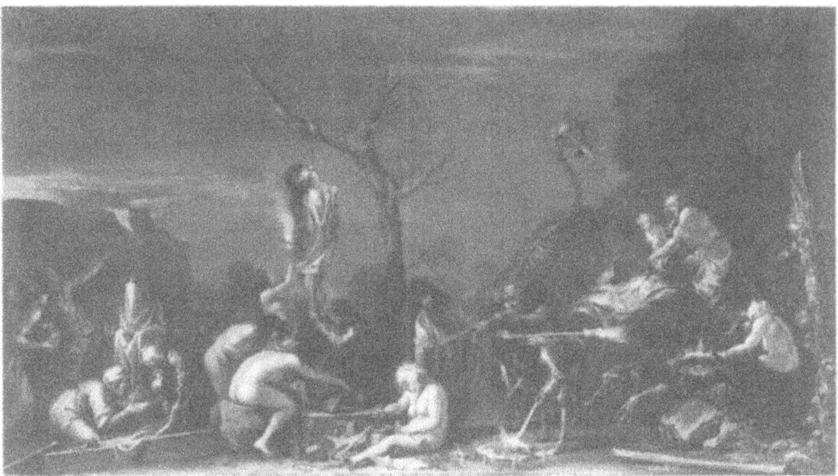

Figure 6.10. Salvator Rosa, *Witches at Their Incantations*, ca. 1646. Oil on canvas, 72.5 × 132.5 cm. National Gallery, London.

fin as a ghostly figure with covered face (to protect his identity?) holds a ring of candles. To the right of center, a soldier and a wreathed figure (a poet?) seem to collaborate on a spell involving a white rabbit in a magic circle, a broom, and a heart, plucked off a sword held by a magician. At the right is a diabolic procession reminiscent of *Lo stregozzo* (see figure 2.3) with a hag carrying a child for sacrifice. At the lower right, a witch rides a demon looking much like the one lurking beneath St. Margaret in Hugo van der Goes's *Portinari Altarpiece* in Florence (Uffizi, 1474). Full of quotations from his own and others' works—as if to drive home the function of these motifs as signs of invention—the painting is indeed a collection of *diversi capricci*, and cannot be read as a single event such as a sabbath (compare the fold-out engraving from Pierre de Lancre's treatise, figure 4.1). It also lacks the turbulent atmosphere that lends unity to the prodigious detail in de Gheyn's engraving or Francken's paintings (compare especially figure 4.2); its additive episodes need to be "read" from left to right.[60] There is a hint here of the motley groupings of figures focused on enigmatic magical activities of Giovanni Battista Tiepolo's etchings a century later (see figure 6.14).

Rosa's stylistic and compositional choices here are pointedly anticlassical to match the grotesque and scatological subject matter. And, as Sohm makes clear, seventeenth-century artistic style resonated with moral and cultural meaning. Rosa's *tenebroso* lighting cuts through figural integrity; his composition is an aggregate of incongruous building-blocks, defying an Albertian model in which the artist, gifted with *ingenium*, composes a meaningful unity by means of his understanding of beauty, decorum, narrative, and naturalistic illusion. In contrast, Sohm observes, Baldinucci, in his *Vocabulario degli Accademici della Crusca*, which expanded the *Crusca*'s Tuscan dictionary with artistic terms, defined composition loosely as a "combination and mix of things"—terms that suggested indiscriminate mixture and confusion. Critics of compositional heterogeneity and fragmentation, Sohm suggests, used style to bemoan the state of Italian culture. They tended to be historians, literary critics, and theologians; defenders of works like Rosa's tended to be artists and patrons.[61]

Wendy Wassyng Roworth interprets the Corsini and London pictures in part as Rosa's satires on the *Bamboccianti*.[62] In his satirical poem, *Pittura*, Rosa also lambasted these painters for their concentration on what he interpreted as vulgar trivia:

street porters, ragamuffins, petty thieves
vineyards and carts, limekilns and hostelries
a crowd of drunken sots and greedy-guts
gypsies, tobacco-touts and stable boys,
mudlarks, eavesdroppers and day-labourers,
activities like catching bugs and fleas
or dishing out porkpies to the canailles,
or pissing, shitting, selling tripe for cats,
or making music fit to wake the dead,
or patching broken pots or backless shoes. . . .[63]

By such satirical means, it seems, Rosa expurgated his own background, for he was known for such pictures even at the time of his impolitic mocking, recounted by Passeri, of Bernini's staging for *Chi soffre, speri* through the character of Formica: "I don't want us to act comedies like some people who spread dirt about all and sundry, because, in due course, you can see that the dirt spreads faster than the poet's ink. And I don't want us to bring on stage couriers, brandy-sellers, goatherds and rubbish of that sort, which are the folly of an ass."[64] Much to his dismay, collectors who favored *Bambocciate* also collected his own paintings (for example, the Corsini of Florence).

There is much irony here, of course. In describing the vulgar trivia of the *Bamboccianti* in the verses above, Rosa uses a verbal heterogeneity as well as scatology. At the level of style, there is not much to distinguish the "rubbish" of Rosa's witchcraft pictures and that of the painters he excoriates. At the level of subject matter, however, there is a difference. Not only were witches as a theme sanctioned by the ancient poets, but they also had an erudite pedigree in the early modern period that no ragamuffin, tripe-seller, or goatherd could compete with. Moreover, the conceptual analogy between sympathetic magic and artistic mimesis that forms the core of Roworth's argument elevates the subject through allegory. Like the *Bamboccianti*, the witches and magicians in

Rosa's Corsini and London paintings (and possibly in the Cleveland tondi as well) seek to "out-do nature with their waxen images and mirrors, anatomies, animals and recipes."[65] The mirror in particular, held as a symbol of self-knowledge in preliminary versions of the toga-clad figure of Stoic Equability in the *Genius* etching (see figure 6.1), is used in these paintings to reflect ephemera like boiling cauldrons or melting wax figurines.[66] Without the proper knowledge, the misguided efforts of witches and charlatan magicians are doomed to failure, just as the *Bamboccianti* produce nothing of significance, no paintings worthy of the gilded frames that hold them.[67] Witchcraft is a degraded magic performed largely by ignorant women and false magicians who mistakenly believe they understand and command nature; *Bambocciate* are similarly based on a false understanding of nature and ignorance of the philosophical and moral content for which Rosa sought recognition. In this sense, we might read the satire of all these paintings more broadly in terms of any artist's or poet's proper use of their creative powers. Roworth also implies that Rosa satirized witchcraft beliefs themselves by treating them in the same facetious, burlesque tone as Horace portrayed Canidia and Sagana.[68]

It is doubtful that Rosa had any deep knowledge of the intellectual arguments surrounding witchcraft and its persecution. More likely, Ricciardi transmitted these arguments to him. Rosa probably would not have had the patience to plumb the pages of demonological and skeptical texts; he was known more for his breadth and glibness. Passeri's comment comes to mind: "When people were talking about the maxims of learned subjects and sciences, he [Rosa] never went in for detail but kept to broad generalities and, when he recognized the right occasion, he plunged into the midst of things and made his contribution in a way that showed that he was not a *tabula rasa* and he did this with great skill."[69] Rosa seems to have appropriated the theme of witchcraft so thoroughly into his self-fashioning as a satiric and an inventive artist-poet during the last half of his Florentine period that issues and concerns inherent in witchcraft beliefs were subsumed under this process.

So, while we can perceive contemporary intellectual and religious positions on witchcraft—one emerging from the emphasis on tolerance and restraint in liberal Dutch circles; the other emerging from an urgent Counter-Reformation Catholicism—underneath the artistic swagger of de Gheyn's and Francken's images, no such deep intellectual engagement underlies Rosa's images of witches and magicians. It is also significant that he was not a religious man; he utterly lacked the intense religiosity of many of his artistic contemporaries such as Bernini or Reni. And, although he had friends and patrons from the clergy, Rosa had an anticlerical streak that we have seen in the preparatory drawing for the Corsini picture and that also emerges in his letters.

Rosa engaged with the artistic questions raised by the subject of witchcraft and with the masculine rivalry of self and style in which it served as a weapon. We are moving closer to an eighteenth-century notion of the *capriccio* in which subject matter is secondary to the liberty of the artist or, perhaps more accurately, his liberty in the form of fantastic invention *becomes* subject matter. In short, witchcraft was part of a role performed by a master thespian on the stage of Florentine intellectual society in the 1640s. I might borrow from Stephen Greenblatt who asserts, in his important essay, "Shakespeare and the Exorcists," that "performance kills belief; or rather acknowledging theatricality kills the credibility of the supernatural."[70]

Envy, Fortune, and Honor: Rosa's Late Career in Rome

Rosa, then, his former *Bamboccianti* self ostensibly purged, returned to Rome in 1649. As in 1639, his entry was a performance calculated to pique his audience's interest. Although his finances had been jeopardized by his extravagant spending in Florence, he knew he had to make a grand entrance, so he paraded the streets in fine dress with a liveried servant and a silver-hilted sword, a portent, perhaps, of the satirical and artistic "brawls" that would engage him in the eternal city.[71]

Rosa's move back to Rome put an end to the kind of witchcraft scenes he had painted for Florentine clients. The pendant panels of a *Witch* and *Soldier* owned by Cardinal Pio are remarkably demure.[72] Undoubtedly, fear of censorship by the Roman Inquisition was part of this. Jacob Isaacsz. van Swanenburgh, Rembrandt's early teacher, had been censured by the Inquisition in 1608 for displaying a painting of dancing witches in his booth next to Santa Maria della Carità, an incident indicating that such scenes were regarded in Rome as capricious titillations rather than antiwitchcraft propaganda.[73] But Rosa's main impetus for dropping witchcraft as a theme probably came from within. The witchcraft paintings he produced in Florence were perhaps meant to satirize the *Bamboccianti* and, more broadly, artists and poets who misuse their powers, along with witchcraft beliefs themselves. These paintings, though, despite their pedigree in learned demonological and poetic discourse, were vulnerable, ironically, to the very same charges. No matter how skilled he was at painting vulgarities, Rosa longed to distance himself from anything vulgar.

Along with the *Genius* etching, two large pictures of 1650–52 and their related etchings, *Diogenes Casting Away his Bowl* and *Democritus in Meditation* (figure 6.11) construct the self that Rosa wanted to present to Rome. Upon seeing a boy use his hands to drink from a stream, Diogenes, the Cynic philosopher and hero of the Stoics, throws away his drinking cup to express his contempt for possessions and wealth. Democritus sits in a landscape strewn with

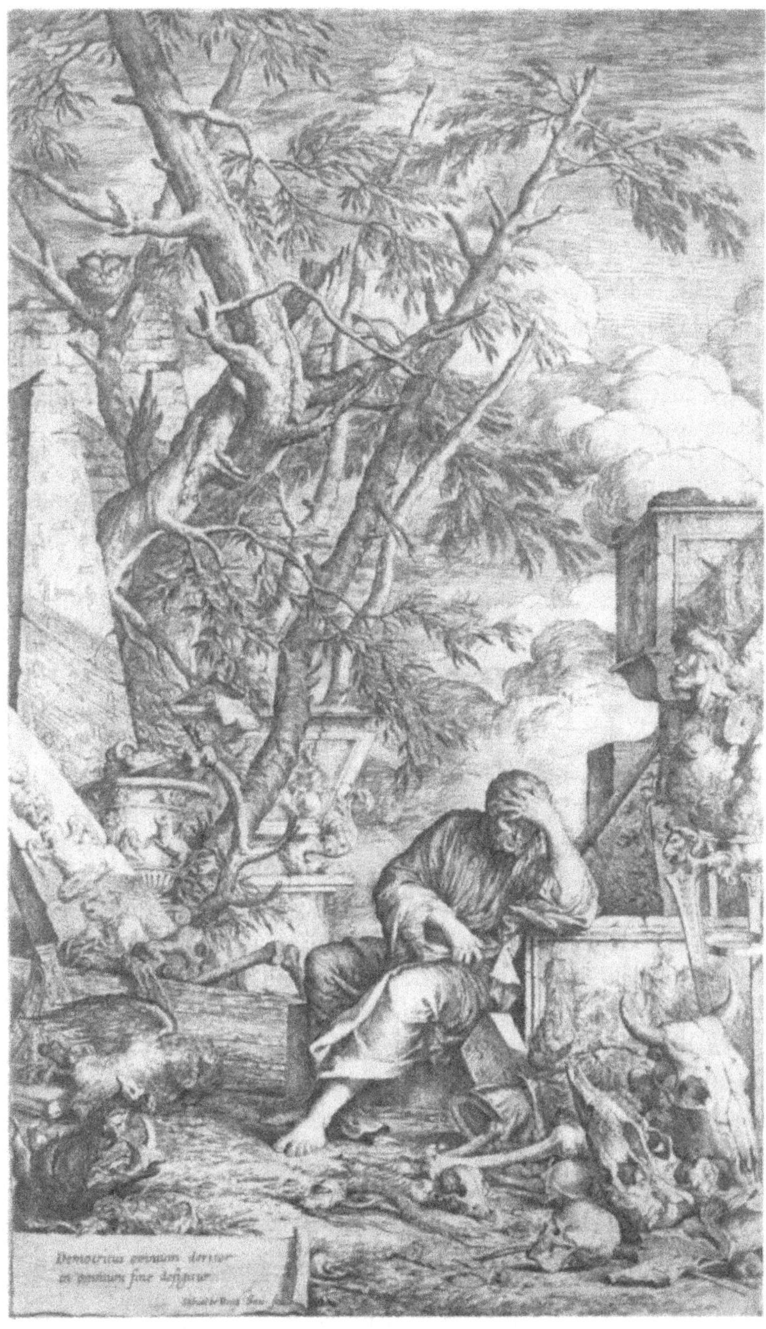

Figure 6.11. Salvator Rosa, *Democritus in Meditation*, 1662. Etching after Rosa's painting of the same name of 1651, 456 × 276 mm. National Gallery of Art, Washington, D.C. Ailsa Mellon Bruce Fund.

an array of *vanitas* symbols and contemplates a book on melancholy and madness.

As Richard Wallace has discussed in detail, Rosa's *Democritus* proclaims the Stoic values that Rosa found important but difficult to achieve. Although Democritus was characterized by Seneca as the "laughing philosopher" and paired with the weeping Heraclitus, Rosa reversed this characterization to show him in a state of profound grief about the vanity of all things. Rosa may also have been aware of additional literary accounts of Hippocrates' visit to Democritus in the midst of his intense studies, or his harassment by pranksters as he studied in a tomb. In both accounts, the presumed insanity of the philosopher disguises the depth and seriousness of his studies. Democritus was regarded in classical literature as an excellent scholar in areas ranging from ethics to mathematics to medicine, and he was also described as a magician and seer. For Rosa, then, he was an appropriate symbol of the artist-poet, here immersed in mournful meditation on the ephemeral nature of human endeavors, including his own work. The etching's inscription reads: "Democritus, the mocker of all things, is here stopped by the ending of all things."[74]

The artistic pedigree of Rosa's image, of course, goes back to Dürer's *Melencolia I* (1514), filtered through Italian treatments of the theme by Domenico Fetti and Giovanni Benedetto Castiglione. As Wallace points out, Rosa probably did not intend the philosophical subtlety of Dürer's print; his main point was a grim *memento mori*.[75] Nevertheless, the visual connection to an erudite image of artist's melancholy adds another layer to Rosa's self-characterization. It is clear that he thought *Democritus* was an extremely important painting. It was shown in 1651 in a public venue: the annual exhibition in the portico of the Pantheon during the festival of St. Joseph, sponsored by the *Congregazione dei Virtuosi* (Congregation of virtuosi), a charitable confraternity comprising many artists. *Democritus* fetched offers of 100 *scudi*, but—pace Diogenes' contempt for wealth—Rosa told Ricciardi that he wanted to hold out for two hundred, based on the painting's inventive subject.[76]

When the pendant work of *Diogenes* was exhibited at the same festival the following year, the pair of pictures was sold to the Venetian ambassador to Rome. Scott points out that public festivals suited Rosa well as means of marketing his works. Fellow exhibitors' works were often inferior, and Rosa accentuated the superiority of his with elaborate gilt frames. Interested buyers would appear and Rosa held out for the highest prices he could obtain. Related etchings, of course, also publicized his paintings; moreover, Rosa sold them in bound sets that buyers could not break up. He retained the plates and limited the numbers of prints he sold to dealers, ensuring continuing production (even after his death) and high prices. Such techniques allowed Rosa to remain independent.[77]

Despite such clever strategies, however, Rosa's career in Rome was mixed.

Unlike Poussin, he found it hard to establish a market for his history paintings, and clients were still attracted to his landscapes, much to his chagrin. Also, as Scott makes so clear, Rosa was his own worst enemy. Although he realized that he needed to be more circumspect in Rome than in relatively tolerant Florence, he was drawn irresistibly to verbal quarrels, and he lacked the protection of a steady, powerful patron. Rosa's behavior is illuminated by the singular importance of oral culture in early modern Italy and the Mediterranean concepts of honor and shame to which it was linked. Peter Burke has characterized early modern Italians as "linguistically self-conscious" to an unprecedented degree. A rich vocabulary of defamation, nuanced by locale, social status, and gender, was enhanced by a wide repertory of gestures and ritualized actions, such as house-scorning, graffiti, and the posting of libelous verses. Rome, in particular, had a thriving tradition of insult and libel.[78]

In 1654, Rosa became embroiled in a controversy over his poetic satire *Invidia*, which reprised the old theme of artists' envy that Mantegna had allegorized in his *Battle of the Sea Gods* (see figure 2.1). In the poem, Rosa's entrance into the temple of Immortality is blocked by the figure of Envy, whom the artist engages in an argument about the merits of his works. So far, so good. But Rosa made the mistake of identifying Envy, portrayed as a loathsome, randy, reptilian creature, by the pseudonym of Agostino Favoriti, an influential cleric and one of the literati belonging to the same Roman academies as Rosa. Although the poem was not published, those who heard it memorized the most scandalous lines (and undoubtedly Rosa's accompanying gestures and facial expressions); after that, the rumor that Rosa had not written his own poetry—Favoriti's revenge—haunted him.[79]

In 1655, more trouble came in the form of harassment by the Inquisition—intent on carrying out the stricter ecclesiastical oversight of marriage decreed by the Council of Trent—for living unmarried with Lucrezia.[80] In fact, they could not marry because they were unable to locate her first husband, who had abandoned her, to obtain a divorce. Having no powerful patrons who could deter the unwanted attentions of the Holy Office, Rosa sent his beloved Lucrezia and their son Rosalvo, born in Florence in 1641, to Naples to the care of his brother Giuseppe. Tragically, Giuseppe and Rosalvo, along with Rosa's sister Giovanna, his artist brother-in-law, and five of their children, were to die in a plague that killed a quarter of a million people; a grieving Lucrezia returned to Rome when the quarantine was lifted.[81] In the pitiful letter of 1656 to Ricciardi outlining the reasons for sending his wife and son to Naples, Rosa lamented the loss of "the comfort and dear company of women like Lucrezia (if there are any others like her in this world—which I don't believe)." The separation was a drastic measure, but Rosa had good reason to be afraid. In this same letter, he described his desperation over the departure of his wife and son, his fear of imprisonment, and his hatred of the Inquisition: "And all this comes of being afraid of running into some misfortune in prison or into some damned cuckold of a spy from the Holy Office—and a thousand curses on the soul of whoever devised it."[82] In 1664 and 1665, we learn that Lucrezia, now in poor health, and their last son Augusto, born in 1657, were once again forced to live apart from Rosa also because of Inquisitorial surveillance. Rosa's last years in Rome were marked by bitterness and sorrow, for both artistic and personal reasons. The problem of his illicit union with Lucrezia had dogged the couple from the beginning of their relationship. Never able to find her husband, they at last obtained a license to marry in 1672, shortly before Rosa's death in 1673.

The much sparser details of Lucrezia's life provide an interesting foil to Rosa's self-revelation, his braggadocio, and his battles for status and autonomy. Both husband and wife's paths were partly shaped by gendered concepts of honor and shame, partly by their genuine love for each other, and partly by their evident determination to live outside convention. Abandoned as a young wife, Lucrezia faced the humiliating possibility of having to return to her family or, saving that, being institutionalized as a woman of marginal status, fitting clearly in no category, in one of the Tuscan institutions for female *malmaritate* (the unhappily married or abused).[83] Her work as an artist's model could not have provided much of a living. Becoming a mistress to an artist she loved was the superior choice for Lucrezia.

In a culture in which the conquest and exchange of women constituted a mark of masculinity, it is notable that Rosa, who was so steeped in artistic and poetic machismo, evidently lived in chaste fidelity to Lucrezia. His letters are full of deep affection for her. Nevertheless, we wince at his behavior regarding their offspring. The birth of their first son Rosalvo had been followed by several more, and all these infants were dispensed to the foundling home. Not long after their move to Rome, Rosa mentioned Lucrezia's indignation as her child was taken away. He stated that he could not support more children, but this claim might be countered by what we know of his finances. He had earned nine thousand *scudi* in Florence, but he had spent so much on entertaining the *Percossi* that he and Lucrezia came to Rome with only three hundred remaining. However, he left a substantial estate when he died in Rome: 12,000 *scudi* (compared to Poussin's 15,000).[84]

Disguising his unconventional relationship, which would have been made even more obvious by the presence of children, was a powerful motivation for keeping only one child (Rosalvo and, after his death, Augusto). Nevertheless, Lucrezia's trials put Rosa's fear of Inquisitorial reprisal and damage to his honor in a larger perspective. Deserted by her first husband, Lucrezia experienced illegitimate pregnancies, forced abandonment of her children, and the death of the one child she was allowed to keep, followed quickly by the birth of another. She endured the social stigma of adultery and the fear of Inquisitorial reprisal and separation along with Rosa, but with the knowledge that her honor and shame were based solely on her sexual status. In Daniela Lombardi's words, female honor in early modern Italy was "almost a material possession," which men could take away or give back through marriage or the payment of dowry.[85] Female honor, as Sharon Strocchia explains, was unaffected by the homosocial and corporate bonds that provided multiple and more flexible models for masculine identity and approval.[86] In the case of artists, this honor was in large part professional. Rosa had fashioned his own distinctive model of masculinity; he asserted and defended his poetic and artistic prowess and autonomy so ferociously because these constituted his identity and honor. Amid the *Percossi* in Florence and his circle of friends and supporters in Rome, he was honorable despite his cohabitation with Lucrezia.

However unfairly weighted by gender, the determination of both Lucrezia and Rosa's honor was more nuanced. Although adultery was still considered a serious sin and crime, historians of early modern Italy have noted the difficulty of enforcing the Council of Trent's regulation of marriage, the leniency often exercised by Church authorities, the growing acceptance of sexuality as an essential aspect of the human condition, and, perhaps most importantly, the malleability of codes of honor by individual circumstances.[87] No one exemplifies this last observation better than Rosa and Lucrezia: Their families and circle of friends and supporters clearly accepted them as husband and wife.

Rosa's images of Lucrezia range from *The Personification of Poetry* to a plain and mournful portrait after the death of Rosalvo (Galleria Nazionale d'Arte Antica, Rome), to the maternal figure seated on the globe of Fortune in the dismal *Human Frailty* (Fitzwilliam Museum, Cambridge, 1657). In this last work, her hair woven with roses to signify her status as Rosa's wife, Lucrezia holds a plump baby who, guided by a skeleton, writes "Conception is Sin, Birth a Pain, Life Toil, Death a Necessity" on a parchment. In the same year, feeling slighted by his exclusion from Pope Alexander VII's commission for frescoes in the Quirinal Palace, Rosa also completed two other allegories of Fortune. The more impolitic of the two, now in the Getty Museum in Malibu, shows a blonde goddess distributing her wealth indiscriminately to animals, including an ass and a pig trampling on symbols of the artist (a palette, a book with Rosa's name on the spine, a rose). The pope's brother, Don Mario Chigi, heard of the picture and Rosa had to write an apology, explaining away his satirical meaning to escape papal reprisal.[88] While *Human Frailty* appropriates Lucrezia's loss to express Rosa's own indirectly in an inventive allegory, the Getty *Fortune* is a defiant, macho assertion of artistic autonomy. The juxtaposition of these two highly unusual pictures says much about how gender, as well as Fortune, shaped Rosa and Lucrezia's lives differently.

Istoria's Failure; *Capriccio*'s Triumph

We encounter witchcraft one more time in Rosa's oeuvre in *Saul and the Witch of Endor*, displayed at the festival of San Giovanni Decollato in 1668, patronized by the Rospigliosi family to celebrate their son Giulio's election to the papacy as Clement IX (figure 6.12). *Saul* and Rosa's *St. George* were the only works by a living artist exhibited—a considerable honor, although to Rosa, of course, it seemed belated.

The painting is divided along the middle axis, where the focus is the absurd mini-pyrotechnics of the witch setting fire to a branch. The canvas practically diagrams the tensions in Rosa's art. Its left side teems with grotesque forms, chopped up by tenebrism and violent movement, while the right is dominated by the indignant, stolid righteousness of the spirit of Samuel (I Samuel 28: 7–25). Depicted in precise profile, the volumes of his yellow robe monumental in their clarity, Samuel's ghost is almost Poussinesque. Despite this gloss of *istoria*, however, one senses (to borrow Sohm's term) its "failure."[89] The vulgarity of Rosa's shrieking hag (does she still function as a symbol of artists Rosa despised, pandering to ignorant patrons embodied in the cowering figure of Saul?) is countered by the edifying message of the iconography, in which Saul asks a "woman that hath a familiar spirit" to conjure up the dead Samuel to inquire about the outcome of an imminent battle with the Philistines. Saul is the antithesis of the good ruler. Despite his earlier banishment of diviners from the realm (I Samuel 3), he now backslides. In contemporary terms, Saul's use of white witchcraft such as divination was equivalent to placing the devil before God, for which he is punished by his downfall and death. The story of the Witch of Endor was often adduced to argue against forms of popular magic that did not result in evident harm,[90] an appropriate message in papal Rome. Despite this noble moral, however, the grotesque is only tenuously contained in Rosa's picture by the stern prophet's shade.

Rosa's witches were rarely echoed: Several paintings by Genoese artist Alessandro Magnasco (1667–1749), done out of an Enlightened skepticism about superstition and as part of his commitment to the fantastic, grotesque, and the satirical, are their most immediate progeny.[91] But the quest for artistic autonomy underlying Rosa's witchcraft paintings took a new and more influential form in the sixty-two etchings of his *Figurine* series (1656–57). Undertaken in his despair after the death of his son and much of his family in Naples, it served as a direct ancestor to Tiepolo's *Capricci* and *Scherzi* etchings, which in turn inspired Goya's *Caprichos*. The title page of Rosa's series features a figure derived from Cesare Ripa's personification in his *Iconologia* (1630) of *Capriccio* as a young man wearing multicolored clothes and a hat with various feathers, signifying that his variety of actions have their origins in his fantasy (figure 6.13). Ripa's figure holds a bellows, its nozzle still visible in Rosa's final

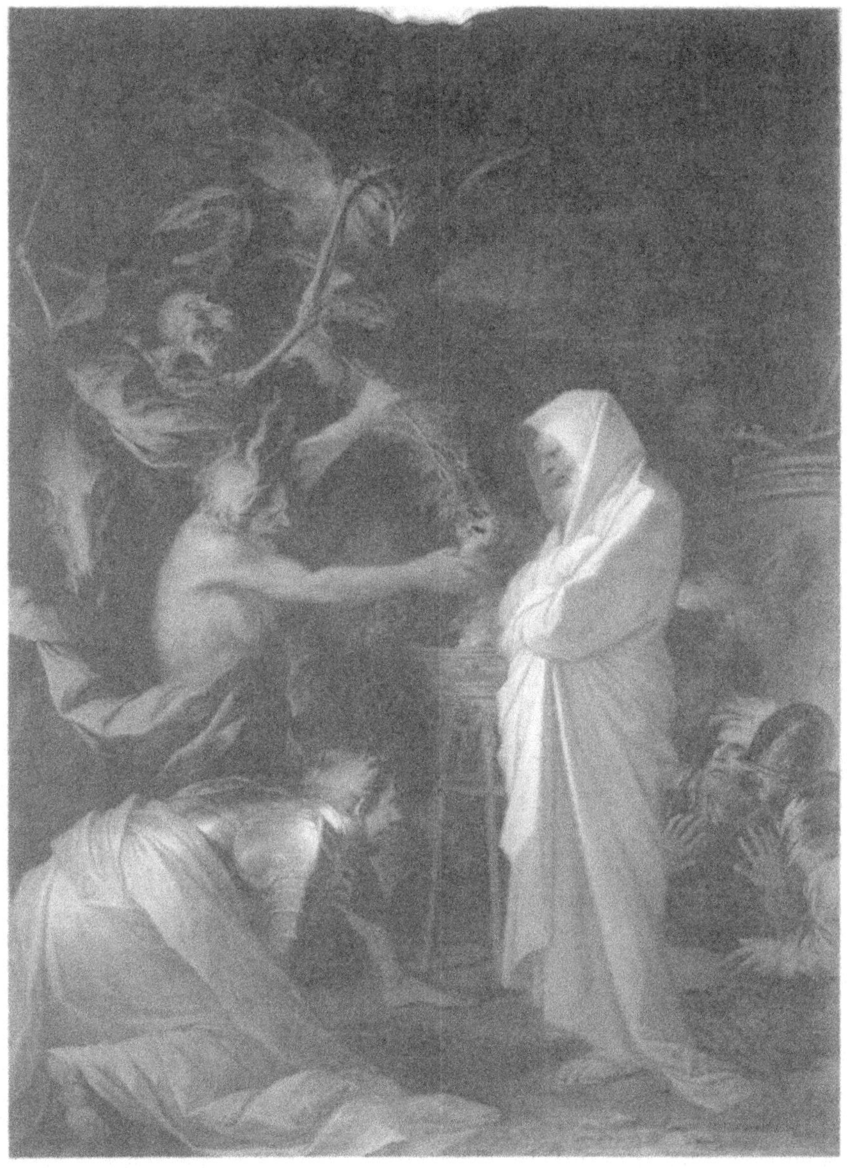

Figure 6.12. Salvator Rosa, *Saul and the Witch of Endor*, 1668. Oil on canvas, 275 × 191 cm. Musée du Louvre, Paris. Erich Lessing/Art Resource, New York.

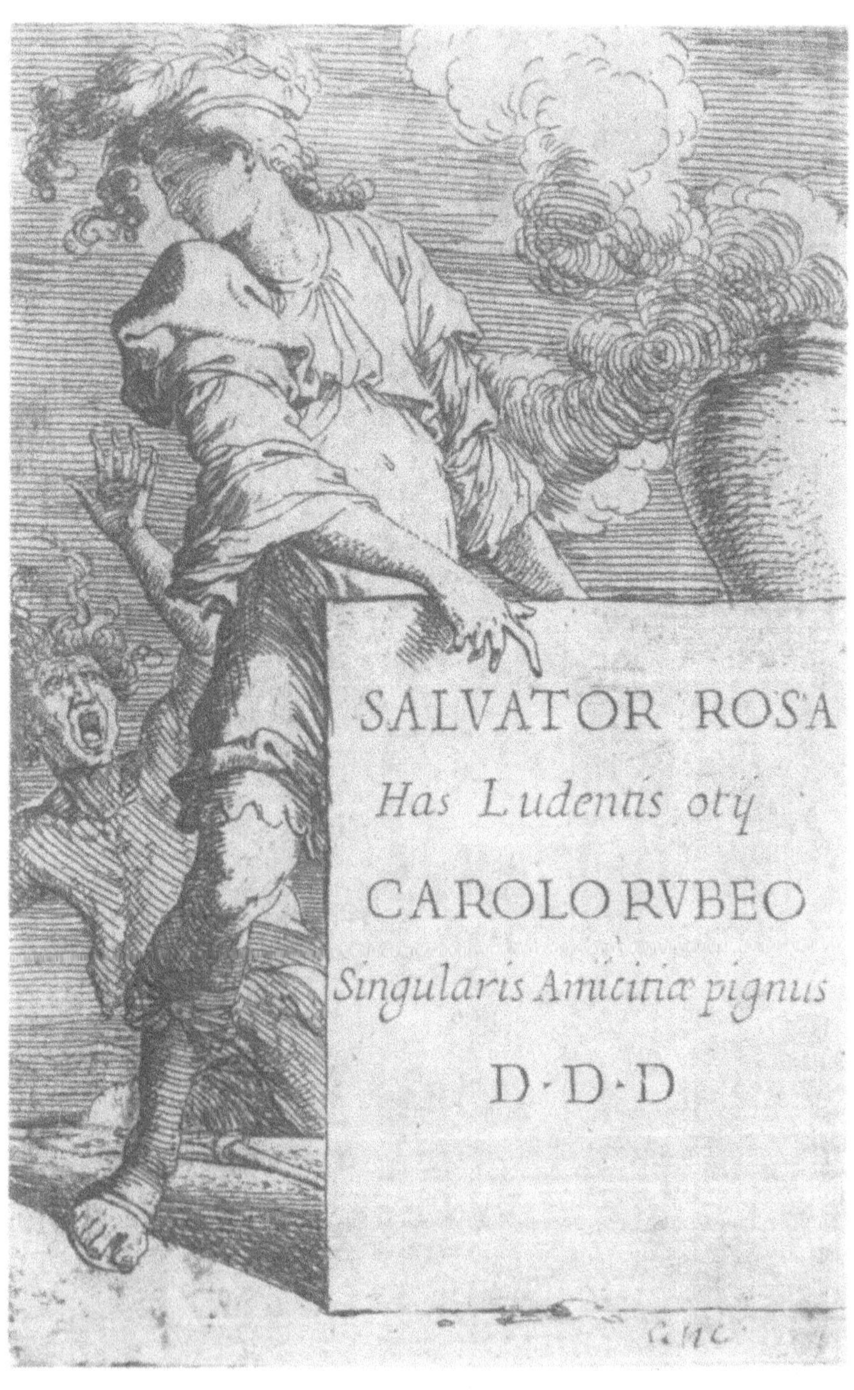

Figure 6.13. Salvator Rosa, frontispiece to the *Figurine* series, 1656–67. Etching, 143 × 93 mm. © The British Museum, London.

etching, and spur, to praise virtue or prick vice, respectively. In painting, music and elsewhere, Ripa asserts, caprices are ideas that are "out of the ordinary." Rosa's altered *Capriccio* points toward the Latin dedication to de' Rossi, in friendship and "playful leisure." The artistic intrigues, petty rivalries, jealousies, and rumors that plagued Rosa in Rome are symbolized by the figure of Envy, kept at bay here by the capricious, inventive artist. In a discarded variant of this title page, printed from the back of the plate, the figure of *Pittura* is also included, her garment draped with the tendrils of a vine and holding paintbrush and thrysus, symbol of satiric poetry in Ripa, and, in Rosa's poem *Pittura*, the implement that touches the painter's head to inspire his fiery creativity. The bacchic nature of the vine and thrysus allude to the ardent, inspired nature of Rosa's invention in the *Figurine* and elsewhere. In the *Genius* etching, Wallace emphasizes, the figure of genius is crowned with bacchic ivy to characterize Rosa's creativity as "intuitive, irrational, inspired and mysterious."[92]

In his thorough discussion of the *Figurines*, Wallace emphasizes Rosa's striking innovation. Although foreshadowed by print series such as Jacques Callot's *Varie Figure* (Various figures, 1617–23), the etchings go beyond their sources in their suggestion of a larger narrative beyond the viewer's grasp. The array of exotic and archaic garments; the sense of the figures having been excerpted from other contexts; and their "elusive, restless and fugitive" formal quality—all this makes the *Figurine* etchings particularly apt expressions of Rosa's mature talent. Moreover, any lingering sense of *Bamboccianti* painting is dispensed by the rhetorical flourish of gestures and the decorous poses. These are no longer coarse low-life figures caught off-guard in insignificant actions (compare figure 2.7). No wonder the English Romantics were so prone to speculation about the content of the series.[93]

Epilogue: Tiepolo's *Scherzi di Fantasia*

Scholars have long sought an explanation for Tiepolo's two major etched series, the ten *Capricci* (1740–42) and the twenty-three *Scherzi di Fantasia* (1740; 1757–58; figure 6.14).[94] As an etcher, Tiepolo was inspired by Castiglione and Stefano della Bella, and, above all, Rosa's *Figurine* series. More broadly, the concern for *diversi capricci* manifested in works by Rosa and other seventeenth-century artists found its fruition in these prints populated by magicians, soldiers, nymphs, satyrs, *commedia dell'arte* characters, and others who might lend ambience to an artist's *istorie*. In Keith Christiansen's apt words, the motley figures, "like extras in some theatrical production," seem to have "wandered onto the copperplates from another context."[95]

Although the *Capricci* are truly diverse and capricious in the sense of hav-

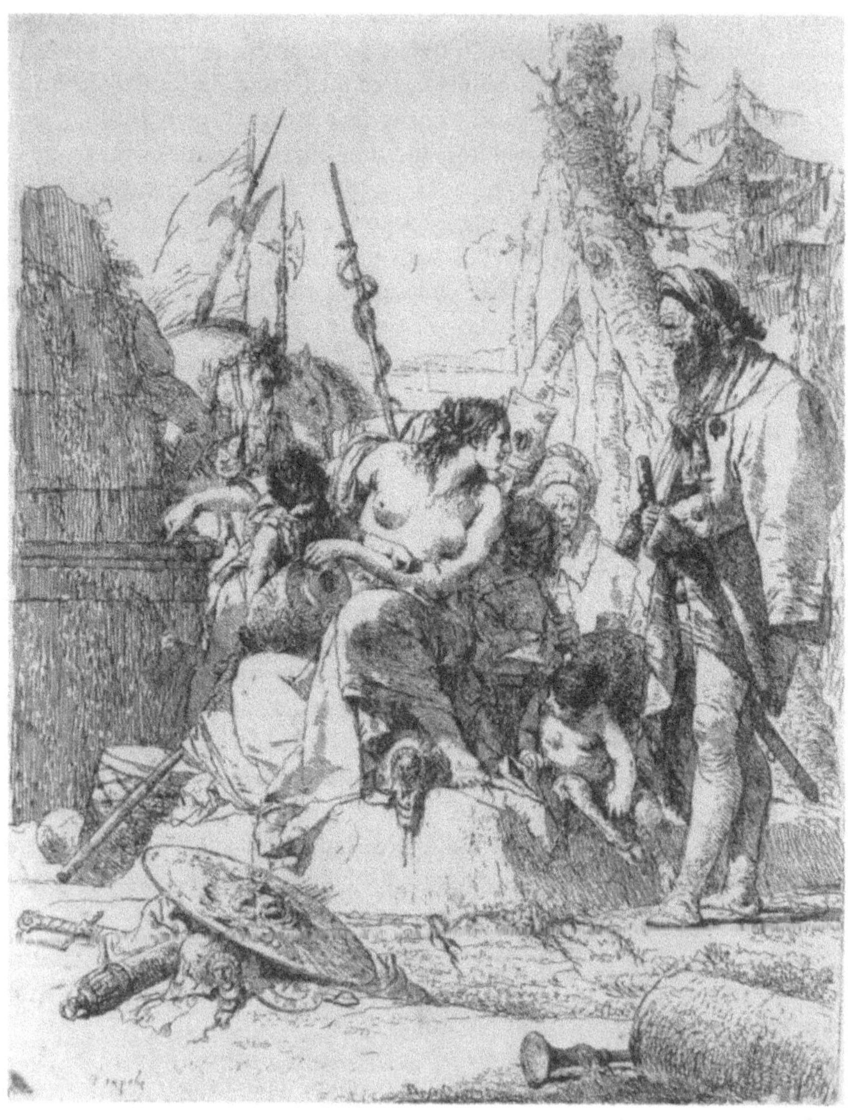

Figure 6.14. Giovanni Battista Tiepolo, *A Sorceress (?) Giving Audience* from *The Scherzi di Fantasia*, ca. 1743–57. Etching, 222 × 175 mm. Metropolitan Museum of Art, New York. Purchase, The Elisha Whittelsey Collection, The Elisha Whittelsey Fund; Dodge and Pfeiffer Funds; Joseph Pulitzer bequest; Gift of Bertina Suida Manning and Robert L. Manning, 1976 (1976.37.11). All rights reserved, The Metropolitan Museum of Art.

ing no discernible unity apart from the style and mood, the more detailed *Scherzi* appear to cling loosely to an iconographic thread of magic. In an exhibition review from 1972, Charles Dempsey argued persuasively that the *Scherzi*—evoking ancient Egypt and Babylonia with costumes, ruined architecture, sculptural ornament, and paraphernalia—concern Gnosticism, the heretical worldview adopted by the magician Simon Magus. From an early Christian viewpoint, the dualism of the Gnostics (their acknowledgment of an evil God who created the world and whose power equaled that of the good God who lay beyond the world) constituted Satan-worship. As demonized by Christianity, the Gnostics, much like the later Cathars, were mired in the senses and the world; their purported knowledge, gained from practices such as astrology, necromancy, and numerology, was false. The evil connotations of Tiepolo's figures, according to Dempsey, are conveyed by the continuing presence of owls, by devil's faces, and by serpents. The male protagonists may even represent specific magicians.[96] This sense of false knowledge and evil may explain why Tiepolo's son Domenico included etchings of St. Joseph with the Christ Child and the Adoration of the Magi along with the series.[97]

However, reception of the etchings by eighteenth-century print connoisseurs such as Antonio Maria Zanetti and Jean-Paul Mariette does not focus on subject matter but on Tiepolo's fertile imagination, revealed in his uniquely light, unfettered handling of the etcher's needle.[98] And, according to Andrea Gottdang, the main import of these etchings is not to be found in any esoteric theme but in their profound implications for art theory. She places the *Scherzi* in the context of a contemporary Venetian interest in dreams; Tiepolo is the dreamer from whose fantasy the discrepant characters of the etchings emerge. For Gottdang, the *Scherzi* completely overthrow the Albertian concept of *istoria*. Their chief significance is a precocious modernity that makes clear the limits of reason and the preeminence of the artist's fantasy.[99] We will encounter this tension again in Goya, and witchcraft is once again its vehicle.

Chapter 7

Between Enlightenment and Horror: Goya's Reinvention of the Witch

Introduction: The Waning of Belief

In hindsight, the Dutch attitude toward witchcraft discussed in Chapter 5 appears as a very early manifestation of a pan-European decline of witch-hunting that was complete, with local variation, by the early eighteenth century. Why witch-hunting ended is almost as complex as why it began.

European governments, aware that many innocent people had died, were loath to repeat the horrific excesses of large-scale hunts like those in Bamberg or Cologne, although the prosecution of witchcraft continued in some areas on an individual and much more cautious basis. Legal changes such as the growing critique of torture as inhumane and ineffective, and stricter parameters for proof (for example, disallowing the "devil's mark" as evidence in England) made executions far less frequent. The diminishing or outright abolition of torture made the spiraling mass accusations of the past impossible. In recognition of the social dysfunction, economic cost, and sheer human suffering that witch-hunting had caused, courts and judges might simply refuse to try such cases. The religious and political tensions of the age of confessionalization and state-building diminished greatly after the mid seventeenth century. As Brian Levack states, Europe after 1660 entered a period of relative stability in which absolutist powers ceased to use witch-hunting as a means of asserting hegemony: States were built; witchcraft lost its force as a metaphor for anti-kingdom.[1]

Among the social reasons for the demise of witch-hunting were changing attitudes toward women and sexuality. The idea that misogyny alone drove witch-hunting has been questioned for good reasons, as we saw in Chapter 1, but its importance is confirmed by the coincidence of witch-hunting's end with a more positive, if ultimately ambivalent, understanding of woman's nature, and the acceptance of sexuality itself as a human need that was, at its base, morally neutral. The *Malleus*'s anxious assumption—so basic to the theory underpinning the witch-hunts—that women were carnal beyond all reason and that innumerable demons exploited that carnality to wage war against

Christendom no longer made sense. In Enlightenment thought, as we shall explore in this chapter, women might be conceived as naturally more sensual and emotional than men, or naturally purer and more moral, but their fundamental attraction or vulnerability to diabolic evil were no longer intellectual commonplaces.[2]

Ultimately, however, it was belief in witchcraft itself that expired. It is true that witchcraft beliefs continued among the uneducated—after all, they had been taught well on this score through sermons, trials, and public executions, even though a persistent strain of common sense and skepticism often surfaces in trial records. Improving economic and climatic conditions and the growth of towns and cities made the kind of accusations that typically emerged from rural village culture much less frequent, even though witchcraft beliefs were still a part of this culture.[3] Among the middle and upper classes, however, a decisive change in worldview took place. It is this shift, many historians agree, that really sounded the death knell of witch-hunting.

Skeptics in the sixteenth and early seventeenth centuries voiced many of the ideas that finally coalesced into a complete denial of witchcraft. Johann Weyer's insistence that many supposed witches were really actually mentally ill was an important caution that authorities in Protestant territories took to heart; Friedrich Spee's moving account of the inhumanity of torture, and the utter failure of the trials to ascertain guilt, had a dampening effect on witch-hunting, especially in Catholic contexts. Reginald Scot's scathing and remarkably advanced critique of credulity struck the first blows to the core beliefs that fueled the persecutions. Most eloquently perhaps, Michel de Montaigne called for a humble acceptance of the limitations of our knowledge before we decide to roast people alive. But it was the development of a materialistic, empirical, and mechanistic worldview—drastically undermining or negating the possibility of demonic interference in nature and society—that had been missing from early modern skepticism. This perspective implied that causes for events were not occult but were discoverable through observation and reasoned investigation. The Cartesian notion that nature ran like an orderly machine left no room for the manipulations of demons. If the world were understood as fundamentally constant and accessible to reason, demonic dissimulation and evil could no longer drive the inconstancy that so tormented Pierre de Lancre and many of his contemporaries.[4]

The desire of the bourgeoisie and the aristocracy to distinguish themselves from the lower classes fostered the acceptance of the new philosophical and scientific ideas. The superstitions of the ignorant became a widespread target of satire. For example, in his wonderful farcical novel published in 1710, *The History of the Ridiculous Extravagancies of Monsieur Oufle*—an anagram for *le fou* (the fool)—Abbé Laurent Bordelon recounts his wealthy protagonist's prolific superstitious beliefs, culminating in a description of the sabbath, accompanied by an engraved illustration that mocks the fold-out print in de Lancre's text, at the end. Monsieur Oufle's pathetic gullibility is bolstered by his vast library of demonological texts and, interestingly for our purposes, his large collection of paintings with demons, phantoms, magicians, and the like. Oufle's eldest son, Abbé Doudon, shares his father's obsession, but Oufle's brother Noncrède (i.e., unbeliever) tries vainly to persuade him of the benefits of reason. For her part, Madame Oufle, moved mainly by a wifely spirit of contradiction, and despite women's traditional affinity for superstition, Bordelon notes, will have nothing of her husband's conceits.[5]

Goya's interest in the theme of witchcraft stems from this skeptical and satirical attitude toward superstition, absorbed into his broader project of exposing the follies of Spanish society and humanity as a whole. He may very well have known Bordelon's book with its preposterous parody of de Lancre's illustration, in which the spatial and conceptual scope of the sabbath is reduced to a circus-like affair, complete with a master of ceremonies. Witches leap like acrobats, children herd their toads like animal tamers, confined to compositional "rings" along with the obligatory diners and cauldron-stirring hags. Monsieur Oufle appears in the lower left, in exactly the same position as Frans Francken's male observer in figure 4.2, introduced to the marvelous spectacle by a jester.

Along with Tiepolo's *Capricci* and *Scherzi*, which do not deal directly with witchcraft, Goya undoubtedly knew many of the prints I have discussed in this book, from early German examples to eighteenth-century French reproductions after David Teniers's paintings. Gillot's *Witches' Sabbath*, this version etched by Jacques-Gabriel Huquier, is one composition Goya very likely knew (figure 7.1).[6] Best known as the teacher of Jean-Antoine Watteau, Gillot was a fascinating artist in his own right with an unconventional manner entirely his own, and themes, like the *commedia dell'arte*, that lacked the prestige of histories. Watteau's contemporary admirers cited Gillot's "fertile and unusual genius," and the taste for the grotesque, the comical and the modern he bequeathed to the younger painter.[7] Both Watteau and Gillot did elegant, whimsical, ornamental designs for walls—Rococo versions of *grotteschi*—that place them within the tradition of invention and *capriccio* traced in this book. According to Joachim Rees, however, these new, Rococo grotesques took decisive steps toward modernity. They no longer depended on antiquity for legitimacy but used contemporary motifs, and they took their place alongside history paintings on the walls of urban *hôtels* (mansions) rather than country houses. They began, as Rees puts it, a "dismantling of the high style."[8]

The panoramic and additive qualities of Gillot's composition recall Salvator Rosa's *Witches at their Incantations* (see figure 6.10). Scanning from the left, we encounter stock characters of the witchcraft genre: a chimeric animal, a skeletal mount, hags in flight, a cadaver seated on his tombstone, a necroman-

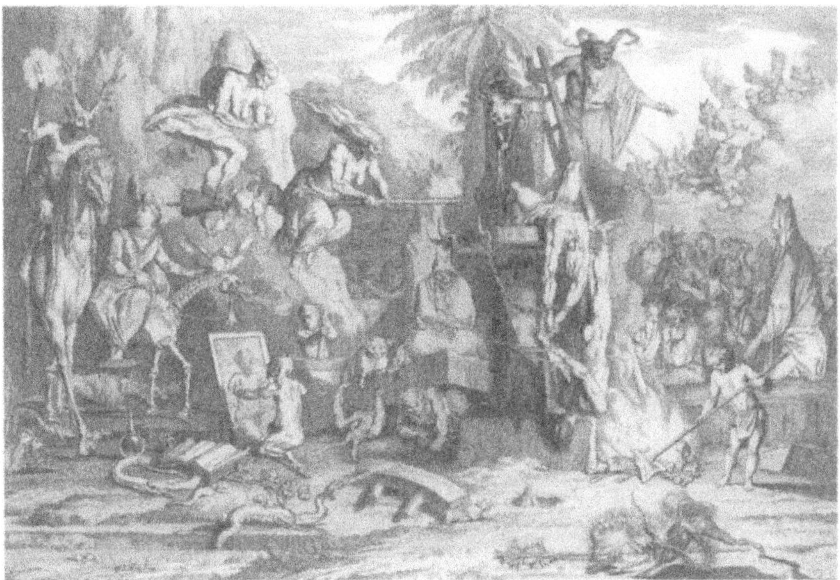

Figure 7.1. After Claude Gillot, *Witches' Sabbath*, undated. Etching by Jacques-Gabriel Huquier, 178 × 210 mm. Photograph © 2004, Museum of Fine Arts, Boston. Ellen Page Hall Fund, 34.832.

cer and male corpses chained and hung, and, at the far right, a spectral devil adored by a crowd of demons and people. Throughout, incongruous, often repugnant or scary, elements and motifs jostle for attention, as they will later in Tiepolo's *Scherzi* and Goya's *Caprichos*. The print's inscription poses a question (Is it an enchantment? Is it an illusion?), but the answer is already clear. This image is indeed an enchantment, an illusion, a tableau with costumed players, sets, and props. What Goya will do with this Rococo heritage in the course of his career, however, is to reinvigorate the *capriccio* with the weight of *istoria* and, finally, with horror—not for demons and witches but for their human creators.

The Witch and Goya's Other Muses

Goya's engagement with the theme of witchcraft both culminates and radically revises the visual tradition I have traced in this study. It is inextricably bound to his self-presentation at two significant moments during his career: the late 1790s, when he sought increased independence from commissioned work; and the early 1820s, when he summarized his views of Spanish society and the human condition in the deeply personal statement of the Black Paintings.

Goya came from a modest background, and his rise was scarcely meteoric. Born in Saragossa in 1746 to a master gilder and the daughter of the minor nobility of Aragon, he was apprenticed to a local painter, José Luzán, who taught his pupil by having him draw after prints, undoubtedly an important experience for the young artist. He moved to Madrid in 1763 and began work in the studio of painters Ramón and Francisco Bayeu, travelling to Italy in the early 1770s. In 1773, Goya married the Bayeus' sister, Josefa—a shadowy figure whose life was filled with pregnancies, miscarriages, and deliveries, but who seems to have had a stable marriage with the painter.[9] The following year, Goya was summoned by Neoclassical painter Anton Raphael Mengs to work on cartoons for the Royal Tapestry Factory, work that continued through the 1780s. Appointed as a painter to the king by Carlos III in 1786, Goya was promoted under Carlos IV to *pintor de cámara* (court painter) in 1789 and *primer pintor de cámara* (first court painter) in 1799, the year the eighty etchings of the *Caprichos* were published. With the exception of some religious commissions, Goya spent much of his career before this point producing tapestry cartoons and portraits of the royal family and a diverse group of nobles, officials, and literati. Within the framework of these conventional tasks, however, Goya strove for originality. His tapestry cartoons, in particular, show his efforts to invent within this decorative art form; when he was asked for further designs upon his promotion to First Court Painter in 1799, Goya stated that he was a painter of histories, and so could not comply.[10]

The length of the period between his first appointment by Mengs in 1774 and the life-threatening, still unknown illness Goya suffered in late 1792 and early 1793—generally thought to be a turning point for the artist—is important to consider. Goya was well into middle age before he changed direction. Whatever the illness was (lead poisoning from the white paint used to prime tapestry cartoons, meningitis, syphilis?), it left him deaf and made teaching so awkward that he had to resign his position at the Academy of San Fernando in Madrid in 1797.[11] There is clearly a downturn in Goya's normally optimistic mood revealed in letters to his childhood friend Martín Zapater written during his recovery.[12]

The change in Goya's artistic direction is not due solely to his brush with death, for he had shown earlier signs of dissatisfaction. In letters to Zapater from the 1780s, Goya gives frequent indications that he felt harried and resented his duties; indeed, he fell ill after he had received permission from the king to take a leave from court to travel to Andalusia and Cadiz.[13] In the mid 1790s, this malaise emerged in works that mark Goya's determination to construct and present himself differently.

In January of 1794, Goya sent eleven remarkable cabinet pictures on tin to the Academy of San Fernando along with a letter to Vice-Protector Bernardo de Iriarte, explaining their genesis:

In order to occupy my imagination, which had been depressed through dwelling on my misfortunes, and to compensate at least in part for some of the considerable expenses I have incurred, I set myself to painting a series of cabinet pictures in which I have been able to depict themes that cannot usually be addressed in commissioned works, where *capricho* and invention have little part to play. I thought of sending them to the Academy, since your Excellency knows the advantages I might expect to derive from submitting my work to the artists' criticism.[14]

A few days later, Goya wrote about his addition of *Yard with Lunatics* to the eleven pictures, informing Iriarte that he could keep the pictures in his home. The small paintings had been well received by the assembled artists. They were a bravado demonstration of Goya's undiminished painterly ability after his illness and his fertile imagination.[15] He would be appointed Director of Painting at the Academy in 1795. As Sarah Symmons points out, the pictures are also evidence of Goya's bid for a small exclusive clientele interested in eroticism and violence as expressed in art and literature—for example, Marquis de Sade's *Justine*, republished since its first appearance in 1791.[16]

Among the themes treated in the paintings were the bullfight and the *commedia dell'arte*, but *Attack by Robbers*, *Fire at Night*, *Interior of a Prison*, *Shipwreck*, and *Yard with Lunatics* confronted viewers with dismal accounts of human vulnerability and cruelty. Like the witchcraft scenes in the *Caprichos*, the pictures engage us by their grotesque subjects and intimate size. Henceforth, cabinet paintings, prints, and drawings were Goya's means to express capricious, inventive themes that also corresponded to his own tastes and concerns.

Goya's understanding of *capricho* derives from, but reformulates the Italian usage exhibited by Rosa and Tiepolo. As an artistic (or musical or poetic) conceit that was out of the ordinary, without rules, characterized by bizarre extravagance, and expressing the artist's free fantasy and *ingenium*, the *capriccio* could be relegated to triviality or frivolity. Goya's friend, dramatist Leandro Fernández de Moratín (Moratín the Younger) condemned certain Roman monuments for their capriciousness and superfluous ornament, their ingenuity badly employed, and their lack of reason or taste. As Paul Ilie has discussed, the capricious and the grotesque existed in tension with neoclassical decorum in eighteenth-century Spanish literature and theory.[17] The *capriccio* could also be fraught with moral and mental dangers, the stance taken by neoclassical critics such as Francesco Milizia, writing in 1797, who likened it to mental illness or delerium.[18] For Goya, the *capriccio* not only allowed him to exercise free fantasy, but also to better society—a role normally ceded to history painting. As Werner Hofmann states, Goya synthesized mere capricious extravagances with the "harmful beliefs commonly held," noted in the inscription on the preparatory drawing for *Capricho* 43 (figure 7.2). In doing so, he used his own invention to turn potential trivialities into parables; he formulated a new

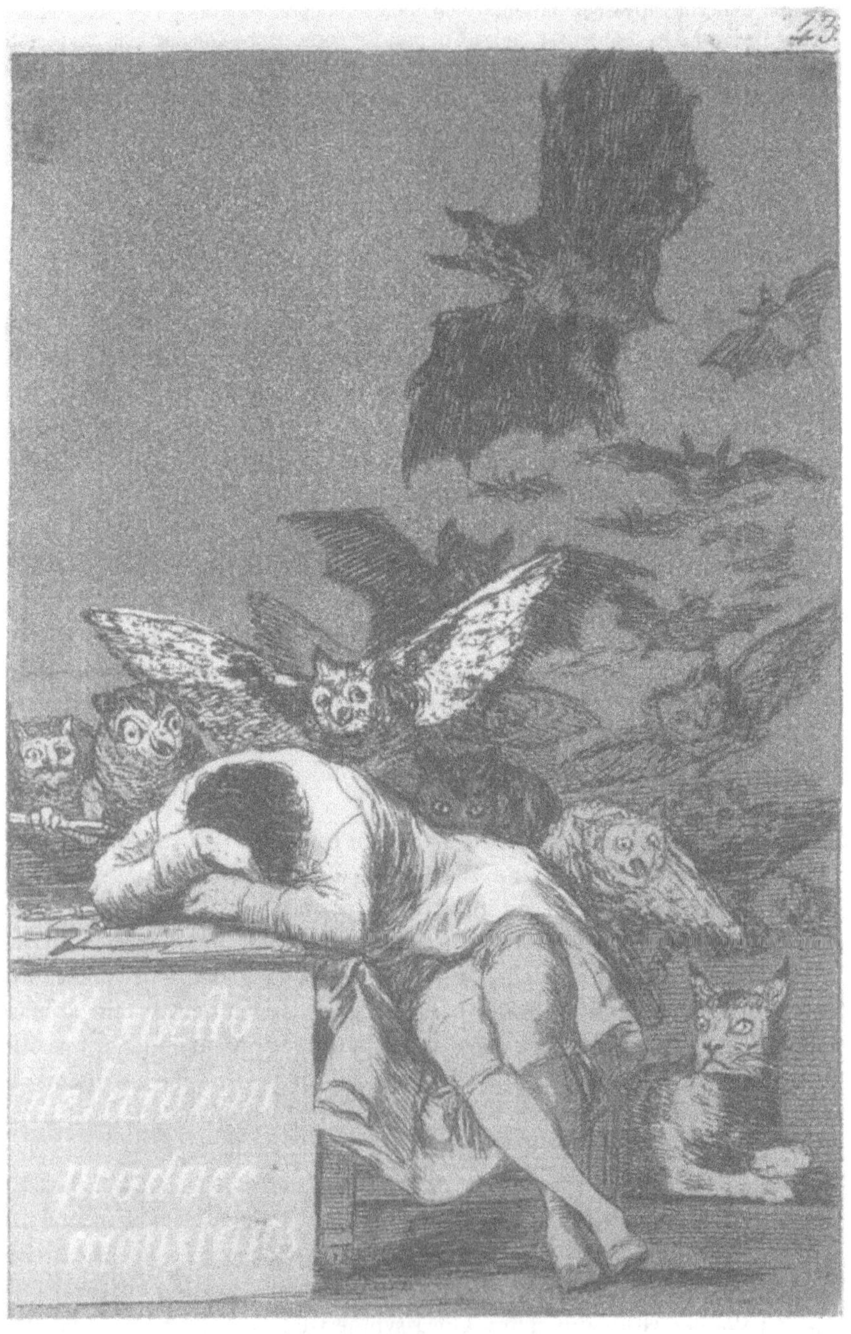

Figure 7.2. Francisco Goya, *The Sleep of Reason Produces Monsters* (*Capricho* 43), 1799. Etching and aquatint, 216 × 152 mm. Image © 2004 Board of Trustees, National Gallery of Art, Washington, D.C. Rosenwald Collection.

kind of history painting that "bears all the distinguishing marks of the *capriccio* as we know it."[19]

The potential for reform through satirical art, incorporating grotesque and extravagant elements, was part of Rosa's self-fashioning, as we remember. But Rosa's ire was channeled mostly into debates about artistic and poetic practice or philosophical ideas, and when he wanted to be taken more seriously, he turned to allegorical works and histories as they were understood in the seventeenth century. For him, as for Tiepolo, the *capriccio* was a demonstration of free creativity existing *alongside* works of serious moral or religious content. Goya, however—rather than abandoning the inventive freedom of the *capriccio* entirely or validating its licentious character in and for itself—insisted on its *social* relevance. It, and not the history painting, became the most difficult test of an artist's *ingenium*. According to Edith Helman, Goya's idea of the *capricho* is indebted to poet José de Cadalso (1741–82) who likewise transferred the notion of extravagance lacking reason from the artist's creation to the society he endeavored to improve. This constituted more than an apology for the artist's imaginative depiction of grotesque persons or actions, it valorized that depiction.[20]

Witchcraft, along with the other violent, disturbing themes of the cabinet pictures of 1793–94, helped Goya reposition himself after his illness within the circle of intelligentsia and collectors he most valued, and perhaps beyond Spain to France and England.[21] He refashioned himself not just as a tapestry designer and portrait artist but as a provocative observer of Spanish society and of human nature itself. His continual production of uncommissioned print series and cabinet paintings after 1799 confirms the success of this refashioning. It is not surprising, then, that the theme of witchcraft reappears in Goya's Black Paintings for his home in Madrid. These frescoes, begun around 1820, presented the aged artist to an intimate circle of friends and family, confirmed his role as insightful satirist, and enveloped them (and the artist himself) in his melancholic *aura*. The Black Paintings are at once a meditation on a career that was coming to an end and an affirmation of the still prodigious imagination of the artist.

Witchcraft and an Enlightened Duchess: The Osuna Paintings

Helman's fundamental research, amplified by subsequent scholars, allows us to reconstruct the intellectual and political context for Goya's interest in witchcraft, expressed first in the paintings for the country house of the Duke and Duchess of Osuna.[22] These canvasses of witchcraft are contemporary with the preparatory stages of the *Caprichos*, but the overall tone of the paintings is more humorous and theatrical, in keeping with the Duchess's strong interest in and patronage of theatre.[23] Indeed, two of the scenes (one now lost) came directly from popular early eighteenth-century comedies by Antonio Zamora (1660–1728?). The moment Goya chose from *El hechizado por fuerza* (The forcibly bewitched, first performed in 1698 and frequently in the eighteenth century) is discernible from the text at the bottom right where a prompter would sit. The preposterous superstition of the miserly, gluttonous priest Don Claudio, who believes his life depends on perpetually refilling an oil lamp kept in the bedroom of a supposed witch, is exposed. His superstitious folly is conveyed not only by his gesture (covering his mouth so that the devil cannot enter) but also by a grotesque backdrop of murky wall paintings of dancing donkeys, and by the wooden goat that holds the lamp.[24]

Although theatrical sources have not been found for the other four paintings, lighting, composition, and space also evoke stage settings. In *The Conjurors*, or *The Spell*, another hapless victim of superstition cowers in her nightgown as witches, with their sacrificial babies and *grimoire*, hover menacingly over her (figure 7.3). She has perhaps offered up her own child—a witch pricks one tiny figure with a large pin—perhaps in the fantasy of her dreams.[25] In contrast to what seem to be feminine protagonists in this painting, *The Witches' Kitchen* (a scene of metamorphosis into animal form and levitation through a chimney) and *Witches in the Air* seem to show males, although the ambiguity of gender of Goya's witches is already apparent in this latter work. Goya also blurs the distinctions between unholy witches and Christian institutions. As the witches vampirize their victim above terrified witnesses, they wear the conical *corozas* placed on defendants by the Inquisition—but here their caps are cleaved, suggesting bishops' miters, and their bare backs and short pants suggest flagellants.[26]

In *The Witches' Sabbath* (figure 7.4), in which babies, corpses, and fetuses seem to be brought to the devil as sacrifices, a Rococo composition compromises the gruesome subject, and the great he-goat lacks the glowering ferocity he acquires in *Capricho* 60 (see figure 7.6). Helman connected the actions depicted here to the Younger Moratín's account of the confessions of accused witches during the famous trials at Logroño in 1610.[27] It may be that in this domestic context Goya dampened the grotesque impact of his subject, but one can also read the work as embracing yet transforming the pictorial vocabulary of the tapestry cartoon and therefore as emblematic of Goya's own shift in artistic direction.

The presence of a theme normally so steeped in misogyny in the Duchess's private quarters seems anomalous, but it is explicable once we understand what she wanted to accomplish with her country house and grounds, *La Alameda* (also called, significantly, *El Capricho*). The essence of this house and its grounds was its wide variety of diverting and illuminating experiences; witchcraft is but one element in an intriguing collage. The Duchess's English friend,

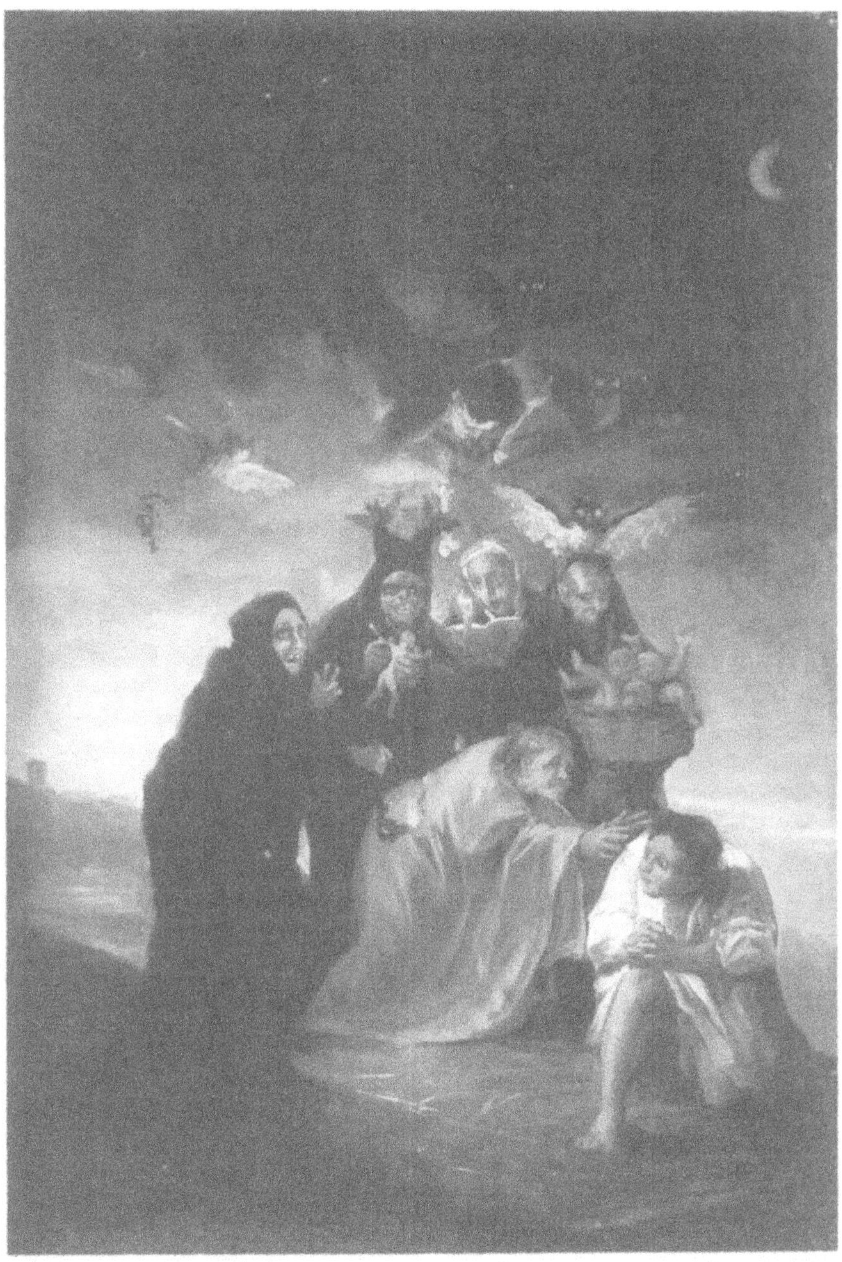

Figure 7.3. Francisco Goya, *The Conjurors* (or *The Spell*), 1797–98. Oil on canvas, 43.5 × 30.5 cm. Museo Lázaro Galdiano, Madrid. Scala/Art Resource, New York.

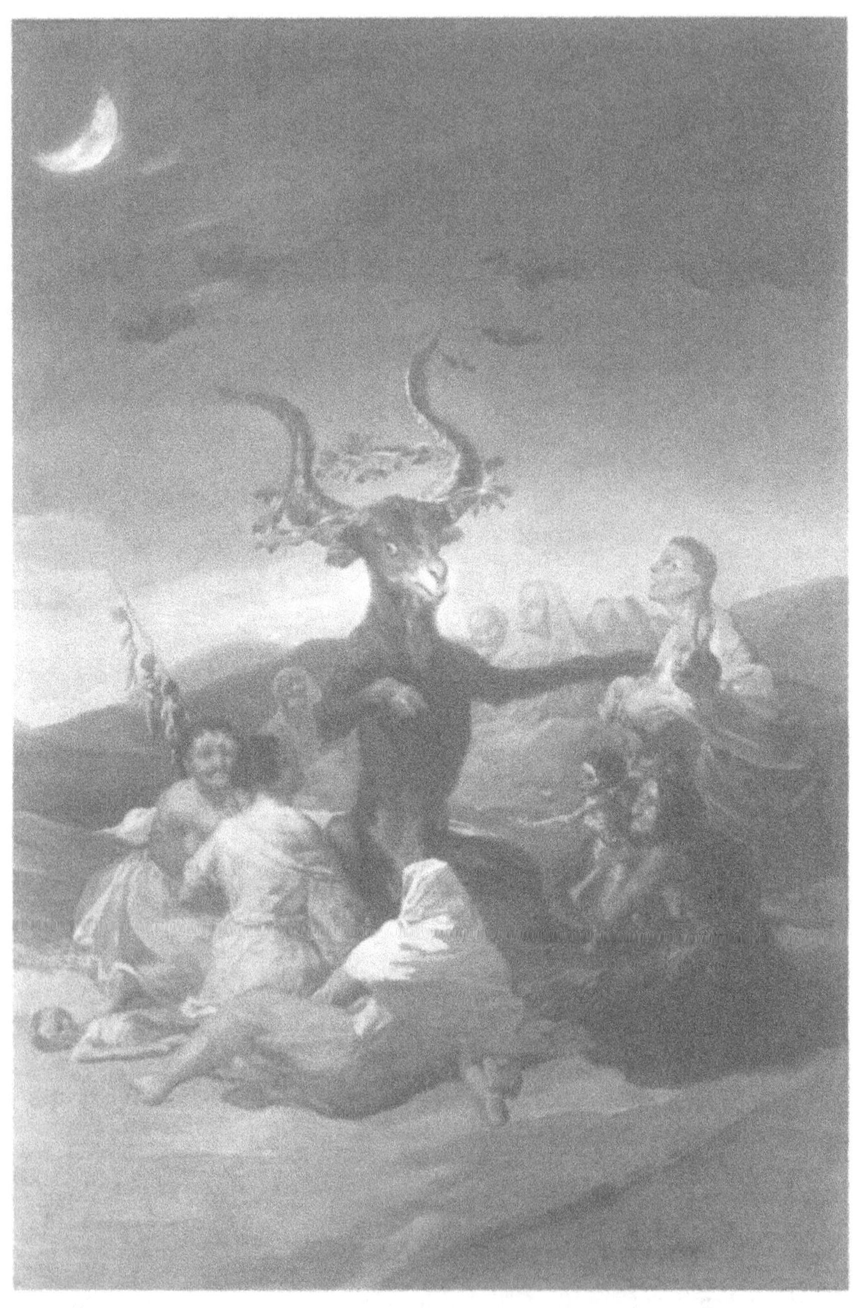

Figure 7.4. Francisco Goya, *The Witches' Sabbath*, 1797–98. Oil on canvas, 44 × 31 cm. Museo Lázaro Galdiano, Madrid. Scala/Art Resource, New York.

Lady Holland, visited *El Capricho* in 1804, when it had reached a form that satisfied its owners, and noted that it was "crowded with a profusion of different ornaments, some in the German sentimental taste, others in a tawdry, citizen-like style." There were "grottoes, temples, chaumières [thatched cottages], hermitages, excavations, canals, ports, pleasure boats, islands, mounts, etc."[28] It is clear that the Alameda's hostess enjoyed surprising, provoking, delighting, and edifying her guests in the course of *tertulias* (salons), outings on gaily decorated pleasure boats floating on the lake, or picnics on the extensive grounds.

María Josefa Alonso Pimentel, known as the Countess-Duchess of Benavente, was one of the most important and enlightened noblewomen in Spain. She acquired the title of the Duchess of Osuna when she married the ninth Duke of Osuna in 1771. Like her friend the tempestuous Duchess of Alba, with whom Goya was apparently romantically involved in 1796–97, she was one of the most fashionable women in Spain. Unlike Alba, however, she took an activist approach to the reform of Spanish society based on principles of the French Enlightenment. Goya's exquisite and innovative portrait of the Osunas and their children (Prado Museum, 1787–88) reveals the couple's interest in new Enlightenment ideals of the family.[29] The Duchess's most important social contribution was her leadership of the *Junta des Damas* (women's council), female wing of the progressive Economic Society of Madrid. The *Junta* sought economic and educational progress and addressed specific issues such as the improvement of conditions in orphanages and women's prisons, and teaching working-class girls the trade of textile manufacturing. In addition, her patronage of art, theater, and literature reveals her interest in satire as a catalyst to social and economic change. The dramatist Ramón de la Cruz; the poet Juan Meléndez Valdés, founder of the radical journal *El Censor*; and Goya all benefited from her support. The Osunas's purchase of four sets of the *Caprichos* strongly suggests their encouragement of Goya in his satirical project. As Symmons points out, the Duchess in particular was a liberal patron who allowed artists and writers great imaginative freedom, and Goya must have felt especially grateful as he sought to fashion himself along these lines.[30]

The Duchess had no pretense of being a woman of the people; her activism was rooted in inherited privilege. Like other themes concerning rural settings, practices, and beliefs, witchcraft was consciously adopted from this aristocratic perspective as part of the scheme of her country house (recall the reception of engravings of David Teniers's witchcraft images in eighteenth-century France as part of a quaint rural genre). The seven paintings by Goya purchased by the Duke for his wife's private quarters at *La Alameda* in 1786–87, most of which are now in the collection of the Duque de Montellano in Madrid, featured rural themes, such as the lighthearted *Greasy Pole*, a village game. But sometimes in these earlier paintings the countryside holds danger: a woman enjoying an outing in the country falls from a donkey, an injured mason is carried on a stretcher. One of the most surprising works, in ravishing Rococo colors that belie its theme, depicts an attack by rural bandits on a coach. Two aristocratic victims, dressed as *maja* and *majo* (i.e., adopting a lower-class Spanish dress) and about to be tied up by the bandits, plead for mercy, as two coachmen and a soldier lie dead in front of them. Such incidents were a real danger for aristocrats like the Osunas while they traveled in the country. Carlos III's plan to repopulate the mountainous regions of Spain had included measures against highwaymen, who were nevertheless regarded popularly as "Robin Hoods" who gave to the poor what they took from the rich.[31] However, Peter Klein notes that in experiencing the Osuna painting, viewers would have sublimated their fears about real violence under a safe, aesthetic response to a picturesque scene.[32] Later, Goya would reprise the theme of rural bandits in his pictures sent to the Madrid Academy in 1794 and again even more grimly in paintings of robbery, rape, and murder done between 1798 and 1800, probably for Don Juan de Salas, a Mallorcan art connoisseur.[33]

In short, *La Alameda* provided the Osunas and their guests with an orchestrated experience of immersion in the countryside—with its natural beauties, simple delights, provocative danger, and violence couched in picturesque terms, as well as its rusticity and poverty, also observed at a safe, aesthetic distance. The Hermitage was equipped with real, aged hermits (and then with an automaton). A rustic house by Milanese theatrical designer Ángel Maria Tadey and Madrid architect Mateo Medina also contained automata, *trompe l'oeil* paintings of food and household implements and a room hung with moss. In her planning of the gardens of *La Alameda*, the Duchess also understood her guests' experience of nature in didactic terms. The production of honey by the bees in her apiary—an example of how human society might learn industry and cooperation from nature—could be viewed through a glass wall.[34] Given the combination of didacticism, delight, and surprise in the Duchess's own rural *Capricho*, the witchcraft scenes in her private quarters are probably to be understood both as titillating, theatrically inspired caprices as well as satirical essays. Witchcraft is viewed as a preposterous belief fostered by the Inquisition to which ignorant Spanish peasants were vulnerable.

Contemporary critiques of witchcraft beliefs also reveal an awareness of the way accusations fell primarily on old peasant women. In his critical history of the Holy Office, former Inquisitorial official Juan Antonio Llorente (whom Goya painted between 1810 and 1812) commented on the irony of the devil's taste for old, poor, and ugly women, as opposed to those who were young, beautiful, and noble.[35] Goya's witchcraft scenes on the Duchess's private walls in her country house may have been *caprichos* that amused her, but also they are connected to her progressive stances on education and improving the lot of the poor. Her activism on behalf of Spanish women also suggests she may well have been aware that misogyny was inherent in the witchcraft stereotype, and that lower-class women were historically the primary victims of that stereotype.

Reason Dreams of Witches: The *Caprichos*

The iconography of Goya's individual images of witches in the *Caprichos* and their preparatory drawings is also fairly well established by research on his visual and literary sources and the linguistic nuances of captions and various verbal glosses. There is the Prado commentary on the *Caprichos*, apparently written in Goya's hand but not necessarily composed by him. Helman believed its author was the Younger Moratín—an important figure for understanding contemporary views of witchcraft, as we shall see below—or an imitator, perhaps Goya himself. However, there are doubts that the Prado commentary gives a fully reliable access to the *Caprichos*; Helman thought that its softened political critique suggests that it may have been written to accompany the plates Goya gave to the King in 1803.[36] A more explicit manuscript commentary owned by Adelardo López de Ayala was published in 1887; its text was elaborated in further commentaries. Taken together, the Prado, Ayala, and other glosses give clues about Goya's own attitude toward witchcraft and the meaning of individual images.

However, this accumulated evidence seems inadequate when faced with the simultaneous subtlety and expressive clout of these images, which are even more remarkable in the light of the pictorial tradition I have traced in this study. Goya's perspective on witchcraft was both broader and more complex than that of any artist I have discussed. The theme provided him with a uniquely powerful lens to view the tension between our reason and fantasy, our perennial fascination with horror, and our capacity for cruelty. The distance between what Goya would call ignorant superstition and the enlightened skepticism of the liberal audience he addressed is certainly apparent in his critique of witchcraft beliefs and witch-hunting. However, his weaving of witchcraft beliefs into a single, grotesque, and disconcertingly *un*reasonable tapestry made up of timeless human flaws and continuing social and political problems in Spain leaves doubt whether enlightened skepticism can triumph. Enlightenment principles ascendant during the reign of Carlos III (1759–88) had shown their vulnerability in the 1790s, retreating before conservative forces, poised to resist any incursions on their power by Carlos IV (1789–1808).[37] Ronald Paulson has argued that Goya's use of the serial format in the *Caprichos* was ideal for expressing the incoherence of the Spanish world in 1799. For Goya in 1799, Paulson states, "experience can be represented only in a series of fragmentary, even contradictory images."[38] For Janis Tomlinson, the shifting perspectives and "perpetual flux" of the *Caprichos* marks a pluralism that characterizes

Goya's oeuvre as a whole.[39] Hofmann emphasizes the role Goya's seemingly arbitrary juxtapositions force on the viewer, who is compelled "to make leaps of perception, and hence also of association, looking here, there and everywhere, for all perspectives are interchangeable."[40]

Although the viewer might find guilty and innocent defined clearly enough within each *Capricho*, collectively the etchings indict widening circles of people until viewers themselves are finally implicated. We linger over the grotesque details of these images, forced to contemplate their interdependence and ambiguity. We cannot extract ourselves from the deeper motives that the idea of witchcraft and its persecution expose: fear and hatred of difference and disorder and our construction of intricate belief systems that justify the most inhumane actions. We are introduced to black magic simply, by the image of a woman gleaning materials for a love spell from a hanged man in *Capricho* 12 (*Out Hunting for Teeth*; figure 7.5). It coexists with other kinds of superstition such as belief in bogey-men in *The Bogey-Man Is Coming* in *Capricho* 3. But after *Capricho* 43, *The Sleep of Reason* (see figure 7.2), we are no longer confronted with mere superstition. Even though prosecutions for magic of various kinds far outnumbered those for diabolical witchcraft in Goya's time, the ignorant woman in *Hunting for Teeth* is not the prime target of Goya's satire.[41] Rather, it is the demonological world view: its near-dualism; its siege mentality; its perverse fascination with cannibalism, infanticide, and sexual taboos; its misogynistic fantasy cloaked in theology.

In Chapter 3, we saw how Hans Baldung Grien implicated his audience and himself in the cycle of lust, sin, and death embodied in the figure of the witch. Similarly, Goya demanded from viewers this kind of intense engagement, but its parameters are much larger. In the past—whether witchcraft was viewed with skepticism, credulity, or some combination of the two—it had always revolved around women. Either their innate evil enabled the devil to use them as instruments or their innate gullibility caused them to believe this was so, or both. Although women are present in Goya's images of witches, they are no longer at the center of the social and political problem represented by witchcraft. Moreover, it is evident from his relationship with the Duchess of Osuna that Goya consciously considered educated women as part of his audience—a factor irrelevant or incidental to earlier images. Certainly the *tertulias* held in the Osunas's palace in Madrid, which Goya must have attended, addressed the social and political issues explored in the series.[42]

Gerlinde Volland has argued forcefully for Goya as an exemplary misogynist, whose depiction of women in the *Caprichos* as witches, objects of desire rather than desiring subjects, and prostitutes conforms completely to the venerable western tradition of woman-hating.[43] However, in keeping with the profound ambiguities in contemporary discussions of woman's nature and her proper role in society, Goya cannot be described accurately as misogynist or

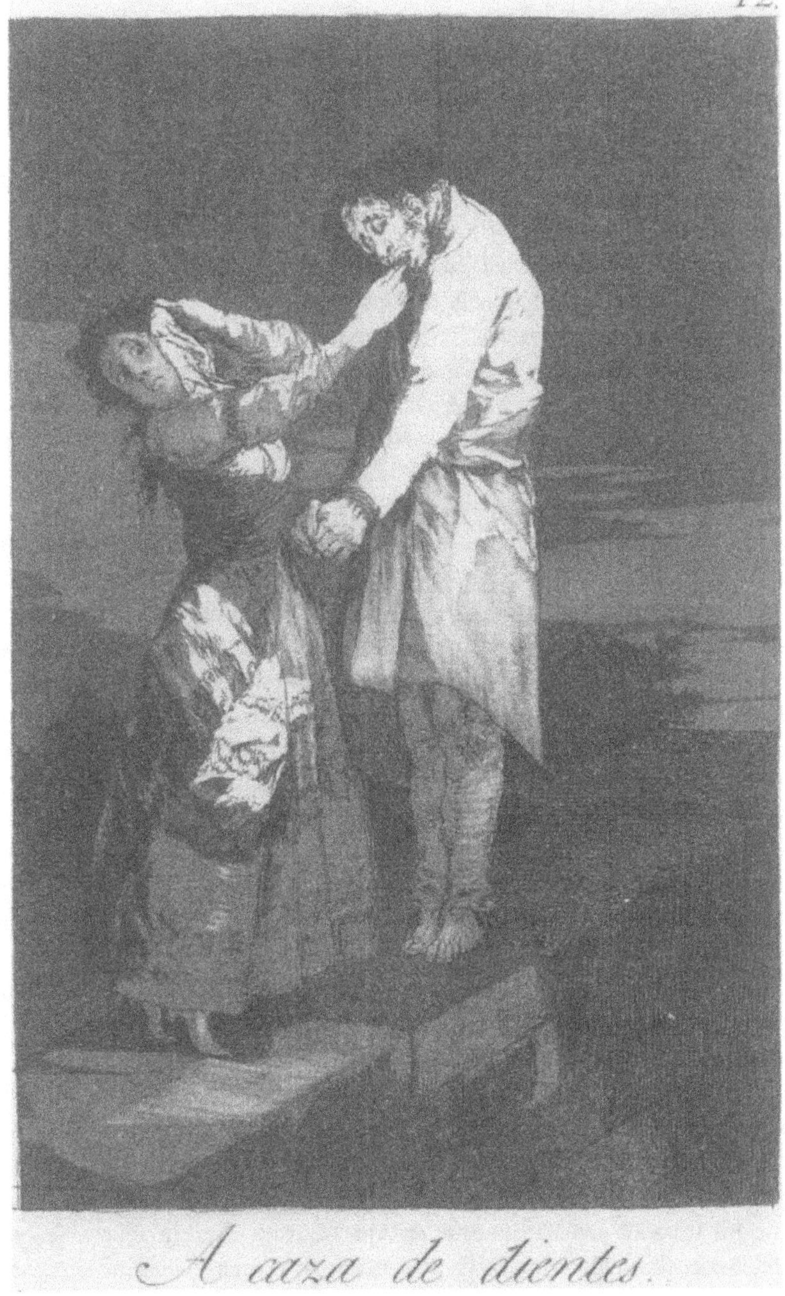

Figure 7.5. Francisco Goya, *Out Hunting for Teeth* (*Capricho* 12), 1799. Etching, burnished aquatint, and burin, 218 × 151 mm. Image © 2004 Board of Trustees, National Gallery of Art, Washington, D.C. Rosenwald Collection.

feminist.[44] Opinions surrounding the admission of women to the Economic Society of Madrid, for instance, varied widely, from patriarchal traditionalism to sexual egalitarianism. The contributions of Gaspar Melchor de Jovellanos, the leading liberal intellectual in Spain and Goya's patron and friend, are particularly disappointing and are based on traditional ideas of women's modesty and their proper place in the domestic sphere. Although Jovellanos recognized that women should be included, he held strong reservations about their full participation and was especially concerned about the potential disruptiveness of their presence at meetings. His relegation of women to auxiliary status is in fact what occurred. However, Pedro Rodriguez de Campomanes argued that women should be admitted not just because of the benefits that would come from their work but because it was their right. One of the most remarkable essays came from Josefa Amar y Borbón, already a female member of the Aragonese society, whose systematic argument centered on women's fundamental equality and the relationship between denying them an education and their lack of political power.[45]

To be sure, Goya often focused on conventionally defined female vices and folly, an attitude corroborating Jovellanos's concerns about women's frivolity, extravagance, and concupiscence contributing to a general decline of Spanish morals: the primary reason why *exemplary* women should be associated with the Madrid Economic Society. Goya also constructed his artistic identity in the masculine terms of genius and melancholy that had excluded women in the past, but he did not condemn women unequivocally to the realms of evil and unreason. Like the companion of his later years, Leocadia Zorilla—depicted in the Black Paintings as the old artist's mournful Muse; as an ironic observer of a witches' sabbath; and in allegorical guise as the patriot, heroine and seductress Judith (see figures 7.16 and 7.17)—women in Goya's art are poised ambivalently between past and future. Goya's critique of contemporary social mores included but did not center on women: He viewed both sexes as subject to education and reform. As Ronald Paulson notes, the "predatory aspect [of human sexual behavior] is shifted from one sex to the other. This man preys on that woman, and then vice versa."[46]

Goya's insistence on shared guilt explains his reinvention of the visual tradition I have traced in this book. By appropriating witchcraft so thoroughly into his broader project of social critique, Goya robbed it of its misogynistic lifeblood. Although some of the *Caprichos* of witches, when isolated, clearly belong within the misogynist tradition (a good example is *Pretty Teacher!*, *Capricho* 68, see figure 7.8), Goya deliberately obscured the sex of his witches in many others (for example, *Blow*, see figure 7.9). As he deflated the longstanding theoretical link between witchcraft and women, he also exposed the corruption of the male institutions—in particular, the Inquisition—that persecuted witches.

Like Italy, Spain experienced comparatively few instances of large-scale witch-hunting even during the peak years between 1580 and 1650: The Spanish and Roman Inquisitions discouraged executing witches, although they were not always willing or able to stop secular authorities from doing so.[47] Witch-hunts were anachronistic in Goya's time (there were only four trials between 1780 and 1820[48]), but they became topical as part of current controversy about the Spanish Inquisition, its history, and its potential reform or dissolution. In the late 1790s, there was a disturbing rapprochement between the Spanish monarchy, alarmed by the recent events of the French Revolution, and the Holy Office that could serve the crown by exposing dissent.[49] When he published the *Caprichos*, Goya tried to sidestep the censorship of the Inquisition. He sold the prints in a shop offering perfumes and liqueurs rather than books and prints. He denied that his critique had specific targets when he advertised the sale of the etchings in the *Diario de Madrid*, an advertisement perhaps written for him by a literary friend.[50] Much later in 1825, Goya stated that he withdrew the *Caprichos* from sale because of the threat of Inquisitorial censorship.[51]

Although some Spaniards argued passionately for the importance of the Holy Office for Spain, Goya was an unremitting critic, and not just because of the censorship that touched him personally. From his Album C—dated by Eleanor Sayre to the period of the Peninsular War (1808–14) and the Cadiz Constitution (1812–14)—there remain twenty-nine drawings about the Inquisition. In these extraordinary works, Goya denounced its use of torture (the rack, the strappado) and prolonged imprisonment, its persecution of innocent people such as the descendents of *conversos* (converts to Christianity), and, most important, its suppression of religious and intellectual freedom.[52] In the context of Spanish debates about the Holy Office in the late eighteenth and early nineteenth centuries, its historical role in formulating the idea of witchcraft and in persecuting witches was highly charged, even though, as we have seen, it acted moderately with respect to witchcraft compared to many secular courts. In fact, the confessions resulting in the Logroño auto-da-fé were brilliantly critiqued on rationalistic grounds from within the Holy Office itself by Alonso de Salazar Frias, the youngest inquisitor at the district tribunal of Logroño.[53] Nevertheless, for Goya's circle, in particular Jovellanos and Moratín, the Holy Office was an obstacle to progress, and witch-hunting exemplified its backwardness and corruption. Both men could have provided the artist access to the literature on witchcraft at the time he was formulating the *Caprichos* in 1797–98.

In 1795, Jovellanos noted purchase of a copy of the *Malleus maleficarum* in his journal, an indication of his interest in the sources of witchcraft belief.[54] In November 1797, Prime Minister Manuel Godoy made Jovellanos Minister of Justice—a surprising appointment bound to turn sour because of the latter's passion for economic, judicial, and educational reform. Jovellanos was to retreat in defeat to Asturias by August 1798. Goya painted him during his ministry, but with his decline made clear; he is in the pose of melancholy with a statue of Minerva offering him solace (Prado Museum, Madrid).[55] Probably contributing to his loss of the ministry were Jovellanos's plans to enact reforms of the Holy Office recommended by Llorente, who had been named commissary of the Inquisition at Logroño in 1782, and Secretary-General of the Inquisition at Madrid in 1789. Although the project of reform that Jovellanos and Llorente desired was cut short, the latter would later write a critical history of the institution, published in French in Paris in 1817, and contribute to its eventual dissolution under King José I. Llorente was careful to distinguish the Spanish Inquisition of the eighteenth century from its notorious past embodiment, but he was rigorously critical of its abuse of power, its hindrance of scientific progress in Spain, as well as its fostering of the delusion of witchcraft.[56]

In 1797, Moratín, also a close friend of the Duchess of Osuna who advised her voracious reading and purchases for their large library, including books forbidden to most Spaniards by Inquisitorial censure,[57] probably began to annotate a seventeenth-century pamphlet on the 1610 auto-de-fé at Logroño, which involved fifty-three delinquents accused of various crimes (e.g., blasphemy and bigamy) along with witchcraft. Eleven people were accused of this last offense, five in effigy because they had died in prison while the Inquisition conducted its slow investigation.[58] Moratín apparently did not know about Salazar Frias's debunking of the trials—the Inquisition did not make those documents public—and so his satire was uncomplicated on that score.[59] Although Moratín's annotations were not published until 1811, Helman concluded that he must have shared his manuscript with Goya as the artist developed the Osuna pictures and the *Caprichos*. The similarities between the commentaries on the witchcraft images of the *Caprichos* in the Prado manuscript and Moratín's sarcastic notes on the Logroño trial, Helman argued, are too great to ignore.[60]

The first ten images of Goya's drawing series *Sueños* (Dreams), comprising at least twenty-eight ink sketches preparatory to the *Caprichos* etchings, constitute a meditation on witchcraft belief inspired by Moratín's critique. Led by the initial stages of *The Sleep of Reason* that eventually became the famous *Capricho* 43 (see figure 7.2), *Sueños* 2 through 10 are scenes of witchcraft that (except for *Sueño* 6) Goya refined into the etched compositions for *Caprichos* 60, 62, 63, 65, 66, 67, 68, 69, and 70.[61] These constitute the most sustained sequence of related images in the second half of the series, akin to the donkey sequence in the first half (*Caprichos* 37–42). Other images depicting witches or demons explicitly (44, 45, 46, 47, 48, 51, 64) fleshed out this sequence, although identifying demonic beings and witches in Goya's works is sometimes difficult, as we will see.

Goya's use of the term "*sueño*" as a title for these preparatory drawings and especially within the title of *Capricho* 43 has generated much scholarly commentary. First, it refers to the seventeenth-century satirist Francisco Gómez de Quevedo y Villegas, who, in his *Sueños* (1607–35), dreamed of descending into a hell populated with foolish, sinful people and also those who simply annoyed him. There is a thin line between humans and demons in Quevedo's inferno. Whereas demons acknowledge their actions as sins, humans persist in condoning what they do.[62] Goya's caustic statement in a letter to Zapater in 1785 is analogous in its denigration of humans: "I'll have you know that I'm not afraid of witches, phantoms, boastful giants, rogues, knaves, etc., nor do I fear any other kind of beings except human ones."[63] Goya's use of the term "*sueños*" to recall Quevedo explains to some extent the extraordinary blurring of the human and demonic in the series for the purpose of heightening satire.

The double meaning of *sueño* as "sleep" and "dream" presents further complexity, especially with regard to *Capricho* 43 and the images that follow it, including the witchcraft sequence. What exactly does Goya mean by "*El Sueño de la razon produce monstruos*" written on the desk in *Capricho* 43? Is it the more straightforward alternative of the Prado commentary? When the artist allows reason to sleep and thus to abandon his imagination, he produces only impossible monsters—those foreshadowed by the bats, owls, and felines, but emerging in full grotesqueness in the plates following. Only when united with reason can imagination be constructive.[64] This meaning coincides with the sense of the advertisement for the *Caprichos* in the *Diario de Madrid* that stated the series' goal to reform society and only secondarily to exercise the artist's imagination.[65] It also coincides with the inscription on the second sketch for *Capricho* 43 (*Sueño* 1) proclaiming the author's purpose to be the banishing of harmful, commonly held beliefs to perpetuate the solid testimony of Truth. Does this more straightforward sense—the cooperation of reason and imagination to make images that, like poetry, can reform society—disguise a different intent? Are we to understand that reason, paradoxically, has *dreamed* its own monsters; that is, the Enlightenment has failed?[66]

In terms of witchcraft and its persecution, this ambiguity is pertinent. Given Goya's unswerving, anti-Inquisition stance, the dominant sense of "*sueño*" with respect to witchcraft and its persecution is probably the "sleep" of reason. Goya asked the same question early scholars of the European witch-hunts emerging out of the Enlightenment asked: How could such otherwise learned and thoughtful men have displayed the credulity and inhumanity? Clearly, reason did sleep, yielding the diabolical phantasms of demonological literature as well as the grim spectacle of the auto-da-fé and the stake. And we must not forget that at the end of the *Caprichos*, dawn (reason) does come, banishing goblins in its wake. However, this dominant sense of "*sueño*" carries a latent fracture. The fact that the Spanish Enlightenment had not overcome the populace's belief in witches, ghosts, and goblins but now transformed such beliefs into satirical entertainment could have been, for Goya, one indication of the failure of reason, now dreaming of what it should abhor. As Barbara Benedict points out in her study of curiosity in early modern English culture, a fascination with the occult, the curious, and the marvelous was a sign of social prestige sanctified "under the proclamation of empirical purity."[67] This commodification of the occult was intense among enlightened Spaniards, who embraced its satiric potential.[68] There can be no doubt that Goya addressed the *Caprichos* to this elite audience—they were expensive, even overpriced prints.[69] But he did not address them as a sycophant, and he also implicated himself in his own critique.

That the first ten *Sueños* and the etchings that resulted from them are based on the Logroño trials seen through his friend Moratín's eyes is significant. Although the number of victims was not large, the Logroño trials nevertheless exemplified the mature concept of witchcraft in its most colorfully embellished form, influenced by magistrate Pierre de Lancre's witch-hunting campaign in the nearby Basque-speaking Pays de Labourd. Goya knew the illustration for de Lancre's account of the trials (see figure 4.1), for the great he-goat turns up in the *Caprichos* (for example in Plate 60, figure 7.6, *Trials*) and in the Osuna pictures.

Goya's images echo many elements of the confessions that led to the Logroño auto-da-fé. Men were occasionally involved, despite the usual preponderance of women—for example, *Trials* seems to show a female witch initiating a male into flight. With its unspecified setting, intimacy, and triangular composition, this etching uncannily recalls Baldung's Freiburg drawings of witches attempting to fly (compare figures 3.7 and 3.8), even though Goya would not have seen them. The common source for both artists, of course, was the centrality of flight and the unguent to the concept of witchcraft. Both artists seized on the visual and satiric potential of this motif. The idea of highly ranked senior witches was also important at Logroño (see *Where Is Mama Going?*, *Capricho* 65), as were levitation and transformation through use of the unguent (*Trials* again; *Wait til You've Been Anointed*, *Capricho* 67; and *Look How Solemn They Are!*, *Capricho* 63, figure 7.7). The notion of witchcraft being passed from the old to the young also occurred (see *Pretty Teacher*! *Capricho* 68, figure 7.8), and there was frequent molestation, vampirizing (sucking), and murder of children (see *Blow*, *Capricho* 69, figure 7.9). The Logroño witches gave extremely detailed accounts of their sacrifices of children, their worship of the devil, and their inversions of Christian worship, suggested in *Devout Profession*, *Capricho* 70; figure 7.10).[70] In short, the ten etchings developed from

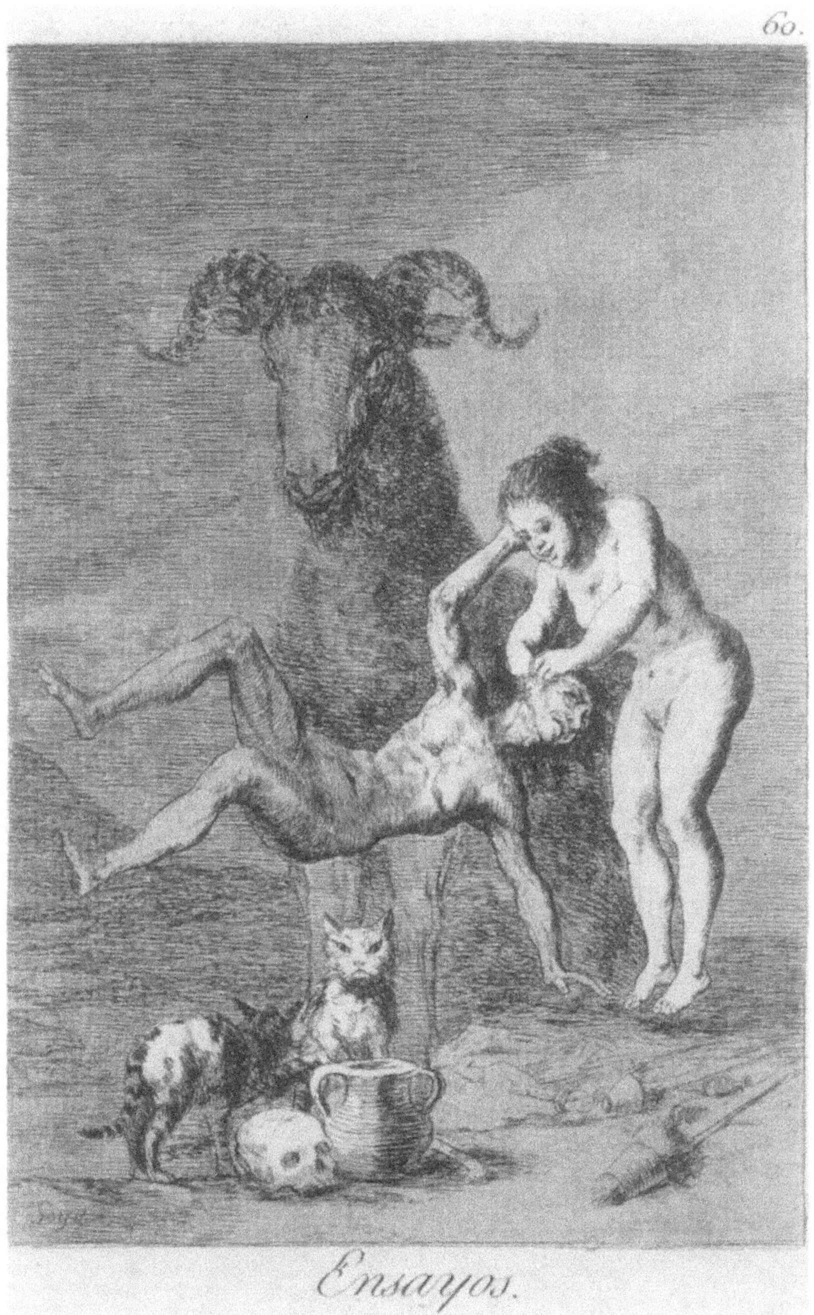

Figure 7.6. Francisco Goya, *Trials* (*Capricho* 60), 1799. Etching, aquatint, and burin. Image © 2004 Board of Trustees, National Gallery of Art, Washington, D.C. Rosenwald Collection.

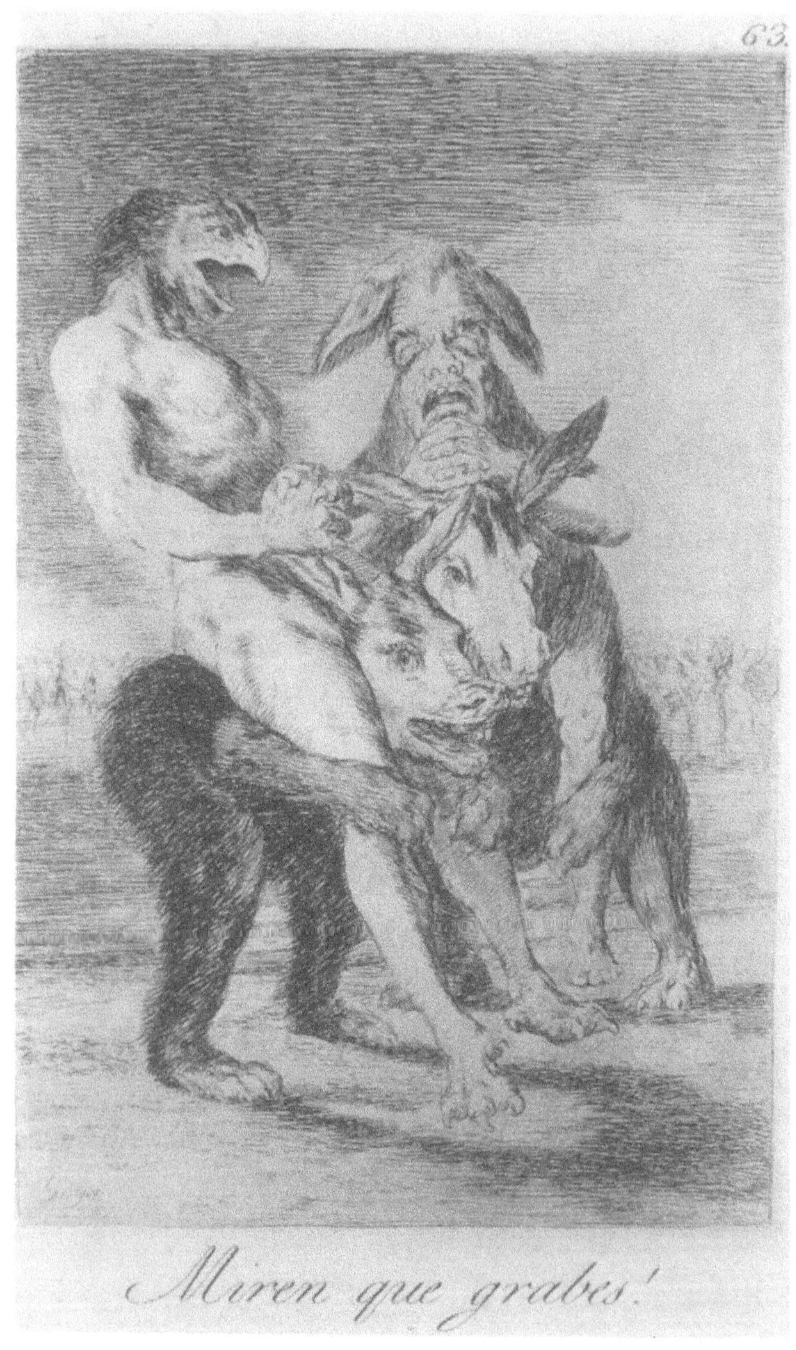

Figure 7.7. Francisco Goya, *Look How Solemn They Are!* (*Capricho* 63), 1799. Etching, aquatint, and drypoint, 215 × 163 mm. Image © 2004 Board of Trustees, National Gallery of Art, Washington, D.C. Rosenwald Collection.

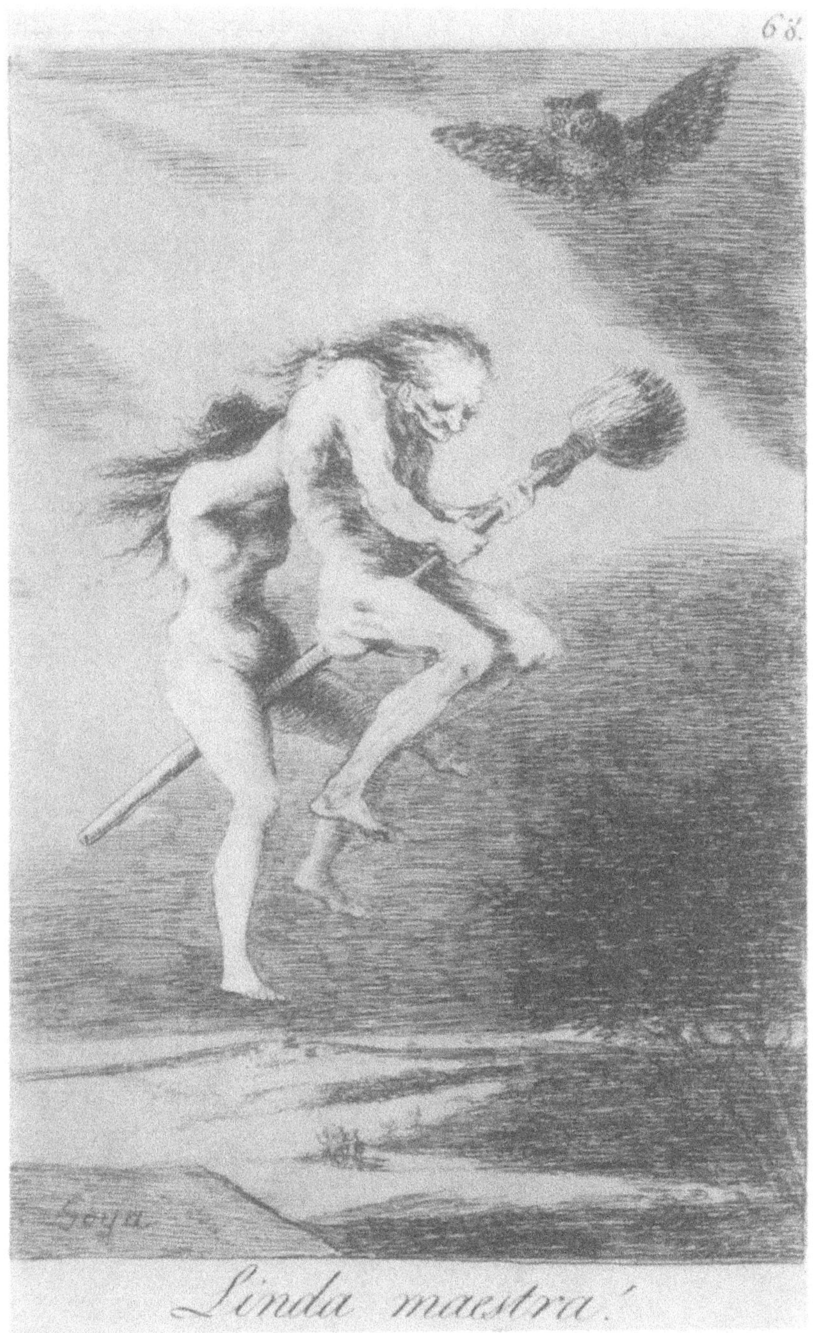

Figure 7.8. Francisco Goya, *Pretty Teacher!* (*Capricho* 68), 1799. Etching, burnished aquatint, and drypoint, 213 × 150 mm. Image © 2004 Board of Trustees, National Gallery of Art, Washington, D.C. Rosenwald Collection.

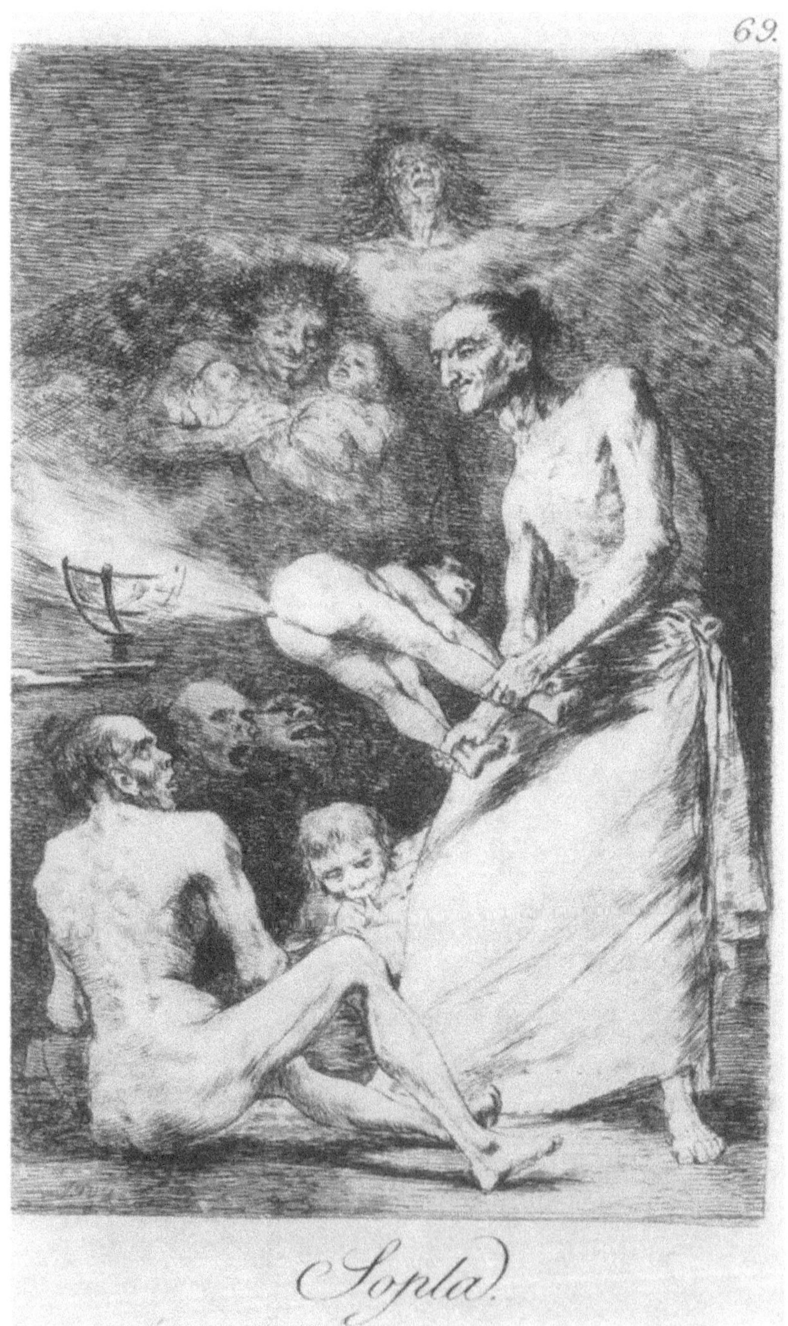

Figure 7.9. Francisco Goya, *Blow* (*Capricho* 69), 1799. Etching, aquatint, drypoint, and burin, 213 × 148 mm. Image © 2004 Board of Trustees, National Gallery of Art, Washington, D.C., Rosenwald Collection.

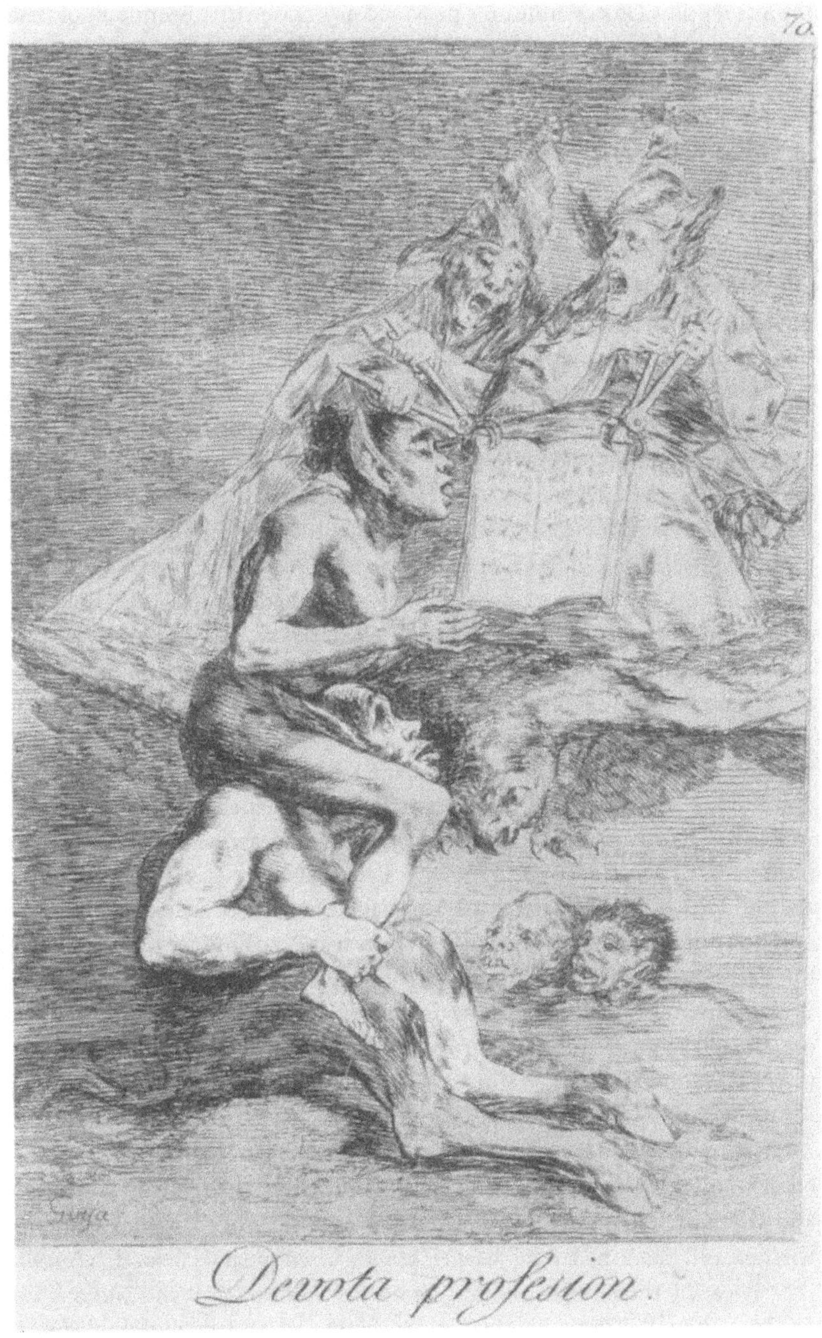

Figure 7.10. Francisco Goya, *Devout Profession* (*Capricho* 70), 1799. Etching, aquatint, and drypoint, 210 × 166 mm. Image © 2004 Board of Trustees, National Gallery of Art, Washington, D.C. Rosenwald Collection.

the *Sueños* plus Goya's additions provided a concise visual summary of mature demonological beliefs as these were manifested in the Logroño trials. When reorganized into the *Capricho* sequence, these images culminated appropriately in *Devout Profession*, an image of heresy, core of the "exceptional crime" of witchcraft as understood by the Inquisition. After this, with *Capricho* 71, *If Day Breaks, We Will Go*, Goya's exploration of witchcraft winds down, as we begin to sense the light of embattled reason reemerging at the end of the cycle. Finally, the minor goblins of Plate 80 (*Time Is Up*) yawn and stretch themselves to disappear. As a complex print series, however, with details buried in the aquatint and requiring close study, and cross-references and contradictions appearing everywhere, the *Caprichos* offered no easy or complete closure.

Pretty Teacher!, *Blow*, and *Devout Profession* illustrate the ambiguity and cross-referentiality of all Goya's images in the *Caprichos*. Carefully pared down from their preparatory drawings, each image offers an ironic, challenging gloss on something we have seen before in the series. The caption of *Devout Profession* cannot help but recall the images of the clergy and the Inquisition, in particular *Caprichos* 23 and 24, *Those Specks of Dust*, and *Nothing Could Be Done about It* (figures 7.11 and 7.12), as well as the brainless adoration of academic authority in *Capricho* 53, *What a Golden Beak!*

The two infernal, mitered bishops of *Devout Profession* hold a book with pincers as a satyr (i.e., Lust) lifts up a devotee on his shoulders. Goya developed this curious image with significant changes through Madrid Album B, to the *Sueños* album, to the *Caprichos* etching. Initially, in the Album B drawing, the devotee was female, wearing a fox-mask—thus identifying her as a prostitute (*zorra* or vixen) as well as a young witch—and on the altar supporting the bishops were devils' faces. In the *Sueños*, the devotee became a male with ass's ears, and the bishops floated on a huge snake, a symbol of heresy. Behind this new altar of heresy were now shadowy creatures reminiscent of those behind the sleeper in *The Sleep of Reason*. In the final etching, the bishops ride an owl with a serpent's tail (false wisdom that is really heresy?), the gender of the devotee is ambiguous, and there are two coarse-featured figures floating up to their necks in water at the right.[71]

Any simple reading of this image in terms of the traditional idea of witchcraft is impossible. Goya's obscuring of the gender of the devotee, especially, breaks down the theoretical link between women, their uncontrollable lust, and witchcraft. He also complicated the inversion of Christian worship by witches and demons by his earlier scenes of Inquisitorial justice, in which those wearing the miters are clearly innocent victims. *Dust* and *Nothing Could Be Done* show the same heretic (or two heretics?) on trial and public display, and a humiliating procession through mocking crowds on a donkey. The victim or victims wear the *coroza* and, in *Dust*, the *sanbenito* tunic on which crimes were written, but it is not clear from the images what crime is being

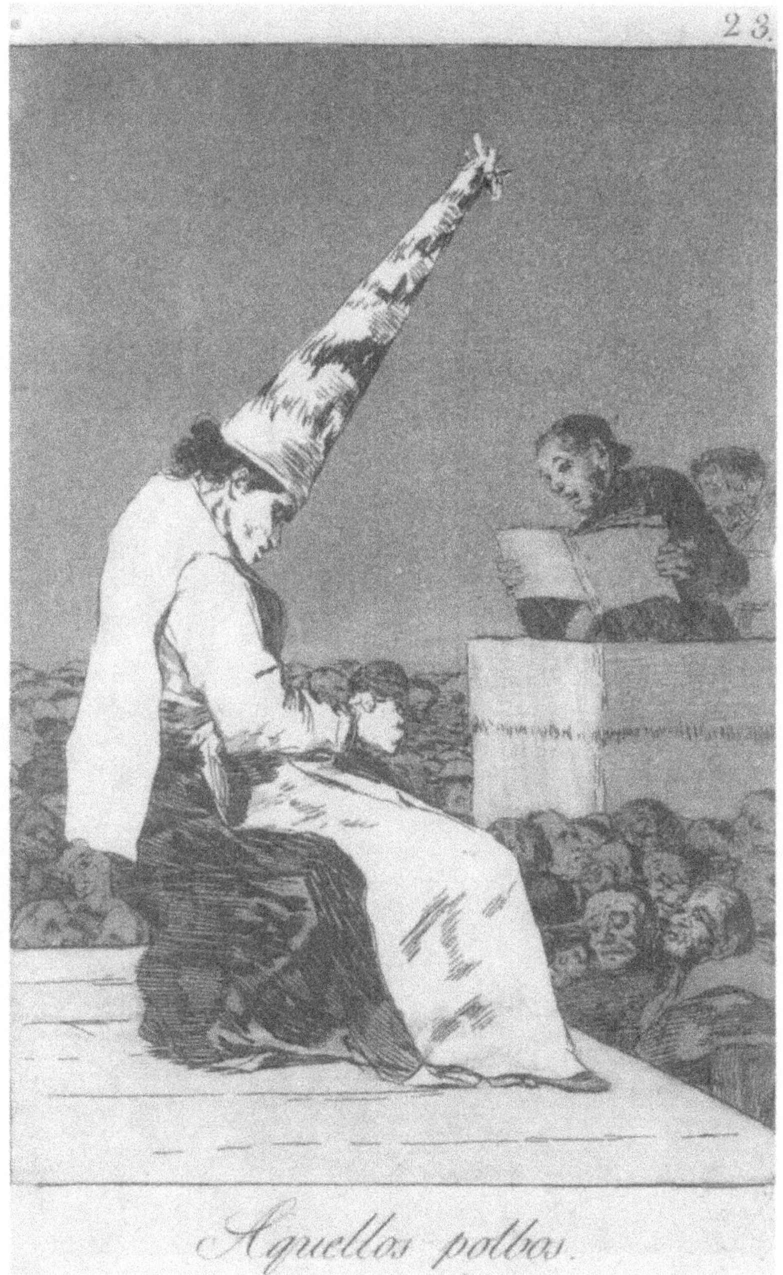

Figure 7.11. Francisco Goya, *Those Specks of Dust* (*Capricho* 23), 1799. Etching, burnished aquatint, drypoint, and burin, 217 × 148 mm. Image © 2004 Board of Trustees, National Gallery of Art, Washington, D.C. Rosenwald Collection.

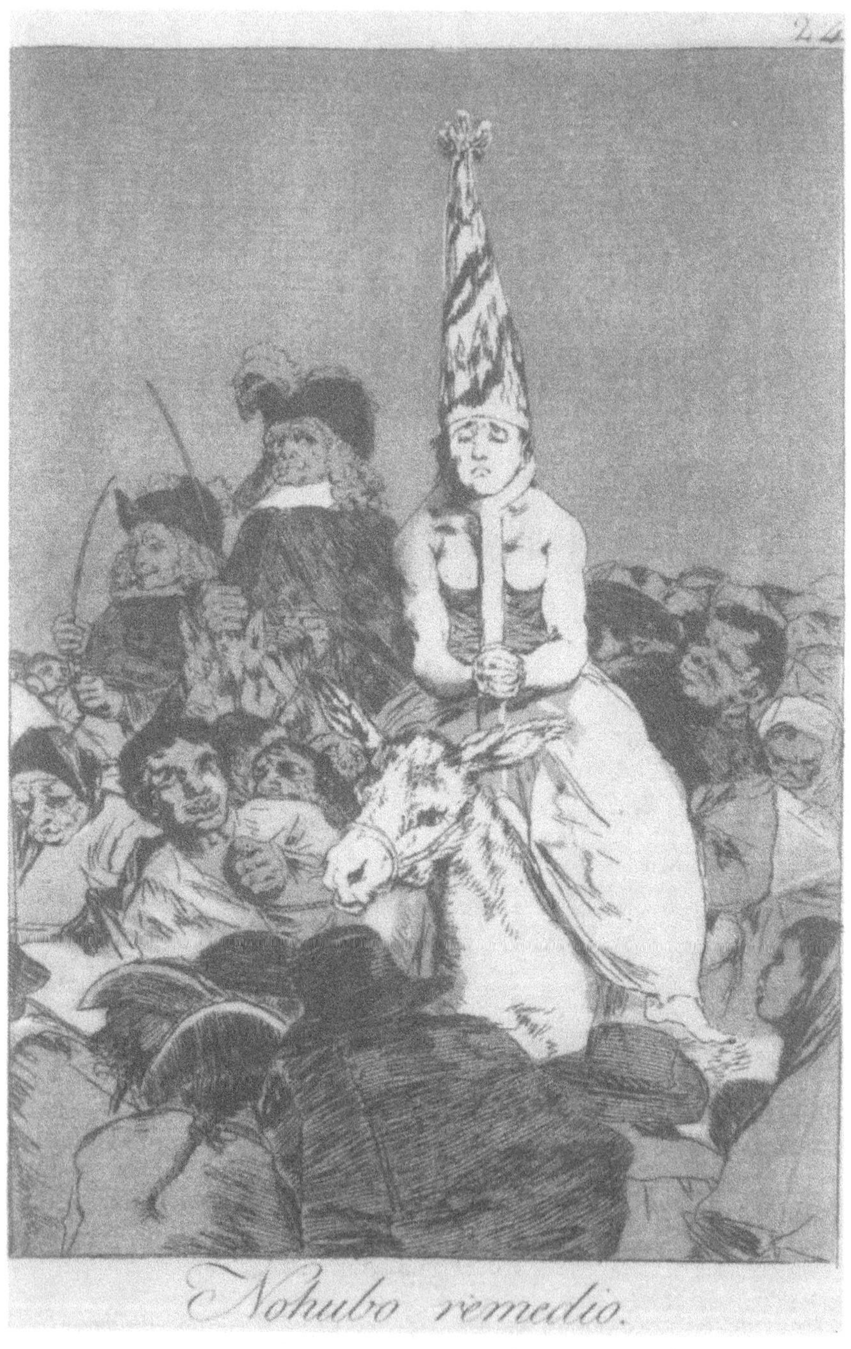

Figure 7.12. Francisco Goya, *Nothing Could Be Done about It* (*Capricho* 24), 1799. Etching and burnished aquatint, 217 × 152 mm. Image © 2004 Board of Trustees, National Gallery of Art, Washington, D.C. Rosenwald Collection.

punished. The more explicit Ayala commentary, however, identifies the figure in *Dust* as a crippled male beggar, Perico, who helped two women sell love powders—much the same offense described in *Hunting for Teeth* (see figure 7.5). The term *polbos* in the caption and the proverb from which the caption derives ("From that dust comes this mud") could also refer to magic powders used in amatory magic.[72]

The confusion of guilt and innocence as we turn from these images of Inquisitorial justice and the witchcraft it punished goes further. The motif of the book held by pincers in *Devout Profession* has been interpreted in terms of theologians' attempts to "torture" meanings from scripture that cannot be found there. Sayre relates this more broadly to the movement toward greater lay access to the Bible through vernacular translations, long forbidden by the Inquisition, which had recently culminated in Padre Felipe Scio de San Miguel's Spanish translation (Valencia, 1790–93). We might interpret the two floating figures beneath the bishops not simply as potential witches, then, but as Christians needing the solace and salvation of a Bible that is kept from them; following a Spanish saying, they are "in water up to their necks"—that is, they are in danger.[73] As viewers acknowledge these meanings, the false bishops can no longer be distinguished from the true ones, and the idea of witchcraft is castigated as just another convoluted if especially pernicious invention of theologians. An even more caustic compromising of ecclesiastical authority, though, is Goya's use of the pincers, instruments of torture used to mutilate heretics before execution. It is on the foundation of mutilated scripture *and* bodies that the punishment of witches and heretics is sustained.

Alongside the clearly female, condemned victim in *Nothing Could Be Done* (see figure 7.12) are constables; the Inquisition itself, of course, did not torture or execute heretics but "relaxed" them to secular authorities. The feline faces of these constables relate them to another who helps a notary devour a prostitute in *Capricho* 21, *How They Pluck Her!* (figure 7.13). Whether cooperating with secular authorities to punish prostitutes or with the Inquisition to punish heretics, the constables seek their own reward, because they are "cats" (*gatos*), cunning petty thieves. Volland's interpretation of *Capricho* 21 is that the whore—an embodiment of Dionysiac sensuality—receives her just punishment from the representatives of Apollonian Reason.[74] To understand the print in this way, however, viewers would have to disregard or to identify with the smugness Goya gave the supervising magistrate, and the relish of the animalistic constable and notary as they bite into their imploring prey.[75] *Capricho* 21 is better understood as the culmination of a sequence of images of prostitution in the first half of the series in which predatory behavior is shifted from one sex to the other. In *Caprichos* 19 and 20, *All Will Fall*, and *There They Go, Plucked*, the whores and procuresses had plucked their customers and chased them away, making room for more. In *There They Go*, one of the pro-

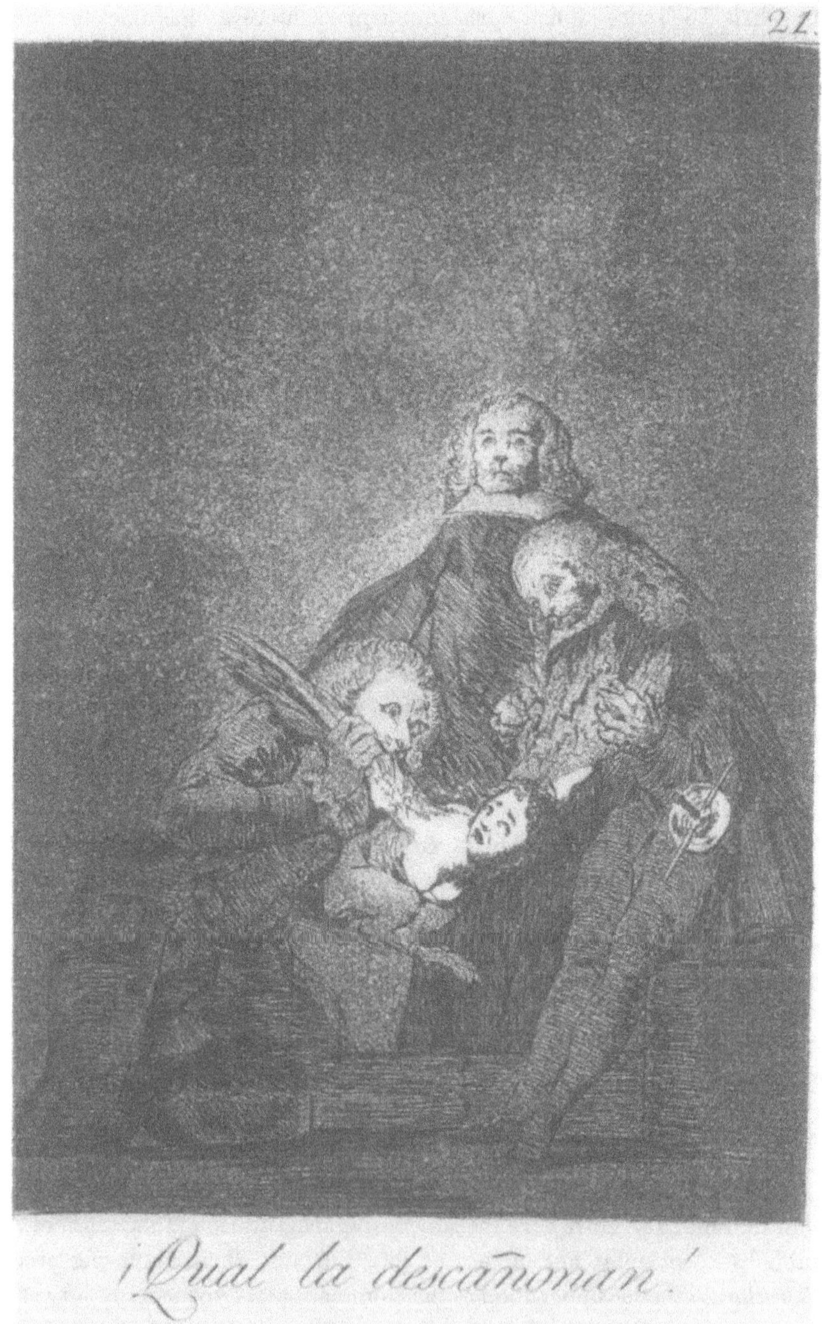

Figure 7.13. Francisco Goya, *How They Pluck Her!* (*Capricho* 21), 1799. Etching and burnished aquatint, 217 × 148 mm. Image © 2004 Board of Trustees, National Gallery of Art, Washington, D.C. Rosenwald Collection.

curesses behind the whores wielding brooms appears male and was indeed read by some contemporaries as a friar.[76] *Capricho* 22, *Poor Little Things!*, then appears as a denouement for the climax of 21: Whores, covering their heads, are followed by sinister male figures, and the whole process will continue.

Throughout the sequence of witchcraft images in the second half of the *Caprichos*, we find an analogy between the delusion of witchcraft and the social reality of prostitution, a great concern to Goya's circle, depicted earlier.[77] *Pretty Teacher!* (see figure 7.8) relies partly on the figures' resemblance to a young whore and her old procuress and partly on idiomatic verbal connotations. The old witch is teaching her protégée to fly (*volar*): to have an orgasm, as an owl (*búho*, meaning "streetwalker") hovers above and tiny gesticulating figures watch from below. Goya emphasized his meaning by the intense concentration of the younger witch and the spread of both witches' legs across the broomstick. We may assume that, as in the Logroño confessions, the old witch has oiled her pupil with the loathsome unguent before the flight.[78] Goya's satirical method here is similar to that of *Capricho* 17, *It's Pulled Tight*, in which a young whore with legs spread wide pulls up a stocking in front of her old procuress, with the stocking and the brazier on which she rests her foot as metaphors for the whore's vagina.[79]

Then, male sexuality is indicted immediately in *Capricho* 18, *And He's Burning the House Down*, in which a drunken man (in an early drawing, a priest) pulls on his trousers after a sexual encounter, both his lust and his house are burning.[80] Similarly, *Pretty Teacher!*—ostensibly an old-fashioned misogynistic projection of human sexuality onto women—is followed by the much more complicated *Blow* (see figures 7.8 and 7.9). Here, witches collect children as a demon with outspread wings shields their gathering. The Prado commentary suggests a routine interpretation: that the children will be eaten at a feast ("There must have been a fine catch of little children last night! The banquet being prepared will be splendid. Fall to."). But the image concerns more than diabolical cuisine: A simian witch in central foreground sucks on a child's penis. This is also the subject of Plate 45, *There's a Lot to Suck*, and was one way the Logroño witches vampirized children.[81] It also inevitably suggests fellatio. Similarly, the main motif of a witch using a child as a bellows to start a fire is one form of witches' abuse of children (in *Sueño* 6, a witch uses a child's body as a trumpet, blowing in its mouth to force air from its anus), but it also refers to the inflaming of lust. The Ayala manuscript commentary states the subject of Plate 69 succinctly and directly: "Children are the target of a thousand obscenities on the part of old and licentious men."[82]

Furthermore, the gender of the sucking and blowing witches is unclear, in contrast to the unequivocal females of *Pretty Teacher!* In *Blow*, the witch at the far left has a topknot and apparently breasts but also massive shoulders that appear male. The witch with the "bellows" appears male despite hair bunched in a loose knot at the back of her head. As the protagonist of the etching holding the instrument enflaming perverse sexual desire, this figure like so many others calls into question the perennial association of women and lust that seemed to be confirmed in *Pretty Teacher!* Taken together, *Caprichos* 68, 69, and 70 (*Pretty Teacher!*, *Blow*, and *Devout Profession*) move from female lust, to perverted male lust, to a catechism of witches' faith that parodies the faith of inquisitors, and links the "torturing" of scripture to the literal torture of the Inquisition's victims. It becomes impossible to disentangle the promiscuous or perverse sexual content of witches' confessions from their core crime of heresy, and both of these for Goya are created and sustained by the Inquisition. When we realize that "blow" also had the connotation of "inform" (as to the Inquisition, which relentlessly pressured accused witches, often under torture, to name accomplices), we cannot separate the accused from the accusers—exactly Goya's point.[83] Indeed, one of the strongest arguments against the autos-da-fé, or indeed any public sentencing of witches by reading the contents of confessions, was that they spread the filth they purportedly wished to stamp out. Salazar Frias advised as little publicity as possible: "in the diseased state of the public mind, every agitation about the matter is harmful and increases the evil. I deduce the importance of silence and reserve from the experience that there were neither witches nor bewitched until they were talked and written about."[84]

Such rich entanglements—seamless movements between witchcraft and other social ills, between witches, demons, and their archenemy the Church—may be found throughout the *Caprichos*. The main result is a total breakdown of the demonological worldview, now stunningly exposed as a human construction with no basis in reality. Another result is the subversion of the complacency of Goya's enlightened audience. For witchcraft is not seen here as an aberrant, past phenomenon, apprehended comfortably from a position of historical (or aesthetic) distance. Nor could it be safely viewed from a condition of maleness or elite status. Those who felt safe initially would have been paradoxically yet surely drawn into the abhorrent web Goya spun. The obfuscation of figures' identities and the muddying of conceptual categories throughout the *Caprichos* are central to Goya's purpose. His witches look like procuresses and whores so that we can identify the promiscuous sexuality central to the idea of witchcraft and, conversely, so that we can perceive the evil of prostitution by its analogy to witchcraft. Witches, demons, and their cohort goblins resemble clerics in form, social organization, and action so we do not mistake who created whom. At the same time, such creatures must be sustained by many segments of society as well or they die ("From that dust comes this mud"). Both men and women and all classes bear responsibility for the unreason they support.

Take, for instance, Plate 63, *Look How Solemn They Are!* (see figure 7.7).

The Prado manuscript commentary tells us these are two witches out for a ride, and the nearly identical *Sueño* 8 is captioned "The Witches' Drones." We notice that the witches are only partly transformed, that their mounts are decidedly earthbound, and that the image is disconcertingly similar to *Capricho* 42, *Thou Who Canst Not* (figure 7.14). Positioned at the end of the donkey sequence debunking Spanish elite (the nobility, doctors, and literati), *Thou Who Canst Not* brilliantly depicts the economic exploitation of the Spanish peasantry by the nobility, the Church, and numerous other segments of society. It has been convincingly tied to Jovellanos's program for the reform of Spanish agriculture.[85] The caption refers to a proverb, "You who cannot do it, lift me up on your shoulders," implying that the oppressed who cannot resist must bear their oppressors. The similarity between Plates 42 and 63 gives another side to the image of the people: the sympathetic, burdened human forms of *Thou Who Canst Not* are altered into the malformed donkeys of *Look How Solemn*. The "witches," who can also be seen as a rapacious, beaked government and a hypocritically pious Church with folded hands, ride a debased *burro-pueblo*, in Gwyn Williams's words, as "brutalized and inhuman as its riders."[86] The comparison between the two images describes unhealthy symbiotic relationships between low and high segments of society. As witchcraft beliefs require the people's compliance to stay alive, so perhaps do other forms of social and economic exploitation.

Goya's views of witchcraft and witch-hunting as epitomes of unreason are aligned with a skeptical tradition and enriched by his vehemently anti-Inquisition stance. If he had stopped there, his witchcraft images would be simple to interpret. Instead of isolating the theme, however, he wove it inextricably into the rest of his social critique, making it transparent to his understanding of both Spanish society and human nature, including the fascination with the grotesque and the horrific that pervaded his own circle. Goya's choice of the witchcraft theme has much in common with his interest in insanity and violence in the cabinet paintings of the mid-1790s that provoked and played to the tastes of patrons he wanted to attract in order to alter the trajectory of his career dramatically. In the Black Paintings, begun when he was seventy-four, Goya reflected on his career and on events in the intervening period. Much had happened in Spain, but very little to bolster faith in reason.

Mourning and Melancholy: The Black Paintings

Early in 1819, Goya purchased a house in suburban Madrid near the Manzanares River that came to be called the *Quinta del Sordo* (House of the deaf man). The location figures in the iconography of the Black Paintings. In the vicinity of the property was a house where witches' mysterious activities sup-

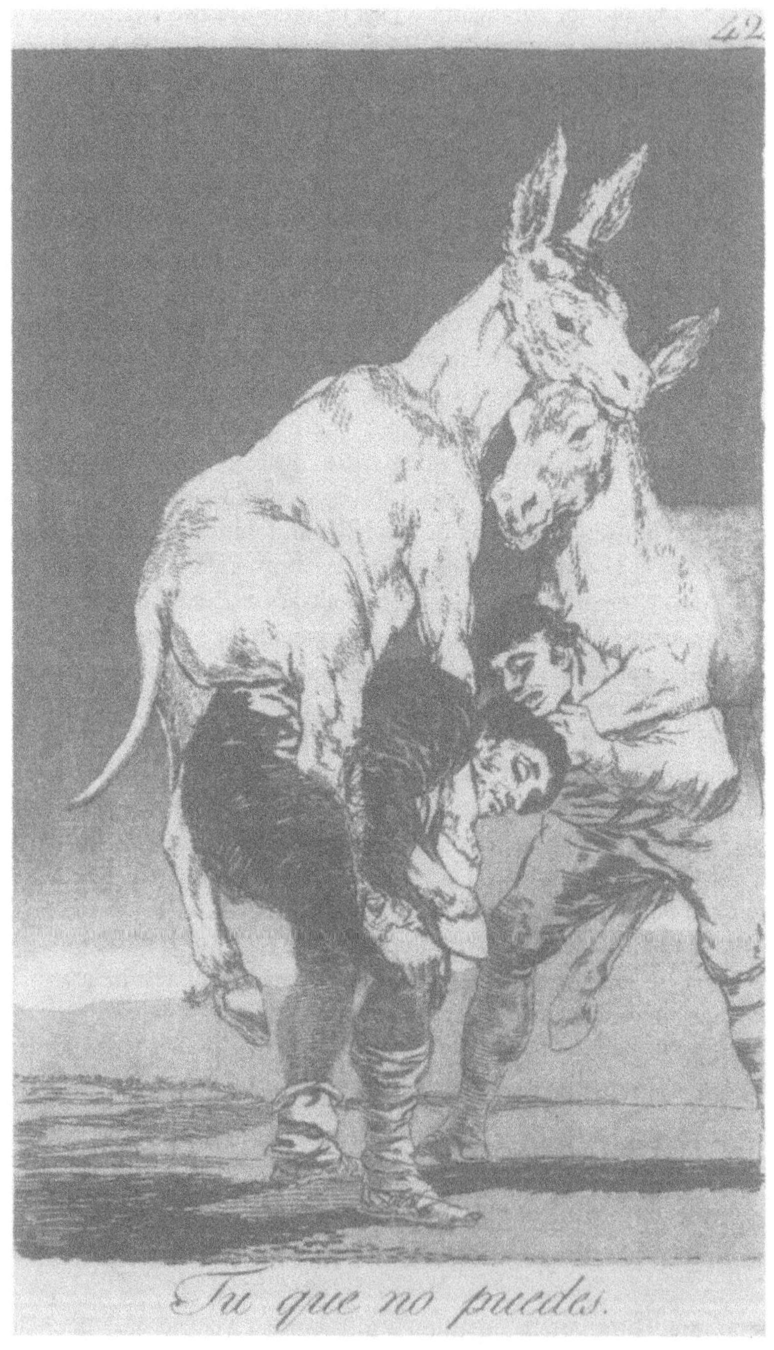

Figure 7.14. Francisco Goya, *Thou Who Canst Not* (*Capricho* 42), 1799. Etching and burnished aquatint, 217 × 151 mm. Image © 2004 Board of Trustees, National Gallery of Art, Washington, D.C. Rosenwald Collection.

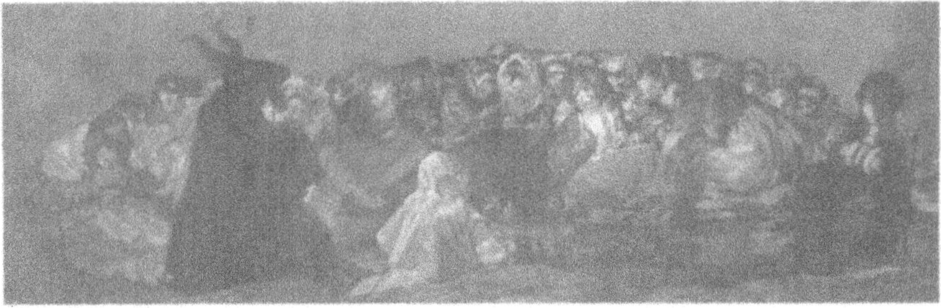

Figure 7.15. Francisco Goya. *The Witches' Sabbath*, from the Black Paintings, 1820–23. Oil fresco, transferred to canvas, 140 × 438 cm. Museo del Prado, Madrid. Erich Lessing/Art Resource, New York.

posedly took place, and this local folklore may have been known to Goya's guests.[87] Moreover, the festival of San Isidro, the patron saint of Madrid, took place in the Manzanares valley in May. Goya had painted the festival in 1788 in a delightful sketch, now in the Prado but once owned by the Osunas, for a tapestry cartoon: In a bright meadow by the River, Madrilenians socialize and watch their fellow citizens. But when Goya painted the pilgrimage to San Isidro on the wall of the ground floor room of the *Quinta*, of course, the expressive tone was dramatically altered.

Later in 1819, he experienced what seems to have been another episode of his earlier illness. The moving *Self-Portrait with Doctor Arrieta* (1819; Minneapolis Institute of Arts) was apparently painted in gratitude to his friend, shown ministering to his severely weakened patient in a secularized version of the Spanish tradition of the ex-voto. Significantly, it is a friend and physician, not Mary or a saint, who saves the patient. Goya's recovery may have inspired him to begin in 1820 to cover the walls of two major rooms on the ground and first floors in his newly acquired house. Radiographic evidence tells us that his first thoughts were of warm, pastoral landscapes with low horizons, but something—perhaps disillusionment as the fragile constitutional government of 1820–23 showed signs of failure—changed his mind. Goya revised his plan to arrive at the extraordinary cycle of oil frescoes later named for their predominant color and mood. The tension between patronage and artistic freedom inherent in painting decorative *capricci* for aristocratic residences such as *La Alameda*, Rees points out, was finally resolved in the artist's own house.[88]

As the explicit subject of one of the largest paintings (figure 7.15), and a subject alluded to in others, witchcraft plays a major part in the iconographic scheme of the *Quinta*. But because of Goya's merging of witchcraft with other manifestations of superstition, vice, and folly (already evident in the *Caprichos*), it is impossible to pluck witchcraft neatly out of the whole context. Moreover, Goya did not give titles to these frescoes. Rather, the current captions derive primarily from a summary inventory made around 1828 by his pupil Antonio de Brugada, and from Charles Iriarte's discussion of the paintings from his 1867 book on Goya. Both sources contain ambiguities.[89] For example, the red-mantled figure of the so-called *Asmodea* on the upper floor is perhaps a feminized form of the deceitful lame, male devil of Spanish folklore whom Goya had depicted earlier with a crutch in *Capricho* 66, *There It Goes*.[90] We might conclude that *Asmodea*, even with the soldiers and refugees depicted below, refers in part to flight to a sabbath that will take place on the mountain in the distance. But scholars have seen a wide variety of references in the painting, from Dante's Mount Purgatory to a patriotic poem written during the Peninsular War by Juan Bautista Arriaza (1808).[91]

I will concentrate on images in the ground-floor room that articulate Goya's rejection of demonological beliefs and suggest women's ambivalent position within Enlightenment thought. The large *Sabbath* is a scene of devil-worship. Its detached female observer—probably Leocadia Zorilla, Goya's companion during his late years and his exile—is also depicted allegorically in *Judith Decapitating Holofernes* on the wall opposite the entrance, and more literally in the majestic mourning figure at the entrance of the ground-floor room (figures 7.16 and 7.17).[92] A focused discussion of these works, however, requires an overview of the interpretation of the Black Paintings as a whole cycle.

Within an oeuvre replete with problematic imagery, the Black Paintings are the most enigmatic of Goya's works, with an extraordinary range of interpretations. Fred Licht and Priscilla Muller represent two polarized approaches. In *Goya: The Origins of the Modern Temper in Art* (1979), Licht proposes that the paintings represent a "complete break with every tradition of art as communication."[93] In a sustained effort to annex Goya for the twentieth century, Licht argues for the impenetrably mysterious, private expression of the paintings: They are, for him, the vision of the utter purposelessness of all experience that Goya sustained during his illness. With their "paralyzing, nullifying nature," they show us why Goya resisted (Licht thinks) Arrieta's help.[94]

At the opposite end of the spectrum, Muller's *Goya's "Black" Paintings: Truth and Reason in Light and Liberty* (1984) is a Herculean effort to discover a coherent iconographic scheme based on principles of the Enlightenment and political freedom in the Black Paintings. In contrast to Licht's dependence on the notions of private catharsis and incommunicable enigma, Muller's thesis arises from what she sees as Goya's complex layering of mythological, literary, and national political iconographies in the paintings and, ultimately, their function as painted theater. The last part of her book is a detailed but not entirely convincing comparison of the visual effects and iconography of the paintings to technical developments in contemporary theater, in particular Belgian artist Étienne Gaspard Robertson's "phantasmagoria" that Goya could

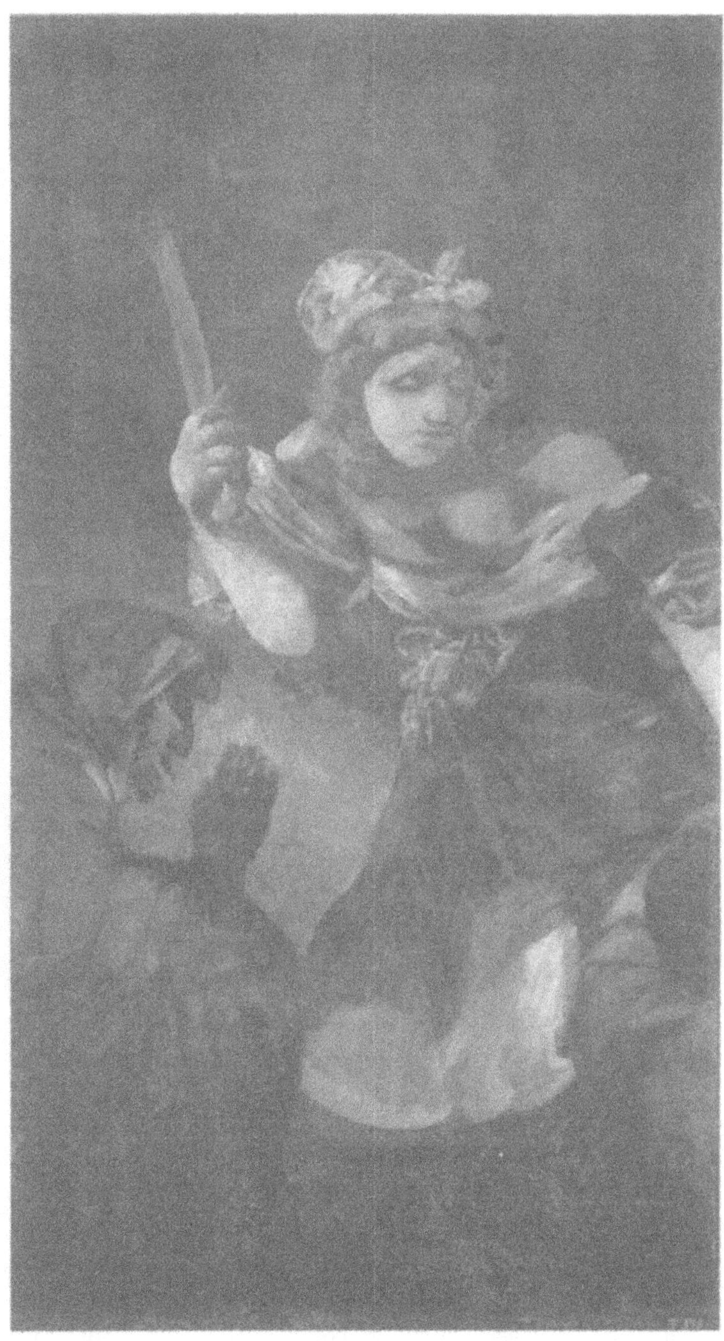

Figure 7.16. Francisco Goya, *Judith Decapitating Holofernes*, from the Black Paintings, 1820–23. Oil fresco, transferred to canvas, 146 × 84 cm. Museo del Prado, Madrid. Erich Lessing/Art Resource, New York.

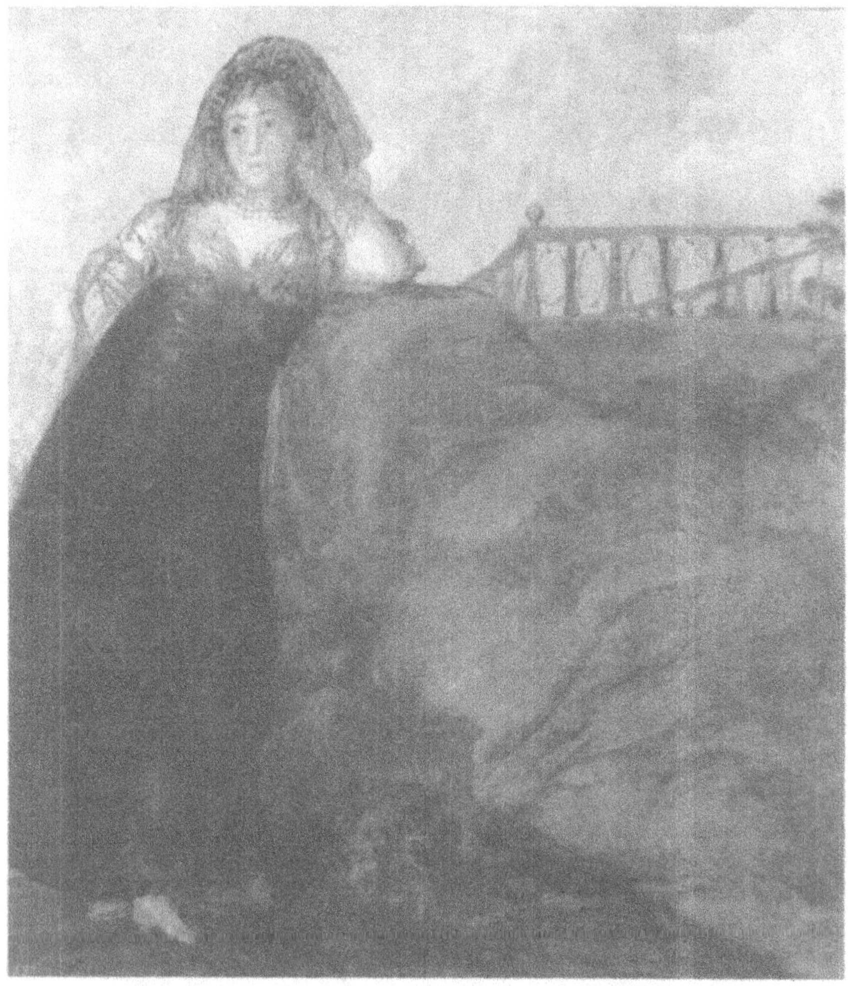

Figure 7.17. Francisco Goya, *Doña Leocadia*, from the Black Paintings, 1820–23. Oil fresco, transferred to canvas, 147 × 132 cm. Museo del Prado, Madrid. Erich Lessing/ Art Resource, New York.

have seen in Madrid in the early 1820s. In such productions, sublimely spectral images and tableaus derived from history or contemporary Romantic literature were projected on surfaces as the audience watched in a profoundly darkened room. Muller believes that Goya wanted to convey intelligible meaning and a sublime experience, engaging emotions of both terror and relief, to what was literally an "audience." Now, he could use his own house to do this, because the paintings were made during another brief period of constitutional government in Spain from 1820 to 1823. When that government collapsed,

Goya gave up trying to reform Spain and lived out his life in exile with Leocadia in France.[95]

How do we negotiate between these two divergent approaches? One might argue that the comparison is meaningless because the two publications are so different. Licht's book muses on the significance of Goya's entire oeuvre for modern art, while Muller's is an exhaustive, fully annotated study of the Black Paintings alone. However, this asymmetry is exactly to the point: Can we understand Goya by traditional, thorough iconographic and contextual analyses, or are these tools worthless because the artist himself threw both tradition and context aside? Did he want to communicate with contemporary Spaniards, or was he by this time so alienated that only twentieth-century viewers can penetrate the depths of these paintings?

The space between these interpretations holds much promise. Licht does not take adequate account of the paintings' poor state of preservation, early photographic evidence of their appearance, and alterations made by the restorer, Martínez Cubells, upon the transfer of the paintings to canvas between 1874 and 1878.[96] For example, to maintain his thesis of Goya's nihilistic destabilization of meaning, Licht argues that the famous *Saturn* on the ground floor "isn't a figure at all," ignoring changes made to both the devourer and the devoured by Cubells (see figure 7.20).[97] But *Saturn* is indeed a figure of an old man related to the mythological Saturn who dominates the melancholic temperament, although his identity is not limited to a traditional iconography (he has no scythe or hourglass, and he devours an adult not an infant). Similarly, *The Dog*, which ends the cycle on the upper floor, is for Licht a "tragic emblem of meaningless"—an interpretation that is less convincing when one realizes that originally the dog may have been looking at some spectral thing or being, long since disappeared from the paint surface.[98] In that case, the dog's quixotic, hopeful stare may have expressed some dumbly misplaced faith or loyalty, which is not the same as meaninglessness.

Muller's analysis takes account of the damage and restoration of the paintings, but sometimes her conclusions seem hallucinatory, as Lawrence Gowing points out in his review of her book. Where Licht sees meaning destabilized and negated, Muller finds it overflowing and so expansive or convoluted that her analysis often strains credibility. The most crucial difference between the two approaches, however, is undoubtedly the assumption of privacy by Licht versus Muller's postulation of an audience, engaged with Goya's images like the audience of phantasmagoria.

The very location and free form of the Black Paintings suggest that, as the deeply personal expressions of an old man, they are not subject to the kind of meticulous iconographic dissection that Muller sustains; as Rees asserts, the thematic variability of eighteenth-century grotesque decoration stimulated salon conversation based on free association of ideas rather than any stringent iconographic program.[99] In his review of Muller's book, Gowing notes that there is no evidence to suggest there was any kind of "audience" at all for these paintings, and that they really may have been done largely for Goya himself.[100] Indeed, in 1831, Goya's son Francisco Javier wrote not only of his father's sense of the *magia* of art but also of the private pleasure he derived from viewing these free works that demonstrated his own genius daily.[101]

However skeptical we may be about an "audience," though, it is worth remembering that the *Quinta* was the home of an artist of great professional stature (the "Apelles of Spain," according to the *Diario de Madrid* in 1801).[102] Muller is undoubtedly correct that Goya did not make the Black Paintings as a total recluse, with no intention of communicating meaning. Rather, the frescoes functioned not only for Goya's own meditation but also as his self-presentation to family, friends, and admirers. It is also reasonable to assume that they formed a backdrop for small *tertulias* (held in the evening when dim light would have augmented their fantastic qualities) and indulged the early Romantic, "Gothick" tastes of Goya and Leocadia's intimate guests. The painted rooms of the *Quinta* were a hybrid of domestic (feminine) and public (masculine) spaces, when that public is understood as limited and sympathetic. The allegorical roles of Leocadia and Goya in the paintings, as well as the investment of the fantastic with political meaning, make sense only then.

The ground-floor room was probably used for dining, and its paintings carry out that theme perversely (Judith decapitated Holofernes after dining; Saturn devoured his children; witches' sabbaths included feasting on revolting fare; and on a small over-door, Goya depicted two hideous characters eating soup).[103] Clearly the frescoes on both floors sustained a mood of grotesque humor and of sarcastic meditation on the follies and tragedies of Spanish history and society that only Goya could have produced. The *magia* noted by Goya's son is equivalent to *aura*, the pictorial ambience that reveals a great artist's hand and mind (his *ingenium*, his *fantasia*). As *caprichos*, the Black Paintings do not admit dissection into minute component parts: Their meaning lies precisely in this charisma generated by their freedom of execution and subject matter. Goya's self-construction as a melancholic genius and his acerbic vision of his society and of human nature surrounded the artist himself and his *Quinta* visitors. The self-referential nature of the paintings also encompassed self-mockery, so that the theme of age and approaching death is followed throughout. As John Ciofalo has aptly described it, the *Quinta* was a "house of mirrors."[104]

Francisco Javier also wrote that the frescoes proved to his father that he had conquered everything there was to conquer in painting.[105] Goya's impetus for making the Black Paintings, unlike that for the *Caprichos*, was not to change his career path but to reflect on that path. Josefa had died in 1812, and

Goya lived in the *Quinta* with Leocadia and her daughter María del Rosario, to whom he was devoted: She was almost certainly his child. How long the relationship had gone on is difficult to say, but Isidoro Weiss, Leocadia's husband since 1807, registered complaints against her in 1811 and again in 1812 for "infidelity, illicit relations and misconduct," and a "high-handed and threatening disposition."[106] At that time, Leocadia was in her early twenties and had two sons.

Leocadia's image welcomed visitors as they entered the ground floor room, opposite a mocking "portrait" of Goya with a companion that bears a clear resemblance to his late drawing of an old man walking with a cane, inscribed "*Aun aprendo*"—I am still learning (figures 7.17 and 7.18). Apparently, in the course of painting *Doña Leocadia*, Goya decided to augment the image by plastering over the door's lintel and painting a tomb-like mound over it. This modification, the image of the aged man on the other side of the door, and Leocadia's unmistakable melancholic pose, chin in hand, convey the notion of Goya's old age and the mourning of his death in the not-too-distant future.[107] Perhaps he wanted to evoke an elegiac sentiment in his guests as had the Duchess of Osuna with the inclusion of a pyramidal tomb on the grounds of her Hermitage.[108]

The mournful Muse Leocadia is also very likely the demure young woman with a muff who appears at the far right end of the witches' sabbath depicted on the long wall to the left of the entrance (see figure 7.15). Goya conceived this sabbath as a group of hideous devotees, mostly of uncertain gender. The attractive Leocadia, a discerning consumer of this occult spectacle, is set somewhat apart from the main group that huddles around a looming he-goat, seen in shadow except for his glowering eye and possibly intended, as Ciofalo suggests, as the alter-ego of the artist.[109] Characteristically, Goya opposed this image of absurd demonic devotion to the fresco of religious pilgrimage on the opposite wall in which a shabby throng of fanatics follow a wailing guitar player and a blind man to the Hermitage of San Isidro (figure 7.19). The obvious significance of pairing the *Sabbath* with the *Pilgrimage* is to suggest parallel realms of unreason: one demonic and one religious, with the Church implicated in the creation and perpetuation of both.

During transfer of the paintings to canvas and restoration, Cubells removed large, murky sections to the left and right of the main sabbath group, but he restored the group itself fairly faithfully.[110] As Muller notes, many witches glance to the left, as if responding to something outside their gathering, possibly lost when the painting was cut down. She suggests that they respond anxiously to the coming of light and Reason, or to threatening inquisitors, but Goya's clever conceit could simply have been that the witches look toward the door, surprised by those entering the room. Cubells may not have removed iconography but ambience.[111]

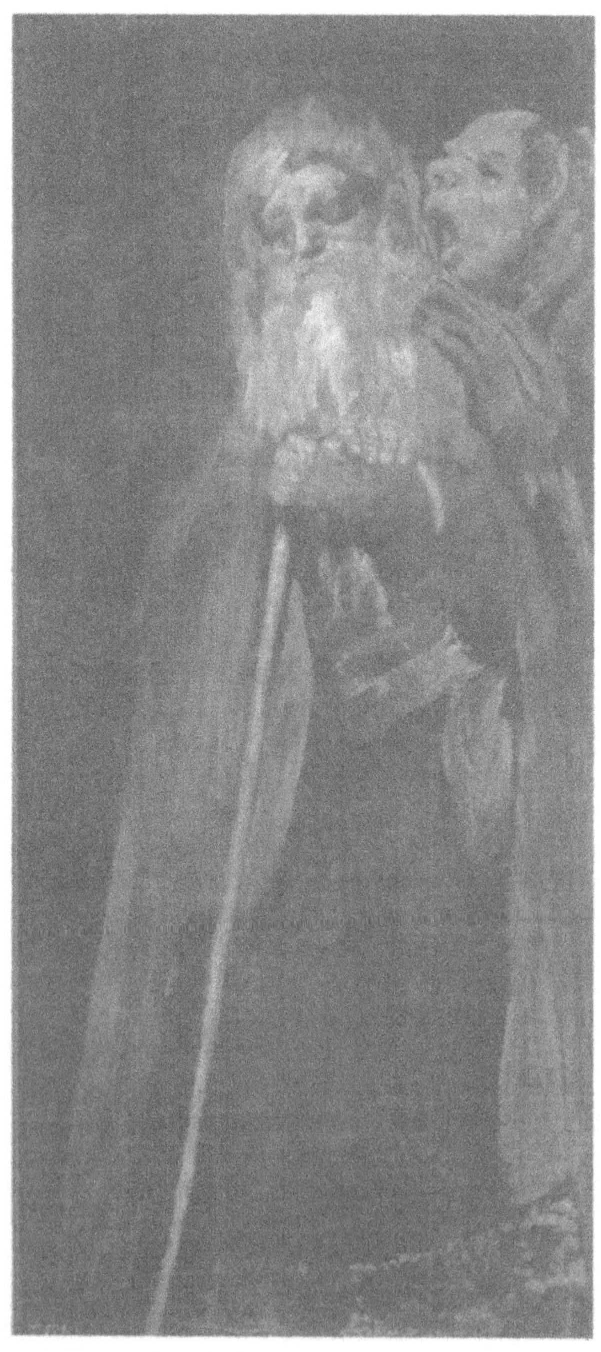

Figure 7.18. Francisco Goya, *Two Old Men*, from the Black Paintings, 1820–23. Oil fresco, transferred to canvas, 144 × 66 cm. Museo del Prado, Madrid. Erich Lessing/Art Resource, New York.

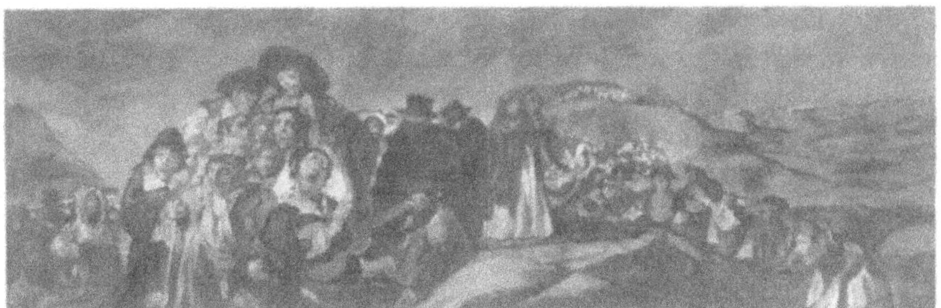

Figure 7.19. Francisco Goya, *The Pilgrimage of San Isidro*, from the Black Paintings, 1820–23. Oil fresco, transferred to canvas, 140 × 438 cm. Museo del Prado, Madrid. Scala/Art Resource, New York.

The grotesque humor of this sabbath hinged not only on its placement in a dining room but also on its inclusion of the woman who would have hosted the meals and the host himself in the guise of the presiding he-goat. But it is Leocadia's distance from the gathering, more psychological than literal, that is important for our purposes. In her aloof figure, watching the witches' sabbath, Goya undermined once again the misogynistic underpinning of witchcraft theory; she is unaffected by the lasciviousness and demented female melancholy that supposedly drew women to witchcraft. Leocadia is also characterized on the ground floor of the *Quinta* in conventional terms as conquering seductress (*Judith*) and faithful companion and soon-to-be widow, *Doña Leocadia*, a faithful Penelope, sign of the absent Odysseus. To borrow from Juliana Schiesari's analysis discussed in Chapter 2, Leocadia's melancholy is of a lesser order than that of her famous "husband."[112] Hers reflects the ancient role of women as mourners; his is the complex and elevated melancholy of the artistic genius and the Dionysiac creative furor of the *cabrón*, or he-goat, associated in Spain, Ciofalo asserts, with the concept of *capricho*.[113] The evidence of Goya's genius filled the walls of the *Quinta*, but we glean little about Leocadia from her gently inserted presence.

This should not surprise us. As reflected in the debates about the admission of women to the Madrid Economic Society discussed earlier, Enlightenment thought was deeply conflicted about women's nature and role. Centuries of misogyny were undermined in aspects of its scientific and social theory, yet ultimately women were limited to their roles as mothers and companions to their husbands.[114] René Descartes's declaration of reason as the defining human capacity had the potential to be radically liberating for women. A gender-less reason, operating independent of bodies, implied in theory that there should be no obstacle to women's full education or to their participation in politics, philosophy, literature, and art. Nevertheless, the bar for women was continually raised. Their theoretically possible participation was severely circumscribed as individual Enlightenment thinkers made their contributions to the *querelle des femmes*, and the shift from a Cartesian to what might be called a sensualist position occurred. In his *Système physique et moral de la femme* (Systematic overview of woman as physical and moral being, 1775), physician Pierre Roussel wrote: "The difficulty of shedding the tyranny of her sensations constantly binds her to the immediate causes which call them [the sensations] forth, preventing her from rising to those heights which would afford her a view of the whole."[115]

Thus, as they developed, eighteenth-century views of women took multiple and contradictory forms. Some feminists such as the Marquis de Condorcet and Mary Wollstonecraft took their cues from Cartesian François Poulain de la Barre's *De l'égalité des deux sexes* (On the equality of the two sexes, 1673) to assert women's equal intellectual capacity and the corresponding need for full female education. However, Jean-Jacques Rousseau and the quintessential *philosophe* Denis Diderot—both widely read in Spain despite Inquisitorial prohibitions—were capable of conservative and even reactionary positions on women, grounded in an ideologically loaded definition of "nature" and in beliefs in women's biological destiny.[116] In Diderot's essay "*Sur les femmes*" (On women, 1772), and in articles in the *Encyclopédie* (1751–65) of which he was the primary editor, an ostensibly sympathetic yet paternalistic stance toward women, embracing some traditional misogynistic views and described charitably by Mary Seidman Trouille as "pseudo-feminist," emerged.[117]

Although women's sexuality and biological functions were no longer discussed in entirely derogatory terms (the Enlightenment's exaltation of breastfeeding is perhaps the most striking example of this), Diderot retained age-old misogynistic concepts such as the wandering womb and hysteria. He grounded women's supposed proclivities toward superstition and religious fanaticism in their assumed sexual volatility,[118] a point with which Goya would seem to take issue both by Leocadia's aloofness at the *Witches' Sabbath*, and the predominance of men in the *Pilgrimage of San Isidro* on the opposite wall.

Ultimately, woman's sexuality and biological functions, although they did not make her less than human (a mere not-quite-man, or *homme manqué*), dictated her irreducible difference from man, and that in turn determined her social utility as wife and mother. For Diderot, women's sexuality made them incapable of any depth of moral convictions; such thoughts, maliciousness as well as kindness, were always superficial in women.[119] Although Rousseau's works contained a great variety of female characters who could be read differently, ultimately for him women's heightened sensitivity, compassion, and nonegoistic morality made them "the moral sex" whose destined sphere of influence was the bourgeois home, place of refuge from the cold, unrelenting competition and strife of the public realm.[120] In his fictionalized educational discourse *Émile*, the work in which Rousseau most reveals his traditionalism according to Trouille, the education of the primary female exemplar Sophie is restricted to those subjects that will make her a suitable companion for Émile. A woman's education, according to Rousseau, should help women help men by advising, consoling, and sustaining them from infancy through adulthood. Despite the complexities of Rousseau's views of women, Trouille concludes it was their relegation to the senses, the passions, and the domestic sphere that took hold across Europe.[121] Spain is a excellent example. Lively debates about women continued in Spanish journals of the 1790s, but the conservatives gained ground by the early nineteenth century. Sally-Ann Kitts observes a waning of the varied, optimistic discussion about women in the eighteenth century and a return to traditional values supported by an increasingly repressive government.[122]

On the walls of the *Quinta*, Leocadia still seems to dwell in an eighteenth-century limbo, even though we can "know" her even less than we can "know" Goya. No longer an innate witch, she is not yet men's equal. Women's "natural" utility as wives and mothers kept them from the public sphere in which men acted: Both literature and art, for instance, still held both theoretical and social obstacles for women (the curse of the "bluestockings"). A paradox of the Enlightenment is that, although women's imagination was considered vivid, especially when it came to superstition, it was not considered productive. Rousseau-follower Antoine Léonard Thomas is particularly instructive on this point in his *Essai sur le caractère, les moeurs et l'esprit des femmes dans les différents siècles* (Essay on the character, mores and spirit of women in the different centuries, 1772). The greater mobility of women's imaginations made them unsuited for the depth of philosophical thought; women's imagination is at best contemplative.[123]

In the figure of Leocadia mourning at his fictional tomb, Goya seems to likewise follow Rousseau and other *philosophes* in an apparent endorsement of the companionate woman of the bourgeois marriage.[124] But as Rousseau's position on women, dispersed through his popular novel *Julie, ou la Nouvelle Héloïse* and through his discourses such as *Émile*, carried a subversive undercurrent, according to Trouille, so does Goya's problematic image of Judith on the wall opposite the entrance of the ground floor room, paired with the self-referential *Saturn* (figure 7.20). Isidoro's description of his wife as "high-handed" and "threatening" seems to be evoked by this image of the seductive shrew, also paradoxically virtuous, heroic and patriotic. The ambiguity that had always existed in the figure of Judith—her relevance both for the Power of Women topos and for a variety of patriotic discourses—is undiminished here.[125] In the period of the Cadiz constitution, Judith/Leocadia may very well have suggested Spain's determination to throw off various forms of tyranny, from Napoleon to Ferdinand VII and its own reactionary institutions.

As Gowing has noted, the two sides of the ground-floor room suggest

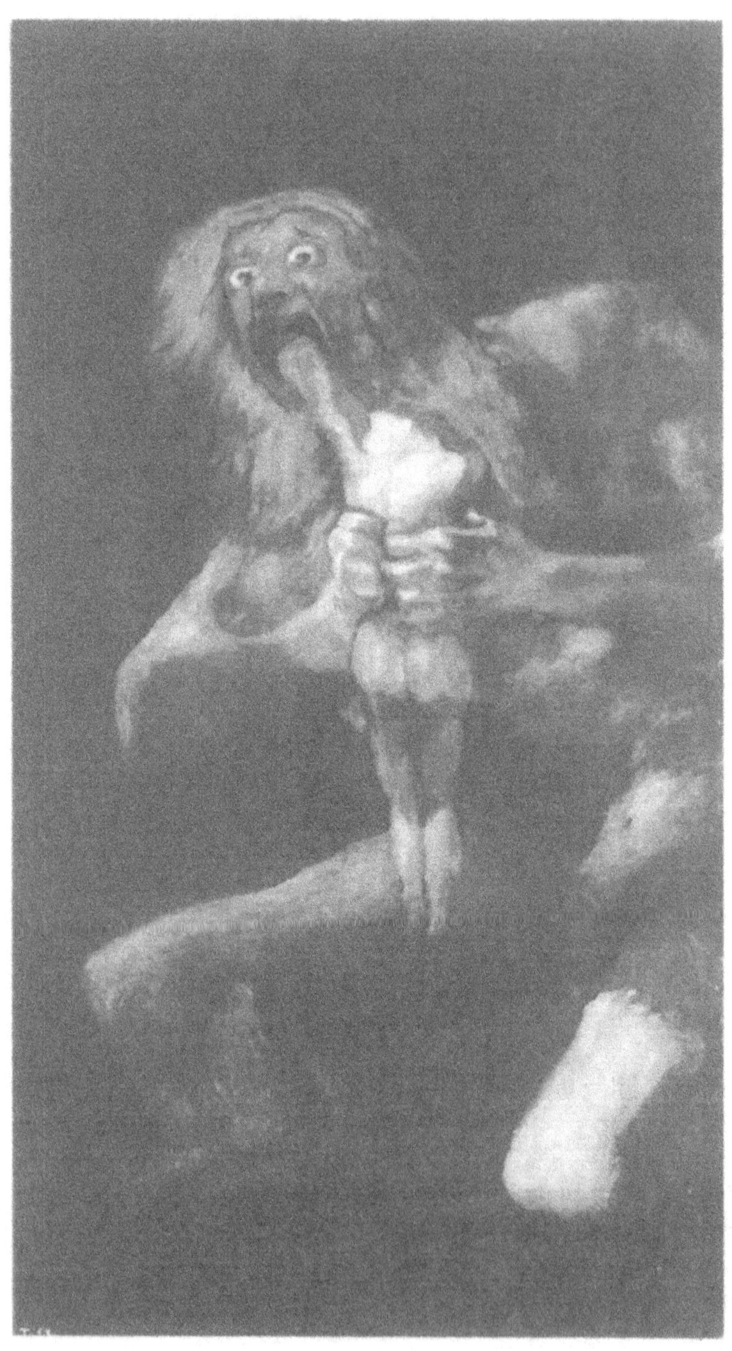

Figure 7.20. Francisco Goya, *Saturn Devouring His Children*, from the Black Paintings, 1820–23. Oil fresco, transferred to canvas, 146 × 83 cm. Museo del Prado, Madrid. Erich Lessing/Art Resource, New York.

predominantly male and female realms, especially if we assume that *Saturn* and *Judith* were on the right and left of the wall opposite the door, despite Brugada's and Iriarte's contrary descriptions.[126] Their compositions—Judith facing right toward the center of the wall; Saturn facing left—also suggest this placement along with the disposition of light in the room, hitting the right side of Saturn's frame in an old photograph.[127] Whatever their positioning, however, *Saturn* and *Judith* may be read in allegorical terms as references to Goya and Leocadia, and in general they represent masculine and feminine forms of aggression. Earlier, as he worked on the *Caprichos*, Goya had drawn both characters on related sheets: Saturn, white-bearded, greedily consumes two bodies, and Judith, more capriciously, wields her sword extravagantly as she collects an entire tentful of severed heads, one of which might be Goya's.[128] Although Goya depicted the Saturn of the *Quinta* somewhat unconventionally, without his usual attributes of scythe, crutch, or hourglass, both Brugada and Iriarte named him, and there is no compelling iconographic or visual reason to reinterpret him as the devil, as Muller suggests.[129] The association of Saturn with the temperament of melancholy, in turn associated with both witchcraft and with the creativity of the artist and with devouring Time in his Greek guise as Chronos, make it virtually certain that Goya intended to evoke Saturn by this gruesome figure. If Goya believed his illness was caused by lead poisoning (*saturnismo*), this would add yet another layer to the figure's associations. Muller argues that, by the eighteenth century, artists were aware of the dangers of exposure to lead and that both Goya and Ramón Bayeu could have realized the hazards involved in the priming of canvasses for tapestry cartoons, influencing their resistance to these assignments.[130]

The mythological Saturn was a savage god who consumed his own children to avoid their supplanting him; only Zeus survived after castrating his father to make the transition to the ordered cosmos represented by the Olympian gods. But chaos and bestiality are not Saturn's only meanings; he developed a complex array of associations—for example, with the cannibalism of the natives of the New World and witches.[131] Time itself is one of the most significant; as Saturn devoured his own offspring, so Time (Chronos) inexorably consumes human life. Saturn thus becomes a *vanitas* symbol appropriate for an aged artist. In this notorious, bloody image, Goya expressed his sense of being consumed by time; as a melancholic, he was one of Saturn's children.

In his book *Goya, Saturn and Melancholy*, published in 1962, Folke Nordström traced the considerable impact of this concept throughout Goya's art. Goya drew upon the humanist transformation of melancholy initiated by Marsilio Ficino, associating the temperament with great heights of intellectual or creative achievement. As we have seen in earlier chapters, melancholy *in males* worked in tow with the concepts of imagination, fantasy, *ingenium*, and *aura* to valorize the profession of artist. But it also held dangers of depression and insanity—dangers that are perhaps suggested in the Black Paintings' nightmarishness and indeterminacy—qualities even more prominent in the enigmatic images of the upper room.

In the conclusion of her study of Enlightenment views on women, on which I have relied heavily, Lieselotte Steinbrügge asserts that however oppressive these views ended up being for women, they did not emerge simply from a patriarchal "will to power." Rather, the same sexless reason that held the potential to liberate women came to be understood as itself problematic: "at the very moment when society put its trust in the power of reason, reason was quickly coming to smack of utilitarianism, egoism, coldness, calculation, and inhumanity."[132] At least part of the function of the Enlightenment's definition of women's natures was a critique of reason itself—a critique in which Goya was also engaged. For Diderot, women's alleged mystery and sensuality could in part function to voice his suspicion of reason. And when Rousseau defined women as the moral sex, exemplifying common sense as well as sensibility, they were positioned as opponents of this revised definition of reason; they critiqued it with their very natures. So perhaps we may locate Goya's characterization of Leocadia in the Black Paintings partly in this fading of Enlightenment optimism and the failure of reason. In this sense, my inquiry comes full circle, for questions of the essential nature of woman, it seems, are never separable from the deepest anxieties of an age.

Notes

Chapter 1

1. This political subtlety is particularly evident in Wolfgang Behringer's study, *Witchcraft Persecutions in Bavaria: Popular Magic, Religious Zealotry and Reason of State in Early Modern Europe*, trans. J. C. Grayson and David Lederer (Cambridge: Cambridge University Press, 1997).

2. Heide Wunder, *He Is the Sun, She Is the Moon: Women in Early Modern Germany*, trans. Thomas Dunlap (Cambridge, Mass.: Harvard University Press, 1998), 147.

3. Brian P. Levack, *The Witch-Hunt in Early Modern Europe* (New York: Longman, 1987), 19–22; Andrea Dworkin, *Woman Hating* (New York: Dutton, 1974), 130; Mary Daly, *Gyn/Ecology: The Metaethics of Radical Feminism* (Boston: Beacon Press, 1978), 208; Anne Llewellyn Barstow, *Witchcraze: A New History of the European Witch Hunts* (San Francisco: Pandora, 1994), 22; William Monter, "Witch Trials in Continental Europe, 1560–1660" in *Witchcraft and Magic in Europe: The Period of the Witch Trials*, ed. Bengt Ankarloo, Stuart Clark, and William Monter (Philadelphia: University of Pennsylvania Press, 2002), 13.

4. Diane Purkiss, *The Witch in History: Early Modern and Twentieth-Century Representations* (London: Routledge, 1996), 7–29.

5. Stuart Clark, *Thinking with Demons: The Idea of Witchcraft in Early Modern Europe* (Oxford: Oxford University Press, 1997), provides an indispensable bibliography of studies up to 1997.

6. E. William Monter, "The Historiography of European Witchcraft: Progress and Prospects," *Journal of Interdisciplinary History* 2 (1974): 435.

7. Levack, *The Witch-Hunt*, 77–82.

8. Hugh Trevor-Roper, *The European Witch-Craze of the Sixteenth and Seventeenth Centuries and Other Essays* (New York: Harper and Row, 1969), 116.

9. Levack, *The Witch-Hunt*, 93–113, argues against religious conflict as the primary cause of witch-hunting.

10. Monter, "The Historiography of European Witchcraft," 441.

11. Joseph Klaits, *Servants of Satan: The Age of the Witch-Hunts* (Bloomington: Indiana University Press, 1985), 49.

12. Clark, *Thinking with Demons*, preface.

13. Trevor-Roper, 105–8, especially 106.

14. Jonathan Barry, "Introduction: Keith Thomas and the Problem of Witchcraft," in *Witchcraft in Early Modern Europe: Studies in Culture and Belief*, ed. Jonathan Barry, Marianne Hester, and Gareth Roberts (Cambridge: Cambridge University Press, 1996), 3.

15. Norman Cohn, *Europe's Inner Demons: An Enquiry Inspired by the Great Witch-Hunt* (New York: Basic Books, 1975), preface.

16. Ibid., 126–46; Richard Kieckhefer, *European Witch Trials: Their Foundations*

in Popular and Learned Culture, 1300–1500 (Berkeley: University of California Press, 1976), 16–18.

17. Levack, *The Witch-Hunt*, 49–50. A particularly important precedent for the *Malleus* was the *Formicarius* (The ant colony) by Dominican inquisitor Johannes Nider (Basel, 1435–38). On Nider, see Michael David Bailey, *Battling Demons: Witchcraft, Heresy and Reform in the Late Middle Ages* (University Park: Pennsylvania State University Press, 2003).

18. Carlo Ginzburg, *Ecstasies: Deciphering the Witches' Sabbath*, trans. Raymond Rosenthal (New York: Pantheon Books, 1991).

19. Purkiss, 8.

20. Jules Michelet, *La Sorcière*, with chronology and preface by Paul Viallaneix (Paris: Garnier-Flammarion, 1966), 328; trans. in Cohn, 105.

21. Purkiss, 37.

22. Cohn, 107–15. For an excellent account of the opposition to and the appeal of Murray, see Jacqueline Simpson, "Margaret Murray: Who Believed Her, and Why?" *Folklore* 105 (1994): 89–96.

23. See the discussion of confessionalization in Heinz Schilling, *Religion, Political Culture and the Emergence of Early Modern Society: Essays in German and Dutch History* (Leiden: E. J. Brill, 1992), 205–45.

24. John Martin, "Journeys to the World of the Dead: The Work of Carlo Ginzburg," *Journal of Social History* 25 (1992): 613–26.

25. Ginzburg, *Ecstasies*, 8–9.

26. Martin, 623.

27. Ibid., 616.

28. Clive Holmes, "Popular Culture? Witches, Magistrates and Divines," in *Understanding Popular Culture: Europe from the Middle Ages to the Nineteenth Century*, ed. Steven L. Kaplan (New York: Mouton Publishers, 1984), 85–111.

29. Levack, *The Witch-Hunt*, 67–69.

30. Barry, 3–4, acknowledges this while proposing in his essay a "more cultural model" for the history of witchcraft, 4.

31. Alan Macfarlane, *Witchcraft in Tudor and Stuart England: A Regional and Comparative Study* (New York: Harper and Row, 1970), 30, 211–40.

32. See Jeffrey Bowman, review of *Oedipus and the Devil: Witchcraft, Sexuality and Religion in Early Modern Europe*, by Lyndal Roper, *Journal of Social History* 32 (1999): 740–42.

33. Robert Rowland, "'Fantasticall and Devilishe Persons': European Witch-Beliefs in Comparative Perspective," in *Early Modern European Witchcraft: Centres and Peripheries*, ed. Bengt Ankarloo and Gustav Henningsen (Oxford: Clarendon Press, 1991), 176–77.

34. Ibid., 171–81; quote, 179.

35. Christina Larner, *Enemies of God: The Witch-Hunt in Scotland* (Baltimore: Johns Hopkins University Press, 1981), 192.

36. For example, see Robert Muchembled, "The Witches of the Cambrésis: The Acculturation of the Rural World in the Sixteenth and Seventeenth Centuries," in *Religion and the People, 800–1700*, ed. James Obelkevich (Chapel Hill: University of North Carolina Press, 1979), 221–76; "Lay Judges and the Acculturation of the Masses (France and the Southern Low Countries, Sixteenth to Eighteenth Centuries)," in *Religion and Society in Early Modern Europe, 1500–1800*, ed. Kaspar von Greyerz (Boston: Allen and Unwin, 1984), 56–65; *Le roi et la sorcière: L'Europe des bûchers XVe-XVIIIe siècles* (Paris:

Desclée, 1993); "Terres de contrastes: France, Pays-Bas, Provinces-Unies," in *Magie et sorcellerie en Europe: du Moyen Age à nos jours*, ed. Robert Muchembled and Bengt Ankarloo (Paris: A. Colin, 1994), 99–132.

37. Robert Muchembled, "Satanic Myths and Cultural Reality," in Ankarloo and Henningsen, 156–57.

38. Ibid., 148–49.

39. Brian P. Levack, "State-Building and Witch Hunting in Early Modern Europe," in Barry, Hester, and Roberts, 99–107.

40. Alfred Soman, *Sorcellerie et justice criminelle: Le Parlement de Paris (16e-18e siècles)* (Aldershot, Hants, U.K.: Ashgate, 1992).

41. Behringer, *Witchcraft Persecutions*, 389.

42. See Barstow's discussion of gender as a category of analysis in scholarship on the witch-hunts, 1–13; see Purkiss on how the witch-hunts have functioned for the radical feminist movement.

43. Barstow, 23; see Robin Briggs, *Witches and Neighbors: The Social and Cultural Context of European Witchcraft* (Harmondsworth, Middlesex, U.K.: Penguin Books, 1996), 259–65, on proportions of women and men accused of witchcraft and acting as deponents.

44. Larner, 92.

45. Briggs, *Witches and Neighbors*, 259–60.

46. Heinrich Kramer and Jacob Sprenger, *Malleus maleficarum*, trans. Montague Summers (New York: Dover, 1971), 47.

47. Barstow, 7–8.

48. Daly, 28, 190–97.

49. Lyndal Roper, *Oedipus and the Devil: Witchcraft, Sexuality and Religion in Early Modern Europe* (London: Routledge, 1994), 199–225; quote, 202.

50. William Monter, "Toads and Eucharists: The Male Witches of Normandy, 1564–1660," *French Historical Studies* 20 (1997): 563–95. In "Women as Victims? Witches, Judges, and the Community," *French History* 5 (1991): 438–50, Robin Briggs cites male witches as part of his argument against any grand theory of witch-hunting as hunting women. Although he acknowledges women's vulnerability to accusation and witch-hunting's correspondence with an increasing criminalization of women, he sees no programmatic effort to accuse women. The underlying reasons for women being disproportionately prosecuted, he speculates, were the need to justify male dominance and the fundamental love/hate maternal relationship.

51. Rossell Hope Robbins, *Encyclopedia of Witchcraft and Demonology* (New York: Bonanza Books, 1959), s.v. "Junius, Johannes."

52. See Clark, *Thinking with Demons*, 313–434, on the impact of eschatological thought on early modern demonology and witch-hunting.

53. Barstow, 24–25.

54. Robbins, s.v. "Bamberg," and "Junius, Johannes."

55. Monter, "Toads and Eucharists," 592.

56. Eva Labouvie, "Men in Witchcraft Trials: Towards a Social Anthropology of 'Male' Understandings of Magic and Witchcraft," in *Gender in Early Modern German History*, ed. Ulinka Rublack (Cambridge: Cambridge University Press, 2002), 55; and Luisa Accati, "The Spirit of Fornication: Virtue of the Soul and Virtue of the Body in Friuli, 1600–1800," in *Sex and Gender in Historical Perspective*, ed. Edward Muir and Guido Ruggiero (Baltimore: Johns Hopkins University Press, 1990), 115–16.

57. Marianne Hester, "Patriarchal Reconstruction and Witch Hunting," in Barry, Hester, and Roberts, 301.

58. Clive Holmes, "Women: Witnesses and Witches," *Past and Present* 140 (1993), 76.

59. Labouvie, 63.

60. Keith Thomas, *Religion and the Decline of Magic: Studies in Popular Beliefs in Sixteenth and Seventeenth Century England* (London: Weidenfeld and Nicolson, 1971), 520, 562–68; Muchembled, "Satanic Myths," 150–51.

61. Hester, 288–93.

62. Clark, *Thinking with Demons*, 133.

63. Ibid., 115–16.

64. Walter Stephens, *Demon Lovers: Witchcraft, Sex, and the Crisis of Belief* (Chicago: University of Chicago Press, 2002).

65. Ibid., 32–57.

66. Clark distinguishes between past attempts to explain witchcraft away and more recent scholarship that seeks to read or interpret early modern history from the "eyes, minds, and imaginations of those involved." I see my own study as being very much a reading rather than an explanation. See Clark's Introduction to *Languages of Witchcraft: Narrative, Ideology and Meaning in Early Modern Culture*, ed. Stuart Clark (London: Macmillan, 2001). Also see Robin Briggs, "'Many Reasons Why': Witchcraft and the Problem of Multiple Explanation," in Barry, Hester, and Roberts, 49–63.

67. Barstow, 11.

68. Ibid., 176–77; Clark, *Thinking with Demons*, 198–203.

69. Joan Wallach Scott, "Women's History," in *American Feminist Thought at Century's End: A Reader*, ed. Linda S. Kaufman (Cambridge, Mass.: Blackwell, 1993), 234–35.

70. Joan Wallach Scott advanced the concept of gender history in "Gender: A Useful Category of Analysis," an essay of 1986 republished in her *Gender and the Politics of History* (New York: Columbia University Press, 1988), 28–50. Critiques of Scott's essay were vigorous and numerous: See those discussed by Kathleen Canning, "Feminist History after the Linguistic Turn: Historicizing Discourse and Experience," in *Feminist Approaches to Theory and Methodology: An Interdisciplinary Reader*, ed. Sharlene Hesse-Biber, Christina Gilmartin, and Robin Lydenberg (Oxford: Oxford University Press, 1999), 66–67, n. 9. I concur with Scott that the dichotomy between a feminist women's history and a nonfeminist gender history is false; see "Women's History," 235–36, 248–49.

71. Merry E. Wiesner, *Women and Gender in Early Modern Europe*, 2nd ed. (Cambridge: Cambridge University Press, 2000), 276–77.

72. See Klaits, 48–85.

73. Whitney Chadwick, *Women, Art, and Society* (New York: Thames and Hudson, 1990), provides an excellent overview. A few exemplary focused studies within this burgeoning literature are Wendy Wassyng Roworth, ed., *Angelica Kauffmann: A Continental Artist in Georgian England* (London: Reaktion Books, 1993); Mary D. Sheriff, *The Exceptional Woman: Elisabeth Vigée-Lebrun and the Cultural Politics of Art* (Chicago: University of Chicago Press, 1996); and Fredrika H. Jacobs, *Defining the Renaissance Virtuosa: Women Artists and the Language of Art History and Criticism* (Cambridge: Cambridge University Press, 1997). It is perhaps Artemisia Gentileschi whose work has elicited the most varied assessments of the relationship between artistic production and gender: See Mary D. Garrard, *Artemisia Gentileschi: The Image of the Female Hero in Italian Art* (Princeton, N.J.: Princeton University Press, 1989); and R. Ward Bissell's rejoinder, *Artemisia Gentileschi and the Authority of Art* (University Park: The Pennsyl-

vania State University Press, 1999). The essays in Keith Christiansen and Judith W. Mann, *Orazio and Artemisia Gentileschi* (New York and New Haven, Conn.: Metropolitan Museum of Art and Yale University Press, 2001), provide a highly nuanced assessment of the issues.

74. Clark Hulse, *The Rule of Art: Literature and Painting in the Renaissance* (Chicago: University of Chicago Press, 1990), 7–114.

75. See Susan L. Smith, *The Power of Women: A Topos in Medieval Art and Literature* (Philadelphia: University of Pennsylvania Press, 1995); H. Diane Russell with Bernadine Barnes, *Eva/Ave: Woman in Renaissance and Baroque Prints* (Washington, D.C., and New York: The National Gallery of Art in association with the Feminist Press at the City University of New York, 1990); and Annette Dixon, ed., *Women Who Ruled: Queens, Goddesses, Amazons in Renaissance and Baroque Art* (London and Ann Arbor: Merrill in association with the University of Michigan Museum of Art, 2002).

76. For an excellent survey of the theory of the grotesque, including Bakhtin's work on Rabelais, see Wilson Yates, "An Introduction to the Grotesque: Theoretical and Theological Considerations," in *The Grotesque in Art and Literature: Theological Reflections*, ed. James Luther Adams and Wilson Yates (Grand Rapids, Mich.: William B. Eerdmans Publishing Co., 1997), 1–68; on Bakhtin's grotesque body, see Peter Stallybrass, "Patriarchal Territories: The Body Enclosed," in *Rewriting the Renaissance: The Discourses of Sexual Difference in Early Modern Europe*, ed. Margaret W. Ferguson, Maureen Quilligan, and Nancy J. Vickers (Chicago: University of Chicago Press, 1986), 123–42.

77. Mary Russo, *The Female Grotesque: Risk, Excess, and Modernity* (London: Routledge, 1994); and Elizabeth Grosz, *Volatile Bodies: Toward a Corporeal Feminism* (Bloomington: Indiana University Press, 1994), 187–210.

78. Accati, 120. For an account of the Renaissance understanding of woman's nature (physiological, moral, intellectual), see Ian Maclean, *The Renaissance Notion of Woman: A Study in the Fortunes of Scholasticism and Medical Science in European Intellectual Life* (Cambridge: Cambridge University Press, 1980; reprint, 1988).

79. Margaret A. Sullivan, "The Witches of Dürer and Hans Baldung Grien," *Renaissance Quarterly* 53 (2000): 332–401.

80. On old age and witchcraft, see Edward Bever, "Old Age and Witchcraft in Early Modern Europe," in *Old Age in Pre-Industrial Society*, ed. Peter Stearns (New York: Holmes and Meier, 1982), 150–90; and Alison Rowlands, "Witchcraft and Old Women in Early Modern Germany," *Past and Present* 173 (2001): 50–89. Rowlands emphasizes the importance of understanding the complexities of individual biographies before making an inherent connection between old age and witchcraft accusations.

81. Charles Zika, *Exorcising Our Demons: Magic, Witchcraft, and Visual Culture in Early Modern Europe* (Leiden: E. J. Brill, 2003), 305–32; Charmian Mesenzeva, "Zum Problem. Dürer und die Antike: Albrecht Dürer's Kupferstich, 'Die Hexe,'" *Zeitschrift für Kunstgeschichte* 46 (1983): 187–202.

82. Jane P. Davidson, *The Witch in Northern European Art, 1470–1750* (Freren, Ger.: Luca Verlag, 1987), 26, doubts her identity as a witch.

83. Manuel's training and contacts are difficult to trace, but he does seem to have been exposed to graphic works by Dürer and Baldung. See Hugo Wagner, "Niklaus Manuel—Leben und künsterlisches Werk," in *Niklaus Manuel Deutsch: Maler, Dichter, Staatsmann*, ed. Cäsar Menz and Hugo Wagner (Bern: Kunstmuseum, 1979), 21.

84. Carl Koch, *Die Zeichnungen Hans Baldung Griens* (Berlin: Deutscher Verein für Kunstwissenschaft, 1941), cat. no. 61, 99.

85. Ibid., cat. no. 59, 98.

86. Mary Douglas, *Purity and Danger: An Analysis of the Concepts of Pollution and Taboo* (London: Routledge & Kegan Paul, 1966).

87. Julia Kristeva, *The Powers of Horror: An Essay on Abjection*, trans. Leon S. Roudiez (New York: Columbia University Press, 1982), 4.

88. Ibid., 210.

89. See Joan Wallach Scott's critique of the loss of historical specificity and variability and the essentialism inherent in psychoanalytic analysis in "Gender: A Useful Category of Analysis," 38–41.

90. Hélène Cixous and Catherine Clément, *The Newly Born Woman*, trans. Betsy Wing (Minneapolis: University of Minnesota Press, 1986), 36; quoted in Purkiss, 81.

91. Kristeva, 3–4.

92. Purkiss, 120.

93. Douglas, 126.

94. Purkiss, 125–30.

95. Ibid., 130–39.

96. Gareth Roberts, "The Descendants of Circe: Witches and Renaissance Fictions," in Barry, Hester, and Roberts, 183–206. Also see his article in *The Spenser Encyclopedia*, ed. Albert Charles Hamilton (Toronto: University of Toronto Press, 1990), s.v. "Circe."

97. Hulse, 105.

98. Ian Bostridge, "Witchcraft Repealed," in Barry, Hester, and Roberts, eds., 310.

99. Clark, *Thinking with Demons*, 195–213.

100. Stephen Greenblatt, *Renaissance Self-Fashioning: From More to Shakespeare* (Chicago: University of Chicago Press, 1980).

101. Hulse, 1.

102. Purkiss, 179–230.

103. Jane Campbell Hutchison, *Albrecht Dürer: A Biography* (Princeton, N.J.: Princeton University Press, 1990), 32, 83.

104. For example, Roper, *Oedipus and the Devil*; Purkiss, 145–96; and Sally Scully, "Marriage or a Career?: Witchcraft as an Alternative in Seventeenth-Century Venice," *Journal of Social History* 28 (1995): 857–76.

105. Purkiss, 26; Hester, 291–300.

106. Natalie Zemon Davis, *Society and Culture in Early Modern France: Eight Essays* (Stanford, Calif.: Stanford University Press, 1975), 133.

107. Merry E. Wiesner-Hanks, *Christianity and Sexuality in the Early Modern World: Regulating Desire, Reforming Practice* (London: Routledge, 2000), 260 and *passim*.

108. E. William Monter, "The Pedestal and the Stake: Courtly Love and Witchcraft," in *Becoming Visible: Women in European History*, ed. Renate Bridenthal and Claudia Koontz (Boston: Houghton Mifflin, 1977), 133–35.

Chapter 2

1. Martin Kemp, "From 'Mimesis' to 'Fantasia': The Quattrocento Vocabulary of Creation, Inspiration and Genius in the Visual Arts," *Viator* 8 (1977): 375.

2. Anthony Blunt, *Artistic Theory in Italy, 1450–1600* (Oxford: Clarendon Press,

1940; reprint, 1963), 14–15; Moshe Barasch, *Theories of Art from Plato to Winckelmann* (New York: New York University Press, 1989), 114–15, 123–24.

3. M. Barasch, 123–27.

4. On ornamental *grotteschi*, see Frances K. Barasch, *The Grotesque: A Study in Meanings* (The Hague, Moutin, 1971), 1–31; André Chastel, *La grottesque* (Paris: Le Promeneur, 1988).

5. Blunt, 21–22.

6. Leonbattista Alberti, *On Painting*, trans. John R. Spencer, rev. ed. (New Haven, Conn.: Yale University Press, 1956), 90–91.

7. Margaret A. Sullivan, "The Witches of Dürer and Hans Baldung Grien," *Renaissance Quarterly* 53 (2000): 332–401.

8. Alberti, 90–91.

9. Francis Ames-Lewis, *The Intellectual Life of the Early Renaissance Artist* (New Haven, Conn.: Yale University Press, 2000), 193–95.

10. David Cast, *The Calumny of Apelles: A Study in the Humanist Tradition* (New Haven, Conn.: Yale University Press, 1981), 39–41.

11. Ronald W. Lightbown, *Sandro Botticelli: Life and Work*, 2 vols. (New York: Abbeville Press, 1987), vol. 1, 125.

12. Cast, 33.

13. Evelyn Lincoln, *The Invention of the Italian Renaissance Printmaker* (New Haven: Yale University Press, 2000), 17–43.

14. Kemp, "From 'Mimesis' to 'Fantasia,'" 359.

15. Michael Vickers, "The Sources of *Invidia* in Mantegna's *Battle of the Sea Gods*," *Apollo* 106 (1977): 270–73; Phyllis Pray Bober, "An Antique Sea-Thiasos in the Renaissance," in *Essays in Memory of Karl Lehmann*, ed. Lucy Freeman Sandler (New York: New York University Press, 1964), 43–48.

16. Ronald W. Lightbown, *Mantegna: With a Complete Catalogue of the Paintings, Drawings, and Prints* (Berkeley: University of California Press, 1986), 240–41.

17. Michael Jacobsen, "The Meaning of Mantegna's *Battle of the Sea Monsters*," *Art Bulletin* 64 (1982): 623–29.

18. Patricia A. Emison, "The Raucousness of Mantegna's Mythological Engravings," *Gazette des Beaux-Arts* 124 (1994): 168.

19. Jacobsen, 624, n. 3.

20. Lincoln, 30.

21. For a summary of interpretations, see Jay A. Levenson, Konrad Oberhuber, and Jacquelyn L. Sheehan, *Early Italian Engravings from the National Gallery of Art* (Washington, D.C.: National Gallery of Art, 1973), cat. no. 13, 66–71.

22. Patricia A. Emison, "The Word Made Naked in Pollaiuolo's *Battle of the Nudes*," *Art History* 13 (1990): 261–75.

23. Ames-Lewis, 254.

24. Louise Richards, "Antonio Pollaiuolo: *Battle of Naked Men*," *Bulletin of the Cleveland Museum of Art* 55 (1968): 61–70.

25. Kemp, "From 'Mimesis' to 'Fantasia,'" 362–63.

26. Ibid., 368–75.

27. Ibid., 379.

28. Ibid., 377–78.

29. Ibid., 377.

30. Erwin Panofsky, *The Life and Art of Albrecht Dürer*, 4th rev. ed. (Princeton, N.J.: Princeton University Press, 1971), 279.

31. Ibid., 271, 279–80, 283.

32. Juliana Schiesari, *The Gendering of Melancholia: Feminism, Psychoanalysis, and the Symbolics of Loss in Renaissance Literature* (Ithaca, N.Y: Cornell University Press, 1992), 42–43.

33. Mark Breitenberg, *Anxious Masculinity in Early Modern England* (Cambridge: Cambridge University Press, 1996), 35–68.

34. David Summers, *Michelangelo and the Language of Art* (Princeton, N.J.: Princeton University Press, 1981), 66, 231.

35. These sources on Michelangelo's theory of art are summarized by M. Barasch, 190–92.

36. Summers, 234–41.

37. Ellen Oliensis, *Horace and the Rhetoric of Authority* (Cambridge: Cambridge University Press, 1998), 215–23.

38. Ibid., 200.

39. Gareth Roberts, "The Descendants of Circe: Witches and Renaissance Fictions," in *Witchcraft in Early Modern Europe: Studies in Culture and Belief*, ed. Jonathan Barry, Marianne Hester, and Gareth Roberts (Cambridge: Cambridge University Press, 1996), 183–206; quote, 206.

40. This double identity is also noted by Jacob Rabinowitz in *The Rotting Goddess: The Origin of the Witch in Classical Antiquity* (Brooklyn, N.Y.: Autonomedia, 1998), 80–81,

41. C. E. Manning, in "Canidia in the *Epodes* of Horace," *Mnemosyne* 23 (1970): 393–401, emphasizes Horace's concern with actual as opposed to literary witchcraft. For Greek and Roman legal repression of magical practices, see Richard Gordon, "Imagining Greek and Roman Magic, in *Witchcraft and Magic in Europe: Ancient Greece and Rome*, ed. Bengt Ankarloo and Stuart Clark (Philadelphia: University of Pennsylvania Press, 1999), 243–66.

42. Daniel Ogden, "Binding Spells: Curse Tablets and Voodoo Dolls in the Greek and Roman Worlds," in Ankarloo and Clark, 62–63.

43. John W. Winkler, *The Constraints of Desire: The Anthropology of Sex and Gender in Ancient Greece* (London: Routledge, 1990), 71–98.

44. Ellen Oliensis, "Canidia, Canicula, and the Decorum of Horace's *Epodes*," *Arethusa* 24 (1991): 107–35.

45. Amy Richlin, *The Garden of Priapus: Sexuality and Aggression in Roman Humor* (Oxford: Oxford University Press, 1992), 113.

46. Oliensis, *Rhetoric of Authority*, 76.

47. George Luck, "Witches and Sorcerers in Classical Literature," in Ankarloo and Clark, 112–13, 137–38.

48. Richlin, 115; also see her "Invective Against Women in Roman Satire," *Arethusa* 17 (1984): 67–80.

49. Richard Gordon, "Lucan's Erichtho," in *Homo Viator: Classical Essays for John Bramble*, ed. Michael Whitby, Philip Hardie, and Mary Whitby (Oak Park, Ill.: Bristol Classical, 1984), 234.

50. Giorgio Vasari, *Lives of the Most Eminent Painters, Sculptors, and Architects*, trans. Gaston du C. de Vere, 10 vols. (London: Macmillan, 1912–15), vol. 6, 210, quoted in F. Barasch, 20.

51. Paul Barolsky, *Infinite Jest: Wit and Humor in Italian Renaissance Art* (Columbia: University of Missouri Press, 1978), 51–74.

52. Summers, 138.

53. F. Barasch, 25–31.

54. Chastel, 32.

55. Maria Ruvoldt, *The Italian Renaissance Imagery of Inspiration* (Cambridge: Cambridge University Press, 2004), 122–40.

56. Stephen J. Campbell, "Michelangelo, Rosso, and the (Un)Divinity of Art," *Art Bulletin* 84 (December 2002): 596–620.

57. Patricia A. Emison, "Truth and *Bizzarria* in an Engraving of *Lo stregozzo*," *Art Bulletin* 81 (1999): 623–33.

58. Tamar Herzig, "The Demons' Reaction to Sodomy: Witchcraft and Homosexuality in Gianfrancesco Pico della Mirandola's *Strix*," *The Sixteenth Century Journal* 34 (2003): 58.

59. For an English translation, see Alan Charles Kors and Edward Peters, eds., *Witchcraft in Europe, 400–1700: A Documentary History*, 2nd ed. (Philadelphia: University of Pennsylvania Press, 2001), 239–45.

60. Herzig, 66–69; and Walter Stephens, *Demon Lovers: Witchcraft, Sex, and the Crisis of Belief* (Chicago: University of Chicago Press, 2002), 87–99.

61. Emison, "Truth and *Bizzarria*," 633.

62. For summaries of attributions, see ibid., 635, n. 31; and Bruce Davis, *Mannerist Prints: International Style in the Sixteenth Century* (Los Angeles: Los Angeles County Museum of Art, 1988), 110–13.

63. David Landau, "From Collaboration to Reproduction in Italy," in David Landau and Peter Parshall, *The Renaissance Print, 1470–1550* (New Haven, Conn.: Yale University Press, 1994), 120–46.

64. Davis, 113.

65. Janet Cox-Rearick, ed., *Giulio Romano: Master Designer* (New York: Hunter College, City University of New York, Bertha and Karl Leubsdorf Gallery, 1999), 17.

66. Ibid., 17.

67. Giorgio Vasari, *The Lives of the Artists*, ed. and trans. Julia Conaway Bondanella and Peter Bondanella (Oxford: Oxford University Press, 1991; reprint, 1998), 359–76.

68. Cox-Rearick, 19.

69. Landau, 144–45.

70. Davis, 112; Landau, 145; Emison, "Truth and *Bizzarria*," 627–28, proposes a different sequence of states.

71. Bette Talvacchia, *Taking Positions: The Erotic in Renaissance Culture* (Princeton, N.J.: Princeton University Press, 1999), 8–9.

72. Emison, "Truth and *Bizzarria*," 632.

73. Kors and Peters, 245–47.

74. Herzig, 70.

75. Jacobsen, 624.

76. Talvacchia, 96–100.

77. Frederick Hartt, *Giulio Romano* (New Haven, Conn.: Yale University Press, 1958), 7.

78. Manfredo Tafuri et al., *Giulio Romano*, trans. Fabio Barry (Cambridge: Cambridge University Press, 1998), 16.

79. See the discussion of Mannerist theory in M. Barasch, 271–309.

80. Walter S. Melion, *Shaping the Netherlandish Canon: Karel Van Mander's Schilder-Boek* (Chicago: University of Chicago Press, 1991), 29, 55.

81. M. Barasch, 232.

82. Melion, 63–66.

83. On Rudolf II's patronage in Prague, see Thomas DaCosta Kaufmann, *The School of Prague: Painting at the Court of Rudolf II* (Chicago: University of Chicago Press, 1988); and "Princely Patronage of the Later Sixteenth and Early Seventeenth Centuries: The Example and Impact of the Court of Rudolf II," in *Court, Cloister and City: The Art and Culture of Central Europe, 1450–1800* (Chicago: University of Chicago Press, 1995), 185–203.

84. Karel van Mander, *The Lives of the Illustrious Netherlandish and German Painters*, trans. and with commentary by Hessel Miedema, 6 vols. (Doornspijk, Neth.: Davaco, 1994–99), vol. 1, 341.

85. Summers, 137–38.

86. Svetlana Alpers, *The Art of Describing: Dutch Art in the Seventeenth Century* (Chicago: University of Chicago Press, 1983), 40–41; Melion, 243, n. 10.

87. Emil Karl Josef Reznicek, "Realism as a 'Side Road or Byway' in Dutch Art," in *Studies in Western Art: Acts of the Twentieth International Congress of the History of* Art, vol. 2, The *Renaissance and Mannerism*, ed. Ida Ely Rubin (Princeton, N.J.: Princeton University Press, 1963), 247–53; Hessel Miedema, "Over het realisme in de Nederlandse schilderkunst van de zeventiende eeuw, naar aanleidung van een tekening van Jacques de Gheyn II (1565–1632)," *Oud Holland* 89 (1975): 2–18; and Claudia Swan, "*Ad vivum, naer het leven*, from the Life: Defining a Mode of Representation," *Word and Image* 11 (1995): 353–72.

88. Walter S. Gibson discusses the terminology surrounding Bosch in "Bosch's Dreams: A Response to the Art of Bosch in the Sixteenth Century," *Art Bulletin* 74 (1992): 205–18

89. For a survey, see Gerd Unverfehrt, *Hieronymus Bosch: Die Rezeption seiner Kunst im frühen 16. Jahrhundert* (Berlin: Gebr. Mann, 1980).

90. Jane L. Carroll, "The Paintings of Jacob Cornelisz. van Oostsanen" (Ph.D. diss., University of North Carolina at Chapel Hill, 1987), 73–76, and cat. no. 3, 90–104.

91. Larry Silver, "Second Bosch: Family Resemblance and the Marketing of Art," *Nederlands kunsthistorisch Jaarboek* 50 (1999): 30–56.

92. Lampsonius, quoted in Gibson, 206, 217.

93. James Snyder, ed. *Bosch in Perspective* (Englewood Cliffs, N.J.: Prentice Hall, 1973), 28–30; also see Unverfehrt, 67–69; and Silver, "Second Bosch," 33–34.

94. Larry Silver, "Imitation and Emulation: Goltzius as Evolutionary Reproductive Engraver," in *Graven Images: The Rise of Professional Printmakers in Antwerp and Haarlem, 1540–1640*, ed Timothy Riggs and Larry Silver (Evanston, Ill.: The Mary and Leigh Block Gallery, Northwestern University, 1993), 21.

95. Charles D. Cuttler, "Witchcraft in a Work by Bosch," *Art Quarterly* 20 (1957): 129–40; and Lène Dresen-Coenders, "De demonen bij Jeroen Bosch: Zoektocht naar bronnen en betekenis," in *Duivelsbeelden: Een cultuurhistorisches speurtocht door de Lage Landen*, ed. Gerard Rooijakkers, Lène Dresen-Coenders, and Margaret Geerdes (Baarn, Neth.: Uitgeverij Ambo, 1994), 168–97 (English summary, 421–22).

96. Charles de Tolnay, *The Drawings of Pieter Bruegel the Elder, with a Critical Catalogue*, trans. Charles Sleeth (New York: Twin Editions, 1953), cat. no. 66, 75.

97. Nadine Monica Orenstein, ed., *Pieter Bruegel the Elder: Drawings and Prints* (New York: Metropolitan Museum of Art, 2001), cat. nos. 101, 102, pp. 230–34.

98. Ibid., cat. no. 102, 234.

99. For an excellent discussion of Bellori's significance and the critical literature on his theory, see Janis Bell, introduction to *Art History in the Age of Bellori: Scholarship*

and Cultural Poetics in Seventeenth-Century Rome, ed. Janis Bell and Thomas Willette (Cambridge: Cambridge University Press, 2002).

100. Elizabeth Cropper, "'La più bella antichità che sappiate desiderare': History and Style in Giovan Pietro Bellori's 'Lives,'" in *Kunst und Kunsttheorie 1400–1900*, ed. Peter Ganz et al. (Wiesbaden: Otto Harrassowitz, 1991), 160. Also see her fundamental study of Italian art theory in the seventeenth century, *The Ideal of Painting: Pietro Testa's Düsseldorf Notebook* (Princeton, N.J.: Princeton University Press, 1984).

101. M. Barasch, 324–36; on Bellori's *ekphrases*, see Cropper, "La più bella antichità," 171–73.

102. Thomas Puttfarken reviews the issues presented by Poussin's statements about art and the interpretations of various art historians in "Poussin's Thoughts on Painting," in *Commemorating Poussin: Reception and Interpretation of the Artist*, ed. Katie Scott and Genevieve Warwick (Cambridge: Cambridge University Press, 1999), 53–75.

103. Ibid., 63–69.

104. M. Barasch, 330–36.

105. Cast, 31.

106. Roland Kanz, "Capriccio und Grotteske," in *Kunstform Capriccio: von der Groteske zur Spieltheorie der Moderne*, ed. Ekkehard Mai and Joachim Rees (Cologne: Walter König, 1998), 23–25; John L. Ciofalo, *The Self-Portraits of Francisco Goya* (Cambridge: Cambridge University Press, 2001), 41–42.

107. Werner Hofmann, "Unending Shipwreck," in *Goya: Truth and Fantasy, the Small Paintings*, ed. Juliet Wilson-Barreau and Manuela B. Mena Marqués (New Haven, Conn.: Yale University Press, 1994), 48.

108. Werner Busch, "Das Capriccio und die Erweiterung der Wirklichkeit," in Mai and Rees, 58.

109. Hofmann, 48–50.

110. Andrea Gottdang, "Tiepolo's *Scherzi di Fantasia*: Begriff und Bedeutung," in Mai and Rees, 84–89.

Chapter 3

1. See Wolfgang Behringer, "Allemagne, 'mère de tant des sorcières," in *Magie et sorcellerie en Europe: Du moyen age à nos jours*, ed. Robert Muchembled and Bengt Ankarloo (Paris: A. Colin, 1994), 59; and William Monter, "Witch Trials in Continental Europe, 1560–1660," in *Witchcraft and Magic in Europe: The Period of the Witch Trials*, ed. Bengt Ankarloo, Stuart Clark, and William Monter (Philadelphia: University of Pennsylvania Press, 2002), 13.

2. Rossell Hope Robbins, *Encyclopedia of Witchcraft and Demonology* (New York: Bonanza Books, 1959), s.v. "Germany, Witchcraft in."

3. Ibid.

4. Norman Cohn, preface to *Europe's Inner Demons: An Enquiry Inspired by the Great Witch-Hunt* (New York: Basic Books, 1975).

5. Behringer, "Allemagne," 61.

6. Brian P. Levack, *The Witch-Hunt in Early Modern Europe* (New York: Longman, 1987), 86–87, 176–79.

7. Behringer, "Allemagne," 70.

8. Ibid., 90; Monter, "Witch Trials in Continental Europe," 16.

9. Robin Briggs, *Witches and Neighbors: The Social and Cultural Context of European Witchcraft* (Harmondsworth, Middlesex, U.K.: Penguin Books, 1996), 328; Monter, "Witch Trials in Continental Europe," 28.

10. Behringer, "Allemagne," 80; Monter, "Witch Trials in Continental Europe," 21.

11. Wolfgang Behringer, *Witchcraft Persecutions in Bavaria: Popular Magic, Religious Zealotry and Reason of State in Early Modern Europe*, trans. J. C. Grayson and David Lederer (Cambridge: Cambridge University Press, 1997).

12. Behringer, "Allemagne," 84–87.

13. See Andreas Blauert, "Frühe Hexenverfolgungen in der Schweiz, am Bodensee und am Oberrhein," in *Hexen und Hexenverfolgungen im deutschen Südwesten*, ed. Sönke Lorenz, 2 vols. (Karlsruhe: Badisches Landesmuseum, 1994), vol. 1, 60; and Michael David Bailey, *Battling Demons: Witchcraft, Heresy, and Reform in the Late Middle Ages* (University Park: Pennsylvania State University Press, 2003), 28.

14. Bailey, 48–53; 119–38; 124.

15. Blauert, 62.

16. Alan Charles Kors and Edward Peters, eds., *Witchcraft in Europe, 400–1700: A Documentary History*, 2nd ed. (Philadelphia: University of Pennsylvania Press, 2001), 177–80.

17. Letter by Bishop Golser, quoted in Blauert, 64 (my translation); for an especially dismissive critique of the *Malleus*, see Sidney Anglo, "Evident Authority and Authoritative Evidence: The *Malleus Maleficarum*," in *The Damned Art: Essays in the Literature of Witchcraft*, ed. Sidney Anglo (London: Routledge & Kegan Paul, 1977), 1–31.

18. Duke Sigmund had employed the father of Willibald Pirckheimer, Dürer's best friend, as legal counsel. See Jane Campbell Hutchison, *Albrecht Dürer: A Biography* (Princeton, N.J.: Princeton University Press, 1990), 52.

19. Stuart Clark, *Thinking with Demons: The Idea of Witchcraft in Early Modern Europe* (Oxford: Oxford University Press, 1997), 452, 521.

20. On early editions of the *Malleus*, see Henry Charles Lea, *Materials Toward a History of Witchcraft*, ed. Arthur C. Howland, 3 vols. (Philadelphia: University of Pennsylvania Press, 1939), vol. 1, 306. Walter Stephens, in *Demon Lovers: Witchcraft, Sex, and the Crisis of Belief* (Chicago: University of Chicago Press, 2002), 33, 377, n. 7, corrects Anne Llewellyn Barstow, *Witchcraze: A New History of the European Witch Hunts* (San Francisco: Pandora Press, 1994), 171, for misstating the countries of publication as languages. Having misread Lea, who notes sixteen German, eleven French, and two Italian editions, I made the same error in "Dürer's Four Witches Reconsidered," in *Saints, Sinners and Sisters: Gender and Northern Art in Medieval and Early Modern Europe*, ed. Jane L. Carroll and Alison G. Stewart (Aldershot, Hants, U.K.: Ashgate, 2003), 102. On the uncertainty of early statistics on witchcraft trials for southwest Germany, see Wolfgang Behringer, "Witchcraft Studies in Austria, Germany and Switzerland," in Jonathan Barry, Marianne Hester, and Gareth Roberts, eds., *Witchcraft in Early Modern Europe: Studies in Culture and Belief* (Cambridge: Cambridge University Press, 1996), 81.

21. Charles Zika, *Exorcising Our Demons: Magic, Witchcraft, and Visual Culture in Early Modern Europe* (Leiden: E. J. Brill, 2003), 240.

22. Joachim von Sandrart, *Teutsche Academie der edlen Bau-, Bild, und Mahlerey-Künste*, ed. A. R. Pelzer (Munich: G. Hirth's Verlag, 1925), 63.

23. Erwin Panofsky, *The Life and Art of Albrecht Dürer*, 4th revised ed. (Princeton, N.J.: Princeton University Press, 1971), 71.

24. For various copies, see *Vorbild Dürer: Kupferstiche und Holzschnitte Albrecht Dürers im Spiegel der europäische Druckgraphik des 16. Jahrhunderts*, ed. Leonie van Wilckens and Peter Strieder (Munich: Prestel Verlag, 1978), cat. nos. 32–34. On the Judgment of Paris, see James Hall, *Dictionary of Subjects and Symbols in Art*, rev. ed. (New York: Harper and Row, 1979), 180–81.

25. The most important source for Dürer's arrangement is a Roman marble group of the Graces that copies a Hellenistic original (Piccolomini Library, Siena Cathedral). See Phyllis Pray Bober and Ruth Rubenstein, *Renaissance Artists and Antique Sculpture: A Handbook of Sources* (London: H. Miller, 1986), cat. no. 60, 96–97. The *pudica* pose of Venus descended ultimately from the *Knidian Aphrodite* of Praxiteles and was reflected in works like the *Capitoline* and *Medici Venuses*: see Bober and Rubenstein, 59–60; also Francis Haskell and Nicholas Penny, *Taste and the Antique: The Lure of Classical Sculpture 1500–1900* (New Haven, Conn.: Yale University Press, 1981), cat. no. 84, 318–20, and cat. no. 88, 325–28. On Dürer's interest in the Praxitilean Aphrodite figure, see Jane Campbell Hutchison, "Forum: Dürer's Praxitelean Aphrodite," *Drawing* 13 (1991): 55–56. On the attributes of Venus, see Hall, 318–20; on myrtle and Venus, see Jesse Poesch, "Sources for Two Dürer Enigmas," *Art Bulletin* 46 (1964): 78, n. 5.

26. Poesch, 78–82; Eugene Dwyer, "The Subject of Dürer's *Four Witches*," *Art Quarterly* 34 (1971): 470, for summary; and Fedja Anzelewsky, *Dürer-Studien: Untersuchungen zu den ikonographischen und geistesgeschichtlichen Grundlagen seiner Werke zwischen den beiden Italienreisen* (Berlin: Deutscher Verein für Kunstwissenschaft, 1983), 29–44. Anzelewsky wants to stress Dürer's ambiguity corresponding to the multileveled erudition and fluid symbolism of mythological subjects in a humanistic, especially Neoplatonic, context.

27. Margaret A. Sullivan, "The Witches of Dürer and Hans Baldung Grien," *Renaissance Quarterly* 53 (2000): 332–401.

28. Zika, 305.

29. Stephens, 32–57.

30. Panofsky, 62–89. On Pirckheimer and his circle, see Hutchison, *Dürer*, 48–56, especially 55–56, for the impact of this friendship on Dürer's early engravings. On the broader woodcut audience, see Alison G. Stewart, "Paper Festivals and Popular Entertainments: Beham's Kermis Woodcuts," *The Sixteenth-Century Journal* 24 (1993): 343–50.

31. For introductions to the social and political structure of Nuremberg, see Guy Fitch Lytle, "The Renaissance, the Reformation, and the City of Nuremberg," in *Nuremberg: A Renaissance City, 1500–1618*, by Jeffrey Chipps Smith (Austin: Archer M. Huntington Art Gallery, University of Texas, and University of Texas Press, 1983), 17–22; and Alfred Wendenhorst, "Nuremberg, the Imperial City: From its Beginnings to the End of its Glory," in Metropolitan Museum of Art, *Gothic and Renaissance Art in Nuremberg, 1300–1550* (New York: Metropolitan Museum of Art, 1986), 11–26; for Dürer's connections with the patrician families, see Hutchison, *Dürer*, 4, 14, 27, 34, 39, 48–56, 61, 66, 78–97, 103, 110, 114, 121, 123, 130, 140, 142, 148, 150, 153–54, 159, 167, 171–72, 180.

32. Hutchison, *Dürer*, 57.

33. On the distinction between women's power and patriarchal authority, see Michelle Rosaldo and Louise Lamphere, Introduction to *Woman, Culture and Society*, ed. Michelle Rosaldo and Louise Lamphere (Stanford, Calif.: Stanford University Press, 1974); Michele Rosaldo, "Theoretical Overview,“ in *Woman, Culture and Society*, 17–42;

James Brain, "An Anthropological Perspective on the Witchcraze," in *The Politics of Gender in Early Modern Europe*, ed. Jean R. Brink, Allison P. Coudert, and Maryanne C. Horowitz (Kirksville, Mo.: Sixteenth Century Journal Publishers, 1989), 16–17; and Constance Jordan, *Renaissance Feminism: Literary Texts and Political Models* (Ithaca, N.Y.: Cornell University Press, 1990), 4–6.

34. Cohn, 206–224. For the shaping influence of inquisitors and judges on folk beliefs, see the classic study by Carlo Ginzburg, *Night Battles: Witchcraft and Agrarian Cults in the Sixteenth and Seventeenth Centuries*, trans. John and Anne Tedeschi (Baltimore: Johns Hopkins University Press, 1983).

35. Poesch, 80; Erwin Panofsky, *Studies in Iconology: Humanistic Themes in the Art of the Renaissance* (New York: Oxford University Press, 1939), 142–45; Hutchison, *Dürer*, 52, 71.

36. Poesch, 78–80. On *The Dream of the Doctor*, see Panofsky, *Dürer*, 71–72.

37. Charmian Mesenzeva, "Zum Problem. Dürer und die Antike: Albrecht Dürers Kupferstich, 'Die Hexe,'" *Zeitschrift für Kunstgeschichte* 46 (1983): 187–202.

38. Walter L. Strauss, *The Complete Drawings of Albrecht Dürer*, 6 vols. (New York: Abaris Books, 1974), vol. 1, cat. no. 1496/17, 426–27.

39. Clark, *Thinking with Demons*, 315–434.

40. Protestantism augmented the role of apocalyptic thought in witch-hunting. See Allison P. Coudert, "The Myth of the Improved Status of Protestant Women: The Case of the Witchcraze," in Brink, Coudert, and Horowitz, 66–67.

41. Sigrid Brauner, *Fearless Wives and Frightened Shrews: The Construction of the Witch in Early Modern Germany*, ed. Robert H. Brown (Amherst: University of Massachusetts Press, 1995), 7, 32–33.

42. Anzelewsky, 104; Brauner, 33; and Hartmut Kunstmann, *Zauberwahn und Hexenprozess in der Reichsstadt Nürnberg* (Nuremberg: Korn and Berg, 1970), 11–12. For a facsimile and German transcription of Kramer's handwritten advice to local authorities, see Günter Jerouschek, ed. and trans., *Nürnberger Hexenhammer 1491 von Heinrich Kramer (Institoris)* (Hildesheim, Ger., and New York: Georg Olms Verlag, 1992); for the impact of this text, also see Rudolf Endres, "Heinrich Institoris, sein Hexenhammer und der Nürnberger Rat," in *Der Hexenhammer: Entstehung und Umfeld des* Malleus *maleficarum von 1487*, ed. Peter Segl (Köln: Böhlau Verlag, 1988), 195–216.

43. Lea, vol. 1, 344.

44. Ibid., 343.

45. Richard Kieckhefer, *European Witch Trials: Their Foundations in Popular and Learned Culture, 1300–1500* (Berkeley: University of California Press, 1976), 144–47.

46. See Hutchison, *Dürer*, 27–39, on Dürer's journeyman travels.

47. Kunstmann, 202; Sullivan, 352.

48. Anzelewsky, 105; Kunstmann, 30–35, and quote, 34 ("*wider christnliche ordnung*").

49. For a summary of Molitor's views, see Lea, vol. 1, 348–53.

50. Zika, 326–27; Sullivan, 353.

51. Gerhild Scholz Williams, "On Finding Words: Witchcraft and the Discourses of Dissidence and Discovery," in *The Graph of Sex and the German Text: Gendered Culture in Early Modern Europe, 1500–1700*, ed. Lynne Tatlock (Atlanta, Ga.: Rodopi, 1994), 61.

52. Cohn, 1–59, 206–24; Zika, 333–74. Geiler mentions "Venusberg" in his Strasbourg sermons when discussing the illusory character of witches' flight. See Kors and Peters, 236–39. The transformation of these beliefs into the full-blown myth of the sab-

bath, a powerful propagandistic tool for later witch-hunters (see Levack, *The Witch-Hunt*, 35–40), is an interesting and difficult problem. Carlo Ginzburg, *Ecstasies: Deciphering the Witches' Sabbath*, trans. Raymond Rosenthal (New York: Pantheon Books, 1991), continues to pursue what he believes are the complex mythological roots of the sabbath. For a convincing argument that the sabbath is, more simply, an inversion invented by the demonologists and imposed on the populace, see Robert Muchembled, "Satanic Myths and Cultural Reality," in *Early Modern European Witchcraft: Centres and Peripheries*, ed. Bengt Ankarloo and Gustav Henningsen (Oxford: Clarendon Press, 1991), 139–60.

53. "And so in this twilight and evening of the world, when sin is flourishing on every side and in every place, witches and their iniquities superabound." Heinrich Kramer and Jacob Sprenger, *Malleus maleficarum*, trans. Montague Summers (New York: Dover, 1971), 16 and *passim*.

54. On how this eschatological attitude affected the political views possibly expressed in Dürer's *Apocalypse*, see Rudolf Chadraba, *Dürers Apocalypse: Eine ikonologische Deutung* (Prague: Verlag der Tschechoslowakischen Akademie der Wissenschaften, 1964).

55. Poesch, 79.

56. Bober and Rubenstein, 59–60.

57. Lyndal Roper, *Oedipus and the Devil: Witchcraft, Sexuality and Religion in Early Modern Europe* (London: Routledge, 1994), 59.

58. Peter Stallybrass, "Patriarchal Territories: The Body Enclosed," in *Rewriting the Renaissance: The Discourses of Sexual Difference in Early Modern Europe*, ed. Margaret W. Ferguson, Maureen Quilligan, and Nancy J. Vickers (Chicago: University of Chicago Press, 1986), 123–42; Patricia Simons, "Women in Frames: The Gaze, the Eye, the Profile," in *The Expanding Discourse: Feminism and Art History*, eds. Norma Broude and Mary D. Garrard (Boulder, Colo.: Westview Press, 1993), 39–57; Joseph Leo Koerner, *The Moment of Self-Portraiture in German Renaissance Art* (Chicago: University of Chicago Press, 1993), 323–57.

59. Margaret R. Miles, *Carnal Knowing: Female Nakedness and Religious Meaning in the Christian West* (Boston: Beacon Press, 1989), 81–82; Scholz Williams, "On Finding Words," 48–49.

60. Roper, *Oedipus*, 68.

61. Kramer and Sprenger, 111; Sophie Houdard, *Les sciences du diable: Quatre discours sur la sorcellerie, XVe-XVIIe siècle* (Paris: Les Éditions du Cerf, 1992), 40. This view contrasts with that of Nider, who discussed witches involved with incubi against their wills. For a summary of Nider's views, see Kors and Peters, 155–59; for an in-depth analysis, see Bailey.

62. H. C. Erik Midelfort, *Witch-Hunting in Southwestern Germany: The Social and Intellectual Foundations* (Stanford, Calif.: Stanford University Press, 1972), 20–21.

63. Dwyer, 469–70; Anzelewsky, 33–37. On the Fates, see Hall, 302–3.

64. Gerhild Scholz Williams, *Defining Dominion: The Discourses of Magic and Witchcraft in Early Modern France and Germany* (Ann Arbor: University of Michigan Press, 1995), 45–63, citation from Paracelsus' *De Sagis* on page 59; and her "On Finding Words," 55.

65. Kramer and Sprenger, 44.

66. Ibid., 47, 109–14; Anglo, "Evident Authority," 17–18; Stephens, 32–57.

67. Kramer and Sprenger, 114.

68. Alison G. Stewart, "Sebald Beham's *Fountain of Youth-Bathhouse* Woodcut:

Popular Entertainment and Large Prints by the Little Masters," *Register of the Spencer Museum of Art* 6 (1989): 75–76; Linda C. Hults, "Dürer's *Four Witches* Reconsidered," 108–13.

69. Anne Röver-Kann, *Albrecht Dürer: Das Frauenbad von 1496* (Bremen: Kunsthalle, 2001), 28–32.

70. Sigrid Schade, "Kunsthexen—Hexenkünste," in *Hexenwelten: Magie und Imagination vom 16–20 Jahrhundert*, ed. Richard van Dülmen (Frankfurt: Fischer Taschenbuch Verlag, 1987), 183.

71. Scholz Williams, *Defining Dominion*, 27.

72. Kramer and Sprenger, 48.

73. Ibid., 96–98; Lène Dresen-Coenders, "Witches as Devils' Concubines," in *Saints and She-Devils: Images of Women in the* 15th and 16th Centuries, ed. Lène Dresen-Coenders (London: Rubicon Press, 1987), 62, 69; on Kramer's intense concern about the demonic assault on the sacrament of matrimony, also see Houdard, 47–51; and Stephens, 312–21.

74. See Max Allihn, *Dürer-Studien: Versuch einer Erklärung schwer zu deutender Kupferstiche A. Dürers* (Leipzig: Rudolf Weigels Buchhandlung, 1871), 52–53; Rudolf Wustmann, "Von einigen Tieren und Pflanzen bei Dürer," *Zeitschrift für bildende Kunst* 22 (1911): 112–16; Gustav Friedrich Hartlaub, "Albrecht Dürers Aberglaube," *Zeitschrift für deutschen Verein für Kunstwissenschaft* 7 (1940): 195; Dwyer, 467; Walter L. Strauss, "The Wherewithal of Witches," *Source* 2 (1980): 20; Anzelewsky, 37.

75. Wustmann, 115; Hartlaub, 195.

76. Wustmann, 115. For a detailed account of the uses of the mandrake, see S. Killermann, "Der Alraun (Mandragora)," *Naturwissenschaftliche Wochenschrift* 15 (18 March 1917): 137–44; also Jane P. Davidson, "Plantes médicinales et vénéneuses: Le sabbat des sorcières et ses préparatifs dans la peinture néerlandais du XVIIe siècle," trans. Catherine Bernard, in *Le sabbat des sorciers en Europe (XVe-XVIIIe siècles): Colloque international E. N. S. Fontenay-Saint-Cloud (4–7 Novembre 1992)*, ed. Nicole Jacques-Chaquin and Maxime Préaud (Grenoble, Fr.: Jérôme Millon, 1993), 422–24. Because witches sacrificed children to the devil and midwives had many opportunities to do this, Kramer and Sprenger, 140–44, singled them out as particular targets of persecution. Barstow, 109–28, gives a good summary of why female healers and midwives might have been especially suspect, but historians have recently debunked the notion that midwives were frequent victims of accusations. See Briggs, *Witches and Neighbors*, 77–78, 279–81.

77. Patricia A. Emison, "The Word Made Naked in Pollaiuolo's *Battle of the Nudes*," *Art History* 13 (1990): 261–75. Also see Mark Meadow, "The Observant Pedestrian and Albrecht Dürer's *Promenade*," *Art History* 15 (1992): 197–222, for a similar assessment of the viewer's role.

78. Martin Kemp, *Leonardo da Vinci: The Marvelous Works of Nature and Man* (Cambridge, Mass.: Harvard University Press, 1981), 156–59.

79. Barstow, 27–29; for a thorough study of witchcraft accusations and age, see Alison Rowlands, "Witchcraft and Old Women in Early Modern Germany," *Past and Present* 173 (2001): 50–89.

80. See Anzelewsky, 101–28; Mesenzeva, "Zum Problem."

81. Zika, 318, 396.

82. Ruth Mellinkoff, "Riding Backwards: Theme of Humiliation and Symbol of Evil," *Viator* 4 (1973): 153–86.

83. Zika, 312–13.

84. Mesenzeva, "Zum Problem," 191–94; Zika, 313–15.

85. Joseph Leo Koerner, "Albrecht Dürer: A Sixteenth-Century *Influenza*," in *Albrecht Dürer and His Legacy: The Graphic Work of a Renaissance Artist*, by Giulia Bartrum, with contributions by Günter Grass, Joseph Leo Koerner, and Ute Kuhlemann (Princeton, N.J.: Princeton University Press), 26–27.

86. Alan Shestack, "An Introduction to Hans Baldung Grien," in *Hans Baldung Grien: Prints and Drawings*, ed. James Marrow and Alan Shestack (Washington, D. C.: National Gallery of Art, 1981), 6.

87. Fritz Baumgarten, *Der Freiburger Hochaltar: Kunstgeschictlich gewürdigt* (Strasbourg: J. H. Heitz and Mündel, 1904), 10; Thomas A. Brady Jr., "The Social Place of a German Renaissance Artist: Hans Baldung Grien (1484/85–1545) at Strasbourg," *Central European History* 8 (1975): 295–315.

88. Gustav Radbruch, "Hans Baldungs Hexenbilder," in *Elegantiae juris criminalis: Vierzehn Studien zur Geschichte des Stafrechts* (Basel: Verlag für Recht und Gesellschaft, 1950), 44, n. 51.

89. Koerner, *Moment of Self-Portraiture*, 323–62.

90. Linda C. Hults, "Hans Baldung Grien and Albrecht Dürer: A Problem in Northern Mannerism" (Ph.D. diss., University of North Carolina at Chapel Hill, 1978); on relationships between older and younger artists, see, in particular, Norman Bryson, *Tradition and Desire: From David to Delacroix* (Cambridge: Cambridge University Press, 1984).

91. Thomas A. Brady Jr., *Ruling Class, Regime and Reformation at Strasbourg, 1520–1555* (Leiden: E. J. Brill, 1978), 94–122.

92. Gerald Strauss, *Sixteenth Century Germany: Its Topography and Topographers* (Madison: University of Wisconsin Press, 1959), 69–72.

93. Hutchison, *Dürer*, 39.

94. Brady, "The Social Place," 298–303.

95. Brady, *Ruling Class*, 123–62.

96. Christopher S. Wood, *Albrecht Altdorfer and the Origins of Landscape* (Chicago: University of Chicago Press, 1993), 66–80.

97. Ibid., 77; Sigrid Schade, *Schadenzauber und die Magie des Körpers: Hexenbilder der frühen Neuzeit* (Worms, Ger.: Werner'sche Verlagsgesellschaft 1983), 62, and 142, n. 308.

98. See Larry Silver, "Forest Primeval: Albrecht Altdorfer and the German Wilderness Landscape," *Simiolus* 13 (1983): 4–43; and "Nature and Nature's God: Landscape and Cosmos of Albrecht Altdorfer," *Art Bulletin* 81 (1999): 194–214.

99. See Larry Silver, "Germanic Patriotism in the Age of Dürer," in *Dürer and his Culture*, ed. Dagmar Eichberger and Charles Zika (Cambridge: Cambridge University Press, 1998), 38–68.

100. Silver, "Forest Primeval," 5–18.

101. Ibid., 21–27.

102. Zika, 33–74.

103. Wood, *Altdorfer*, 179.

104. I disagree with Wood that landscape was primarily an absence of subject into which the artist asserted the inimitable graphic trace of his individuality. The artist's choice of subject matter also seems to me a distinctive sign of inventiveness, an irreducible indication of his uniqueness. The poetic license Wood finds in Altdorfer's landscapes, analogous to the rhetorical category of topothesia (description of fictive places) is evident outside or without the forest as well. See Wood, 160, on topothesia.

105. On the female body as the locus of evil, see Schade, *Schadenzauber*, 79–80; on numbers of witchcraft trials in Alsace, see Monter, "Witch Trials in Continental Europe," 38.

106. Peter Parshall, "The Cultivation of the Woodcut in the North," in David Landau and Peter Parshall, *The Renaissance Print, 1470–1550* (New Haven, Conn.: Yale University Press, 1994), 191–202.

107. Ibid., 184–87.

108. Ibid., 393, n. 56.

109. Sullivan, 369.

110. Schade, *Schadenzauber*, 57–59.

111. Radbruch, a historian and philosopher of law interested in Baldung's familial connections, offered a fundamental iconographic explanation of the objects and activities. Oddly, given his legal interests, he concluded that Baldung used the theme of witchcraft primarily for aesthetic purposes. Another early interpretation of Baldung's witches is Gustav Friedrich Hartlaub, *Hans Baldung Grien: Hexenbilder* (Stuttgart: Philipp Reclam Jr., 1961). Hartlaub argued that Baldung was influenced by Neoplatonic nature mysticism, the witches being nonhuman nature spirits. Also see Linda C. Hults, "Baldung and the Witches of Freiburg: The Evidence of Images, *Journal of Interdisciplinary History* 18 (1987): 249–76.

112. Schade, *Schadenzauber*, 60.

113. Kramer and Sprenger, 19–20.

114. Clark, *Thinking with Demons*, 281–93.

115. On the situation in Freiburg, see Ronnie Po-Chia Hsia, *The Myth of Ritual Murder: Jews and Magic in Reformation Germany* (New Haven, Conn.: Yale University Press, 1988), 86–110.

116. Steven W. Rowan, *Ulrich Zasius: A Jurist in the German Renaissance, 1461–1535* (Frankfurt am Main: Vittorio Klostermann, 1987), 44–67, 62.

117. Ibid., 95.

118. On Reuchlin, see Eckhard Bernstein, *German Humanism* (Boston: Twayne, 1983), 68–78; Hsia, 111–35; Heiko A. Oberman, "Discovery of Hebrew and Discrimination against the Jews: The *Veritas Hebraica* as Double-Edged Sword in Renaissance and Reformation," in *Germania Illustrata: Essays on Early Modern Germany Presented to Gerald Strauss*, ed. Andrew C. Fix and Susan C. Karant-Nunn (Kirksville, Mo.: Sixteenth Century Journal Publishers, 1992), 19–34; and Zika, 21–97.

119. Zika, 69–97; Hsia, 135.

120. Ibid., 146, 159.

121. Richard Kieckhefer, "Avenging the Blood of Children: Anxiety over Child Victims and the Origins of the European Witch-Trials," in *The Devil, Heresy, and Witchcraft in the Middle Ages: Essays in Honor of Jeffrey B. Russell*, ed. Alberto Ferreiro (Leiden: E. J. Brill, 1998), 91–109.

122. Trans. in Kors and Peters, 157.

123. Cohn, 1–59; Kors and Peters, 157–61; Valerie Flint, "The Demonisation of Sorcery in Late Antiquity," in *Witchcraft and Magic in Europe: Ancient Greece and Rome*, ed. Bengt Ankarloo and Stuart Clark (Philadelphia: University of Pennsylvania Press, 1999); Sprenger and Kramer, 100, 107.

124. Schade, *Schadenzauber*, 107–8.

125. Trans. in Kors and Peters, 237–38.

126. Ibid., 238.

127. Kramer and Sprenger, 121.

128. Brady, "The Social Place," 29.

129. On the history of Freiburg from the Middle Ages to 1500, see Tom Scott, *Freiburg and the Breisgau: Town-Country Relations in the Age of Reformation and the Peasants' War* (Oxford: Clarendon Press, 1986), 15–46.

130. Rowan, 23–67.

131. Gerald Strauss, *Law, Resistance, and the State: The Opposition to Roman Law in Reformation Germany* (Princeton, N.J.: Princeton University Press, 1986).

132. Rowan, 77–81.

133. Ibid., 34–38.

134. Naomi Zack, *Bachelors of Science: Seventeenth-Century Identity, Then and Now* (Philadelphia, Pa.: Temple University Press, 1996), 182–92.

135. For copies, see Carl Koch, *Die Zeichnungen Hans Baldung Griens* (Berlin: Deutscher Verein für Kunstwissenschaft, 1941), cat. nos. A16, A17, A17a, A17b, A19, pp. 196–98; and Hults, "Witches of Freiburg," fig. 5, by Monogrammist Hans Frank (not catalogued by Koch).

136. For Zasius, the law is *sanctissima*; for Melanchthon, a "holy office." See G. Strauss, *Law, Resistance, and the State*, 91.

137. See Monter, "Witch Trials in Continental Europe," 32–33, on the *Reichskammergericht*'s influence on witch trials.

138. Levack provides a particularly clear summary of legal changes, *The Witch-Hunt*, 64–92; also see John H. Langbein, *Prosecuting Crime in the Renaissance: England, Germany, France* (Cambridge, Mass.: Harvard University Press, 1974), 129–39; on prosecutory procedures, see Richard van Dülmen, *Theatre of Horror: Crime and Punishment in Early Modern Germany*, trans. Elisabeth Neu (Cambridge, U.K.: Polity Press, 1990), 5–42.

139. Zika, 245.

140. Koch, cat. nos. 62 and 63, pp. 99–101; The Louvre sheet may be dated from Urs Graf's Albertina copy, Koch, cat. no. A16, 196–97.

141. The "HF" monogram on this copy seems to me distinct from the "HF" on the witches' spell in the Louvre image, possibly a reference to "Hexenfahrt" or "Hexenflucht"—witches' flight: Hults, "Witches of Freiburg," 258–60, and n. 13.

142. Koerner, *Moment of Self-Portraiture*, 335.

143. Baumgarten, *Der Freiburger Hochaltar*, 14–15.

144. Merry E. Wiesner, *Gender, Church, and State in Early Modern Germany* (New York: Longman, 1998), 163–96.

145. Schade, *Schadenzauber*, 112–18; Koerner, 346; Robert Norman Swanson, "Angels Incarnate: Clergy and Masculinity from Gregorian Reform to Reformation," in *Masculinity in Medieval Europe*, ed. Dawn M. Hadley (New York: Longman, 1995), 160–77.

146. Ruth Mazo Karras, *From Boys to Men: Formations of Masculinity in Late Medieval Europe* (Philadelphia: University of Pennsylvania Press, 2003), 67–108.

147. Koerner, *Moment of Self-Portraiture*, 336.

148. François Rabelais, *Gargantua and Pantagruel*, trans. Burton Raffel (New York: Norton, 1990), 327.

149. Koch, cat. no. 246, 183–84; Marrow and Shestack, cat. no. 82, 260–61.

150. On Baldung and the Reformation, see Fritz Baumgarten, "Hans Baldungs Stellung zur Reformation," *Zeitschrift für die Geschichte des Oberrheins*, new series 19 (1904): 245–64; Brady, "The Social Place," 307–11; and Linda C. Hults, "Baldung and the Reformation," in Marrow and Shestack, 38–59.

151. Lorna Jane Abray, *The People's Reformation: Magistrates, Clergy, and Commons in Strasbourg, 1500–1598* (Ithaca, N.Y.: Cornell University Press, 1985), 48–49.

152. Brady, *Ruling Class*, 199–335.

153. Gert von der Osten, *Hans Baldung Grien: Gemälde und Dokumente* (Berlin: Deutscher Verein für Kunstwissenschaft, 1983), cat. no. 53, 160.

154. W. Strauss, *Dürer*, vol. 1, cat. no. 1945/10, 280.

155. For the formal background of Baldung's figures, see Linda C. Hults, "Baldung's *Weather Witches* in Frankfurt," *Pantheon: Internationale Zeitschrift für Kunst* 40 (1982): 124–30.

156. Koch, cat. no. 126, 138–39.

157. Trans. in Kors and Peters, 339–45.

158. Rodolphe Reuss, *La sorcellerie au seizième et au dix-septième siècle, particulièrement en Alsace* (Paris: Cherbuliez, 1871), 78–79.

159. Eva Labouvie, "Men in Witchcraft Trials: Towards a Social Anthropology of 'Male' Understandings of Magic and Witchcraft," in *Gender in Early Modern German History*, ed. Ulinka Rublack (Cambridge: Cambridge University Press, 2002), 53.

160. Abray, 85.

161. Koch, cat. no. 143, 150–51.

162. Charmian Mesenzeva, "'Der Behexte Stallknecht' des Hans Baldung Griens," *Zeitschrift für Kunstgeschichte* 44 (1981): 57–61; Dale Hoak, "Art, Culture, and Mentality in Renaissance Society: The Meaning of Hans Baldung Grien's *Bewitched Groom*," *Renaissance Quarterly* 38 (1985): 488–509.

163. Linda C. Hults, "Baldung's *Bewitched Groom* Revisited: Artistic Temperament, Fantasy and the 'Dream of Reason,'" *The Sixteenth-Century Journal* 15 (1984): 260–79.

164. Koerner, *Moment of Self-Portraiture*, 437–47; quote, 444.

165. Quoted, Sullivan, 386.

166. Marrow and Shestack, cat. nos. 83–84, pp. 264–66.

167. Koerner, 426–27; Schade, *Schadenzauber*, 82.

168. Mark Breitenberg, *Anxious Masculinity in Early Modern England* (Cambridge: Cambridge University Press, 1996), 50.

169. Ibid., 90.

170. Zika, 333–74.

171. Gianfrancesco Pico della Mirandola, *On the Imagination*, trans. Harry Caplan (Ithaca, N.Y.: Cornell University Press, 1930), 57, 79.

172. On Graf, see Christiane Andersson, *Dirnen, Krieger, Narren: Ausgewählte Zeichnungen von Urs Graf* (Basel: G. S. Verlag, 1978); on Manuel, see Cäsar Menz, ed. *Niklaus Manuel Deutsch: Maler, Dichter, Staatsmann* (Bern: Kunstmuseum Bern, 1979).

173. Christiane Andersson, "Das Bild der Frau in der oberrheinischen Kunst um 1520," in *Die Frau in der Renaissance*, ed. Paul Gerhardt Schmidt (Wiesbaden, Ger.: Harrassowitz, 1994), 246.

174. On the relationship of this work to Agrippa's essay on original sin, which emphasized the role of sexuality, see A. Kent Hieatt, "Hans Baldung's Ottawa *Eve* and Its Context,"*Art Bulletin* 65 (1983): 290–304.

175. For the social context of war in the early modern period, see Frank Tallett, *War and Society in Early Modern Europe* (London: Routledge, 1992). On the genre of military imagery and women and early modern armies, see John R. Hale, *Artists and Warfare in the Renaissance* (New Haven, Conn.: Yale University Press, 1990), especially 34–41; also Barton C. Hacker, "Women and Military Institutions in Early Modern Europe: A Reconnaissance," *Signs* 6 (1981): 643–71.

176. Andersson, "Das Bild der Frau," 244; in contrast, Hale, without a great deal of justification to my mind, asserts the "steadiness" and "sympathy" with which these artists portrayed women, 41.

Chapter 4

1. Brian P. Levack, *The Witch-Hunt in Early Modern Europe* (New York: Longman, 1987), 172–73.

2. Ibid., 173–74; Jean Bodin, *On the Demon-Mania of Witches*, trans. Randy A. Scott (Toronto: Centre for Reformation and Renaissance Studies, 1995), 35–44 and passim.

3. Jonathan L. Pearl, *The Crime of Crimes: Demonology and Politics in France, 1560–1620* (Waterloo, Ont.: Wilfred Laurier University Press, 1999), 133.

4. On de Lancre's relating of inconstancy, political turmoil, demons, and women's passions, see ibid., 130–31; and Sophie Houdard, *Les sciences du diable: Quatre discours sur la sorcellerie, XVe-XVIIIe siècle* (Paris: Les Éditions du Cerf, 1992), 161–71. On the profound resonance of Lipsius's Neostoicism for contemporaries, see Mark Morford, *Stoics and Neostoics: Rubens and the Circle of Lipsius* (Princeton, N.J.: Princeton University Press, 1991).

5. Pearl, *The Crime of Crimes*, 127–47.

6. Gerhild Scholz Williams, *Defining Dominion: The Discourses of Magic and Witchcraft in Early Modern France and Germany* (Ann Arbor: University of Michigan Press, 1995), 89–119; Houdard, 171–79, 195–201.

7. Pierre de Lancre, *Tableau de l'inconstance des mauvais anges et démons*, ed. Nicole Jacques-Chaquin (Paris: Éditions Aubier, 1982), 42, quoted in Scholz Williams, *Defining Dominion*, 111.

8. Ibid., 111–12, 115–16.

9. Pearl, *The Crime of Crimes*, 59–101.

10. Robert Bireley, *The Counter-Reformation Prince: Anti-Machiavellianism or Catholic Statecraft in Early Modern Europe* (Chapel Hill: University of North Carolina Press, 1990), 221–22.

11. Pearl, *The Crime of Crimes*, 143–44; Houdard, 169–70.

12. Francesco-Maria Guazzo, *Compendium maleficarum*, ed. and notes by Montague Summers, trans. E. A. Ashwin (New York: Barnes and Noble, 1970). For an English translation of de Lancre's legend, see Rossell Hope Robbins, *Encyclopedia of Witchcraft and Demonology* (New York: Bonanza Books, 1959), 300–301.

13. Houdard, 210–16.

14. For biographical details about Francken, see Ursula Alice Härting, *Frans Francken der Jüngere (1581–1642): Die Gemälde mit kritischem Oeuvrekatalog* (Freren, Ger.: Luca Verlag, 1989), 9–12.

15. Ibid., 12.

16. On Francken's development of the Antwerp tradition of gallery pictures and their iconography, see Zirka Zaremba Filipczak, *Picturing Art in Antwerp, 1550–1700* (Princeton, N.J.: Princeton University Press, 1987); Härting, *Francken*, 83–91; and idem, "'Doctrina et pietas': Über frühe Galeriebilder," *Jaarboek van het Koninklijk Museum voor Schone Kunsten Antwerpen* (1993): 95–133.

17. Härting, *Francken*, 68–71; cat. nos. 405 through 410, p. 360; fig. 67, p. 69.

18. On the practice of copying, see Elizabeth Alice Honig, "The Beholder as Work

of Art: A Study in the Location of Value in Seventeenth-Century Flemish Painting," *Nederlands kunsthistorisch Jaarboek* 46 (1995): 269.

19. Sigrid Schade, "Kunsthexen—Hexenkünste," in *Hexenwelten: Magie und Imagination vom 16–20 Jahrhundert*, ed. Richard van Dülmen (Frankfurt: Fischer Taschenbuch Verlag, 1987), 196; Härting, *Francken*, 68; Jane P. Davidson, *The Witch in Northern European Art, 1470–1750* (Freren, Ger.: Luca Verlag, 1987), 40; Marijke S. Lucas, "Het heksengeloof verbeeld 17de eeuwse voorstellingen in de Nederlanden," *Jaarboek van het Koninklijk Museum voor Schone Kunsten Antwerpen* (1996): 116.

20. Arnout Balis, "Antwerp, Foster-Mother of the Arts: Its Contribution to the Artistic Culture of Europe in the Seventeenth Century," in *Antwerp: Story of a Metropolis, 16th-17th* Century, ed. Jan van der Stock (Ghent: Snoeck-Ducaju and Zoon, 1993), 118–20.

21. Reginald Howard Wilenski, *Flemish Painters, 1430–1830*, 2 vols. (New York: Viking, 1960), vol. 1, 212.

22. On the history of the Vienna collections, see Wolfgang Prohaska, *Kunsthistorisches Museum, Vienna: The Paintings*, trans. Judith Hayward (London: Philip Wilson Publishers, 1997), 6–15.

23. Gerard l'Estrange Turner has identified three goals for the private collection: self-advertisement, economic advantage and utility, and intellectual satisfaction. See "The Cabinet of Experimental Philosophy," in *The Origins of Museums: The Cabinet of Curiosities in Sixteenth- and Seventeenth-Century Europe*, ed. Oliver Impey and Arthur MacGregor (Oxford: Oxford University Press, 1985), 214.

24. Thomas DaCosta Kaufmann, *The Mastery of Nature: Aspects of Art, Science and Humanism in the Renaissance* (Princeton, N.J.: Princeton University Press, 1995), 180–81.

25. Elizabeth Alice Honig, *Painting and the Market in Early Modern Antwerp* (New Haven, Conn.: Yale University Press, 1998), 205.

26. Robert Muchembled, *Le roi et la sorcière: L'Europe des bûchers, XVe-XVIIIe siècle* (Paris: Desclée, 1993).

27. Alain Boureau, preface to *Les sciences du diable*, by Sophie Houdard.

28. Marie Tanner, *The Last Descendant of Aeneas: The Hapsburgs and the Mythic Image of the Emperor* (New Haven, Conn.: Yale University Press, 1993).

29. Ibid., 191–93.

30. Ibid., 196–97.

31. Ibid., 215.

32. Norman Cohn, *Europe's Inner Demons: An Enquiry Inspired by the Great Witch-Hunt* (New York: Basic Books, 1975), 16–59.

33. Walter Stephens, *Demon Lovers: Witchcraft, Sex, and the Crisis of Belief* (Chicago: University of Chicago Press, 2002), 180–240.

34. Stuart Clark, *Thinking with Demons: The Idea of Witchcraft in Early Modern Europe* (Oxford: Oxford University Press, 1997), 534.

35. On the integration of demonology into Bodin's political thought, see Houdard, 57–103; Clark, 668–82; and Jonathan Pearl, introduction to *On the Demon-Mania of Witches*, by Jean Bodin.

36. Jean Bodin, *The Six Bookes of a Commonweale*, trans. Richard Knolles, ed. K. D. McRae (Cambridge: Cambridge University Press, 1962), 793–94, quoted in Clark, *Thinking with Demons*, 681.

37. Pearl, *The Crime of Crimes*, 70–71.

38. Ronnie Po-Chia Hsia, *The World of Catholic Renewal, 1540–1770* (Cambridge: Cambridge University Press, 1998), 64–66.

39. Härting, *Francken*, 71; also idem, " 'Doctrina et pietas.' "

40. Clark, *Thinking with Demons*, 587; Robert Muchembled, "Lay Judges and the Acculturation of the Masses (France and the Southern Low Countries, Sixteenth to Eighteenth Centuries)," in *Religion and Society in Early Modern Europe, 1500–1800*, ed. Kaspar von Greyerz (Boston: Allen and Unwin, 1984), 56–65.

41. Clark, *Thinking with Demons*, 572–601.

42. On the Habsburg decrees, see Marie-Sylvie Dupont-Bouchat, "La répression de la sorcellerie dans le duché de Luxembourg aux XVIe et XVIIe siècles," in *Prophètes et sorciers dans le Pays-Bas, XVe- XVIIIe siècle*, ed. Marie-Sylvie Dupont-Bouchat, Willem Frijhoff, and Robert Muchembled (Paris: Hachette, 1978), 86–90.

43. On the water ordeal, see Marijke Gijswijt-Hofstra, "Six Centuries of Witchcraft in the Netherlands: Themes, Outlines and Interpretations," in *Witchcraft in the Netherlands from the Fourteenth to the Twentieth Century*, ed. Marijke Gijswijt-Hofstra and Willem Frijhoff, trans. Rachel M. J. van der Wilden-Fall (Rotterdam: University Press, 1991), 21.

44. For the text of the 1595 edict, see Josef Bernaert Cannaert, *Olim: Procès des sorcières en Belgique sou Philippe II et le gouvernement des Archiducs* (Ghent: C. Annoot-Braeckman, 1847), 7–9.

45. Clark, *Thinking with Demons*, 673.

46. Scholz Williams, *Defining Dominion*, 19–20.

47. Hans de Waardt, "Prosecution or Defense: Procedural Possibilities Following a Witchcraft Accusation in the Province of Holland before 1800," in Gijswijt-Hofstra and Frijhoff, 86–89.

48. Martín Del Rio, *Martín Del Rio: Investigations into Magic*, ed. and trans. P. G. Maxwell-Stewart (Manchester, U.K.: Manchester University Press, 2000), 159.

49. Ibid., 91–92.

50. Cannaert, 48–51.

51. Härting, *Francken*, cat. no. 410, 360 , contains a burning church as a reference to heresy.

52. Lukas, 119–20.

53. Del Rio, 27–29.

54. Clark, *Thinking with Demons*, 536.

55. Schade, "Kunsthexen-Hexenkünste," 195–97. Without knowing the rooms in which the paintings hung, we cannot know whether and how often women might have seen them. Women's viewing may have been restricted by placement in rooms frequented by men, and we know that Salvator Rosa's panorama of witchcraft now in London was kept covered, to be savored when unveiled as an epitome of inventiveness within a male collector's cabinet (see figure 6.10). On domestic spaces and the display of art in the Southern Netherlands, see Jeffrey M. Muller, "Private Collections in the Spanish Netherlands: Ownership and Display of Paintings in Domestic Interiors," in Peter C. Sutton, *The Age of Rubens* (Boston: Museum of Fine Arts, 1994), 195–206.

56. Del Rio, 28.

57. Pearl, *The Crime of Crimes*, 145; on de Lancre's views of Basque witchcraft as an infection spread through families, see Scholz Williams, *Defining Dominion*, 117–18.

58. See Hugo Soly, "Social Relations in Antwerp in the Sixteenth and Seventeenth Centuries," in van der Stock, 39; the theme of class tensions is also addressed throughout Honig's study of Antwerp market scenes (as in note 25 above).

59. Jonathan Brown, *Kings and Connoisseurs: Collecting in Seventeenth-Century Europe* (Princeton, N.J.: Princeton University Press, 1995), 153.

60. Honig, *Painting and the Market*, 115–69.

61. Alison Rowlands, "Witchcraft and Old Women in Early Modern Germany," *Past and Present* 173 (November 2001): 70–71.

62. Cannaert, 57–60 (my translations).

63. Härting, "'Doctrina et pietas,'" 109.

64. Pearl, *The Crime of Crimes*, 131.

65. Barbara M. Benedict, *Curiosity: A Cultural History of Early Modern Inquiry* (Chicago: University of Chicago Press, 2001); on the distinction between curiosity and wonder, also see Katie Whitaker, "The Culture of Curiosity," in *Cultures of Natural History*, ed. Nicholas Jardine, James A. Secord, and Emma C. Spary (Cambridge: Cambridge University Press, 1998), 75–90.

66. Christopher S. Wood, "'Curious Pictures' and the Art of Description," *Word and Image* 11 (1995): 332–52.

67. Trans. in Pearl, *The Crime of Crimes*, 99.

68. Ibid., 67.

69. Franciscus Junius, *The Painting of the Ancients*, trans. Keith Aldrich, Philipp Fehl, and Raina Fehl (Berkeley: University of California Press, 1991), 300, 65, quoted in Wood, "Curious Pictures," 347–48.

70. Kaufmann, *The Mastery of Nature*, 185–87.

71. Schade, "Kunsthexen-Hexenkünste," 196–97; Machteld Löwensteyn, "Peindre le pandémonium païen: Images du sabbat des sorcières aux Pays-Bas," in *Le sabbat des sorciers en Europe (XVe-XVIIIe siècles): Colloque international E. N. S. Fontenay-Saint-Cloud (4–7 Novembre 1992)*, ed. Nicole Jacques-Chaquin and Maxime Préaud (Grenoble, Fr.: Jêrome Millon, 1993), 427–37.

72. Lucas, 118.

73. Härting, *Francken*, 69–71.

74. H. Diane Russell with Bernadine Barnes, *Eva/Ave: Women in Renaissance and Baroque Prints* (Washington, D.C. and New York: National Gallery of Art in association with the Feminist Press at the City University of New York, 1990), cat. nos. 99–101, pp. 162–64.

75. For overviews of the impact of the Counter Reformation on women, see Susan C. Karant-Nunn, "The Reformation of Women," in *Becoming Visible: Women in European History*, 3rd ed., ed. Renate Bridenthal, Susan Mosher Stuard, and Merry E. Wiesner (Boston: Houghton Mifflin, 1998), 186–90; Merry Wiesner, *Women and Gender in Early Modern Europe*, 2nd ed. (Cambridge: Cambridge University Press, 2000), 231–40. For a detailed account of the Counter-Reformation's regulation of sexuality and marriage, see Merry E. Wiesner-Hanks, *Christianity and Sexuality in the Early Modern World: Regulating Desire, Reforming Practice* (London: Routledge, 2000), 102–40.

76. Wiesner, *Women and Gender*, 238.

77. Ibid., 236–37.

78. Wiesner-Hanks, 128.

79. Wiesner, *Women and Gender*, 149–51.

80. Filipczak, 31–39.

81. Ibid., 33–34.

82. Ibid., 115–16.

83. Karel van Mander, *The Lives of the Illustrious Netherlandish and German Painters*, trans., ed., and with introduction by Hessel Miedema, 6 vols. (Doornspijk, Neth.: Davaco, 1994–99), vol. 1, 126–27.

84. Ibid., 341.

85. On the School of Prague, see Thomas DaCosta Kaufmann, *The School of Prague: Painting at the Court of Rudolf II* (Chicago: University of Chicago Press, 1988); and idem, "Princely Patronage of the Later Sixteenth and Early Seventeenth Centuries: The Example and Impact of Art at the Court of Rudolf II," in *Court, Cloister and City: The Art and Culture of Central Europe, 1450–1800* (Chicago: University of Chicago Press, 1995), 185–203.

86. Härting, *Francken*, 89; Filipczak, 51–53.

87. Härting, *Francken*, 86, and cat. no. 361, 342.

88. Honig, "The Beholder," 268; also see Muller on Antwerp collections and self-presentation.

89. Honig, *Painting and the Market*, 190–92.

90. Margret Klinge, *David Teniers the Younger: Paintings, Drawings*, trans. David R. McLintock (Ghent: Snoeck-Ducaju and Zoon, 1991), 19.

91. Ibid., 21–22.

92. Ibid., 22–23.

93. Ibid., cat. no. 11, 50–51.

94. Clifford S. Ackley, "Printmaking in the Age of Rembrandt: The Quest for Printed Tone," *Printmaking in the Age of Rembrandt* (Boston: Museum of Fine Arts, 1981), xxv.

95. Linda Stone-Ferrier, *Dutch Prints of Daily Life: Mirrors of Life or Masks of Morals?* (Lawrence: Spencer Museum of Art, University of Kansas, 1983), cat. no. 24, 106–09.

96. Jane P. Davidson, "Plantes médicinales et vénéneuses: Le sabbat des sorcières et ses préparatifs dans la peinture néerlandais du XVIIe siècle," in Jacques-Chaquin and Préaud, 424–25; Diedrich Roskamp, "Eine 'Hexenszene' von David Teniers d. J.," *Jahrbuch der Hamburger Kunstsammlungen* 8 (1963): 31–32.

97. Clark, *Thinking with Demons*, 526–45.

98. See Reindert L. Falkenburg, "De duivel buiten beeld: Over duivelafwerende krachten en motieven in de beeldende kunst rond 1500," in *Duivelsbeelden: Een cultuurhistorische speurtocht door de Lage Landen*, ed. Gerard Rooijakkers, Lène Dresen-Coenders, and Margaret Geerdes (Baarn, Neth.: Uitgeverij Ambo, 1994), 107–22 (English summary, 420).

99. Norbert Schneider, *The Art of the Still Life: Still Life Painting in the Early Modern Period* (Cologne: Benedikt Taschen Verlag, 1990), 151–53.

100. Jane P. Davidson, *David Teniers the Younger* (Boulder, Colo.: Westview Press, 1979), 42–43; Lucas, 95.

101. Davidson, *The Witch*, 49.

102. On the reception of Teniers's rural scenes in France, see Vivian Lee Atwater, "A Catalogue and Analysis of Eighteenth-Century French Prints after Netherlandish Baroque Painters," 2 vols. (Ph.D. diss., University of Washington, 1988), vol. 1, 80, and idem, "Les graveurs et la vogue néerlandais dans le Paris du XVIIIe siècle: Le Bas, Teniers et l'idéalisation de la vie paysanne," *Nouvelles de l'estampe*, no. 142–43 (1995): 3–12.

103. Davidson, *The Witch*, 49; Lucas, 111.

104. Klinge, 21.

105. See Levack, *The Witch-Hunt*, 170–75, on the chronology of the witch-hunts.

106. Dupont-Bouchat, 145; also see Marcus Hellyer, introduction to *Cautio Criminalis, or, a Book on Witch Trials*, by Friedrich Spee, trans. Marcus Hellyer (Charlottesville: University of Virginia Press, 2003), especially xxxii–xxxiii.

107. Cannaert, 12.

Chapter 5

1. I. Q. van Regteren Altena, *Jacques de Gheyn: Three Generations, I-III*, 3 vols. (The Hague: Martinus Nijhoff, 1983), vol. 1, 86.

2. J. Richard Judson, *The Drawings of Jacques de Gheyn II* (New York: Grossman, 1973), 29.

3. Machteld Löwensteyn, "Helse hebzucht en wereldse wellust: een iconografische interpretatie van enkele heksenvoorstellingen van Jacques de Gheyn II," *Volkskundig Bulletin* 12 (1986): 241–61; Jane P. Davidson, *The Witch in Northern European Art, 1450–1750* (Freren, Ger.: Luca Verlag, 1987), 57–64; Sigrid Schade, "Kunsthexen-Hexenkünste," in *Hexenwelten: Magie und Imagination vom 16–20 Jahrhundert*, ed. Richard van Dülmen (Frankfurt: Fischer Taschenbuch Verlag, 1987), 192–94.

4. Marijke Gijswijt-Hofstra, "Six Centuries of Witchcraft in the Netherlands: Themes, Outlines, and Interpretations," in *Witchcraft in the Netherlands from the Fourteenth to the Twentieth Century*, ed. Marijke Gijswijt-Hofstra and Willem Frijhoff, trans. Rachel M. J. van Wilden-Fall (Rotterdam: University Press, 1991), 3, 30; Marijke Gijswijt-Hofstra, "The European Witchcraft Debate and the Dutch Variant," *Social History* 15 (1990): 181–94; and Robert Muchembled, *Le roi et la sorcière: L'Europe des bûchers, XVe-XVIIIe siècle* (Paris: Desclée, 1993), 93–95. For the Dutch expression of demonological theory in the sixteenth century, see Herman Beliën's remarks on Philips Wielant and Joost de Damhouder, "Judicial Views on the Crime of Witchcraft," in Gijswijt-Hofstra and Frijhoff, 56–59.

5. Benjamin J. Kaplan, "'Dutch' Religious Tolerance: Celebration and Revision," in *Calvinism and Religious Toleration in the Dutch Golden Age*, ed. Ronnie Po-Chia Hsia and Henk van Nierop (Cambridge: Cambridge University Press, 2002), 8–26; and Willem Frijhoff, " Religious Toleration in the United Provinces: From 'Case' to Model," in Hsia and Frijhoff, 27–52.

6. Muchembled, *Le roi et la sorcière*, 94; Gijswijt-Hofstra, "Six Centuries," 32–33.

7. Frijhoff, "Religious Toleration," 31–35.

8. Heinz Schilling, *Religion, Political Culture and the Emergence of Early Modern Society: Essays in German and Dutch History* (Leiden: E. J. Brill, 1992), 388–401.

9. On Coornhert, see Gerrit Voogt, *Constraint on Trial: Dirck Volckertsz Coornhert and Religious Freedom* (Kirksville, Mo.: Truman State University Press, 2000).

10. Kaplan, "'Dutch' Religious Toleration," 25–26.

11. Judith Pollmann, "The Bond of Christian Piety: The Individual Practice of Tolerance and Intolerance in the Dutch Republic," in Hsia and van Nierop, 53–71; also see idem, *Religious Choice in the Dutch Republic: The Reformation of Arnoldus Buchelius (1565–1641)* (Manchester, U.K.: Manchester University Press, 1999), 95–101.

12. Beliën, 61.

13. For fundamental discussions of how these terms are translated, see Emil Karl Josef Reznicek, "Realism as a 'Side Road or Byway' in Dutch Art," in *Studies in Western Art: Acts of the Twentieth International Congress of the History of Art*, vol. 2, *The Renaissance and Mannerism*, ed. Ida Ely Rubin (Princeton, N.J.: Princeton University Press, 1963), 252; Karel van Mander, *Den grondt der edel vry schilder-const*, trans. and with commentary by Hessel Miedema (Utrecht: Haentjens Dekker and Gumbert, 1973), vol. 2, 437–38; Svetlana Alpers, *The Art of Describing: Dutch Art in the Seventeenth Century* (Chicago: University of Chicago Press, 1983), 40–41, 242–43, n. 30; and Walter S. Melion, *Shaping the Netherlandish Canon: Karel van Mander's Schilder-Boek* (Chicago: University of Chicago Press, 1991), 63–66, 243, n. 10.

14. Karel van Mander, *The Lives of the Illustrious Netherlandish and German Painters*, trans. and with commentary by Hessel Miedema (Doornspijk, Neth.: Davaco, 1994–99), vol. 1, 435–37.

15. Reznicek, "Realism as a 'Side Road or Byway'"; van Mander, *Grondt*, vol. 2, 438; and Claudia Swan, "*Ad vivum, naer het leven*, from the Life: Defining a Mode of Representation," *Word and Image* 11 (1995): 354.

16. Van Mander, *Netherlandish and German Painters*, vol. 1, 190.

17. Quoted in Melion, *Netherlandish Canon*, 29.

18. Ibid., 51–55.

19. See Melion's discussion of Goltzius's development of his own as well as other artists' *handelingh* in ibid., 44–50, 54–59.

20. Ibid., 59.

21. Paula Findlen, "Courting Nature," in *Cultures of Natural History*, ed. Nicholas Jardine, James A. Secord, and Emma C. Spary (Cambridge: Cambridge University Press, 1998), 57–73.

22. For an introduction to the issues in gender and early modern science, see especially Evelyn Fox Keller, *Reflections on Gender and Science* (New Haven, Conn.: Yale University Press, 1985), especially 33–42; and Mark Breitenberg, *Anxious Masculinity in Early Modern England* (Cambridge: Cambridge University Press, 1996), 69–96.

23. Claudia Swan, "Jacques de Gheyn II and the Representation of the Natural World in the Netherlands ca. 1600" (Ph.D. diss., Columbia University, 1997), 48–49, 89, 92.

24. Lawrence O. Goedde, "Naturalism as Convention: Subject, Style, and Artistic Self-Consciousness in Dutch Landscape," in *Looking at Seventeenth-Century Dutch Art: Realism Reconsidered*, ed. Wayne Franits (Cambridge: Cambridge University Press, 1997), 140.

25. On the pluralistic religious milieu of Utrecht, see Benjamin J. Kaplan's detailed study, *Calvinists and Libertines: Confession and Community in Utrecht, 1578–1620* (Oxford: Clarendon Press, 1995).

26. Van Regteren Altena, *de Gheyn*, vol. 2, cat. no. 693, 113.

27. In addition to Melion's discussion of Goltzius throughout *Shaping the Netherlandish Canon*, see his "Karel van Mander's 'Life of Goltzius': Defining the Paradigm of Protean Virtuosity in Haarlem around 1600," *Studies in the History of Art* 27 (1989): 113–33.

28. Larry Silver, "Imitation and Emulation: Goltzius as Evolutionary Reproductive Engraver," in *Graven Images: The Rise of Professional Printmakers in Antwerp and Haarlem, 1540–1640*, ed. Timothy Riggs and Larry Silver (Evanston, Ill.: The Mary and Leigh Block Gallery, Northwestern University, 1993), 74–76.

29. Melion, *Netherlandish Canon*, 34–35, 43–51.

30. Silver, "Imitation and Emulation," 76–77. For a catalog of Goltzius's graphic oeuvre, see Walter L. Strauss, *Hendrik Goltzius, 1558–1617: The Complete Engravings and Woodcuts*, 2 vols. (New York: Abaris Books, 1977).

31. Silver, "Imitation and Emulation," 89.

32. Jan Piet Filedt Kok, "Jacques de Gheyn II: Engraver, Designer and Publisher—I and II," *Print Quarterly* 7 (1990): 259.

33. Judson, *The Drawings*, 34–35, argues for de Gheyn's Calvinism. Constantijn Huygens reported that no priest was present at de Gheyn's death. See Van Regteren Altena, *de Gheyn*, vol. 1, 152.

34. Van Regteren Altena, *de Gheyn*, vol. 1, 42–45.

35. Willem Frijhoff, "What Is an Early Modern University? The Conflict between Leiden and Amsterdam in 1631," in *European Universities in the Age of Reformation and Counter-Reformation*, ed. Helga Robinson-Hammerstein (Dublin: Four Courts Press, 1998), 149–68.

36. Van Regteren Altena, *de Gheyn*, vol. 1, 45–46; 66–69.

37. Filedt Kok, 275.

38. Van Regteren Altena, *de Gheyn*, vol. 1, 73.

39. Filedt Kok, 261, 275.

40. De Gheyn's project of engravings for a book on weaponry was commissioned in 1597 but not completed until 1607, when the truce was in sight. Van Regteren Altena, *de Gheyn*, vol. 2, nos. 342–464, pp. 64–78.

41. Van Mander, *Netherlandish and German Painters*, vol. 1, 434. 42. Emil Karl Josef Reznicek, "Two 'Masters of the Pen,'" in Museum Boymans-van Beuningen, *Jacques de Gheyn II: Drawings* (Rotterdam: Museum Boymans-van Beuningen, 1986), 16.

43. Ilja M. Veldman, "Images of Labor and Diligence in Sixteenth-Century Netherlandish Prints: The Work Ethic Rooted in Civic Morality or Protestantism," *Simiolus* 21 (1992): 242.

44. See *The New Interpreter's Bible* (Nashville, Tenn.: Abingdon Press, 1994–98), vol. 8, 306–12, on the parable of the tares.

45. Johann Weyer, *De praestigiis daemonum*, trans. John Shea (Binghamton, N.Y.: Medieval and Renaissance Texts and Studies, 1991), 529.

46. Friedrich Spee, *Cautio Criminalis, or, a Book on Witch Trials*, trans. Marcus Hellyer (Charlottesville: University of Virginia Press, 2003), 45–46.

47. Michel de Montaigne, *The Essays of Michel de Montaigne*, ed. and trans. Jacob Zeitlin (New York: Knopf, 1936), vol. 3, 235.

48. Stuart Clark, *Thinking with Demons: The Idea of Witchcraft in Early Modern Europe* (Oxford: Oxford University Press, 1997), 203–8.

49. Gijswijt-Hofstra, "Six Centuries," 9.

50. Hans de Waardt, *Toverij en samenleving: Holland 1500–1800* (The Hague: Stichting Hollandse Historisiche Reeks, 1991), 156–64.

51. Van Regteren Altena, *de Gheyn*, vol. 1, 86; on the water ordeal, see Gijswijt-Hofstra, "Six Centuries," 20–21.

52. Pollmann, *Religious Choice*, 95–101.

53. Van Regteren Altena, *de Gheyn*, vol. 1, 45.

54. On Weyer's and Bodin's arguments, see Christopher Baxter, "Johann Weyer's *De praestigiis daemonum*: Unsystematic Psychopathology," in *The Damned Art: Essays in the Literature of Witchcraft*, ed. Sidney Anglo (London: Routledge & Kegan, Paul, 1977), 76–105; and idem, "Jean Bodin's *De la démonomanie des sorciers*: The Logic of Persecution," in *The Damned Art*, 76–105. Also see Clark, *Thinking with Demons*, 198–203, 668–82.

55. Weyer, 499, 548.

56. Ibid., 263–65, 541.

57. Ibid., 541.

58. Ibid., 490.

59. Clark, 211–12.

60. Jan A. van Dorsten, *Thomas Basson, 1553–1613: English Printer at Leiden* (Leiden: University of Leiden, 1961), 48, 50.

61. Trans. in Beliën, 60–61.

62. On the drawing's date, see van Regteren Altena, *de Gheyn*, vol. 1, 87.

63. This curious process of "inspissation" is explained by Heinrich Kramer and Jacob Sprenger, *Malleus maleficarum*, trans. Montague Summers (New York: Dover, 1971), 109–10.

64. For a study of this iconographic conceit, see Alison G. Stewart, *Unequal Lovers: A Study of Unequal Couples in Northern Art* (New York: Abaris Books, 1977).

65. Van Regteren Altena, *de Gheyn*, vol. 2, cat. no. 874, 136.

66. For *Orpheus*, see ibid., vol, 2, cat. no. 131, 37.

67. Machteld Löwensteyn, "Helse hebzucht en wereldse wellust," 257–58.

68. Charles Zika, *Exorcising Our Demons: Magic, Witchcraft, and Visual Culture in Early Modern Europe* (Leiden: E. J. Brill, 2003), 406–09; Valerie Traub, "Gendering Mortality in Early Modern Anatomies," in *Feminist Readings of Early Modern Culture: Emerging Subjects*, ed. Valerie Traub, M. Lindsay Kaplan, and Dympna Callaghan (Cambridge: Cambridge University Press, 1996), 44–99. For a discussion of the iconography of de Gheyn's *Anatomical Lesson*, and the identity of the observers, see van Regteren Altena, *de Gheyn*, vol. 2, cat. no. 154, 43–44.

69. Traub, 50.

70. Van Regteren Altena, *de Gheyn*, vol. 2, cat. no. 895, 139; and vol. 2, cat. no. 1002, 152.

71. Ibid., vol. 2, cat. no. 888, 138.

72. Ibid., vol. 2, cat. no. 867, 135–36.

73. Anne Llewellyn Barstow, *Witchcraze: A New History of the European Witch Hunts* (San Francisco: Pandora, 1994), 177.

74. Reginald Scot, *The Discoverie of Witchcraft* (Carbondale: Southern Illinois University Press, 1964), 29.

75. Weyer's Preface is not included in Shea's English translation of *De praestigiis daemonum*, but it is quoted in Clark, *Thinking with Demons*, 199; for women's inclinations toward melancholy, see Weyer, 181–83; and Scot, 68–69.

76. Weyer, 540.

77. Naomi Zack, *Bachelors of Science: Seventeenth-Century Identity, Then and Now* (Philadelphia, Pa.: Temple University Press, 1996), 182–92.

78. Judson, *The Drawings*, 29; Institut Néerlandais, *Le héraut du dix-septième siècle: Dessins et gravures de Jacques de Gheyn II et III de la Fondation Custodia Collection Frits Lugt* (Paris: Institut Néerlandais, 1985), cat. no. 13, pp. 38–44.

79. On the preparatory drawing, see van Regteren Altena, *de Gheyn*, vol. 2. cat. no. 519, 84–85; Museum Boymans-van Beuningen, *de Gheyn*, cat. no. 68, 71–72; and Claudia Swan, "*The Preparation for the Sabbath* by Jacques de Gheyn II: The Issue of Inversion," *Print Quarterly* 16 (1999): 327–39.

80. Filedt Kok, 279.

81. Löwensteyn, "Helse hebzucht en wereldse wellust," 250–51.

82. Filedt Kok, 280, and cat. nos. 105, 108, 287–92, pp. 377, 379–80; Clifford S. Ackley, *Printmaking in the Age of Rembrandt* (Boston: Museum of Fine Arts, 1981), 43.

83. Nadine Monica Orenstein, *Hendrick Hondius and the Business of Prints in Seventeenth-Century Holland* (Rotterdam: Sound and Vision Interactive, 1996), 135. See also her "Print Publishers in the Netherlands," in *Dawn of the Golden Age: Northern Netherlandish Art, 1580-1620*, ed. Ger Luijten, Ariane van Suchtelen et al. (Amsterdam: Rijksmuseum, 1993), 168.

84. Van Regteren Altena, *de Gheyn*, vol. 2, nos. 466–90, pp. 78–80.

85. Ibid., vol. 2, 78.

86. Löwensteyn, "Helse hebzucht en wereldse wellust," 259.

87. Scot, 400.

88. Quoted and trans., van Dorsten, 50–51.

89. Another speculation about the meaning of the cupid might emerge from David Wootten's recent discussion of the rapport between Scot's positions on witchcraft and the theological principles of the Anglo-Dutch "Family of Love," with its emphasis on self-perfection, mutual love, the origins of good and evil *within* the human spirit, toleration of confessional differences, and Nicodemism. Wootten interprets Scot's use of a Latin poem on love at the end of his book, among other features of the text, as a cryptic indication of his membership. Because Basson was also demonstrably Familist, Wootten's analysis of Scot's text bears close consideration: see "Reginald Scot/Abraham Fleming/The Family of Love," in *Languages of Witchcraft: Narrative, Ideology and Meaning*, ed. Stuart Clark (London: Macmillan, 2001), 119–38. On Basson and Familism, see van Dorsten, 64–68.

90. Van Regteren Altena, *de Gheyn*, vol. 1, 103–4; vol. 2, cat. no. 667, pp. 105–06.

91. Clark, *Thinking with Demons*, 457–88. Gijswijt-Hofstra urges a broader consideration of diabolical witchcraft with other forms of magic and counter-magic in the Northern Netherlands: see "European Witchcraft Debate," 184; and "Six Centuries," 14–15.

92. Clark, *Thinking with Demons*, 139–42, 144–45; Walter Stephens, *Demon Lovers: Witchcraft, Sex, and the Crisis of Belief* (Chicago: University of Chicago Press, 2002), 180–240.

93. Van Regteren Altena, *de Gheyn*, vol. 1, 148.

94. On the grotto design, see van Regteren Altena, *de Gheyn*, vol. 1, 139–42; and his "Grotten in de tuinen der Oranjes," *Oud Holland* 85 (1970): 33–44.

95. Zack, 188.

96. For overviews of women in the Dutch Republic, see Simon Schama, *The Embarrassment of Riches: An Interpretation of Dutch Culture in the Golden Age* (New York: Knopf, 1987), 375–480; and Rudolf Michel Dekker, "Getting to the Source: Women in the Medieval and Early Modern Netherlands," *Journal of Women's History* 10 (1998): 165–88.

97. Van Regteren Altena, *de Gheyn*, vol. 1, 11.

98. Pieter J. J. van Thiel, "*Poor Parents, Rich Children*, and *Family Saying Grace*: Two related Aspects of the Iconography of Late Sixteenth- and Seventeenth-Century Dutch Domestic Morality," *Simiolus* 17 (1987): 128–45.

99. J. Richard Judson, "Rembrandt and Jacob de Gheyn II," in *Album Amicorum J. G. van Gelder*, ed. Joshua Bruyn et al. (The Hague: Martinus Nijhoff, 1974), 207.

100. Hessel Miedema, "Over het realisme in de Nederlandse schilderkunst van de zeventiende eeuw, naar aanleidung van een tekening van Jacques de Gheyn II (1565–1632)," *Oud Holland* 89 (1975): 2–18 (English summary, 16–18).

101. Ibid.; Alpers, 93–99; 253, n. 45.

102. Leigh Ann Whaley, *Women's History as Scientists: A Guide to the Debates* (Santa Barbara, Calif: ABC-Clio, 2003), 64–67.

103. Van Regteren Altena, *de Gheyn*, vol. 1, 115.

104. On the goals of women's education in early modern Europe and learned women, see Merry E. Wiesner, *Women and Gender in Early Modern Europe*, 2nd ed. (Cambridge: Cambridge University Press, 2000), 143–74.

105. Erika Rummel, *Erasmus on Women* (Toronto: University of Toronto Press, 1996), 9–10.

106. On van Beverwijk, see A. Agnes Sneller, "'If She Had Been a Man . . .':

Anna Maria van Schurman in the Social and Literary Life of her Age," in *Choosing the Better Part: Anna Maria van Schurman (1606–1678)*, ed. Mirjam de Baar et al. (Dordrecht, Neth.: Kluwer Academic Publishers, 1996), 143–47.

107. On Anna Maria van Schurman, see the essays in de Baar et al.

108. Laurinda S. Dixon, *Perilous Chastity: Women and Illness in Pre-Enlightenment Art and Medicine* (Ithaca, N.Y: Cornell University Press, 1995), especially 197–220.

109. Wiesner, *Women and Gender*, 175–210.

Chapter 6

1. On Ricciardi, see Jonathan Scott, *Salvator Rosa: His Life and Times* (New Haven, Conn.: Yale University Press, 1995), 67–73.

2. The main sources for Rosa's written remains are publications by Uberto Limentani, *Poesie e lettere inedite di Salvator Rosa* (Florence: Limentani, 1950); "Salvator Rosa: nuovi studi e ricerche," *Italian Studies* 8 (1953): 29–58; "Salvator Rosa: nuovi studi e ricerche," *Italian Studies* 10 (1954): 46–55; and "Salvator Rosa: nuovi contributi al Epistolario," *Studi Secenteschi* 8 (1972): 255–73. In all my quotations from Rosa's writings, I have used the English translations of the scholar cited.

3. Richard W. Wallace, *The Etchings of Salvator Rosa* (Princeton, N.J.: Princeton University Press, 1979), 84–92. Wendy Wassyng Roworth, *"Pictor Succensor": A Study of Salvator Rosa as Satirist, Cynic, and Painter* (New York: Garland, 1978), 74, translates *pictor succensor* as "Painter-Satirist" or "Painter who inflames with indignation."

4. Rosa's letter of June 21, 1664, to Ricciardi, quoted in Wallace, 83.

5. Wallace, 82–92.

6. Giovanni Battista Passeri, *Vite de' pittore, scultori, ed architetti che hanno lavorato in Roma, morti dal 1641 fino al 1673*, ed. Jacob Hess (Leipzig and Vienna: H. Keller, 1934), 387, trans. and quoted in Scott, *Rosa*, 8.

7. Helen Langdon, in *Caravaggio: A Life* (Boulder, Colo.: Westview Press, 2000), 33–50, gives an account of late sixteenth-century Rome; also see Elizabeth S. Cohen, "Honor and Gender in the Streets of Early Modern Rome," *Journal of Interdisciplinary History* 22 (1992): 597–625. On Rosa and the Roman Carnival, see Scott, *Rosa*, 19–22.

8. On Gian Carlo de' Medici and his patronage, see Silvia Mascalchi, "Giovan Carlo de' Medici," *Apollo* 120 (1984): 268–72; on art patronage and art theory in late Medici Florence, including that of Gian Carlo, see Edward L. Goldberg, *After Vasari: History, Art, and Patronage in Late Medici Florence* (Princeton, N.J.: Princeton University Press, 1988).

9. Scott, *Rosa*, 27.

10. Wallace, 15.

11. Scott, *Rosa*, 239–40, notes 13 and 14; Wendy Wassyng Roworth, in "The Consolations of Friendship: Salvator Rosa's Self-Portrait for Giovanni Battista Ricciardi," *Metropolitan Museum Journal* 23 (1988): 103–22, doubts that these are portraits.

12. Scott, *Rosa*, 61–64; Helen Langdon, "Salvator Rosa in Florence, 1640–1649," *Apollo* 100 (1974): 190.

13. Rosa's *La poesia*, quoted in Wallace, 90.

14. Richard Spear, *The "Divine" Guido: Religion, Sex, Money, and Art in the World of Guido Reni* (New Haven, Conn.: Yale University Press, 1997), 44–50.

15. For an overview of witchcraft and witch persecutions in Italy, see Francisco Bethencourt, "Un univers saturé de magie: L'Europe méridionale," in *Magie et sorcelle-*

rie en Europe: du moyen age à nos jours, ed. Robert Muchembled and Bengt Ankarloo (Paris: A. Colin, 1994), 159–94; on the Inquisition in Italy, see Ruth Martin, *Witchcraft and the Inquisition in Venice, 1550–1650* (Oxford: Basil Blackwell, 1989); and especially John Tedeschi, *The Prosecution of Heresy: Collected Studies on the Inquisition of Early Modern Italy* (Binghamton, N.Y.: Medieval and Renaissance Texts and Studies, 1991).

16. Scott, *Rosa*, 28, 42–43; quote from Rosa's letter of May 24, 1646, to Giulio Maffei, 43.

17. Scott, *Rosa*, 28–54; also see Francis Haskell, *Patrons and Painters: Art and Society in Baroque Italy* (New Haven, Conn.: Yale University Press, 1980), 11, 22–23.

18. Scott, *Rosa*, 93.

19. Filippo Baldinucci, *Notizie de' professori del disegno* (Florence: V. V. Batelli, 1847), 441, quoted in ibid., 55.

20. Goldberg, 15–47.

21. Scott, *Rosa*, 57.

22. Langdon, "Rosa in Rome," 193–95.

23. Scott, *Rosa*, 58.

24. Ibid., 59–60.

25. Ibid., 90–91.

26. Peter Humfrey and Mauro Lucco, *Dosso Dossi: Court Painter in Renaissance Ferrara* (New York: Metropolitan Museum of Art, 1999), cat. nos. 3 and 12, pp. 89–92, 114–18.

27. On Castiglione's interest in this theme, see Ann Percy, *Giovanni Benedetto Castiglione: Master Draughtsman of the Italian Baroque* (Philadelphia: Philadelphia Museum of Art, 1971), cat. nos. 70, 71, and E. 23, pp. 98–99, 145.

28. Humfrey and Lucco, cat. no. 12, 114.

29. Ibid., 118.

30. See Valeria Finucci's study of Ariosto's and Baldassare Castiglione's strategies to contain the power of female characters, *The Lady Vanishes: Subjectivity and Representation in Castiglione and Ariosto* (Stanford, Calif.: Stanford University Press, 1992).

31. Humfrey and Lucco, cat. no. 12, 114.

32. Gareth Roberts, s.v. "Circe," in *The Spenser Encyclopedia*, ed. Albert Charles Hamilton (Toronto: University of Toronto Press, 1990).

33. Gareth Roberts, "The Descendants of Circe: Witches and Renaissance Fictions," in *Witchcraft in Early Modern Europe: Studies in Culture and Belief*, ed. Jonathan Barry, Marianne Hester, and Gareth Roberts (Cambridge: Cambridge University Press, 1996), 187–94.

34. Stuart Clark, *Thinking with Demons: The Idea of Witchcraft in Early Modern Europe* (Oxford: Oxford University Press, 1997), 634–54.

35. Roberts, "The Descendants of Circe."

36. See Patricia A. Parker's fundamental analysis of this episode in *Literary Fat Ladies: Rhetoric, Gender, Property* (London: Methuen, 1987), 54–66.

37. See David Leinweber, "Witchcraft and Lamiae in 'The Golden Ass,'" *Folklore* 105 (1994): 77–82.

38. Mark Breitenburg, *Anxious Masculinity in Early Modern England* (Cambridge: Cambridge University Press, 1996), 52.

39. Carlo Ginzburg, *The Night Battles: Witchcraft and Agrarian Cults in the Sixteenth and Seventeenth Centuries*, trans. John and Anne Tedeschi (Baltimore: Johns Hopkins University Press, 1983).

40. Brian P. Levack, *The Witch-Hunt in Early Modern Europe* (New York: Longman, 1987), 54–57.

41. Roworth, "*Pictor Succensor*," 136.

42. Rosa's letter of September 16, 1662, to Ricciardi, quoted in Wallace, 83.

43. Scott, *Rosa*, 75–76.

44. Rosa's *La Strega*, quoted in Scott, *Rosa*, 51; for the Italian text, see Limentani, *Poesie e lettere*, 48–50.

45. On the art-theoretical implications of compositional disorder and tenebrist light that obfuscates details, see Philip Sohm's insightful essay, "Baroque Piles and Other Decompositions," in *Pictorial Composition from Medieval to Modern Art*, ed. François Quiviger and Paul Taylor (London: Warburg Institute Colloquia, 2000), 58–90.

46. R. Martin, 4–5, 80–147.

47. On Agrippa and della Porta, see Clark, *Thinking with Demons*, 237–38.

48. Rosa's *Invidia*, quoted in Wallace, 83.

49. Clark, *Thinking with Demons*, 195–250.

50. On Spenser's Merlin, see William Blackburn, "Spenser's Merlin," *Renaissance and Reformation* 4, new series (1980): 179–98.

51. Wallace, 85–86.

52. Ibid., 57.

53. Philip Sohm, *Style in the Art Theory of Early Modern Italy* (Cambridge: Cambridge University Press, 2001), 12–42.

54. For comparison, see Richard Spear, "Scrambling for *Scudi*: Notes on Painters' Earnings in Early Baroque Rome," *Art Bulletin* 85 (2003): 310–20.

55. Luigi Salerno, *L'opera completa di Salvator Rosa* (Milan: Rizzoli, 1975), cat. no. 72, 90.

56. Michael Mahoney, *The Drawings of Salvator Rosa*, 2 vols. (New York: Garland, 1977), vol. 1, cat. no. 28.4, 335–36.

57. R. Martin, 226.

58. Carlo Cesare Malvasia, *Scritti originali del Conte Carlo Cesare Malvasia*, ed. Lea Marzocchi (Bologna: ALFA, 1984), 135, quoted in Scott, *Rosa*, 111.

59. Rosa's letter of December 15, 1666 to Ricciardi, quoted in Luigi Salerno, "Four Witchcraft Scenes by Salvator Rosa," *Cleveland Museum Bulletin* 65 (1978): 231, n. 11; for a comparative perspective, see Spear, "Scrambling for *Scudi*." Spear, 314, notes that Giulio Mancini wrote that a good painter could average 3 to 6 *scudi* a day; extrapolating from that, Spear estimates that the annual salary of an artist in demand would be over 1,000 *scudi*.

60. Langdon, "Rosa in Florence," 197.

61. Filippo Baldinucci, *Vocabulario degli Accademici della Crusca* (Florence, 1681), 38, trans. and quoted in Sohm, "Baroque Piles," 61–62; on the cultural antagonists and defenders of this perspective, see idem, 69.

62. Roworth, "*Pictor Succensor*," 111–41. Rosa's contemporary Pietro Testa was also angered by the *Bamboccianti*'s success, particularly among upper-class patrons. See Elizabeth Cropper, *The Ideal of Painting: Pietro Testa's Düsseldorf Notebook* (Princeton, N.J.: Princeton University Press, 1984), 104–5.

63. Rosa's *Pittura*, quoted in Scott, *Rosa*, 86–87; for the Italian text of *Pittura*, see Limentani, *Poesie et lettere*, 48–50.

64. Passeri, trans. and quoted in Scott, *Rosa*, 21.

65. Roworth,"*Pictor Succensor*," 139.

66. Wallace, 88–89.

67. Rosa notes the discrepancy between the pictures and their frames in *Pittura*, cited by Scott, *Rosa*, 87.

68. Roworth, "*Pictor Succensor*," 136.

69. Passeri, trans. and quoted in Scott, *Rosa*, 72–73.

70. Stephen Greenblatt, "Shakespeare and the Exorcists," in *Critical Essays on Shakespeare's King Lear*, ed. Jay Halio (New York: G. K. Hall, 1996), 100.

71. Scott, *Rosa*, 94. This kind of conspicuous consumption would have helped to establish status in Rosa's new social milieu; see Peter Burke, *The Historical Anthropology of Early Modern Italy: Essays on Perception and Communication* (Cambridge: Cambridge University Press, 1987), 132–49.

72. Salerno, *L'opera completa*, cat. nos. 80, 81, p. 90.

73. J. Richard Judson, "Jacob Isaacsz. van Swanenburgh and the Phlegraean Fields," in *Essays in Northern European Art Presented to Egbert Haverkamp-Begemann on His Sixtieth Birthday* (Doornspijk, Neth.: Davaco, 1983), 119.

74. See Wallace, 55–69, for a comprehensive discussion of the iconography of the two etchings.

75. Ibid., 65.

76. Scott, *Rosa*, 98.

77. Ibid., 98, 133–34, 151.

78. Burke, 79–109; also see Cohen, "Honor and Gender"; Edward Muir, "The Double Binds of Manly Revenge in Renaissance Italy," in *Gender Rhetoric: Postures of Dominance and Submission in History*, comp. Richard C. Trexler (Binghamton, N.Y.: Medieval and Renaissance Texts and Studies, 1994), 65–82; and Sharon T. Strocchia, "Gender and the Rites of Honour in Italian Renaissance Cities," in *Gender and Society in Renaissance Italy*, ed. Judith C. Brown and Robert C. Davis (New York: Longman, 1998), 39–60.

79. Scott, *Rosa*, 105–6.

80. On Trent's *Tametsi* decree on marriage, see Merry E. Wiesner-Hanks, *Christianity and Sexuality in the Early Modern World: Regulating Desire, Reforming Practice* (London: Routledge, 2000), 106–8.

81. Scott, *Rosa*, 110.

82. Rosa's letter of February 1656 to Ricciardi, quoted in ibid., 108–10; for the full Italian text of this important letter, see Limentani, *Poesie et lettere*, 111.

83. For a history of these institutions in Tuscany, see Sherrill Cohen, *The Evolution of Women's Asylums Since 1500: From Refuges for Ex-Prostitutes to Shelters for Battered Women* (Oxford: Oxford University Press, 1992).

84. Scott, *Rosa*, 64–65; for Rosa's finances, see idem, 94, 220–21.

85. Daniela Lombardi, "Intervention by Church and State in Marriage Disputes in Sixteenth- and Seventeenth-Century Florence," in *Crime, Society and the Law in Renaissance Italy*, ed. Trevor Dean and Kate J. P. Lowe (Cambridge: Cambridge University Press, 1994), 153.

86. Strocchia, 47–48.

87. Ibid., 42; Wiesner-Hanks, 115; Nicholas Davidson, "Theology, Nature and the Law: Sexual Sin and Sexual Crime in Italy from the Fourteenth to the Seventeenth Century," in Dean and Lowe, 74–98; and Sandra Cavallo and Simona Cerutti, "Female Honor and the Social Control of Reproduction in Piedmont between 1600 and 1800," in *Sex and Gender in Historical Perspective*, ed. Edward Muir and Guido Ruggiero (Baltimore: Johns Hopkins University Press, 1990), 73–109.

88. Scott, *Rosa*, 120–24.

89. Sohm, "Baroque Piles," 67.

90. Clark, *Thinking with Demons*, 457–525.

91. The best recent account of Magnasco's artistic and intellectual context is Fausta Franchini Guelfi, "La pittura di Alessandro Magnasco dalle fonti figurative e culturali alle tenebre della realtà," in *Alessandro Magnasco* (Milan: Palazzo Reale, 1996), 17–38; for her remarks on his attitude toward witchcraft, see idem, 32–34.

92. Wallace, 17–19, 91.

93. Ibid., 12–36; quote on p. 36.

94. Keith Christiansen, ed. *Giambattista Tiepolo, 1696–1770* (New York: Metropolitan Museum of Art, 1996), cat. nos. 59a-j; 60a-w, pp. 348–60.

95. Ibid., 350.

96. Charles Dempsey, "Tiepolo Etchings at Washington," *Burlington Magazine* 114 (1972): 503–7; on Gnosticism, see Valerie Flint, "The Demonisation of Magic and Sorcery in Late Antiquity," in *Witchcraft and Magic in Europe: Ancient Greece and Rome*, ed. Bengt Ankarloo and Stuart Clark (Philadelphia: University of Pennsylvania Press, 1999), 298–300.

97. H. Diane Russell, *Rare Etchings by Giovanni Battista and Giovanni Domenico Tiepolo* (Washington, D.C.: National Gallery of Art, 1972), 27.

98. Christiansen, 348.

99. Andrea Gottdang, "Tiepolo's *Scherzi di Fantasia*: Begriff und Bedeutung," in *Kunstform Capriccio: von der Groteske zur Spieltheorie der Moderne*, ed. Ekkehard Mai and Joachim Rees (Cologne: Walter König, 1998), 81–96.

Chapter 7

1. Brian P. Levack, *The Witch-Hunt in Early Modern Europe* (New York: Longman, 1987), 227.

2. Joseph Klaits, *Servants of Satan: The Age of the Witch-Hunts* (Bloomington: Indiana University Press, 1985), 172–73.

3. Levack, *The Witch-Hunt*, 213, 225–27.

4. Alan Charles Kors and Edward Peters, eds., *Witchcraft in Europe, 400–1700: A Documentary History*, 2nd ed. (Philadelphia: University of Pennsylvania Press, 2001), 392–94.

5. Laurent Bordelon, *A History of the Ridiculous Extravagancies of Monsieur Oufle*, English ed. (1711; reprint, New York: Garland, 1973).

6. Eleanor A. Sayre, *The Changing Image: Prints by Francisco Goya* (Boston: Museum of Fine Arts, 1974), cat. no. 86, 115. On Gillot's two major witchcraft prints, see Bernard Populus, *Claude Gillot: Catalogue de l'oeuvre gravé* (Paris: Société pour l'Étude de la Gravure Française, 1930), cat. nos. 9 and 10, pp. 82–84.

7. For Gillot's relationship to Watteau, see Marianne Roland Michel, *Watteau, an Artist of the Eighteenth Century* (Secaucus, N.J.: Chartwell Books, 1984), 17–21.

8. Joachim Rees, "Das Capriccio und die Privatisierung der Bildwelt in Interieurs des 18. Jahrhunderts," in *Kunstform Capriccio: von der Groteske zur Spieltheorie der Moderne*, ed. Ekkehard Mai and Joachim Rees (Cologne: Walter König, 1998), 117–21, quote, 119 (my translation).

9. Francisco Calvo Serraller, "Goya's Women in Perspective," in *Goya: Images of Women*, ed. Janis A. Tomlinson (Washington, D.C. and New Haven, Conn.: National Gallery of Art in association with Yale University Press, 2003), 35.

10. Janis A. Tomlinson, *Francisco Goya: The Tapestry Cartoons and Early Career at the Court of Madrid* (Cambridge: Cambridge University Press, 1989), 6.

11. Priscilla E. Muller, *Goya's 'Black' Paintings: Truth and Reason in Light and Liberty* (New York: Hispanic Society of America, 1984), 23–25, 171.

12. Manuela B. Mena Marqués, "Must It Be So? It Must Be So!," in *Goya: Truth and Fantasy, the Small Paintings*, ed. Juliet Wilson-Bareau and Manuela B. Mena Marqués (New Haven, Conn.: Yale University Press, 1994), 32–33.

13. Ibid., 32.

14. Goya's letter of January 4, 1794, to Iriarte, quoted in Nigel Glendinning, *Goya and His Critics* (New Haven, Conn.: Yale University Press, 1977), 46–47.

15. Wilson-Bareau and Mena Marqués, 190.

16. Sarah Symmons, *Goya in Pursuit of Patronage* (London: Gordon Fraser Gallery, 1988), 24–25.

17. Edith Helman, "*Caprichos* and *Monstruos* of Cadalso and Goya," *Hispanic Review* 26 (1958): 202; Paul Ilie, "Concepts of the Grotesque before Goya," *Studies in Eighteenth-Century Culture* 5 (1976): 185–201.

18. Francesco Milizia, *Dizionario delle belle arti* (Dictionary of the fine arts, Bassano, 1797), cited in Werner Hofmann, "Unending Shipwreck," in Wilson-Bareau and Mena Marqués, 50.

19. Hofmann, 50, 55.

20. Helman, "*Caprichos* and *Monstruos*."

21. On the taste for Goya in England, see Nigel Glendinning, "Goya and England in the Nineteenth Century," *Burlington Magazine* 106 (1964): 4–14.

22. Helman, "*Caprichos* and *Monstruos*"; idem, "The Elder Moratín and Goya," *Hispanic Review* 23 (1955): 219–30; idem, "The Younger Moratín and Goya: On *Duendes* and *Brujas*," *Hispanic Review* 27 (1959): 103–22; and idem, *Trasmundo de Goya* (Madrid: Rivista de Occidente, 1963).

23. Symmons, 140; Alfonso E. Pérez Sánchez and Eleanor A. Sayre, eds., *Goya and the Spirit of Enlightenment*, with contributions by Gonzalo Anes, Michael Armstrong Roche, Jeannine Baticle, Nigel Glendinning, Fred Licht, et al. (Boston: Museum of Fine Arts, 1989), cat. nos. 25–27, pp. 58–64.

24. Pérez Sánchez and Sayre, 60.

25. Folke Nördstrom, *Goya, Saturn and Melancholy: Studies in the Art of Goya* (Stockholm: Almkvist and Wiksell, 1962), 168.

26. Pérez Sánchez and Sayre, 62.

27. Helman, "Younger Moratín."

28. Elizabeth Vassall, *The Spanish Journal of Elizabeth, Lady Holland*, ed. The Earl of Ilchester (London: Longmans, Green and Co., 1910), 143, 149, quoted in Juan F. Remón Menéndez, "The Alameda of the Duchess of Osuna: A Garden of Ideas," *Journal of Garden History* 4 (1993): 231.

29. Tomlinson, *Images of Women*, cat. no. 27, 162–64.

30. Symmons, 138; Pérez Sánchez and Sayre, cat. no. 6, 14; also see Andrew Schulz, "Goya's Portraits of the Duchess of Osuna: Fashioning Identity in Enlightenment Spain," in *Women, Art and the Politics of Identity in Eighteenth-Century Europe*, ed. Melissa Hyde and Jennifer Milam (Aldershot, Hants, U.K: Ashgate, 2003), 263–83.

31. Pérez Sánchez and Sayre, cat. no. 11, 24–26.

32. Peter Klein, "'La fantasía abandonada de la razón': Zur Darstellung des Wahnsinns in Goya's 'Hof der Irren,'" in *Goya, neue Forschungen: Das internationale Symposium 1991 in Osnabrück*, ed. Jutta Held (Berlin: Gebr. Mann, 1994), 182.

33. Wilson-Bareau and Mena Marqués, 276–81.

34. Remón Menéndez, 231–32.

35. Juan Antonio Llorente, *Historia crítica de la Inquisición en España* (Critical history of the Inquisition in Spain, Madrid, 1822), vol. 3, 260, cited in Pérez Sánchez and Sayre, 60; on Goya's portrait of Llorente, see idem, cat. no. 73, 164–67.

36. Helman, "Younger Moratín," 109–11, 121.

37. Janis A. Tomlinson, *Goya in the Twilight of Enlightenment* (New Haven, Conn.: Yale University Press, 1992), 16–27.

38. Ronald Paulson, *Representations of Revolution (1789–1820)* (New Haven, Conn.: Yale University Press, 1983), 294.

39. Tomlinson, *Twilight of Enlightenment*, 8.

40. Werner Hofmann, *Goya: "To Every Story There Belongs Another"* (London: Thames and Hudson, 2003), 104.

41. Pérez Sánchez and Sayre, 225.

42. Ibid., 40.

43. Gerlinde Volland, *Männermacht und Frauenopfer: Sexualität und Gewalt bei Goya* (Berlin: Reiner, 1993).

44. See especially Calvo Serraller's balanced essay.

45. See Sally-Ann Kitts's discussion of this controversy in *The Debate on the Nature, Role, and Influence of Woman in Eighteenth-Century Spain* (Lewiston, N.Y.: E. Mellen Press, 1995), 139–72.

46. Paulson, 306. Also see Reva Wolf's essay on sexual and social ambiguity in Goya's masked images in terms of carnival and contemporary uneasiness about gender indeterminacy: "Sexual Identity, Mask and Disguise in Goya's 'Los Caprichos,'" in Held, 89–110.

47. William Monter, "Witch Trials in Continental Europe, 1560–1660," in *Witchcraft and Magic in Europe: The Period of the Witch Trials*, ed. Bengt Ankarloo, Stuart Clark, and William Monter (Philadelphia: University of Pennsylvania Press, 2002), 44–49.

48. Pérez Sánchez and Sayre, 225.

49. Jeannine Baticle, *Goya* (Paris: Fayard, 1992), 236.

50. Pérez Sánchez and Sayre, xcix.

51. Ibid., ci. For doubts about the timing and seriousness of the Inquisitorial threat, see Janis A. Tomlinson, *Graphic Evolutions: The Print Series of Francisco Goya* (New York: Columbia University Press, 1989), 13–14.

52. Peréz Sánchez and Sayre, cv-cviii, and cat. nos. 98–106, pp. 217–37.

53. The major account of the Logroño trials is Gustav Henningsen, *The Witches' Advocate: Basque Witchcraft and the Spanish Inquisition (1609–1614)* (Reno: University of Nevada Press, 1980); for Salazar Frias's critique, see Kors and Peters, 407–18.

54. Helman, "Younger Moratín," 121, n. 20.

55. On this portrait, see Pérez Sánchez and Sayre, cat. no. 30, 69–71; on the portrait's influence on *Capricho* 43, see Steven A. Mansbach, "Goya's Liberal Iconography: Two Images of Jovellanos," *Journal of the Warburg and Courtauld Institutes* 41 (1978): 340–44.

56. Pérez Sánchez and Sayre, 166.

57. The Osunas intended to open their library to the public, but its content made that impossible; see Schulz, 272–73.

58. Henningsen, 186.

59. Julio Caro Baroja, *The World of the Witches*, trans. Nigel Glendinning (Chicago: University of Chicago Press, 1964), 172.

60. Helman, "Younger Moratín," 10–11.

61. To see these drawn and etched compositions together, see Pierre Gassier and Juliet Wilson, *The Life and Complete Works of Francisco Goya* (New York: Harrison House, 1971), cat. nos. 536–38, 571–72, 575–76, 577–78, 581–82, 583–84, 585–86, 587–88, 589–90, 591–92, pp. 181, 183–84.

62. Pérez Sánchez and Sayre, xcviii–xcix.

63. Goya's letter of February 19, 1785, to Zapater, quoted in Mena Marqués, 24.

64. For the text of the Prado commentary, see Pérez Sánchez and Sayre, cat. no. 52, 116.

65. Ibid., xcix–c.

66. Paul Ilie, "Goya's Teratology and the Critique of Reason," *Eighteenth-Century Studies* 18 (1984): 35–56; John L. Ciofalo, "Goya's Enlightenment Protagonist—A Quixotic Dreamer of Reason," *Eighteenth-Century Studies* 30 (1997): 421–36.

67. Barbara M. Benedict, *Curiosity: A Cultural History of Early Modern Inquiry* (Chicago: University of Chicago Press, 2001), 246.

68. Gwyn A. Williams, *Goya and the Impossible Revolution* (New York: Pantheon, 1976), 54–58; Paulson, 330–31.

69. Symmons, 162–63.

70. Caro Baroja, 171–79.

71. Pérez Sánchez and Sayre, cat. nos. 60 and 61, pp. 130–35.

72. Sayre, *The Changing Image*, cat. nos. 58–59, pp. 85–86.

73. Pérez Sánchez and Sayre, cat. no. 61, 132–34.

74. Volland, 95–97.

75. Pérez Sánchez and Sayre, cat. no. 45, 98–101.

76. Ibid., cat. no. 44, 96–98.

77. On the contemporary concern about prostitution and venereal disease, see ibid.; and Helman, "Elder Moratín."

78. Helman, "Younger Moratín," 118.

79. Sayre, *The Changing Image*, cat. nos. 50–52, pp. 78–79.

80. Ibid., cat. nos. 53–54, pp. 80–81.

81. Henningsen, 88.

82. Pérez Sánchez and Sayre, cat. no. 58, 127–28.

83. Paulson, 328.

84. Kors and Peters, 410.

85. Pérez Sánchez and Sayre, cat. no. 49, 107–10.

86. Williams, 59.

87. P. E. Muller, 47, n. 72.

88. Rees, 118.

89. P. E. Muller, 61–72.

90. Ibid., 125–26; Eleanor A. Sayre, "Goya's Caprichos: A Sampling of Witches," in Held, 74–77.

91. Nigel Glendinning, "Goya and Arriaza's *Profecia del Pirineo*," *Journal of the Warburg and Courtauld Institutes* 26 (1963): 363–66; Muller, 127–30.

92. John L. Ciofalo, *The Self-Portraits of Francisco Goya* (Cambridge: Cambridge University Press, 2001), 165, identifies her as Alba, but the painting surface has been altered, and this seems a difficult thesis to sustain given that Goya was living with Zorilla.

93. Fred Licht, *Goya: The Origins of the Modern Temper in Art* (New York: Universe Books, 1979), 159. Also see his later, lavishly illustrated account of Goya's art, *Goya* (New York: Abbeville Press, 2001).

94. Licht, *Origins of the Modern Temper*, 164.

95. See P. E. Muller, 217–36, on the relationship between the Black Paintings and Robertson's horror shows.

96. Nigel Glendinning, "The Strange Translation of Goya's Black Paintings," *Burlington Magazine* 117 (1975): 465–79.

97. Licht, *Origins of the Modern Temper*, 170.

98. Ibid., 179; Glendinning, "Strange Translation," 479.

99. Rees, 121.

100. Lawrence Gowing, review of *Goya's "Black Paintings": Truth and Reason in Light and Liberty*, by Patricia Muller, in *Burlington Magazine* 128 (1986): 507.

101. P. E. Muller, 35.

102. Ibid., 32.

103. Nigel Glendinning and Rolfe Kentish, "Goya's Country House in Madrid: The Quinta del Sordo," *Apollo* 123 (1986): 108, n. 31.

104. Ciofalo, *Self-Portraits of Francisco Goya*, 146.

105. Muller, 35.

106. Isodoro Weiss's complaint, quoted in Gassier and Wilson, 248.

107. P. E. Muller, 145–46; Gowing, 507.

108. Remón Menéndez, 231.

109. Ciofalo, *Self-Portraits of Francisco Goya*, 153–57.

110. Glendinning, "Strange Translation," 473.

111. P. E. Muller, 160–67.

112. Juliana Schiesari, *The Gendering of Melancholia: Feminism, Psychoanalysis, and the Symbolics of Loss in Renaissance Literature* (Ithaca, N.Y.: Cornell University Press, 1992); also see Angela Rosenthal's essay on Angelica Kauffman's subversion of the Penelope myth in her history paintings to express her own identity as a narrative painter, "Angelica's Odyssey: Kauffman's Paintings of Penelope and the Weaving of Narrative," in Hyde and Milam, 211–36.

113. Ciofalo, *Self-Portraits of Francisco Goya*, 41–42.

114. For overviews, see Michèle Crampe-Casnabet, "A Sampling of Eighteenth-Century Philosophy," in *Renaissance and Enlightenment Paradoxes*, ed. Natalie Zemon Davis and Arlette Farge, vol. 3 of *A History of Women in the West*, 5 vols., ed. Georges Duby and Michelle Perrot (Cambridge, Mass.: Belknap, 1992–94), 314–47; and Dena Goodman, "Women and the Enlightenment," in *Becoming Visible: Women in European History*, 3rd ed., ed. Renate Bridenthal, Susan Mosher Stuard, and Merry E. Wiesner (Boston: Houghton Mifflin, 1998), 233–62.

115. Pierre Roussel, *Système physique et moral de la femme* (Paris, 1775), 30, quoted in Lieselotte Steinbrügge, *The Moral Sex: Woman's Nature in the French Enlightenment*, trans. Pamela E. Selwyn (Oxford: Oxford University Press, 1995), 37.

116. The Inquisition reluctantly allowed prestigious laypeople like the Osunas to apply for government permission to have banned books, and they were also obtained clandestinely: see Jeannine Baticle's essay, "Goya and the Link with France at the End of the Old Regime," in Pérez Sánchez and Sayre, l, and lxii, n. 1; and Schulz, 272–73. On Rousseau's pervasive influence among Spanish intellectuals, see Jefferson Rea Spell, *Rousseau in the Spanish World before 1833: A Study in Franco-Spanish Literary Relations* (Austin: University of Texas Press, 1938; reprint, New York: Gordian Press, 1969).

117. Mary Seidman Trouille, *Sexual Politics in the Enlightenment: Women Writers Read Rousseau* (Albany: State University of New York Press, 1997), 44.

118. Steinbrügge, 44–45.

119. Ibid., 44.

120. Ibid., 68–70.

121. Trouille, 13–72; on views of women's education in *Émile*, idem, 35–37.

122. Kitts, 231.

123. Steinbrügge, 38–39, 98–99.

124. Ibid., 30–33.

125. H. Diane Russell with Bernadine Barnes, *Eva/Ave: Woman in Renaissance and Baroque Prints* (Washington, D.C., and New York: National Gallery of Art in association with the Feminist Press at the City University of New York, 1990), 32–33.

126. P. E. Muller, 61.

127. Glendinning and Kentish, 106.

128. Gassier and Wilson, cat. nos. 635 and 636, pp. 186–87.

129. P. E. Muller, 172–77; Gowing, 507.

130. P. E. Muller, 24–25.

131. Charles Zika, in *Exorcising our Demons: Magic, Witchcraft, and Visual Culture in Early Modern Europe* (Leiden: E. J. Brill, 2003), 375–479, deals extensively with Saturn's associations with sexual aggression, violence, and cannibalism, drawing together the iconography of Saturn and his children with the imagery of witchcraft and the New World.

132. Steinbrügge, 106.

Bibliography

Abray, Lorna Jane. *The People's Reformation: Magistrates, Clergy, and Commons in Strasbourg, 1500–1598.* Ithaca, N.Y.: Cornell University Press, 1985.

Accati, Luisa. "The Spirit of Fornication: Virtue of the Soul and Virtue of the Body in Friuli, 1600–1800." In Muir and Ruggiero, 110–40.

Ackley, Clifford S. *Printmaking in the Age of Rembrandt*, Boston: Museum of Fine Arts, 1981.

———. "Printmaking in the Age of Rembrandt: The Quest for Printed Tone." In Ackley, xix–xxvi.

Alberti, Leonbattista. *On Painting.* Trans. John R. Spencer. Rev. ed. New Haven, Conn.: Yale University Press, 1956.

Allihn, Max. *Dürer-Studien: Versuch einer Erklärung schwer zu deutender Kupferstiche A. Dürers.* Leipzig: Rudolf Weigels Buchhandlung, 1871.

Alpers, Svetlana. *The Art of Describing: Dutch Art in the Seventeenth Century.* Chicago: University of Chicago Press, 1983.

Ames-Lewis, Francis. *The Intellectual Life of the Early Renaissance Artist.* New Haven, Conn.: Yale University Press, 2000.

Andersson, Christiane. "Das Bild der Frau in der oberrheinischen Kunst um 1520." In *Die Frau in der Renaissance*, ed. Paul Gerhardt Schmidt, 243–59. Wiesbaden, Ger.: Harrassowitz, 1994.

———. *Dirnen, Krieger, Narren: Ausgewählte Zeichnungen von Urs Graf.* Basel: G. S. Verlag, 1978.

Anglo, Sydney. "Evident Authority and Authoritative Evidence: The *Malleus Maleficarum.*" In Anglo, 1–31.

Anglo, Sidney, ed. *The Damned Art: Essays in the Literature of Witchcraft.* London: Routledge & Kegan Paul, 1977.

Ankarloo, Bengt, and Gustav Henningsen, eds. *Early Modern European Witchcraft: Centres and Peripheries.* Oxford: Clarendon Press, 1991.

Ankarloo, Bengt, and Stuart Clark, eds. *Witchcraft and Magic in Europe: Ancient Greece and Rome.* Philadelphia: University of Pennsylvania Press, 1999.

Anzelewsky, Fedja. *Dürer-Studien: Untersuchungen zu den ikonographischen und geistesgeschichtlichen Grundlagen seiner Werke zwischen den beiden Italienreisen.* Berlin: Deutscher Verein für Kunstwissenschaft, 1983.

Ariosto, Ludovico. *Il negromante* (The necromancer). In *The Comedies of Ariosto*, trans. and ed. Edmond M. Beame and Leonard G. Sbrocchi. Chicago: University of Chicago Press, 1975.

———. *Orlando Furioso.* Trans. Guido Waldman. Oxford: Oxford University Press, 1983.

Atwater, Vivian Lee. "A Catalogue and Analysis of Eighteenth-Century French Prints after Netherlandish Baroque Painters." 2 vols. Ph.D. diss., University of Washington, 1988.

———. "Les graveurs et la vogue néerlandais dans le Paris du XVIIIe siècle: Le Bas, Teniers et l'idéalisation de la vie paysanne." *Nouvelles de l'estampe* no. 142–43 (1995): 3–12.

Bailey, Michael David. *Battling Demons: Witchcraft, Heresy, and Reform in the Late Middle Ages.* University Park: Pennsylvania State University Press, 2003.

Baldinucci, Filippo. *Notizie de' professori del disegno.* Florence: V. V. Batelli, 1847, 441. Quoted in Scott, 55.

———. *Vocabulario degli Accademici della Crusca.* Florence, 1681, 38. Quoted in Sohm, "Baroque Piles," 61–62

Balis, Arnout. "Antwerp, Foster-Mother of the Arts: Its Contribution to the Artistic Culture of Europe in the Seventeenth Century." In van der Stock, 115–17.

Barasch, Frances K. *The Grotesque: A Study in Meanings.* The Hague: Moutin, 1971.

Barasch, Moshe. *Theories of Art from Plato to Winckelmann.* New York: New York University Press, 1989.

Barolsky, Paul. *Infinite Jest: Wit and Humor in Italian Renaissance Art.* Columbia: University of Missouri Press, 1978.

Barry, Jonathan. "Introduction: Keith Thomas and the Problem of Witchcraft." In Barry, Hester, and Roberts, 1–45.

Barry, Jonathan, Marianne Hester, and Gareth Roberts, eds. *Witchcraft in Early Modern Europe: Studies in Culture and Belief.* Cambridge: Cambridge University Press, 1996.

Barstow, Anne Llewellyn. *Witchcraze: A New History of the European Witch Hunts.* San Francisco: Pandora, 1994.

Baticle, Jeannine. *Goya.* Paris: Fayard, 1992.

———. "Goya and the Link with France at the End of the Old Regime." In Pérez Sánchez and Sayre, l–lxiii.

Baumgarten, Fritz. *Der Freiburger Hochaltar: Kunstgeschichtlich gewürdigt.* Strasbourg: Heitz and Mündel, 1904.

———. "Hans Baldungs Stellung zur Reformation." *Zeitschrift für die Geschichte des Oberrheins*, new series 19 (1904): 245–64.

Baxter, Christopher. "Jean Bodin's *De la démonomanie des sorciers*: The Logic of Persecution." In Anglo, 76–105.

———. "Johann Weyer's *De praestigiis daemonum*: Unsystematic Psychopathology." In Anglo, 53–75.

Behringer, Wolfgang. "Allemagne, 'mère de tant de sorcières' au coeur des persecutions." In Muchembled and Ankarloo, 59–98.

———. *Witchcraft Persecutions in Bavaria: Popular Magic, Religious Zealotry and Reason of State in Early Modern Europe.* Trans. J. C. Grayson and David Lederer. Cambridge: Cambridge University Press, 1997.

———. "Witchcraft Studies in Austria, Germany and Switzerland." In Barry, Hester, and Roberts, 64–95.

Beliën, Herman. "Judicial Views on the Crime of Witchcraft." In Gijswijt-Hofstra and Frijhoff, 53–78.

Bell, Janis. Introduction to *Art History in the Age of Bellori: Scholarship and Cultural Poetics in Seventeenth-Century Rome.* Ed. Janis Bell and Thomas Willette. Cambridge: Cambridge University Press, 2002.

Benedict, Barbara M. *Curiosity: A Cultural History of Early Modern Inquiry.* Chicago: University of Chicago Press, 2001.

Bernstein, Eckhard. *German Humanism.* Boston: Twayne, 1983.

Bethencourt, Francisco. "Un univers saturé de magie: L'Europe méridionale." In Muchembled and Ankarloo, 159–94.

Bever, Edward. "Old Age and Witchcraft in Early Modern Europe." In *Old Age in Pre-Industrial Society*, ed. Peter Stearns, 150–90. New York: Holmes and Meier, 1982.

Bireley, Robert. *The Counter-Reformation Prince: Anti-Machiavellianism or Catholic Statecraft in Early Modern Europe.* Chapel Hill: University of North Carolina Press, 1990.

Bissell, R. Ward. *Artemisia Gentileschi and the Authority of Art.* University Park: Pennsylvania State University Press, 1999.

Blackburn, William. "Spenser's Merlin." *Renaissance and Reformation* 4, new series (1980): 179–98.

Blauert, Andreas. "Frühe Hexenverfolgungen in der Schweiz, am Bodensee und am Oberrhein." In Lorenz, 59–66.

Blunt, Anthony. *Artistic Theory in Italy, 1450–1600.* Reprint ed. Oxford: Clarendon Press, 1963.

Bober, Phyllis Pray, and Ruth Rubenstein. *Renaissance Artists and Antique Sculpture: A Handbook of Sources.* London: H. Miller, 1986.

Bober, Phyllis Pray. "An Antique Sea-Thiasos in the Renaissance." In *Essays in Memory of Karl Lehmann*, ed. Lucy Freeman Sandler, 43–48. New York: New York University Press, 1964.

Bodin, Jean. *On the Demon-Mania of Witches.* Trans. Randy A. Scott. Toronto: Centre for Reformation and Renaissance Studies, 1995.

———. *The Six Bookes of a Commonweale.* Trans. Richard Knolles, ed. K. D. McRae. Cambridge: Cambridge University Press, 1962, 793–94. Quoted in Clark, *Thinking with Demons*, 681.

Bordelon, Laurent. *A History of the Ridiculous Extravagancies of Monsieur Oufle.* English edition, 1711. Reprint, New York: Garland, 1973.

Bostridge, Ian. "Witchcraft Repealed." In Barry, Hester and Roberts, 309–34.

Boureau, Alain. Preface to *Les sciences du diable*, by Sophie Houdard.

Bowman, Jeffrey. Review of *Oedipus and the Devil: Witchcraft, Sexuality and Religion in Early Modern Europe*, by Lyndal Roper. *Journal of Social History* 32 (Spring 1999): 740–42.

Brady, Thomas A., Jr. *Ruling Class, Regime and Reformation at Strasbourg, 1520–1555.* Leiden: E. J. Brill, 1978.

———. "The Social Place of a German Renaissance Artist: Hans Baldung Grien (1484/85–1545) at Strasbourg." *Central European History* 5 (1975): 295–315.

Brain, James. "An Anthropological Perspective on the Witchcraze." In Brink, Coudert, and Horowitz, 15–27.

Brauner, Sigrid. *Fearless Wives and Frightened Shrews: The Construction of the Witch in Early Modern Germany.* Ed. Robert H. Brown. Amherst: University of Massachusetts Press, 1995.

Breitenberg, Mark. *Anxious Masculinity in Early Modern England.* Cambridge: Cambridge University Press, 1996.

Bridenthal, Renate, Susan Mosher Stuard, and Merry E. Wiesner, eds. *Becoming Visible: Women in European History.* 3rd ed. Boston: Houghton Mifflin, 1998.

Briggs, Robin. "'Many Reasons Why': Witchcraft and the Problem of Multiple Explanation." In Barry, Hester, and Roberts, 49–63.

———. *Witches and Neighbors: The Social and Cultural Context of European Witchcraft.* Harmondsworth, Middlesex, U.K.: Penguin Books, 1996.

———. "Women as Victims? Witches, Judges and the Community." *French History* 5 (1991): 438–50.

Brink, Jean R., Allison P. Coudert, and Maryanne C. Horowitz, eds. *The Politics of Gender in Early Modern Europe.* Kirksville, Mo.: Sixteenth Century Journal Publishers, 1989.

Brown, Jonathan. *Kings and Connoisseurs: Collecting in Seventeenth-Century Europe.* Princeton, N.J.: Princeton University Press, 1995.

Brown, Judith C., and Robert C. Davis, eds. *Gender and Society in Renaissance Italy.* New York: Longman, 1998.

Bryson, Norman. *Tradition and Desire: From David to Delacroix.* Cambridge: Cambridge University Press, 1984.

Burke, Peter. *The Historical Anthropology of Early Modern Italy: Essays on Perception and Communication.* Cambridge: Cambridge University Press, 1987.

Busch, Werner. "Das Capriccio und die Erweiterung der Wirklichkeit." In Mai and Rees, 53–79.

Calvo Serraller, Francisco. "Goya's Women in Perspective." In Tomlinson, *Goya: Images of Women*, 25–49.

Campbell, Stephen J. "Michelangelo, Rosso, and the (Un)Divinity of Art." *Art Bulletin* 84 (2002): 596–620.

Cannaert, Josef Bernaert. *Olim: Proces des sorcières en Belgique sou Philippe II et le gouvernement des Archiducs.* Ghent: C. Annoot-Braeckman, 1847.

Canning, Kathleen. "Feminist History after the Linguistic Turn: Historicizing Discourse and Experience." In *Feminist Approaches to Theory and Methodology: An Interdisciplinary Reader*, ed. Sharlene Hesse-Biber, Christina Gilmartin, and Robin Lydenberg, 45–78. Oxford: Oxford University Press, 1999.

Caro Baroja, Julio. *The World of the Witches.* Trans. Nigel Glendinning. Chicago: University of Chicago Press, 1964.

Carroll, Jane L. "The Paintings of Jacob Cornelisz. van Oostsanen." Ph.D. diss., University of North Carolina at Chapel Hill, 1987.

Cast, David. *The Calumny of Apelles: A Study in the Humanist Tradition.* New Haven, Conn.: Yale University Press, 1981.

Cavallo, Sandra, and Simona Cerutti. "Female Honor and the Social Control of Reproduction in Piedmont between 1600 and 1800." In Muir and Ruggiero, 73–109.

Chadraba, Rudolf. *Dürers Apocalypse: Eine ikonologische Deutung.* Prague: Verlag der Tschechoslowakischen Akademie der Wissenschaften, 1964.

Chadwick, Whitney. *Women, Art, and Society.* New York: Thames and Hudson, 1990.

Chastel, André. *La grottesque.* Paris: Le Promeneur, 1988.

Christiansen, Keith, ed. *Giambattista Tiepolo, 1696–1770.* New York: Metropolitan Museum of Art, 1996.

Christiansen, Keith, and Judith W. Mann. *Orazio and Artemisia Gentileschi.* New York and New Haven, Conn.: Metropolitan Museum of Art and Yale University Press, 2001.

Ciofalo, John L. "Goya's Enlightenment Protagonist—A Quixotic Dreamer of Reason." *Eighteenth-Century Studies* 30 (1997): 421–36.

———. *The Self-Portraits of Francisco Goya.* Cambridge: Cambridge University Press, 2001.

Cixous, Hélène, and Catherine Clément. *The Newly Born Woman.* Trans. Betsy Wing. Minneapolis: University of Minnesota Press, 1986.

Clark, Stuart. Introduction to *Languages of Witchcraft: Narrative, Ideology and Meaning in Early Modern Culture.* Ed. Stuart Clark. London: Macmillan, 2001.

———. *Thinking with Demons: The Idea of Witchcraft in Early Modern Europe*. Oxford: Oxford University Press, 1997.

Cohen, Elizabeth S. "Honor and Gender in the Streets of Early Modern Rome." *Journal of Interdisciplinary History* 22 (1992): 597–625.

Cohen, Sherrill. *The Evolution of Women's Asylums Since 1500: From Refuges for Ex-Prostitutes to Shelters for Battered Women*. Oxford: Oxford University Press, 1992.

Cohn, Norman. *Europe's Inner Demons: An Enquiry Inspired by the Great Witch-Hunt*. New York: Basic Books, 1975.

Coudert, Allison P. "The Myth of the Improved Status of Protestant Women: The Case of the Witchcraze." In Brink, Coudert, and Horowitz, 61–89.

Cox-Rearick, Janet, ed. *Giulio Romano: Master Designer*. New York: Hunter College, City University of New York, Bertha and Karl Leubsdorf Gallery, 1999.

Crampe-Casnabet, Michèle. "A Sampling of Eighteenth-Century Philosophy." In *Renaissance and Enlightenment Paradoxes*, ed. Natalie Zemon Davis and Arlette Farge, 314–47. Vol. 3, *A History of Women in the West*, 5 vols., ed. Georges Duby and Michelle Perrot. Cambridge, Mass.: Belknap Press, 1992–94.

Cropper, Elizabeth. *The Ideal of Painting: Pietro Testa's Düsseldorf Notebook*. Princeton, N.J.: Princeton University Press, 1984.

———. "'La più bella antichità che sappiate desiderare': History and Style in Giovan Pietro Bellori's 'Lives.'" In Ganz et al., 145–73.

Cuttler, Charles D. "Witchcraft in a Work by Bosch." *Art Quarterly* 20 (1957): 129–40.

Daly, Mary. *Gyn/Ecology: The Metaethics of Radical Feminism*. Boston: Beacon Press, 1978.

Davidson, Jane P. *David Teniers the Younger*. Boulder, Colo.: Westview Press, 1979.

———. "Plantes médicinales et vénéneuses: Le sabbat des sorcières et ses préparatifs dans la peinture néerlandais du XVIIe siècle." In Jacques-Chaquin and Préaud, 419–25.

———. *The Witch in Northern European Art, 1470–1750*. Freren, Ger.: Luca Verlag, 1987.

Davidson, Nicholas. "Theology, Nature and the Law: Sexual Sin and Sexual Crime in Italy from the Fourteenth to the Seventeenth Century." In Dean and Lowe, 74–98.

Davis, Bruce. *Mannerist Prints: International Style in the Sixteenth Century*. Los Angeles: Los Angeles County Museum of Art, 1988.

Davis, Natalie Zemon. *Society and Culture in Early Modern France: Eight Essays*. Stanford, Calif.: Stanford University Press, 1975.

de Baar, Mirjam, et al., eds. *Choosing the Better Part: Anna Maria van Schurman (1606–1678)*. Dordrecht, Neth.: Kluwer Academic Publishers, 1996.

de Montaigne, Michel. *The Essays of Michel de Montaigne*. Ed. and trans. Jacob Zeitlin. 3 vols. New York: Knopf, 1936.

de Tolnay, Charles. *The Drawings of Pieter Bruegel the Elder, with a Critical Catalogue*. Trans. Charles Sleeth. New York: Twin Editions, 1953.

de Waardt, Hans. "Prosecution or Defense: Procedural Possibilities Following a Witchcraft Accusation in the Province of Holland before 1800." In Gijswijt-Hofstra and Frijhoff, 79–90.

———. *Toverij en samenleving: Holland 1500–1800*. The Hague: Stichting Hollandse Historische Reeks, 1991.

Dean, Trevor, and Kate J. P. Lowe, eds. *Crime, Society and the Law in Renaissance Italy*. Cambridge: Cambridge University Press, 1994.

Dekker, Rudolf Michel. "Getting to the Source: Women in the Medieval and Early Modern Netherlands." *Journal of Women's History* 10 (1998): 165–88.

Del Rio, Martín. *Martín Del Rio: Investigations into Magic.* Ed. and trans. P. G. Maxwell-Stewart. Manchester, U.K.: Manchester University Press, 2000.

Dempsey, Charles. "Tiepolo Etchings at Washington." *Burlington Magazine* 114 (1972): 503–07.

Dixon, Annette, ed. *Women Who Ruled: Queens, Goddesses, Amazons in Renaissance and Baroque Art.* London and Ann Arbor, Mich.: Merrill in association with the University of Michigan Museum of Art, 2002.

Dixon, Laurinda S. *Perilous Chastity: Women and Illness in Pre-Enlightenment Art and Medicine.* Ithaca, N.Y.: Cornell University Press, 1995.

Douglas, Mary. *Purity and Danger: An Analysis of the Concepts of Pollution and Taboo.* London: Routledge & Kegan Paul, 1966.

Dresen-Coenders, Lène. "De demonen bij Jeroen Bosch: Zoektocht naar bronnen en betekenis." In Rooijakkers, Dresen-Coenders and Geerdes, 168–97.

———. "Witches as Devils' Concubines." In *Saints and She-Devils: Images of Women in the 15th and 16th Centuries*, ed. Lène Dresen-Coenders, 59–82. London: Rubicon Press, 1987.

Dupont-Bouchat, Marie-Sylvie. "La répression de la sorcellerie dans le duché de Luxembourg aux XVIe et XVIIe siècles." In *Prophètes et sorciers dans les Pays-Bas, XVIe–XVIIe siècle*, ed. Marie-Sylvie Dupont-Bouchat, Willem Frijhoff, and Robert Muchembled, 43–154. Paris: Hachette, 1978.

Dworkin, Andrea. *Woman Hating.* New York: Dutton, 1974.

Dwyer, Eugene. "The Subject of Dürer's *Four Witches.*" *Art Quarterly* 34 (1971): 456–72.

Emison, Patricia A. "The Raucousness of Mantegna's Mythological Engravings." *Gazette des Beaux-Arts* 124 (1994): 159–76.

———. "Truth and *Bizzarria* in an Engraving of *Lo stregozzo.*" *Art Bulletin* 81 (1999): 623–33.

———. "The Word Made Naked in Pollaiuolo's *Battle of the Nudes.*" *Art History* 13 (1990): 261–75.

Endres, Rudolf. "Heinrich Institoris, sein Hexenhammer und der Nürnberger Rat." In *Der Hexenhammer: Entstehung und Umfeld des Malleus maleficarum von 1487*, ed. Peter Segl, 195–216. Cologne: Böhlau Verlag, 1988.

Falkenburg, Reindert L. "De duivel buiten beeld: Over duivelafwerende krachten en motieven in de beeldende kunst rond 1500." In Rooijakkers, Dresen-Coenders, and Geerdes, 107–22.

Filedt Kok, Jan Piet. "Jacques de Gheyn II: Engraver, Designer and Publisher—I and II." *Print Quarterly* 7 (1990): 248–81, 370–95.

Filipczak, Zirka Zaremba. *Picturing Art in Antwerp, 1550–1700.* Princeton, N.J.: Princeton University Press, 1987.

Findlen, Paula. "Courting Nature." In Jardine, Secord, and Spary, 57–73.

Finucci, Valeria. *The Lady Vanishes: Subjectivity and Representation in Castiglione and Ariosto.* Stanford, Calif.: Stanford University Press, 1992.

Flint, Valerie. "The Demonisation of Magic and Sorcery in Late Antiquity." In Ankarloo and Clark, 279–348.

Frijhoff, Willem. "Religious Toleration in the United Provinces: From 'Case' to 'Model.'" In Hsia and van Nierop, 27–52.

———. "What Is an Early Modern University? The Conflict between Leiden and Amsterdam in 1631." In *European Universities in the Age of Reformation and*

Counter-Reformation, ed. Helga Robinson-Hammerstein, 149–68. Dublin: Four Courts Press, 1998.

Ganz, Peter, et al., eds. *Kunst und Kunsttheorie, 1400–1900*. Wiesbaden: Otto Harrassowitz, 1991.

Garrard, Mary D. *Artemisia Gentileschi: The Image of the Female Hero in Italian Art.* Princeton, N.J.: Princeton University Press, 1989.

Gassier, Pierre, and Juliet Wilson. *The Life and Complete Works of Francisco Goya.* New York: Harrison House, 1971.

Gibson, Walter S. "Bosch's Dreams: A Response to the Art of Bosch in the Sixteenth Century." *Art Bulletin* 74 (1992): 205–18

Gijswijt-Hofstra, Marijke. "The European Witchcraft Debate and the Dutch Variant." *Social History* 15 (1990): 181–94.

———. "Six Centuries of Witchcraft in the Netherlands: Themes, Outlines, and Interpretations." In Gijswijt-Hofstra and Frijhoff, 1–36.

Gijswijt-Hofstra, Marijke, and Willem Frijhoff, eds. *Witchcraft in the Netherlands from the Fourteenth to the Twentieth Century.* Trans. Rachel M. J. van der Wilden-Fall. Rotterdam: University Press, 1991.

Ginzburg, Carlo. *Ecstasies: Deciphering the Witches' Sabbath.* Trans. Raymond Rosenthal. New York: Pantheon Books, 1991.

———. *The Night Battles: Witchcraft and Agrarian Cults in the Sixteenth and Seventeenth Centuries.* Trans. John and Anne Tedeschi. Baltimore: Johns Hopkins University Press, 1983.

Glendinning, Nigel. "Goya and Arriaza's *Profecia del Pirineo.*" *Journal of the Warburg and Courtauld Institutes* 26 (1963): 363–66.

———. "Goya and England in the Nineteenth Century." *Burlington Magazine* 106 (1964): 4–14.

———. *Goya and His Critics.* New Haven, Conn.: Yale University Press, 1977.

———. "The Strange Translation of Goya's Black Paintings." *Burlington Magazine* 117 (1975): 465–79.

Glendinning, Nigel, and Rolfe Kentish. "Goya's Country House in Madrid: The Quinta del Sordo." *Apollo* 123 (1986): 102–09.

Goedde, Lawrence O. "Naturalism as Convention: Subject, Style, and Artistic Self-Consciousness in Dutch Landscape." In *Looking at Seventeenth-Century Dutch Art: Realism Reconsidered*, ed. Wayne Franits, 129–43. Cambridge: Cambridge University Press, 1997.

Goldberg, Edward L. *After Vasari: History, Art, and Patronage in Late Medici Florence.* Princeton, N.J.: Princeton University Press, 1988.

Goodman, Dena. "Women and the Enlightenment." In Bridenthal, Stuard, and Wiesner, 233–62.

Gordon, Richard. "Imagining Greek and Roman Magic." In Ankarloo and Clark, 161–275.

———. "Lucan's Erichtho." In *Homo Viator: Classical Essays for John Bramble*, ed. Michael Whitby, Philip Hardie, and Mary Whitby, 231–41. Oak Park, Ill.: Bristol Classical, 1984.

Gottdang, Andrea. "Tiepolo's *Scherzi di Fantasia*: Begriff und Bedeutung." In Mai and Rees, 81–96.

Gowing, Lawrence. Review of *Goya's "Black Paintings": Truth and Reason in Light and Liberty*, by Patricia Muller. *Burlington Magazine* 128 (1986): 506–08.

Greenblatt, Stephen. *Renaissance Self-Fashioning: From More to Shakespeare.* Chicago: University of Chicago Press, 1980.

———. "Shakespeare and the Exorcists." In *Critical Essays on Shakespeare's King Lear*, ed. Jay Halio, 88–121. New York: G. K. Hall, 1996.

Grosz, Elizabeth. *Volatile Bodies: Toward a Corporeal Feminism*. Bloomington: Indiana University Press, 1994.

Guazzo, Francesco-Maria. *Compendium maleficarum*. Ed. and notes by Montague Summers, trans. E. A. Ashwin. New York: Barnes and Noble, 1970.

Guelfi, Fausta Franchini. "La pittura di Alessandro Magnasco dalle fonti figurative e culturali alle tenebre della realtà." In *Alessandro Magnasco*, 17–38. Milan: Palazzo Reale, 1996.

Hacker, Barton C. "Women and Military Institutions in Early Modern Europe: A Reconnaissance." *Signs* 6 (1981): 643–71.

Hale, John R. *Artists and Warfare in the Renaissance*. New Haven, Conn.: Yale University Press, 1990.

Hall, James. *Dictionary of Subjects and Symbols in Art*. Rev. ed. New York: Harper and Row, 1979.

Härting, Ursula Alice. "'Doctrina et pietas': Über frühe Galeriebilder." *Jaarboek van het Koninklijk Museum voor Schone Kunsten Antwerpen* (1993): 95–133.

———. *Frans Francken der Jüngere (1581–1642): Die Gemälde mit Kritischem Oeuvrekatalog*. Freren, Ger.: Luca Verlag, 1989.

Hartlaub, Gustav Friedrich. "Albrecht Dürers Aberglaube." *Zeitschrift für deutschen Verein für Kunstwissenschaft* 7 (1940): 167–96.

———. *Hans Baldung Grien: Hexenbilder*. Stuttgart: Philipp Reclam Jr., 1961.

Hartt, Frederick. *Giulio Romano*. New Haven, Conn.: Yale University Press, 1958.

Haskell, Francis, and Nicholas Penny. *Taste and the Antique: The Lure of Classical Sculpture, 1500–1900*. New Haven, Conn.: Yale University Press, 1981.

Haskell, Francis. *Patrons and Painters: Art and Society in Baroque Italy*. New Haven, Conn.: Yale University Press, 1980.

Held, Jutta, ed. *Goya, neue Forschungen: Das internationale Symposium 1991 in Osnabrück*. Berlin: Gebr. Mann, 1994.

Helman, Edith. "*Caprichos* and *Monstruos* of Cadalso and Goya." *Hispanic Review* 26 (1958): 200–222.

———. "The Elder Moratín and Goya." *Hispanic Review* 23 (1955): 219–30.

———. *Trasmundo de Goya*. Madrid: Revista de Occidente, 1963.

———. "The Younger Moratín and Goya: On *Duendes* and *Brujas*." *Hispanic Review* 27 (1959): 103–22.

Henningsen, Gustav. *The Witches' Advocate: Basque Witchcraft and the Spanish Inquisition (1609–1614)*. Reno: University of Nevada Press, 1980.

Herzig, Tamar. "The Demons' Reaction to Sodomy: Witchcraft and Homosexuality in Gianfrancesco Pico della Mirandola's *Strix*." *The Sixteenth Century Journal* 34 (2003): 53–72.

Hester, Marianne. "Patriarchal Reconstruction and Witch Hunting." In Barry, Hester, and Roberts, 288–306.

Hieatt, A. Kent, "Hans Baldung's Ottawa *Eve* and Its Context." *Art Bulletin* 65 (1983): 290–304.

Hoak, Dale. "Art, Culture, and Mentality in Renaissance Society: The Meaning of Hans Baldung Grien's *Bewitched Groom*." *Renaissance Quarterly* 38 (1985): 488–509.

Hofmann, Werner. *Goya: "To Every Story There Belongs Another."* London: Thames and Hudson, 2003.

———. "Unending Shipwreck." In Wilson-Bareau and Mena Marqués, 43–64.

Holmes, Clive. "Popular Culture? Witches, Magistrates and Divines." In *Understanding Popular Culture: Europe from the Middle Ages to the Nineteenth Century*, ed. Steven L. Kaplan, 85–111. New York: Mouton Publishers, 1984.

———. "Women: Witnesses and Witches." *Past and Present* 140 (1993): 45–78.

Honig, Elizabeth Alice. "The Beholder as Work of Art: A Study in the Location of Value in Seventeenth-Century Flemish Painting." *Nederlands kunsthistorisch Jaarboek* 46 (1995): 252–93.

———. *Painting and the Market in Early Modern Antwerp*. New Haven, Conn.: Yale University Press, 1998.

Horace. *The Complete Odes and Epodes with the Centennial Hymn*. Trans. W. G. Shepherd. Harmondsworth, Middlesex, U.K.: Penguin, 1983.

———. *Satires, Epistles and Ars Poetica*. Trans. H. Rushton Fairclough. Cambridge, Mass.: Harvard University Press, 1978.

Houdard, Sophie. *Les sciences du diable: Quatre discours sur la sorcellerie, XVe–XVIIe siècle*. Paris: Les Éditions du Cerf, 1992.

Hsia, Ronnie Po-Chia. *The Myth of Ritual Murder: Jews and Magic in Reformation Germany*. New Haven, Conn.: Yale University Press, 1988.

———. *The World of Catholic Renewal, 1540–1770*. Cambridge: Cambridge University Press, 1998.

Hsia, Ronnie Po-Chia, and Henk van Nierop, eds. *Calvinism and Religious Toleration in the Dutch Golden Age*. Cambridge: Cambridge University Press, 2002.

Hulse, Clark. *The Rule of Art: Literature and Painting in the Renaissance*. Chicago: University of Chicago Press, 1990.

Hults, Linda C. "Baldung and the Reformation." In Marrow and Shestack, 38–59.

———. "Baldung and the Witches of Freiburg: The Evidence of Images. *Journal of Interdisciplinary History* 18 (1987): 249–76.

———. "Baldung's *Bewitched Groom* Revisited: Artistic Temperament, Fantasy and the 'Dream of Reason.'" *The Sixteenth-Century Journal* 15 (1984): 260–79.

———. "Baldung's *Weather Witches* in Frankfurt." *Pantheon: Internationale Zeitschrift für Kunst* 40 (1982): 124–30.

———. "Dürer's *Four Witches* Reconsidered." In *Saints, Sinners and Sisters: Gender and Northern Art in Medieval & Early Modern Europe*, ed. Jane L. Carroll and Alison G. Stewart, 94–126. Aldershot, Hants, U.K.: Ashgate, 2003.

———. "Hans Baldung Grien and Albrecht Dürer: A Problem in Northern Mannerism." Ph.D. diss., University of North Carolina at Chapel Hill, 1978.

Humfrey, Peter, and Mauro Lucco. *Dosso Dossi: Court Painter in Renaissance Ferrara*. New York: Metropolitan Museum of Art, 1999.

Hutchison, Jane Campbell. *Albrecht Dürer: A Biography*. Princeton, N.J.: Princeton University Press, 1990.

———. "Forum: Dürer's Praxitelean Aphrodite." *Drawing* 13 (1991): 55–56.

Hyde, Melissa, and Jennifer Milam, eds. *Women, Art and the Politics of Identity in Eighteenth-Century Europe*. Aldershot, Hants, U.K.: Ashgate, 2003.

Ilie, Paul. "Concepts of the Grotesque before Goya." *Studies in Eighteenth-Century Culture* 5 (1976): 185–201.

———. "Goya's Teratology and the Critique of Reason." *Eighteenth-Century Studies* 18 (1984): 35–56.

Institut Néerlandais. *Le héraut du dix-septième siècle: Dessins et gravures de Jacques de Gheyn II et III de la Fondation Custodia Collection Frits Lugt*. Paris: Institut Néerlandais, 1985.

Jacobs, Fredrika H. *Defining the Renaissance Virtuosa: Women Artists and the Language of Art History and Criticism*. Cambridge: Cambridge University Press, 1997.

Jacobsen, Michael. "The Meaning of Mantegna's *Battle of the Sea Monsters*." *Art Bulletin* 64 (1982): 623–29.

Jacques-Chaquin, Nicole, and Maxime Préaud, eds. *Le sabbat des sorciers en Europe (XVe–XVIIIe siècles): Colloque international E. N. S. Fontenay-Saint-Cloud (4–7 Novembre 1992)*. Grenoble, Fr.: Jérôme Millon, 1993.

Jardine, Nicholas, James A. Secord, and Emma C. Spary, eds. *Cultures of Natural History*. Cambridge: Cambridge University Press, 1998.

Jerouschek, Günter, ed. *Nürnberger Hexenhammer 1491 von Heinrich Kramer (Institoris)*. Hildesheim, Ger. and New York: Georg Olms Verlag, 1992.

Jordan, Constance. *Renaissance Feminism: Literary Texts and Political Models*. Ithaca, N.Y.: Cornell University Press, 1990.

Judson, J. Richard. *The Drawings of Jacques de Gheyn II*. New York: Grossman, 1973.

———. "Jacob Isaacsz. van Swanenburgh and the Phlegraean Fields." In *Essays in Northern European Art Presented to Egbert Haverkamp-Begemann on His Sixtieth Birthday*, 119–22. Doornspijk, Neth.: Davaco, 1983.

———. "Rembrandt and Jacob de Gheyn II." In *Album Amicorum J. G. van Gelder*, ed. Joshua Bruyn et al., 207–10. The Hague: Martinus Nijhoff, 1974.

Junius, Franciscus. *The Painting of the Ancients*. Trans. Keith Aldrich, Philipp Fehl, and Raina Fehl. Berkeley: University of California Press, 1991.

Kanz, Roland. "Capriccio und Grotteske." In Mai and Rees, 13–32.

Kaplan, Benjamin J. *Calvinists and Libertines: Confession and Community in Utrecht, 1578–1620*. Oxford: Clarendon Press, 1995.

———. "'Dutch' Religious Tolerance: Celebration and Revision." In Hsia and van Nierop, 8–26.

Karant-Nunn, Susan C. "The Reformation of Women." In Bridenthal, Stuard, and Wiesner, 175–201.

Karras, Ruth Mazo. *From Boys to Men: Formations of Masculinity in Late Medieval Europe*. Philadelphia: University of Pennsylvania Press, 2003.

Kaufmann, Thomas DaCosta. "The *Kunstkammer* as a Form of *Representatio*." *Art Journal* 38 (1978): 22–28.

———. *The Mastery of Nature: Aspects of Art, Science and Humanism in the Renaissance*. Princeton, N.J.: Princeton University Press, 1995.

———. "Princely Patronage of the Later Sixteenth and Early Seventeenth Centuries: The Example and Impact of Art at the Court of Rudolf II." In *Court, Cloister and City: The Art and Culture of Central Europe, 1450–1800*, 185–203. Chicago: University of Chicago Press, 1995.

———. *The School of Prague: Painting at the Court of Rudolf II*. Chicago: University of Chicago Press, 1988.

Keller, Evelyn Fox. *Reflections on Gender and Science*. New Haven, Conn.: Yale University Press, 1985.

Kemp, Martin. "From 'Mimesis' to 'Fantasia': The Quattrocento Vocabulary of Creation, Inspiration and Genius in the Visual Arts." *Viator* 8 (1977): 347–98.

———. *Leonardo da Vinci: The Marvelous Works of Nature and Man*. Cambridge, Mass.: Harvard University Press, 1981.

Kieckhefer, Richard. "Avenging the Blood of Children: Anxiety over Child Victims and the Origins of the European Witch Trials." In *The Devil, Heresy and Witchcraft in the Middle Ages: Essays in Honor of Jeffrey B. Russell*, ed. Alberto Ferreiro, 91–109. Leiden: E. J. Brill, 1998.

———. *European Witch Trials: Their Foundations in Popular and Learned Culture, 1300–1500*. Berkeley: University of California Press, 1976.

Killermann, S. "Der Alraun (Mandragora)." *Naturwissenschaftliche Wochenschrift* 15 (18 March 1917): 137–44.

Kitts, Sally-Ann. *The Debate on the Nature, Role, and Influence of Woman in Eighteenth-Century Spain* (Lewiston, N.Y.: E. Mellen Press, 1995.

Klaits, Joseph. *Servants of Satan: The Age of the Witch-Hunts*. Bloomington: Indiana University Press, 1985.

Klein, Peter. "'La fantasía abandonada de la razón': Zur Darstellung des Wahnsinns in Goya's 'Hof der Irren.'" In Held, 161–94.

Klinge, Margret. *David Teniers the Younger: Paintings, Drawings*. Trans. David R. McLintock. Ghent: Snoeck, Ducaju and Zoon, 1991.

Koch, Carl. *Die Zeichnungen Hans Baldung Griens*. Berlin: Deutscher Verein für Kunstwissenschaft, 1941.

Koerner, Joseph Leo. "Albrecht Dürer: A Sixteenth-Century Influenza." In *Albrecht Dürer and his Legacy: The Graphic Work of a Renaissance Artist*, by Giulia Bartrum, with contributions by Günter Grass, Joseph Leo Koerner, and Ute Kuhlemann, 18–38. Princeton, N.J.: Princeton University Press, 2002.

———. *The Moment of Self-Portraiture in German Renaissance Art*. Chicago: University of Chicago Press, 1993.

Kors, Alan Charles, and Edward Peters, eds. *Witchcraft in Europe, 400–1700: A Documentary History*. 2nd ed. Philadelphia: University of Pennsylvania Press, 2001.

Kramer, Heinrich, and Jacob Sprenger. *Malleus maleficarum*. Trans. Montague Summers. New York: Dover, 1971.

Kristeva, Julia. *The Powers of Horror: An Essay on Abjection*. Trans. Leon S. Roudiez. New York: Columbia University Press, 1982.

Kunstmann, Hartmut. *Zauberwahn und Hexenprozess in der Reichsstadt Nürnberg*. Nuremberg: Korn und Berg, 1970.

Labouvie, Eva. "Men in Witchcraft Trials: Towards a Social Anthropology of 'Male' Understandings of Magic and Witchcraft." In *Gender in Early Modern German History*, ed. Ulinka Rublack, 49–68. Cambridge: Cambridge University Press, 2002.

Lancre, Pierre de. *Tableau de l'inconstance des mauvais anges et démons*. Ed. Nicole Jacques-Chaquin. Paris: Éditions Aubier, 1982. Quoted in Scholz Williams, 111.

Landau, David. "From Collaboration to Reproduction in Italy." In Landau and Parshall, 103–68.

Landau, David, and Peter Parshall. *The Renaissance Print, 1470–1550*. New Haven, Conn.: Yale University Press, 1994.

Langbein, John H. *Prosecuting Crime in the Renaissance: England, Germany, France*. Cambridge, Mass.: Harvard University Press, 1974.

Langdon, Helen. *Caravaggio: A Life*. Boulder, Colo.: Westview Press, 2000.

———. "Salvator Rosa in Florence, 1640–1649." *Apollo* 100 (1974): 190–97.

Larner, Christina. *Enemies of God: The Witch-Hunt in Scotland*. Baltimore: Johns Hopkins University Press, 1981.

Lea, Henry Charles. *Materials Toward a History of Witchcraft*. 3 vols. Philadelphia: University of Pennsylvania Press, 1939.

Leinweber, David. "Witchcraft and Lamiae in 'The Golden Ass.'" *Folklore* 105 (1994): 77–82.

Levack, Brian P. "State-Building and Witch Hunting in Early Modern Europe." In Barry, Hester, and Roberts, 99–107.

———. *The Witch-Hunt in Early Modern Europe*. New York: Longman, 1987.

Levenson, Jay A., Konrad Oberhuber, and Jacquelyn L. Sheehan. *Early Italian Engravings from the National Gallery of Art*. Washington, D.C.: National Gallery of Art, 1973.

Licht, Fred. *Goya*. New York: Abbeville Press, 2001.

———. *Goya: The Origins of the Modern Temper in Art*. New York: Universe Books, 1979.

Lightbown, Ronald W. *Mantegna: With a Complete Catalogue of the Paintings, Drawings, and Prints*. Berkeley: University of California Press, 1986.

———. *Sandro Botticelli: Life and Work*. 2 vols. New York: Abbeville Press, 1987.

Limentani, Uberto. *Poesie e lettere inedite di Salvator Rosa*. Florence: Limentani, 1950.

———. "Salvator Rosa: Nuovi contributi al Epistolario." *Studi Secenteschi* 8 (1972): 255–73.

———. "Salvator Rosa: Nuovi studi e ricerche." *Italian Studies* 8 (1953): 29–58.

———. "Salvator Rosa: Nuovi studi e ricerche." *Italian Studies* 10 (1954): 46–55.

Lincoln, Evelyn. *The Invention of the Italian Renaissance Printmaker*. New Haven, Conn.: Yale University Press, 2000.

Llorente, Juan Antonio. *Historia crítica de la Inquisición en España*. Madrid, 1822, vol. 3, 260. Cited in Pérez Sánchez and Sayre, 60.

Lombardi, Daniela. "Intervention by Church and State in Marriage Disputes in Sixteenth- and Seventeenth-Century Florence." In Dean and Lowe, 142–56.

Lorenz, Sönke, ed. *Hexen und Hexenverfolgung im Deutschen Südwesten*. 2 vols. Karlsruhe: Badisches Landesmuseum, 1994.

Löwensteyn, Machteld. "Helse hebzucht en wereldse wellust: een iconografische interpretatie van enkele heksenvoorstellingen van Jacques de Gheyn II." *Volkskundig Bulletin* 12 (1986): 241–61.

———. "Peindre le pandémonium païen: Images du sabbat des sorcières aux Pays-Bas." In Jacques-Chaquin and Préaud, 427–37.

Lucan. *Civil War*. Trans. Paul Frederick Widdows. Bloomington: Indiana University Press, 1988.

Lucas, Marijke S. "Het heksengeloof verbeld 17de eeuwse voorstellingen in de Nederlanden." *Jaarboek van het Koninklijk Museum voor Schone Kunsten Antwerpen* (1996): 91–140.

Lucian. *Luciana Opera*. Ed. M. D. MacLeod. Oxford: Oxford University Press, 1972.

Luck, George. "Witches and Sorcerers in Classical Literature." In Ankarloo and Clark, 91–158.

Lytle, Guy Fitch. "The Renaissance, the Reformation, and the City of Nuremberg." In *Nuremberg: A Renaissance City, 1500–1618*, by Jeffrey Chipps Smith, 17–22. Austin: Archer M. Huntington Art Gallery, the University of Texas, and University of Texas Press, 1983.

Macfarlane, Alan. *Witchcraft in Tudor and Stuart England: A Regional and Comparative Study*. New York: Harper and Row, 1970.

Maclean, Ian. *The Renaissance Notion of Woman: A Study in the Fortunes of Scholasticism and Medical Science in European Intellectual Life*. Cambridge: Cambridge University Press, 1980. Reprint, 1988.

Mahoney, Michael. *The Drawings of Salvator Rosa*. 2 vols. New York: Garland, 1977.

Mai, Ekkehard, and Joachim Rees, eds. *Kunstform Capriccio: Von der Groteske zur Spieltheorie der Moderne*. Cologne: Walter König, 1998.

Malvasia, Carlo Cesare. *Scritti originali del Conte Carlo Cesare Malvasia*. Ed. Lea Marzocchi. Bologna: ALFA, 1984, 135. Quoted in Scott, 111.

Manning, C. E. "Canidia in the *Epodes* of Horace." *Mnemosyne* 23 (1970): 393–401.

Mansbach, Steven A. "Goya's Liberal Iconography: Two Images of Jovellanos." *Journal of the Warburg and Courtauld Institutes* 41 (1978): 340–44.

Marrow, James, and Alan Shestack, eds. *Hans Baldung Grien: Prints and Drawings.* Washington, D.C.: National Gallery of Art, 1981.

Martin, John. "Journeys to the World of the Dead: The Work of Carlo Ginzburg." *Journal of Social History* 25 (1992): 613–26.

Martin, Ruth. *Witchcraft and the Inquisition in Venice, 1550–1650.* Oxford: Basil Blackwell, 1989.

Martineau, Jane, Susan Boorsch, et al., eds. *Andrea Mantegna.* London and New York: Royal Academy of Arts and the Metropolitan Museum of Art, 1992.

Mascalchi, Silvia. "Giovan Carlo de' Medici." *Apollo* 120 (1984): 268–72.

Meadow, Mark. "The Observant Pedestrian and Albrecht Dürer's *Promenade.*" *Art History* 15 (1992): 197–222.

Melion, Walter S. "Karel van Mander's 'Life of Goltzius': Defining the Paradigm of Protean Virtuosity in Haarlem around 1600." *Studies in the History of Art* 27 (1989): 113–33.

———. *Shaping the Netherlandish Canon: Karel Van Mander's Schilder-Boek.* Chicago: University of Chicago Press, 1991.

Mellinkoff, Ruth. "Riding Backwards: Theme of Humiliation and Symbol of Evil." *Viator* 4 (1973): 153–86.

Mena Marqués, Manuela B. "Must It Be So? It Must Be So!" In Wilson-Bareau and Mena Marques, 19–41.

Menz, Cäsar, ed. *Niklaus Manuel Deutsch: Maler, Dichter, Staatsmann.* Bern: Kunstmuseum Bern, 1979.

Mesenzeva, Charmian. "'Der Behexte Stallknecht' des Hans Baldung Griens." *Zeitschrift für Kunstgeschichte* 44 (1981): 57–61.

———. "Zum Problem. Dürer und die Antike: Albrecht Dürer's Kupferstich, 'Die Hexe.'" *Zeitschrift für Kunstgeschichte* 46 (1983): 187–202.

Michel, Marianne Roland. *Watteau, an Artist of the Eighteenth Century.* Secaucus, N.J.: Chartwell Books, 1984.

Michelet, Jules. *La Sorcière.* With chronology and preface by Paul Viallaneix. Paris: Garnier-Flammarion, 1966.

Midelfort, H. C. Erik. *Witch-Hunting in Southwestern Germany: The Social and Intellectual Foundations.* Stanford, Calif.: Stanford University Press, 1972.

Miedema, Hessel. "Over het realisme in de Nederlandse schilderkunst van de zeventiende eeuw, naar aanleidung van een tekening van Jacques de Gheyn II (1565–1632)." *Oud Holland* 89 (1975): 2–18.

Miles, Margaret R. *Carnal Knowing: Female Nakedness and Religious Meaning in the Christian West.* Boston: Beacon Press, 1989.

Milizia, Francesco. *Dizionario delle belle arti.* Bassano, 1797. Cited in Hofmann, "Unending Shipwreck," 50.

Monter, William. "The Historiography of European Witchcraft: Progress and Prospects." *Journal of Interdisciplinary History* 2 (1974): 435–51.

———. "The Pedestal and the Stake: Courtly Love and Witchcraft." In *Becoming Visible: Women in European History,* ed. Renate Bridenthal and Claudia Koontz, 119–36. Boston: Houghton Mifflin, 1977.

———. "Toads and Eucharists: The Male Witches of Normandy, 1564–1660." *French Historical Studies* 20 (1997): 563–95.

———. "Witch Trials in Continental Europe, 1550–1660." In *Witchcraft and Magic in Europe: The Period of the Witch Trials*, ed. Bengt Ankarloo, Stuart Clark, and William Monter, 3–52. Philadelphia: University of Pennsylvania Press, 2002.

Morford, Mark. *Stoics and Neostoics: Rubens and the Circle of Lipsius*. Princeton, N.J.: Princeton University Press, 1991.

Muchembled, Robert. "Lay Judges and the Acculturation of the Masses (France and the Southern Low Countries, Sixteenth to Eighteenth Centuries)." In *Religion and Society in Early Modern Europe, 1500–1800*, ed. Kaspar von Greyerz, 56–65. Boston: Allen and Unwin, 1984.

———. *Le roi et la sorcière: L'Europe des bûchers, XVe–XVIIIe siècle*. Paris: Desclée, 1993.

———. "Satanic Myths and Cultural Reality." In Ankarloo and Henningsen, 139–60.

———. "Terres de contrastes: France, Pays-Bas, Provinces Unies." In Muchembled and Ankarloo, 99–132.

———. "The Witches of the Cambrésis: The Acculturation of the Rural World in the Sixteenth and Seventeenth Centuries." In *Religion and the People, 800–1700*, ed. James Obelkevich, 221–76. Chapel Hill: University of North Carolina Press, 1979.

Muchembled, Robert, and Bengt Ankarloo, eds. *Magie et sorcellerie en Europe: Du moyen age à nos jours*. Paris: A. Colin, 1994.

Muir, Edward. "The Double Binds of Manly Revenge in Renaissance Italy." In *Gender Rhetoric: Postures of Dominance and Submission in History*, comp. Richard C. Trexler, 65–82. Binghamton, N.Y.: Medieval and Renaissance Texts and Studies, 1994.

Muir, Edward, and Guido Ruggiero, eds. *Sex and Gender in Historical Perspective*. Baltimore: Johns Hopkins University Press, 1990.

Muller, Jeffrey M. "Private Collections in the Spanish Netherlands: Ownership and Display of Paintings in Domestic Interiors." In *The Age of Rubens*, by Peter C. Sutton, 195–206. Boston: Museum of Fine Arts, 1994.

Muller, Priscilla E. *Goya's "Black" Paintings: Truth and Reason in Light and Liberty*. New York: Hispanic Society of America, 1984.

Murray, Margaret Alice. *The Witch-Cult in Western Europe: A Study in Anthropology*. Oxford: Oxford University Press, 1921.

Museum Boymans-van Beuningen. *Jacques de Gheyn II: Drawings*. Rotterdam: Museum Boymans-van Beuningen, 1986.

The New Hollstein Dutch and Flemish Etchings, Engravings and Woodcuts, 1450–1700. Comp. Ilja Veldman; ed. Ger Luijten. Roosendaal, Neth.: Koninklijke Van Poll in cooperation with the Rijksprentenkabinet, Rijksmuseum, Amsterdam, 1993–.

The New Interpreter's Bible. 12 vols. Nashville, Tenn.: Abingdon Press, 1994–98.

Nordström, Folke. *Goya, Saturn and Melancholy: Studies in the Art of Goya*. Stockholm: Almkvist and Wiksell, 1962.

Oberman, Heiko A. "Discovery of Hebrew and Discrimination against the Jews: The *Veritas Hebraica* as Double-Edged Sword in Renaissance and Reformation." In *Germania Illustrata: Essays on Early Modern Germany Presented to Gerald Strauss*, ed. Andrew Fix and Susan C. Karant-Nunn, 19–34. Kirksville, Mo.: Sixteenth Century Journal Publishers, 1992.

Ogden, Daniel. "Binding Spells: Curse Tablets and Voodoo Dolls in the Greek and Roman Worlds." In Ankarloo and Clark, 3–90.

Oliensis, Ellen. "Canidia, Canicula, and the Decorum of Horace's *Epodes*." *Arethusa* 24 (1991): 107–35.

———. *Horace and the Rhetoric of Authority*. Cambridge: Cambridge University Press, 1998.

Orenstein, Nadine Monica. *Hendrik Hondius and the Business of Prints in Seventeenth-Century Holland*. Rotterdam: Sound and Vision Interactive, 1996.

———. "Print Publishers in the Netherlands." In *Dawn of the Golden Age: Northern Netherlandish Art, 1580–1620*, ed. Ger Luijten, Ariane van Suchtelen, et al., 167–200. Amsterdam: Rijksmuseum, 1993.

Orenstein, Nadine Monica, ed. *Pieter Bruegel the Elder: Drawings and Prints*. New York: Metropolitan Museum of Art, 2001.

Panofsky, Erwin. *The Life and Art of Albrecht Dürer*. 4th rev. ed. Princeton, N.J.: Princeton University Press, 1971.

———. *Studies in Iconology: Humanistic Themes in the Art of the Renaissance*. New York: Oxford University Press, 1939.

Parker, Patricia A. *Literary Fat Ladies: Rhetoric, Gender, Property*. London: Methuen, 1987.

Parshall, Peter. "The Cultivation of the Woodcut in the North." In Landau and Parshall, 169–259.

Passeri, Giovanni Battista. *Vite de' pittore, scultori, ed architetti che hanno lavorato in Roma, morti dal 1641 fino al 1673*. Ed. Jacob Hess. Leipzig and Vienna: H. Keller, 1934, 387. Trans. and quoted in J. Scott, 8, 21, 72–73.

Paulson, Ronald. *Representations of Revolution (1789–1820)*. New Haven, Conn.: Yale University Press, 1983.

Pearl, Jonathan L. Introduction to *On the Demon-Mania of Witches*, by Jean Bodin.

———. *The Crime of Crimes: Demonology and Politics in France, 1560–1620*. Waterloo, Ont.: Wilfred Laurier University Press, 1999.

Percy, Ann. *Giovanni Benedetto Castiglione: Master Draughtsman of the Italian Baroque*. Philadelphia: Philadelphia Museum of Art, 1971.

Pérez Sánchez, Alfonso E., and Eleanor A. Sayre, eds. *Goya and the Spirit of Enlightenment*. With contributions by Gonzalo Anes, Michael Armstrong Roche, Jeannine Baticle, Nigel Glendinning, Fred Licht, et al. Boston: Museum of Fine Arts, 1989.

Pico della Mirandola, Gianfrancesco. *On the Imagination*. Trans. Harry Caplan. Ithaca, N.Y.: Cornell University Press, 1930.

Poesch, Jesse. "Sources for Two Dürer Enigmas." *Art Bulletin* 46 (1964): 78–86.

Pollmann, Judith. "The Bond of Christian Piety: The Individual Practice of Tolerance and Intolerance in the Dutch Republic." In Hsia and van Nierop, 53–71.

———. *Religious Choice in the Dutch Republic: The Reformation of Arnoldus Buchelius (1565–1641)*. Manchester, U.K.: Manchester University Press, 1999.

Populus, Bernard. *Claude Gillot: Catalogue de l'oeuvre gravé*. Paris: Société pour l'Étude de la Gravure Française, 1930.

Prohaska, Wolfgang. *Kunsthistorisches Museum, Vienna: The Paintings*. Trans. Judith Hayward. London: Philip Wilson Publishers, 1997.

Purkiss, Diane. *The Witch in History: Early Modern and Twentieth-Century Representations*. London: Routledge, 1996.

Puttfarken, Thomas. "Poussin's Thoughts on Painting." In *Commemorating Poussin: Reception and Interpretation of the Artist*, ed. Katie Scott and Genevieve Warwick, 53–75. Cambridge: Cambridge University Press, 1999.

Rabelais, François. *Gargantua and Pantagruel*. Trans. Burton Raffel. New York: Norton, 1990.

Rabinowitz, Jacob. *The Rotting Goddess: The Origin of the Witch in Classical Antiquity*. Brooklyn, N.Y.: Autonomedia, 1998.

Radbruch, Gustav. "Hans Baldungs Hexenbilder." In *Elegantiae juris criminalis: Vierzehn Studien zur Geschichte des Stafrechts*, 30–48. Basel: Verlag für Recht und Gesellschaft, 1950.

Rees, Joachim. "Das Capriccio und die Privatisierung der Bildwelt in Interieurs des 18. Jahrhunderts." In Mai and Rees, 113–37.

Remón Menéndez, Juan F. "The Alameda of the Duchess of Osuna: A Garden of Ideas." *Journal of Garden History* 13 (1993): 224–40.

Reuss, Rodolphe. *La sorcellerie au seizième et au dix–septième siècle, particulièrement en Alsace*. Paris: Cherbuliez, 1871.

Reznicek, Emil Karl Josef. "Realism as a 'Side Road or Byway' in Dutch Art." In *Studies in Western Art: Acts of the Twentieth International Congress of the History of Art*. Vol. 2, *The Renaissance and Mannerism*, ed. Ida Ely Rubin, 247–53. Princeton, N.J.: Princeton University Press, 1963.

———. "Two 'Masters of the Pen.'" In Museum Boymans-van Beuningen, 13–18.

Richards, Louise. "Antonio Pollaiuolo: *Battle of Naked Men*." *Bulletin of the Cleveland Museum of Art* 55 (1968): 61–70.

Richlin, Amy. *The Garden of Priapus: Sexuality and Aggression in Roman Humor*. Oxford: Oxford University Press, 1992.

———. "Invective against Women in Roman Satire." *Arethusa* 17 (1984): 67–80.

Robbins, Rossell Hope. *Encyclopedia of Witchcraft and Demonology*. New York: Bonanza Books, 1959.

Roberts, Gareth. s.v. "Circe." In *The Spenser Encyclopedia*, ed. Albert Charles Hamilton. Toronto: University of Toronto Press, 1990.

———. "The Descendants of Circe: Witches and Renaissance Fictions." In Barry, Hester, and Roberts, 183–206.

Rooijakkers, Gerard, Lène Dresen-Coenders, and Margaret Geerdes, eds. *Duivelsbeelden: Een cultuurhistorisches speurtocht door de Lage Landen*. Baarn, Neth.: Uitgeverij Ambo, 1994.

Roper, Lyndal. *Oedipus and the Devil: Witchcraft, Sexuality and Religion in Early Modern Europe*. London: Routledge, 1994.

Rosaldo, Michele. "Theoretical Overview." In Rosaldo and Lamphere, 17–42.

Rosaldo, Michele, and Louise Lamphere. Introduction to Rosaldo and Lamphere.

———, eds. *Woman, Culture and Society*. Stanford, Calif.: Stanford University Press, 1974.

Rosenthal, Angela. "Angelica's Odyssey: Kauffman's Paintings of Penelope and the Weaving of Narrative." In Hyde and Millam, 211–36.

Roskamp, Diedrich. "Eine 'Hexenszene' von David Teniers d.j." *Jahrbuch der Hamburger Kunstsammlungen* 8 (1963): 7–32.

Roussel, Pierre. *Système physique et moral de la femme* (Paris, 1775), 30. Quoted in Steinbrügge, 37.

Röver-Kann, Anne, ed. *Albrecht Dürer: Das Frauenbad von 1496*. Bremen: Kunsthalle, 2001.

Rowan, Steven W. *Ulrich Zasius: A Jurist in the German Renaissance, 1461–1535*. Frankfurt am Main: Vittorio Klostermann, 1987.

Rowland, Robert. "'Fantasticall and Devilishe Persons': European Witch-Beliefs in Comparative Perspective." In Ankarloo and Henningsen, 161–90.

Rowlands, Alison. "Witchcraft and Old Women in Early Modern Germany." *Past and Present* 173 (2001): 50–89.

Roworth, Wendy Wassyng. "The Consolations of Friendship: Salvator Rosa's Self-

Portrait for Giovanni Battista Ricciardi." *Metropolitan Museum Journal* 23 (1988): 103–22.

———. *"Pictor Succensor": A Study of Salvator Rosa as Satirist, Cynic, and Painter.* New York: Garland, 1978.

Roworth, Wendy Wassyng, ed. *Angelica Kauffmann: A Continental Artist in Georgian England.* London: Reaktion Books, 1993.

Rummel, Erika. *Erasmus on Women.* Toronto: University of Toronto Press, 1996.

Russell, H. Diane. *Rare Etchings by Giovanni Battista and Giovanni Domenico Tiepolo.* Washington, D.C.: National Gallery of Art, 1972.

Russell, H. Diane, with Bernadine Barnes. *Eva/Ave: Woman in Renaissance and Baroque Prints.* Washington, D.C. and New York: National Gallery of Art in association with the Feminist Press at the City University of New York, 1990.

Russo, Mary. *The Female Grotesque: Risk, Excess, and Modernity.* London: Routledge, 1994.

Ruvoldt, Maria. *The Italian Renaissance Imagery of Inspiration.* Cambridge: Cambridge University Press, 2004.

Salerno, Luigi. "Four Witchcraft Scenes by Salvator Rosa." *Cleveland Museum Bulletin* 65 (1978): 224–31.

———. *L'opera completa di Salvator Rosa.* Milan: Rizzoli, 1975.

Sayre, Eleanor A. *The Changing Image: Prints by Francisco Goya.* Boston: Museum of Fine Arts, 1974.

———. "Goya's Caprichos: A Sampling of Witches." In Held, 67–87.

Schade, Sigrid. "Kunsthexen-Hexenkünste." In *Hexenwelten: Magie und Imagination vom 16–20 Jahrhundert*, ed. Richard van Dülmen, 170–207. Frankfurt: Fischer Taschenbuch Verlag, 1987.

———. *Schadenzauber und die Magie des Körpers: Hexenbilder der frühen Neuzeit.* Worms, Ger.: Werner'sche Verlagsgesellschaft, 1983.

Schama, Simon. *The Embarrassment of Riches: An Interpretation of Dutch Culture in the Golden Age.* New York: Knopf, 1987.

Schiesari, Juliana. *The Gendering of Melancholia: Feminism, Psychoanalysis, and the Symbolics of Loss in Renaissance Literature.* Ithaca, N.Y.: Cornell University Press, 1992.

Schilling, Heinz. *Religion, Political Culture and the Emergence of Early Modern Society: Essays in German and Dutch History.* Leiden: E. J. Brill, 1992.

Schneider, Norbert. *The Art of the Still Life: Still Life Painting in the Early Modern Period.* Cologne: Benedikt Taschen Verlag, 1990.

Scholz Williams, Gerhild. *Defining Dominion: The Discourses of Magic and Witchcraft in Early Modern France and Germany.* Ann Arbor: University of Michigan Press, 1995.

———. "On Finding Words: Witchcraft and the Discourses of Dissidence and Discovery." In *The Graph of Sex and the German Text: Gendered Culture in Early Modern Europe, 1500–1700*, ed. Lynne Tatlock, Atlanta, Ga.: Rodopi, 1994.

Schulz, Andrew. "Goya's Portraits of the Duchess of Osuna: Fashioning Identity in Enlightenment Spain." In Hyde and Milam, 263–83.

Scot, Reginald. *The Discoverie of Witchcraft.* Carbondale: Southern Illinois University Press, 1964.

Scott, Joan Wallach. "Gender: A Useful Category of Analysis." In *Gender and the Politics of History*, 28–50. New York: Columbia University Press, 1988.

———. "Women's History." In *American Feminist Thought at Century's End: A Reader*, ed. Linda S. Kaufmann, 234–57. Cambridge, Mass.: Blackwell, 1993.

Scott, Jonathan. *Salvator Rosa: His Life and Times*. New Haven, Conn.: Yale University Press, 1995.

Scott, Tom. *Freiburg and the Breisgau: Town-Country Relations in the Age of Reformation and the Peasants' War*. Oxford: Clarendon Press, 1986.

Scully, Sally. "Marriage or a Career?: Witchcraft as an Alternative in Seventeenth-Century Venice." *Journal of Social History* 28 (1995): 857–76.

Sheriff, Mary D. *The Exceptional Woman: Elisabeth Vigée-Lebrun and the Cultural Politics of Art*. Chicago: University of Chicago Press, 1996.

Shestack, Alan. "An Introduction to Hans Baldung Grien." In Marrow and Shestack, 3–18.

Silver, Larry. "Forest Primeval: Albrecht Altdorfer and the German Wilderness Landscape." *Simiolus* 13 (1983): 4–43.

———. "Germanic Patriotism in the Age of Dürer." In *Dürer and His Culture*, ed. Dagmar Eichberger and Charles Zika, 38–68. Cambridge: Cambridge University Press, 1998.

———. "Imitation and Emulation: Goltzius as Evolutionary Reproductive Engraver." In *Graven Images: The Rise of Professional Printmakers in Antwerp and Haarlem, 1540–1640*, ed. Timothy Riggs and Larry Silver, 71–99. Evanston, Ill.: The Mary and Leigh Block Gallery, Northwestern University, 1993.

———. "Nature and Nature's God: Landscape and Cosmos of Albrecht Altdorfer." *Art Bulletin* 81 (1999): 194–214.

———. "Second Bosch: Family Resemblance and the Marketing of Art." *Nederlands kunsthistorisch Jaarboek* 50 (1999): 30–56.

Silver, Larry, and Susan L. Smith. "Carnal Knowledge: The Late Engravings of Lucas van Leyden." *Nederlands Kunsthistorisch Jaarboek* 29 (1978): 239–98.

Simons, Patricia. "Women in Frames: The Gaze, the Eye, the Profile." In *The Expanding Discourse: Feminism and Art History*, ed. Norma Broude and Mary D. Garrard, 39–57. Boulder, Colo.: Westview Press, 1993.

Simpson, Jacqueline. "Margaret Murray: Who Believed Her, and Why?" *Folklore* 105 (1994): 89–96.

Smith, Susan L. *The Power of Women: A Topos in Medieval Art and Literature*. Philadelphia: University of Pennsylvania Press, 1995.

Sneller, A. Agnes. "'If She Had Been a Man . . .': Anna Maria van Schurman in the Social and Literary Life of her Age." In de Baar et al., 133–49.

Snyder, James, ed. *Bosch in Perspective*. Englewood Cliffs, N.J.: Prentice Hall, 1973.

Sohm, Philip. "Baroque Piles and Other Decompositions." In *Pictorial Composition from Medieval to Modern Art*, ed. François Quiviger and Paul Taylor, 58–90. London: Warburg Institute Colloquia, 2000.

———. *Style in the Art Theory of Early Modern Italy*. Cambridge: Cambridge University Press, 2001.

Soly, Hugo. "Social Relations in Antwerp in the Sixteenth and Seventeenth Centuries." In van der Stock, 37–47.

Soman, Alfred. *Sorcellerie et justice criminelle: Le Parlement de Paris (16e–18e siècles)*. Aldershot, Hants, U.K.: Ashgate, 1992.

Spear, Richard. *The "Divine" Guido: Religion, Sex, Money, and Art in the World of Guido Reni*. New Haven, Conn.: Yale University Press, 1997.

———. "Scrambling for *Scudi*: Notes on Painters' Earnings in Early Baroque Rome." *Art Bulletin* 85 (2003): 310–20.

Spee, Friedrich. *Cautio Criminalis, or, a Book on Witch Trials*. Trans. Marcus Hellyer. Charlottesville: University of Virginia Press, 2003.

Spell, Jefferson Rea. *Rousseau in the Spanish World before 1833: A Study in Franco-Spanish Literary Relations*. Austin: University of Texas Press, 1938. Reprint, New York: Gordian Press, 1969.

Spenser, Edmund. *The Faerie Queene*. Ed. Thomas P. Roche Jr., with the assistance of C. Patrick O'Donnell Jr. New Haven, Conn.: Yale University Press, 1981.

Stallybrass, Peter. "Patriarchal Territories: The Body Enclosed." In *Rewriting the Renaissance: The Discourses of Sexual Difference in Early Modern Europe*, ed. Margaret W. Ferguson, Maureen Quilligan, and Nancy J. Vickers, 123–42. Chicago: University of Chicago Press, 1986.

Steinbrügge, Lieselotte. *The Moral Sex: Woman's Nature in the French Enlightenment*. Trans. Pamela E. Selwyn. Oxford: Oxford University Press, 1995.

Stephens, Walter. *Demon Lovers: Witchcraft, Sex, and the Crisis of Belief*. Chicago: University of Chicago Press, 2002.

Stewart, Alison G. "Paper Festivals and Popular Entertainments: Beham's Kermis Woodcuts." *The Sixteenth-Century Journal* 24 (1993): 343–50.

———. "Sebald Beham's *Fountain of Youth-Bathhouse* Woodcut: Popular Entertainment and Large Prints by the Little Masters." *Register of the Spencer Museum of Art* 6 (1989): 64–88.

———. *Unequal Lovers: A Study of Unequal Couples in Northern Art*. New York: Abaris Books, 1977.

Stone-Ferrier, Linda. *Dutch Prints of Daily Life: Mirrors of Life or Masks of Morals?* Lawrence: Spencer Museum of Art, University of Kansas, 1983.

Strauss, Gerald. *Law, Resistance, and the State: The Opposition to Roman Law in Reformation Germany*. Princeton, N.J.: Princeton University Press, 1986.

———. *Sixteenth Century Germany: Its Topography and Topographers*. Madison: The University of Wisconsin Press, 1959.

Strauss, Walter L. *The Complete Drawings of Albrecht Dürer*. 6 vols. New York: Abaris Books, 1974.

———. *Hendrik Goltzius, 1558–1617: The Complete Engravings and Woodcuts*. 2 vols. New York: Abaris Books, 1977.

———. "The Wherewithal of Witches." *Source* 2 (1980): 16–22.

Strocchia, Sharon T. "Gender and the Rites of Honour in Italian Renaissance Cities." In Brown and Davis, 39–60.

Sullivan, Margaret A. "The Witches of Dürer and Hans Baldung Grien." *Renaissance Quarterly* 53 (2000): 332–401.

Summers, David. *Michelangelo and the Language of Art*. Princeton, N.J.: Princeton University Press, 1981.

Swan, Claudia. "*Ad vivum, naer het leven*, from the Life: Defining a Mode of Representation." *Word and Image* 11 (1995): 353–72.

———. "Jacques de Gheyn II and the Representation of the Natural World in the Netherlands ca. 1600." Ph.D. diss., Columbia University, 1997.

———. "*The Preparation for the Sabbath* by Jacques de Gheyn II: The Issue of Inversion," *Print Quarterly* 16 (1999): 327–39.

Swanson, Robert Norman. "Angels Incarnate: Clergy and Masculinity from Gregorian Reform to Reformation." In *Masculinity in Medieval Europe*, ed. Dawn M. Hadley, 160–77. New York: Longman, 1995.

Symmons, Sarah. *Goya in Pursuit of Patronage*. London: Gordon Fraser Gallery, 1988.

Tacitus. *The Agricola and the Germania*. Trans. H. Mattingly. Harmondsworth, Middlesex, U.K.: Penguin Books, 1970.

Tafuri, Manfredo, et al. *Giulio Romano*. Trans. Fabio Barry. Cambridge: Cambridge University Press, 1998.

Tallett, Frank. *War and Society in Early Modern Europe*. London: Routledge, 1992.

Talvacchia, Bette. *Taking Positions: The Erotic in Renaissance Culture*. Princeton, N.J.: Princeton University Press, 1999.

Tanner, Marie. *The Last Descendant of Aeneas: The Hapsburgs and the Mythic Image of the Emperor*. New Haven, Conn.: Yale University Press, 1993.

Tedeschi, John. *The Prosecution of Heresy: Collected Studies on the Inquisition of Early Modern Italy*. Binghamton, N.Y.: Medieval and Renaissance Texts and Studies, 1991.

Theocritus. *Idylls*. Trans. Anthony Verity. Oxford: Oxford University Press, 2002.

Thomas, Keith. *Religion and the Decline of Magic: Studies in Popular Beliefs in Sixteenth and Seventeenth Century England*. London: Weidenfeld and Nicolson, 1971.

Tomlinson, Janis A. *Francisco Goya: The Tapestry Cartoons and Early Career at the Court of Madrid*. Cambridge: Cambridge University Press, 1989.

———. *Goya in the Twilight of Enlightenment*. New Haven, Conn.: Yale University Press, 1992.

———. *Graphic Evolutions: The Print Series of Francisco Goya*. New York: Columbia University Press, 1989.

Tomlinson, Janis A., ed. *Goya: Images of Women*. Washington, D.C., and New Haven, Conn.: National Gallery of Art in association with Yale University Press, 2001.

Traub, Valerie. "Gendering Mortality in Early Modern Anatomies." In *Feminist Readings of Early Modern Culture: Emerging Subjects*, ed. Valerie Traub, M. Lindsey Kaplan, and Dympna Callaghan, 44–92. Cambridge: Cambridge University Press, 1996.

Trevor-Roper, Hugh. *The European Witch-Craze of the Sixteenth and Seventeenth Centuries and Other Essays*. New York: Harper and Row, 1969.

Trouille, Mary Seidman. *Sexual Politics in the Enlightenment: Women Writers Read Rousseau*. Albany: State University of New York Press, 1997.

Turner, Gerard l'Estrange. "The Cabinet of Experimental Philosophy." In *The Origins of Museums: The Cabinet of Curiosities in Sixteenth and Seventeenth-Century Europe*, ed. Oliver Impey and Arthur MacGregor, 214–22. Oxford: Oxford University Press, 1985.

Unverfehrt, Gerd. *Hieronymus Bosch: Die Rezeption seiner Kunst im frühen 16 Jahrhundert*. Berlin: Gebr. Mann, 1980.

van der Stock, Jan, ed. *Antwerp: Story of a Metropolis, 16th–17th Century*. Ghent: Snoeck-Ducaju and Zoon, 1993.

van Dorsten, Jan A. *Thomas Basson, 1553–1613: English Printer at Leiden*. Leiden: University of Leiden, 1961.

van Dülmen, Richard. *Theatre of Horror: Crime and Punishment in Early Modern Germany*. Trans. Elisabeth Neu. Cambridge, U.K.: Polity Press, 1990.

van Mander, Karel. *Den Grondt der edel vry schilder-const*. Trans. and with commentary by Hessel Miedema. 2 vols. Utrecht: Haentjens Dekker and Gumbert, 1973.

———. *The Lives of the Illustrious Netherlandish and German Painters*. Trans. and with commentary by Hessel Miedema. 6 vols. Doornspijk, Neth.: Davaco, 1994–99.

van Regteren Altena, I. Q. "Grotten in de tuinen der Oranjes." *Oud Holland* 85 (1970): 33–44.

———. *Jacques de Gheyn: Three Generations, I–III*. 3 vols. The Hague: Martinus Nijhoff, 1983.

van Thiel, Pieter J. J. "*Poor Parents, Rich Children*, and *Family Saying Grace*: Two Related Aspects of the Iconography of Late Sixteenth- and Seventeenth-Century Dutch Domestic Morality." *Simiolus* 17 (1987): 90–149.

van Wilckens, Leonie, and Peter Strieder, eds. *Vorbild Dürer: Kupferstiche und Holzschnitte Albrecht Dürers im Spiegel der europäische Druckgraphik des 16. Jahrhunderts.* Munich: Prestel Verlag, 1978.

Vasari, Giorgio. *Lives of the Most Eminent Painters, Sculptors, and Architects.* Trans. Gaston du C. de Vere, 10 vols. London: Macmillan, 1912–15, vol. 6, 210, quoted in F. Barasch, 20.

———. *The Lives of the Artists.* Ed. and trans. Julia Conaway Bondanella and Peter Bondanella. Oxford: Oxford University Press, 1991. Reprint, 1998.

Vassall, Elizabeth. *The Spanish Journal of Elizabeth, Lady Holland.* Ed. The Earl of Ilchester. London: Longmans, Green and Co., 1910. Quoted in Remón Menéndez, 231.

Veldman, Ilja M. "Images of Labor and Diligence in Sixteenth-Century Netherlandish Prints: The Work Ethic Rooted in Civic Morality or Protestantism." *Simiolus* 21 (1992): 227–64.

Vickers, Michael. "The Sources of *Invidia* in Mantegna's *Battle of the Sea Gods.*" *Apollo* 106 (1977): 270–73.

Virgil. *Eclogues, Georgics, Aeneid I–V.* Trans. H. Rushton Fairclough. Cambridge, Mass: Harvard University Press, 1916; reprint, 1978.

Volland, Gerlinde. *Männermacht und Frauenopfer: Sexualität und Gewalt bei Goya.* Berlin: Reiner, 1993.

von der Osten, Gert. *Hans Baldung Grien: Gemälde und Dokumente.* Berlin: Deutscher Verein für Kunstwissenschaft, 1983.

von Sandrart, Joachim. *Teutsche Academie der Edlen Bau-, Bild, und Mahlerey-Künste.* Ed. A. R. Pelzer. Munich: G. Hirth's Verlag, 1925.

Voogt, Gerrit. *Constraint on Trial: Dirck Volckertsz Coornhert and Religious Freedom.* Kirksville, Mo.: Truman State University Press, 2000.

Wagner, Hugo. "Niklaus Manuel—Leben und künsterlisches Werk," In *Niklaus Manuel Deutsch: Maler, Dichter, Staatsman*, ed. Cäsar Menz and Hugo Wagner, 17–41. Bern: Kunstmuseum, 1979.

Wallace, Richard W. *The Etchings of Salvator Rosa.* Princeton, N.J.: Princeton University Press, 1979.

Wendenhorst, Alfred. "Nuremberg, the Imperial City: From its Beginnings to the End of its Glory." In Metropolitan Museum of Art. *Gothic and Renaissance Art in Nuremberg, 1300–1550*, 11–26. New York: Metropolitan Museum of Art, 1986.

Weyer, Johann. *De praestigiis daemonum.* Trans. John Shea. Binghamton, N.Y.: Medieval and Renaissance Texts and Studies, 1991.

Whaley, Leigh Ann. *Women's History as Scientists: A Guide to the Debates.* Santa Barbara, Calif: ABC-Clio, 2003.

Whitaker, Katie. "The Culture of Curiosity." In Jardine, Secord, and Spary, 75–90.

Wiesner, Merry E. *Gender, Church, and State in Early Modern Germany.* New York: Longman, 1998.

———. *Women and Gender in Early Modern Europe.* 2nd ed. Cambridge: Cambridge University Press, 2000.

Wiesner-Hanks, Merry E. *Christianity and Sexuality in the Early Modern World: Regulating Desire, Reforming Practice.* London: Routledge, 2000.

Wilenski, Reginald Howard. *Flemish Painters, 1430–1830.* 2 vols. New York: Viking, 1960.

Williams, Gwyn A. *Goya and the Impossible Revolution*. New York: Pantheon, 1976.

Wilson-Bareau, Juliet, and Manuela B. Mena Marqués, eds. *Goya: Truth and Fantasy, the Small Paintings*. New Haven, Conn.: Yale University Press, 1994.

Winkler, John W. *The Constraints of Desire: The Anthropology of Sex and Gender in Ancient Greece*. London: Routledge, 1990.

Wolf, Reva. "Sexual Identity, Mask and Disguise in Goya's 'Los Caprichos.'" In Held, 89–110.

Wood, Christopher S. *Albrecht Altdorfer and the Origins of Landscape*. Chicago: University of Chicago Press, 1993.

———. "'Curious Pictures' and the Art of Description." *Word and Image* 11 (1995): 32–52.

Wootten, David. "Reginald Scot/Abraham Fleming/The Family of Love." In Clark, *Languages of Witchcraft*, 119–38.

Wunder, Heide. *He Is the Sun, She Is the Moon: Women in Early Modern Germany*. Trans. Thomas Dunlap. Cambridge, Mass.: Harvard University Press, 1998.

Wustmann, Rudolf. "Von einigen Tieren und Pflanzen bei Dürer." *Zeitschrift für bildende Kunst* 22 (1911): 109–16.

Yates, Wilson. "An Introduction to the Grotesque: Theoretical and Theological Considerations." In *The Grotesque in Art and Literature: Theological Reflections*, ed. James Luther Adams and Wilson Yates, 1–68. Grand Rapids, Mich.: William B. Eerdmans Publishing Co., 1997.

Zack, Naomi. *Bachelors of Science: Seventeenth-Century Identity, Then and Now*. Philadelphia, Pa.: Temple University Press, 1996.

Zika, Charles. *Exorcising Our Demons: Magic, Witchcraft, and Visual Culture in Early Modern Europe*. Leiden: E. J. Brill, 2003.

Index

Page numbers in italics refer to illustrations.

Acknowledgments

As readers will discern from my notes and bibliography, *The Witch as Muse* owes much to many scholars—from art historians to historians, literary critics, and theorists of gender. I hope I have done justice to their efforts as I incorporated them into this book. In these acknowledgments, I would like to recognize some of the most significant influences on my scholarship.

My major professors in graduate school (John Dixon, Jaroslav Folda, Frances Huemer, and Donald Kuspit, among others) exemplified the interpretive richness and depth of a broadly contextual form of art history, and their instruction is still very much a part of this book. For me, despite recent theoretical enrichments, the best art history remains grounded in works of art and the myriad aspects of their historical contexts. The art historians whose exemplary work in that vein is woven into this book are too numerous to name individually, but their influence is amply evident.

The earliest study by a historian that shaped my approach is Norman Cohn's *Europe's Inner Demons* (1975), which alerted me to witchcraft's utility as a rhetorical construction with a wide range of political, religious and social implications. The most important recent book for this kind of understanding is surely Stuart Clark's *Thinking with Demons* (1997), which confirms the profound importance of the idea of witchcraft for early modern thought, history, and culture. Of the many historians whose specific regional or topical studies of the witch-hunts have shaped my analysis of the images, those who center their inquiries on early modern women—such as Marianne Hester, Anne Barstow, and Lyndal Roper—have repeatedly brought me back to a focus on women and gender amid the daunting complexity of this topic.

Literary studies provided me with indispensable interpretive models that I adapted to this endeavor. A postdoctoral seminar on the careers of early modern writers at the Pennsylvania State University in the summer of 1993, directed by Frederick de Armas and Patrick Cheney, helped me think about the relationship between artists' use of the witchcraft theme and their artistic self-presentation. Diane Purkiss's *The Witch in History* (1996), emerging from her work on English drama, exemplified for me a rich understanding of witchcraft that is both diachronic and synchronic, takes account of social reality as well as cultural expression, and maintains a focus on gender. The feminist criticism of classical scholars Amy Richlin and Ellen Oliensis provided me with a way of conceptualizing early modern artists' interest in ancient literary accounts of witches. In addition, Mark Breitenberg's *Anxious Masculinity in Early Modern England* (1996) represented a major turning point at which I began to see the importance of masculine identity for my own research on witchcraft images.

I also owe a professional debt of gratitude to the College of Wooster for helping me complete this project. Faculty Development Funds enabled me to attend the Penn State seminar mentioned above and a variety of other professional conferences that enriched my thinking. Monies from the Henry Luce III Fund for Distinguished Scholarship went toward the completion of the index. Most significantly, the college provided two essential sabbatical leaves, one for a full year in 1998–99 and one for the fall semester of 2003. At a deeper level, the interdisciplinary inquiry fostered by Wooster's curriculum and exemplified in the work of its faculty and students, especially in the Department of Art and the Women's Studies Program, has decisively shaped and sustained this text.

The scholars of the Midwest Art History Society have attended a number of my papers on witchcraft images over the years. I am grateful for their responses to my ideas and for the perennially congenial, supportive fellowship of this organization. I also thank Larry Silver for suggesting that I submit my manuscript to the University of Pennsylvania Press and for his invaluable encouragement of scholarship in the field of Northern Renaissance art. The initial (anonymous) reader for the University of Pennsylvania Press also gave me some excellent suggestions that I have tried to incorporate into the final version of my text.

Many people helped to facilitate the process of acquiring images: Joyce Fuell, administrative assistant for the College of Wooster Department of Art; Claudia Ponton at Art Resource, New York; Matthew Percival at the Witt Library of the Courtauld Institute in London; Peter Huestis at the National Gallery of Art in Washington; Lizabeth Dion at the Museum of Fine Arts, Boston; Monica Wolf at the Cleveland Museum of Art; and many others. At the University of Pennsylvania Press, I would like to thank Jo Joslyn for her optimistic reception of my prospectus, Theodore Mann and Erica Ginsburg for their help, and Kathleen Benn McQueen for her skilled copyediting.

I would also like to acknowledge some personal debts, even though they are not directly related to this project. First of all, I am grateful to my sisters, Judy Hults and Nancy Hargrove, who cared for our mother during her long illness, something I was not able to help with much because of distance. They met this difficult challenge with strength and courage. I was recently reminded at an idyllic wedding in Berkeley, California, of how lucky I am to have meaningful longtime friendships. So, to all the dear friends I have acquired from my childhood in Indianapolis, my college days in Bloomington, Indiana, my years of teaching at Northern Illinois University, the University of Tulsa, and the College of Wooster, thank you for your abundant humor and your unwavering encouragement.

Finally, I thank my husband, Bill Munger, for proofreading, for listening, for making bank transfers to pay for photographs, for cleaning the house, for taking my car to the shop and our cats to the vet, and for managing hundreds of other things while I completed this manuscript. Most of all, I thank him for his unfailing love and support for me in this and all my endeavors, and for being the man he is. Although I often write about the oppressive workings of gender roles, he proves to me on a daily basis that human beings can do much better.

www.ingramcontent.com/pod-product-compliance
Lightning Source LLC
Chambersburg PA
CBHW072129170526
45158CB00004BA/1308
9780812221459